# Beginning PHP 4

Wankyu Choi
Allan Kent
Chris Lea
Ganesh Prasad
Chris Ullman
with
Jon Blank
Sean Cazzell

**wrox**

Programmer to Programmer

# Beginning PHP 4

Published by
**Wiley Publishing, Inc.**
10475 Crosspoint Boulevard
Indianapolis, IN 46256
www.wiley.com

Copyright © 2003 by Wiley Publishing, Inc., Indianapolis, Indiana

Published simultaneously in Canada

Library of Congress Card Number: 2003107058

ISBN: 0-7645-4364-4

Manufactured in the United States of America

10 9 8 7 6 5 4 3 2 1

1B/QW/QW/QT/IN

# Trademark Acknowledgements

Wrox has endeavored to provide trademark information about all the companies and products mentioned in this book by the appropriate use of capitals. However, Wrox cannot guarantee the accuracy of this information.

## Credits

**Authors**
Wankyu Choi
Allan Kent
Chris Lea
Ganesh Prasad
Chris Ullman

**Contributing Authors**
Jon Blank
Sean Cazzell

**Additional Material**
Simon Cozens
John Kauffman
Dan Squier

**Technical Architect**
James Hart

**Technical Editors**
David Mercer
Christian Peak
Dan Squier
Julia Gilbert
Mark Waterhouse

**Category Manager**
Viv Emery

**Author Agent**
Lynne Bassett

**Index**
Alessandro Ansa

**Project Administrator**
Nicola Phillips

**Technical Reviewers**
Luis Argerich
Darren Beale
Mark Fehrenbacher
Dario Ferreira Gomes
Chris Harshman
Andrew Hill
Mark Mamone
Jurgen Prins
Mark Roedel
Bart Ssyszka
Rick Stones
Travis Swicegood
Kevin Yank

**Production Manager**
Laurent Lafon

**Production Project Co-Ordinator**
Pip Wonson

**Figures/Illustrations**
Shabnam Hussain

**Cover**
Shelley Frazier

**Chapter Divider**
Dan Squier

**Proofreaders**
Fiona Berryman
Odette Randall

# About the Authors

## Wankyu Choi

Wankyu holds a Master's degree in English/Korean interpretation and translation from the Graduate School of Translation & Interpretation. He is the president/CEO of NeoQuest Communications, Inc. running a PHP-powered English language education portal (http://www.neoqst.com) in the Republic of Korea. He is independently working on an open source PHP project called NeoBoard (http://www.neoboard.net), a feature-rich web discussion board.

*I'd like to thank my parents for their encouragement and guidance, the dedicated staff at Wrox and technical reviewers for all their hard work, the staff at NeoQuest for their support while working on the book, and last but not the least, my wife, Yonsuk Song for her patience and love for this particular computer nerd.*

## Allan Kent

Allan has been programming seriously for the last 7 years and other than the single blemish when he achieved a Diploma in Cobol programming, is entirely self-taught. He started his career working at the local University and now runs his own company. Allan lives in Cape Town, South Africa with his girlfriend and 5 cats.

## Chris Lea

Chris is one of the co-founders of Lucid Designs (http://www.luciddesigns.com), a Venice, CA based web design and development firm. He received a BS in Physics with Highest Honors and Distinction from UNC-CH in 1997, and has been hacking away with lots of (mostly open source) software since then. During his tenure with Lucid, he has worked on a wide variety of web site development projects ranging from the entertainment industry to the financial sector. When he's not staring at his monitor, you can usually find him swing dancing somewhere in the Los Angeles area. For more information, you can always check out his personal site at http://www.chrislea.com/.

## Ganesh Prasad

Ganesh has worked in IT for 13 years, specializing in applications software design and development, in a number of countries including India, the United Arab Emirates, and Australia. He currently works for Reply2 Ltd., Australia, an e-CRM service provider. His experience covers IBM mainframes, VAX and UNIX minis, as well as Windows client/server and Web-based programming. Interests include Java and Open Source software, and his hope is that Open Source software will bring cheap computing to the masses and kick-start Third World economies. He is an Australian citizen, and lives in Sydney with his wife Sashi and son Lalit.

*I'd like to thank my wife Sashi for her patience, support and encouragement. She took all my other responsibilities off my shoulders, allowing me to concentrate on the task of writing.*

## Chris Ullman

Chris Ullman is a Computer Science graduate who came to Wrox five years ago, when 14.4 modems were the hottest Internet technology and Netscape Navigator 2.0 was a groundbreaking innovation. Since then he's applied his knowledge of HTML, server-side web technologies, Java, and Visual Basic to developing, editing, and authoring books. When not trying to reconstruct the guts of his own PC or trying to write extra chapters in a hurry, he can be found either playing keyboards in psychedelic band, The Bee men, tutoring his cats in the way of eating peacefully from their own food bowl and not the one next to theirs, or hoping against hope that this is the year his favorite soccer team, Birmingham City, can manage to end their exile from the Premier League.

*Thanks to James and Sarah B for getting me involved on this project and Christian, David, and Dan for deciphering, organizing, and improving my work, and most importantly thanks to my wife Kate, for being there.*

## Jon Blank

Jon Blank has been a part of the Linux world since before "Linux" was a buzzword, and has been programming (much to the detriment of his social life) in various languages for the better part of his life. He came to the PHP world by way of Perl, and came to Perl by way of The Web Union, an experimental Web hosting provider for students and non-profit organizations that he runs in his spare time. He currently lives in the New York City area, where he is trying to craft a stable career in a field where tempting offers are always around the corner. He doesn't think he'll succeed.

Jon's interests include online role-playing, vintage computers and video games, and graphics arts, as well as many sorts of programming. His primary focus as a programmer is on automation – convincing the computer to do the sort of boring and/or repetitive work that only a computer can stand.

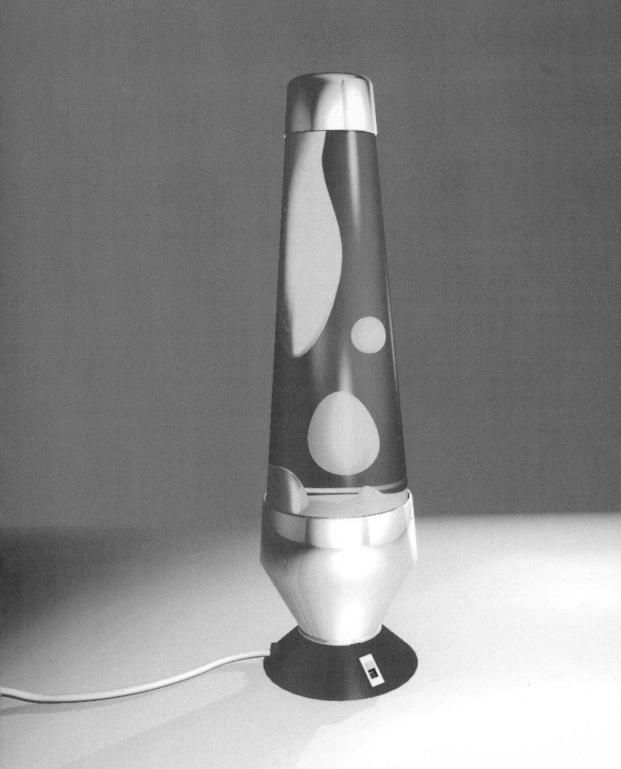

# Table of Contents

## Introduction

**1**

### Why PHP4?
**2**

The Prompt

2

### What Do I Need To Use This Book?
**3**

PHP4 Resources

4

### Conventions
**4**

Downloading the Source Code

5

### Support & Errata
**5**

### Online Forums at p2p.wrox.com
**6**

### Checking the Errata Online at www.wrox.com
**6**

Wrox Developer's Membership

6

Finding Errata on the Web Site

8

### Adding Errata and Obtaining e-Mail Support
**9**

Customer Support

9

Editorial

9

The Authors

9

What We Can't Answer

9

### How to Tell Us Exactly What You Think
**9**

## Chapter 1: Installation

**11**

### Installing PHP4 on Windows 95 and 98
**13**

Obtaining PWS

13

Setting Up PWS

15

Installing PHP4 Alongside PWS

17

### Installing PHP4 on Windows NT and 2000
**19**

Installing PHP4 Alongside IIS

24

### Installing PHP4 on Linux and Other UNIXes
**28**

Choosing Your Installation Method

29

Obtaining RPMs

29

Which Packages Do We Need?

30

Configuring and Starting Apache with PHP4

31

### Testing Your Installation
**34**

# Table of Contents

## Chapter 2: Writing PHP Programs     39

### An Example PHP Program     40

### Viewing a Web Page     44
Client-Server     44
    Internet Protocols     44
    The HTTP Protocol     45
    The HTTP Request     46
    The HTTP Response     48

### Where PHP Comes Into This     49
Server-Side Scripting     50
    Identifying a PHP Script     51

### Caching     51

### Variables     52
Data Types     55
    String Data Type     55
    Numeric Data Types     58
Constants     63
    The Define Keyword     64
Initialization     64
Conversions     65
    Type Casting     67
    gettype and settype     67
    isset, unset, and empty     68
Environment Variables     68

### Summary     69

## Chapter 3: Getting Data from the Client     71

### Web Forms     72
The FORM Tag     72
Attributes of FORM     72
    ACTION     72
    METHOD     73
HTML Form Controls and PHP     76
    Text Fields (Text Boxes)     76
    Text Areas     80
    Check Boxes     82
    Radio Buttons     88
    List Boxes     91
    Hidden Controls     95
    Passwords     99
    Submit Buttons and Reset Buttons     99
Using Values Returned From Forms In Your PHP Scripts     100

### Summary     106

## Chapter 4: Decision Making     109

### Conditional or Branching Statements     110
An Example of Branching in Day to Day Life     110
If Statements     111
    Boolean Values     112
    Boolean operators     112
    Combining Operators     123

Multiple Conditions – else and elseif                                                   127
    Nesting If Statements                                                              129
  Switch Statements                                                                    135

**Form Validation**                                                                   **140**

**Summary**                                                                            **144**


## Chapter 5: Loops and Arrays                                                          147

### Loops                                                                               148
  while Loops                                                                  148
  do while Loops                                                               155
  for Loops                                                                    159

### Arrays                                                                              165
  Initialization of Arrays                                                     165
  Iterating Through an Array                                                   167
    Iterating Through Non-Sequential Arrays                          172
    Iterating Through String-Indexed Arrays                          176
  Sorting Arrays                                                               177
    sort()                                                           177
    asort()                                                          178
    rsort() and arsort()                                             179
    ksort()                                                          179
  Miscellaneous Array Functions                                               180
    array_push() and array_pop()                                     180
    Implode and Explode                                              180
    HTTP_GET_VARS and HTTP_POST_VARS                                 182
  Multi-dimensional Arrays                                                     182
  Practical Demonstration of Arrays                                            183

### New Loop and Array Features in PHP4                                                 188
  Array Multisorting                                                           188
  foreach Loops                                                                189

### Summary                                                                             191


## Chapter 6: Organizing Your Code                                                      193

### What's So Great About Code Reuse?                                                   194
  Modularization                                                               194

### Functions                                                                           194
  Defining and Calling Functions                                               195
  Switching Functions                                                          201
    Assigning the Value Returned by Functions to Variables           202
  Passing Values                                                               203
    Passing By Value                                                 203
    Passing By Reference                                             203
    Setting Default Parameter Values                                 204

### Scope of Variables                                                                  206
  Global and Local Variables                                                   207
    Using Global Variables Inside Functions                           208
    Getting Local Variables to Retain their Value                     209

### Nesting                                                                             213
  Recursion                                                                    215

# Table of Contents

**Include Files**      **218**

Common Uses of Include Files      221

**Summary**      **224**


## Chapter 7: Handling and Avoiding Errors      227

**Error Handling in PHP**      **228**

Insecure Information      228

Unsightly Web Pages      228

Invisible Error Messages      228

**Error Types**      **229**

Syntax Errors      229

Logical Errors      232

Runtime Errors      232

Unexpected Output Errors      235

Errors In the Program Assumptions      235

**Good Coding Practice**      **236**

Indent Your Code      237

Comment Your Code      237

Use Functions      238

Use Include Files      239

Use Sensible Variable Names      239

**Trying to Break your Code**      **240**

More Form Validation      241

Thinking Like Your Users      241

Protection From Mischievous or Malicious Users      242

**Receiving Input from Users**      **243**

Regular Expressions      243

Patterns      243

Special Characters      244

**Debugging PHP Script**      **255**

Use echo()      256

Check the HTML Source      257

Suppressing Error Messages      257

Checking The Error Log      257

Doing the Hard Work Manually      258

**Summary**      **258**


## Chapter 8: Working With the Client      261

**Making the Most of a Stateless Protocol**      **262**

Talking to the User – HTTP, HTML, PHP and Interactivity      262

Native Sessions in PHP4      264

**'Do It Yourself' Persistence**      **265**

Hidden Form Fields Revisited      265

Query Strings      272

Cookies      280

**Sessions**      **287**

PHP4 Sessions      288

**Summary**      **292**

## Chapter 9: Objects

**295**

### Object-Oriented Terminology

**296**

### Using Pre-Defined Classes

**297**

Why Use Objects?

300

Giving the Calculator a Memory

304

Exploring Our Simple Class Further

307

Passing By Value And By Reference

307

### Creating Classes Of Our Own

311

Creating a Class From Scratch

311

Extending an Existing Class

314

### A Useful Object

**317**

### Summary

**321**

## Chapter 10: File and Directory Handling

**323**

### Working with Files

**324**

Opening and Closing Files

325

Reading and Writing to Files

327

Reading and Writing Characters in Files

331

Reading Entire Files

333

Random Access to File Data

335

Getting Information on Files

339

Time-related Properties

340

Ownership and Permissions

342

Splitting the Name and Path from a File

347

Copying, Renaming and Deleting Files

347

Building a Text Editor

350

### Working with Directories

**358**

Other Directory Functions

359

Traversing a Directory Hierarchy

361

Creating a Directory Navigator

363

### Uploading Files

**367**

### Putting it All Together – A Web Text Editor

**371**

### Resources

**377**

### Summary

**377**

## Chapter 11: PHP Database Connectivity

**379**

### Databases

**379**

Data Models

380

Normalization and Relational Databases

380

Database Architecture

382

Standalone Model

383

Client/Server Model

383

### Why MySQL?

**384**

Installing MySQL

385

Installing On Windows

385

Installing On Linux

386

Setting Up The Root Account

387

Testing Our MySQL Server

388

# Table of Contents

Introduction to SQL    388
    Data Types    388
    Indexes and Keys    390
    Queries    391

**A Quick Play with MySQL**    **393**
    Running the MySQL Client    393
    Selecting a Database to Use    394
    Taking a Peek at Data in a Database    394
    Manipulating Data in a Database    396
    Using GRANT and REVOKE commands    398
        GRANT    398
        REVOKE    399
    Summing Up    399

**PHP MySQL Connectivity**    **400**
    Basic Connection Functions    400
        Handling Server Errors    403

**Creating Databases and Tables from MySQL**    **407**
    Creating the Sample Database and Tables with PHP    411
    Altering Tables    415
    Inserting Data Into a Table    417
        Escaping Quotes    418
        Populating our Database Tables    419

**Resources**    **421**

**Summary**    **421**

**Chapter 12: Retrieving Data from MySQL Using PHP**    **423**

**Retrieving Data Using PHP**    **423**

**SQL Statements for Retrieving Data**    **426**
    Server Functions    426
    Retrieving Fields    427
        Limiting the Number of Results Returned    428
        Ordering the Results    430
        Pattern Matching    431
    Getting Summaries    432
    More Complex Retrievals    433
        Retrieving Fields from More Than One Table    435

**Putting It All Together**    **437**
    Using the User Viewer    446

**Resources**    **447**

**Summary**    **447**

**Chapter 13: Manipulating Data in MySQL Using PHP**    **449**

**Inserting Records Using PHP**    **449**
    Special Characters    450

**Updating and Deleting Records in Tables**    **452**

**Working with Date and Time Type Fields**    **454**

**Getting Information on Database Tables**    **458**
    ENUM Options and Field Defaults    464

**Creating a User Registration Script**     **468**

**Creating an Access Logger Script**     **474**

**Creating a User Manager**     **482**

**Resources**     **491**

**Summary**     **491**

## Chapter 14: XML     **493**

**What is XML?**     **493**

**XML Document Structure**     **496**

**Well-Formed XML**     **496**

**DTDs**     **499**

**Event Driven Parsing**     **501**

**Parsing the Example File**     **502**

**Parsing an External File**     **508**

**Summary**     **512**

## Chapter 15: e-Mail Handling     **515**

**Sending e-mails in PHP**     **515**

**Anatomy of an e-Mail**     **518**

**Handling Attachments**     **525**

Anatomy of e-Mail Revisited     525

    Content-type     526

    Content-transfer-encoding     527

    MIME-Version     527

    Multiple Mail Components     528

Attaching Files to e-Mail     529

**A Newsletter Mailing List Manager**     **536**

**Resources**     **552**

**Summary**     **553**

## Chapter 16: Generating Graphics     **555**

**Laying a Foundation**     **555**

Creating an Image     556

    Setting up Colors     556

    The Image Coordinate System     557

Drawing on our Image     558

    Lines     558

    Circles     560

    Rectangles     562

Putting it all Together     563

# Table of Contents

**Practical Application**                                    **566**

Interactive Maps                                                566
Getting Started                                                 567
   Creating the database                         568
   Adding data                                   568
   Testing our data                              569
Building a Framework                                            573
   Drawing the Layout                            574
Further Interactivity                                           579
Showing the Shop Detail                                         581

**Advanced Graphics Manipulation**                          **585**

A Stylized Map                                                  585
Palette Limitations                                            589

**Summary**                                                 **591**


**Chapter 17: Case Study – A URL Directory Manager**       **593**

**Introducing the URL Directory Manager**                   **593**

**Designing the Directory Manager**                         **594**

User Requirements                                              594
   Users vs Administrators                       595
   User Authentication                           596
User Interface                                                 596
Data Storage                                                   596
   Connecting to the Database                    597
   Database Schema                               597
   Database Tables                               600
Other Design Considerations                                    601
Code Layout                                                    601
   Security Issues                               601
   Directory Functions                           602

**Code Implementation**                                     **604**

Common Code – php_directory.inc                               604
   directory_header()                            606
   directory_footer()                            606
   db_connect()                                  607
   sql_error()                                   607
   error_message()                               608
   user_message()                                608
   get_category_info()                           609
   get_url_info()                                615
   search_form()                                 616
   show_list()                                   617
   add_url_form()                                631
   add_url()                                     634
   modify_url_form()                             637
   modify_url()                                  640
   go_url()                                      642
   list_sites()                                  643
User Code – php_directory.php                                  645
Administration Code – dir_manager.php                          646
   list_categories()                             646
   add_category_form()                           649
   add_category()                                651
   edit_category_form()                          652
   edit_category()                               653

delete_category() 654
update_db() 655
view_new() 657
edit_new_form() 660
edit_new() 662
delete_url() 664
top_menu() 665

**User Feedback** 667

**Summary** 667

## Appendix A: ODBC 669

**What is ODBC?** 669

**What ODBC Isn't** 670

**PHP and ODBC** 674

**Connecting to a Data Source** 674

**Executing SQL commands** 674

**Handling Query Results** 675

## Appendix B: PHP Functions 683

**Apache-Specific Functions** 683

**Array Functions** 683

**Aspell Functions** 687

**Calendar Functions** 687

**Class/Object Functions** 688

**CURL, Client URL Library Functions** 689

**Database Functions** 689
Database Abstraction Layer Functions 689
dBase Functions 690
DBM Functions 691
Informix Functions 692
InterBase Functions 694
Microsoft SQL Server Functions 695
mSQL Functions 696
MySQL Functions 699
Unified ODBC Functions 701
Oracle 8 Functions 704
Oracle Functions 706
PostgreSQL Functions 707
Sybase Functions 709

**Date and Time Functions** 710

**Directory Functions** 711

**DOM XML Functions** 712

# Table of Contents

Error Handling and Logging Functions     **712**

Filesystem Functions     **713**

Forms Data Format Functions     **716**

Function Handling Functions     **717**

HTTP Functions     **718**

Image Functions     **718**

Mail Functions     **722**

Mathematical Functions     **722**

Miscellaneous Functions     **724**

Network Functions     **725**

Output Control Functions     **726**

PHP Options and Information     **727**

POSIX Functions     **728**

Program Execution Functions     **730**

Pspell Functions     **730**

Perl-Compatible Regular Expression Functions     **731**

Regular Expression Functions (POSIX Extended)     **732**

Session Handling Functions     **733**

String Functions     **734**

URL Functions     **738**

Variable Functions     **739**

WDDX Functions     **740**

XML Parser Functions     **740**

Zlib Functions     **742**

Function Index     **745**

Index     **755**

A Guide to the Index     755

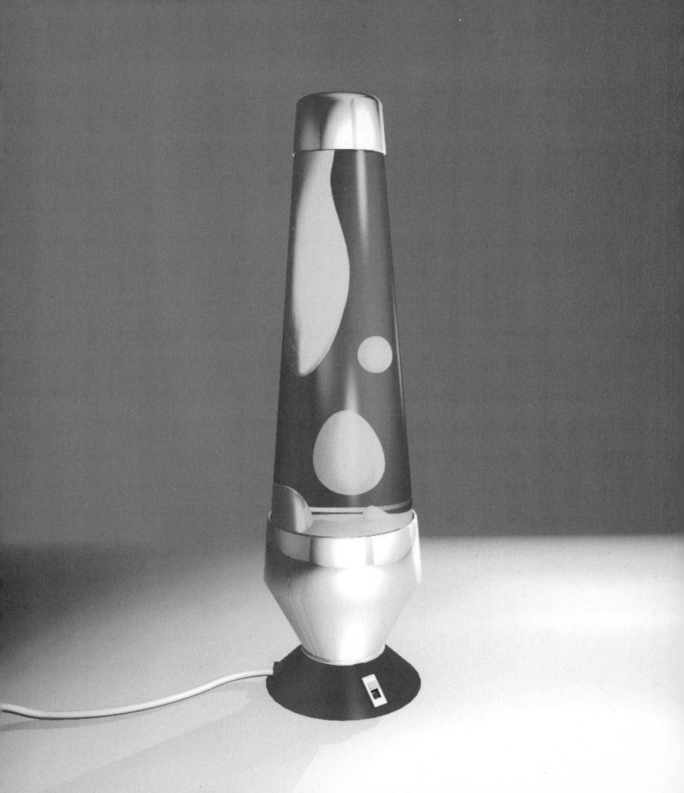

# Introduction

PHP4 is the latest incarnation of PHP – the "PHP Hypertext Preprocessor". It's a programming language for building dynamic, interactive web sites, originally devised by Rasmus Lerdorf way back in 1994. Since then it's been through a great many changes, and has been adopted by web programmers all around the world. So what exactly is it?

In technical terms, PHP4 is a cross-platform, HTML-embedded, server-side web scripting language. Let's take a moment to define these terms:

❑ **Cross-platform**

You can run most PHP4 code, without alteration, on computers running many different operating systems. A PHP4 script that runs on Linux will generally run on Windows as well.

❑ **HTML-embedded**

PHP4 code is written in files containing a mixture of PHP instructions and HTML code.

❑ **Server-side**

The PHP4 programs we write are run on a server – specifically, a web server.

❑ **A web scripting language**

We run PHP4 programs via a web browser. We access the web server on which they reside, and this runs the program, sending any resulting output back to the browser.

This means that we're going to be writing programs that mix PHP4 code and HTML together, using the former to control and format the latter. We'll then need to put those programs onto a web server to run them. Finally, we're going to access them from a web browser, which displays the resulting HTML. This means our programs can be made available for other people to access across the Web, simply by placing them on a public web server.

You're probably already familiar with HTML – "HyperText Markup Language". This is the language used to write web pages, combining plain text and special tags that tell a browser how to treat that text. We use HTML to describe how different elements in a web page should be displayed, how pages should be linked, where to put images, and so on.

Pure HTML documents, for all their versatility, are little more than static arrangements of text and pictures, albeit nicely presented ones; but the majority of sites you can find on the Web aren't static, but **dynamic**, even **interactive**. They show you a list of sites containing words that you've specified, present you with the latest news, even greet you by name when you log on. They allow you to **interact**, and present different web pages according to your choices.

You can't build a web site like that using raw HTML, and that's where PHP4 comes in. So what sort of things can we do with it? Well, we can program sites that will:

❑    Present data from a wide variety of different sources, such as databases, or files

❑    Incorporate interactive elements, such as search facilities, message boards, and straw-polls

❑    Allow the user to perform actions, such as sending e-mail, or buying something

In other words, PHP4 can be used to write the kind of web sites which anyone familiar with the Web uses every day. From e-commerce sites, to search engines, to information portals, most major web sites on the Internet incorporate some or all of these sorts of programming. In the course of this book, we'll be using it to build, among other things:

❑    A browser-based text editor, which lets us create and edit files on the web server from our web browser

❑    A web site for a shopping mall, which allows us to search for stores which sell a certain item, and displays the stores on a map

❑    An online word game

❑    A directory-based web search engine, which allows people to search all the web sites in the directory, or find web sites by navigating through a hierarchical topic structure

❑    A mailing-list service, which allows users to subscribe to different mailing lists, and allows the list administrators to then send out e-mails to the subscribers

So, PHP4 can be used for a diverse range of applications, from utilities like the text editor, to powerful web sites such as the shopping mall and directory examples. In this book, we're going to try and equip you with the necessary knowledge to build any kind of web site you want using PHP4. You'll learn some useful coding techniques along the way, and we'll hopefully give you some ideas that you can incorporate into your own applications.

# Why PHP4?

One of the best things about PHP4 is that it is supported by a large number of Internet Service Providers (ISPs), which means that once you've written an application in PHP4, you can easily put it on the Web for anyone to use.

You can find a list of ISPs who can help you with hosting PHP-based websites at http://hosts.php.net/.

# The Prompt

When we start looking at databases in Chapter 11, we'll be introducing the MySQL database manager, and making extensive use of its command line interface. If you're primarily using your computer in a graphical environment like Windows or X, you may not be familiar with using the command line interface, or "shell". Before these graphical environments came into common use, users had to start a new program not by finding its icon and clicking on it, but by typing its name. The "shell" is the program that takes the name from you – the "shell prompt" (or just "prompt") refers specifically to the text that prompts you to enter a new program name, and more generally to working with the shell instead of using a graphical interface. Some people still find working with the shell much easier, and many sophisticated shells have been developed to simplify common tasks.

To get to a prompt in Windows, look for **Command Prompt** or **DOS Prompt** in the **Start Menu**. UNIX users should look for a program called something like `console`, `terminal`, `konsole`, `xterm`, `eterm`, or `kterm`. You'll then usually be faced with a black screen with a small amount of text on it that says various things like:

```
$
%
C:\>
#
bash$
```

For the purposes of this book, however, we'll use a prompt that looks like this:

```
>
```

We'll show text for you to enter in bold, and the text the computer generates in a lighter typeface, like this:

```
> mysqlshow
+-----------+
| Databases |
+-----------+
| mysql     |
| test      |
+-----------+
```

# What Do I Need To Use This Book?

We will be focusing on using PHP4 on Windows and UNIX platforms. As we shall see in the first chapter, we can install it on Windows 95 and 98, and NT and 2000. It will also run on virtually any flavor of UNIX, although our instructions only detail installation from RPM files.

As well as the actual PHP4 libraries, you'll need a text editor to create and edit your scripts. We'll look at a number of options in Chapter 1.

You'll need a web server. Apache is a good bet on UNIX machines – it's included in most Linux distributions, and you can obtain it from http://www.apache.org. Windows users can also use Apache, or alternatively Microsoft's Personal Web Server (for 95 and 98) or Internet Information Server (for NT and 2000). Chapter 1 explains how to get up and running.

To get the most out of certain chapters, you'll need to have an Internet connection. However, don't panic if you haven't got one – as long as you have the necessary software installed, you can run most of the examples in the book on a single machine, acting as both client *and* server.

# PHP4 Resources

Your first stop for information should be the official PHP site, which you can find at www.php.net. This not only features news, downloads, and complete documentation (including user feedback), but it also features a complete searchable index of all the above.

PHP4 is based on the Zend scripting engine, owned by Zend Technologies, whose site can be found at www.zend.com. Here you'll find information specific to PHP4, as well as articles, case studies, and news about the different uses PHP4 is currently being put to in business environments.

Another very useful resource is the www.phpbuilder.com site, a community-driven forum for PHP programmers. It's a good place for useful tips and tutorials, and generally finding out what's happening in the PHP programming community.

# Conventions

We have used various styles of text and layout in the book to help differentiate between different kinds of information. Here are examples of the styles we use and an explanation of what they mean:

## Try It Out – A 'Try It Out' Example

'Try It Out' is our way of presenting a practical example.

### How It Works

Then the 'How It Works' section explains what's going on.

*Advice, hints and background information come in an indented, italicized font like this.*

---

**Important bits of information that you shouldn't ignore come in boxes like this!**

---

- ❑ **Important Words** are in a bold typeface.
- ❑ Words that appear on the screen in menus like the File or Window menu are in a similar font to that which you see on screen.
- ❑ Keys that you press on the keyboard, like *Ctrl* and *Enter*, are in italics.

Code is presented in two formats. If it's a word that we're talking about in the text, for example, when discussing the fopen() function, it's in a distinctive font. If it's a block of code that you can type in as a program and run, then it's shown in a gray box like this:

```
$fp = fopen("./data.txt", "r");
```

Sometimes you'll see code in a mixture of styles, like this:

```
$fp = fopen("./data.txt", "r");
if(!$fp) die ("Cannot open the file");
```

This is meant to draw your attention to code that's new, or relevant to the surrounding discussion (in the gray box), whilst showing it in the context of the code you've seen before (on the white background).

Where we show text to be entered at a command prompt, this will be shown as follows:

> **mysqlshow**

Any output will be shown in the same font, only lighter:

```
+-----------+
| Databases |
+-----------+
| mysql     |
| test      |
+-----------+
```

# Downloading the Source Code

As you work through the examples in this book, you might decide that you prefer to type all the code in by hand. Many readers prefer this because it's a good way to get familiar with the coding techniques that are being used.

Whether you want to type the code in or not, we have made all the source code for this book available at our web site, at the following address:

http://www.wrox.com

If you're one of those readers who likes to type in the code, you can use our files to check the results you should be getting – they should be your first stop if you think you might have typed in an error. If you're one of those readers who doesn't like typing, then downloading the source code from our web site is a must! Either way, it'll help you with updates and debugging.

# Support & Errata

One of the most irritating things about any programming book is when you find that bit of code that you've just spent an hour typing out simply doesn't work. You check it a hundred times to see if you've set it up correctly and then you notice the spelling mistake in the variable name on the book page. Of course, you can blame the authors for not taking enough care and testing the code, the editors for not doing their job properly, or the proofreaders for not being eagle-eyed enough, but this doesn't get around the fact that mistakes do happen.

We try hard to ensure no mistakes sneak out into the real world, but we can't promise that this book is 100% error free. What we can do is offer the next best thing by providing you with immediate support and feedback from experts who have worked on the book and try to ensure that future editions eliminate these gremlins. We also now commit to supporting you not just while you read the book, but once you start developing applications as well through our online forums where you can put your questions to the authors, reviewers, and fellow industry professionals.

In this section we'll look at how to:

- ❏ Enroll in the peer to peer forums at p2p.wrox.com
- ❏ Post and check for errata on our main site, www.wrox.com
- ❏ e-mail technical support a query or feedback on our books in general

Between these three support procedures, you should get an answer to your problem in no time at all.

# Online Forums at p2p.wrox.com

Join the PHP mailing list for author and peer support. Our system provides **Programmer to Programmer™ support** on mailing lists, forums and newsgroups all in addition to our one-to-one e-mail system, which we'll look at in a minute. Be confident that your query is not just being examined by a support professional, but by the many Wrox authors and other industry experts present on our mailing lists.

# Checking the Errata Online at www.wrox.com

The following section will take you step by step through the process of posting errata to our web site to get that help. The sections that follow, therefore, are:

- ❏ Wrox Developer's Membership
- ❏ Finding a list of existing errata on the web site
- ❏ Adding your own errata to the existing list
- ❏ What happens to your errata once you've posted it (why doesn't it appear immediately)?

There is also a section covering how to e-mail a question for technical support. This comprises:

- ❏ What your e-mail should include
- ❏ What happens to your e-mail once it has been received by us

So that you only need view information relevant to yourself, we ask that you register as a Wrox Developer Member. This is a quick and easy process, that will save you time in the long-run. If you are already a member, just update membership to include this book.

## *Wrox Developer's Membership*

To get your FREE Wrox Developer's Membership click on Membership in the top navigation bar of our home site – http://www.wrox.com. This is shown in the screenshot on the opposite page:

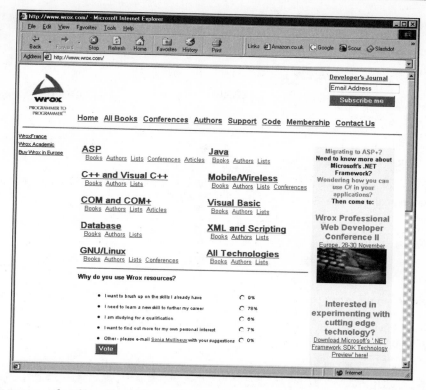

On the next screen, select New User. This will display a form. Fill in the details on the form and submit the details using the Register button at the bottom. Before you can say "The best read books come in Wrox Red" you will get the following screen:

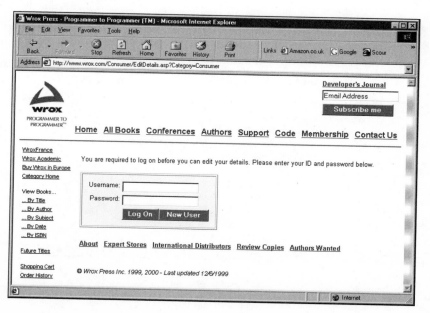

Type in your password once again and click **Log On**. The following page allows you to change your details if you need to, but now you're logged on, you have access to all the source code downloads and errata for the entire Wrox range of books.

## Finding Errata on the Web Site

Before you send in a query, you might be able to save time by finding the answer to your problem on our web site: http:\\www.wrox.com.

Each book we publish has its own page and its own errata sheet. You can get to any book's page by clicking on **Support** from the top navigation bar.

Halfway down the main support page is a drop down box called **Title Support**. Simply scroll down the list until you see **Beginning PHP4**. Select it and then hit **Errata**.

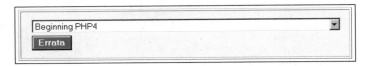

This will take you to the errata page for the book. Select the criteria by which you want to view the errata, and click the **Apply criteria** button. This will provide you with links to specific errata. For an initial search, you are advised to view the errata by page numbers. If you have looked for an error previously, then you may wish to limit your search using dates. We update these pages daily to ensure that you have the latest information on bugs and errors.

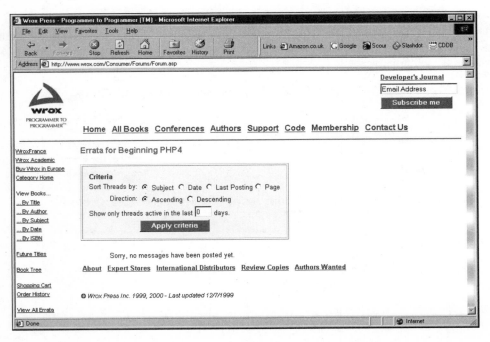

# Adding Errata and Obtaining e-Mail Support

If you wish to point out errata to put up on the website, or directly query a problem in the book page with an expert who knows the book in detail then e-mail support@wrox.com with the title of the book and the last four numbers of the ISBN in the subject field. A typical e-mail should include the following things:

The **book title**, **last four digits of the ISBN,** and **page number** of the problem in the Subject field.

Your **name**, **contact info,** and the **problem** in the body of the message.

We won't send you junk mail. We need the details to save your time and ours. If we need to replace a disk or CD we'll be able to get it to you straight away. When you send an e-mail it will go through the following chain of support:

## Customer Support

Your message is delivered to one of our customer support staff who are the first people to read it. They have files on most frequently asked questions and will answer anything general immediately. They answer general questions about the book and the web site.

## Editorial

Deeper queries are forwarded to the technical editor team responsible for that book. They have experience with the programming language or particular product and are able to answer detailed technical questions on the subject. Once an issue has been resolved, the editor can post any errata which have been discovered to the web site.

## The Authors

Finally, in the unlikely event that the editor can't answer your problem, s/he will forward the request to the author. We try to protect the authors' time, since they are busy professionals with wide ranging commitments. However, we are quite happy to forward specific requests to them. All Wrox authors help with the support on their books. They'll mail the customer and the editor with their response, and again all readers should benefit.

## What We Can't Answer

Obviously with an ever-growing range of books and an ever-changing technology base, there is an increasing volume of data requiring support. While we endeavor to answer all questions about the book, we can't answer bugs in your own programs that you've adapted from our code. So, while you might have loved the chapters on file handling, don't expect too much sympathy if you cripple your company with a routine which deletes the contents of your hard drive. But do tell us if you're especially pleased with a routine you developed with our help.

# How to Tell Us Exactly What You Think

We understand that errors can destroy the enjoyment of a book and can cause many wasted and frustrated hours, so we seek to minimize the distress that they can cause.

You might just wish to tell us how much you liked or loathed the book in question, or you might have ideas about how this whole process could be improved. In which case you should e-mail feedback@wrox.com. You'll always find a sympathetic ear, no matter what the problem is. Above all you should remember that we do care about what you have to say and we will do our utmost to act upon it.

# Installation

To run the code in this book you will need at least the following software:

### Server software

- ❑ A PHP-compatible web server
- ❑ PHP4
- ❑ For most of the examples from Chapter 11 onwards, a relational database system

### Client software

- ❑ A web browser
- ❑ A text editor, such as Notepad, Emacs, vi, BBEdit, and so on.

You can run all of these programs on the same computer for development purposes. If you have access to several networked computers, you may want to install all of your server software on one (typically either a UNIX or Windows NT/2000 computer), and use another networked computer as your client machine. For the purposes of this book, we will generally assume you are running all of the software on a single computer. This is the configuration used by most web developers.

Don't panic if you don't have a web server. Most people don't. In this first chapter, we're going to explain how to set up a web server on an ordinary desktop PC. You'll be able to run your PHP4 programs on either a UNIX machine (we'll use Linux – you could use FreeBSD, or Solaris) or a Windows box (Windows 95, 98, NT or 2000), so we'll explain how to install a popular web server on each of these platforms.

In case you're worried, a computer doesn't need to be attached to the Internet, or even to a network, to run web server software. If you install a web server on a computer, it's always possible to access that web server from a web browser running on the same machine, even if it doesn't have a network card or modem. Of course, to download and install the software we need, you'll have to have access to an Internet connection. But you don't need it to be active just because you're running your web server.

Once we have a web server, we'll install PHP4 alongside it. There's some configuration required to tell the web server how to run PHP programs, and we'll walk through that process.

As well as a web server and PHP4, we'll also need a database system for some of our examples. One of the most powerful uses for web scripting tools, such as PHP4, is to present information stored in a database to people accessing them across the Web. All the examples presented in Chapter 11 onwards, which use databases, are written to work with the popular free database system, MySQL. There's information in Appendix A on how to convert the information presented for MySQL to apply to ODBC databases, which might be of interest to Windows users who would prefer to be able to play with their databases using a visual tool such as Microsoft Access. Versions of most of the database code presented in the book, converted for use with ODBC, will be available as part of the code download for the book at http://www.wrox.com/.

However, on either Windows or Linux, installing MySQL is relatively painless, and you'll find it much easier to run the examples if you simply install MySQL. Full instructions are included at the start of Chapter 11.

In this chapter, then, we'll explain how to set up the most basic development environment which you'll need to run all of the examples in this book.

### What If It All Goes Wrong?

The README and INSTALL files which are included in most PHP downloads, as well as the PHP manual at http://www.php.net/manual/, provide detailed information which may be more up to date than the information here, which covers the PHP 4.0.2 release.

## Where Do I Start?

There are three main installation paths to choose from, and it should be fairly easy to work out which one you need to follow. It simply depends which operating system you're using:

❑     Installing PHP4 with Microsoft Personal Web Server on Windows 95 or 98

❑     Installing PHP4 with Microsoft Internet Information Server on Windows NT4 or 2000

❑     Installing PHP4 with the Apache Web Server on Linux (or another UNIX)

*PHP4 can be installed on a great variety of web server/operating system combinations, including under Apache on Windows. However, the three systems we have suggested are the easiest to get working. If you don't think any of these three will suit you, feel free to install whatever other configuration you want – you should still be able to run all of the examples in the book. Refer to the PHP4 manual for more general installation instructions.*

The three paths are covered separately over the next few pages. We'll all join up again at the end to test our system is working properly.

*Microsoft recently released the latest version of their Windows 95/98 operating system series, Windows Me. At the time of going to press, we were able to verify that it is possible to install PWS on the newer operating system using the procedure shown below for Windows 95 users. It is possible that final release Windows Me CDs will include PWS on the install CD, in the add-ons folder, just like Windows 98 does, but we weren't able to verify this at time of writing.*

# Installing PHP4 on Windows 95 and 98

First of all, let's install Microsoft Personal Web Server (PWS). It should be noted PWS is really only suitable for running your development machine on – it's not up to the job of running a real web site. However, it provides a convenient and inexpensive development environment for pre-Windows 2000 machines, without the need for powerful hardware. One of the main drawbacks of PWS is that it can be awkard to install and get up and running correctly. Let's try and get over this by following these steps:

## Obtaining PWS

The version of PWS you need to install is version 4.0, which was first released in NT 4 Option Pack of Dec 1997 as part of IIS 4.0. It is available from several sources, as follows.

### Visual InterDev

Microsoft's Visual InterDev version 6.0 includes PWS. It can be installed at the time VID is set up or can be installed afterwards as an option from a custom set-up.

### Windows 98

The Windows 98 CD contains an installer for PWS. Most people who have installed PWS from the Windows 98 CD onto a Windows 98 installation seem to have fewer problems then those who use other sources.

### FrontPage

FrontPage, FrontPage 97 and FrontPage 98 included PWS, although in different flavors.

> *The early releases of FrontPage had a program named HTTPD which was sold as Front Page Server. The functionality was the same as PWS, but it was an entirely different set of code. As far as we are aware, it's not possible to run PHP under this server.*

FrontPage 97 contained PWS 1.0, and FrontPage 98 contains PWS 4.0, the current incarnation of PWS.

### Download

Microsoft offers PWS as a download, but with a strange nomenclature. It is actually a component of the Windows NT option pack for Windows 95. If you run the Windows NT Option Pack on a Windows 9x machine, the option pack will recognize that this is not an NT OS and will install PWS instead of IIS.

"Wait A Minute! Run the Windows NT Option Pack on Windows 9x?" Many people have a hard time believing that one possible technique to install PWS was to run the NT Option Pack on their Windows 9x machines. But it does work and is the recommended method for Windows 95 users. We'll show you how to do it shortly.

## Which Source To Use

You'll generally have the fewest problems when installing PWS on Windows 98 from the Windows 98 CD. The second least-problematic source seems to be the NT download which is good for Windows 95 as well as Windows 98. Another strategy with minimum complaints has been the installation from NT 4 Option pack onto NT workstation. Folks that are installing from Visual InterDev and FrontPage CD-ROMs seem to have the most problems. It is also recommended that if you are considering moving from Windows 95 to Windows 98, you do so *before* attempting to install PWS.

## Installing From NT Option Pack Onto Windows 95

This is the best option for Windows 95. However, keep in mind that a much higher percentage of users have had problems with PWS on Windows 95 then PWS on Windows 98. If you are considering upgrading to Windows 98 we suggest you do it prior to installing PWS.

**1.** Close all applications.

**2.** Download Windows NT Option Pack for Windows 95 from http://www.microsoft.com/ntserver/nts/downloads/recommended/NT4OptPk/. You'll find the link at the bottom of the web page.

**3.** Select option 1 of the download options, and then on the next page select the operating system you are running on. On the next page click on download.exe for the site nearest to you.

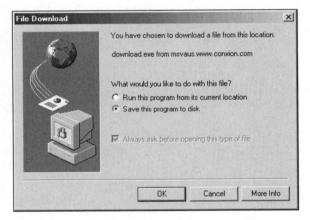

**4.** Save the program to disk.

**5.** Go to the directory where you saved download.exe and run it, and the wizard will first ask you to agree to the licensing terms, and then present you with the following screen:

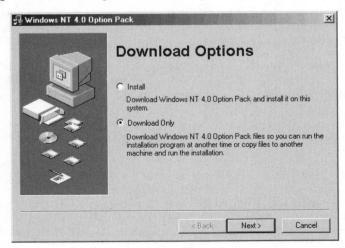

**6.** Choose to download only, as, if the install option quits halfway through, it can mess up your machine's configuration.

**7.** Click Next and choose x86: Windows 95 for the operating system and click Next.

**8.** Choose the Typical Installation and click Next.

**9.** Choose a location on your hard drive of where to download the pack to, and click Next.

**10.** Choose a location from where to download the pack.

**11.** Accept the verification certificate that appears and then the option pack will download.

**12.** Finally go to the location where you saved it, and run the newly downloaded setup.exe.

## Installing From The Windows 98 CD Onto Windows 98

This is the safest option for installing PWS, but is only possible if using Windows 98. The steps are as follows:

**1.** Ensure that the Windows 98 CD is in the drive. When you insert the CD, a splash screen will normally appear. Click the button marked Browse this CD.

**2.** In the explorer window for your CD-ROM, you should find a directory called add-ons. Inside, there will normally be a single directory called pws. Open this up.

**3.** Run the program in this folder called setup.exe.

# Setting Up PWS

Having downloaded or located PWS's setup tool and run it, you will be greeted with a splash screen similar to the following:

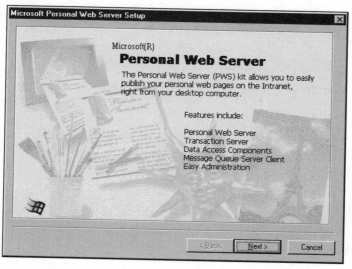

For most users, the typical install will work fine. If you choose to do a custom install, then ensure that at least the following components are selected:

- ❑ Common Program Files
- ❑ Personal Web Server

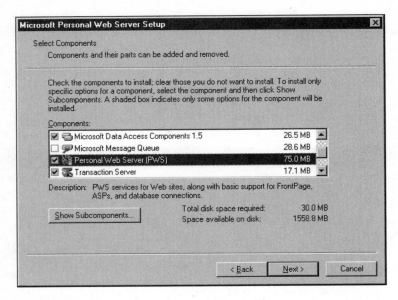

You will then be prompted for your default web publishing home directory. The normal one to choose is C:\Inetpub\wwwroot, although you can choose anywhere. Later in this chapter, if we refer to C:\Inetpub\wwwroot, you should remember to substitute it with the path we used here.

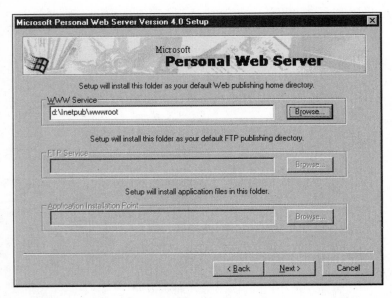

# Installing PHP4 Alongside PWS

Now you've installed PWS, and your computer has rebooted, let's get PHP4 installed. First of all you need to download it. While you would normally obtain the latest version of PHP4 from http://www.php.net/, unfortunately the version of PHP distributed via that site is only a basic installation, and doesn't support all the features we need. Instead, we recommend you go to http://php4win.de/, and download their latest, non-development, stable release. You'll end up with a ZIP file, which you should save somewhere on your hard drive. Create a folder for your PHP software to live in – somewhere like C:\php is good – and unzip the file you downloaded into this directory.

Now, this directory contains several sub-directories, and a few text files. Also, a program file called php.exe, which we won't actually be using, and a library file called php4ts.dll. To start off, you need to copy this .dll to your C:\Windows\System directory. Now open up the dlls subdirectory, and copy *all* of the files from here to your C:\Windows\System directory as well. If Windows complains that you've already got a file by one or other of these names, then keep your old one – don't overwrite it with the newly downloaded files.

Now, back in the top of our PHP directory, there should be a file called php.ini. Copy this file to C:\Windows, and open it up with Notepad. Note that the download from http://php4win.de doesn't contain "php.ini" with Win 98, but does contain "php.ini-dist" and "php.ini-optimized". Rename one of thses as "php.ini". Scroll down the document until you find a line that looks like:

```
extension_dir = "C:\php\extens~1" ; directory in which the loadable extensions
(modules) reside
```

Now, make sure that this path is the correct path to the extensions directory of the unzipped PHP4 installation. If it isn't, change it to point to the right place. (The extensions directory is the one which contains a large number of files whose names begin with php_ and end with .dll.

The next section tells PHP which extensions to load. You should put semi-colons at the beginning of all the lines which load extensions we don't need – the semi-colons mean that PHP will ignore the directive on that line. You can put semi-colons before all of them, except before extension=php_gd.dll, so that you have text like this:

```
;extension=php_filepro.dll
extension=php_gd.dll
;extension=php_dbm.dll
;extension=php_mssql.dll
```

This means you will have access to the functionality of the GD library, which allows us to generate images using PHP programs. We'll look at how in Chapter 16. You should now save your modified php.ini file.

Now, also in Notepad, you need to create a new file, and enter the following text:

```
REGEDIT4

[HKEY_LOCAL_MACHINE\SYSTEM\CurrentControlSet\Services\w3svc\parameters\Script Map]
".php"="C:\\php\\sapi\\php4isapi.dll"
```

Note that this script is included in the code download for this book from http://www.wrox.com/, and is called PWS-php4.reg.

If you didn't unzip the download into C:\php, you need to edit this so it knows where your php4isapi.dll file is. If you unzipped the download into E:\Stuff\php4, then the location will be E:\Stuff\php4\sapi\php4isapi.dll. Because of the way the file will be interpreted, you should double up all the backslashes, and insert the path in the file where it says C:\\php\\sapi\\php4isapi.dll. For example:

```
REGEDIT4

[HKEY_LOCAL_MACHINE\SYSTEM\CurrentControlSet\Services\w3svc\parameters\Script Map]
".php"="E:\\Stuff\\php4\\sapi\\php4isapi.dll"
```

Save the edited file somewhere convenient, as PWS-php4.reg, close Notepad, and double-click PWS-php4.reg to set up PWS with PHP4 support. You should get a dialog box asking you if you want to make changes to your registry. You should click **Yes**.

*If double-clicking* PWS-php4.reg *just starts up Notepad, rather than making changes to your system, make sure that the file is really called* PWS-php4.reg, *not* PWS-php4.reg.txt, *and try again.*

## Finishing off the Installation

Now, you need to launch the Personal Web Manager, which is a graphical program used to configure PWS. You can find it in Start | Programs | Accessories | Internet Tools | Personal Web Server | Personal Web Manager. When you've launched it, check that PWS is started. If it's not, click the start button. You should have a screen like this:

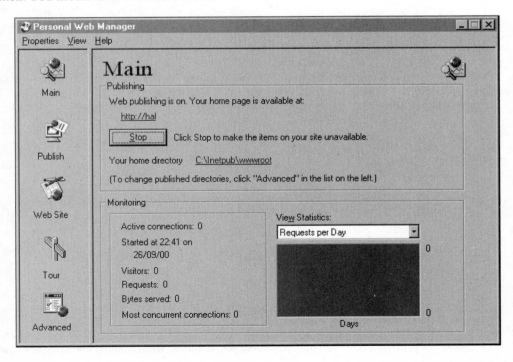

Select the **Advanced** option from the list of icons on the left. On the following screen, make sure that the top item in the hierarchical list, <Home>, is selected.

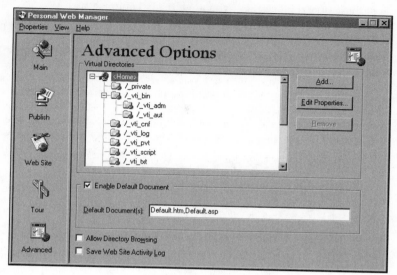

Click **Edit Properties**, and make sure the **Execute** check box is selected in the dialog box.

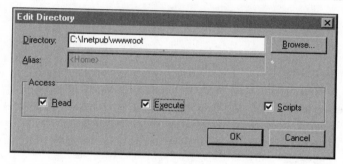

Now, you have configured PWS to run PHP4 programs. You need to restart your computer to get PWS to load the PHP4 component.

The root directory of your web server is, unless you configured it differently, C:\Inetpub\wwwroot. Remember this – it's important. You can now skip on to the *Testing Your Installation* section later in the chapter.

# Installing PHP4 on Windows NT and 2000

On either Windows NT or 2000, we'll be using Internet Information Server, which is Microsoft's industrial strength web server. An NT or 2000 machine running IIS is actually a suitable environment for running a production web server, although you should make sure you know what you're doing if you're planning on setting up any computer as a server on the public Internet – security should be your biggest concern. IIS running on a Windows NT or 2000-powered desktop computer is also a perfectly good development environment.

Some versions of Windows 2000 (specifically the three server versions – Server, Advanced Server and Datacenter) come with IIS 5.0 installed by default. Unless you elected not to install the web server when you installed one of these operating systems, you are already equipped with IIS.

We'll now show you how to install IIS onto either Windows NT 4.0 or Windows 2000 Professional.

## Installing From Windows NT 4.0 Option Pack onto Windows NT 4.0

To install IIS 4.0, we need to install the Microsoft Windows NT 4.0 Option Pack. You can download the Option Pack from http://www.microsoft.com/ntserver/nts/downloads/recommended/NT4OptPk/.

**1.** Select Option 1 of the download options, and then on the next page select the operating system you are running on. On the next page click on `download.exe` for the site nearest to you.

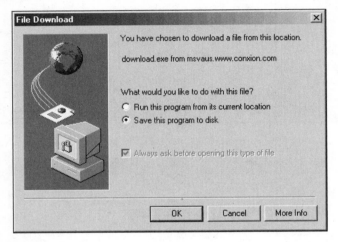

**2.** Save the program to disk. Go to the directory where you saved `download.exe` and run it, and the wizard will first ask you to agree to the licensing terms, and then present you with the following screen:

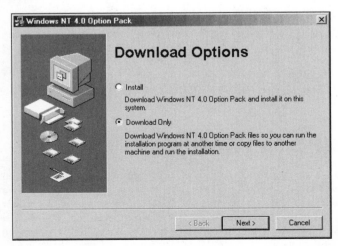

**3.** Choose to download only, as, if the install option quits halfway through, it can mess up your machine's configuration. After some initialization the Option Pack installation wizard will run.

**4.** The first screen of the wizard is a splash screen that describes the features that can be installed. Click Next and you'll be presented with the licensing agreement. If you agree with the licensing of the Windows NT 4.0 Option Pack, then click Accept and then Next. Now you'll be offered the three types of installation: Minimum, Typical and Custom:

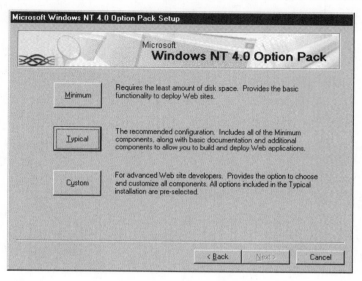

**5.** You need to perform a Custom installation, so click Custom and you will be presented with all the installation options:

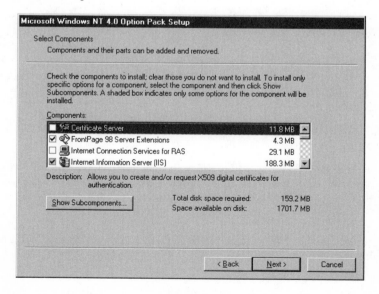

**6.** You do not want to install the FrontPage 98 Server Extensions, so uncheck the FrontPage 98 Server Extensions option.

At this point you should have as a minimum the following options **checked**:

❑ Internet Information Server (IIS)
❑ Microsoft Management Console
❑ NT Option Pack Common Files

**7.** Click Next to continue the installation, and you'll be presented with the folder locations for web and FTP publishing, and the folder location for the application files. The defaults are fine:

❑ The WWW service root is C:\Inetpub\wwwroot
❑ The FTP service root is C:\Inetpub\ftproot
❑ The application install directory is C:\Program Files

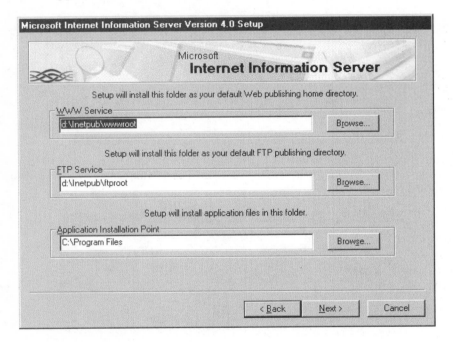

**8.** Click Next and the installation will proceed. It may take several minutes depending on the speed of your machine, but you'll be presented with a progress bar so that you can monitor the installation and estimate when it might complete.

**9.** Upon completion, click Finish to exit the installation and the Option Pack setup will finalize the settings. You'll be asked if you want to restart to complete the installation, so choose Yes and the computer will restart.

## Installing Internet Information Server 5.0 on Windows 2000

IIS 5.0 is located on the Windows 2000 installation CD, so you'll need access to this CD to install the server. Have it ready, but don't put it into the CD-ROM drive yet.

**1.** Go to the control panel (Start | Settings | Control Panel) and select the Add/Remove Programs icon. The following dialog will appear, displaying a list of your currently installed programs:

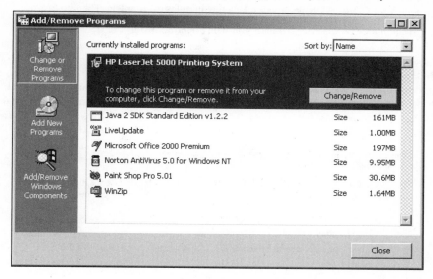

**2.** Select the Add/Remove Windows Components icon on the left side of the dialog, to get to the screen that allows you to install new Windows components.

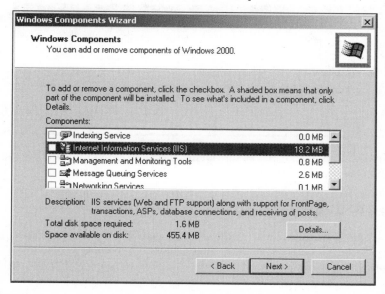

**3.** Locate the Internet Information Services (IIS) entry in the dialog, and note the check box that appears to its left. Unless you installed Windows 2000 Professional via a custom install and specifically requested IIS, it's most likely that the check box will be unchecked (as shown above). If you installed Windows 2000 Server, the chances are it is already checked.

    **a.** If the checkbox is *cleared*, then place a check in the check box and click on Next to install Internet Information Services 5.0. You should be prompted to place your Windows 2000 installation disk into your CD-ROM drive. It will take a few minutes to complete. Then go to Step 4.

    **b.** If the check box is *checked* then you won't need to install the IIS 5.0 component – it's already present on your machine. Go to Step 4.

**4.** Click on the Details button – this will take you to the dialog shown below. There are a few options here, for the installation of various optional bits of functionality. For example, if the World Wide Web Server option is checked then our IIS installation will be able to serve and manage web pages and applications. The Internet Information Server Snap-In is very desirable, as you'll see later in the chapter – so ensure that is checked too.

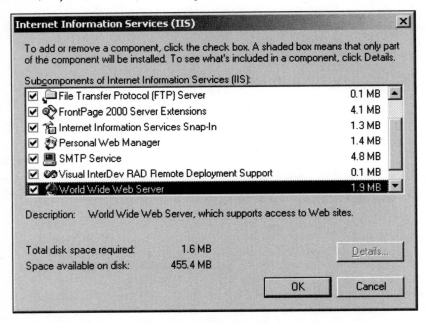

For the purposes of this installation, make sure all the check boxes in this dialog are checked; then click on OK to return to the previous dialog.

# Installing PHP4 Alongside IIS

If you've followed the instructions so far, you'll now find that IIS's Web Services start up automatically as soon as your installation is complete, and thereafter whenever you boot up Windows – so you don't need to run any further startup programs, or click on any short-cuts as you would to start up Word or Excel.

Now you need to download PHP4. While you would normally obtain the latest version of PHP4 from http://www.php.net/, unfortunately the version of PHP distributed by that site is only a basic installation, and doesn't support all the features we need. Instead, we recommend you go to http://php4win.de/, and download their latest, non-development, stable release. You'll end up with a ZIP file, which you should save somewhere on your hard drive. Create a folder for your PHP software to live in – somewhere like C:\php is good – and unzip the file you downloaded into this directory.

Now, this directory contains several sub-directories, and a few text files. It also contains a program file called php.exe, which we won't actually be using, and a library file called php4ts.dll. To start off, you need to copy this .dll to your C:\WINNT\System32 directory. Now open up the dlls subdirectory, and copy *all* of the files from here to your C:\WINNT\System32 directory as well. If Windows complains that you've already got a file by one or other of these names, then keep your old one – don't overwrite it with the newly downloaded files.

Now, back in the top of our PHP directory, there should be a file called php.ini. Copy this file to C:\WINNT, and open it up with Notepad. Scroll down the document until you find a line that looks like:

```
extension_dir = C:\php\extensions ; directory in which the loadable extensions
(modules) reside
```

Now, make sure that this path is the correct path to the extensions directory of the unzipped PHP4 installation. If it isn't, change it to point to the right place. (The extensions directory is the one which contains a large number of files whose names begin with php_ and end with .dll.

The next section tells PHP which extensions to load. You should put semi-colons at the beginning of all the lines which load extensions we don't need – the semi-colons mean that PHP will ignore the directive on that line. You can put semi-colons before all of them, except before extension=php_gd.dll, so that you have text like this:

```
;extension=php_filepro.dll
extension=php_gd.dll
;extension=php_dbm.dll
;extension=php_mssql.dll
```

This means you will have access to the functionality of the GD library, which allows us to generate images using PHP programs. We'll look at how in Chapter 16. You should now save your modified php.ini file.

Now you need to start up your Internet Services Manager. On Windows NT, you should find it under Windows NT 4.0 Option Pack in your Start menu. On Windows 2000, it will be under Start | Programs | Administrative Tools. The services manager is shown overleaf.

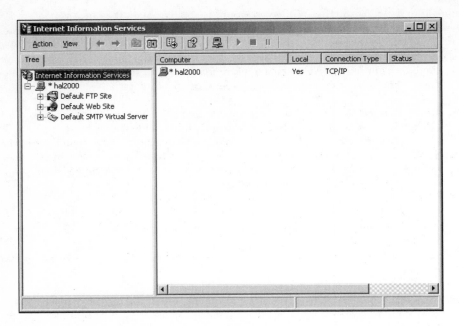

Right-click on Default Web Site, and bring up its Properties. There are two changes we need to make. First of all, we need to register the PHP4 ISAPI filter. Click on the ISAPI Filters tab. Click the Add button, and create a new filter called PHP. The folder of PHP files we downloaded contains a PHP ISAPI filter in the `sapi` directory, called `php4isapi.dll`. Put in the correct path for your `php4isapi.dll` file (if you've been following our instructions to the letter, it will be `C:\php\sapi\php4isapi.dll`).

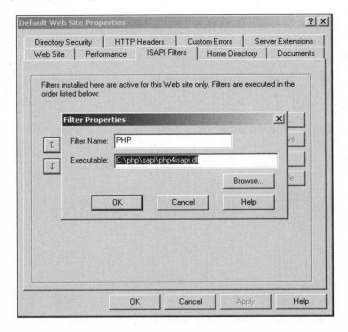

Next we need to tell IIS which files to apply the PHP4 filter to. We want it to treat all files that end .php as PHP programs. Go to the Home Directory tab, and click on Configuration.

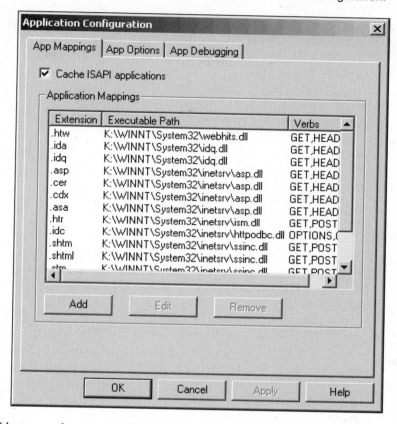

Click the Add button and, again specify the path to php4isapi.dll. Tell IIS to apply it to .php files, and click OK.

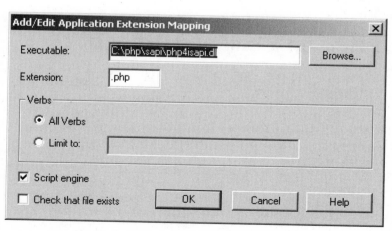

Now we need to completely restart IIS. The best way to completely shut down IIS and bring it up again is to bring up a command prompt, and enter the following commands:

```
> net stop iisadmin
The following services are dependent on the IIS Admin Service service.
Stopping the IIS Admin Service service will also stop these services.

   World Wide Web Publishing Service
   Simple Mail Transport Protocol (SMTP)
   FTP Publishing Service

Do you want to continue this operation? (Y/N) [N]: y
The World Wide Web Publishing Service service is stopping.
The World Wide Web Publishing Service service was stopped successfully.

The Simple Mail Transport Protocol (SMTP) service is stopping.
The Simple Mail Transport Protocol (SMTP) service was stopped successfully.

The FTP Publishing Service service is stopping.
The FTP Publishing Service service was stopped successfully.

The IIS Admin Service service is stopping...
The IIS Admin Service service was stopped successfully.


> net start w3svc
The World Wide Web Publishing Service service is starting....
The World Wide Web Publishing Service service was started successfully.


>
```

Provided the message at the end reports that the World Wide Web Publishing service was started successfully, you now have PHP4 installed. Remember your web site's root directory: it should be C:\Inetpub\wwwroot, if you've installed IIS exactly the way we showed you. You can proceed to the *Testing Your Installation* section later in the chapter.

# Installing PHP4 on Linux and Other UNIXes

Apache is the most popular web server in the world, so it's fitting that we're going to be installing PHP4 on UNIX onto an Apache system. First of all, though, we need to make sure we have some support libraries in place, then we can begin installing the server software.

The combination of Linux, Apache, MySQL and PHP is probably the most common production environment for running PHP web servers. This combination of open source software has been referred to by the acronym "LAMP", and if you run the same combination of software, you'll be able to benefit from the experiences of the many other people who've also used this setup. The PHP developers work very closely with the Apache and MySQL teams to ensure that advances in the three server systems are fully supported by the other components.

# Choosing Your Installation Method

As with other open source software, PHP and Apache give us the option of downloading the source code (which, in both cases, is written in the C programming language), and compiling the programs ourselves. If that sounds daunting (it's not actually as scary as it sounds), you can obtain pre-compiled versions in one of two forms. Binary downloads are pre-compiled versions of the software, which typically come with installation scripts to put all the required pieces into the necessary parts of our file system. Binary packages are available for systems which have a software package management system, like the Red Hat Package Manager (RPM) for Linux, and are the easiest to install. Here's a quick overview of the three methods:

| Installation Method | Advantages | Disadvantages |
| --- | --- | --- |
| Source | Most flexible solution for custom installations. Additional tests and examples are included in the source distribution. | Needs to be compiled. Slightly more difficult than the other options. Harder to remove once it's been done. |
| Binary (compiled) | No need to mess around with trying to compile the server. Takes less time to install. | Less flexible than doing an installation from source. |
| Binary RPMs | Fastest and easiest installation method. Very easy to uninstall or upgrade later. | Must be using an RPM based Linux distribution such as Red Hat. Least flexible installation method. |

In this chapter, we're going to explain how to obtain and install the components we need using RPMs.

*A number of popular Linux distributions use the Red Hat Package Manager, including Red Hat, SuSE, Mandrake, Definite, TurboLinux, Caldera and Yellow Dog. We'll be explaining how to install RPM packages throughout. If your system uses an alternative package management system, such as Debian's deb packages, refer to your distribution's manual for installation instructions.*

# Obtaining RPMs

The best place to get RPMs from is almost always the disks you installed your Linux system from. Red Hat 7 and SuSE 7 both include PHP4 (although it isn't installed by default) – by the time you read this, the same should be true of most current Linux distribution versions.

If your distribution doesn't include PHP4, or it doesn't include all the required functionality or support RPMs, then the next place to check is your distribution vendor's web site. They should have a download area or FTP site from which you can obtain the latest RPMs.

Finally, www.rpmfind.net provides a comprehensive search service for RPMs. Make sure that when you download RPMs, though, that they are compatible with your Linux distribution, and your computer hardware. Different distributions put important files in different places, and this can lead to RPMs from different vendors not working on other systems. Most RPMs are available compiled to run on the different hardware systems Linux supports. The following table shows the most common abbreviations used in RPM names:

| Abbreviation | Compatible with |
|---|---|
| i386 | PCs based on Intel and 100% compatible processors – Intel 80386, 486, Pentium, Pentium II, Pentium III, and Celeron, AMD 5x86, K-series and Athlon, Cyrix 6x86 |
| i586 | PCs based on Intel Pentium and 100% compatible processors – Intel Pentium II, III, Celeron, AMD K-Series and Athlon, Cyrix 6x86 |
| PPC | Computers built around Motorola PowerPC (and compatible) chips, such as Apple's Power Macs, G3s, G4s, and iMacs. You can still only use the RPMs on Macintosh hardware with Linux installed, though. |
| alpha | Servers and workstations running the Compaq Digital 64 bit Alpha processor |
| sparc | Servers and workstations running the processors which use the 64 bit SPARC architecture, such as Sun Microsystems' UltraSPARC. |
| m68k | Computers built around Motorola's older 68000 series processors, such as Amigas, and older Apple Macintoshes, for which various Linux ports exist. |

Refer to your distribution's manual if you want to use the graphical installation tools that come with your specific distribution. These differ widely, so we can't cover all of them here. However, any RPM based system can be controlled using the rpm command-line tool, so we will explain how to install the required components using this interface.

# Which Packages Do We Need?

The RPM packages you will need are:

- ❑ zlib
- ❑ libpng
- ❑ libjpeg
- ❑ gd
- ❑ gd-devel
- ❑ apache
- ❑ mod_php4

You can find out which of them are already installed on your system by typing the following at a command prompt, substituting in the name of each of these packages in turn:

```
> rpm -q zlib
zlib-1.1.3-6-i386
> rpm -q libpng
Package libpng is not installed
```

As you can see, if the package is installed, it gives us a random-looking string. If it isn't installed, we get a helpful error message. The random looking string actually tells us which version of the software we installed using the package (1.1.3 in this case), which release of the package this is (we have the sixth public release installed), and the architecture for which the RPM was compiled (Intel 386 compatible, which is just as well, since we've got this package installed on a Pentium III).

Note down which of the packages you have already got, and which versions they are (the version number is more important than the release number).

Only a few of our packages have to be of a minimum version. We need gd and gd-devel to be at least version 1.8 to provide support for the graphics formats we need. apache should be version 1.3.12 if you can get it, although 1.3.6 or newer should be fine. mod_php4, obviously, needs to be version four point something. The current version at time of going to press was 4.0.2.

You should now try to locate suitably up-to-date versions of all the packages which you don't have already, or have old versions for. As we suggested, try your install CDs, your distributor's web site, and www.rpmfind.net.

Having obtained sufficiently current versions of all the packages, you can install them. The command for upgrading an existing installation, or installing a package which has never been installed before, is exactly the same. Navigate your command prompt to the location of the files on CD, or the directory into which you downloaded the RPMs. As root, type:

```
> rpm -Uh libpng-1.0.5-3-i386.rpm
############################
```

Substituting in the name of the package file you downloaded for each package you need to upgrade or install. The line of # signs extends across the screen as each installation progresses.

If you install the packages in the order we listed them above, you should find that all the prerequisite files are installed in the necessary order.

# Configuring and Starting Apache with PHP4

The first thing to do is locate your Apache server's various files. The standard location for an Apache installation is /usr/local/apache. However, as we've noted before, some Linux distributors like to put files in different locations, so your Apache server may well not be there.

## Finding Apache

rpm provides a neat way of finding out what files a given package created on your system. You just need to type rpm -ql, followed by the name of the package you're interested in. Let's do that with Apache:

```
> rpm -ql apache
```

Okay, that generated a *long* list of files. We can find the ones we're looking for with a little UNIX shell magic. Let's find the location Apache uses to store its web site files:

```
> rpm -ql apache | grep /htdocs$
/usr/local/apache/htdocs
```

Obviously, the path returned may differ. For example, on a freshly installed SuSE 7 Linux system, the result is:

```
> rpm -ql apache | grep /htdocs$
/usr/local/httpd/htdocs
```

The `htdocs` directory is the web server's root directory. Note down this location, as you'll be needing it later. Now you'll need to locate Apache's configuration file. Use the following variation on the previous command:

```
> rpm -ql apache | grep /httpd.conf$
/usr/local/apache/conf/httpd.conf
```

Again, different systems will use different paths. Our SuSE 7 system does this:

```
> rpm -ql apache | grep /httpd.conf$
/etc/httpd/httpd.conf
```

## Gathering Information

Now, you'll need to know the **host name** of your machine. Normally it appears in your command prompt, which might be something like:

```
myhost:~#
root@myhost:~ >
```

or similar. In both of these, the host name is `myhost`. Alternatively, type the following command to find out what your computer thinks it's called:

```
> echo $HOSTNAME
myhost
```

## Configuring Apache

Now, armed with the host name, as the system's root user, you need to edit the `httpd.conf` file. Use a command like:

```
> kedit /usr/local/apache/conf/httpd.conf
```

or:

```
> gnp /usr/local/apache/conf/httpd.conf
```

to launch a KDE or GNOME based text editor respectively.

First, let's ensure that PHP4 is enabled on this Apache server. Look for a lot of lines that begin with the word `LoadModule`. In amongst them, after installing Apache with most RPM systems, you should find a line like:

```
LoadModule php4_module /usr/local/apache/lib/libphp4.so
```

If there isn't such a line, we'll need to add one. First, let's find out where the PHP RPM put our `libphp4.so` file:

```
> rpm -ql php | grep /libphp4.so$
/usr/local/apache/lib/libphp4.so
```

This information is going to be necessary to tell Apache how to run PHP scripts. Back in the Apache configuration file, `httpd.conf`, we need to add the instruction to load PHP4. Let's put it before any of the other `LoadModule` lines, using the path we obtained from the `rpm` command:

```
LoadModule php4_module /usr/local/apache/lib/libphp4.so
```

Now that Apache knows how to load PHP4, we need to activate it. There's a section further down the file consisting of a lot of lines beginning `AddModule`. We need to add the following to the *top* of it:

```
Addmodule mod_php4.c
```

Finally, now Apache knows what to do with a PHP program, we need to tell it how to recognize one. Further down the document, you'll find some directives that begin `AddType`. To the end of these, add the following line:

```
AddType application/x-httpd-php .php
```

This tells Apache that all files that end in `.php` are PHP programs. Finally, search back up the file for a line like:

```
#ServerName www.foo.com
```

and change it to the following, substituting your host name (which we looked up earlier) for the word `myhost`.

```
ServerName myhost
```

Save the file.

## Starting or Restarting Apache

Now, try typing this command (still as root) to get Apache working. We use a special controller program called `apachectl`:

```
> apachectl restart
```

If you get a `command not found` error, we need to find the `apachectl` program, again using a command like:

```
> rpm -ql apache | grep /apachectl$
/usr/local/apache/bin/apachectl
```

If that doesn't work, you might find a program called rcapache instead.

```
> rpm -ql apache | grep / rcapache $
/usr/sbin/rcapache
```

Use the full path of either of these programs in place of apachectl to restart Apache, with a command like one of these:

```
> /usr/local/apache/bin/apachectl restart
> /usr/sbin/rcapache restart
```

If all's well, Apache will start up, and you can move on to testing your installation.

# Testing Your Installation

Okay, now we've got PHP4 and our web server up and running, we can test our installation. Recall that we told you to remember your web server's root directory? This is where you'll need it. The root directory of a web server is the directory the web server looks in for files. For example, when you go to a web site and type in a URL like http://www.wrox.com/mypage.html the web server is going to look in its root directory for a file called mypage.html. If it finds such a file, it will then send the contents of that file back to you. Similarly, if you asked for http://www.wrox.com/somewhere/mypage.html, the web server looks in its root directory for a directory called somewhere, and then looks in this directory for a file called mypage.html. So, you might get the file /usr/local/apache/htdocs/somewhere/mypage.html if your request was served by an Apache server with a default configuration, or C:\Inetpub\wwwroot\somewhere\mypage.html if it was served by IIS or PWS.

We need to be aware of this because the web server applies the same logic to PHP programs. We save our PHP programs as files which end .php, in the directory structure under the web server's root directory – the same place it looks for web pages. So, for example, if we saved a file called myprogram.php in the www.wrox.com web server's root directory, that program would be run when we called up http://www.wrox.com/myprogram.php in our browser.

So what are we going to enter into our browser to call up PHP programs on our newly installed web server? As we said before, you can always access a web server from a browser running on the same machine. How? Well, from your computer's perspective, the name it uses to refer to itself is **localhost**. That's kind of the computer networking word for "me". So, if you type http://localhost/ into a web browser, the browser tries to connect to the computer it's running on. Normally, that doesn't work, because most computers aren't running web server software. But since we've just installed a web server, we should find that connecting to http://localhost/ brings up a standard holding page put there by the web server to let us know it's there.

If your computer is attached to a network then you'll find it probably has a name on the local network as well. You can use this name to refer to your computer from the web browser of other connected machines. If you're not sure of its name, try using the following commands at a command prompt on the web server machine:

On Windows:

```
> echo %COMPUTERNAME%
```

On UNIX:

```
> echo $HOSTNAME
```

Try using this name in a web browser on a networked machine, and you should see the same web page you got when you connected to localhost. For example, if your machine name was mycomputer, you could type http://mycomputer/ into a web browser, and hopefully find yourself viewing web pages served from your newly installed web server.

> Note that IIS provides a different page by default for users connecting from the same computer as the web server than it does for people who connect from networked computers.

Now, we're ready to write our first PHP program, and test it out.

## Try it Out – Is Our PHP4-Powered Web Server Working?

**1.** Open up a text editor – any program which creates plain text files will do. Notepad is ideal on Windows; you could use vi or emacs on a UNIX machine, if you're used to either of their interfaces. Alternatively, most Linux distributions come with a selection of good quality graphical text editors. Try Gnotepad+, which comes with GNOME (type gnp at a command prompt), or KEdit, which comes with KDE (kedit at the command prompt).

**2.** Enter the following text, *exactly* as it appears here, into a blank text file.

```
<?php
phpinfo();
?>
```

**3.** Save the file in your web server's root directory as phpinfo.php. If the editor you have chosen gives you any choice as to which format to save in, make sure you choose plain text.

> If you're using Notepad on Windows, you need to watch out for an annoying habit it has of putting .txt onto the end of the name of any files you save. The easiest way to stop it from doing this is to remember, when saving files in Notepad, to select **All files** from the **Save as type** pull-down menu (below the file listing in the save dialog), before entering the filename you want to save the file as, with .php on the end.

**4.** Double check that you've saved the file in the right place, with the right name. It should be in your web server's root directory (normally C:\Inetpub\wwwroot or /usr/local/apache/htdocs/) and that it really is called phpinfo.php. In Windows, you might want to uncheck **Hide file extensions for known file types** in the **View** tab of the Explorer window's **Folder Options...** dialog, since this sometimes prevents you from seeing the exact name files are saved as in Explorer (and elsewhere in Windows).

**5.** We're ready to connect to our web server. Bring up your web browser on the web server machine, and type in http://localhost/phpinfo.php to its address bar. As we've said, that should make the browser connect to the web server, and the web server look in the default directory for a program called phpinfo.php. If all goes to plan, you should soon see the following screen in your browser.

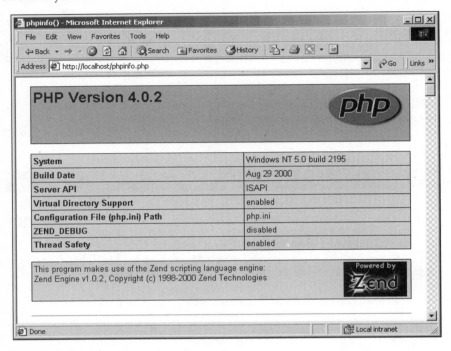

If so, congratulations – PHP4 is up and running on your web server. You're now ready to move on to the rest of the book. If not, then you shouldn't panic.

- ❏ Go back and double-check that you followed the instructions correctly. It's easy enough to miss out one crucial step.

- ❏ Try to narrow down the problem to work out what the cause is. Is it your web server? Is PHP set up correctly? Is there a problem with the file?

- ❏ If you're having trouble following the instructions we've given here, then you can e-mail Wrox's book support staff on support@wrox.com. Unfortunately, due to the vast number of possible system configurations PHP4 can run on, we aren't necessarily able to offer support if you aren't setting up the basic system we cover here in the book. Instead, you should...

- ❏ Take a look at the archives of the moderated PHP mailing lists at http://p2p.wrox.com/, to see if anyone else has encountered your problem, using your particular set up. If not, sign up and post a question to the developer community. There's a good chance someone out there will have some idea of how to fix your problem.

- ❏ Above all, don't give up. PHP4 is sometimes tricky to get up and running, but it's worth persevering.

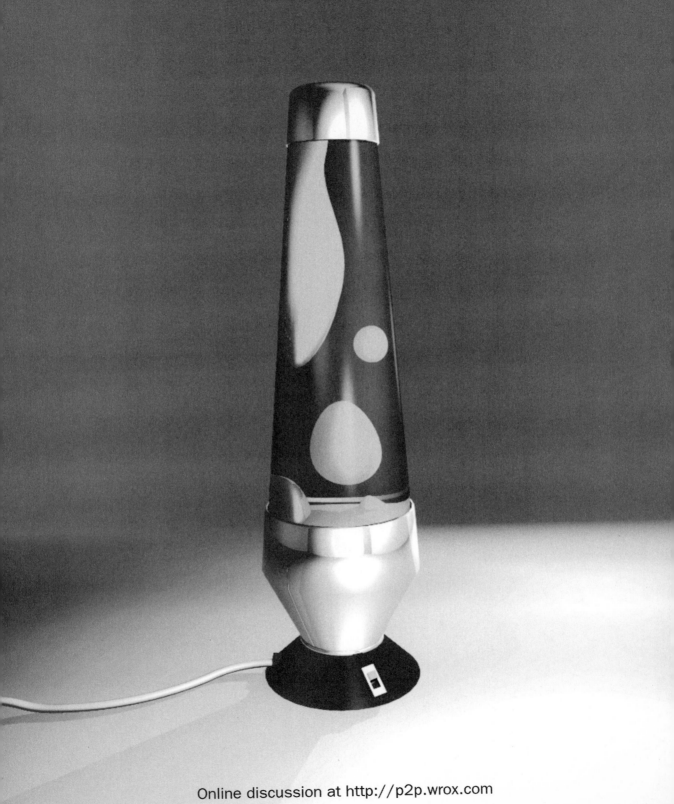

# Writing PHP Programs

In the first chapter, we introduced PHP and went through the decidedly non-trivial process of installing it on your web server, and getting PHP itself up and running. What we didn't do in any detail is look at an example of PHP code in action, other than to test that our installation was functioning correctly. The first thing that we will look at in this chapter is how to write a very basic PHP page and get it functioning on our web server, while answering questions about how it works and what the code is doing. Once we've worked through this, we'll examine the role of the web server and find out, in greater detail, how PHP actually works.

Once we've established, at a fairly basic level, what goes on under the hood of PHP, we will take a look at some of the principal building blocks of the language, and how we can use PHP to store information in our web pages. Every programming language requires a mechanism for storing information and attaching it to an identifier, which you can then reference for later use. For example, how do you store dates, such as a set of people's birthdays? How can you come back to that list and know which date matches which birthday? This is done in PHP, and in most programming languages, by using the concept of variables. The final part of the chapter will be spent looking at variables and how we can use them to perform mathematical operations, or simple manipulations of text.

The itinerary for this chapter is:

- ❑ Write and examine a very short PHP program
- ❑ Discuss some of the Internet Protocols
- ❑ Talk about the role of the PHP engine and the web server
- ❑ Define what we mean by interpretation and execution
- ❑ Variables – what are they?
- ❑ Data Types – we will discuss the different data types that variables can have
- ❑ Operations you can perform on variables
- ❑ Constants
- ❑ Converting variables from one data type to another
- ❑ Environment variables

# An Example PHP Program

This chapter starts with almost the simplest one line example possible – we aim to demonstrate that PHP pages are a mixtures of three things, namely text, HTML code, and PHP script. Pages containing PHP script are different from pages that contain only HTML, and in order to identify them to the PHP engine, they are saved with the `.php` suffix (or something similar) on the web server and are executed by the PHP engine running on the server.

> *The* `.php` *suffix is something that is dependent on your particular configuration of PHP. If you wanted to, when setting up PHP, you could change it to almost anything, even something like* `.groovysuffix`. *In this book we will be using the suffix* `.php` *in lower case only.*

The results of this are returned to the browser in HTML. We'll see more on this shortly, but let's get started on an example.

## Try It Out – First Example Program

**1.** Open your web page editor of choice and type the following in:

```
<HTML>
<BODY>
The date at the moment is
<?php echo gmdate("M d Y");
?>
</BODY>
</HTML>
```

**2.** Save this as `example1.php` in the document root (on UNIX systems) or root directory (on Windows systems) of your web server.

**3.** Next, open up your browser of choice, type in the full URL of your web server and web page, mine would be `http://chrisu/example1.php`. You should see something similar to the following in Navigator 6:

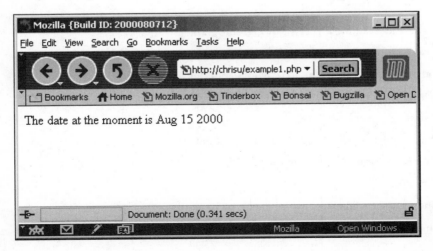

## The Different Types of Code

As we said before this example, we are aiming first and foremost to demonstrate the three different types of code used on this page. So let's look at the code we just typed in, and assign it into each of the three categories:

```
<HTML>
<BODY>
The date at the moment is
<?php echo gmdate("M d Y");
?>
</BODY>
</HTML>
```

The code with the clear background isn't really code at all; it's just plain **text**. There's really nothing more to say about it.

The code with the light gray background is **HTML markup**. Markup of any type is easy to spot because it's denoted by opening and closing angled brackets known as **tags**. It isn't really programming code in the traditional sense, as you will see, hence we will use the term markup to describe our HTML tags. You should be familiar with HTML so we're not going to discuss it much further here.

One thing to note though is that we're going to capitalize the HTML tags throughout this book, despite the fact that strictly speaking it's against the standards (the HTML 4.0 standard suggests that all HTML tags should be in lower case). The reason for this is that we don't want to continue using the awkward color scheme shown above throughout the book, and all browsers are case-insensitive (they don't care whether the tags are in upper or lower case) anyway.

*Bright sparks who know about XHTML, will know that this language is a rendering of the HTML 4.01 standard (the most recent standard in XML), and will also probably know that XHTML is intolerant of a lot of aspects of HTML that browsers tend to ignore. What this means is that XHTML will not allow you to get away with using obsolete tags, or without closing tags properly, and it also requires HTML to be in lower case. As yet, there are no XHTML-only browsers in mainstream use, so for this reason we're not going to worry about the upper case.*

The code with the dark gray background is **PHP script**. The PHP script denoted by angled brackets, and question marks as well. So, anytime you see a portion of code that starts with < ?php and ?> tags you know that everything inside must be PHP script.

As you can see from the results output to the browser, the three types of content quite happily co-exist in the web page, despite the fact that the PHP script must be processed by the web server (which may be on a different machine from your browser).

## How the Code Works

Having established the nature of the different types of code on the page, we've so far neglected to explain what the one line of PHP code in the program does. So let's rectify that now – the only actual PHP script in the page was the following:

```
echo gmdate("M d Y");
```

Three things are going on here. Firstly, the word `echo()` is a PHP command, which takes whatever is fed into it and displays it on the web page. So if we had the line:

```
echo "Hello world";
```

you would see the words Hello world on the screen when you browsed that web page. However, you may have noticed that in our example the date appeared on the screen, yet we only fed the **function** `gmdate("M d Y")` to the `echo()` command – this is the second thing that is going on, and we'll look at it in a moment.

> **PHP has a large library of these reserved words, known as functions, and they perform popular tasks such as returning the date or time, sending e-mail, executing some of the more complex mathematical operations, or pausing the execution of a script for a few seconds. There is a list of all the functions in Appendix D. You don't need to know these off by heart, but you will find that time and time again throughout the book we will be making use of them.**

The final issue is the semi-colon; PHP requires that every line of code (there are one or two exceptions to this rule as we shall see), when completed, should be terminated with a semi-colon to denote where that particular line ends.

You might have noticed that the word `gmdate()` wasn't enclosed by quotation marks. In our "Hello world" example, by enclosing the text we want to display in quotation marks, we are telling the PHP engine that we want to display everything between the quotation marks exactly as written. In our case, when we don't include quotation marks, we are telling the engine to use a special function of PHP's called `gmdate()` to run an operation for us. The function retrieves today's date and time in Greenwich Mean Time. Let's discuss how `gmdate()` works in greater detail.

You may have noticed that in our example we displayed the date as follows:

Aug 15 2000

However, there are many different formats for displaying today's date. For example, you could have:

15/8/00 09-30AM

or

Tuesday 15th August

These are both valid formats of today's date, yet PHP has no idea which version you want it to use, or whether you want it to use an entirely different version altogether. So, you need to tell it what to do, and that's exactly what the section in parentheses and quotation marks after `gmdate()` does. We specify that we want the month first, followed by the day and then the year. The fact that we use upper case and lower case D's, M's, and Y's is also significant. PHP attaches different meanings to each as shown in the table that follows:

| Option | Result |
|--------|--------|
| a | Displays "am" or "pm". |
| A | Displays "AM" or "PM". |
| d | Gives the day of the month, 2 digits with leading zeros; that is, "01" to "31". |
| D | Shows day of the week, textual, 3 letters; for example, "Fri". |
| F | Displays month, textual, long; for example, "January". |
| h | Shows the hour, 12-hour format; that is, "01" to "12". |
| H | Shows the hour, 24-hour format; that is, "00" to "23". |
| g | Shows the hour, 12-hour format without leading zeros; that is, "1" to "12". |
| G | Shows the hour, 24-hour format without leading zeros; that is, "0" to "23". |
| i | Displays the minutes; that is, "00" to "59". |
| j | Gives the day of the month without leading zeros; that is, "1" to "31". |
| l | Gives the day of the week, textual, long; for example, "Friday". |
| L | Boolean for whether it is a leap year; that is, "0" or "1". |
| m | Shows the month; that is, "01" to "12". |
| n | Shows the month without leading zeros; that is, "1" to "12". |
| M | Gives the month, textual, 3 letters; that for example, "Jan". |
| s | Displays the seconds; that is, "00" to "59". |
| S | English ordinal suffix, textual, 2 characters; for example, "th", "nd". |
| t | The number of days in the given month; that is, "28" to "31". |
| T | Timezone setting of this machine; for example, "MDT". |
| U | Displays the seconds since the epoch. |
| w | Shows the day of the week, numeric, that is, "0" (Sunday) to "6" (Saturday). |
| Y | Displays the year, 4 digits; for example, "1999". |
| y | Displays the year, 2 digits; for example, "99". |
| z | Shows the day of the year; that is, "0" to "365". |
| Z | Gives the timezone offset in seconds (that is, "-43200" to "43200"). |

As you can see, this is quite a comprehensive list. Once again, we're not going to reproduce a table every time we want to outline the workings of a new PHP function, so you will need to refer to the appendices. Equally, we could have changed our previous example to:

```
echo gmDate("D");
```

This would display:

Tue

Alternatively, we could have changed it to:

```
echo gmDate("d m Y");
```

We leave this last example as an exercise to the reader to workout what will be displayed. Now we have a better understanding of what the code is actually doing, we can move on...

# Viewing a Web Page

Let's step back from our example, and take an overhead view of what's going on with our web page between writing it and viewing it. When we installed PHP in Chapter 1, the installation was broken down into stages because we installed several different pieces of software.

One of these pieces of software was the web server, which makes your web pages available to all and sundry. Another job of the web server is to provide an area (typically in a directory or folder structure) in which to organize and store your web pages or whole web site. There are many commercial and freeware web servers available, but two companies' web servers predominate and take up over 70% of the market. The two products are Apache's web server and Microsoft's Internet Information Server. We will assume that you are using one of these two web servers to perform the task of making your web pages available.

When you use the Web to view a web page, you will automatically be making contact with a web server. The process of submitting your URL is called as making a **request** to the server. The server interprets the URL, locates the corresponding page, and sends back the page as part of what is called the **response** to the browser. The browser then takes the code it has received from the web server and compiles a viewable page from it. The browser is referred to as a **client** in this interaction, and the whole interaction as a **client-server relationship**.

# Client-Server

This term describes effectively the workings of the web by outlining the distribution of tasks. The server (the web server) stores, interprets, and distributes data, and the client (browser) accesses the server to get at the data. From now on whenever we use the term client, we are just referring to the browser. As you'll come to see in later chapters, the term client-server is an oversimplification of the process – it's quite an abstract description of a physical process. To understand what is going on in greater detail, we need to briefly discuss the workings of the Internet itself.

## Internet Protocols

We won't go through the entire history of the Internet here; the important point is that it is a network of interconnected nodes. The Internet is designed to carry *information* from one place to another. It uses a suite of networking protocols (known as **TCP/IP**) to transfer information around the network.

> *A **networking protocol** is simply a method of describing information packets so that they can be sent down your telephone-, cable-, or T1-line from node to node, until they reach their intended destination.*

One advantage of the TCP/IP protocol is that it can re-route information very quickly if a particular node or route is broken or slow. When the user tells the browser to fetch a web page, the browser parcels up this instruction using a protocol called the **Transmission Control Protocol** (or **TCP**). TCP is a transport protocol, which provides a reliable transmission format for the instruction. It ensures that the entire message is packaged up correctly for transmission (and also that it is correctly unpacked and put back together after it reaches its destination). The networking protocol TCP/IP is a method of describing your information packets so that they can be sent down a telephone line, cable, or T1-line from node to node.

Before the parcels of data are sent out across the network, they need to be addressed. So a second protocol called **HyperText Transfer Protocol** (or **HTTP**) puts an address label on it, so that TCP/IP knows where to direct the information. HTTP is the protocol used by the World Wide Web in the transfer of information from one machine to another – when you see a URL prefixed with `http://`, you know that the internet protocol being used is HTTP. You can think of TCP/IP as the postal service that does the routing and transfer, while HTTP is the stamp and address on the letter (data) to ensure it gets there.

The message passed from the browser to the web server is known as an **HTTP request**. When the web server receives this request, it checks its stores to find the appropriate page. If the web server finds the page, it parcels up the HTML contained within (using TCP), addresses these parcels to the browser (using HTTP), and sends them back across the network. If the web server cannot find the requested page, it issues a page containing an error message (in this case, the dreaded Error 404: Page Not Found) – and it parcels up and dispatches that page to the browser. The message sent from the web server to the browser is called the **HTTP response**.

Here's an illustration of the process as we understand it so far:

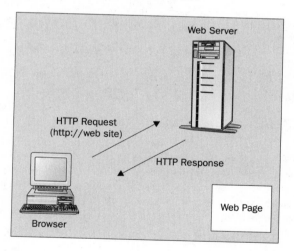

## The HTTP Protocol

There is still quite a lot of technical detail missing here, so let's dig further down and look more closely at exactly how HTTP works. When a request for a web page is sent to the server, this request contains more than just the desired URL. There is a lot of extra information that is sent as part of the request. This is also true of the response – the server sends extra information back to the browser. It's these different types of information that we'll look at in this next section.

A lot of the information that is passed within the HTTP message is generated automatically, and the user doesn't have to deal with it directly, so you don't need to worry about transmitting such information yourself. While you don't have to worry about creating this information yourself, you should be aware that this extra information is being passed between machines as part of the HTTP request and HTTP response – because the PHP script that we write can allow us to have a direct effect on the exact content of this information.

Every HTTP message assumes the same format (whether it's a client request or a server response). We can break this format down into three sections: the **request/response line**, the **HTTP header**, and the **HTTP body**. The content of these three sections is dependent on whether the message is an HTTP request or HTTP response – so we'll take these two cases separately.

Let's just pause and illustrate our understanding of the process now:

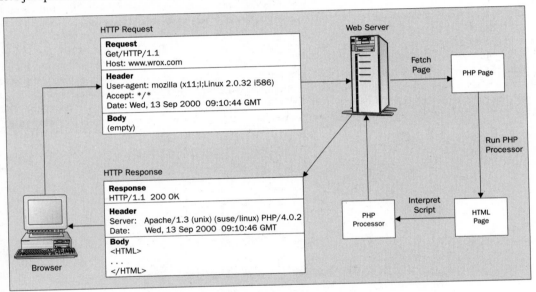

We can see that the HTTP request and HTTP response have broadly similar structures, and that there is information common to both that is sent as part of the HTTP header. There are other pieces of information that can only be known to either the browser or the server, and are only sent as part of either the request or response, so it makes sense to examine their constituent parts in greater detail.

## The HTTP Request

The browser sends the HTTP request to the web server and it contains the following:

### The Request Line

The first line of every HTTP request is the **request line**, which contains three pieces of information:

- ❏   An HTTP command known as a **method**
- ❏   The path from the server to the resource that the client is requesting
- ❏   The version number of HTTP.

So, an example request line might look like this:

```
GET /testpage.htm HTTP/1.1
```

The method is used to tell the server how to handle the request. Here are three of the most common methods that might appear in this field:

| Method | Description |
| --- | --- |
| GET | This is a request for information residing at a particular URL. The majority of HTTP requests made on the Internet are GET requests. The information required by the request can be anything from an HTML or PHP page, to the output of a JavaScript or PerlScript program, or some other executable. You can send some limited data to the browser, in the form of an extension to the URL. |
| HEAD | This is the same as the GET method, except that it indicates a request for the HTTP header only and no data. |
| POST | This request indicates that data will be sent to the server as part of the HTTP body. This data is then transferred to a data-handling program on the web server. |

There are a number of other methods supported by HTTP – including PUT, DELETE, TRACE, CONNECT, and OPTIONS. As a rule, you'll find that these are less common; they are therefore beyond the scope of this discussion. If you want to know more about these, take a look at RFC 2068, which you can find at http://www.rfc.net.

### The HTTP Header

The next bit of information sent is the HTTP **header**. This contains details of what document types the client will accept back from the server, like the type of browser that has requested the page, the date, and general configuration information. The HTTP request's header contains information that falls into three different categories:

❑ **General**: contains information about either the client or server, but not specific to one or the other

❑ **Entity**: contains information about the data being sent between the client and server

❑ **Request**: contains information about the client configuration and different types of acceptable documents

An example HTTP header might look like this:

```
Accept: */*
Accept-Language: en-us
Connection: Keep-Alive
Host: www.wrox.com
Referer: http://webdev.wrox.co.uk/books/SampleList.php?bookcode=3730
User-Agent: Mozilla (X11; I; Linux 2.0.32 i586)
```

As you can see, the HTTP header is composed of a number of lines; each line contains the description of a piece of HTTP header information, and its value.

There are many different lines that can comprise a HTTP header, and most of them are optional, so HTTP has to indicate when it has finished transmitting the header information. To do this, a blank line is used. In HTTP 1.1, a request must comprise of at least a request line and a HOST header.

### The HTTP Body

If the `POST` method was used in the HTTP request line, then the HTTP request **body** will contain any data that is being sent to the server – for example, data that the user typed into an HTML form (we'll see examples of this later in the book). Otherwise, the HTTP request body will be empty.

## The HTTP Response

The HTTP response is sent by the server back to the client browser, and contains the following.

### The Response Line

The **response line** contains only two bits of information:

❑ The HTTP version number

❑ An HTTP request code that reports the success or failure of the request

An example response line might look like this:

```
HTTP/1.1 200 OK
```

This example returns the HTTP status code 200, which represents the message "OK". This denotes the success of the request, and that the response contains the required page or data from the server. You may recall that we mentioned the status code 404 a few pages ago – if the response line contains a 404 then the web server failed to find the requested resource. Error code values are three-digit numbers, where the first digit indicates the class of the response. There are five classes of response:

| Code class | Description |
|------------|-------------|
| 100-199 | These codes are informational – they indicate that the request is currently being processed. |
| 200-299 | These codes denote success – that the web server received and carried out the request successfully. |
| 300-399 | These codes indicate that the request hasn't been performed, because the information required has been moved. |
| 400-499 | These codes denote a client error – that the request was incomplete, incorrect, or impossible. |
| 500-599 | These codes denote a server error – that the request appeared to be valid, but that the server failed to carry it out. |

### The HTTP Header

The HTTP response **header** is similar to the request header, which we discussed above. In the HTTP response, the header information again falls into three types:

❑ **General**: contains information about either the client or server, but not specific to one or the other

❑ **Entity**: contains information about the data being sent between the client and the server

❑ **Response**: contains information about the server sending the response and how it can deal with the response

Once again, the header consists of a number of lines, and uses a blank line to indicate that the header information is complete. Here's a sample of what a header might look like, and the name of each line down the side:

```
HTTP/1.1 200 OK
Date: Mon, 1st Nov 1999, 16:12:23 GMT
Server: Apache/1.3.12 (Unix) (SUSE/Linux) PHP/4.0.2
Last-modified: Fri, 29th Oct 1999, 12:08:03 GMT
```

– the status line
– the general header
– the response header
– the entity header

The first line we've already discussed, the second is self-explanatory. On the third line, "Server", indicates the type of software the web server is running, and as we are requesting a file somewhere on the web server, the last bit of information refers to the last time the page we are requesting was modified.

*The header can contain much more information than this, or different information, depending on what is requested. If you want to know more about the different types of information contained in the three parts of the header, you'll find them listed in RFC 2068 (Sections 4.5, 7.1 and 7.2).*

### The HTTP Body

If the request was successful, then the HTTP response **body** contains the HTML code (together with any script that is to be executed by the browser), ready for the browser's interpretation.

# Where PHP Comes Into This

So now we have a better understanding of how a browser sends a web page request, and how the web server sends the page back to the browser. Let's sum up the 6-step process for delivering a web page:

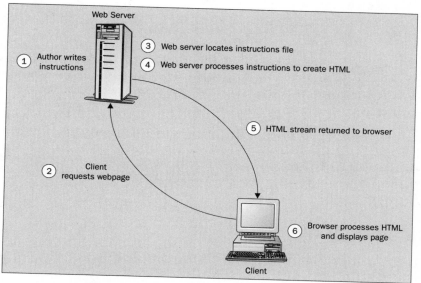

The web server needs to locate the page that was requested (Step 3); and, if it's a PHP page, then the web server will need to process the PHP, in order to generate the HTML that is returned to the browser (Step 4). At this stage, if the name of the web page is suffixed with .php, the server sends it to the PHP script engine (which is attached to the web server) for processing.

Well, we've studied many of the necessary aspects surrounding PHP, but our understanding of the PHP processing itself is still rather sketchy. Up to now, for simplification, we've discussed as though the PHP script engine were like a sausage machine – the web server feeds in the raw PHP code (meat) at one end, and out comes a neatly packaged pure HTML page – it's time to demystify this process.

We mentioned earlier in this chapter that PHP pages are divided into text, HTML markup, and PHP script. The nuggets of programming capability embedded within our HTML are referred to as **scripts**. As HTML can't really be described as a programming language, and has limited capabilities outside displaying static text and images, it becomes necessary to write commands in other languages to add extra features. We use the term **scripting language** to describe the languages in which these extra features are written. There are many scripting languages, and you are probably familiar with some of them such as JavaScript. However, what makes PHP different to JavaScript, or just plain HTML, is the fact that it is executed on the server, not the browser.

HTML allows us to include scripts at (almost) any point in our HTML code – it does this by providing us with legal ways of inserting scripts, which we'll come to shortly. So, when the page has been requested and its HTML is being generated, each script within the page is sent to a **script engine** for interpretation, and to generate the equivalent HTML.

Script is the basis of PHP! We use script to write the instructions that allow pages to be created dynamically. There are a lot of advantages to generating a page dynamically; you can return information to the user based on their responses in a form, you can customize web pages for a particular browser, you can personalize information, and utilize a particular profile for each individual, and, much more beyond the static text and you can generate graphics that pure HTML returns. This is all down to the fact that script we write must be interpreted at the time it is requested.

### The Concepts of Parsing and Execution (A Quick Digression)

The interpretation of your PHP script can be split into two sub-processes. When a web page is sent to the PHP engine, two things happen. The PHP script is first checked for correctness in a process known as **parsing**. This is the equivalent of having your sentences checked for grammar and spelling mistakes. This doesn't ensure that the PHP script is correct, it just checks the script to see if it conforms to a set of predefined rules. The second process called **execution** takes place once a script has been parsed. This is where you find out if your script makes sense. Execution is the process of taking a single line of PHP script and turning it into the equivalent HTML. It is done in a linear fashion unless otherwise directed in the PHP script.

There are two places that the PHP engine can return errors, during parsing and during execution. If this happens the errors will be returned to the browser. If not, a dynamically created HTML page will be returned to the browser.

## Server-Side Scripting

What difference does the introduction of scripts make to the way the page is processed? For the most part, our model of the browser making a connection to the web server, sending a request, receiving a response, and then interpreting the received HTML to construct a web page still holds true.

The only difference comes when, in the act of preparing a page to be sent to the browser, the server comes across a script. The first thing the server must do is identify the machine responsible for processing the script. This is an important point because, when we write a script, we can choose whether it is to be processed by the server or by the browser. Let's make this difference more precise:

❑ A script that is interpreted by the web server is called a **server-side script**. A server-side script is an instruction set that is processed by the server, and generates HTML. The resulting HTML is sent as part of the HTTP response to the browser. The browser lays out the HTML and displays it accordingly.

❑ A pure HTML page is interpreted by the browser. HTML is *not* processed by the web server. Instead, it is sent to the browser (as part of the HTTP response) and is processed by the browser; the result is then displayed by the browser.

## Identifying a PHP Script

We've just been talking about how the web server identifies on which machine a script must be processed. But, how do we identify a script when it is embedded in a small or large amount of pure HTML? In fact, we have already answered this question earlier this chapter – PHP (which is destined to be processed on the web server) is enclosed in special `<?php ... ?>` tags, like this:

```
The number of days since the beginning of the year is:
<?php echo gmDate("z"); ?>
```

Here, everything contained within the `<?php` and the `?>` is assumed to be PHP, and is sent to the PHP script engine for processing. So, in our example, once the PHP is processed it is returned to the browser as HTML, and indeed if you look on your browser's View Source option you should see that your program has been returned to you in pure HTML:

```
<HTML>
<BODY>
The number of days since the beginning of the year is:
263</HTML>
```

In this way, you can see that the traditional problem of browser reliance is bypassed. In particular, features such as components embedded with the `<OBJECT>` tag would only function on Internet Explorer. Also, new features such as style sheets were dependent on a particular browser's capabilities and rendering, for instance IE3 barely supported style sheets; IE4 did to a large extent, while IE5 supported them completely.

PHP is most categorically not like this – you're not reliant on the browser understanding PHP, as the browser only ever needs to understand HTML. The only browser issue which affects you is how well the browser supports different HTML features, and if you're using an up-to-date version of Netscape Navigator, Internet Explorer, or Opera, then this won't be a problem.

# Caching

Before we get into looking at how you actually program in PHP, this is a good time to mention the existence of an item on the browser known as a **cache**. You may already be aware of this item; it stores web pages that have already been viewed. To speed up the process of viewing pages, the browser will drag up the old version of the page. The location of the cache on your machine varies according to two different things – the type of browser that you're using, and the platform you are browsing on.

On Windows (98/NT and 2000), you'll typically find your cache for Netscape Navigator under something like `C:\Program Files\Netscape\Users\Cache`. On Internet Explorer it resides in the `Temporary Internet Files` folder which resides under Windows or WinNT in Windows 98 and NT 4.0 respectively, or in Windows 2000 under the `Documents and Settings` folder with a separate version of the cache for each user profile on the machine.

In Linux you can find it under `~/.netscape/cache` (where ~ represents the home directory).

When you're relying on the PHP engine on the server to do processing of pages before you, the existence of caching becomes significant. If you're using cached results from a previous execution of the page, then you won't be using the dynamic code at all, and the information returned will be incorrect. You will notice this if you try and use the browser's back button to backtrack through a series of old PHP pages. Sometimes even pressing the refresh button isn't enough, as even then the cache isn't refreshed and the page isn't properly reloaded because the browser doesn't think that the page is out of date. In this event, to force a refresh on Internet Explorer 5 you should press *CTRL+F5* together, while on Netscape Navigator you should hold down the *Shift* key and click on Reload.

This is important because if you run an example, you might get the same set of results from a previous execution of the example, if the browser is using the cached version of the page. You must then ensure the browser gets a new page by refreshing it (or by altering the browser's settings) if you are in any doubt.

> *There is also a set of HTTP headers that can be used to prevent a web page from being cached. The following 3 lines of PHP code (if used at the **beginning** of a PHP script) prevent Explorer or Navigator from caching a page; users should use them to prevent undesired results, or the tiring process of refreshing the document "n" times.*

```
<?
header("Cache-Control: no-cache, must-revalidate");
header("Pragma: no-cache");
header("Expires: Mon,26 Jul 1997 05:00:00 GMT");
?>
```

# Variables

Having looked at how to insert PHP script into your web pages, and how the web server treats the pages once it receives them, it's time to start looking at the various parts of the language you will need to know about in order to program in PHP. Perhaps the most basic unit of currency in programming is the **variable**. A variable is most simply explained as an area of memory set aside to store information, and it is assigned a particular identifier by the programmer. In PHP all variables begin with a dollar ' $ ' sign. To assign a value to a variable, you use the equals sign or assignment ' = ' operator. So to create a variable in PHP and assign it a value you can do the following:

```
$author = "William Shakespeare";
```

The variable identifier is `$author` and it has been assigned the text value William Shakespeare. You can also assign numbers to variables.

```
$number_of_digits_on_one_hand = 5;
```

Here we have a rather convoluted variable name `$number_of_digits_on_one_hand`, but apart from that it's not much different to the assignation we made before. The difference is that the numeric value now has no quotation marks surrounding it. This tells PHP that it should be treated as a numeric value; no further intervention is required on the part of the user to tell PHP to treat the value as a number.

Once you've created a variable, you're free to use it within your program however you like. To display it on the screen using our old friend the `echo()` command, you'd do the following:

```
echo $author;
```

### Limitations on Variable Naming

There are a few limits on what you can and can't call your variables. In many languages there is a limit on size of the variable name, typically such as 255 characters or 1000 characters; PHP, however, has no such limit. You'll probably find though that you never need to go beyond 50 characters, and 20-30 is ample for most people.

The first actual limit is that all variable names must start with a letter or underscore (ignoring the dollar sign, which isn't strictly part of the variable name). The second is that the variable name must be made up out of a selection of numbers, letters, and underscores. Other characters such as +, -, *, and & aren't allowed and will cause an error in your web page. Apart from that you're pretty much free to name variables as you please. However, we will be looking at a sensible naming convention for variables later in this chapter.

### Case-Sensitivity in Variable Names

Variables aren't quite as straightforward as they first appear. One problem that often snares the newcomer in PHP is that of case-sensitive variable names. The easiest way to explain this is with a quick bit of code:

```
$author = "William Shakespeare";
$Author = "James Joyce";
```

The above two lines of code actually create two separate variables, one called `$author` and another called `$Author`. These two variables have the two different values and are really as different as if you'd used the following code:

```
$famous_english_author = "William Shakespeare";
$famous_irish_author = "James Joyce";
```

Quite often it impacts on the final output of the results on a web page if you unintentionally use a capital letter where you haven't been using one before. If you did intend to only use one variable, then following code should have been used:

```
$author = "William Shakespeare";
$author = "James Joyce";
```

The first line would set the contents of `$author` to William Shakespeare, while the second line would completely alter the contents of `$author` to the text James Joyce. Only one variable would be created and used by this section of code.

Now let's have a look at a quick example which creates a variable and then displays the contents of the variable on the web page.

## Try It Out – Assigning a Value to a Variable and Displaying It

**1.** Open up your text editor of choice and type in the following:

```
<HTML>
<BODY>

<?php
$actor = "Marlon Brando";
echo $actor;
?>
</BODY>
</HTML>
```

**2.** Save this code as `variable.php`.

**3.** Open up this page on your browser.

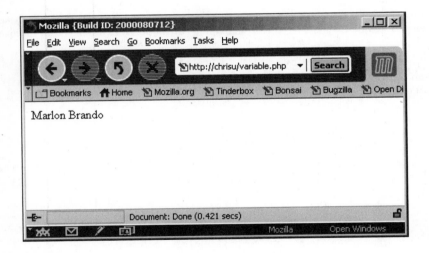

### How It Works

The code required is only two lines long. The first line:

```
$actor = "Marlon Brando";
```

assigns the string `Marlon Brando` to our variable `$actor`. The second line:

```
echo $actor;
```

supplies the contents of our `$actor` variable to the `echo()` command. You can see that when we sent the contents of the variable `$actor` to the web page, we didn't use quotation marks. However, if we had written the following:

```
echo "$actor";
```

the display would *still* have been **Marlon Brando**. This is because to tell PHP *not* to substitute in the value of the variable, you would have to use single quotes instead of double quotes.

> *Those from a Windows background might be slightly confused here. You might expect the above line to have displayed the actual text $actor. The reason for this is because when PHP was written, the authors took some elements from Perl and some elements from UNIX shell scripts, and in shell scripts the user of the dollar-sign as a variable name actually "overrides" the quotation marks. To actually display a dollar sign followed by a letter (or set of letters) you have to resort to other means which we will look at in later chapters.*

# Data Types

We mentioned earlier that we were going to concentrate on two types of variables, those that contain numeric values, and those that contain text values. There are actually several more types of variable, known as **data types**, that PHP uses, such as arrays and objects, which we will defer discussion of until later chapters. For the record a whole list of data types is as follows:

- ❑ string (text)
- ❑ integer (numeric)
- ❑ double (numeric)
- ❑ array
- ❑ object
- ❑ unknown type

Data types are not set by the programmer, rather PHP decides for you when interpreting the web page, what data type a variable should be and assigns them accordingly. These different data types are used by PHP to denote the different types of information that can be stored, and the different operations that can be performed upon this information.

## String Data Type

The string data type is the one that holds textual information or words, and can even hold full sentences. Everything stored inside quotation marks automatically becomes text, even numeric data. For example the following are both strings:

```
$CarType = "Cadillac";
$EngineSize = "2.6";
```

It doesn't matter that the second value is purely numeric, as once enclosed by quotation marks, it automatically becomes a string. If you nominate a certain value as a string, then to perform mathematical operations on it, PHP will have to perform some sort of conversion on it, in order to convert it to a number.

The result of this is that adding strings together as though they are numbers might produce some unexpected results. However, strings do have a form of addition, which can be performed on them. This operation is known as **concatenation**.

### String Concatenation

String concatenation is the process of adding one string to another, that is, attaching one string to the end of another. You use the . (period) as the concatenation operator, to perform this operation. This line:

```
$Car = $CarType . $EngineSize;
```

would yield the result Cadillac2.6, assuming we used the variables in the previous example.

Aesthetically speaking the fact that there is no space between the two strings might displease the designers among us. So we create a variable to contain a space character as well:

```
$Space = " ";
```

You should note that this quite different from having an empty string. An empty string contains nothing at all, while a string with a space contains a character, albeit an invisible one. Spaces of course can be concatenated just like any other text:

```
$Car = $CarType . $Space . $EngineSize;
```

This would produce the desired, nicely spaced-out text Cadillac 2.6.

Of course, there's no reason why you can't concatenate variables with actual text phrases as well:

```
$Car = "Buick" . $Space . "2.0";
```

Here we added text to a variable to more text, which produces the response Buick 2.0. There would also have been nothing wrong with the following line either:

```
$Car = "Buick" . " " . "2.0";
```

This would have had the same effect. There's only one thing to remember when using spaces that are displayed as HTML, if you display them as part of a line of text, and have more than one space, HTML will display only one space on the web page.

In PHP, there is one more way to concatenate variables, and that is actually within the echo() command. Remember that we mentioned earlier that if you tried to print a variable name on the web page, you couldn't do it, and it just displayed the contents of the variable? For example:

```
$CarType = "Cadillac";
echo "$CarType";
```

will still print out Cadillac. However, this does give us the ability to use the variable name within text in order to concatenate text, for example:

```
echo "Duke's $CarType";
```

This would produce Duke's Cadillac. There are extra knock-ons to consider here as well, the first is that you can use escape characters between double quotes but not single quotes. You should also consider what happens if you have two variables such as $Car and $Cars. How would you go about displaying the following?

```php
echo "Click here for the $Carsale";
```

It might look obvious to you, because you can see what is intended – you wish to use the variable $Car and not $Cars, but how can PHP know this? In fact PHP would be looking for a variable called $Carsale. To get around this, you would use parentheses around the variable name as follows:

```php
echo "Click here for the ${Car}sale";
```

You might also notice that we've been careful to space out the period from the variable names in our examples. This isn't just for readability's sake; it can actually have an effect on the output. The two lines might look functionally the same, but they actually produce different results:

```php
echo 2 . 2;
echo 2.2;
```

Respectively, 22 and 2.2! OK, we've cheated here slightly in that none of the numbers are encased by quotation marks, so they aren't actually strings. However, the point is still valid because the number 2 in the example above is treated as a string character by the concatenation operator. So, to ensure that it isn't treated as a number, you need to add spaces between it and the concatenation operator. The important message here is that spacing of your code can, in certain situations, alter the output you receive on your web page.

It's time to see an example of some of these features in a PHP page. Let's create a couple of strings with values and use the echo() command to display them on the web page.

## Try It Out – Using String Variables

**1.** Open up your trusty web page editor and type the following in:

```php
<HTML>
<BODY>
<?php
$CarType = "Pontiac";
$EngineSize = "3.0";
$Space = " ";
$Car = $CarType . $Space . $EngineSize;
echo $Car . $Car;
?>
</BODY>
</HTML>
```

**2.** Save this as string.php.

**3.** Open it up in your web browser, it should look something like this:

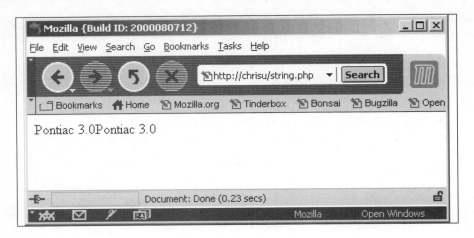

### How It Works

We've mulled over very similar code to this example quite extensively already. The first three lines create three string variables, $CarType, $EngineSize, and $Space and assign them three different values.

```
$CarType = "Pontiac";
$EngineSize = "3.0";
$Space = " ";
```

Then on the next line, we concatenate our three values and place the result in a newly created variable called $Car:

```
$Car = $CarType . $Space . $EngineSize;
```

Finally, we can concatenate our answer to itself in the echo() statement:

```
echo $Car . $Car;
```

Hence the answer is repeated twice, but without a space between the two $Car variables. It looks a bit odd, but we've done this just to demonstrate that concatenating a variable to itself is actually possible.

### It Didn't Work!

If you're seeing something along the following lines of Parse error in C:\inetpub\wwwroot\string.php on line *n*, then most likely you have not remembered to add the semi-colon to the end of each line. If some of the output is displayed as in the above screenshot, but not all, then most likely you have mistyped the name or the case in the name of one of the variables. Make sure that both the names and capitalization are consistent for each variable name throughout the example. If not, you could have inadvertently created a new variable with nothing in it.

## Numeric Data Types

There are two different numeric data types, **integers**, and **doubles**. Integers are whole numbers, while doubles are floating point numbers. Here are some examples of both:

```
$an_integer = 33;
$another_integer = -5797;

$a_double = 4.567;
$another_double = -23.2;
```

So, you should be able to deduce from the above that any whole number is automatically an integer, while anything with a fraction becomes a double data type.

These two data types also have differences in the range of values they can hold, but this is generally dependent on the operating system/platform you are running on. So, in Windows 98 for example a PHP integer could hold a value between –32,768 up to 32,767. A PHP double in Windows 98 can hold – 1.79769313486232E308 to -4.94065645841247E-324 (for negative values), and 4.94065645841247E-324 to 1.79769313486232E308 (for positive values), and it can also contain the zero value.

> *The E-notation (exponential notation) mentioned here is the method that PHP, and indeed any programming language, uses to easily represent very small and very large numbers, The number is written as a base number times ten to the power (exponent) of another number. For example, 2.5E3 represents $2.5 \times 10^3$ or 2500.*

Once again this is where PHP is different from other programming languages, as there are generally far fewer data types in PHP, and these are the only two numeric data types in the language. In general, this makes things a lot simpler, as it's usually fairly easy to see when you want a whole number, or one with a decimal point.

### Simple Mathematical Operations

There are a set of numerical operators that you can use in PHP to perform mathematical operations. These are all very common operators and should be familiar to anybody who has done math at school. They are as follows:

| Operator | Operation |
|----------|-----------|
| + | The addition operator |
| * | The multiplication operator |
| – | The subtraction operator, and also the unary operator depicting negatives for example, –6 |
| / | The division operator |
| % | The modulus operator (works out the remainder left by division) for example, 8 % 5 = 3 |

Their use is pretty much intuitive. For example, we could use the addition operator to compile the total of today's shopping bill:

```
$Bread = 1.5;
$Milk = 0.8;
$ShoppingTotal = $Bread + $Milk;
```

The shopping total is the addition of the contents of the bread variable to the contents of the milk variable. You should be able to see that $ShoppingTotal will contain the total 2.3, which corresponds to 2 dollars and 30 cents, although nowhere does the program make this connection for you. The other operators work pretty much in the same way, so if you'd bought two loaves of bread only, it could be reflected as follows:

```
$Bread = 1.5;
$ShoppingTotal = $Bread * 2;
```

Of course you can combine the mathematical operators in an expression as you see fit, like this:

```
$Bread = 1.5;
$Milk = 0.8;
$DiscountCoupon = 0.5;
$ShoppingTotal = $Bread + $Milk - $DiscountCoupon;
```

### Adding a Variable to Itself

One other thing you're allowed to do in PHP is the following statement which might baffle mathematicians:

```
$ShoppingTotal = $ShoppingTotal + $Bread;
```

It doesn't actually mean $ShoppingTotal is equal to $ShoppingTotal plus $Bread, which implies $Bread equals zero. The equals, or assignment operator, actually means $ShoppingTotal is assigned the OLD value of $ShoppingTotal plus the value of $Bread. So, the following line:

```
$ShoppingTotal = $ShoppingTotal + 1;
```

actually means add one to the variable $ShoppingTotal. There is also a shorthand for incrementing a variable by one, and it is done like this:

```
$ShoppingTotal++;
```

This has an identical effect to the previous line. Another shorthand trick is as follows:

```
$ShoppingTotal += 2;
```

which is the same as saying:

```
$ShoppingTotal = $ShoppingTotal + 2;
```

You could even say:

```
$ShoppingTotal += $ShoppingTotal;
```

Try this out, and see what you get.

There are more mathematical operators in PHP than just the ones discussed here. For starters, there is a set of PHP functions specifically for performing operations such as calculating trigonometric functions or logarithms. We won't be looking at these elsewhere in this book; we suggest that you refer to Appendix C for a full list of them. Secondly, there is also a set of comparison, logical, and bitwise operators that we'll be looking at in later chapters – they require features we have yet to look at. For the time being, the operators we saw above will be more than adequate.

### Precedence

These simple mathematical operations still have to conform to the rules of precedence that we use in mathematics. For instance, the following sum can produce two different results depending on which order you calculate the operators:

```
$Sum = 5+3*6;
```

If you calculate it in strict order as it appears, you'll end up with the total 48. However, if you follow the mathematical order of precedence, where multiplication is calculated before addition then you'll come up with the total 23. Clearly you need some sort of rule to sort out which operation is performed first.

> *In mathematics BODMAS is the acronym used to help you remember the order of operator precedence, which stands for Brackets, Division, Multiplication, Addition, and Subtraction.*

As in mathematics, PHP uses parentheses to enforce these rules of precedence. So, if you wanted to ensure the addition in the above sum was calculated before the multiplication, you'd need to add parentheses as follows:

```
$Sum = (5+3)*6;
```

Let's look now at a quick example which makes use of some of these operators, and after performing a small calculation, displays the result on a web page. In this example we'll take a basic salary and calculate the salary after a 20% tax deduction. After that tax deduction, from the post tax salary figure, we will calculate a 3% pension deduction and display the final salary figure, and the pre-pension deduction salary figure on the same page.

### Try It Out – Numeric Types

**1.** Open up your web page editor of choice once more and type in the following:

```
<HTML>
<BODY>
<?php
$Salary = 15000;
$TaxRate = 20;
$Pension = 3;
$BeforePensionIncome = $Salary - (($Salary / 100) * $TaxRate);
$AfterPensionIncome = $BeforePensionIncome -
(($BeforePensionIncome/100)*$Pension);
echo "Before Pension Deductions:$BeforePensionIncome<BR>";
echo "After Pension Deductions:$AfterPensionIncome";
```

```
?>
</BODY
</HTML>
```

**2.** Save it as `calculation.php`.

**3.** Open it up in your browser of choice. You should see the following result:

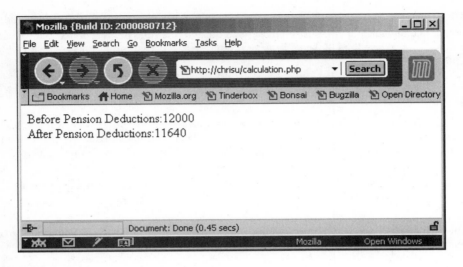

### How It Works

The code is pretty straightforward. The first line creates a salary variable and sets its value to 15000:

```
$Salary = 15000;
```

The second line creates a `$TaxRate` variable and sets its value to 20:

```
$TaxRate = 20;
```

The third line creates a `$Pension` variable and sets its value to 3:

```
$Pension = 3;
```

Now we're ready to start doing some calculations. To calculate the salary figures we first have to calculate what 20% of the salary is. To do this we take the salary variable, divide it by a hundred, and multiply it by 20. This gives us our 20% value, but we still need to subtract this from the salary total for the final figure. However, we must make sure that the 20% figure is calculated first, so we stick this calculation within parenthesis. Then we can subtract from the full salary figure and assign it to the `$BeforePensionIncome` variable:

```
$BeforePensionIncome = $Salary - (($Salary / 100) * $TaxRate);
```

Next, we need to get a figure that is 3% of the post-tax salary figure which is held in $BeforePensionIncome. To do this we need to perform the same calculation as before, but with different variables. This time we need to divide the post tax figure by 100 and multiply it by 3, to get the 3% figure – we use the $Pension variable to supply the 3% figure. Then we subtract this from our post tax figure ($BeforePensionIncome) and store it in the variable $AfterPensionIncome:

```
$AfterPensionIncome = $BeforePensionIncome -
(($BeforePensionIncome/100)*$Pension);
```

Now we've got both of our figures calculated, we can display them on the screen. The following two lines state by displaying the text **Before Pension Deductions:**, followed by the contents of the $BeforePensionIncome variable. Notice that we've also supplied an HTML tag in the echo() statement. It's easy to forget that the PHP is generating HTML, so this is why we supply HTML tags, and not just the special character codes such as CR or CRLF – this is a trick we will be using a lot. This time the <BR> or line break tag is interpreted exactly as though it is in a pure HTML page, and creates a new line for our second calculation figure to be displayed on.

```
echo "Before Pension Deductions:$BeforePensionIncome<BR>";
echo "After Pension Deductions:$AfterPensionIncome";
```

Also note, that we've been very careful to supply semi-colons at the end of every line. Without these the program would generate an error.

## Constants

So far we've looked at figures that we could change or alter in some way after we've assigned them to variables. For instance the variable $author we created earlier with the value "William Shakespeare", can be changed at the drop of the hat to "Herman Melville". For example:

```
$author = "William Shakespeare";
echo $author;
$author = "Herman Melville";
echo $author;
```

If you placed the above code snippet into a full web page and executed it, the echo() statements would produce two different answers, one on top of the other as the variable changes values:

William Shakespeare
Herman Melville

What if you didn't want this to happen though? Certain values will never need to change, such as:

```
$FreezingPointCentigrade = 0;
$IndependenceDay = "4th July";
$FirstPresident = "George Washington";
```

Also you may wish to define certain values within your code that aren't obviously fixed, but are nevertheless unchanging. For example:

```
$ChrisFaveNFLTeam = "Eagles";
```

In which case, you don't want anybody else messing around with your code, changing the values, and introducing errors. Fortunately, PHP has a special facility which allows you to create an identifier, which takes a value that cannot be changed. These identifiers are known as **constants,** which allow you to create variables and assign them values that can never change. The way constants are created is slightly different to the way normal variables are created.

## The Define Keyword

Constants actually require a special keyword `define` to create them. They also don't need to be prefixed with a dollar sign. So, to create a constant for the `FreezingPointCentigrade` variable, we'd need to use `define` as follows:

```
define("FREEZINGPOINTCENTIGRADE", 0);
```

Constant names are by convention all in upper case. The first value is the constant name; the second is the constant value. To create a constant that contains text, you'd just enclose the constant value with quotation marks, just as we do for variables:

```
define("INDEPENDENCEDAY","4th July");
define("FIRSTPRESIDENT,"George Washington");
```

Constants can then be used in exactly the same way as variables. So, you can display them on web pages using the `echo()` statement:

```
echo "Independence Day is the " . INDEPENDENCEDAY;
```

We can append them to text, as above, by using the concatenate operator. However, one difference is that as constants are not preceded by the $ sign, there is no way that PHP can distinguish them from normal text as with normal variables. So the following:

```
echo "Independence Day is the INDEPENDENCEDAY";
```

will display the text Independence Day is the INDEPENDENCEDAY. To avoid displaying constants incorrectly, you need to make sure that the constant name always appears *outside* the quotation marks.

PHP also has its own built-in constants which are used to reflect values such as the operating system that PHP is running on or the version of PHP. For example:

```
echo PHP_OS;
```

will return the current operating system that your server is running on.

# Initialization

Anybody with experience of programming languages other than PHP might be getting a little disconcerted at this point. We've talked about variables in length, yet it's common in most programming languages for variables to have to undergo a process known as **declaration** or **initialization** first. This process is common in many languages such as Java or Visual Basic. In these languages you must declare/initialize a variable before you use them. Declaration or initialization just means that before you can use a variable, you must first declare that variable to exist. For example, this is done with the `Dim` keyword in Visual Basic, for example:

```
Dim newVariable
newVariable = "Hello"
```

*The above code is not PHP, and will ONLY work in Visual Basic.*

However, in PHP you don't have to do this at all. It isn't required, and in fact once you use a variable name for the first time, it is automatically created for you:

```
$newVariable = "Hello";
```

However, there is one advantage of initialization that PHP misses out on. We mentioned earlier that each variable has a data type, and that PHP automatically assigns a data type on creation of a variable type. With variable initialization in other programming languages you could typically specify which data type you wanted that variable to have – for example, in Visual Basic:

```
Dim newVariable As String
newVariable = "Hello"
```

*The above code is not PHP, and will ONLY work in Visual Basic.*

In PHP you can't. This can lead to one problem – what happens in PHP when it automatically assigns a data type, but assigns a type you didn't want? What happens if you want to change the data type of a variable halfway through a calculation? For example, you could get the user to supply some information such as the size and make of their car – a Volkswagen Golf 2.0CL, say. This would have to be treated as text. Then, what if you just wanted to extract the engine size, and use the actual number in some mathematical calculations? You should be able to imagine plenty of other tricky situations like this.

In each case you will need to convert the data type of the variable from one to another.

# Conversions

PHP does provide a set of built in functions to help you not only convert the data type of a variable from one to another, but also to determine exactly what data type of variable PHP has assigned it in the first place. In fact, a lot of the hard work is saved, because PHP commonly performs this process for you. Once again this is totally different to most other programming languages, which typically only allow operations between two or more variables of the same type. In PHP though you could do the following:

```
$EngineType = "2.0L";
$TaxRate = 3;
$TaxPaid = $EngineType * $TaxRate;
```

This doesn't change the contents of any variables. In fact let's run this example right now to prove everything is as it seems:

## Try It Out – Implicit Conversions

**1.** Open your web page editor and type in the following:

```
<HTML>
<BODY>
<?php
$EngineType = "2.0L";
$TaxRate = 3;
$TaxPaid = $EngineType * $TaxRate;
echo "Engine Type: $EngineType<BR>";
echo "Tax Rate: $TaxRate<BR>";
echo "Tax Paid: $TaxPaid";
?>
</BODY>
</HTML>
```

**2.** Save it as `convert.php`

**3.** Open it and view it in your browser:

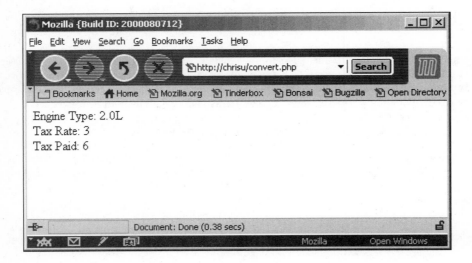

### How It Works

It's no different to our earlier examples using mathematical operations. The first three lines create three variables. The first `$EngineType` is a string:

```
$EngineType = "2.0L";
```

The second `$TaxRate` is a number:

```
$TaxRate = 3;
```

The third performs our calculation for us, by multiplying the contents of $EngineType and $TaxRate and placing them in the variable $TaxPaid:

```
$TaxPaid = $EngineType * $TaxRate;
```

Here, PHP is actually saying, "I don't care that there is an L in the variable $EngineType, I can see the number and I can use the number in the multiplication sum." The last three lines display the contents of our variables to prove that there has been no sleight of hand:

```
echo "Engine Type: $EngineType<BR>";
echo "Tax Rate: $TaxRate<BR>";
echo "Tax Paid: $TaxPaid";
```

## Type Casting

PHP up until now has done the conversion of data types itself, but if you want to specify the data type of a variable when you create it, you can do this as well. All you need to do is set the variable to equal itself, then specify the data type you want in parentheses before the second occurrence of the variable name. This is known as a **cast**:

```
$NewVariable =  13;
$NewVariable = (string) $NewVariable;
```

The code has assigned our variable a numeric value. Then it has taken the numeric value and turned it into a text value on the second line. You could then convert the variable back again if so required:

```
$NewVariable =  13;
$NewVariable = (string) $NewVariable;
$NewVariable = (integer) $NewVariable;
```

## gettype and settype

We also alluded to the ability that PHP has in determining the current data type of a variable. This is via a preset function that PHP provides called gettype(). It works by providing the variable in parentheses to the function as follows:

```
gettype($number);
```

To get it to display anything, you'd need to feed it to the echo() statement as follows:

```
$number = 5;
echo gettype($number);
```

This would display the result Integer on a web page. There is also a related function that PHP provides called settype() which, like type casting, allows you to specifically set the data type. It takes two parameters within the parentheses – the variable you wish to set the data type of, and the data type you wish to set it to. It works as follows:

```
$number=10;
settype($number, "string");
```

To demonstrate that this has changed the data type, you can show the value returned by the `gettype` function to the screen as follows:

```
echo gettype($number);
```

Before it displayed the result number, now it returns the word string.

### isset, unset, and empty

There are three more PHP functions that will be of use to you when you use variables. The first function, `isset()`, allows you to see whether a variable with a certain name has been created or not. You just supply one parameter to it – the name of the variable itself. If you supplied it to the `echo()` statement:

```
echo isset($number);
```

This would display a number 1 if there was a variable named `$number` already in existence. Otherwise it wouldn't return any value at all, not even a zero.

The second function, `unset()`, is used to completely destroy a variable and release any memory that has been allocated to it. Again, it takes just one parameter – the variable name:

```
unset($number);
```

However, make sure this is really what you want to do to the variable, because both the name and the value are destroyed when it is used.

The third of the three functions, `empty()`, is the logical opposite of `isset()`. It is used in exactly the same way as `isset()`, returning 1 if there is no variable `$number`, or if `$number` equals 0 or "" (the empty string), and nothing at all if this variable exists:

```
echo empty($number);
```

This almost brings to a close our introduction to variables. However, there is still one more type that PHP provides that we haven't talked about yet.

# Environment Variables

Environment variables (also termed PHP variables) are variables that have been set outside PHP scripts, but are available within any PHP script. These variables typically provide information about the client-server transaction that we described earlier in the chapter. They can be information about the HTTP request or the HTTP response, and they take the same format as variables you have created yourself, since they also begin with a dollar sign. The only difference is that they have already been created, and need no kind of intervention from the user. You can see them by using the function `phpinfo()`, which we used in the first chapter.

You can also reference these individually, with the `echo()` statement, such as:

```
echo $HTTP_COOKIE_DATA;
```

This line will display the contents of any cookies currently in use. Another useful environment variable is $HTTP_USER_AGENT which contains the user browser type:

```
echo $HTTP_USER_AGENT;
```

You can then use the value of this in your own programs and tailor make them to a specific browser or set of browsers. There are other very useful variables such as $HTTP_FROM which contains the email address of the user making the request, or $HTTP_ACCEPT which contains a list of the different media types that the user's browser can accept.

The difference between environment variables and the PHP defined constants we detailed earlier is that you can change or influence the contents of these variables yourself. However, they are there more for reference rather than setting, and you will see them used throughout this book.

# Summary

This chapter has covered a lot of ground in a short space, so to make sure everyone keeps up, we have kept things relatively short and simple. We started the chapter with an introductory PHP example, and demonstrated that PHP pages are a mixture of three things, text, HTML markup, and PHP script. We noted that the PHP script is sent to the web server for processing. We made a brief mention of the process of interpretation that the script has to undergo. The PHP script engine then returns the page as pure HTML markup, so that the browser can understand it. We looked at the interaction between web server and browser more closely, and the way that HTTP sends messages back and forth.

We saw how to delimit PHP scripts in your pages, and briefly reviewed the process of caching, before moving out into programming territory. We started programming by introducing the concept of variables – the method by which PHP stores and retrieves information (as indeed do most programming languages). We looked at the different types of data you could store, and examined in greater depth the storage of numerical and textual information.

We looked at the process of converting a variable of one data type to another, and also introduced constants, which are variables with never-changing values. We looked at some tools PHP offers to perform fairly basic manipulation of this information. Finally, we took a brief look at some environment variables.

# Getting Data from the Client

In the last chapter we went through a lot of practical examples, setting information in a variable and then displaying the contents of the variable in a web page. We didn't actually ask for any input from the user, or require any interaction from them whatsoever, and as such we didn't really provide more than HTML offers already. Fear not though, the last chapter was preparing the ground for us to be able to get information from the user, store it, and then act on the information supplied and return it to the user as part of a web page.

We will start by looking at HTML forms – these are the most common method via which a user can enter information. We'll then look at the two different methods HTML uses to transmit information from one page to another, and the pros and cons involved with each. We'll see how PHP can easily pick up and use the values transmitted by pure HTML markup. There are many different methods that HTML forms can use to encapsulate data, from text boxes and text areas, to check boxes, password fields, and radio buttons. We're also going to look at examples of how you can use PHP to get information back from all of these types of controls in this chapter.

The last part of the chapter deals with using values to produce a response to the form input when necessary. The order of topics in this chapter is:

- ❑ Two different ways of sending form information  – GET and POST
- ❑ Text fields
- ❑ Checkboxes
- ❑ Radio buttons
- ❑ Listboxes
- ❑ Hidden form fields
- ❑ Passwords
- ❑ Submit and Reset buttons
- ❑ Returning a result based on information provided by the user

# Web Forms

Probably the one area of HTML that causes the most confusion and difficulty is the subject of forms. This is mainly due to the fact that, in order to manipulate data passed by a form, you have to use some other technology to pick up the data. This can range from a simple scripting language such as JavaScript, or a "glue" technology like Active Server Pages, an application such as CGI, or a fully-fledged language feature such as Java Servlets. To properly implement client-server processing, it isn't feasible to just take information from the user and reply to them at a later date. A proper client-server interface needs to process information and return information to the user while they are waiting.

If you think of it, all you're doing when you send a URL to a web server is asking for the web page at a particular address. If the web server can find it, it will package it up and send it back to your browser. The browser has the hard job of understanding the package sent to it by the web server, and the process of translating it into a web page. If the server can't find the page it will send back an error, usually of the form HTTP Error 404 Page not found.

When you send a form off to a server, what you are doing is sending it a load of code that it doesn't actually understand! To be able to understand your form, the web server has to have an additional application or module bolted on to perform the task. PHP is one such application that performs the task for you.

We're going to begin this chapter with a discussion of the HTML <FORM> tag. The <FORM> tag's attributes are used directly by PHP to make sense of what it has been sent.

## The FORM Tag

What happens when you send a form in HTML? The user fills out the various text boxes and clicks a submit button when ready; the information that is supplied is then bundled up in one of two ways and sent to the web server. The web server can then pull out this information, and supply it to the PHP script engine. PHP manipulates this information and sends it back as part of the HTTP response to the browser. All you need to do to make a form is create a pure HTML web page with opening and closing <FORM> tags. Any controls such as text field, check boxes, and radio buttons that are placed between the <FORM> tags, automatically become part of the form that is sent to the web server.

## Attributes of FORM

The <FORM> tag has a whole host of attributes, but we can get by using only two of them, ACTION and METHOD. Other attributes, such as ID, CLASS, DIR, LANG, LANGUAGE, NAME, STYLE, and TITLE are universal to most or all HTML tags, and shouldn't need further explanation. The more obscure attributes ACCEPT-CHAR and ENCTYPE, which specify the character sets and the MIME-TYPE of the form data are outside the scope of this overview - we will be looking specifically at the second of these in Chapter 10. There is also a TARGET attribute that, like its namesake in the <A HREF> tag, allows you to specify a frame or window in which to display the Web page that is sent back in response to the form's submission.

### ACTION

The ACTION attribute tells the server which page to go to once the user has clicked a submit button on the form. It doesn't matter whether this page is pure HTML, PHP, or uses any server-side technology, as long as the page exists on the web server. It can be used as follows to link to an HTML page:

```
<FORM ACTION="test.html">
...
</FORM>
```

or, for a PHP page it would read as follows:

```
<FORM ACTION="test.php">
...
</FORM>
```

However, when we supply a PHP page as part of the ACTION attribute, what we're actually doing is sending the information entered into this form to the PHP script engine for processing. The ACTION attribute just tells the server which page to go to next – if you saved the above page as test.html instead of test.php, then the page wouldn't be sent to the PHP script engine and nothing at all would be displayed unless PHP has been configured to parse .html files. Shortly, we'll look at what the PHP script engine does when it receives the form, but before we do that, we need to look at the second FORM attribute, METHOD.

## METHOD

The METHOD attribute controls the way that information is sent to the server. As we mentioned previously, it can do this in one of two ways. These are GET and POST methods, and you use them as follows:

```
<FORM ACTION="test.php" METHOD=GET>
```

or

```
<FORM ACTION="test.php" METHOD=POST>
```

> *There are actually more than two values you can supply to the METHOD attribute, HEAD, PUT, LINK, UNLINK, OPTIONS, DELETE, TRACE and CONNECT. However, these options are not commonly used, and you will rarely have call to use them, so we will discuss them no further.*

Let's now examine the main two settings of METHOD more closely.

### GET

We'll start with the GET value of METHOD. This tells the browser to append the values the user placed on the form to the URL. To do this the browser adds a question mark to the end of the URL to denote where the URL finishes and the form information starts. The information on the form is then transmitted in the form of **name/value pairs**. It is easier to look at some examples than to explain in detail.

A name/value pair works in a very similar way to a variable. The first part is the name, which acts as an identifier. The second part is the value that you wish to store. For example:

```
?animal=cat
```

Here "animal" is the name, while "cat" is the value. This can be appended to the URL as follows:

```
http://www.nonexistentserver.com/test.php?animal=cat
```

The browser automatically appends the information to the URL when it sends the page request to the web server. You can add more than one name/value pair to a URL if you separate each pair with an ampersand (&). With two name/value pairs the end of the URL might look like this:

```
?furryanimal=cat&spikyanimal=porcupine
```

As part of the URL it would look like this:

```
http://www.nonexistentserver.com/test.php?furryanimal=cat&spikyanimal=porcupine
```

The part appended to the URL is known as a **query string**. We mentioned earlier that name/value pairs are very similar to variables. In fact, once they have been passed to the web server for processing, PHP makes them available as variables. So, if you submitted your form to the web server, and moved to another page, the name/value pairs would be available in the PHP script as variables.

Occasionally, you might wish to pass spaces in the values that make up the query string. For instance, if you had a form that had a <TEXTAREA> tag, and someone had typed in the following reply:

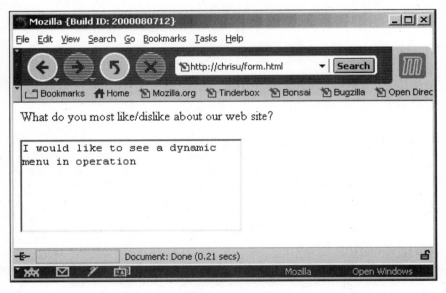

The line "I would like to see a dynamic menu in operation" contains several spaces that need to be represented. In which case the addition operator replaces the spaces:

```
http://chrisu/form.php?TextArea=I+would+like+to+see+a+dynamic+menu+in+operation
```

Some of you will be thinking, "But what happens if you want to put an addition operator in the <TEXTAREA>? How is that represented within a query string?" In this case, the character or operator in question has to be replaced by a code, which signifies this particular character. This is known as **URL encoding**.

## URL Encoding

There is a set of characters that can't appear in a URL, and therefore by association, can't appear in a query string either, so they have to be URL encoded.

The encoding process requires you, the user or developer, to do precisely nothing. It's all done for you. The web browser takes the offending character, whether a bracket or an addition sign, and replaces it with a **code value**. The code is always the same and we have listed the most common characters and their code values for you in the table beneath:

| Character | URL Encoding |
|-----------|--------------|
| Tab | %09 |
| Space | %20 |
| ! | %21 |
| " | %22 |
| # | %23 |
| % | %25 |
| & | %26 |

| Character | URL Encoding |
|-----------|--------------|
| ( | %28 |
| ) | %29 |
| + | %2B |
| , | %2C |
| . | %2E |
| / | %2F |
| : | %3A |

| Character | URL Encoding |
|-----------|--------------|
| ; | %3B |
| < | %3C |
| > | %3E |
| = | %3D |
| ? | %3F |
| @ | %40 |
| \ | %5C |

Some of the above characters have to be encoded, or they would adopt another meaning in the query string – as we saw above, the addition operator is used to denote a space in the query string, and the question mark denotes the start of a query string.

The previous query string with the URL code value for a space in place of the addition operator would look like this:

```
http://chrisu/form.php?TextArea=I%20would%20like%20to%20see%20a%20dynamic%20menu%2
0in%20operation
```

We won't look at an example of GET in action just yet; instead we'll look at POST.

## POST

One disadvantage you might have discerned from query strings is the rather public nature of their transmission. If you don't want the information sent to appear in the URL, then you will have to rely on the POST method instead. This works almost identically to the GET method; the difference is that the information in the form is sent in the body of the HTTP request, rather than as part of the URL. This means that it isn't visible to everybody, because it isn't attached to the URL. POST can also allow a greater amount of information to be transmitted – there is a physical limit to the amount you can transmit as part of a URL.

## Do I Use GET or POST?

There's a mixture of opinion on this one; some people say you should almost never use the GET method, due to its insecurity and limit on size; others maintain that you can use GET to retrieve information, while POST should be used whenever you modify data on the web server. There are no hard and fast rules though, and these are just guidelines.

One disadvantage of POST is that pages loaded with POST cannot be properly book-marked, whereas pages loaded with GET contain all the information needed to reproduce the request right in the URL. In many cases you can bookmark the result of a form submission (a search on Alta Vista, for example) by using the GET method, and this is why most search engines use GET. As well as this, the POST method itself isn't secure – while the information is placed in the HTTP body and isn't immediately visible, the information isn't encrypted and is still easily obtained by a hacker. To make sure it is secure, you would need to use a secure connection to a secure server.

Which method you use depends on what you want to the form to do. If you do use GET, be aware of its shortcomings and its indiscreet nature. If you use POST, beware that it can't be book-marked by search engines, and just because it is more discreet doesn't mean it is more secure.

# HTML Form Controls and PHP

Now we've explained the process in some detail, let's take a look at the most common HTML controls you can use to collect information in a form, and see how we can use PHP to get at this information afterwards. All of the following examples in this section will require two web pages. The first page retrieves information posted by the user, and the second sends the information from the web server and scripting engine back to the browser.

The first web page doesn't have to contain any PHP script at all. In fact, on a large number of sites, the web page that contains the form will be pure HTML and will have the suffix .htm or .html. We will be observing this format in all of the following examples. Obviously there is no need to send any information to the PHP scripting engine, because if it contains no PHP, then this will just add extra time to the amount of time it takes to generate the web page to be returned to the browser

Let's get started by looking at the most common HTML form controls.

## Text Fields (Text Boxes)

Text fields or text boxes are probably one of the most familiar controls you will come across on any form. They are created using the <INPUT> element and by setting the TYPE attribute to text.

```
<INPUT TYPE="Text" NAME="TextBox1">
```

Their advantage is that they can take whole sentences of text from the user. This makes them ideal for open-ended questions, where there can be a vast and unpredictable range of possible answers. A typical text box looks like this:

> Who is your favourite author? [                    ]

> To pass variables between PHP scripts you must make sure that the expression
> register_globals = On is uncommented in your php.ini file. Remember that
> if you adjust anything in the php.ini file, to apply changes, you must reboot.

We've kept away from the practical side of things long enough, so let's move onto an example. We'll explain what's going on after we've run the example. In this example we'll just take the user's favorite author and display it to the screen on the next page.

## Try It Out – Using Text Fields

**1.** Open up your text editor and type in the following HTML:

```
<HTML>
<HEAD></HEAD>
<BODY>
```

```
<FORM METHOD=GET ACTION="text.php">
Who is your favourite author?
<INPUT NAME="Author" TYPE="TEXT">
<BR>
<BR>
<INPUT TYPE=SUBMIT>
</FORM>
</BODY>
</HTML>
```

**2.** Save this as `text.html`

**3.** Close this file and start a new file in your editor and type the following code:

```
<HTML>
<HEAD></HEAD>
<BODY>
Your favorite author is:
<?php
echo $Author;
?>
</BODY>
</HTML>
```

**4.** Save this file as `text.php`.

**5.** Open up `text.html` in your browser and type a name:

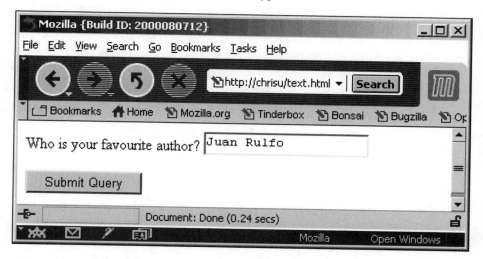

**6.** Click on the **Submit Query** button and you should see the author name you supplied displayed as shown overleaf:

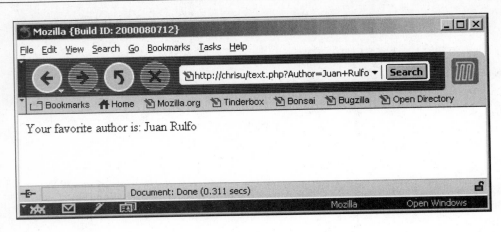

### How It Works

First of all, before we look at the code, take note of the URL in the previous screenshot (the second page we created). Appended to the end of the page name `text.php` is a query string. This is something that has been added by the web browser, because we instructed it to do this in the program `text.html`, with the following highlighted HTML line:

```
<HTML>
<HEAD></HEAD>
<BODY>
<FORM METHOD=GET ACTION="text.php">
Who is your favourite author?
...
```

Setting the attribute to GET has passed our form information on as a query string, rather than hiding it. Let's examine the query string now. In the example in the screenshot it reads:

```
?Author=Juan+Rulfo
```

We've already said that query strings are made up from name/value pairs. You don't have to be Sherlock Holmes to deduce that `Author` is the name and `Juan Rulfo` is the value in this example. The query string picks up `Author` as its name from the following highlighted line in our first program, `text.html`:

```
Who is your favourite author?
<INPUT NAME="Author" TYPE="TEXT">
<BR>
```

The NAME attribute of the `<INPUT>` tag has set this control to have the name Author. I added the value when I entered the name of my favorite author in the text field.

This deals with our first program, so let's look at the second program `text.php`. It's actually one line of text, followed by one line of PHP:

```
Your favorite author is:
```

```
<?php
echo $Author;
?>
```

The line of PHP displays the contents of the variable called $Author. Nowhere within our code have we physically created a variable called $Author. What we have done is created an HTML text box and given it the name Author. When we sent the form to the web server and the PHP script engine, it created a variable with the name $Author. If we'd called our text box "Name" then our variable would have been called $Name. That's all our example program does.

### Why This Example Might Not Be Working For You

If you're just seeing the following picture without any author name, but with the author name passed as a query string:

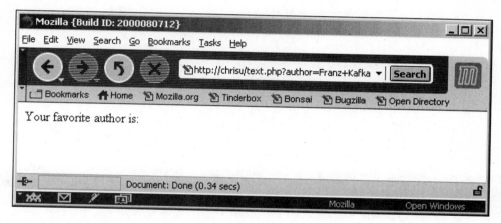

then, most likely you have confused the cases in your two programs. If you had the following line in text.html, with a lower case "a":

```
Who is your favourite author?
<INPUT NAME="author" TYPE="TEXT">
<BR>
```

while in text.php you had $Author with an upper case "A":

```
<?php
echo $Author;
?>
```

this would be enough to break the program because variable names in PHP are case-sensitive. While HTML itself isn't case-sensitive, PHP is taking the variable name from the name you assigned to the HTML text field, so it is creating the PHP variable $author, not $Author. You must make sure that the name of the HTML text field and the name you use in your PHP script are absolutely identical, cases and all. Let's move onto our next example.

## Text Areas

If you want to have a text field that allows multiple lines to be typed, as opposed to having a multiple number of separate text fields on your page, then you need a completely different HTML control. You don't even use the HTML <INPUT> tag; instead you use the <TEXTAREA> tag. The <TEXTAREA> tag takes a different set of attributes to <INPUT>, which allow you to set the size and number of rows and columns of the control, among other features. For example:

```
<TEXTAREA NAME="WebSites" ROWS="30" COLS="50">
```

Once again it's designed to take whole sentences from the user. The advantage of <TEXTAREA> is that you can set the size, so it can take many lines of text. <TEXTAREA> requires a closing tag, so you can also place default text for each line between the tags. For example:

Let's take a look at another example. In this one, we will do the same as we did in the previous example, and display all the web sites the user fills in. However, we will be making one crucial change to the method of transmission, as you shall see.

### Try It Out – Using Text Area

**1.** Yet again poke your trusty web page editor in the ribs to start it up and type the following:

```
<HTML>
<HEAD></HEAD>
<BODY>
<FORM METHOD=POST ACTION="textarea.php">
What are your favourite web sites?
<TEXTAREA NAME="WebSites" COLS="50" ROWS="5">
http://
http://
http://
http://
</TEXTAREA>
<BR>
<BR>
<BR>
<INPUT TYPE=SUBMIT>
</FORM>
</BODY>
</HTML>
```

**2.** Save this as textarea.html.

**3.** Close the previous file and start a completely new one and type the following in:

```
<HTML>
<HEAD></HEAD>
<BODY>
Your favorite web sites are:
<?php
echo $WebSites;
?>
</BODY>
</HTML>
```

**4.** Save this as `textarea.php`.

**5.** Open up `textarea.html` in your browser and type in the names of some of your favorite web sites:

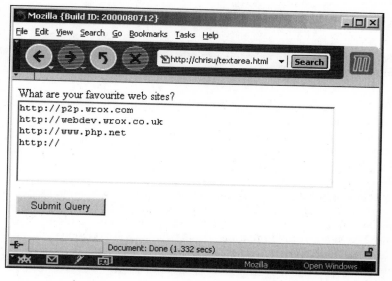

**6.** Click on Submit Query once you have typed in the names of your sites. You don't have to fill in all four sites; we've even left one blank above. You should see something like the screen shown below:

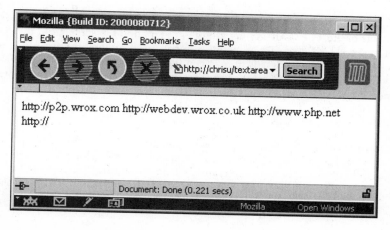

### How It Works

Not quite as neat and tidy as our previous example, is it? However, don't let this distract you from an important point, which is the URL that reads:

```
http://chrisu/textarea.php
```

There's no query string attached. This is because in the first of the two programs we have now set METHOD to equal POST.

```
<HTML>
<HEAD></HEAD>
<BODY>
<FORM METHOD=POST ACTION="textarea.php">
What are your favourite web sites?
...
```

This is the only change we need to make to ensure that our form details aren't freely visible. There's little else of particular interest on the web page, apart from the <TEXTAREA> tag:

```
<TEXTAREA NAME="WebSites" COLS="50" ROWS="5">
http://
http://
http://
http://
</TEXTAREA>
```

We set it to be 5 rows high, and 50 columns across to get it to the size we require. The text inside the <TEXTAREA> tag, unlike in normal HTML, doesn't require line breaks (the <BR> tag), it's enough to start it on a new line, to get it displayed on a new line. We set the name of the TEXTAREA control to be "WebSites", and then in our second program textarea.php, we reference this variable in PHP as $WebSites, once again taking care to ensure the cases are identical:

```
...
Your favorite web sites are:
<?php
echo $WebSites;
?>
...
```

The whole contents of the <TEXTAREA> tag are then dumped to the screen, but the carriage returns that separated them in the HTML page are automatically collapsed by the browser, along with any extra white space, in order to make the details fit in. Even though we've used the POST method instead of GET, the PHP variable is exactly the same, and there's no way of telling just by looking at the variable name, which method of transmission was used. Let's move onto another control now.

## Check Boxes

Check boxes are, like text fields, created in HTML using the <INPUT> tag. They provide a single box, which can be ticked or not ticked, depending on the option chosen. This doesn't require any data from the user, other than to click on the checkbox, so any data this control contains will be quite different from the text field. Superficially in HTML it looks very similar, all that's different is the type:

```
<INPUT NAME="Choice" TYPE="Checkbox">
```

It is suitable for use when you have a question that requires a strict yes/no answer with no room for maneuver:

Have you ever eaten haggis before? ☐

Check boxes also have a CHECKED attribute (which takes no value). If you supply this attribute in the control, then the checkbox will be checked by default:

```
<INPUT NAME="Choice" TYPE="Checkbox" CHECKED>
```

It will also have a VALUE attribute set to "on" by default.

Some of the advantages of checkboxes over other forms of input control aren't immediately obvious, but they will become clear once we have used several of them. However, to get the hang of them, let's do a quick example, which utilizes just one checkbox and returns the contents of it to the screen.

## Try It Out – Using a Check Box

**1.** Dust off your web page editor again and type the following code in:

```
<HTML>
<HEAD></HEAD>
<BODY>
<FORM METHOD=POST ACTION="checkbox.php">
Have you ever eaten haggis before?
<INPUT NAME="Choice" TYPE="Checkbox">
<BR>
<BR>
<INPUT TYPE=SUBMIT>
</FORM>
</BODY>
</HTML>
```

**2.** Save it as checkbox.html.

**3.** Close this file and start a new one; then type in the following:

```
<HTML>
<HEAD></HEAD>
<BODY>
<?php
echo $Choice;
?>
</BODY>
</HTML>
```

**4.** Save this as checkbox.php.

**5.** Open up `checkbox.html` in your browser of choice:

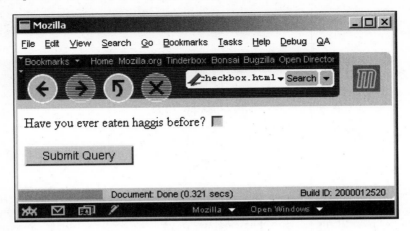

Depending on whether you check the box or not before you submit the query, you will get one of two results. Hit the back button, and go back and select the opposite choice to the one you made earlier and hit submit again:

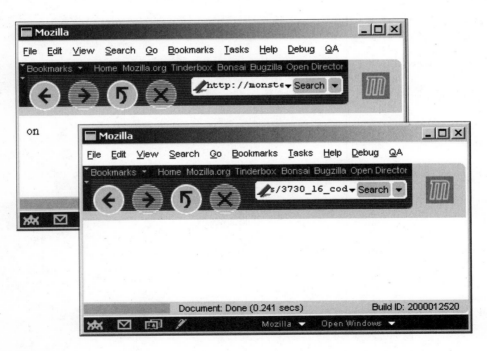

### How It Works

You're probably getting used to this ritual now. Once again, if you look at the URL you will see there is no query string. This is because we have used the POST method to pass our form information to the web server. This is set in the first of our two programs, `checkbox.html`:

```
<HTML>
<HEAD></HEAD>
<BODY>
<FORM METHOD=POST ACTION="checkbox.php">
```

Our form control is a checkbox, so it is created with the `<INPUT>` tag once again:

```
Have you ever eaten haggis before?
<INPUT NAME="Choice" TYPE="Checkbox">
```

This is all there is to comment on in our first program. In the second one, `checkbox.php`, we call the PHP variable, which once again has exactly the same name as the control we set in `checkbox.html`:

```
<?php
echo $Choice;
?>
```

The only difference is that the variable is now created with a value that wasn't assigned by us. If the checkbox was ticked then it contains the value 'on'. If it wasn't checked then it contains nothing at all.

### Multiple Check Boxes

What happens if you want to use more than one check box? If you're familiar with radio buttons, you'll know that selecting one radio button in a group of radio buttons, will automatically move the choice from whatever button was selected before to your current selection. Checkboxes don't work like that. Their advantage is that each checkbox is counted as an individual entity. So you can have several checkboxes ticked altogether, or you can have none checked at all. For example we could modify our previous example to look like this:

```
Have you ever eaten haggis before? ☑
Have you ever eaten snails before? ☑
Have you ever eaten locusts before? ☐
```

In fact, let's do that; we will go back and modify our previous example to include several checkboxes, to reflect these choices.

## Try It Out – Using Multiple Checkboxes

**1.** Open up your web page editor, load `checkbox.html`, and add the following lines to it:

```
<HTML>
<HEAD></HEAD>
<BODY>
<FORM METHOD=POST ACTION="checkboxes.php">
Have you ever eaten haggis before?
<INPUT NAME="Choice1" TYPE="Checkbox" VALUE="Haggis">
<BR>
Have you ever eaten snails before?
<INPUT NAME="Choice2" TYPE="Checkbox" VALUE="Snails">
<BR>
```

```
Have you ever eaten locusts before?
<INPUT NAME="Choice3" TYPE="Checkbox" VALUE="Locusts">
<BR>
<BR>
<INPUT TYPE=SUBMIT>
</FORM>
</BODY>
</HTML>
```

**2.** Save this as `checkboxes.html`.

**3.** Close this and create a new file and type in the following:

```
<HTML>
<HEAD></HEAD>
<BODY>
<?php
echo "$Choice1<BR>";
echo "$Choice2<BR>";
echo "$Choice3<BR>";
?>
</BODY>
</HTML>
```

**4.** Save this as `checkboxes.php`.

**5.** Open `checkboxes.html` on your browser.

**6.** Click on a couple of the options and submit your query, you should see something like this:

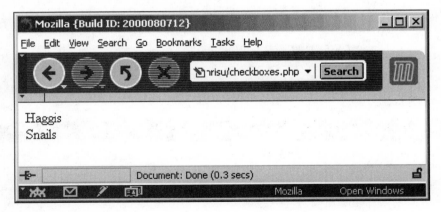

### How It Works

We set the VALUE attribute for each checkbox in the first program:

```
Have you ever eaten haggis before?
<INPUT NAME="Choice1" TYPE="Checkbox" VALUE="Haggis">
```

```
<BR>
Have you ever eaten snails before?
<INPUT NAME="Choice2" TYPE="Checkbox" VALUE="Snails">
<BR>
Have you ever eaten locusts before?
<INPUT NAME="Choice3" TYPE="Checkbox" VALUE="Locusts">
```

This has the effect of setting a value for each checkbox once it has been checked. So, if the Choice1 checkbox is ticked, it will have the value of Haggis (rather than the default 'on'), and this in turn will be passed on to the $Choice1 variable in our checkboxes.php page. If the checkbox isn't ticked then once again, nothing is passed on to the PHP variable of the same name. In our second program, checkboxes.php, we display the contents of the three variables set independently in the first program like so:

```
echo "$Choice1<BR>";
echo "$Choice2<BR>";
echo "$Choice3<BR>";
```

From the display screen above, you should be able to deduce that the Haggis and Snails checkboxes were ticked, while the locusts one wasn't.

### An Additional Note

We mentioned that each of three checkbox controls was named and set independently. It is possible to set all three inputs to have the same name. However, this might not yield the results you expect. If you changed the following code in the program checkboxes.html:

```
Have you ever eaten haggis before?
<INPUT NAME="Choice" TYPE="Checkbox" VALUE="Haggis">
<BR>
Have you ever eaten snails before?
<INPUT NAME="Choice" TYPE="Checkbox" VALUE="Locusts">
<BR>
Have you ever eaten locusts before?
<INPUT NAME="Choice" TYPE="Checkbox" VALUE="Snails">
```

If you run the program again and select more than one option, you will only get one answer, which will be the last selected option in the list. For example:

What has happened here is that, as with variables, PHP stores each occurrence of the variable over whatever the variable contained before. Whichever was the last checkbox to be set, this is the last value the variable is set to. In this case it is changed to "Snails" and this is what is displayed as a result. What you can do though, is add a couple of square brackets to the name of each HTML control:

```
Have you ever eaten haggis before?
<INPUT NAME="Choice[]" TYPE="Checkbox" VALUE="Haggis">
<BR>
Have you ever eaten snails before?
<INPUT NAME="Choice[]" TYPE="Checkbox" VALUE="Snails">
<BR>
Have you ever eaten locusts before?
<INPUT NAME="Choice[]" TYPE="Checkbox" VALUE="Locusts">
```

This creates what is known as an **array**. This means that PHP stores the three different values seemingly in the same variable. An array is just a set of variables which all have the same name. To distinguish the different variables, PHP adds a number to the end of each variable name, which acts a unique identifier. The first version of the variable has a zero in square brackets added to the end, the second has a one in square brackets, and third version has a two in square brackets.

To get PHP to display the contents of these variables you would need to refer to the variable explicitly with its full name, such as $Choice[0]. In $Choice[0] you will find the value "Haggis" if Haggis has been selected first. In variable $Choice[1] you will find the value "Snails" if Snails has been selected second, and so on for the rest of the HTML controls that share the same name. For the time being, treat each occurrence in our array $Choice[] as though it was different variables entirely.

Without the square brackets, you can't create an array. We will be coming across this again later on in the chapter, but will actually be covering this unusual behavior in lot more detail in Chapter 5 when we discuss arrays. Until then, when naming check boxes, or indeed other controls such as text fields, make sure they all have different NAME attributes to prevent anything unexpected happening.

## Radio Buttons

Radio buttons are the selfish cousins to checkboxes. If you have a selection of answers or options but only one of the options can be selected at a time, then you should use radio buttons. For example a multiple-choice answer to a question would require radio buttons:

What is the capital of Portugal?

○ Porto
○ Lisbon
○ Madrid

Once again, radio buttons are created using the <INPUT> tag, setting the TYPE attribute to Radio.

```
<INPUT NAME="Question1" TYPE="Radio" VALUE="Porto">
```

Radio buttons, like checkboxes, also have a CHECKED attribute in HTML, which again takes no value. If you supply this attribute in the control, then checkbox will be checked by default:

```
<INPUT NAME="Question1" TYPE="Radio" CHECKED>
```

If you supply no value for the VALUE attribute, it will be set to "on" by default.

To connect a set of radio buttons, completely contrary to our recommendations for checkboxes, you must supply each radio button in your group with the same name. For example:

```
<INPUT NAME="Question1" TYPE="Radio" VALUE="Porto">
<INPUT NAME="Question1" TYPE="Radio" VALUE="Lisbon">
<INPUT NAME="Question1" TYPE="Radio" VALUE="Madrid">
```

Via this method you are telling the web server that all of these buttons are connected. If you give each radio button control a different name, you will find that you can select each option independently, just like a checkbox.

Let's do an example now, and put the above into code.

## Try It Out – Using Radio Buttons

**1.** Open your web page editor and, you've guessed it, type in the following code:

```
<HTML>
<HEAD></HEAD>
<BODY>
<FORM METHOD=GET ACTION="radio.php">
What is the capital of Portugal?
<BR>
<BR>
<INPUT NAME="Question1" TYPE="Radio" VALUE="Porto">
Porto
<BR>
<INPUT NAME="Question1" TYPE="Radio" VALUE="Lisbon">
Lisbon
<BR>
<INPUT NAME="Question1" TYPE="Radio" VALUE="Madrid">
Madrid
<BR>
<BR>
<INPUT TYPE=SUBMIT>
</FORM>
</BODY>
</HTML>
```

**2.** Save this as radio.html.

**3.** Close this file and create a new one in your web page editor, then type in the following:

```
<HTML>
<HEAD></HEAD>
<BODY>
<?php
echo "You selected the answer: $Question1";
?>
</BODY>
</HTML>
```

**4.** Save this as `radio.php`.

**5.** Open up `radio.html` in your browser and select an answer:

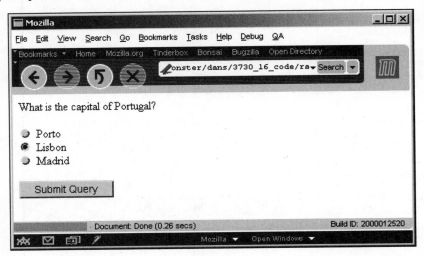

**6.** Click on **Submit Query** and view the results of the choice you have made:

### How It Works

We've switched our method of transmission to GET again, so the query string is visible once more. A questionnaire is actually the one time when this might be useful. It confirms which answer we have selected, which would admittedly be more useful if the answer wasn't already displayed in the body of the page. This aside, we'll take a quick look at the programs. The first program, `radio.html`, sets three radio button controls. They all have the same name, `Question1`, but with three different values to reflect the different answers:

```
<INPUT NAME="Question1" TYPE="Radio" VALUE="Porto">
Porto
<BR>
<INPUT NAME="Question1" TYPE="Radio" VALUE="Lisbon">
Lisbon
<BR>
<INPUT NAME="Question1" TYPE="Radio" VALUE="Madrid">
Madrid
```

Then in our second program, `radio.php`, we only need to display the contents of the one variable because there can only ever be one answer to our question:

```php
<?php
echo "You selected the answer: $Question1";
?>
```

There are only two more form controls that we wish to consider, so let's move quickly onto them.

## List Boxes

Listboxes or dropdown listboxes are controls that typically display several items in a list. Sometimes they have an arrow next to them that will allow you to scroll down to further items. They work a little different in HTML because they're created with two tags, the `<SELECT>` and `<OPTION>` tags. Essentially, they provide the same functionality as the radio buttons, given that usually you can only select one item from a predetermined list of options. For example:

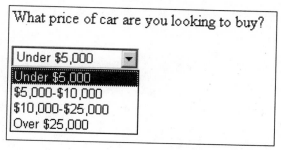

The `<SELECT>` tag that creates the list box encloses a number of `<OPTION>` tags. The `<OPTION>` tags each contain the text that corresponds to an item on the dropdown list.

```
<SELECT NAME="Price">
    <OPTION>Under $5,000</OPTION>
    <OPTION>$5,000-$10,000</OPTION>
    <OPTION>$10,000-$25,000</OPTION>
    <OPTION>Over $25,000</OPTION>
</SELECT>
```

However, there are times when being able to select several items is appropriate:

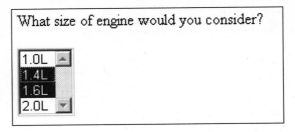

You can allow multiple items to be selected by adding the MULTIPLE attribute to the <SELECT> tag. This gives PHP two things to think about. In fact let's deal with these both of these options in the following example. We'll get information on the user about the price of car they wish to purchase and its engine size. The first question will only allow single answers; the second will allow multiple items, which can be selected by holding down the *Shift* key.

## Try It Out – Using a ListBox

**1.** Open up your web page editor and type in the following:

```
<HTML>
<HEAD></HEAD>
<BODY>
<FORM METHOD=GET ACTION="listbox.php">
What price of car are you looking to buy?
<BR>
<BR>
<SELECT NAME="Price">
     <OPTION>Under $5,000</OPTION>
     <OPTION>$5,000-$10,000</OPTION>
     <OPTION>$10,000-$25,000</OPTION>
     <OPTION>Over $25,000</OPTION>
</SELECT>
<BR>
<BR>
What size of engine would you consider?
<BR>
<BR>
<SELECT NAME="EngineSize[]" MULTIPLE>
     <OPTION>1.0L</OPTION>
     <OPTION>1.4L</OPTION>
     <OPTION>1.6L</OPTION>
     <OPTION>2.0L</OPTION>
</SELECT>
<BR>
<BR>
<INPUT TYPE=SUBMIT>
</FORM>
</BODY>
</HTML>
```

**2.** Save this as `listbox.html`.

**3.** Close this file and create another new file and type in the following:

```
<HTML>
<HEAD></HEAD>
<BODY>
<?php
echo "Price Range: $Price";
echo "<BR>Engine Size(s): $EngineSize[0]";
echo "$EngineSize[1]";
echo "$EngineSize[2]";
echo "$EngineSize[3]";
?>
</BODY>
</HTML>
```

**4.** Save this as `listbox.php`.

**5.** Open `listbox.html` up in your browser now and select one option from the top box, and one or more from the bottom listbox:

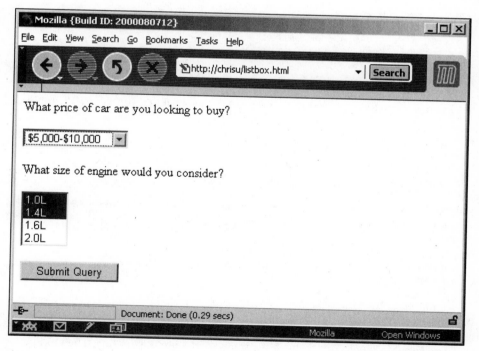

**6.** Click on Submit Query:

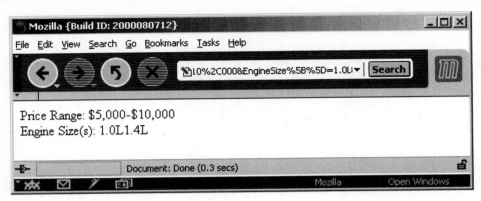

### How It Works

Let's split up the explanation of how our two different listboxes work. In our first program `listbox.html`, we have created a listbox with four items; multiple items may not be selected. We set the `<SELECT>` tag's NAME attribute to price:

```
<SELECT NAME="Price">
        <OPTION>Under $5,000</OPTION>
        <OPTION>$5,000-$10,000</OPTION>
        <OPTION>$10,000-$25,000</OPTION>
        <OPTION>Over $25,000</OPTION>
</SELECT>
```

In our second program, `listbox.php`, we referred to this attribute with the PHP variable `$Price`.

```
<?php
echo "Price Range: $Price";
echo "<BR>Engine Size(s): $EngineSize[0]";
...
```

There's absolutely nothing out of the ordinary going on here, and it should look very familiar up to this point. It's on the second listbox in our first program, `listbox.html`, that things depart from the norm:

```
<SELECT NAME="EngineSize[]" MULTIPLE>
        <OPTION>1.0L</OPTION>
        <OPTION>1.4L</OPTION>
        <OPTION>1.6L</OPTION>
        <OPTION>2.0L</OPTION>
</SELECT>
```

Well actually everything looks pretty much the same apart from the top line. The top line sets the NAME attribute to be `EngineSize[]`. We said in our checkbox example that this is a cue to PHP to treat this as an array. Hopefully, now the code in our second program, `listbox.php`, makes a little more sense.

```
echo "Price Range: $Price";
echo "<BR>Engine Size(s): $EngineSize[0]";
echo "$EngineSize[1]";
echo "$EngineSize[2]";
echo "$EngineSize[3]";
```

We said that during the creation of an array, PHP creates a new variable of the same name with an index number bolted on. We've got four items on the list, so there are four index numbers. We have to display the contents of each one, as each index number refers to an item in the array. Array indexes always start at zero, so $EngineSize[0] refers to the first option in the list, 1.0L. It will only contain this item if we have selected that option, otherwise it will contain the contents of the first <SELECT> option chosen on that page.

In this case we have selected this option in the screenshots above, so $EngineSize[0] does indeed contain the value 1.0L. The same goes for $EngineSize[1] which relates to the second option. $EngineSize[2] and $EngineSize[3] don't contain anything because we didn't select any more values on the listbox. If we selected only one option, then only $EngineSize[0] would contain a value. Only if we selected all four options would $EngineSize[2] and $EngineSize[3] contain any values. If we had only selected the last two items, then the variables $EngineSize[0] and $EngineSize[1] would contain 1.6L and 2.0L respectively. $EngineSize[2] and $EngineSize[3] still wouldn't contain any values. We're not going to go any further with arrays here, as we will be covering them in a lot of detail in Chapter 5 – hopefully we have laid some of the groundwork for them.

*We've kept the method of transmission of the FORM data in GET, so you can study it just to confirm that the items have actually been passed across.*

## Hidden Form Fields

There are times when you want to take information contained in a web page, and pass it to another web page without requiring any input from the user. There is another setting for the <INPUT> control that allows you to pass information in a field (while keeping the control and its contents hidden), just as though it was a text box. This is known as a **hidden form field** (or **hidden control**).

Hidden form fields come into play in a slightly different manner to the controls we have already demonstrated. They're probably more useful on PHP pages that contain forms because you can use them to send information contained within PHP variables. A typical hidden form field on a form might look like this:

```
<INPUT TYPE=HIDDEN NAME=Hidden1 VALUE="Secret Message">
```

We can't display a screenshot of this, because this control wouldn't appear on the page. Any form that submitted it though would have a variable called $Hidden1 that contains the text "Secret Message". To use the hidden form field in a PHP page, you can write the whole HTML form in echo() statements – in this way you can transfer the contents of PHP variables via HTML controls as shown below:

```
<?php
$Message1="This message is invisible";
echo "<FORM>";
echo "<INPUT TYPE=HIDDEN NAME=Hidden2 VALUE='$Message1'>";
```

```
echo "<INPUT TYPE=SUBMIT>";
echo "</FORM>";
?>
```

Here the entire HTML form is written in PHP statements and it enables us to create a variable called $Hidden2 and transfer the contents of $Message1 into it.

Let's do an example now that takes the contents of a <SELECT> listbox and displays the user's choice on the next page as well as all of the other options. We'll use the process outlined above to write the HTML form in PHP echo() statements as well.

## Try It Out – Using the Hidden Form Field Field

**1.** Open your web page editor and type the following:

```
<HTML>
<HEAD></HEAD>
<BODY>
<?php
$Message1="Bugs Bunny";
$Message2="Homer Simpson";
$Message3="Ren & Stimpy";
echo "<FORM METHOD=GET ACTION='hidden2.php'>";
echo "Which of the following would win in a shootout?";
echo "<SELECT NAME='ListBox'>";
echo "<OPTION>$Message1</OPTION>";
echo "<OPTION>$Message2</OPTION>";
echo "<OPTION>$Message3</OPTION>";
echo "</SELECT><BR><BR>";
echo "<INPUT TYPE=HIDDEN NAME=Hidden1 VALUE='$Message1'>";
echo "<INPUT TYPE=HIDDEN NAME=Hidden2 VALUE='$Message2'>";
echo "<INPUT TYPE=HIDDEN NAME=Hidden3 VALUE='$Message3'>";
echo "<INPUT TYPE=SUBMIT>";
echo "</FORM>";
?>
</BODY>
</HTML>
```

**2.** Save this as hidden.php.

**3.** Close this file and start a new one and type in the following:

```
<HTML>
<HEAD></HEAD>
<BODY>
<?php
echo "The three options were:<BR>";
echo "$Hidden1<BR>";
echo "$Hidden2<BR>";
echo "$Hidden3<BR>";
echo "<BR>You selected:<BR>";
echo "$ListBox";
```

```
?>
</BODY>
</HTML>
```

**4.** Save this as `hidden2.php`.

**5.** Close this and open up `hidden.php` in your browser and make a selection:

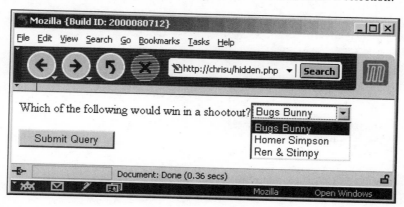

**6.** Click on **Submit Query** to view the results:

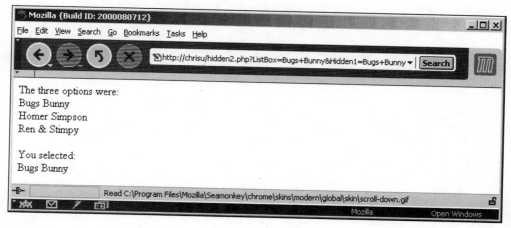

### How It Works

Once you get over the process of creating the HTML form in `echo()` statements rather than straight HTML code, this is really very straightforward. We start by creating our three variables that will form the basis of the `<SELECT>` listbox:

```
$Message1="Bugs Bunny";
$Message2="Homer Simpson";
$Message3="Ren & Stimpy";
```

They are respectively $Message1, $Message2, and $Message3. Next we create the HTML form using echo() statements. Absolutely nothing differs from a normal HTML form, except when we want to use quotation marks in the HTML – we have to use single quotation marks and not double ones. The first line just tells us to send the form contents to hidden2.php via the GET method:

```
echo "<FORM METHOD=GET ACTION='hidden2.php'>";
```

We display some explanatory text and start the <SELECT> listbox:

```
echo "Which of the following would win in a shootout?";
echo "<SELECT NAME='ListBox'>";
```

We give it three options, the contents of the variables $Message1, $Message2, and $Message3 respectively.

```
echo "<OPTION>$Message1</OPTION>";
echo "<OPTION>$Message2</OPTION>";
echo "<OPTION>$Message3</OPTION>";
```

We then close the <SELECT> box and add a couple of line breaks:

```
echo "</SELECT><BR><BR>";
```

Next we take the three variables we've already used and pass them as hidden form fields to our form also:

```
echo "<INPUT TYPE=HIDDEN NAME=Hidden1 VALUE='$Message1'>";
echo "<INPUT TYPE=HIDDEN NAME=Hidden2 VALUE='$Message2'>";
echo "<INPUT TYPE=HIDDEN NAME=Hidden3 VALUE='$Message3'>";
```

The three variables will turn up on the form as $Hidden1, $Hidden2, and $Hidden3 respectively. We can then add a Submit button to the form, and close the form:

```
echo "<INPUT TYPE=SUBMIT>";
echo "</FORM>";
```

The second PHP page just displays the contents of the controls created in the first page. We display the contents of the three hidden form fields first.

```
echo "The three options were:<BR>";
echo "$Hidden1<BR>";
echo "$Hidden2<BR>";
echo "$Hidden3<BR>";
```

This is useful because normally the contents of the whole listbox aren't transferred across. Only the option selected by the user will be passed over to the next PHP page. However, sometimes you want to have all of the listbox contents available in your PHP page. This is one effective method for transferring this type of information.

The last lines just display the contents of selection made by the user.

```
echo "<BR>You selected:<BR>";
echo "$ListBox";
```

We will be using hidden form fields later in this book to perform this type of task.

## Passwords

Passwords are essentially text fields that blank out the input with asterisks when the user types in text. They store and transmit information in the same way as text fields:

```
What is your password?
<INPUT NAME="Password" TYPE="Password">
```

We won't be doing a practical example with them, as there is no difference in the processing between TEXT and PASSWORD type of text fields. If you want to see one in action, just go back to the previous example text.html and change the type to PASSWORD. However, if you choose to transmit this information, using GET, then notice that the password is not encrypted in the query string and will be visible to all and sundry. That isn't to say once again that POST is a secure method of sending data, just that the information isn't as immediately visible. If you want security you will have to use something like SSL (Secure Sockets Layer) to actively encrypt your data.

## Submit Buttons and Reset Buttons

We've already used Submit buttons copiously throughout this chapter, so we're not going to subject you to an example that demonstrates how they work. However, there are a couple of points we wish to note. What happens if you need more than one submit button in a form? In this case you will have to set the NAME and VALUE attributes of the SUBMIT buttons on your page as well. For example:

```
<INPUT VALUE="Button 1 pressed" TYPE="SUBMIT" NAME="Submit1">
<INPUT VALUE="Button 2 pressed" TYPE="SUBMIT" NAME="Submit2">
```

This, as you might expect, creates variables in PHP that PHP can pick up. In fact, the above code would create one variable in PHP depending on which button is pressed. If you press Submit1 then a variable called $Submit1 is created. If you press button 2, then $Submit2 is created. The contents of $Submit1 are "Button 1 pressed", while the contents of $Submit2 are "Button 2 pressed". We can't actually do anything useful with this yet, so we won't show you an example. We're going to look at some new programming features in Chapter 4 that will make this feature useful.

Secondly, the submit button offers no respite if you type in the wrong information. Even though you can't actually undo information sent via the submit button, the reset button control offers a little help as it can be used to set the state of all controls on the form to their initial state.

```
<INPUT TYPE="Reset">
```

Now that we have examined all of the form controls we are going to use throughout the book, we are going to put them together and use them all in one large example.

# Using Values Returned From Forms In Your PHP Scripts

We've demonstrated all manner of controls, and how PHP handles their contents, but we still haven't done anything practical with the contents other than to dump the contents back to another web page. Admittedly, without any of the features that we're going to discuss in the next chapter, manipulating the contents of our variables is hard. However, we learned about mathematical and string operators in the last chapter and so we can combine the things we learned there with the concepts learned in this chapter.

In the last example in this chapter, we're going to create a loan application form that asks for the amount of money that a person wants to borrow, and calculates the amount of money that a fictional bank called NAMLLU can offer a person based on their age, and salary. We give them a simple yes or no answer at the end of the calculation. We'll run through our criteria for accepting a loan now. Although our loan calculation acceptance formula might seem quite complex, it's quite straightforward, and not based on any company's formula.

The loan amount for a person in our program is calculated using three figures, as follows:

- ❑ The first figure is their annual salary divided by 5 to give our Salary Allowance Variable.

- ❑ The second figure is their age divided by 10, with the resulting figure rounded down to the nearest whole number.

- ❑ Next we subtract one from our second figure to arrive at our final second figure, which is our Age Allowance variable.

- ❑ The formula takes this first figure and multiplies by a second figure to get our third and final figure, which is the Loan Allowance, variable.

The age calculation on the second figure means that anybody who is under the age of 20 is automatically excluded, because our formula will always return a zero – the result of dividing zero by any non-zero value is zero. So let's just run through the second part of the formula to demonstrate this.

```
First figure * (19/10 - (19 Modulus 10) /10))-1
```

Remember that the Modulus operator is used to return the remainder from a division sum. This calculation will then work out to

```
First figure * (1.9 - 0.9) -1
```

which in turn changes to

```
First figure * 0
```

So, if you provide an age under 20, the second figure will always revert to zero. This is because no matter what the first figure is, when multiplied by a zero, it will return zero. Once we've multiplied the first figure by the second figure we arrive at a total and if this is more than the amount the person wants to borrow we say yes, otherwise we say no.

Once again we're just going to need two pages in this example. The first one takes the loan details from which we will get the person's first name, second name, age, address, salary, and the amount they want to borrow. We'll use nearly all of the controls we introduced in the chapter to do this. The second page, our PHP page, will do the calculation for us and deliver a verdict.

**Try It Out – Our Loan Application Form**

**1.** Open your web page editor and type in the following:

```
<HTML>
<HEAD></HEAD>
<BODY>
<B>Namllu Credit Bank Loan Application Form</B>
<FORM METHOD=POST ACTION="loan.php">
First Name:
<INPUT NAME="FirstName" TYPE="Text">
Last Name:
<INPUT NAME="LastName" TYPE="Text">
Age:
<INPUT NAME="Age" TYPE="Text" SIZE="3">
<BR>
<BR>
Address:
<TEXTAREA NAME="Address" ROWS=4 COLS=40>
</TEXTAREA>
<BR>
<BR>
What is your current salary?
<SELECT NAME="Salary">
<OPTION VALUE=0>Under $10000</OPTION>
<OPTION VALUE=10000>$10,000 to $25,000</OPTION>
<OPTION VALUE=25000>$25,000 to $50,000</OPTION>
<OPTION VALUE=50000>Over $50,000</OPTION>
</SELECT>
<BR>
<BR>
How much do you want to borrow?<BR><BR>
<INPUT NAME="Loan" TYPE="Radio" VALUE=1000>Our $1,000 package at 8.0% interest
<BR>
<INPUT NAME="Loan" TYPE="Radio" VALUE=5000>Our $5,000 package at 11.5% interest
<BR>
<INPUT NAME="Loan" TYPE="Radio" VALUE=10000>Our $10,000 package at 15.0% interest
<BR>
<BR>
<INPUT TYPE=SUBMIT VALUE="Click here to Submit application">
<INPUT TYPE=RESET VALUE="Reset application form">
</FORM>
</BODY>
</HTML>
```

**2.** Save this as `loan.html`

**3.** Close this file down and create a new one and type the following:

```
<HTML>
<HEAD></HEAD>
<BODY>
```

```
<B>Namllu Credit Bank Loan Application Form</B>
<BR>
<BR>
<?
$SalaryAllowance = $Salary/5;
$AgeAllowance = ($Age/10 - ($Age%10)/10)-1;
$LoanAllowance = $SalaryAllowance * $AgeAllowance;
echo "Loan wanted:$Loan<BR>";
echo "Loan amount we will allow:$LoanAllowance<BR><BR>";
if ($Loan <= $LoanAllowance) echo "Yes, $FirstName $LastName, we are delighted to
accept your application";
if ($Loan > $LoanAllowance) echo "Sorry, $FirstName $LastName, we cannot accept
your application at this time";
?>
</BODY>
</HTML>
```

**4.** Save this as `loan.php`

**5.** Open `loan.html` in your browser and supply some details:

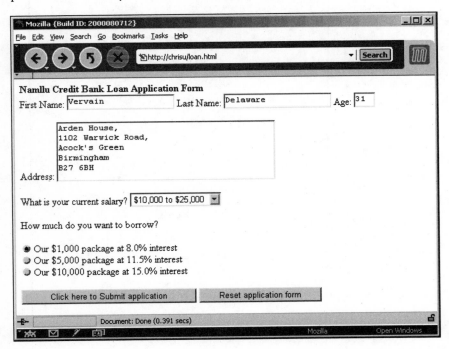

**6.** Click the Submit application button and you should see something like the screenshot opposite:

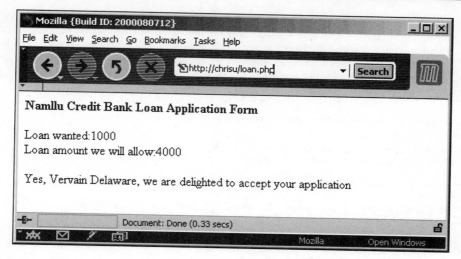

### How It Works

You'll have earned a break after examining these two programs. While the first is quite lengthy, it isn't doing anything out of the ordinary, and certainly nothing we haven't already encountered in this chapter. We have combined a total of eight controls on our loan form in `loan.html`. The first three are as follows:

```
First Name:
<INPUT NAME="FirstName" TYPE="Text">
Last Name:
<INPUT NAME="LastName" TYPE="Text">
Age:
<INPUT NAME="Age" TYPE="Text"SIZE="3">
```

They're all text fields, used for accepting the first name, last name, and age of our applicant. You should be able to see now that they will create the variables `$FirstName`, `$LastName`, and `$Age` on our PHP page. The address is entered into a `<TEXTAREA>` control:

```
<TEXTAREA NAME="Address" ROWS=4 COLS=40>
</TEXTAREA>
```

This in turn creates a PHP variable `$Address`. You should note that we don't actually make use of all of the PHP variables we create in the form, but we will be returning to this example in later chapters and using some of them there.

The next control is a dropdown listbox, which contains a set of salary ranges:

```
<SELECT NAME="Salary">
<OPTION VALUE=0>Under $10000</OPTION>
<OPTION VALUE=10000>$10,000 to $25,000</OPTION>
<OPTION VALUE=25000>$25,000 to $50,000</OPTION>
<OPTION VALUE=50000>Over $50,000</OPTION>
</SELECT>
```

We can't actually store a range as a value, so instead we take the lowest value in the range and assign that as a particular value to each radio button. This creates just one PHP variable, $Salary, which holds the value associated with whichever range has been selected by the user. If there has been no range selected, then the radio button will return no value. Notice that we set the first value to zero, and as before this zero will propagate in our formula, and will ensure that anybody with a salary of under $10,000 will automatically be refused. We're a bit mercenary!

Our next control is a group of three related radio buttons:

```
How much do you want to borrow?<BR><BR>
<INPUT NAME="Loan" TYPE="Radio" VALUE=1000>Our $1,000 package at 8.0% interest
<BR>
<INPUT NAME="Loan" TYPE="Radio" VALUE=5000>Our $5,000 package at 11.5% interest
<BR>
<INPUT NAME="Loan" TYPE="Radio" VALUE=10000>Our $10,000 package at 15.0% interest
<BR>
```

These all have the same name, because the variable only ever needs to contain one value depending on what the user has selected. This group of three buttons creates just one PHP variable, $Loan.

The last two controls are a Submit button and Reset button:

```
<INPUT TYPE=SUBMIT VALUE="Click here to Submit application">
<INPUT TYPE=RESET VALUE="Reset application form">
```

The Submit button utilizes the ACTION attribute that was set right at the top of the form, so it knows where to send the form:

```
<FORM METHOD=POST ACTION="loan.php">
```

### Processing The Claim For a Loan

We've talked about how we've stored and transmitted the information in our form; it's our second program loan.php that takes these values and performs some simple operations on them in order to approve or reject the loan claim. Let's see if you've successfully followed what was going on. The first line creates a new variable, the Salary Allowance, which is the user's salary divided by five:

```
$SalaryAllowance = $Salary/5;
```

The second line calculates our more complex Age Allowance formula. What we want to do in this formula is return a whole number, based on the user's age divided by 10. If there is any remainder left over from the division, then we want to remove it by rounding the answer downwards to the nearest whole number.

*Developers in other programming languages will notice that what we're doing is implementing a DIV function. Unfortunately PHP doesn't have such an operation automatically provided.*

To calculate the remainder we use the modulus operator on the user's age – remember though, we need to divide this by 10. We then subtract one from the total, in line with our formula as we explained earlier. Our final line will return a 0 if we put in a value between 0 and 19 for the user's age, a 1 if we supply a value between 20 and 29, a 2 if we supply a value between and 30 and 39, and so on. The result of this calculation is stored in the new `$AgeAllowance` variable:

```
$AgeAllowance = ($Age/10 - ($Age%10)/10)-1;
```

Fortunately, the next line is much simpler. It takes the two figures we've just calculated, multiplies them together, and stores them in a new variable `$LoanAllowance`, which is our final figure for how large a loan we will allow the user to take out.

```
$LoanAllowance = $SalaryAllowance * $AgeAllowance;
```

The next two lines just `echo()` a confirmation on the web page of the amount supplied by the user for the loan they want, and the amount of loan that we will allow:

```
echo "Loan wanted:$Loan<BR>";
echo "Loan amount we will allow:$LoanAllowance<BR><BR>";
```

If you followed the program this far you've done well, but in the next two lines we cheated a bit and introduced a new feature, the <= (less than equals operator). This allows us to make a decision based on the information we've been given. What the operator does is calculates whether the figure that we want for our loan, is less than or equal to the amount that the bank will allow. If it is then we display a message on the web page, saying that we are delighted to accept the application. We will be looking at this structure in extensive detail in the next chapter; so don't panic if we've only covered it very briefly.

We also personalize this message with the names the user provided on the form:

```
if ($Loan <= $LoanAllowance) echo "Yes, $FirstName $LastName, we are delighted to
accept your application";
```

The last line of PHP script does the opposite to the previous line. If the amount we want for our loan exceeds the amount the bank will authorize, then we display a message saying we have rejected the application.

```
if ($Loan > $LoanAllowance) echo "Sorry, $FirstName $LastName, we cannot accept
your application at this time";
```

That's all there is to our programs. Oh, one tiny little detail – the nature of the information in a real-life application is sensitive, so we use the POST method to transmit it. Once again we must remind you that POST is only more discreet, hackers can still just as easily hijack information sent via this method.

### Possible Improvements to Our Form

That's not to say that our form is perfect; indeed if you try hard enough, you can probably break it, or cause it to display illogical values. This is because we've not performed any kind of validation on the values received by the user. What's to stop a user supplying a totally erroneous value for their age such as 965? We know it can't be true, but we can't stop it. We'll look at ways in the next chapter of tightening this up, by checking the values and only allowing values within a certain range, or even that the user has actually supplied a value, but that's enough for now.

# Summary

This chapter might have seemed a bit pedantic, but the concepts we've run through, while being repetitive, are absolutely vital to PHP. Any kind of form handling in a web site means you have to be comfortable with manipulating the results from a large variety of controls. We've tried to put everybody on a level playing field for later chapters.

We started by looking at the HTML `<FORM>` tag in a lot of detail and saw that there are two distinct methods for submitting your data with it. The first is the GET method, which publicly transmits the information as a query string attached to the end of a URL. The second is the POST method, which sends the form information hidden away as part of the HTTP body in a more discreet but not really more secure format. We saw that the ACTION attribute is used to specify which page we go to once the form is submitted, and the suffix of the destination is used to determine where the form is being sent. The `.php` suffix indicates that we should send the page to the PHP script engine.

We then conducted a tour of the most common HTML form controls, which were text fields, text areas, checkboxes, radio buttons, listboxes, hidden form fields, passwords fields, and the submit and reset buttons. We closed the chapter by using nearly all of these controls in one application, and we performed mathematical operations on input we received from the user. We introduced a new concept at the end of this example, that of a programming structure which can determine a particular course of action in our web page. This decision making structure allows our PHP programs to branch into one of two possible courses of action. This will be the first topic we look at in our next chapter.

# Decision Making

In the last chapter, we started getting to grips with sending form information and receiving some dynamic responses from the web server, which we then incorporated within our web pages. Admittedly, we were still hampered by the amount of things we could do with them, and indeed in the last example of Chapter 3 we had to cheat a bit and introduce a new feature, which made a decision on whether or not to display a line of code based on the truth-value of a certain condition.

We'll be getting to the meat of PHP programming in the next three chapters, starting with the processes that PHP uses in order to make decisions. Prior to this, your PHP code was mostly executed in strict sequence, line one first, line two second, and so on. Decision making code gives you the ability to choose whether you wish to execute a particular line of code, and it allows you to start making comparisons between different variables and values.

It also gives us the opportunity to introduce some Boolean operators (which return a value of "true" or "false"). We could have introduced these alongside the mathematical and string operators in Chapter 2, but we wouldn't have been able to demonstrate their use and effectiveness. You'll find that the features learned in this chapter will enable you to write much more complex PHP scripts, and we'll use them to improve the large example we produced in the last chapter.

We'll be discussing topics in this order:

- ❑ How branching effects the flow of our code
- ❑ An everyday example of branching
- ❑ The `If` statement
- ❑ Comparison operators
- ❑ Equality operators
- ❑ Logical operators
- ❑ The `Switch` statement
- ❑ Include files
- ❑ How to validate the contents of a form

# Conditional or Branching Statements

In its most simple form, a conditional piece of code means either "execute one line of code" or "don't execute it at all", depending on whether or not a specified criterion is met. A more complex variation on this could be either "execute this line of code", or "execute that line of code" depending on which condition is met. You can extend this to execute one complete section of code, or execute another complete section of code. Finally, it's possible to list a whole heap of possible outcomes to a certain condition. If the result of the condition is outcome number 1, then execute section 1 of code; if the result is outcome number 2, then execute section 2; if the result is outcome number 3 then execute section number 3, and so on.

## An Example of Branching in Day to Day Life

We're talking rather abstractly here, so let's clarify this by thinking of an example from day-to-day life. Shopping is probably the most mundane activity that we can think of, but it works rather well in illustrating the type of decision-making your program might have to perform.

Imagine you have to compile a list of items that you will need in order to:

a)   make a cup of tea
b)   make a cheese sandwich
c)   feed the pets

You will also have to go and buy any items you don't have, but let's say that you only have five dollars in your purse. We'll record this process now in English terms:

**1.**   Check the fridge to see if you have any milk, cheese, and butter and if you haven't, add to your list.

**2.**   Check the bread bin to see if you have any bread, and if you haven't, then add this to your list.

**3.**   Check the cupboard to see if you have any tea, and if you haven't, add this to your list.

**4.**   If you have all the items you need to complete these 3 tasks then go to step 7.

**5.**   Go to the supermarket.

**6.**   Buy as many items on the list as you can for five dollars

**7.**   If you have pet food, you can feed the pets. If you haven't skip step 8.

**8.**   Pets are happy

**9.**   If you have milk and tea, you can make a cup of tea. If you haven't skip step 10.

**10.** You aren't thirsty anymore.

**11.** If you have bread, butter, and cheese you can make a cheese sandwich. If this isn't true, then skip step 12.

**12.** You aren't hungry anymore.

**13.** Collapse exhausted in front of the TV!

The first thing to notice is that it is extremely unlikely that you will perform all thirteen steps in this program (even though this isn't a true computer program, we will refer to it as a program because it has the same logical flow). Depending on the results from earlier steps, you can end up skipping individual steps, or if the conditions on lines 1, 2 and 3 are met then you can jump the majority of the program. There is also a list of completely different possible outcomes – you could go hungry if you don't spend your money wisely! This is typical of decision-making statements in PHP. When you write PHP programs, parts of the code will be written to deal with specific situations and if a particular situation doesn't arise, then there is no need to run the PHP code that relates to it.

You could actually represent the entire process above quite easily with a PHP program. We could represent each line of our shopping expedition in code. You could start with line 1, which could be represented in three separate lines. We actually require three separate actions in line 1. Check the fridge for milk, check the fridge for cheese and check the fridge for butter. To represent the first action we just need one if statement that checks a condition, and then performs an action if the condition is true:

```
if ($FridgeHasNoMilk) $ShoppingList = $Shoppinglist . "Milk.";
```

In other words, if the fridge has no milk, then add the item milk to the shopping list. We could then go back and do this for the next two items required in our first action. However, rather than go back and translate each of the lines in our "program" into PHP, let's take a look at the rules that govern how we create an if statement.

# If Statements

We've already mentioned the if statement in the previous chapter, and having touched upon it again you should have a good idea of how it works. Abstractly it works like this:

```
if (a condition is true) execute a line of code
```

The if statement will only execute any code if the condition is true. If the condition isn't met then the code will be completely ignored, and won't get executed by PHP at all. It will then jump onto the next line.

```
if  (weather is rainy) put up umbrella
go outside
```

The second line is executed no matter what, but we only put up our umbrella if it is raining. If you need to execute a whole section of code, then you need to put the code on separate lines after the condition and in between braces.

```
if (a condition is true)
{
   execute the contents of these braces
}
```

So to expand on our umbrella example we could say:

```
if (weather is rainy)
{
    put up umbrella
    put on raincoat
}
go outside
```

Once again the "go outside" clause is always executed, but we only put up the umbrella and put on the raincoat if the condition "weather is rainy" is true.

Let's now take a look at how you can create the conditions within the parentheses to determine if a section or line of code is to be executed or not. It really doesn't matter what the code between the braces does, or how much of it there is, the braces just enable the code they contain to be treated as a separate entity.

## Boolean Values

Before we go any further, we need to introduce the concept of a **Boolean** value. Previously our variables could hold numbers or text, but Boolean values are held in a third type of variable, which can hold one of two absolute values, **true** or **false**. You can set any variable to one of these two values:

```
$Variable = true;
```

However, if you then display the value on the screen, you see a numeric value:

1

The same goes for setting $variable to false, it will then display:

0

So, you can see that Boolean values have both numeric and literal values. On it's own this isn't particularly interesting, but once you start needing to make decisions on the outcome of situations, and having to say either a given condition is true or false, you'll find that you use them a lot.

## Boolean operators

While we've looked at mathematical operators in some detail (and you've probably surmised there aren't that many of them in PHP), there is another set of operators that we've deferred talking about. This is because without branching structures, these operators are useless. In the last chapter, we had to introduce some of them so that we could make a decision in our loan application form. In fact, any time you need to create a condition, in order to make any kind of decision, you will have to use one of these operators. We'll divide them into four broad categories and look at examples of each one in action.

### The > and < Operators

You should already be familiar with the **greater than** and **less than** operators – they're fairly fundamental in even basic math, and equally important in programming. In PHP we can use them to compare two constants, a constant with a variable, or two variables. Depending on what the outcome of the comparison is, a certain course of action can be pursued. With constants the result is self-evident, as you can see:

```
If (5 < 6) echo "Five is smaller than six";
```

However, we still need to dig below the surface to examine what's going on. The conditional part of the if statement is the part contained within parentheses. It can evaluate to one of the two Boolean values, either true or false. In fact, it can only ever evaluate to one of these two values. Either a condition is met or it isn't met. It can't be partially met, and PHP can't return a value like "Maybe", or "I'll know later if you ask me". So the above line returns "true". The if statement will only execute if the condition inside evaluates to true.

The above statement isn't too useful – you already know that five is smaller than six. However, if we compare the contents of a variable to a number, such as our lucky number, then the answer depends upon the value of the variable $LuckyNumber:

```
If  ($LuckyNumber < 6) echo ("Our lucky number is smaller than six");
```

Or we can compare two variables for an outcome:

```
If  ($LuckyNumber < $LotteryNumber) echo ("Our lucky number is too small");
```

And of course, we can use the results of this condition to not just display a message but to determine a particular course of action:

```
If  ($LuckyNumber < $LotteryNumber)
{
    echo ("Our lucky number is too small");
    $LuckyNumber = $LuckyNumber+1;
}
```

Ok, let's do a simple example now where our PHP program "thinks" of a number between one and ten and we have to guess it. To get PHP to "think" of a number, we will use the PHP random number generating function rand. We will explain how it works after we've done the example.

## Try It Out – Using Comparison Operators

1. Open up your web page editor and type in the following:

```
<HTML>
<HEAD></HEAD>
<BODY>
<FORM METHOD=GET ACTION="guessgame.php">
What number between 1 and 10 am I thinking of?
<INPUT NAME="Guess" TYPE="Text">
<BR>
<BR>
<INPUT TYPE=SUBMIT>
</FORM>
</BODY>
</HTML>
```

2. Save this as guessgame.html.

3. Close this down and create a new file, then type the following:

```
<HTML>
<HEAD></HEAD>
<BODY>
<?php
$Number = rand(1,10);
if ($Guess>$Number) {
   echo "Guess is too high";
   echo "<BR>I was thinking of $Number, you don't ";
}
if ($Guess<$Number) {
   echo "Guess is too low";
   echo "<BR>I was thinking of $Number, you don't ";
}
?>
win
</BODY>
</HTML>
```

**4.** Save this as `guessgame.php`.

**5.** Open up `guessgame.html` in your browser and type in a number:

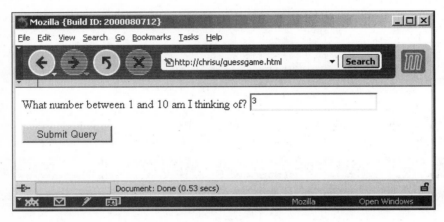

**6.** Hit **Submit Query** and see whether you win or not:

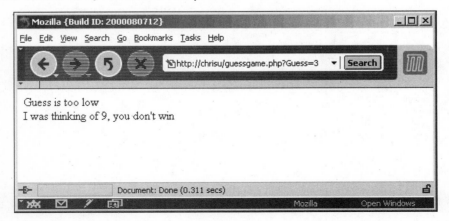

### How It Works

We actually cheat a little bit in this example, in that we don't get PHP to generate a random number until after the user has submitted their guess. This has no effect on the outcome, because the random number we generate is totally uninfluenced by the guess the user has supplied. The first program asks the user for a number, and stores the answer in a text box with the NAME attribute set to Guess.

```
What number between 1 and 10 am I thinking of?
<INPUT NAME="Guess" TYPE="Text">
```

This is then passed to the program guessgame.php, which can access this value because it's stored in the variable $Guess, which has been created by PHP automatically. Let's look at the second program in sequence. The first line in guessgame.php generates a number between 1 and 10:

```
$Number = rand(1,10);
```

The rand function is extremely simple to use, just supply it with a minimum value and a maximum value separated by a comma and it will generate a random number between and including these two values. The result is stored in the $Number variable.

We then take the number that the user supplied, which is stored in $Guess, and compare it to the number that PHP is "thinking" of. We check to see if the value stored in $Guess is higher than the value stored in $Number. If it is, then we execute the code between the next set of braces:

```
if ($Guess>$Number) {
    echo "Guess is too high";
    echo "<BR>I was thinking of $Number, you don't ";
}
```

The code between the braces informs the user that the guess was too high, and tells them what the number should have been. It also adds the incomplete phrase "you don't", which is completed later in the program.

The second if statement checks to see if the guess is too low, and then executes the code contained in the following set of braces:

```
if ($Guess<$Number) {
echo "Guess is too low";
echo "<BR>I was thinking of $Number, you don't ";
}
```

This time we inform the user that their guess was too low, and again we tell them what the number was, and also put in the incomplete phrase "you don't" again.

The next line of code completes our PHP script, and we follow it with the single line of text "win".

```
?>
win
```

This line is always displayed, and you can see that we're using it to complete the phrase, "you don't". However, as you might have guessed, nothing happens if the user guesses the correct number. In this case, neither of the if statements will evaluate to true, so neither are executed. All that will be displayed in fact is the simple message "win".

So, we've actually doctored the program to avoid having to check to see whether the user has won, we merely deduced that if the user's guess isn't too low, or too high then it must be the correct answer. We'll introduce the operator that checks for equality now.

### The == and === Operators

We've used the equals sign already to perform a slightly different task in PHP, so you might have already noted that the equals sign has two different distinct usages in PHP. The single equality sign operator is the **assignment operator**; the double equality sign is the **equality operator**. This is an important difference, if you consider the following:

```
$LuckyNumber = 5;
$LuckyNumber = 7;
```

The above lines sets the value of $LuckyNumber as 5 and then it's says, whatever was previously in the variable $LuckyNumber should be disregarded, and assign to it the new value on the right hand side, which is 7. So the second line here overrides the first line.

What's different is that the equality operator doesn't affect the contents of the variable in any way. In the following line:

```
if ($LuckyNumber == 7) echo ("Your lucky number is seven");
```

the value of $LuckyNumber isn't changed in any way by this comparison, whether or not it is equal to the number 7. The variable is just checked for its value. This is a very important distinction to make and when you use the equals sign, you must be sure that you use single for assignment and double for equality. If you don't you might get slightly unexpected results.

There is a second version of the equality operator that has recently been introduced in PHP 4.01. This takes three signs and will evaluate to true, only if the values are equal and the data types of the variable are also equal:

```
if ($LuckyNumber === $RandomNumber) echo ("Your lucky number is $RandomNumber");
```

### The != and <> Operators

The reverse of the equality operator == is the **inequality** operator !=.

```
if ($LuckyNumber != 7) echo ("Your lucky number most definitely isn't seven");
```

"!=" literally stands for not equal to!

There is a second notation for not equal to, using the less than and greater than operators. It's used in the following way in an if statement:

```
if ($LuckyNumber <> 7) echo ("Your lucky number most definitely isn't seven");
```

The only time that either of these conditions will evaluate to `false` is if the value in $LuckyNumber is 7.

Let's take a look at an example of these two operators in a simple quiz question that we encountered in the previous chapter. We will not only set the question, but we'll also tell the user whether or not they got the answer correct.

## Try It Out – Using the Equality and Inequality Operators

**1.** Start up your web page editor, and if you've still got a copy of `radio.html` from Chapter 2, amend the highlighted line. If you haven't, then just type in all of the following code:

```
<HTML>
<HEAD></HEAD>
<BODY>
<FORM METHOD=GET ACTION="quiz.php">
What is the capital of Portugal?
<BR>
<BR>
<INPUT NAME="Question1" TYPE="Radio" VALUE="Porto">
Porto
<BR>
<INPUT NAME="Question1" TYPE="Radio" VALUE="Lisbon">
Lisbon
<BR>
<INPUT NAME="Question1" TYPE="Radio" VALUE="Madrid">
Madrid
<BR>
<BR>
<INPUT TYPE=SUBMIT>
</FORM>
</BODY>
</HTML>
```

**2.** Save this as `quiz.html`.

**3.** Close this down and then create a new file in your web page editor and type the following:

```
<HTML>
<HEAD></HEAD>
<BODY>
<?php
if ($Question1=="Lisbon") echo "You are correct, Lisbon is the right answer";
if ($Question1!="Lisbon") echo "You are incorrect, Lisbon is not the right answer";
?>
</BODY>
</HTML>
```

**4.** Save this as `quiz.php`.

**5.** Open up `quiz.html` in your browser and supply an answer:

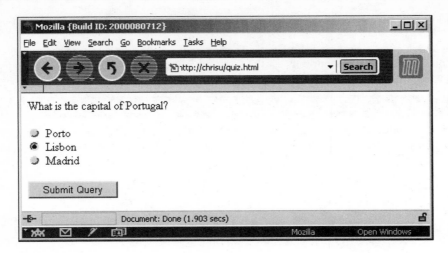

**6.** If you supplied Lisbon, then you will see the following:

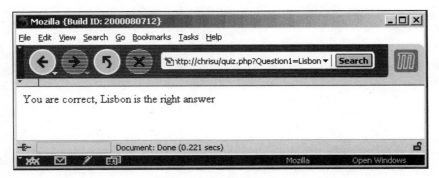

**7.** Go back and try a different answer, to see what the response is.

## How It Works

There is very little to explain in this example. We've covered radio buttons in the previous chapter, and you should be aware that whichever option is selected means that the value assigned is the corresponding NAME attribute to your selection:

```
<INPUT NAME="Question1" TYPE="Radio" VALUE="Porto">
Porto
<BR>
<INPUT NAME="Question1" TYPE="Radio" VALUE="Lisbon">
Lisbon
<BR>
<INPUT NAME="Question1" TYPE="Radio" VALUE="Madrid">
Madrid
```

We then take this value which is now stored in the PHP variable $Question1, and in our second program compare it with our answer "Lisbon" to see if it matches:

```
if ($Question1=="Lisbon") echo "You are correct, Lisbon is the right answer";
```

If it does then we display the "You are correct" message, if it doesn't, nothing happens. Either way PHP moves onto the next line and checks to see if the contents of $Question1 don't match "Lisbon":

```
if ($Question1!="Lisbon") echo "You are incorrect, Lisbon is the right answer";
```

Logically speaking, one of these two statements has to be correct. Either, we did put Lisbon as our answer or we didn't, so we will always see one of those two messages. Given that all possible eventualities have been handled, unlike in our previous example, we don't need to do anything further in our PHP program.

This leaves one last set of Boolean operators to look at.

### Logical Operators (AND, OR, NOT )

The logical operators are a little less fearsome than they sound. In practice, their English usage alerts you to the way they are used in PHP. You can say something like, if the day is Sunday and the weather is sunny, then I will go to the beach. The same goes for PHP:

```
if  ($day == "Sunday" AND $weather == "Sunshine") echo ("Off to the beach then");
```

AND can also be written using the ampersand operator twice (&&), for example:

```
if  ($day == "Sunday" && $weather == "Sunshine") echo ("Off to the beach then");
```

The OR and NOT operators are similarly straightforward. We could rephrase the following PHP code, using the OR operator, to say the opposite thing:

```
if  ($day == "Monday" OR $weather == "rainy") echo ("Not going to the beach today
then");
```

If it is Monday or the weather is raining then we can't got to the beach. The OR operator is also represented by the double || sign. So, you could have written the previous line as:

```
if  ($day == "Monday" || $weather == "rainy") echo ("Not going to the beach today
then");
```

*An interesting note that probably won't affect your code, but one that you should be aware of, is that the && and AND operators have slightly different precedence. The same goes for the || and OR operators. The && and || operators will take precedence over their textual alternatives.*

The final operator we're going to discuss only has one form. You can't actually use the word NOT as an operator. The NOT operator is actually an exclamation mark, if it goes outside parenthesis it reverses, the result inside them. So, if it returns true, then NOT means it is now false and vice versa, if the condition is originally false, then it becomes true. For example, if the day isn't Sunday then we can't go to the beach.

```
if !($day == "Sunday") echo ("Not going to the beach today then");
```

This you might surmise has exactly the same effect as the inequality operator != we introduced earlier. In fact you don't have to have any operators at all in an if statement. You could just place a variable inside a condition part of an if statement:

```
if !($Answer) echo ("There's no answer");
```

The above statement will only print a message if there is no value in the $Answer variable, or if $Answer holds a zero as its value(which in PHP is equivalent to being empty). Can you work out why? It's because the ! operator negates the truth-value of $Answer, so if $Answer returns false, !($Answer) returns true, and the if statement executes.

There's still quite a bit more detail to go into logical operators, but to break it up we'll do an example. It will be a program which a car hire company might use to verify whether somebody can drive one of their cars. To do this, they have to hold a valid driving license, and be aged 21 or over. Our program will check for these details and more.

## Try It Out – Using the Logical Operators

**1.** Open your web page editor and type in the following code:

```
<HTML>
<HEAD></HEAD>
<BODY>
<B>Namllu Car Hire Company</B>
<FORM METHOD=POST ACTION="car.php">
First Name:
<INPUT NAME="FirstName" TYPE="Text">
Last Name:
<INPUT NAME="LastName" TYPE="Text">
Age:
<INPUT NAME="Age" TYPE="Text"SIZE="3">
<BR>
<BR>
Address:
<TEXTAREA NAME="Address" ROWS=4 COLS=40>
</TEXTAREA>
<BR>
<BR>
Do you hold a current driving license?
<INPUT NAME="License" TYPE="Checkbox">
<BR>
<BR>
<INPUT TYPE=SUBMIT VALUE="Click here to Submit application">
</FORM>
</BODY>
</HTML>
```

**2.** Save this as car.html.

**3.** Close this file and start a new file in the editor, then type in the following:

```
<HTML>
<HEAD></HEAD>
<BODY>
<B>Namllu Car Hire Company</B>
<?php
if ($Age>20 AND $License=="on") echo ("Your car hire has been accepted.");
if ($Age<21 OR $License=="") echo ("Unfortunately we cannot hire a car to you.");
?>
</BODY>
</HTML>
```

**4.** Save this as `car.php`.

**5.** Open up `car.html` in your browser and type in some details:

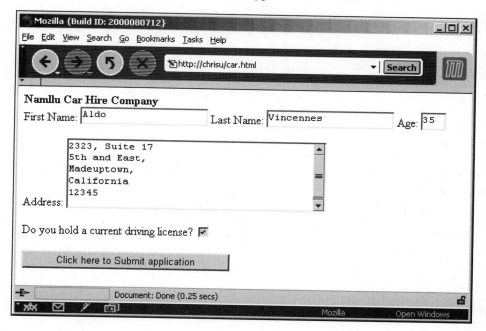

**6.** Click on Submit application to get the results:

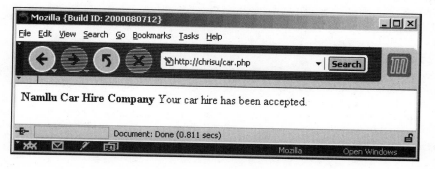

### How It Works

The HTML might be rather lengthy in our first program, but we actually only make use of two of the controls on the screen, those for age, and current driving license:

```
<INPUT NAME="Age" TYPE="Text"SIZE="3">
<BR>
<BR>
Address:
<TEXTAREA NAME="Address" ROWS=4 COLS=40>
</TEXTAREA>
<BR>
<BR>
Do you hold a current driving license?
<INPUT NAME="License" TYPE="Checkbox">
```

The text box has the NAME attribute "Age", so a $Age variable is created to hold the user's age. The second control for driving license is either set to on or off. So the $License variable can either hold the value "on" or it can hold no value at all.

*The value "on" is actually browser dependent, but given that Internet Explorer, Netscape Navigator and Opera all use it, we're sure that you won't encounter any problems using it. If your browser is different and the example doesn't work, then use the echo() statement to interrogate the $License variable, and amend the code accordingly.*

We make use of both these variables within our PHP script in our second program. The first line in car.php says that if the age is greater than 20, and the user is a license holder, then we can accept the car hire:

```
if ($Age>20 AND $License=="on") echo ("Your car hire has been accepted.");
```

The second line says the reverse:

```
if ($Age<21 OR $License=="") echo ("Unfortunately we cannot hire a car to you.");
```

If either the user's age is under 21, or the user isn't a license holder then we refuse the hire. That's all there is to the script.

One last contingency, we haven't taken into account what happens if the user puts in an age between 20 and 21, say 20.5? Unlikely, but something our script should be able to handle. In our script we've actually pushed the boundaries a little, because either condition will accept it and you will get two answers. This needs fixing, but to do this we need to introduce a new, but familiar, set of operators.

### The >= and <= Operators

These operators should sound pretty familiar because they're both just a combination of operators we've already come across. If you want to say that a number must be **less than or equal** to a value, then you use the <= operator. The same goes for the **greater than or equal to** operator >=. Despite only having one equals sign, the equality operator doesn't perform assignments in this context, it is used in a purely comparative sense. To get our last example to work in the way we wanted, we need to amend the first line of car.php as follows:

```
if ($Age>=21 AND $License=="on") echo ("Your car hire has been accepted.");
```

Now you will find that our script works in the way that we want it to.

## Combining Operators

We've already combined the logical operators with the equality operator, but there's actually no restriction on how many operators you can combine in a PHP statement. To reword our first statement – "if the weather is sunny and the day is Sunday then we will go to the beach" – we can say "if the day isn't Monday, Tuesday, Wednesday, Thursday, Friday or Saturday, or it isn't raining, then we will go to the beach":

```
if (($day != "Monday")
OR ($day!="Tuesday")
OR ($day !="Wednesday")
OR ($day !="Thursday")
OR ($day !="Friday")
OR ($day !="Saturday")
OR ($weather!="Rainy")) echo ("Off to the beach then");
```

This is once again similar to the English language, albeit rather drawn out and pedantic. There's no limit to how you can combine these operators or how many you can use, but it can all get quite complicated to read if you use a lot. What do you think the following code is saying?

```
if (($day == "Monday" AND $month != "August")
OR ($day == "Tuesday" AND $time != "12")
OR ($month != "December")) echo ("Board meeting set")
```

This says: if it's a Monday and not in August, or if it's a Tuesday and it's not 12.00, or if it's not in December, then we can have a board meeting. You can work it out, but it takes a little patience and effort.

Let's look at another example that calculates a quote for insurance on a car when given the following four variables – the age of the driver, the value of the car, the car's top speed, and its engine size. For this fictitious insurance company, there are only three possible packages. The top one is the Comprehensive cover at $1500, which is the only one available for the following risk categories:

- ❑ a driver under 25 years of age
- ❑ a car worth more than $10,000
- ❑ a car with an engine size of more than 1.5L
- ❑ a car with a top speed more than 100 miles per hour

The second one is Standard cover, which is $1000 provided you don't fall into any of the risk categories above. The third one is senior persons discount at $750, which is available provided:

- ❑ the driver is over 65,
- ❑ the car either isn't worth more than $5,000, or has a top speed of no more than 80 miles per hour
- ❑ none of the risk categories above apply.

Our page will calculate, given these details, which package should be offered.

## Try It Out – Using a Combination of Operators

**1.** Rev up your web page editor once more and type in the following:

```
<HTML>
<HEAD></HEAD>
<BODY>
<B>Namllu Car Insurance Quoter</B>
<BR>
<BR>
<FORM METHOD=POST ACTION="quote.php">
What age are you?
<INPUT TYPE=TEXT NAME="Age" SIZE=3>
<BR>
<BR>
What is the top speed of your car?
<INPUT TYPE=TEXT NAME="Speed">
<BR>
<BR>
What is the approximate value of your car?
<SELECT NAME="Value">
<OPTION VALUE=5000>Under $5,000</OPTION>
<OPTION VALUE=7000>Between $5,000 and $7,000</OPTION>
<OPTION VALUE=10000>Between $7,000 and $10,000</OPTION>
<OPTION VALUE=25000>Over $10,000</OPTION>
</SELECT>
<BR>
<BR>
What is the engine size of your car?
<SELECT NAME="EngineSize">
<OPTION VALUE=1.0>1.0L</OPTION>
<OPTION VALUE=1.3>1.3L</OPTION>
<OPTION VALUE=1.5>1.5L</OPTION>
<OPTION VALUE=2.0>2.0L</OPTION>
</SELECT>
<BR>
<BR>
<INPUT TYPE=SUBMIT VALUE="Click here to Submit information for quote">
</FORM>
</BODY>
</HTML>
```

*Quick warning, make sure that the cases of the NAME attributes are all typed exactly, otherwise you may inadvertently end up passing some values to a variable $age say, and using the contents of an unset variable called $Age, as I did for a while when writing the example!*

**2.** Save this as quote.html.

**3.** Close this file and open up a new one, then type in the following:

```
<HTML>
<HEAD></HEAD>
```

```
<BODY>
<B>Namllu Car Insurance Quoter</B>
<?php
if ($Age<25 OR $Speed>100 OR $Value>10000 OR $EngineSize>1.5)
{
   echo ("We can offer you the $1500 Comprehensive package");
}
if ($Age>=65 AND ($Value<=5000 OR $Speed<=80) AND $Value<=10000 AND
$EngineSize<=1.5 AND $Speed<=100)
{
   echo ("We can offer you the $750 Senior Citizens Discount Package");
}
if (($Age<65 OR $Value>5000 AND $Speed>80) AND $Age>=25 AND $Speed<=100 AND
$Value<=10000 AND $EngineSize<1.5)
{
   echo ("We can offer you the $1000 Standard Cover Package");
}
?>
</BODY>
</HTML>
```

**4.** Save this as `quote.php`.

**5.** Open up `quote.html` in your browser and fill in some information:

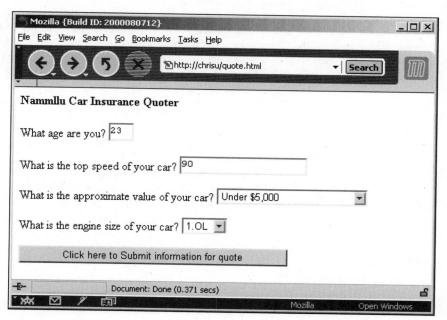

**6.** Click on the Submit button to see your quote:

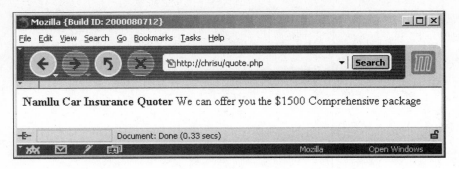

### How It Works

Yes, there are easier ways of doing this than the method used in this example, but we wanted to show you how to combine a large set of conditions in one statement. The first program, `quote.html` is straightforward but lengthy HTML, which takes the four values from the user and stores them. In this example, we do make use of all the values the user has input. We're not going to examine the code in `quote.html` in any more detail, other than to remark that it creates the (self-explanatory) variables `$Age`, `$Speed`, `$EngineSize`, and `$Value` in the HTML code, and passes their values to the server for use in our PHP script in our second program.

What interests us more, are the complex conditions we now have to test for in `quote.php`. We have to perform a total of three tests, and we have to make sure that every candidate who uses this insurance will come out with one quote and only one quote – Namllu aren't in the habit of turning people away without a quote! The first test is the one for comprehensive cover. There are four conditions we are testing for, and if any one of them is "true", then the user can only be recommended the most expensive insurance package. We test the `$Age` variable to see if it's below 25, the `$Speed` variable to see if it's over 100, the `$EngineSize` variable to see if it's over 1.5L, and the car's value to see if it's over $10,000. Then we display the details of the comprehensive package if a match is made.

```
if ($Age<25 OR $Speed>100 OR $Value>10000 OR $EngineSize>1.5)
{
echo ("We can offer you the $1500 Comprehensive package");
}
```

Secondly, we test for the senior citizen's discount. This is applicable when the `$Age` variable is at least 65, and either the `$Value` variable is 5000 or lower, or the `$Speed` variable is 80 or lower. We conduct the second test separately in parentheses, as only one of the two needs to hold true. We also need to check that the user, while being a senior citizen, doesn't encroach into any other risk category, because they will already have been offered the expensive quote:

```
if ($Age>=65 AND ($Value<=5000 OR $Speed<=80) AND $Value<=10000 AND
$EngineSize<=1.5 AND $Speed<=100)
{
echo ("We can offer you the $750 Senior Citizens Discount Package");
}
```

Lastly, to trap anything else that might have come through, we check to see whether the `$Age` variable is between the values of 25 and 64, the car's value is over 5000, and whether the top speed is over 80. This means that our driver can't qualify for the senior citizen's discount, but we also have to check that he/she hasn't exceeded any of the other criteria set and therefore has to be offered a Comprehensive Package. So we check each of the $Speed, $Value, and $EngineSize variables.

```
if (($Age<65 OR $Value>5000 AND $Speed>80) AND $Age>=25 AND $Speed<=100 AND
$Value<=10000 AND $EngineSize<1.5)
{
echo ("We can offer you the $1000 Standard Cover Package");
}
```

To sum up then, the conditions we are testing for in the above lines of code are:

❑ To qualify for the standard package, none of the expense conditions for age, value, speed or engine size can be broached.

❑ However, if you are a senior citizen, but don't meet the criteria for a senior citizen's discount (that is, you have a car that does in excess of 80 miles an hour and is worth more than $5000), then this also qualifies for the Standard coverage.

When you write conditions like this, you must make sure that they cover every eventuality by testing each possible outcome. In conditions like these, where working out in your head might not capture all situations, good design is the best way to work things out. Once you've worked it out on paper and implemented it, you should test it to make sure everything is caught.

This has been a rather complex example and you might be thinking, isn't there any easier way of doing any of this – are there any shortcuts? Well the good news is, there are some, and we'll look at some new features that will make programming PHP a bit easier.

# Multiple Conditions – else and elseif

We've looked at multiple conditions within one `if` statement, but what happens if you want to execute one set of statements if a condition is true, and another set if the condition is false? You could always reverse the condition and do a new `if` statement, but there's a much easier way of doing this. The `else` statement works like this:

```
if (a condition is true)
{
  execute the contents of these braces
}
else
{
  execute the contents of these braces
}
```

We could reformulate our car hire example yet again to say:

```
if ($Age>=21 AND $License=="on")
{
     echo ("Your car hire has been accepted.");
}
else
{
     echo ("Unfortunately we cannot hire a car to you.");
}
```

Notice here that we're indenting the contents of each set of braces. This isn't something necessary to make our example work, but it makes our code easier to read. If a particular set of statements are only executed if the condition is true, then it makes them standout more by indenting them from that condition.

Let's take this one step further, what happens if you want to test a variable against a set of values and have a different outcome for each value? Another feature of the if statement we haven't covered so far is the elseif statement, which allows us to cater for multiple conditions:

```
if (a variable is equal to value1)
{
    execute the contents of these braces
}
elseif (a variable is equal to value2)
{
    execute the contents of these braces
}
else
{
    execute the contents of these braces
}
```

We could amend our car hire company program even further now, taking on the premise that we will grant somebody between the ages of 18 and 21 (with a car license) a car, provided they can give the name of a guarantor:

```
if ($Age>=21 AND $License=="on")
{
    echo ("Your car hire has been accepted.");
}
elseif ($Age>=18 AND $License=="on")
{
    echo ("Your car hire has been accepted, subject to you providing the name of
    a guarantor.");
}
else
{
    echo ("Unfortunately we cannot hire a car to you.");
}
```

This copes with three possible conditions, the third being the else statement, which acts as a catch-all if the conditions in the first two statements aren't satisfied. There's nothing to stop us adding yet more and more elseif statements to your list. For instance, a program that grades examinations, where you could get A, B, C, D or E, could be reflected as follows:

```
if ($grade>70) echo "You got an A";
elseif ($grade > 60) echo "You got a B";
elseif ($grade > 50) echo "You got a C";
elseif ($grade > 40) echo "You got a D";
elseif ($grade > 30) echo "You got an E";
else echo "You failed";
```

This still doesn't cover one course of action; what happens if you want the results of one condition to feed straight into the criteria of another condition? For instance, you want to amend the grades table, to check to see whether a person who got an A grade also deserves a special merit for getting an A grade in their project. In this case, you need to put one `if` statement inside another.

## Nesting If Statements

The process of placing one `if` statement inside another is known as **nesting**. So, if we tweaked our above code we could add a nested `if` statement to our 'A grade' `if` statement.

```
if ($Grade>70)
{
    echo ("You got an A.");
    if ($ProjectGrade>70)
    {
        echo ("You also got a special merit");
    }
}
```

You could also reflect this by using multiple AND statements, but this is much simpler to read. You don't have to stop there either, you can carry on nesting to almost infinite levels, but your code will once again be very awkward to read. We could amend this code further to check whether the attendance record was one hundred percent, in which case we'll award a distinction:

```
if ($Grade>70)
{
    echo ("You got an A.");
    if ($ProjectGrade>70)
    {
        if ($AttendanceRecord==100)
        {
            echo ("You also got a special distinction");
        }
        else
        {
            echo ("You also got a merit");
        }
    }
}
```

As you can see the number of braces needed to open and close all of the `if` statements is increasing, and if you get the number wrong, like having three open braces and only two closing ones, then your code will generate errors. Multiple conditions make it necessary to see which braces are being opened and which are being closed. This makes indentation even more useful, because if all the braces appeared in a straight line like this:

```
if ($Grade>70)
{
echo ("You got an A.");
if ($ProjectGrade>70)
{
if ($AttendanceRecord==100)
```

```
{
echo ("You also got a special distinction");
}
else
{
echo ("You also got a merit");
}
}
```

then you might not notice that I have in fact omitted the last closing brace! Oops!

Let's do an example now that makes use of all of the features discussed above, in order to create a holiday booking form for several destinations. It will calculate a price based on the level of hotel, and your destination. There will be three destinations, Prague, Barcelona, and Vienna, each of which is increasingly more expensive. There are also two grades of hotel in each destination, three star and four star, with four star being more expensive. However, with holiday companies being holiday companies, the price increases for destination and grades aren't uniform. So while the four star hotel might be $1500 more expensive in Barcelona than the three star one, the difference between three star and four star hotels in Vienna is an extortionate $2250! Our PHP program will have to record all of this.

## Try It Out – Using More Complex Conditions

**1.** Open up your web page editor and type in the following:

```
<HTML>
<HEAD></HEAD>
<BODY>
<B>Namllu Holiday Booking Form</B>
<FORM METHOD=GET ACTION="holiday.php">
Where do you want to go on holiday?
<BR>
<BR>
<INPUT NAME="Destination" TYPE="Radio" VALUE="Prague">
Prague
<BR>
<INPUT NAME="Destination" TYPE="Radio" VALUE="Barcelona">
Barcelona
<BR>
<INPUT NAME="Destination" TYPE="Radio" VALUE="Vienna">
Vienna
<BR>
<BR>
What grade of hotel do you want to stay at?
<BR>
<BR>
<INPUT NAME="Grade" TYPE="Radio" VALUE="Three">
Three Star
<BR>
<INPUT NAME="Grade" TYPE="Radio" VALUE="Four">
Four Star
<BR>
<BR>
<INPUT TYPE=SUBMIT>
```

```
</FORM>
</BODY>
</HTML>
```

**2.** Save this as `holiday.html`.

**3.** Close this file and open a new one in your web page editor, then type the following:

```
<HTML>
<HEAD></HEAD>
<BODY>
<B>Namllu Holiday Booking Form</B>
<BR>
<BR>
<?php
$Price=500;
$StarModifier=1;
$CityModifier=1;
if ($Grade=="Three")
{
     if ($Destination=="Barcelona")
     {
          $CityModifier=2;
          $Price = $Price * $CityModifier;
          echo "The cost for a week in $Destination is $Price";
     }
     elseif ($Destination=="Vienna")
     {
          $CityModifier=3.5;
          $Price = $Price * $CityModifier;
          echo "The cost for a week in $Destination is $Price";
     }
     elseif ($Destination=="Prague")
     {
          $Price = $Price * $CityModifier;
          echo "The cost for a week in $Destination is $Price";
     }
     else
     {
          echo ("You've not entered a value for destination, go back and do it
          again");
     }
}
elseif ($Grade=="Four")
{
     $StarModifier=2;
     if ($Destination=="Barcelona")
     {
          $CityModifier=2.5;
          $Price = $Price * $CityModifier * $StarModifier;
          echo "The cost for a week in $Destination is $Price";
     }
     elseif ($Destination=="Vienna")
```

```
        {
            $CityModifier=4;
            $Price = $Price * $CityModifier * $StarModifier;
            echo "The cost for a week in $Destination is $Price";
        }
    elseif ($Destination=="Prague")
        {
            $Price = $Price * $CityModifier * $StarModifier;
            echo "The cost for a week in $Destination is $Price";
        }
else
{
    echo ("You've not entered a value for destination, go back and do it
    again");
        }
}
else
{
    echo ("You've not entered a value for hotel grade, go back and do it
again");
}
?>
</BODY>
</HTML>
```

**4.** Save this as `holiday.php` and check it thoroughly. Make sure you have included the right number of braces otherwise the example won't work.

**5.** Open up `holiday.html` in your browser and make some selections:

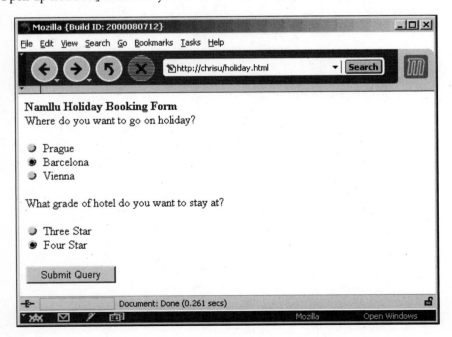

**6.** Click on Submit Query to see a price:

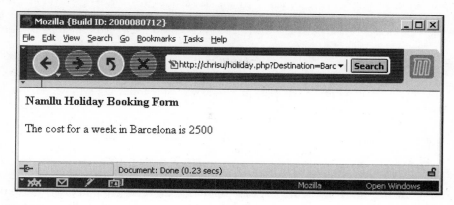

## How It Works

Other than to remark that it creates two variables, $Destination and $Grade, which store the user's choice of destination and grade of hotel, we're going to pay scant attention to the first program that just contains the HTML code. The second program, holiday.php, is by far the longest program we've created in PHP so far. However, it does nothing that we haven't talked about already, and if we go through it step by step, we'll see that it isn't really too difficult to understand.

The first three lines create variables with default values:

```
$Price=500;
$StarModifier=1;
$CityModifier=1;
```

The presence of the two modifier variables is to alter the prices for the more expensive hotels and more expensive destinations. If we're using a four star hotel then we might multiply the price by two. If we're staying in Vienna we might multiply the price by three and so on. To reflect this, we will multiply our price total by the contents of these two variables. The default choice is a week in Prague in a three star hotel at 500 dollars and doesn't require any modifiers so we leave them at value 1; anything else is going to be more expensive. So, our first statement checks to see the grade of the hotel:

```
if ($Grade=="Three")
```

If it's equal to three, then we jump to a second test for the destination:

```
if ($Destination=="Barcelona")
```

We test first to see if it matches Barcelona, and if it does, we take the following course of action:

```
$CityModifier=2;
$Price = $Price * $CityModifier;
echo "The cost for a week in $Destination is $Price";
```

First we changed the value of the variable $CityModifier. When we multiply this by the price in the second line, we get the new increased price. We then display the price for the destination of Barcelona. Note that these lines are only executed if a grade of three stars and a destination of Barcelona is selected. This ends our first nested if statement. The second test checks to see if the destination is Vienna:

```
elseif ($Destination=="Vienna")
```

This is all part of one large nested if statement. We execute the following set of code, only if the hotel grade is three and the destination is Vienna:

```
$CityModifier=3.5;
$Price = $Price * $CityModifier;
echo "The cost for a week in $Destination is $Price";
```

Here the $CityModifier variable is increased to four to reflect the jump in price due to the destination. We multiply it by the $Price variable in the second line and display the results on the screen in the third line. This closes our second course of action.

Our third check is to see if the destination is Prague or not:

```
elseif ($Destination=="Prague")
```

If it is, we multiply the price by the existing $CityModifier variable, which currently contains 1. We also display destination and price, but once again only if the grade is three and the destination is Prague:

```
$Price = $Price * $CityModifier;
echo "The cost for a week in $Destination is $Price";
```

We then include a catch-all to make sure that the user has actually suggested a destination. If they haven't selected Prague, Barcelona or Vienna, then we can deduce they left it blank and they need to fill it in:

```
else
    {
        echo ("You've not entered a value for destination, go back and do it
        again");
    }
```

This completes half the program; however we now need to perform the same operation for grade four hotels in Prague, Barcelona, and Vienna. This time we also have a star rating, which doubles the price:

```
elseif ($Grade=="Four")
{
    $StarModifier=2;
```

Then we check each destination in turn, alter the destination weighting as necessary, and multiply the price by the star modifier too. For example, the code dealing with Barcelona looks like this:

```
if ($Destination=="Barcelona")
    {
```

```
                    $CityModifier=2.5;
                    $Price = $Price * $CityModifier * $StarModifier;
                    echo "The cost for a week in $Destination is $Price";
            }
```

The code for each destination is quite repetitive, so we won't go through it all, but we do have a catch-all at the end:

```
        else
            {
                    echo ("You've not entered a value for destination, go back and do it
                    again");
            }
```

You might be thinking, why is it here, when we've already entered it earlier? This is because the catch-all was only operated if we selected no destination and the three star grade. We now need a catch-all to work if somebody enters a four star grade and no destination.

Lastly, we have a catch-all in case somebody has entered no grading at all.

```
        else
        {
            echo ("You've not entered a value for hotel grade, go back and do it
        again");
        }
```

This has all been long-winded, and required large amounts of braces. If you missed any out, you were probably greeted by unhelpful error messages. However, there is an alternative structure in PHP, which allows you to eliminate the braces when large numbers of conditions are required, and also present your code in a more readable manner.

# Switch Statements

The switch statement performs a similar function to a structure that we met earlier and described, the elseif statement. However, it does it a lot more succinctly, and it again is much easier to read and allows us to leave out nearly all of the irritating braces.

If we look at our grading exams example, we can see that it could have been written to have the same functionality with the switch statement:

```
switch ($Grade) {
      case $Grade>70:
            echo ("You got an A.");
            break;
      case $Grade>60:
            echo ("You got a B.");
            break;
      case $Grade>50:
            echo ("You got a C.");
            break;
```

```
        case $Grade>40:
                echo ("You got a D.");
                break;
        case $Grade>25:
                echo ("You got an E. ");
                break;
        default:
                echo ("You failed");
  }
```

This doesn't save many lines, but does remove some of the code. In place of if and elseif we now have just one case, followed by a condition, and then a set of actions. In each case the PHP program will have something different to execute.

You will have noticed we used a command called break in our switch statement. When PHP encounters break, it stops what it's doing, drops out of the whole switch structure, and picks up the programming thread after the closing brace. It doesn't go on checking for further compliance with other criteria, even though a grade of 80 percent would have met all of these criteria. This is useful because we don't have to write countless little catch-alls for every conceivable situation. If you want all criteria checked, then just omit the keyword break, although you should note that break only works in conjunction with the switch statement, and not the if statement. If you omit the word break, then all statements would evaluate to true, and you would get A, B, C, D, and E:

```
switch ($Grade) {
     case $Grade>70:
             echo ("You got an A.");
     case $Grade>60:
             echo ("You got a B.");
     case $Grade>50:
             echo ("You got a C.");
     case $Grade>40:
             echo ("You got a D.");
     case $Grade>25:
             echo ("You got an E. ");
     default:
             echo ("You failed");
  }
```

The switch statement also introduces an interesting little shorthand:

```
switch ($State) {
     case "IL":
             echo ("Illinois");
             break;
     case "GA":
             echo ("Georgia");
             break;
     default:
             echo ("California");
             break;
     }
```

If you just supply a value next to the `case` keyword, then it automatically checks the variable you supplied in the `switch` parentheses for equality with the value next to case, whether numerical or textual. Note that after the `case` keyword we use a colon and not a semi-colon.

You can also leave occurrences within `switch` empty, and then the `default` clause is activated if that particular case is encountered. All you need to do is include a `case` clause that only contains the `break` statement:

```
switch ($State) {
    case "HH":
        break;
    case "IL":
        echo ("Illinois");
        break;
    case "GA":
        echo ("Georgia");
        break;
    default:
        echo ("California");
        break;
}
```

So, since we have a pretty good idea of what `switch` does already, let's go back to our previous example and see if we can save any code by amending `holiday.php` so that it uses a `switch` statement instead.

## Try It Out – Using Switch Statements

**1.** Go back and open up `holiday.php` and delete the contents and type in the following:

```
<HTML>
<HEAD></HEAD>
<BODY>
<B>Namllu Holiday Booking Form</B>
<BR>
<BR>
<?php
$Price=500;
$StarModifier=1;
$CityModifier=1;
$DestGrade = $Destination.$Grade;
switch($DestGrade) {
    case "BarcelonaThree":
        $CityModifier=2;
        $Price = $Price * $CityModifier;
        echo "The cost for a week in $Destination is $Price";
        break;
    case "BarcelonaFour":
        $CityModifier=2;
        $StarModifier=2;
        $Price = $Price * $CityModifier * $StarModifier;
        echo "The cost for a week in $Destination is $Price";
        break;
```

```
        case "ViennaThree":
            $CityModifier=3.5;
            $Price = $Price * $CityModifier;
            echo "The cost for a week in $Destination is $Price";
            break;
        case "ViennaFour":
            $CityModifier=3.5;
            $StarModifier=2;
            $Price = $Price * $CityModifier * $StarModifier;
            echo "The cost for a week in $Destination is $Price";
            break;
        case "PragueThree":
            $Price = $Price * $CityModifier;
            echo "The cost for a week in $Destination is $Price";
            break;
        case "PragueFour":
            $StarModifier=2;
            $Price = $Price * $CityModifier * $StarModifier;
            echo "The cost for a week in $Destination is $Price";
            break;
        default:
            echo ("Go back and do it again");
            break;
    }
    ?>
    </BODY>
    </HTML>
```

**2.** Save `holiday.php` again.

**3.** Open up `holiday.html` in your browser, enter some details and it will work just like before:

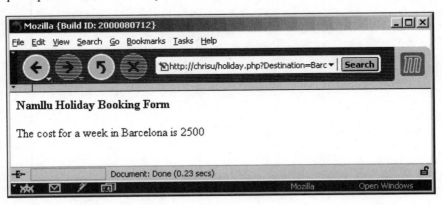

### How It Works

We originally made two boasts about `switch` – first, it's easier to read, and second, it uses less lines of code. The first is subjective. Consider the second; the first program has used 58 lines of PHP script in between the `<?php   ?>` markers, while our new version of `holiday.php` has used just 39 lines, that's roughly a third less. Let's have a look at the program now to see how this was achieved. The first three lines are identical to last time and need no re-explanation:

```
$Price=500;
$StarModifier=1;
$CityModifier=1;
```

The fourth line introduces a new variable, $DestGrade, which is a concatenation of the contents of the $Destination and $Grade variables.

```
$DestGrade = $Destination.$Grade;
```

So, if you chose Barcelona and four star, $DestGrade would contain BarcelonaFour. Note that we could have also have done this on our previous version of holiday.php and it would have saved us a couple of lines of braces. However, it wouldn't have been a huge saving, and it would have prevented us from demonstrating nested if statements in action. The saving we make here is much larger, and we're only feeding one variable to the switch statement:

```
switch($DestGrade) {
```

All we have to do is make sure we capture the seven possible outcomes. (We have to take account of the three hotel choices, multiplied by two star grades to give us six. Anything else that isn't one of these choices must be wrong, whether it's a choice of one hotel and no grade, or no hotel and a grading.) The six possible correct outcomes are Barcelona and three star, Barcelona and four star, Prague and three star, Prague and four star, Vienna and three star, Vienna and four star. This means our possible variables in $DestGrade can only be BarcelonaThree, BarcelonaFour, PragueThree, PragueFour, ViennaThree, and ViennaFour, so we tailor make a case for each.

All of the cases perform a similar action, so we won't explain each one, we'll just take one example of a case and work through it:

```
case "BarcelonaThree":
        $CityModifier=2;
        $Price = $Price * $CityModifier;
        echo "The cost for a week in $Destination is $Price";
        break;
```

In the case of BarcelonaThree, we set the $CityModifier to two and multiply it by the price. We display the price and destination and then break to the end of the program. If the value in $DestGrade doesn't match any correct case, then something must be wrong and we tell the user to go back and do it again.

```
default:
        echo ("Go back and do it again");
        break;
```

In the interests of "good practice" we would add a break at the end, even though it does nothing. It means that your code is less likely to generate errors if you ever add another case after the default.

It's as simple as that. Now we've covered the if statement and the related switch statements, we're going to take a look at a practical application of them in PHP.

# Form Validation

In the last chapter we mentioned that it was possible to break our loan application example by either accidentally or deliberately supplying erroneous or nonsensical information. For instance, in the box that asked for your age, what happens if you type "None of your business". Perfectly acceptable you might think if you were talking to another human being, although perhaps a little rude. How's your PHP program going to deal with this though? You might want to assume that your users will have enough common sense to not type something like this in, but any time you put a program up for public use, you will be amazed by the different possible replies, from a comical "999", to the grammatically correct "forty-four", but to your PHP program it's totally meaningless.

The way you can deal with this is to restrict the values permitted in a certain text box. In our example, we passed the person's age into a variable called $Age. On our PHP page we could then check this against a realistic range:

```
if ($Age<1 or $Age>120)
{
    echo "Incorrect Age value entered";
    break;
}
```

and we can also take the appropriate course of action.

### The exit Statement

You could also add another keyword in place of break, and that is exit.

```
if ($Age<1 or $Age>120)
{
    echo "Incorrect Age value entered";
    exit;
}
```

If we're checking a form, and we know that somebody hasn't supplied a value, there's no point validating the rest of the form, so we can stop it right there with the keyword exit, which is just like our keyword break. No further HTML, PHP code, or text will be executed after an exit is encountered within an if statement. However, the exit keyword does terminate the page rather suddenly and the fact that it doesn't close any remaining HTML tags could mean you get some irregular output. So, while being useful, it should be used very carefully and only in specialist situations.

Let's go back to our loan application example and waterproof it against possible user errors.

## Try It Out – Form Validation

**1.** Go back and open up loan.php and add the following highlighted code:

```
<HTML>
<HEAD></HEAD>
<BODY>
<B>Namllu Credit Bank Loan Application Form</B>
<BR>
```

```
<BR>
<?php
if ($Age<10 OR $Age>140)
{
    echo "Incorrect Age entered - Press back button to try again";
    exit;
}
if ($FirstName=="" or $LastName=="")
{
    echo "You must enter your name - Press back button to try again";
    exit;
}
if ($Address=="")
{
    echo "You must enter your address - Press back button to try again";
    exit;
}
If ($Loan!=1000 and $Loan!=5000 and $Loan!=10000)
{
    echo "You must enter a loan value - Press back button to try again";
    exit;
}
$SalaryAllowance = $Salary/5;
$AgeAllowance = ($Age/10 - ($Age%10)/10)-1;
...
```

**2.** Save this as `loan.php`.

**3.** Now go back and try `loan.html` and attempt to get a loan without entering all of the information required, or by supplying an obviously made up age:

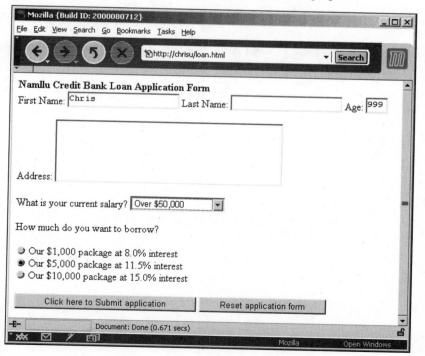

**4.** You should receive a message along these lines:

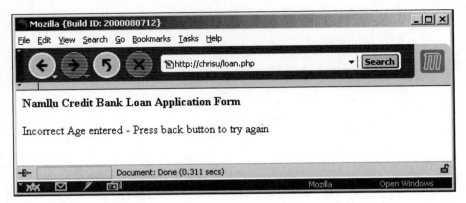

### How It Works

Of course, you could always enter somebody else's address, or enter an age other than your own, but there is no way PHP can check for this. What we do with our new code is make sure that the user hasn't mistakenly forgotten to add a detail, or maliciously supplied obviously wrong information about their age. We do this with four `if` statements. The first checks to see whether the age entered is between 10 and 140, otherwise we can be pretty sure that the person is lying:

```
if ($Age<10 OR $Age>140)
{
    echo "Incorrect Age entered - Press back button to try again";
    exit;
}
```

We display an appropriate message and exit there. We don't need to do anything further if this condition is met.

The second `if` statement checks for first and last names being present. The string "" denotes an empty string variable, and this is how you check for one:

```
if ($FirstName=="" or $LastName=="")
{
    echo "You must enter your name - Press back button to try again";
    exit;
}
```

We do the same for Address to see if the `$Address` variable is empty:

```
if ($Address=="")
{
    echo "You must enter your address - Press back button to try again";
    exit;
}
```

Lastly, we check the contents of the radio buttons, for one of the three possible values:

```
If ($Loan!=1000 and $Loan!=5000 and $Loan!=10000)
{
    echo "You must enter a loan value - Press back button to try again";
    exit;
}
```

If it's not equal to any of them, we know that the user cannot have selected a value.

### Malicious Scripters – HTMLSpecialChars

This doesn't completely "bug proof" our script – if you were to correctly fill in the form but to type in the following in the first name <B>Abel</B>, you would see the following:

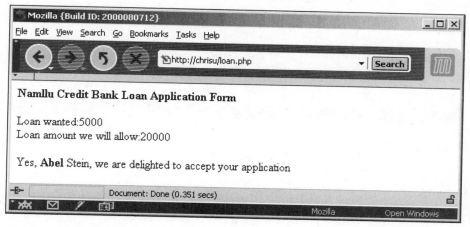

Nothing odd about this you might think, except if you look at the name Abel. It's in bold. This is because the browser hasn't displayed the contents of the text box exactly as we typed it. It's actually interpreted the HTML tags for us. Now, you can see that if someone supplied some malicious HTML, or worse still a script, they could get our program to execute it for them.

Fortunately PHP provides a great function to stop this happening, called HTMLSpecialChars. It just requires a string argument to work:

```
$String = HTMLSpecialChars("<B>This won't display the Bold tags </B>");
```

or a variable name:

```
$String ="<B>This won't display the Bold tags </B>";
$String = HTMLSpecialChars($String);
```

This function converts any HTML tags into the actual text we wish to display, and in doing so, stops any HTML tags entered from being interpreted by the browser as HTML. It also stops any script that has been entered in the text box from being executed. So, if we wanted to stop this from happening we'd have to take each of our text box inputs within loan.php and run them through the function as follows.

```
$FirstName = HTMLSpecialChars($FirstName);
$LastName = HTMLSpecialChars($LastName);
```

```
$Address = HTMLSpecialChars($Address);
$Age= HTMLSpecialChars($Age);
```

We'd have to add this code somewhere early on in `loan.php` and then it would only display:

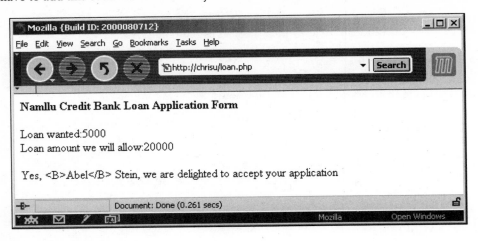

Now our program is a bit more secure.

# Summary

We've introduced a major part of the PHP language in this chapter; decision making. The foundation of this in PHP is the `if` statement. We also took the opportunity to look at the Boolean operators, greater than, less than, equality, inequality, AND, OR, and NOT. We saw that the `if` statement has quite a few different formats and is fairly flexible in that it can be nested, or extended using `elseif`. The `switch` statement offered us a better method of handling multiple conditions, and while there are guidelines for when you should use `if`, `elseif`, or `switch`, ultimately it's the choice of the programmer.

We rounded off the chapter by using form validation to improve the loan application example from the last chapter. Hopefully the techniques introduced will be of use for validating any form you will create in the future. As you might have noticed though, the examples were growing in size by the end of this chapter, and the code contained within them was quite repetitive. In the next chapter, we will see how PHP deals with repetition using loops. One of the main reasons for using loops is that they can cut down on the amount of code written. They can also be used to write code to variables in arrays much more quickly and efficiently than linear code.

# 5

# Loops and Arrays

We introduced a fundamental programming concept in the last chapter: decision making. Instead of moving through our code sequentially, we found that we could avoid executing a line of code, or even miss out whole sections of code. In this chapter we're going to introduce something that computers like doing best – and indeed what they were invented for – performing repetitive tasks. If you have to perform the same task, every day, every hour, over and over, sooner or later you're going to do it wrong. If you give a similar task to a computer, if it does it right the first time, then it'll do it right the hundredth time, the thousandth time and even the millionth time. Concentration, natural wear and tear, and even interest in the task doesn't enter into the equation.

The mechanism that most programming languages, including PHP, use to perform repetition is the **loop**. There are three kinds of loop in PHP, and we're going to spend the first half of the chapter looking at them. Once we've covered loops, we're going to examine another related feature, the **array**. We have already encountered arrays earlier in the book. An array is a set of indexed variables which, especially when coupled with the loop, can prove very useful. Loops coupled with arrays allow you to create hundreds or even thousands of variables using only three or four lines of code. We will spend the rest of the chapter looking at arrays; then we'll finish it off with a practical example that combines loops and arrays.

In this chapter we'll be looking at:

- ❑ The `while` loop
- ❑ The `do while` loop
- ❑ The `for` loop
- ❑ Creating arrays
- ❑ Retrieving values from arrays
- ❑ How arrays are indexed
- ❑ How arrays can be sorted
- ❑ Multi-dimensional arrays
- ❑ A practical example of loops and arrays

# Loops

In the previous chapter we introduced the branching (conditional) statement, which allows us to introduce decision-making into our PHP code. Loops bear certain similarities to branching statements, because in both cases, the next line of code to be executed depends upon whether a condition is true or false.

However, loops differ from conditional statements because the contents of the loop may be executed over and over again. The condition is tested, and the code in the loop is executed if the condition holds. Then the condition is tested again; if it still is correct, the code in the loop is executed again, and maybe again, and so on for many interations. You get the picture. Each passage through the loop is known as an **iteration**.

Actually, loops have something else in common with branching statements. We saw in the last chapter that there are three types of branching statements, and that we choose the type most suited to the task in hand. Similarly, there are three types of loop, each of which is suited to a different situation. We shall now examine each type separately.

## while Loops

We'll start with the `while` loop because it's the simplest of the three loops, and it bears some similarity to the `if` statement. Like the `if` statement, it checks the result of a condition. Depending on whether the condition is true or false, the section of code (placed within braces) after the conditional statement is executed:

```
while (a condition is true)
{
    execute the contents of these braces
}
```

After the contents of the loop are executed, then the condition at the top is tested again, and the code might be executed again, and so on. If the condition is tested and it is found to be false, the code in braces will be ignored, and PHP will proceed to the first line beyond the end of the braces. Let's have a pseudocode example:

```
while (the moon is full)
{
    the coyotes will howl
}
```

So if the moon isn't full, then the coyotes won't be howling, but for the whole duration of the moon being full, they will howl at it. Let's have another example. Say we wanted to inform a user, shopping on an e-commerce site, that their credit limit has been exceeded. We might use something like the following PHP code snippet to display a message when the user's shopping bill exceeds the credit limit:

```
while ($ShoppingTotal > $CreditLimit)
{
    echo ("You have exceeded your credit limit,
                    so the last item from your basket will be removed");
    $ShoppingTotal = $ShoppingTotal - $LastPurchase;
    $LastPurchase = $LastPurchaseButOne;
}
```

So, if the user exceeds his credit limit $CreditLimit, we cancel his last purchase, removing its value ($LastPurchase) from the total bill ($ShoppingTotal). We then change the value of $LastPurchase to be the value of the last purchase but one, $LastPurchaseButOne. In this way, we can iterate through the loop, removing one item at a time from the shopping list, until $ShoppingTotal is below $CreditLimit.

You may have noticed that this loop could continue to iterate indefinitely if $CreditLimit was given a negative value. If you use a condition which might always be true, an infinite loop may occur, in which case your program won't end. It won't generate an error, it will just continue to execute the contents of the loop over and over again. When you write code which uses loops, you should bear this in mind. We'll come back to this issue later.

We're going to write an example now with a `while` loop. It's an extension to our loan application example from the last chapter. If you remember, we asked the user to choose a loan package, and then our PHP program approved or rejected the loan. Now imagine that we've approved several possible loan packages for the user to choose from. There are three different loans: each offers a different amount, and each is loaned at a different interest rate per month. Our new example is going to tell us how long it's going to take to pay the loan back.

Of course, to do this we need another piece of information from the user: the amount of money the user is willing to pay each month. Our loan also requires us to pay interest on the loan each month. In other words, if I borrowed $1000 at 5% interest per month, and I was repaying $100 a month, I'd also have to pay $50 interest for the first month. So really I'd only actually pay $50 of my outstanding loan in the first month. In the second month, I'd owe $950, so if I was repaying another $100 this month, 5% loan interest on $950 would be $47 and 50c. You can see that very quickly the calculations will get quite complex, although the formula to do the calculation will remain the same each month:

```
Payment = Monthly Payment - Interest
Debt = Debt - Payment
```

All we need to do is perform these two calculations over and over until our debt is zero, and count up how many payments were required. We don't know how many months this will take unless we're mathematical whizzes – but we don't need to be, as we can get PHP to use a `while` loop to do the job for us.

## Try It Out – Using a While Loop

**1.** Wake your web page editor from its slumber and type in the following:

```
<HTML>
<HEAD></HEAD>
<BODY>
<B>Namllu Credit Bank Loan Form</B>
<FORM METHOD=POST ACTION="loan2.php">
<BR>
How much do you want to borrow?<BR><BR>
<INPUT NAME="Loan" TYPE="Radio" VALUE=1000>Our $1,000 package at 5.0% interest
<BR>
<INPUT NAME="Loan" TYPE="Radio" VALUE=5000>Our $5,000 package at 6.5% interest
<BR>
<INPUT NAME="Loan" TYPE="Radio" VALUE=10000>Our $10,000 package at 8.0% interest
<BR>
<BR>
```

```
How much do you want to pay a month?
<INPUT NAME=Month TYPE=Text SIZE=5>
<BR>
<BR>
<INPUT TYPE=SUBMIT VALUE="Click here to calculate">
</FORM>
</BODY>
</HTML>
```

**2.** Save this as `loan2.html`.

**3.** Close this file, and open a new one in your web page editor. Type in the following:

```
<HTML>
<HEAD></HEAD>
<BODY>
<?php
$Duration=0;
switch ($Loan) {
case 1000:
   $Interest = 5;
   break;
case 5000:
   $Interest = 6.5;
   break;
case 10000:
   $Interest = 8;
   break;
default:
   echo "You didn't enter a loan package!";
   exit;
}
while ($Loan > 0)
{
   $Duration = $Duration + 1;
   $Monthly = $Month - ($Loan*$Interest/100);
   if ($Monthly<=0)
   {
       echo "You need larger repayments to pay off your loan!";
       exit;
   }
$Loan = $Loan - $Monthly;
}
echo "This would take you $Duration months to pay this off at the interest rate of
$Interest percent.";
?>
</BODY>
</HTML>
```

**4.** Save this as `loan2.php`.

**5.** Close this and open `loan2.html` in your browser. Select the $1000 package, and type in 100:

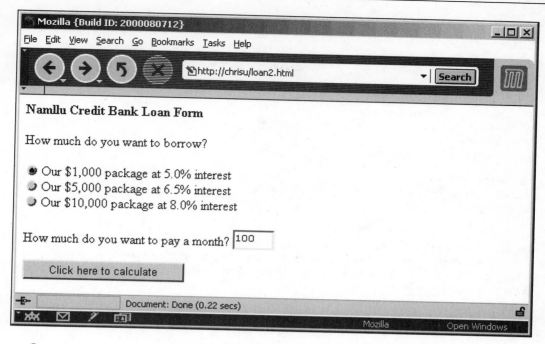

**6.** Click on the Click here to calculate button. You should see something like this:

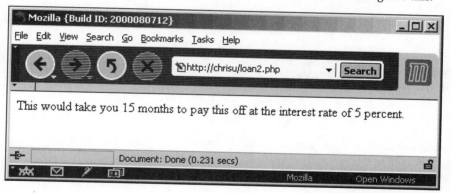

### How It Works

The form generated by `loan2.html` asks the user to make two choices: the amount of their loan, which is then stored in the variable `$Loan`, and the amount they wish to repay per month, which is stored in the variable `$Month`. These two variables are then used in `loan2.php`. It might seem quite a long program, but there are only two structures being used in the PHP script. The first is a `switch` structure, which we introduced in the last chapter. We start by initializing the `$Duration` variable, which will hold a count of the number of monthly repayments which have been made. We then use the `switch` statement to choose the interest rate, because the rate depends on the loan the user selected on the HTML form:

```
$Duration=0;
switch ($Loan) {

case 1000:
   $Interest = 5;
   break;
case 5000:
   $Interest = 6.5;
   break;
case 10000:
   $Interest = 8;
   break;
default:
   echo "You didn't enter a loan package!";
   exit;
}
```

There are only three possible values $Loan could evaluate to: 1000, 5000, and 10000. We use the value of $Loan to set the variable $Interest to the corresponding interest rate, using the switch statement. If none of the three loan values were picked, then we tell the user so, and stop the program right there, because they didn't enter a value.

Okay, now it's time to introduce our while loop. However, before we can enter the loop, the conditional statement must to be validated. Here, the condition is that we can iterate as long as $Loan hasn't reached zero – in other words, as long as the debt hasn't been paid off:

```
while ($Loan > 0)
{
```

This starts the loop, because we know that $Loan must either be 1000, 5000 or 10000, not zero. Next we deal with our month counter, $Duration. $Duration was initially set to zero, so we increment it by one, to indicate that this is the first time around the loop:

```
$Duration = $Duration + 1;
```

Our next line calculates how much money will be repaid towards the loan this month, including interest:

```
$Monthly = $Month - ($Loan*$Interest/100);
```

To get this month's interest payment, we divide the percentage interest by 100 percent, and multiply this by the loan amount. Then, to calculate how much of the loan will be repaid this month, we subtract this month's interest payment from our fixed monthly payment. This provides the answer to the first part of the calculation we mentioned at beginning of the example:

```
Payment = Monthly Payment - Interest
```

However, you might be wondering why we are creating a new variable called $Monthly at this point in the program. Why not just use the following line instead?

```
$Month = $Month - (($Loan/100)*$Interest);
```

The reason is that we want the value of $Month to remain constant over all of the loops, representing the fixed $100 monthly repayment. If we used the line of code above, $Month would change value over each loop, because we would be subtracting the monthly interest from it with each iteration. Therefore we use a different variable, $Monthly, to represent the total amount repaid toward the loan this month. Each time we go around the loop it will hold a different value.

Ignore the next if statement for the moment; it doesn't alter the values of our variables. Now we've got a value for how much to subtract from the loan this month, we can adjust the figure in our overall $Loan:

```
$Loan = $Loan - $Monthly;
```

Let's actually step through the loop now and substitute some values, to see what is really happening. We will use the numbers shown in the screenshot. The first time round the loop, the variables contain their initial values:

```
$Loan = 1000
$Interest = 5
$Duration= 0
$Month= 100
```

So our first line effectively reads:

```
while (1000>0)
```

Yes, 1000 is bigger than 0, so we safely proceed inside the loop to the first line of code, which now reads:

```
$Duration = 0 + 1;
```

So $Duration now equals one. The next line reads:

```
$Monthly = 100 - (1000*5/100);
```

If we calculate the contents of the parentheses we get;

```
$Monthly = 100 - (50);
```

So $Monthly is equal to 50. We reach the final line, which reads:

```
$Loan = 1000 - 50;
```

So $Loan is now $950. Next we encounter the closing brace, meaning the end of the iteration. We jump back to the condition part of the loop: when we test it this time it reads:

```
while (950>0)
```

Our condition still hasn't been met so we venture into the loop once more. $Duration was changed to 1 during the last loop, so this time it reads:

```
$Duration = 1 + 1;
```

So now $Duration has the value 2. The next line is changed slightly from the last loop, because the value of $Loan is different. It now reads:

```
$Monthly = 100 - (950*5/100);
```

This leaves $Monthly with a value of 52.5. This has a knock-on effect to our remaining loan calculation which reads:

```
$Loan = 950 - 52.5;
```

After this, $Loan holds the value 897.5. So the actual interest payments decrease over time because the loan amount decreases. However, the monthly loan payment remains fixed, so effectively the amount of loan being repaid each month increases. For the first month we pay off $50, for the second we pay off $52 and 50c, and so on.

We jump back to the condition at the beginning of the loop and test it again:

```
while (897.5>0)
```

It still hasn't been met, so we're back around the loop a third time. In fact we have to go around it 15 times before the loan is paid off, but you should now have an idea of what is going on. Now it's time to look at the one line of code we have so far ignored.

### Infinite Loops

You probably know that paying back loans at a very slow rate is a bad idea. This is because the interest to be paid outstrips your repayments, so the loan will gradually increase and the loan will never be paid off. This rather frightening prospect could also have lethal implications for our program. If the user enters a value which is too low, then our loop continues indefinitely, because our condition of $Loan>0 will never be false. If PHP is thrown into an infinite loop, by default a PHP script should only execute for 30 seconds, infinite loop or not. However, on Windows 2000 and IIS 5, on some machines your browser will eventually freeze, and if you're not careful your web server will too.

This means that we must make sure that infinite loops don't occur. In the loan example, we can do this by checking for repayment values which are too low; however, this value is entirely dependent on which loan package is selected. Therefore we have to use a little more brainpower and construct a search in the loop itself. Now, the only time an infinite loop will occur is if we're actually adding to our $Loan value each month. Take another look at the relevant line of code in our program:

```
$Loan = $Loan - $Monthly;
```

But we are *subtracting* $Monthly from $Loan, so the only way we can *increase* the $Loan value is if we have a negative value in $Monthly (subtracting a negative value is equivalent to adding a positive value). We therefore perform a check to see if $Monthly is smaller than or equal to zero. As long as it isn't, we can be sure that our $Loan amount is going to decrease with each iteration of the loop, and it can only do this a finite amount of times. It doesn't really matter how many times it takes: PHP can iterate many thousands of times in just one second.

If we encounter an infinite loop condition, then we break out of the loop using the exit command, first displaying a message informing the user of this:

```
if ($Monthly<=0)
    {
        echo "You need larger repayments to pay off your loan!";
        exit;
    }
```

As we don't want to display anything afterwards, we use the `exit` command to prevent further output to the web page.

On the other hand, if we finish iterating correctly, we display the final contents of the `$Duration` variable:

```
echo "This would take you $Duration months to pay this off at the Interest rate of
$Interest percent.";
```

This lets the user know how long it would take them to pay off the loan. Despite our loop only being 5 lines long, we've had to explain it in quite some detail. If you're still not happy with the workings, go back and put some different figures in, work out what should happen on paper, writing out the results of the loop each time, and then check that your results concur with what PHP returns. They should be identical. We'll move on to the next type of loop.

# do while Loops

The `do while` loop is similar in operation to the `while` loop, except for one small point: the conditional statement is tested at the end of the loop, not the beginning. This has a subtle but important implication – the contents of the braces will be executed at least once, even if the condition turns out to be false.

```
do
{
    execute the contents of these parentheses
}
while(a condition is true); - go back and do it again
```

Therefore you could use `do while` if you want to iterate at least once, even if the condition isn't true. This is important. If we go back to our shopping example and change it to `do while`, it alters the whole working of the code:

```
do
{
    echo ("You have exceeded your credit limit,
                        so the last item from your basket will be removed");
    $ShoppingTotal = $ShoppingTotal - $LastPurchase;
    $LastPurchase = $LastPurchaseButOne;
} while ($ShoppingTotal > $CreditLimit);
```

Now we'd print the warning message before we'd even checked to see if the user had exceeded his credit limit. That's not what we wanted to do at all!

Let's see a situation where `do while` might be used. If we had to travel on a highway from Junction 1 to Junction 10, it could be represented as:

```
do
{
    drive until next junction;
} while ($junction != 10);
```

It stands to follow that, if you wanted to get off the highway, you'd have to drive at least until the next junction before scurrying to find the map book, it would be necessary to iterate at least once. Another good example in PHP would be if you definitely need to perform a calculation at least once, but might also need to perform the calculation over and over again, until you get a certain answer. Say for example, we had a prime number checker. To check if a number is a prime, we need to divide it by every number from two up to the value of the number itself minus one. We could let the do while loop do it for us:

```
do
{
    $Remainder = $PossiblePrimeNumber%$Number;
    $Number=$Number+1;
} while ($Remainder!=0 AND $Number<$PossiblePrimeNumber);
```

Here we divide our candidate for a prime number $PossiblePrimeNumber by each number from 2 up to one less than $PossiblePrimeNumber itself, using the modulus operator (%) to determine if there is a remainder from each division. During each iteration we perform one division and test for a remainder. If no remainder is found during an iteration we drop out of the loop, because we know then the number can't be a prime.

We have to do at least one division to find whether our candidate number is divisible by another number, so this is why do while is suitable here. If we reach the value of the candidate number without dropping out of the loop, we know that our candidate number is only divisible by itself or 1, so it must be a prime number. Simple!

Another common situation where do while proves useful is when we need to wait for user input. For example, do you remember the number guessing game in Chapter 4, where we get PHP to produce a random number from 1 to 10? What if we wanted to modify it so that the user has to keep guessing until the right number is picked? One simple option is to place the code in a do while loop, which iterates until the right number is guessed.

Okay, let's reinforce your understanding of do while loops with an example. We'll flesh out the prime number checker code snippet into a proper example in PHP.

## Try It Out – Using do while

**1.** Start up your web page editor and type in the following:

```
<HTML>
<HEAD></HEAD>
<BODY>
<FORM METHOD=POST ACTION="check.php">
What is your Number:
<INPUT NAME="Guess" TYPE="Text">
<BR>
<BR>
```

```
<INPUT TYPE=SUBMIT VALUE="Click here to check if it is prime">
<BR>
</FORM>
</BODY>
</HTML>
```

**2.** Save this as check.html.

**3.** Close this file, open a new one, and type in the following:

```
<HTML>
<HEAD></HEAD>
<BODY>
<?php
$Count=2;
do
{
    $Remainder = $Guess%$Count;
    $Count=$Count+1;
} while ($Remainder!=0 AND $Count<$Guess);
if (($Count<$Guess) || ($Guess==0)) {
    echo ("Your number is not prime");
} else {
    echo ("Your number is prime");
}
?>
</BODY>
</HTML>
```

**4.** Save this as check.php.

**5.** Close this, open up check.html in your browser, and enter a number:

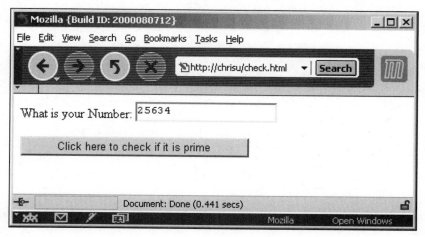

**6.** Click on the button to discover the result:

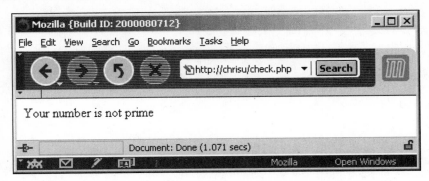

### How It Works

The purpose of check.html is solely to extract a number from the user.

```
What is your Number:
<INPUT NAME="Guess" TYPE="Text">
```

This number is passed to the $Guess variable which is used in check.php. The first task of check.php is to set up a count variable:

```
$Count=2;
```

It is set to 2, as we don't want to start dividing by 1 – after all, every whole number is exactly divisible by 1! Next we start the do loop:

```
do
{
```

Inside the loop we start by checking for a remainder when we divide our $Guess number by the value of the $Count variable. We then increment our $Count variable:

```
$Remainder = $Guess%$Count;
$Count=$Count+1;
```

These two lines form the whole body of the loop. Not bad considering in our example we typed in 25634, and so this loop must be dividing 25634 by 2, 3, 4, 5, 6, 7, 8, and so on, all the way up to 25633. That's a lot of iterations our loop has to do. At the end of every iteration we test to see if two things have happened: whether there is no remainder from the division, and whether the value of $Count has reached our candidate prime number $Guess yet:

```
} while ($Remainder!=0 AND $Count<$Guess);
```

When we drop out of the loop, it must be because one of these two conditions has occurred. If we drop out of the loop but the value of $Count doesn't match $Guess, it must be because the candidate prime number has been divided exactly by the number in $Count, so $Guess isn't prime. We must also take into account a guess of zero, which gives a remainder of zero when divided by any number, but is not prime. Otherwise, if the two variables have matching values, then we must have a prime number.

```
if (($Count<$Guess) || ($Guess==0)) {
    echo ("Your number is not prime");
} else {
    echo ("Your number is prime");
}
```

The last step is to display the results to the user. Now it's time to look at the last type of loop.

# for Loops

The `for` loop is best used when you want to repeat a section of code a specified amount of times. In other words, it gives you the ability to specify the amount of times you iterate around the loop. The condition part of the loop is more complex than in the `while` loop, as it is composed of three parts:

```
for (set loop counter; test loop counter;
add or subtract from the counter)
{
    execute the contents of these braces
}
```

The `for` loop introduces the concept of a loop counter. This is a variable which is used to count the amount of times we have been around the loop (number of iterations), and terminate the loop when the set number of iterations has been exceeded. The third part of the condition ensures that you change the value of the counter with each iteration. These three parts to the condition allow you to construct some complex conditions and loops. None of the parts of the condition are actually compulsory, but to begin with we will be using all three.

Let's see how the `for` loop can be used. First example: what's the best way to print out our name ten times in a row? Well, we could use the `echo` command ten times, but this would get quite tiresome. We could also use the new `while` loop that we have just learned, and create a variable inside it to count the number of iterations, as follows:

```
$counter=0;
while ($counter<10)
{
    echo "My name is Chris!";
    $counter=$counter+1;
}
```

However, how many times does this go around the loop? Is it 9 because when we reach 10, we stop? Is it 11, because we start the loop counter at 0? It is actually 10, but you have to go back, think about it logically, and work it out in your head. The number of iterations is much easier to keep track of with a `for` loop:

```
for ($counter=1; $counter<=10; $counter++)
{
    echo "My name is Chris!";
}
```

You don't have to keep track of the loop counter either, as it's all done for you. You can also make use of the counter within the loop:

```
for ($counter=1; $counter<=10; $counter++)
{
    echo $counter;
}
```

This would produce the output **12345678910**. You may have noticed that there's some terminology here that we have seen before: the increment operator ++ symbols. This is equivalent to saying:

```
$counter=$counter+1;
```

It's just another shorthand.

Let's now try an example that creates a dynamic form. It takes a value from the user, and this value sets the number of HTML controls displayed on a second page. It then displays the contents of these controls on a third page. Give it a try.

## Try It Out – Using a for Loop

**1.** Nudge your web page editor to make sure it's still awake, and type in the following:

```
<HTML>
<HEAD></HEAD>
<BODY>
<FORM METHOD=POST ACTION="dynamic.php">
How many children do you have?
<INPUT NAME="Number" TYPE="Text">
<BR>
<BR>
<INPUT TYPE=SUBMIT>
<BR>
</FORM>
</BODY>
</HTML>
```

**2.** Save this as `dynamic.html`.

**3.** Close this file, create a new one and type in the following:

```
<HTML>
<HEAD></HEAD>
<BODY>
<FORM METHOD=GET ACTION="dynamic2.php">
<?php
for ($Counter=0; $Counter<$Number; $Counter++)
{
    $Offset = $Counter+1;
    echo "<BR><BR>Please enter the name of child number $Offset<BR>";
    echo "<INPUT NAME=Child[] TYPE=TEXT>";
}
if ($Counter==0) echo"Press the button to move on";
?>
<BR>
<BR>
```

```
<INPUT TYPE=SUBMIT>
</FORM>
</BODY>
</HTML>
```

**4.** Save this one as `dynamic.php`.

**5.** Close this file down, and create another new one and type in the following:

```
<HTML>
<HEAD></HEAD>
<BODY>
<?php
$Count=0;
echo "Your children's names are:";
do
{
    echo"<BR><BR>$Child[$Count]";
    $CheckEmpty = "$Child[$Count]";
    $Count=$Count+1;
} while ($CheckEmpty!="");
if ($Count==1) echo "Not Applicable";
?>
</BODY>
</HTML>
```

**6.** Save this as `dynamic2.php`.

**7.** Close this. Then open `dynamic.html` in your browser and enter a number (play along and enter a number greater than zero, even if you don't have any children):

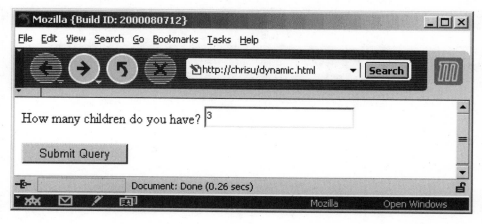

**8.** Click on **Submit Query** and the next page will display the same number of text boxes as you entered for the number of children.

**9.** Enter some names into the browser:

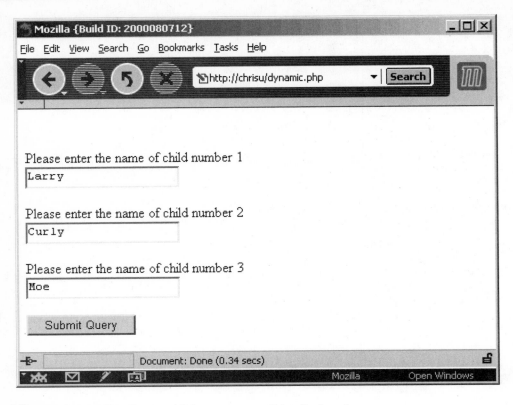

**10.** Click on Submit Query and these names will be displayed.

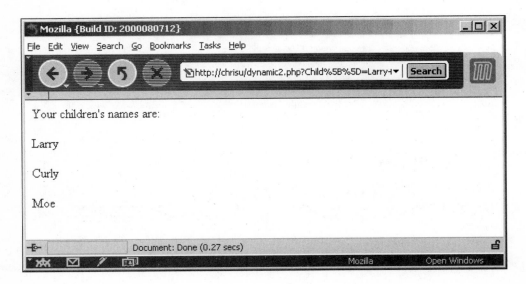

## *How It Works*

This deceptively simple task isn't actually as simple as it first might have seemed. We start with the simple HTML file `dynamic.html`, which takes the number of children as form input. This number is passed as the variable `$Number` to the `dynamic.php` script.

```
How many children do you have?
<INPUT NAME="Number" TYPE="Text">
```

Then in our PHP script, we started by introducing a little trickery. We mentioned in Chapter 1 that if you pass HTML tags along as part of a text statement, the PHP is translated into HTML. The same idea applies to the contents of any statements, so by sending a `<FORM>` tag as part of an `echo` statement, we're telling the browser that we want to create a form.

```
<FORM METHOD=GET ACTION="dynamic2.php">
<?php
echo
```

Once we're inside the `<FORM>` tag, we need to create a number of text boxes. We know how many we need, as the user will have supplied this number on the last page, and it will be contained in the variable `$Number`. This is a perfect time to introduce a `for` loop. We want to display the number of text boxes to match `$Number`, but if the user doesn't have any children, then we don't want to display any text boxes at all. This means we have to start the `$Counter` at zero, and if the value in `$Number` is zero, we want to jump over the loop entirely. Hence the counter starts at zero, and is incremented by one at the end of each loop. The loops continue while the counter is lower than the number of children:

```
for ($Counter=0; $Counter<$Number; $Counter++)
{
```

Inside the loop we're faced with another problem. We need to personalize each text box with a number, yet if we display the current count of the loop, the text box number will be one below what it should be. So we create an 'offset variable' to get around this, which is just `$counter` plus one:

```
$Offset = $Counter+1;
```

Then we start getting to the meat of the script. We display a message instructing the user to enter the name of a child:

```
echo "<BR><BR>Please enter the name of child number $Offset<BR>";
```

We add the text box next. The interesting bit here is that when we set the text box's name attribute, we add brackets after it to denote that it's an array. Then each time a name is passed to `$Child`, it will be stored in a new element of child: `$Child[0]`, `$Child[1]`, `$Child[2]` and so on:

```
echo "<INPUT NAME=Child[] TYPE=TEXT>";
}
```

The loop actually ends there. So all we do each time we iterate through a loop is to display a bit of text and a text box, for as many times as the value of the variable `$Number`. After that we drop out of the loop, display a Submit button, and close the form. Before we can do this though, we need to check the user's input, to see if zero was entered (or a text field which will default to zero) into the number of children field. If it was, we display another message:

```
if ($Counter==0) echo"Press the button to move on";
?>
```

The third script is the one that just prints out the names you've just supplied to the array. Sounds easy enough, but first you must take into account the fact that the variable $Number has not been passed to the new script. It only existed in the last page, dynamic.php. So, we're left with a situation where we know names might have been supplied to the array $Child[], but we don't know how many, if any. This means we resort to our old friend the do while loop, and we have to set the child counter $Count manually. We start it at zero, because it might be zero.

```
$Count=0;
```

We display a text message on the web page:

```
echo "Your children's names are:";
```

We then start a do while loop, as we want the contents of the loop to run at least once:

```
do
{
```

On entering the loop, we display the first item in the array, $Child[0]. If there is nothing in the array, then nothing apart from the line breaks will be displayed. Otherwise it will display the first child's name:

```
echo"<BR><BR>$Child[$Count]";
```

We then alter the contents of the $CheckEmpty variable to be the contents of $Child[0]. If it's empty, $CheckEmpty will trigger the end of the loop later on. If it's not empty we will iterate again.

```
$CheckEmpty = "$Child[$Count]";
```

We increment the count:

```
$Count=$Count+1;
```

Then we check to see if $CheckEmpty is an empty variable. If it is we drop out of the loop; if not we continue:

```
} while ($CheckEmpty!="");
```

Lastly, we have a check to see whether the number of children entered was zero. If it was, we display an appropriate message:

```
if ($Count==1) echo "Not Applicable";
```

The last program has actually introduced the next topic of discussion for this chapter: arrays. The reason that we held back using them until now is that loops make them much more practical to implement. What if you had put in 20 children? Without using loops, our code would have needed 20 lines to read in their names, and 20 more to echo them out. We would also lose flexibility without loops because we would have to fix the number of name fields to read in; loops allow us to be more dynamic.

# Arrays

We briefly encountered arrays already earlier in this book, and have just encountered them again. It's now time to introduce them more formally. Arrays are a set of variables which all have the same name, but each has a different **index**. Each member of the array is called an **element**. You can create arrays in the same way you create variables, as long as you remember to put the square brackets around them to denote the index:

```
$StatesOfTheUSA[1] = "Washington";
$StatesOfTheUSA[2] = "California";
```

You don't have to assign them in order numerically, you can jump as few, or as many entries as you want:

```
$StatesOfTheUSA[49]="Alaska";
$StatesOfTheUSA[13]="Alabama";
```

In fact you can dispense with the numeric indexing completely and use characters instead. Arrays like this are often known as associative arrays:

```
$StateCapital["ca"] = "Sacramento";
$StateCapital["il"] = "Springfield";
```

Note that, if you wish to access the contents of an associative array, you can drop the quotation marks surrounding the index value if you wish. To display Sacremento, you can type either:

```
echo $StateCapital["ca"];
```

or

```
echo $StateCapital[ca];
```

Both get it displayed on the web page.

One last feature of arrays in PHP is that you can actually assign different data types and variables to the values within the array. Here are some examples:

```
$Number[1]=24;
$Number[2]="twenty three";
$Number[2]=$variable;
$Number["ca"]=$variable;
```

However, this poses a couple of questions. How does PHP know how big an array should be? And how much memory should it assign to an array?

# Initialization of Arrays

Setting the initial values of array variables is, surprisingly enough, a process known as initialization. We've come across the first way to initialize arrays in two examples in this book already: we don't worry about the indexing and let PHP do it automatically for us. We create one item in the array, then we create another with the same name:

```
$Author[]="William Shakespeare";
$Author[]="Franz Kafka";
```

Without the square brackets, PHP would not have known that we are dealing with array variables, and would have replaced the first value with the second one: the square brackets indicate that we want to store the values in an array. The lack of an index value lets PHP decide where to put them. You'll find that if the `$Author[]` array hasn't been used before, then the values above will be stored in `$Author[0]` and `$Author[1]`. PHP will carry on assigning new values to the next element in the array.

We have also encountered the second way to initialize an array, using explicit index values:

```
$Author[0]="William Shakespeare";
$Author[1]="Franz Kafka";
```

Here we don't have to abide by the constraints of auto-numbering that PHP would otherwise impose on us – we can assign index values out of sequence, as described earlier. PHP is different from many programming languages, where arrays are concerned, on two counts. First, we don't have to predefine the data type of the array, stating whether it will contain numbers or text. This is consistent with PHP's policy on variables: you don't have to choose a data type, PHP does it for you. Second, you also don't have to specify how large the array is before it is created. Once again, PHP determines how large the maximum index number in the array needs to be; for example `$Author[]` only needs to contain 2 items.

There are two more ways of populating arrays in PHP and both make use of the `array ()` construct. If we take our authors code snippet, it can be redefined as follows:

```
$Author = array ("William Shakespeare", "Franz Kafka");
```

Once again we're asking PHP to automatically generate the index values. Again, the index values start at zero, and new values placed in the array are placed in the unfilled element with the lowest index. If you were to echo the contents of `$Author[1]` after this line of code, it would contain Franz Kafka.

There are no size limits on arrays like these, so you could also write the following line:

```
$StatesOfTheUSA = array ("Alabama", "Alaska", "Arizona", "Arkansas", "California",
"Colorado", "Connecticut", "Delaware", "Florida", "Georgia", "Hawaii", "Idaho",
"Illinois", "Indiana", "Iowa", "Kansas", "Kentucky", "Louisiana", "Maine",
"Maryland", "Massachusetts", "Michigan", "Minnesota", "Mississippi", "Missouri",
"Montana", "Nebraska", "Nevada", "New Hampshire", "New Jersey", "New Mexico", "New
York", "North Carolina", "North Dakota", "Ohio", "Oklahoma", "Oregon",
"Pennsylvania", "Rhode Island", "South Carolina", "South Dakota", "Tennessee",
"Texas", "Utah", "Vermont", "Virginia", "Washington", "West Virginia",
"Wisconsin", "Wyoming");
```

Once again, the first state will start with an index value of zero, while Wyoming will have the value 49. However, this can be a little counter-intuitive, you know there are 50 states in the USA, and if you finish with 49, you will have the niggling feeling that one has been missed out. To get around this, the `array()` function allows you to pick the index you want the array to start at. It makes use of the `=>` operator to do this, as follows:

```
$StatesOfTheUSA = array (1 => "Alabama", "Alaska", "Arizona", "Arkansas",
"California", "Colorado", "Connecticut", "Delaware", "Florida", "Georgia",
"Hawaii", "Idaho", "Illinois", "Indiana", "Iowa", "Kansas", "Kentucky",
"Louisiana", "Maine", "Maryland", "Massachusetts", "Michigan", "Minnesota",
"Mississippi", "Missouri", "Montana", "Nebraska", "Nevada", "New Hampshire", "New
Jersey", "New Mexico", "New York", "North Carolina", "North Dakota", "Ohio",
"Oklahoma", "Oregon", "Pennsylvania", "Rhode Island", "South Carolina", "South
Dakota", "Tennessee", "Texas", "Utah", "Vermont", "Virginia", "Washington", "West
Virginia", "Wisconsin", "Wyoming");
```

In other words, you place the number you want the index to start at, followed by the => operator and then your list of values as normal. Now if you were to echo the contents of $StatesOfTheUSA[50], it would be Wyoming, whereas without this shift of one it would have been empty. It doesn't have to be 1, it equally be 101, and then Wyoming would have the index of 150.

If you wish to index a large associative array, then you have to set each value individually. For example, with our states, it might be as follows:

```
$StatesOfTheUSA = array ("al" => "Alabama", "ak" => "Alaska", "az" => "Arizona",
"ar" => "Arkansas", "ca" => "California", "co" => "Colorado", "ct" =>
"Connecticut", "de" => "Delaware", "fl" => "Florida", "ga" => "Georgia", "hi" =>
"Hawaii", "id" => "Idaho", "il" => "Illinois", "in" => "Indiana", "ia" => "Iowa",
"ks" => "Kansas", "ky" => "Kentucky", "la" => "Louisiana", "me" => "Maine", "md"
=> "Maryland", "ma" => "Massachusetts", "mi" => "Michigan", "mn" => "Minnesota",
"ms" => "Mississippi", "mo" => "Missouri", "mt" => "Montana", "ne" => "Nebraska",
"nv" => "Nevada", "nh" => "New Hampshire", "nj" => "New Jersey", "nm" => "New
Mexico", "ny" => "New York", "nc" => "North Carolina", "nd" => "North Dakota",
"oh" => "Ohio", "ok" => "Oklahoma", "or" => "Oregon", "pa" => "Pennsylvania", "ri"
=> "Rhode Island", "sc" => "South Carolina", "sd" => "South Dakota", "tn" =>
"Tennessee", "tx" => "Texas", "ut" => "Utah", "vt" => "Vermont", "va" =>
"Virginia", "wa" => "Washington", "wv" => "West Virginia", "wi" => "Wisconsin",
"wy" => "Wyoming");
```

Slow, but it does the job.

# Iterating Through an Array

Once you've created an array with lots of entries, you don't want to have to go back and individually retrieve each item in the array. It makes for a lot of extra work. This is where loops work hand-in-hand with arrays. If we want to print out the name of each of these states on our web page, we'd just use the for loop to do it for us. To display all 50 states in the 1 to 50 indexed $StatesOfTheUSA array would take a grand total of 3 lines, excluding the line that creates the array:

```
for ($counter=1; $counter<51; $counter++) {
   echo"<BR>$StatesOfTheUSA[$counter]";
}
```

The line between the braces selects an element from the $StatesOfTheUSA array, by placing the variable $counter between the brackets to use as the index. Since $counter is a variable, the index can then be changed by changing the value of $counter. Our for loop says, "Start the counter at one, and go up to the value 50, in increments of one." So the $counter variable is substituted for 1, 2, 3, and so on, for each iteration (note that <BR> is used to display each state on a new line):

```
echo"<BR>$StatesOfTheUSA[1];
echo"<BR>$StatesOfTheUSA[2];
echo"<BR>$StatesOfTheUSA[3];
etc...
```

There's nothing to preclude us from using while or do while loops, although you'd have to create a loop counter yourself, and set it yourself. The following while loop would do the same as our for loop:

```
$counter=1;
while ($counter<51) {
    echo"<BR> $StatesOfTheUSA[$counter]";
    $counter=$counter+1;
}
```

It just takes an extra couple of lines to do it, that's all.

Let's now do a quick example of iterating through an array. As we've already done this earlier, we're going to spice up this example a little bit to keep your interest. We're going to create two arrays in this example, one that holds all of the states' names, and one that holds all of the states' capitals. You select the name of a state from a dropdown list box, and it searches through the corresponding array of states to find the state capital. However, we're going to employ loops and arrays several times, to ensure that we don't have to create fifty lines of HTML to display any of the answers.

## Try It Out – Iterating Through an Array

**1.** Open your favorite web page editor and type in the following:

```
<HTML>
<HEAD></HEAD>
<BODY>
<FORM ACTION="capitals.php" METHOD=POST>
What state do you want to know the capital of?
<SELECT NAME=State>
<?php

$StatesOfTheUSA = array (1 => "Alabama", "Alaska", "Arizona", "Arkansas",
"California", "Colorado", "Connecticut", "Delaware", "Florida", "Georgia",
"Hawaii", "Idaho", "Illinois", "Indiana", "Iowa", "Kansas", "Kentucky",
"Louisiana", "Maine", "Maryland", "Massachusetts", "Michigan", "Minnesota",
"Mississippi", "Missouri", "Montana", "Nebraska", "Nevada", "New Hampshire", "New
Jersey", "New Mexico", "New York", "North Carolina", "North Dakota", "Ohio",
"Oklahoma", "Oregon", "Pennsylvania", "Rhode Island", "South Carolina", "South
Dakota", "Tennessee", "Texas", "Utah", "Vermont", "Virginia", "Washington", "West
Virginia", "Wisconsin", "Wyoming");
for ($counter=1; $counter<51; $counter++) {
    echo"<OPTION>$StatesOfTheUSA[$counter]</OPTION>";
}
echo "</SELECT><BR><BR>";
for ($counter=1; $counter<51; $counter++) {
    echo"<INPUT TYPE=HIDDEN
NAME='HiddenState[]'VALUE='$StatesOfTheUSA[$counter]'>";
}
```

```
echo "<INPUT TYPE=SUBMIT></FORM>";
?>
</BODY>
</HTML>
```

**2.** Save this script as `states.php`, noting that this is a PHP file, not an HTML file.

**3.** Close this, open a new file, and type the following:

```
<HTML>
<HEAD></HEAD>
<BODY>
<?php
$StateCapital = array (0 => "Montgomery", "Juneau", "Phoenix", "Little Rock",
"Sacramento","Denver","Hartford", "Dover","Tallahasse", "Atlanta", "Honolulu",
"Boise", "Springfield","Indianapolis", "Des Moines", "Topeka", "Frankfort", "Baton
Rouge","Augusta","Annapolis","Boston", "Lansing", "Saint Paul","Jackson",
"Jefferson City", "Helena","Lincoln", "Carson City","Concord", "Trenton","Santa
Fe", "Albany", "Raleigh","Bismarck","Columbus","Oklahoma City", "Salem",
"Harrisburg", "Providence", "Columbia","Pierre", "Nashville", "Austin","Salt Lake
City", "Montpelier","Richmond","Olympia","Charleston", "Madison","Cheyenne");
for ($counter=0; $counter<50; $counter++)
{
   if($HiddenState[$counter]==$State)
   {
      echo"The State capital is $StateCapital[$counter]";
   }
}
?>
</BODY>
</HTML>
```

**4.** Save this as `capitals.php`.

**5.** Open up `states.php` and select a state:

**6.** Click on the Submit Query button to get an answer:

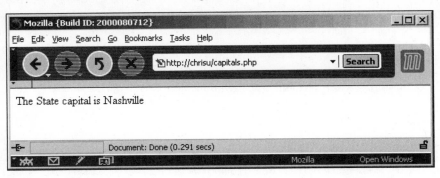

## How It Works

This is an example which demonstrates exactly how much code it is possible to save using loops and arrays. If only it could have saved us typing the data in as well! For this example, we changed the first page into a PHP one as well, so that we could use PHP's `array()` function to avoid typing in 50 lines of HTML in the `<SELECT>` list box. We started by creating an HTML form:

```
<FORM ACTION="capitals.php" METHOD=POST>
What state do you want to know the capital of?
```

Next we created a dropdown list box:

```
<SELECT NAME=State>
```

Then we moved onto our PHP script and started by feeding the names of the states into an array called `$StatesOfTheUSA`, beginning at index 1:

```
<?php
$StatesOfTheUSA = array (1 => "Alabama", "Alaska", "Arizona", "Arkansas",
"California", "Colorado", "Connecticut", "Delaware", "Florida", "Georgia",
"Hawaii", "Idaho", "Illinois", "Indiana", "Iowa", "Kansas", "Kentucky",
"Louisiana", "Maine", "Maryland", "Massachusetts", "Michigan", "Minnesota",
"Mississippi", "Missouri", "Montana", "Nebraska", "Nevada", "New Hampshire", "New
Jersey", "New Mexico", "New York", "North Carolina", "North Dakota", "Ohio",
"Oklahoma", "Oregon", "Pennsylvania", "Rhode Island", "South Carolina", "South
Dakota", "Tennessee", "Texas", "Utah", "Vermont", "Virginia", "Washington", "West
Virginia", "Wisconsin", "Wyoming");
```

We then created a loop which iterated 50 times, placing the name of each state in our list box.

```
for ($counter=1; $counter<51; $counter++) {
    echo"<OPTION>$StatesOfTheUSA[$counter]</OPTION>";
}
echo "</SELECT><BR><BR>";
```

Once the loop was finished we closed the list box. You might have expected the next line to supply a Submit button and to close the form. However, a problem arises here, if you think ahead to the next page. We need all of the states to be available on the next page, not just this page.

Why? Well, consider how we find the state capital of a particular state. We find the index of the state in the $StatesOfTheUSA array, and then look up which state capital is present at the same index of the $StateCapital. For example, the contents of $StatesOfTheUSA[1] is Alabama, so the contents of $StateCapital[1] is Montgomery. We can do this because we have made sure that the capital at any particular index in $StateCapital is the capital of the state located at the same index in $StatesOfTheUSA. In other words the data in the two arrays correspond by index.

Now, if we passed only the state selected from the list box across to the next script, then we wouldn't be passing on the index of this state within $StatesOfTheUSA as well. Without this information, we can't look up the corresponding index of $StateCapital and find the capital of our selected state.

So what can we do? We obviously need to pass some information about the index of the state to the next script. One obvious way to do this is to simply pass the full array of states to the next script. So this is what we do.

We create a second loop, and use it to create an array containing 50 Hidden controls, HiddenState. We fill the array with the states present in $StatesOfTheUSA.

```
for ($counter=1; $counter<51; $counter++) {
echo"<INPUT TYPE=HIDDEN NAME='HiddenState[]' VALUE='$StatesOfTheUSA[$counter]'>";
}
```

After we've read across the names of 50 states, we add a **Submit Query** button and close the form:

```
echo "<INPUT TYPE=SUBMIT></FORM>";
```

Our second PHP page now has two sets of data. The first is obtained from the dropdown list box, and contains the name of the single state that the user selected. It is stored in the variable $State. The second is a whole list of the 50 states, in alphabetical order, stored in the array $HiddenState. However, as PHP populated this array, it now runs from numbers 0 to 49. This isn't a problem though, we just need to make sure we're aware of it. Our first line deals with this. We now create an array with the name of the 50 state capitals. However to match the indexes of the $HiddenState array we need to make our array indexes run from 0 to 49:

```
$StateCapital = array (0 => "Montgomery", "Juneau", "Phoenix", "Little Rock",
"Sacramento","Denver","Hartford", "Dover","Tallahasse", "Atlanta", "Honolulu",
"Boise", "Springfield","Indianapolis", "Des Moines", "Topeka", "Frankfort", "Baton
Rouge","Augusta","Annapolis","Boston", "Lansing", "Saint Paul","Jackson",
"Jefferson City", "Helena","Lincoln", "Carson City","Concord", "Trenton","Santa
Fe", "Albany", "Raleigh","Bismarck","Columbus","Oklahoma City", "Salem",
"Harrisburg", "Providence", "Columbia","Pierre", "Nashville", "Austin","Salt Lake
City", "Montpelier","Richmond","Olympia","Charleston", "Madison","Cheyenne");
```

This means that the array $HiddenState and the array $StateCapital now correspond by index, which makes the rest of the program very straightforward. In fact we just need one loop, which runs from 0 to 49.

```
for ($counter=0; $counter<50; $counter++)
{
```

Inside this we nest a conditional statement, which checks to see if the current state is equal to the state that the user selected. If it is, then we display the contents of the corresponding element of `$StateCapital`, making use of the correspondence between the arrays:

```
if($HiddenState[$counter]==$State)
{
    echo"The State capital is $StateCapital[$counter]";
}
}
```

In other words, if the contents of `$HiddenState` matches the state selected by the user, then this index value can be used to retrieve the state capital from the `$StateCapital` array. If there isn't a match, we carry on iterating through the `for` loop until there is one. Using the listbox, there is only a finite set of choices, so we can guarantee that there will always be a match. This is all our program needs to do.

### Improvements to our Program

In fact, we've been a little unhelpful in this previous example, as we wanted to demonstrate how two separate arrays may be linked by an index number. If you actually wanted to run an example like this, it would be much simpler to use an associative array, where you can link the array items within one array statement as follows:

```
$StateCapital = array ("Alabama" => "Montgomery", "Alaska" => "Juneau", "Phoenix"
=>"Arizona", "Arkansas" => "Little Rock", "California" => "Sacramento","Colorado"
=> "Denver", "Connecticut" => "Hartford", "Delaware" => "Dover", "Florida" =>
"Tallahasse", "Georgia" => "Atlanta", "Hawaii" => "Honolulu", "Idaho" => "Boise",
"Illinois" => "Springfield","Indiana" => "Indianapolis", "Iowa" => "Des Moines",
"Kansas" => "Topeka", "Kentucky" => "Frankfort", "Louisiana" => "Baton
Rouge","Maine" => "Augusta","Maryland" =>"Annapolis","Massachusetts" => "Boston",
"Michigan" => "Lansing", "Minnesota" => "Saint Paul","Mississippi" => "Jackson",
"Missouri" => "Jefferson City", "Montana" => "Helena","Nebraska" => "Lincoln",
"Nevada" => "Carson City","New Hampshire" => "Concord", "New Jersey" =>
"Trenton","New Mexico" => "Santa Fe", "New York" => "Albany", "North Carolina" =>
"Raleigh","North Dakota" => "Bismarck","Ohio" => "Columbus","Oklahoma" =>
"Oklahoma City", "Oregon" => "Salem", "Pennsylvania" => "Harrisburg", "Rhode
Island" => "Providence", "South Carolina" => "Columbia","South Dakota" =>"Pierre",
"Tennessee" => "Nashville", "Texas" => "Austin","Utah" => "Salt Lake City",
Vermont" => "Montpelier","Virginia" => "Richmond","Washington" => "Olympia","West
Virginia" => "Charleston", "Wisconsin" => "Madison","Wyoming" =>"Cheyenne");
```

Then you could output the capital using the state name variable, `$State`, as the index.

## Iterating Through Non-Sequential Arrays

So it's pretty simple to iterate through arrays whose elements have been populated sequentially (first element populated first, then second element second, then third element third, and so on). But is it so simple if the elements weren't populated sequentially? For example:

```
$Array[56993]="absolutely huge";
$Array[1]="quite small";
$Array[499]="quite big";
```

Actually, non-sequential arrays aren't too much of a problem, as our old methods still work. If you store the values out of order, it doesn't matter because PHP considers them to be in the straightforward numerical order of the index values. The only problem is that when you check through all of the elements sequentially, you might find yourself checking a lot of empty space in a large array like one above, which contains only three values!

### Current and Key Functions

PHP uses a **pointer** to keep track of which element it's at when it moves through an array. This pointer will point to the element that is currently being used by the script. You can view which element in the array is currently being used by PHP with the current() function, and you can find out which index value the current element has using the key() function. (Key is another name for index.)

We'll use a quick code snippet to illustrate how the current() and key() functions works. First consider what would happen if you added another item to the following array, and got PHP to add the index value automatically. Which index would PHP choose?

```
$Director[4]="Orson Welles";
$Director[1]="Carol Reed";
$Director[93]="Fritz Lang";
$Director[24]="Jacques Tourneur";
```

We can find out by adding the next couple of lines. These return the current index of $Director[], and echo it:

```
$CurrentIndexValue = key($Director);
echo ($CurrentIndexValue);
```

The key() function returns the value 4. Why? Because it returns the index value of the first item we have placed into the array, which was "Orson Welles" at index 4. If you use the current() function it returns the value "Orson Welles":

```
$CurrentContents = current($Director);
echo ($CurrentContents);
```

Now, if you then added the following line to the array:

```
$Director[]="Alfred Hitchcock";
```

"Alfred Hitchcock" would be placed in the array at the index value 94. How can we test to find out what the index value of the new element is, given that the key() and current() functions return information on the first item to be placed in the array?

### Next() and Prev() Functions

In order to find out the index value of a new element added to an array, you will need to use the next() and prev() functions. These functions allow you to navigate through arrays, by moving the pointer to the next or previous element in the array. They both take the name of the array to navigate through as an argument. Let's now go back to our previous array creation list:

```
$Director[4]="Orson Welles";
$Director[1]="Carol Reed";
$Director[93]="Fritz Lang";
$Director[24]="Jacques Tourneur";
$Director[]="Alfred Hitchcock";
```

We call the `next()` function before checking the current index, and the contents of the current element:

```
next($Director);
$CurrentIndexValue = key($Director);
echo ($CurrentIndexValue);
```

The value displayed is **1**, and the `current()` function would return the name "Carol Reed".

If we call `next()` three more times:

```
next($Director);
next($Director);
next($Director);
next($Director);
$CurrentIndexValue = key($Director);
echo ($CurrentIndexValue);
```

The value **94** is displayed. If we now call the `current()` function:

```
$CurrentContents = current($Director);
echo ($CurrentContents);
```

Our browser now displays **Alfred Hitchcock**.

The `prev()` function is used in a similar way. If we took our previous example and added one occurrence of `prev()` after the four of `next()`:

```
next($Director);
next($Director);
next($Director);
next($Director);
prev($Director);
$CurrentIndexValue = key($Director);
echo ($CurrentIndexValue);
```

This time we see **24**, which is the index value associated with "Jacques Tourneur". This is because we have moved forward through four items of the array and back through one. This is fairly straightforward, although one question that springs to mind is: what happens when you move `next()` beyond the last item in the array, or `prev()` before the first?

```
prev($Director);
$CurrentIndexValue = key($Director);
echo ($CurrentIndexValue);
```

The answer here: is nothing at all. This code snippet would return no value. It won't generate an error (as it would in some programming languages); the pointer would just move beyond the end of the array. However, you wouldn't be able to move it back again:

```
prev($Director);
next($Director);
next($Director);
$CurrentIndexValue = key($Director);
echo ($CurrentIndexValue);
```

This would still return nothing at all.

So, we can see that the order we choose to populate the array in makes no difference to the order they will be navigated in. Any new value placed in the array is placed in the element immediately above the filled element with the highest index. So if the highest filled element had index 34, the next value would be placed in index 35. To navigate through the arrays, we need to use the next() and prev() functions. To display our current position we use current() and key() functions.

### List and Each Functions

If you're iterating through a non-sequential array then you can make life easier for yourself. Rather than having to loop through loads of empty values, the list() and each() functions allow you to return only the elements in the array that contain data. This allows you to display the whole contents of an array with the minimum amount of fuss. You would use the while loop to perform this task for you, like this:

```
while (list(IndexValue, ElementContents) = each(ArrayName))
```

This says: for each element of the array Arrayname, set IndexValue equal to the element's index, and ElementContents equal to the contents of the element. If you only want to return either the index or the contents, then you can just omit the appropriate attribute:

```
while (list(IndexValue) = each(ArrayName))
```

Or:

```
while (list(,ElementContents) = each(ArrayName))
```

For our Directors code snippet we could write the following code, to display each director's name in the array:

```
while (list($ElementIndexValue, $ElementContents) = each($Director))
{
    echo "<BR>$ElementIndexValue - $ElementContents";
}
```

You don't have to call the variables $ElementIndexValue and $ElementContents, we've just done it for clarity's sake here. You could just as easily have called them:

```
while (list($MickeyMouse, $DonaldDuck) = each ($Director))
{
    echo "<BR>$MickeyMouse - $DonaldDuck";
}
```

All you've got to remember is that `list()` returns the index value first and the element contents second. This provides us with some useful tools, which are also applicable if the array doesn't happen to have numerical index.

## Iterating Through String-Indexed Arrays

The rules for navigating through associative arrays are similar to those for numerically indexed ones, but there are some slight differences. The first difference is that the following lines, which would have worked fine if the array was numerically indexed, will now create a numerically indexed array:

```
$StateCapital["ga"]="Atlanta";
$StateCapital["il"]="Springfield";
$StateCapital["ca"]="Sacramento";
$StateCapital[] = "Cheyenne";
```

The value "Cheyenne" will be stored in the array item `$StateCapital[0]`. It's not too surprising, given that PHP will have no idea what you want to create as an index value, which might be "WY", but it might just have easily been "AB" or 4563, so instead it will just try and find the biggest numerical index. As we haven't added a numerical index , it will start at the beginning with zero.

The `current()` and `key()` functions will still work in the way you expect on associative arrays. If you try the following code:

```
$WhatState = current($StateCapital);
$WhatAbbreviation = key($StateCapital);
echo "$WhatAbbreviation - $WhatState";
```

You'll find that it returns the first element to be filled in the array, which was index "ga" containing "Atlanta". And you can also iterate through each list just as before.

```
$StateCapital["ga"]="Atlanta";
$StateCapital["il"]="Springfield";
$StateCapital["ca"]="Sacramento";
$StateCapital[] = "Cheyenne";
next($StateCapital);
$WhatState = current($StateCapital);
$WhatAbbreviation = key($StateCapital);
echo "$WhatAbbreviation - $WhatState";
```

This time we display the result il - Springfield. The functions `list()` and `each()` also function in the same way with associative arrays too. We can set up the following array:

```
$StateCapital = array ("ga" => "Atlanta", "il" => "Springfield",
"ca"=>"Sacramento", "wy" => "Cheyenne");
```

Then we can still feed our array to the `each` function, and use `list()` to display the contents in the same way as before:

```
while (list($StateAbbreviation, $StateName) = each ($StateCapital))
{
    echo "<BR>$StateAbbreviation - $StateName";
}
```

This will produce the list of abbreviations and state names as expected, and display them in the order you created them:

```
ga - Atlanta
il - Springfield
ca - Sacramento
wy - Cheyenne
```

We've looked at iterating through these two different types of arrays, and seen how PHP will navigate them in index order, no matter which order you populate the elements, for both numerically-indexed and associative arrays. What happens though if you want PHP to create or preserve a different order?

# Sorting Arrays

There are several functions that PHP provides for sorting arrays. We're going to look at the five most commonly used. They all work in conjunction with the list() and each() functions which we have just discussed.

## sort()

The sort function is the most basic of the sorting functions. It takes the contents of the array and sorts them into alphabetical order. The sort() function just requires an array name to sort the array:

```
sort(ArrayName)
```

If we create an array of directors using the array structure:

```
$Director = array ("Orson Welles","Carol Reed","Fritz Lang","Jacques Tourneur");
```

Then we can sort them by supplying the array name to the sort() function as follows:

```
sort($Director);
```

To view the effect this function has had on our array, we can use the list() and each() functions again. We've already stated that the order in which the items are stored in the array is also the order that they were created in the array. With the above array we'd expect the following order:

```
$Director[0]= "Orson Welles"
$Director[1]= "Carol Reed"
$Director[2]= "Fritz Lang"
$Director[3]= "Jacques Tourneur"
```

After using sort() though, a different pattern emerges:

```
$Director[0]= "Carol Reed"
$Director[1]= "Fritz Lang"
$Director[2]= "Jacques Tourneur"
$Director[3]= "Orson Welles"
```

You can check this, using our earlier code snippet to display the contents of the list on the screen:

```
while (list($IndexValue, $DirectorName) = each ($Director))
{
    echo "<BR>$IndexValue - $DirectorName";
}
```

So our array has been alphabetically sorted and shuffled around. What happens though if we try to sort an associative array?

## asort()

The function `asort()` takes functions created with a string index and sorts them according to their contents. You are probably asking, "Isn't this just what the sort function did though?" Well, not quite. If you cast your mind back to our state capitals code snippet:

```
$StateCapital = array ("ga" => "Atlanta", "il" => "Springfield",
"ca"=>"Sacramento", "wy" => "Cheyenne");
```

You'd expect the array to be created as follows:

```
$StateCapital["ga"]= "Atlanta"
$StateCapital["il"]= "Springfield"
$StateCapital["ca"]= "Sacramento"
$StateCapital["wy"]= "Cheyenne"
```

If you perform a sort on it though:

```
sort($StateCapital);
```

Then you get the following order:

```
$StateCapital[0]= "Atlanta"
$StateCapital[1]= "Cheyenne"
$StateCapital[2]= "Sacramento"
$StateCapital[3]= "Springfield"
```

In other words, the string index values would be replaced by numerical indexes – not particularly useful. However, if we call the `asort()` function instead:

```
asort($StateCapital);
```

The order would now be:

```
$StateCapital["ga"]= "Atlanta"
$StateCapital["wy"]= "Cheyenne"
$StateCapital["il"]= "Sacramento"
$StateCapital["ca"]= "Springfield"
```

This time, the elements have been sorted alphabetically, but we have retained the string indexes too. Once again you can use `list()` and `each()` to show that this has been the case:

```
while (list($StateAbbreviation, $StateName) = each ($StateCapital))
{
    echo "<BR>$StateAbbreviation - $StateName";
}
```

PHP also offers facilities for reverse sorting. Let's take a look.

## rsort() and arsort()

These two functions work in a similar way to their close relations `sort()` and `asort()`. The only difference is that they return the array elements in reverse alphabetical order. You can use `rsort()` to reverse our list of directors:

```
$Director = array ("Orson Welles","Carol Reed","Fritz Lang","Jacques Tourneur");
rsort($Director);
```

You can call `arsort()` to reverse our list of state capitals:

```
$StateCapital = array ("ga" => "Atlanta", "il" => "Springfield",
"ca"=>"Sacramento", "wy" => "Cheyenne");
arsort($StateCapital);
```

We won't look at the results, as you should be able to work out what they are. If you want to check, you should be able to adapt the previous code to display the answers.

There is one last type of sort we haven't looked at – sorting the contents of an associative array according to the index.

## ksort()

The `ksort()` function can do this type of sorting for you. It's applied in exactly the same way as the other sort functions, but instead it arranges an associative array in alphabetical order of string indexes. In the example of our state capitals:

```
$StateCapital = array ("ga" => "Atlanta", "il" => "Springfield",
"ca"=>"Sacramento", "wy" => "Cheyenne");
ksort($StateCapital);
```

The `ksort()` function would yield the following order:

```
$StateCapital["ca"]= "Sacramento"
$StateCapital["ga"]= "Atlanta"
$StateCapital["il"]= "Springfield"
$StateCapital["wy"]= "Cheyenne"
```

# Miscellaneous Array Functions

There are a vast number of functions which PHP provides, to help you use arrays more efficiently. There are so many that we don't have time to effectively cover them all here, but there are one or two functions that you should know about, because we will be making further use of them in this book.

## array_push() and array_pop()

We noted in a previous section that if you had an array, and you added a new item without specifying an index value, the new item would be placed in the next element up from the filled element with the highest index. In other words, if we add a new entry to the $Director array below:

```
$Director[4]="Orson Welles";
$Director[1]="Carol Reed";
$Director[93]="Fritz Lang";
$Director[24]="Jacques Tourneur";
$Director[]="Alfred Hitchcock";
```

The new item would be placed in the element with index 94. The function array_push() does exactly the same thing. To add "Alfred Hitchcock" to the array, we would use:

```
array_push($Director, "Alfred Hitchcock");
```

It takes two arguments, the first being the name of the array, and the second being the item you wish to place in the array. However you can also use it to "push" many items onto the array, by listing them:

```
array_push($Director, "Alfred Hitchcock", "FW Murnau", "Akira Kurosowa");
```

The array_pop() function does the opposite, removing the last item added to the array. So if we executed the following:

```
$Director[4]="Orson Welles";
$Director[1]="Carol Reed";
$Director[93]="Fritz Lang";
$Director[24]="Jacques Tourneur";
array_pop($Director);
```

This would remove the entry with the index value 24, which contains "Jacques Tourneur", leaving three items in the array. Note that unlike array_push(), array_pop() only takes one argument: the array name. Both functions treat the array as a **stack**: a system where you add items to the top of the pile, and remove them from the top of the pile as well.

## Implode and Explode

These two functions are not as destructive as their names imply! They allow you to store the entire contents of an array as a string, or vice versa: to split one long string up into chunks and place the chunks into the elements of an array.

The implode() function takes an already existing array as its argument, and concatenates the contents of each element in the array into a string. You can also give an extra delimiter argument to the function, which is then used to separate each array item in the string:

```
$StringName = implode("delimiter", $ArrayName);
```

If we take our previous state capitals example, we can glue all of the array items together, with a dash delimiter between each name, as follows:

```
$StateCapital ["ca"]= "Sacramento";
$StateCapital ["ga"]= "Atlanta";
$StateCapital ["il"]= "Springfield";
$StateCapital ["wy"]= "Cheyenne";
$AllCapitalsSeparatedByADash = implode("-", $StateCapital);
echo ($AllCapitalsSeparatedByADash);
```

The echo statement would return the following: Sacramento-Atlanta-Springfield-Cheyenne.

The opposite function is performed by explode(). Say we have a string, which is split into items by a common delimiter, such as a dash, an ampersand, or a space. We can split the string up item by item, and place each item into a new array. Again, explode() takes two arguments: the string (or string variable), and the delimiter:

```
$ArrayName = explode("delimiter", $StringName);
```

We could reverse our previous example:

```
$AllCapitalsSeparatedByADash = "Sacramento-Atlanta-Springfield-Cheyenne";
$Capitals = explode("-", $AllCapitalsSeparatedByADash);
```

To look at the array that has been created, we can tag on the following code that we saw earlier in this chapter:

```
$AllCapitalsSeparatedByADash = "Sacramento-Atlanta-Springfield-Cheyenne";
$Capitals = explode("-", $AllCapitalsSeparatedByADash);
while (list($IndexValue, $CapitalName) = each ($Capitals))
{
    echo "<BR>$IndexValue $CapitalName";
}
```

This should return:

0 Sacramento
1 Atlanta
2 Springfield
3 Cheyenne

So this confirms that an array called Capitals had been created, and that it starts at index zero. Each string item has been added sequentially to the array. In other words, explode() has created an array that is the equivalent of this PHP code:

```
$Capitals[0]="Sacramento";
$Capitals[1]="Atlanta";
$Capitals[2]="Springfield";
$Capitals[3]="Cheyenne";
```

Both of these functions are very useful and will be used in examples later in this book.

## HTTP_GET_VARS and HTTP_POST_VARS

The last two items we're going to look at aren't functions, but arrays. They have already been created by PHP, and are called HTTP_GET_VARS and HTTP_POST_VARS. When we talked about forms in Chapter 3, and mentioned the main two methods for transmitting form information using GET or POST, we implied that PHP automatically creates variables for us which assume the names of the controls on the forms. In other words, the contents of the following form field becomes the variable $TextBox32:

```
<INPUT TYPE=TEXT NAME="TextBox32">
```

This is correct, but there are situations where variables you assume will be automatically created are not. For instance, this often happens if you are using a third party ISP to provide web services. In fact for these variables to be created automatically, a configuration setting called register_globals must be switched on in your php.ini configuration script. This is done automatically on your own web server, enabling you to have access to all of the HTML controls as PHP variables. But for security reasons, some third party ISPs choose to switch register_globals off. The result is that the variable associated with the form field above, $TextBox32, would be empty.

If your ISP does this, don't worry, as the variable information you require is still available, in two arrays called HTTP_GET_VARS and HTTP_POST_VARS. We can access this information as follows. Say we know a variable has been transmitted using the GET method:

```
<FORM METHOD=GET ACTION="transfer.php">
<INPUT TYPE=TEXT NAME="TextBox32">
```

Within the PHP script for the page transfer.php, we can retrieve the contents of the text box, from an associative array called HTTP_GET_VARS. The index name of the element containing the contents of the text box is "TextBox32" – the name of the HTML control we created. So if we wanted to display the contents of the field, we would simply use:

```
echo HTTP_GET_VARS["TextBox32"];
```

This works for both GET and POST transmitted controls. Similarly we can read these values into variables:

```
$TextBox32 = HTTP_GET_VARS["TextBox32"];
```

So with just one extra line, we've got around the problem of not having register_globals switched on. However, there could be a further problem. If your ISP is ultra security-conscious, then they might also switch off a setting called track_vars, which prevents you from using these two arrays. In which case you need to write to your ISP and complain, or perhaps switch to a more considerate ISP!

We'll be using both of these global arrays later on in the book as well.

# Multi-dimensional Arrays

It is possible to create an array of arrays. Such beasts are known as multi-dimensional arrays. They are useful when representing data that needs two sets of indexes, like coordinates on a map or graph. You can carry on nesting arrays until PHP runs out of memory, which probably will be in under 100 nested arrays. (If you can think of a sensible practical use of any more than 10 nested arrays, then you deserve a medal). Multi-dimensional arrays are set up in the same way as normal arrays, except that you call the array structure as an argument to itself, like this:

```
ArrayName = array (index => array (Array contents))
```

An example might be an array in which each element represents one member from a group of people, and each element is also an array, used to store the details for each person:

```
$PhoneDirectory = array ("John Doe" => array ("1 Long Firs Drive","777-000-000"),
                         "Jane Doe" => array ("4 8th and East","777-111-111"));
```

Our array now has entries for "John Doe" and "Jane Doe"; and each element represents an array with two entries, one for an address and one for a phone number. To actually get hold of this information, you have to use a nested loop to get at it:

```
$PhoneDirectory = array ("John Doe" => array("1 Long Firs Drive","777-000-000"),
                         "Jane Doe" => array("4 8th and East","777-111-111"));
while (list($Person) = each($PhoneDirectory))
{
    echo("<BR>$Person");
    while (list(,$PersonalDetails) = each ($PhoneDirectory[$Person]))
    {
        echo (" $PersonalDetails");
    }
}
```

The <BR> character, and the space before $PersonalDetails in the echo statement, are simply used to make the displayed details more presentable. Multi-dimensional arrays aren't encountered very often, so we won't go into them in further detail here.

# Practical Demonstration of Arrays

This chapter has covered a lot of material, so we're not going to go through an extensive example at the end. Instead we'll use quite a short example, but it still covers a lot of the features discussed in this chapter. In it we're going to take a set of mythical students and ask for the grades they got in their Math exam. We're then going to sort them into grade order (A is highest, E is lowest) on the web page.

## Try It Out – Combining Array Features in a Practical Example

**1.** Prod your web page editor into life, and type in the following:

```
<HTML>
<HEAD></HEAD>
<BODY>
<?php
echo"<FORM METHOD=POST ACTION='exam2.php'>";
$Student = array("Albert Einstein","Ivan The Terrible","Napoleon","Simon
Bolivar","Isaac Newton");
while (list(,$Name)=each($Student))
{
    echo "What grade did $Name get in Math?";
    echo"<BR><BR>";
    echo"<SELECT NAME='Math[]'>
            <OPTION>Grade A</OPTION>
```

```
              <OPTION>Grade B</OPTION>
              <OPTION>Grade C</OPTION>
              <OPTION>Grade D</OPTION>
              <OPTION>Grade E</OPTION>
          </SELECT>";
    echo"<BR><BR>";
    echo"<INPUT TYPE=HIDDEN NAME=Student[] VALUE='$Name'>";
}
echo"<INPUT TYPE=SUBMIT></FORM>";
?>
</BODY>
</HTML>
```

**2.** Save this as exam.php.

**3.** Close this file, and create another one, typing the following:

```
<HTML>
<HEAD></HEAD>
<BODY>
In Math the grades were in order:
<BR>
<?php
while (list($Index,$Value)=each($Math))
{
    $GradeStudent[]=$Math[$Index].$Student[$Index];
}
asort($GradeStudent);
while (list($Index,$Value)=each($GradeStudent))
{
    echo "<BR>$Student[$Index] - $Math[$Index]";
}
?>
</BODY>
</HTML>
```

**4.** Save this as exam2.php.

**5.** Open up exam.php on your browser, and type in some grades:

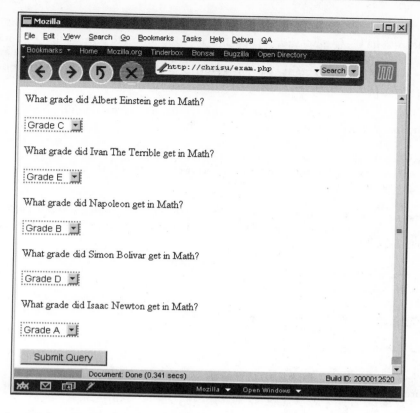

**6.** Click on Submit Query and the grades will have been sorted, not only in order of grade, but also in alphabetical order of students' names where two or more students have the same grade:

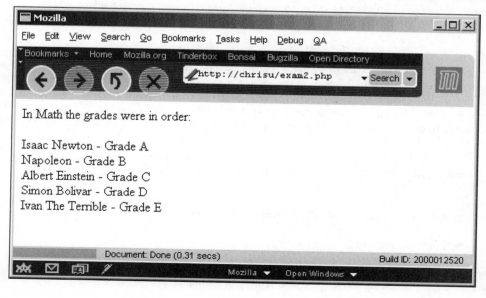

### How It Works

This example, despite being quite short, had a difficult conundrum to sort out that you might have spotted. We wanted to sort the grades array, which corresponds by index to the student array. But how can we relate the *sorted* array of grades back to the array of students? Without too much difficulty, as it turns out, but it needs a little sleight of hand.

The first program `exam.php` creates a dynamically-created form. This one supplies the names of the students from an array called `$Student`:

```
echo"<FORM METHOD=POST ACTION='exam2.php'>";
$Student = array("Albert Einstein","Ivan The Terrible","Napoleon","Simon
Bolivar","Isaac Newton");
```

Now we move on to construct a `while` loop, to iterate through the contents of our newly-created student array As we only want the names in the student array, not the indexes, we only ask `list()` to return the names:

```
while (list(,$Name)=each($Student))
{
```

For each student in the list, we display a question asking for the grade of the student:

```
echo "What grade did $Name get in Math?";
```

Next we create a dropdown listbox which contains five options, each corresponding to a grade from A to E. To store the grades, we create an array `$Math` that PHP can pass to the next script:

```
echo"<SELECT NAME='Math[]'>
```

We display a couple of line breaks between each list box, for presentation's sake.

```
echo"<BR><BR>";
```

However, as we create the array of students' names in this first PHP script, this array won't be available to the second PHP script, which receives the values chosen from the list boxes. What can we do to get around this is? We can pass the values across to the second script via a hidden HTML control. This hidden control has the same name as the array that holds the students' names. We indicate that the control needs to be an array by adding brackets. We pass the control names for each student, and then we end the loop:

```
echo"<INPUT TYPE=HIDDEN NAME=Student[] VALUE='$Name'>";
}
```

At the end of the loop we add a Submit button and close the form:

```
echo"<INPUT TYPE=SUBMIT></FORM>";
```

Our second program `exam2.php`, which receives the form data, is composed of a loop, a sort and another loop. The first loop in our program is used to associate the two arrays received from the form.

We do this by concatenating the grade to the student's name, and storing the result in a new array called $GradeStudent.

```
while (list($Index,$Value)=each($Math))
{
    $GradeStudent[]=$Math[$Index].$Student[$Index];
}
```

We know from examining the first script that the contents of an index in the Math array, relates to the contents of the same index in the $Student array. So this concatenation is a valid way of combining the related values from each array. The resulting $GradeStudent array will contain this:

```
Grade CAlbert Einstein
Grade EIvan The Terrible
Grade BNapoleon
Grade DSimon Bolivar
Grade AIsaac Newton
```

We can now sort $GradeStudent and we should get the order we desire:

```
asort($GradeStudent);
```

However, it still leaves us with the problem of how to display the results, because they look a little unsightly in the format displayed above. We can print out a sorted list of grades side-by-side with the students' names using the following snippet of code:

```
while (list($Index,$Value)=each($GradeStudent))
{
    echo "<BR>$Student[$Index] - $Math[$Index]";
}
```

Can you see how this works? Remember that the $GradeStudent array is sorted on grade. Note that during the sort, the order of the elements is rearranged, but each index still contains the same content as it did before the sort. Also, we have seen that each element in the $GradeStudent array is simply a concatenation of the corresponding elements in the $Math and $GradeStudent array. So, what happens if we echo out elements from the $Math and $Student arrays, but in the order that the indexes occur in sorted $GradeStudent? Since the indexes of all of these arrays correspond, we find that the $Math and $Student arrays are echoed out in grade order too, as the table shows:

| $Index | $Student | $Math | Sorted $GradeStudent |
|--------|----------|-------|----------------------|
| 4 | Isaac Newton | Grade A | "Grade AIsaac Newton" |
| 2 | Napoleon | Grade B | "Grade BNapoleon" |
| 0 | Albert Einstein | Grade C | "Grade CAlbert Einstein" |
| 3 | Simon Bolivar | Grade D | "Grade DSimon Bolivar" |
| 1 | Ivan The Terrible | Grade E | "Grade EIvan The Terrible" |

We know that using `list()` and `each()` will provide index values from the sorted `$GradeStudent` array in the order that they occur in the array. So the code snippet will echo out elements from the `$Math` and `$Student` arrays in grade order too. This completes our second program.

# New Loop and Array Features in PHP4

The arrival of PHP4 has brought with it some new features related to loops and arrays. In this section we will cover two of the most useful.

## Array Multisorting

The first new feature we will describe is the `array_multisort()` function, which actually provides the same functionality as we needed for the previous Math grades example. It takes two arrays as arguments.

The function sorts the first array, and then notes the indexes of any repeated entries in the array. It then sorts these repeated entries according to the contents of the corresponding indexes in the second array. Finally the function sorts the second array into the same order as the sorted first array. Let's take our previous example to illustrate this. We could change our code in `exam2.php` to use `array_multisort()`:

```php
<?php
array_multisort($Math,$Student);
while (list($Index,$Value)=each($Student))
{
    echo "<BR>$Student[$Index] - $Math[$Index]";
}
?>
```

Now consider what would happen if this function was asked to sort the following year's Math grades (stored in the `$Math` array) for our students (whose names are stored in the `$Student` array):

```
Albert Einstein - Grade A
Ivan The Terrible - Grade E
Napoleon - Grade D
Simon Bolivar - Grade D
Isaac Newton - Grade A
```

The `array_multisort()` function first sorts the `$Math[]` array, giving A, A, D, D, E. Since we have two entries for each of A and D, the function then notes the indexes of the two A entries (0 and 4), turns to the second array `$Student[]` and *sub-sorts* elements 0 (Albert Einstein) and 4 (Isaac Newton) alphabetically by name. The same is done for the two D entries. When the function is finished sub-sorting, it notes the final index order of the `$Math` array (0, 4, 2, 3, 1), and sorts `$Student[]` into the same order. Both arrays are now sorted primarily by grade and secondly by name.

However, this is a new feature and there have been problems reported with it, which is why we didn't use it in the main example.

# foreach Loops

There is also an extension to the `for` loop in PHP4. It's the last type of loop that we shall look at: the `foreach` loop. You use a `foreach` loop when you have an array with an unknown number of elements. The `foreach` loop will iterate until the end of the array. It takes two formats. The first is as follows:

```
foreach ($ArrayName As $ArrayItem)
{
    execute the contents of these braces
}
```

This means that for each item in the array, we will iterate around the loop. An example of this would be, say, the crowd attendance at a baseball game. You might want to store the name of each fan in the baseball stadium in a database. But, until the day of the game, you don't know how many fans will actually turn up. In pseudo-code our example would look like this:

```
foreach ($Crowd As $Fan)
{
    Add $Fan to database...
}
```

It would go through the crowd adding a fan at a time. PHP doesn't need to be told how many fans attended the game, as it can work this out from the number of items in the array `$Crowd`.

The second format is:

```
foreach ($ArrayName As $ArrayIndexValue => $ArrayItem)
{
    execute the contents of these braces
}
```

This is the same as the first format, but it makes the array index value available as well. Let's have a quick look at how `foreach` works in the context of an example. We'll use our list of states once more, and just display each state we have in the array, along with the index value that PHP has assigned to each state.

## Try It Out – Using foreach

**1.** Start your web page editor and type in the following code:

```
<HTML>
<HEAD></HEAD>
<BODY>
<?
$StatesOfTheUSA = array ("Alabama", "Alaska", "Arizona", "Arkansas", "California",
"Colorado", "Connecticut", "Delaware", "Florida", "Georgia", "Hawaii", "Idaho",
"Illinois", "Indiana", "Iowa", "Kansas", "Kentucky", "Louisiana", "Maine",
"Maryland", "Massachusetts", "Michigan", "Minnesota", "Mississippi", "Missouri",
"Montana", "Nebraska", "Nevada", "New Hampshire", "New Jersey", "New Mexico", "New
York", "North Carolina", "North Dakota", "Ohio", "Oklahoma", "Oregon",
"Pennsylvania", "Rhode Island", "South Carolina", "South Dakota", "Tennessee",
```

```
   "Texas", "Utah", "Vermont", "Virginia", "Washington", "West Virginia",
   "Wisconsin", "Wyoming");

   foreach($StatesOfTheUSA As $StateIndex => $State)
   {
      echo "<BR>$StateIndex - $State";
   }
   ?>
   </BODY>
   </HTML>
```

**2.** Save this as `foreach.php`.

**3.** View `foreach.php` in your browser:

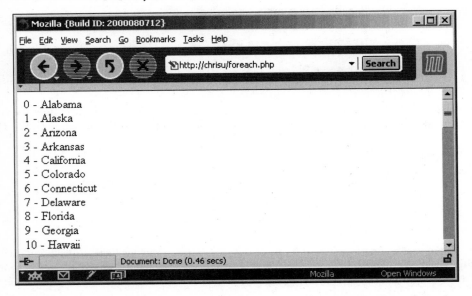

**4.** Scroll down just to check that there are all 50 states, with values running from 0 to 49.

### How It Works

This couldn't be simpler. We first create the array with the names of all 50 states, which is called `$StatesOfTheUSA`:

```
   $StatesOfTheUSA = array ("Alabama", "Alaska", "Arizona", "Arkansas", "California",
   "Colorado", "Connecticut", "Delaware", "Florida", "Georgia", "Hawaii", "Idaho",
   "Illinois", "Indiana", "Iowa", "Kansas", "Kentucky", "Louisiana", "Maine",
   "Maryland", "Massachusetts", "Michigan", "Minnesota", "Mississippi", "Missouri",
   "Montana", "Nebraska", "Nevada", "New Hampshire", "New Jersey", "New Mexico", "New
   York", "North Carolina", "North Dakota", "Ohio", "Oklahoma", "Oregon",
   "Pennsylvania", "Rhode Island", "South Carolina", "South Dakota", "Tennessee",
   "Texas", "Utah", "Vermont", "Virginia", "Washington", "West Virginia",
   "Wisconsin", "Wyoming");
```

We then supply the array name as the first argument to our `foreach` loop:

```
foreach ($StatesOfTheUSA As $StateIndex => $State)
```

The second and third arguments are variable names that we create ourselves here, which hold the index value and the corresponding element in the array respectively. We execute the contents of the braces for each of the 50 members in the array:

```
{
    echo "<BR>$StateIndex - $State";
}
```

This has the effect of displaying each index value and each state in the array on a separate line.

There are two points to note here. The first is that the current array element and array index are available as separate variables. Note that, because each iteration processes a new array element, each time we go around the loop, the variables are effectively assigned a new value.

The second thing to note is that we haven't supplied a count of how many elements there are in the array anywhere in our program. PHP has worked this out for itself, and this is the main advantage of using `foreach`. This factor allows you to iterate through an array that might not be in any numerical or alphabetical order. There might also be missing entries in the array, but it doesn't have to check every index value, only the elements that contain values. We could add the following code which adds a new element to our array of States:

```
$StatesOfTheUSA[100]="Atlantis";
```

Then if we re-performed the `foreach` loop, it would be able to add this value to the end of our web page without needing to check through elements 50-99.

# Summary

This chapter has introduced two distinct, but related topics: loops and arrays. While being conceptually different, loops and arrays are actually closely linked in PHP, as we have demonstrated. You need loops to perform repetitious operations, and one such useful operation is to fill large related sets of indexed variables known as arrays.

In the first section of the chapter we examined the three types of loop, `while`, `do while` and `for`. We concluded that each was suited to different types of task, and so the choice of which one to use depended upon the situation. We then went on to introduce arrays, and demonstrated the methods we can use to populate them. We looked at the features PHP introduces for iterating through arrays, including arrays which don't have sequential or numerical indexes. We also looked at how arrays can be sorted. Finally, we looked at the concept of multi-dimensional arrays, gave a short practical example that made use of arrays, and got a taste of some new loop and array features for PHP4.

In the next chapter we conclude our tour of PHP programming fundamentals, by introducing the touchstone of structured programming, the function.

# Organizing Your Code

Throughout the earlier chapters, we touched on the subject of code reuse – strongly hinting that this is a good thing, without really explaining why. Once again, before we've been able to discuss the features in PHP that allow us to reuse and structure code most effectively, we've had to delve into more fundamental programming structures first. When we first introduced branching, we cited one of the main benefits being that you were no longer constrained by having to execute your code in a linear fashion. This is certainly true, but as your code becomes more complex, you soon discover that branches and loops are far from sufficient in order to write effective code. After a little excursion into a conditional statement or a loop, you return to the first line after the structure. It's only with the introduction of **functions** that you can truly create small independent sections of code that can be called up at any time and in any order.

Functions allow you to encapsulate sections of code, as though they were independent standalone programs. You can pass values into them, and get values out of them. You can call functions at any time during your PHP script, and redirect the flow of execution in this way. Functions also introduce the idea of scope into your programs. The normal process in your PHP programs is that once a variable is created, the name you have assigned to it, and the value, persist until you alter it or until the script ends. However, in functions you have to learn to deal with the idea that variables might only exist inside a function, while outside it they have no value. This raises a whole set of concerns, which we will examine in this chapter. We also look at how one function can be nested inside another, over and over again, and how you can include separate text or PHP scripts within your current web page.

In this chapter we'll be looking at the following topics:

- ❑ What's so great about code reuse?
- ❑ Functions
- ❑ How to call functions in your web pages
- ❑ Passing values to and from functions
- ❑ The scope of variables inside and outside functions
- ❑ Nesting functions
- ❑ Include files

# What's So Great About Code Reuse?

We're not going to give you an extended tutorial about software engineering here, but it needs to be emphasized that writing code with a view to being able to use sections of it a number of times over offers many benefits. First and foremost, there is less code to write, and this means there is less code to check and therefore less code to go wrong. However, it doesn't just stop there. Code reuse allows you to structure your programs with much greater thought.

In the heyday of the microcomputer (the early eighties), most programming languages didn't allow you to write structured programs and certainly didn't include features like functions. They did however allow you to reroute your programs at a whim. Typically, every line of code you wrote had a number, normally in increments of 10, in case you came back later and forgot something and had to add it. There was an infamous statement, GOTO, which told the computer to jump to the line number after GOTO. Most peoples' first programs would read:

```
10 PRINT" HELLO WORLD"
20 GOTO 10
```

This would immediately create an infinite loop, printing HELLO WORLD on the screen until the user intervened forcefully. In a large program with several of these GOTO statements, it got very hard to follow the flow of the program, and so programs written on microcomputers were termed **spaghetti code**. While we're sitting here another twenty years on, feeling very smug and superior, some of the code that we have written so far has been long, tangled, and hard to follow – no different to spaghetti code. How are we better off? Answer is, we're not at the moment, but we can be.

## Modularization

When you come to write a program, hopefully you stop and think about what tasks need to be performed, and you split the program up into several smaller tasks. Think of these tasks as modules. Programmers write code in modern programming languages in modules and compile these modules into one large application. It's easier to test if there's only going to be one task performed in a specific part of the program. There's generally fewer values going in and coming out of a module. Say you know a particular module works without error, and then it's plugged into another new and untested module, producing wrong results, then you can narrow your search down to the untested module straightaway.

Also if a module performs a specific task, then you can call up that module each time you need to perform that task. You can think of these modules as little black boxes, where you put data in, and you get data out, and as long as the data is correct, you don't worry about what's going on inside. In PHP (and any other language), the name given to a "module" of code like this is a **function**.

# Functions

As we have noted, functions are sections of code that are defined by the user to perform a specific task. We have already seen that functions can take values called **arguments** as input, perform some operations, and then may return another value. The function transfers any argument values into new variables, called **parameters**, which can then be used within the function. We have used PHP functions extensively in this book so far; to do things like get the data type of a variable, right through to sorting arrays. In this chapter we are going to build our own functions. Our functions will work on the same principle as the ready-made ones that we have already used, so when we supply them with information, they will perform an operation and return an answer.

# Defining and Calling Functions

To define a function, you have to give it a name. To do this, you use the keyword `function`, followed by the function name. Any parameter names are listed in parentheses after the function name. The code that forms the body of the function is placed in braces after the parameters. Abstractly it works like this:

```
function functionname (parameters)
{
function code goes here...
}
```

Let's have an example now in PHP of a tax-calculating function:

```
function tax ($Salary)
{
    $Salary = $Salary - (($Salary/100)*20);
      return $Salary;
}
```

The function itself can have as many lines of code as you want, but on the last line of the function, to return a value, you need to place the final expression or calculation after the `return` keyword. This tells the function that you've finished doing your working out and that the function ends here. It can also optionally mean that you wish to return a value that was calculated within the function. You don't have to return a value; you can just get the function to alter HTML for example, as follows:

```
function html_header($page)
{
print "\n<HTML>\n<HEAD>\n<TITLE>My Website ::: " . $page . "</TITLE>\n</HEAD>";
print "\n<BODY>";
return;
}
```

The `return` keyword is used here to denote the end of the function, rather than to return any value.

However, if you want to display the value returned by a function, you can do this by using the `echo` statement. The `return` statement doesn't display a value; it just passes the result (if any) to the function. The process of executing the contents of a function within a PHP script is known as **calling** the function. You can supply it directly with a number:

```
echo (tax(1600));
```

or you can supply it with the name of an already created variable:

```
$Salary=1600;
echo (tax($Salary));
```

To make it clearer what is happening, you might want to assign the result of a function to a variable and then display the contents of the variable:

```
$Salary=1600;
$TaxedSalary = tax($Salary);
echo ($TaxedSalary);
```

If you want to supply more than one parameter to the function, then you have to separate each parameter with a comma as follows:

```
function tax ($Salary,$TaxRate)
{
   $Salary = $Salary - (($Salary/100)*$TaxRate);
   return $Salary;
}
```

To call the function here you need to supply two values:

```
echo (tax(1600,25));
```

or two variables:

```
$Salary=1600;
$TaxRate=25;
echo (tax($Salary,$TaxRate));
```

or just a mixture of variables and values:

```
$TaxRate=25;
echo (tax(1600,$TaxRate));
```

You don't have to supply any parameters to a function at all:

```
function tax ()
{
   $Salary = 2500;
   $TaxRate = 15;
   $Salary = $Salary - (($Salary/100)*$TaxRate);
      return $Salary;
}
```

Now you might be wondering about where you put the definitions of variables that we use within a function body, if we do use parameters. They can go before a function:

```
<?php
$Salary=1600;                  ← Execution will start here
$TaxRate=25;
echo (tax($Salary,$TaxRate));  ← Function called here

function tax($Salary,$TaxRate) ← Function defined here
{
   $Salary = $Salary - (($Salary/100)*$TaxRate);
   return;
}
?>
```

But equally as easily, they can also go after the function. If you look at our whole example program:

```php
<?php
function tax($Salary,$TaxRate)    ← Function defined here
{
    $Salary = $Salary - (($Salary/100)*$TaxRate);
    return $Salary;


}
$Salary=1600;                     ← Execution will start here
$TaxRate=25;
echo (tax($Salary,$TaxRate));     ← Function called here
?>
```

Execution will start in the middle of the program, with the first line that isn't contained within a function. Our function isn't used until we call it on the last line. If we remove the last line, then our function will never be used. In fact there's no obligation to use a function if it isn't needed, as we'll demonstrate shortly. Conversely you're free to call a function as many times as you like, using different values or variables:

```php
$Salary=1600;
$TaxRate=25;
echo (tax(2000,$TaxRate));
echo (tax($Salary,30));
echo (tax(2000,30));
echo (tax($Salary,$TaxRate));
```

Lastly, you're not limited to having to call the variables outside the function the same name as the parameters. We have been doing this to keep things straightforward and logical, but you could just as easily have written:

```php
$Thing=1600;
$Blob=25;
echo (tax($Thing,$Blob));
function tax($Salary,$TaxRate)
{
    $Salary = $Salary - (($Salary/100)*$TaxRate);
    return $Salary;
}
```

All that matters is that the function takes on these variables and assigns their values to the names of the variables it is using as parameters inside the brackets. So $Salary takes the value of $Thing inside the function, and $TaxRate takes the value of $Blob.

Before we do an example, let's have a quick recap.

❑　Functions are named by the user

❑　Functions take parameters, which are values or variables supplied by the user in parentheses after the function name

❑　If you have multiple parameters they are separated by commas

❑　The code of the function body is provided in braces after the function name and parameters

❑ You must use the `return` keyword inside the function to return a value that you can use outside the function

❑ If there is no value to return, then the return keyword just denotes the end of the function code

❑ Functions aren't actually executed until called elsewhere within your PHP script

❑ You are free to call a function in your script either before or after it appears in the code, and this means it doesn't matter where you put a function in your code

❑ You can call a function as few or as many times as you need

We'll look at an example now where we go back to our holiday example from earlier chapters and use our function to calculate the expenses for our holiday break week. As you'll see we end up saving quite a few lines of code.

## Try It Out – Using a Simple Function

**1.** Start your web page editor and open up `holiday.html` and amend the highlighted line. If you haven't got `holiday.html` then type in all of the following:

```
<HTML>
<HEAD></HEAD>
<BODY>
<B>Namllu Holiday Booking Form</B>
<FORM METHOD=GET ACTION="holiday3.php">
Where do you want to go on holiday?
<BR>
<BR>
<INPUT NAME="Destination" TYPE="Radio" VALUE="Prague">
Prague
<BR>
<INPUT NAME="Destination" TYPE="Radio" VALUE="Barcelona">
Barcelona
<BR>
<INPUT NAME="Destination" TYPE="Radio" VALUE="Vienna">
Vienna
<BR>
<BR>
What grade of hotel do you want to stay at?
<BR>
<BR>
<INPUT NAME="Grade" TYPE="Radio" VALUE="Three">
Three Star
<BR>
<INPUT NAME="Grade" TYPE="Radio" VALUE="Four">
Four Star
<BR>
<BR>
<INPUT TYPE=SUBMIT>
</FORM>
</BODY>
</HTML>
```

**2.** Save this file as `holiday.html` again.

**3.** Close the file and open up a new one and type in the following:

```
<HTML>
<HEAD></HEAD>
<BODY>
<B>Namllu Holiday Booking Form</B>
<BR>
<BR>
<?php
function Calculator($Price, $CityModifier, $StarModifier)
{
    return $Price = $Price * $CityModifier * $StarModifier;
}
$Price=500;
$StarModifier=1;
$CityModifier=1;
$DestGrade = $Destination.$Grade;
switch($DestGrade) {
    case "BarcelonaThree":
        $CityModifier=2;
        break;
    case "BarcelonaFour":
        $CityModifier=2;
        $StarModifier=2;
        break;
    case "ViennaThree":
        $CityModifier=3.5;
        break;
    case "ViennaFour":
        $CityModifier=3.5;
        $StarModifier=2;
        break;
    case "PragueThree":
        break;
    case "PragueFour":
        $StarModifier=2;
        break;
    default:
        $CityModifier=0;
        echo ("Go back and do it again");
}
if ($CityModifier<>0)
{
    echo "The cost for a week in $Destination is " . "$" .
Calculator($Price,$CityModifier,$StarModifier);
}
?>
</BODY>
</HTML>
```

**4.** Save this as `holiday3.php`.

**5.** Go and open up `holiday.html` in your browser again.

**6.** Select a couple of options and click on Submit.

**7.** You should see the example functions as normal:

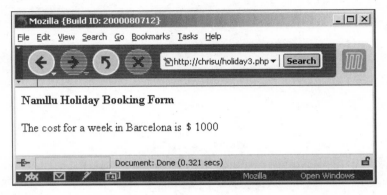

### How It Works

The holiday form will be very familiar, it's just passing two variables the destination (`$Destination`) and the hotel grade (`$Grade`) to the PHP script. We start the PHP script with the function to calculate the cost of our holiday:

```
function Calculator($Price, $CityModifier, $StarModifier)
{
    return $Price = $Price * $CityModifier * $StarModifier;
}
```

It takes three parameters – the basic price of the holiday, the modification to the price made by the city, and the modification made to the price by the star rating of the hotel. It multiplies these three variables together and returns one value, the total price of the hotel. This calculation is repeated throughout the previous examples and here we only need to repeat it once, and call the function when needed. The rest of the program is very familiar, we concatenate the `$Destination` and `$Grade` variables:

```
$DestGrade = $Destination.$Grade;
```

Then depending on what they contain, we switch and execute associated section of code. The code within the case statements now just alters the contents of the `$CityModifier` and `$StarModifier` variables:

```
switch($DestGrade) {
    case "BarcelonaThree":
        $CityModifier=2;
        break;
    case "BarcelonaFour":
```

```
      $CityModifier=2;
      $StarModifier=2;
      break;
   case "ViennaThree":
      $CityModifier=3.5;
      break;
   case "ViennaFour":
      $CityModifier=3.5;
      $StarModifier=2;
      break;
   case "PragueThree":
      break;
   case "PragueFour":
      $StarModifier=2;
      break;
   default:
      $CityModifier=0;
      echo ("Go back and do it again");
}
```

One small change we've made underneath the `default` option is to change the contents of the `$CityModifier` variable to zero, if none of the cases are executed. Before executing the function we check to see whether the `$CityModifier` variable has been set to zero or not, if it hasn't then we can call the function within the `echo()` statement, using the concatenate operator (the period) to add the text to our function result:

```
if ($CityModifier<>0)
{
    echo "The cost for a week in $Destination is " . "$" .
    Calculator($Price,$CityModifier,$StarModifier);
}
```

The function call passes the three variables we generated in the program as parameters to display the results.

# Switching Functions

If you go one step beyond the last example where we used the `switch()` statement, one very useful application of functions is to switch to different functions contained within different cases of a `switch()` statement. Consider an application that, depending on the city you were going to, took the amount of the money you wanted to change, and converted it into the requisite currency of that country. Each converter could get its details from the web, and since the page for each country's currency rate conversion would be different, each function would require a different URL. We can then display the $MoneyAmount as a default case. Also, only one of the set of functions would be required and executed at any one time:

```
switch ($City)
{
case "Oslo":
    echo(Norwegian_converter($MoneyAmount));
    break;
case "Stockholm":
```

```
        echo(Swedish_converter($MoneyAmount));
        break;
    case    "Copenhagen":
        echo(Danish_converter($MoneyAmount));
        break;
    default:
        echo $MoneyAmount;
    }

    function Norwegian_converter($MoneyAmount)
    {
        ... calculates and returns the value in Norwegian currency
    }
    function Swedish_converter($MoneyAmount)
    {
        ... calculates and returns the value in Swedish currency
    }
    function Danish_converter($MoneyAmount)
    {
        ... calculates and returns the value in Danish currency
    }
```

This might make for a large amount of redundant code, but the switch() statement deals with a lot of possibilities and improves the program performance, given that it only ever has to execute one of a set of functions rather than the whole lot. It also improves readability, since the switch/case construct is very easy to read with just one-line function calls in it. We're going to be seeing this example later in the book, where we take the result of a HIDDEN field, and use it to determine a particular course of action on a form that a user has selected. Each course of action is defined in a function, and when the user selects one course of action such as viewing a set of data or adding some data, there is a switch() statement to change to the function that performs that particular action and that action only.

## Assigning the Value Returned by Functions to Variables

You can take this one step further. Functions return values, so it should follow that you are able to assign the value returned by a function to a variable, and indeed you can. You just do it as follows:

```
$HitCounter = number_of_hits();
```

Our variable $HitCounter would then be able to store what ever the function number_of_hits() returned. You can then place the variable within the brackets of the switch() statement.

```
switch ($HitCounter)
{
case $HitCounter <100:
    echo "Not many hits this week";
    break;
case $HitCounter <1000:
    echo "Some hits this week";
    break;
case $HitCounter <10000:
    echo "Loads of hits this week";
    break;
}
```

The function is run once, and depending on the outcome, we perform a difference action.

# Passing Values

We've already described how functions use parameters. The single items that we pass into functions are individually known as **arguments**. The difference between a parameter and an argument is that arguments are what go in the function call, while parameters are what are used in the function body. We haven't examined this process in any detail and we need to look at it further as there are actually two ways to pass arguments into our functions, and depending on which method you use, it could yield a different result.

## Passing By Value

The first method is the one we've already used. Our tax example required us to pass the $Salary variable into it. If we tweak it slightly, so that it physically alters the contents of the $Salary variable, we can use it to illustrate the difference between the two methods.

```
function tax ($Salary)
{
   $Salary = $Salary - (($Salary/100)*20);
   return $Salary;


}
$Salary = 2500;
echo (tax($Salary));      // This will display 2000
echo $Salary;             // This will display 2500
```

This doesn't alter our earlier example in anyway, as the two echoed values would still be different.

What we have done is pass the value of the variable as an argument to the function. In this case the number 2500 was passed, so inside the function it's as though a new variable, also called $Salary, was created and given the value 2500:

```
function tax (2500)
{
   $Salary = 2500 - ((2500/100)*20);
   return $Salary;
}
echo (tax($Salary));   // This will display 2000
echo $Salary;          // This will display 2500
```

This process is known as passing an argument **by value**. No matter how we alter the value within the function, the value we have passed to it in $Salary will remain the same, so if you echo the contents of $Salary after running the function, it will still be 2500. The function is only outputting the figure we have calculated which is 2000, it isn't doing anything else with it. This is the default process that you will use when passing variables to functions. What happens if you want the variable $Salary to actually hold the new figure you have just calculated?

## Passing By Reference

There is a second method that we haven't seen so far which involves the passed value being changed inside the function. This is called passing an argument **by reference**. To indicate to PHP that you wish to use this method, you add an ampersand to the front of the variable you are passing:

```
function tax(&$Salary)
{
    $Salary = $Salary - (($Salary/100)*20);
    return $Salary;
}
$Salary = 2500;
echo (tax($Salary));      // This displays $2000
echo $Salary;             // This also displays $2000
```

In which case, the actual contents of the $Salary variable are changed in this example, so that the $Salary variable will now contain the value 2000, and you can echo the contents of the $Salary variable after the calculation to the screen.

## Setting Default Parameter Values

Just to confuse matters, you can also set the values of your parameters within the arguments themselves. This becomes the default value for when you don't specify any parameters:

```
function tax($Salary=2500)
{
    $Salary = $Salary - (($Salary/100)*20);
    return $Salary;
}
```

This would mean that if you supplied no value in the function call arguments:

```
tax();
```

It would use the value 2500 automatically. However, if you supplied an argument to the function such as:

```
tax(3000);
```

then the value supplied would override the value set in the function itself – 3000 would be used in this case instead of 2500.

### Parameter Order

If you don't set values, or don't pass all of the arguments across in the function call, then PHP 4 will effectively pass a zero across for you. By this we mean if your function accepts two parameters, and you only pass it one in the call, then the one you didn't set is passed as zero. You may get warnings depending on which version of PHP you are using, and PHP's error-reporting configuration. If we take an example where our function takes two parameters:

```
function tax($Salary, $TaxRate)
{
    return $Salary - (($Salary/100)*$TaxRate);
}
```

Now if you only pass to this function one parameter in the function call, such as:

```
echo (tax(3000));
```

it will assume that you are only passing the first parameter across to $Salary, and passing a blank value in $TaxRate. As a result our function will return the same value, because the right hand side of our expression evaluates to zero:

```
3000 - ((3000/100 * 0)
```

This also applies to optional parameters, so if you make the first parameter optional as follows:

```
function tax($Salary=2500, $TaxRate)
{
    return $Salary - (($Salary/100)*$TaxRate);
}
```

and called it in the same way:

```
echo (tax(3000));
```

PHP would still assume that you are passing the value of 3000 to $Salary and passing nothing to the $TaxRate variable, even though $Salary is optional and you are not expected to pass a value to it. It also means that if you place an optional parameter before any non-optional ones, then the optional parameter will become compulsory too. You can't type in the following:

```
echo (tax(,25));
```

> PHP3 users will find this behavior contradicts PHP3's behavior, which assumes that we're automatically omitting the optional parameter.

The lesson in this is – the parameters in your function and your function calls must match each other in both number and position, unless you use optional parameters. If you use optional parameters, then they must come after parameters that don't have any value by default. So this would be perfectly legal:

```
function tax($Salary=2500, $TaxRate)
{
    return $Salary - (($Salary/100)*$TaxRate);
}
```

but you would always have to pass a value to $Salary before $Taxrate. To make it truly optional you would have to pass it like this:

```
function tax($TaxRate, $Salary=2500)
{
    return $Salary - (($Salary/100)*$TaxRate);
}
```

and call it like this:

```
echo(tax(25));
```

### Pitfalls of Parameters with Default Values

There is one last point to be aware of when using parameters; the following line might look fine, but will actually generate an error:

```
function tax(&$Salary)
{
    $Salary = $Salary - (($Salary/100)*20);
    return $Salary;
}
echo (tax(1000));
```

This might look absolutely fine to you, but when you come to call this function you'll receive something looking like this rather nasty message:

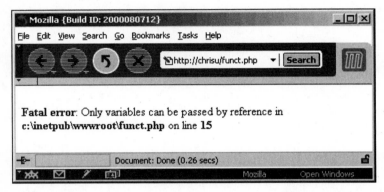

Previous versions of PHP prior to 4, seemed to allow you to do this, and get away with just a warning, but PHP4 stops this dead in its tracks. If you want this code to work, all you need to do is pass a variable across, not a literal value, like this:

```
$Salary = 20;
echo (tax(&$Salary));
```

The reason the previous example caused an error, isn't because PHP is being opaque; it's perfectly sensible. You can't pass a literal number by reference, because it wouldn't make sense for a literal value to change. If you pass 1000 across, you don't want to change this value in any way. The same rule applies for constants also.

Now let's move on to another feature of functions.

# Scope of Variables

We suggested in the introduction of this chapter, that variables inside functions don't necessarily exist outside of them. In fact we need to introduce a whole new concept here, that of the **lifetime** of a variable. The lifetime of a variable is the span from the moment a variable is created to the moment it ceases to exist. Normally for a variable this is the duration of a web page. However, when using variables inside functions, this isn't necessarily true. It might just be for the duration of the function that the variable lasts. The function is called, and the variables inside come into existence. You get to the end of the function, and these variables are closed down. Any reference to them outside of the function is invalid, as they no longer have any values.

# Global and Local Variables

Variables created outside a function still exist for the whole of the duration of the web page. This whole concept is termed **scope**. Variables inside a function are described as having **local scope**. Variables that retain their value throughout the lifetime of the page are described as having **global** scope.

Let's see an example of both of these in action. The following code snippet displays a welcome message either in French or in English:

```php
<?php
$WelcomeMessage = "Hello world";              ← Global Variable
function translate_greeting($WelcomeMessage)
{
    $WelcomeMessage = "Bonjour Tout Le Monde";    ← Local Variable
    return $WelcomeMessage;
}
translate_greeting();
echo $WelcomeMessage;
?>
```

The first occurrence of the $WelcomeMessage sets it to the value "Hello World". This is our global variable. Inside our function we set $WelcomeMessage to "Bonjour Tout Le Monde", and then run the function – $WelcomeMessage is a local variable. If you were to run this code, the words that would be displayed on your web page would be "Hello World". This is because the variable inside the function is in effect a completely different variable; it is local to the function that contains it.

*You should note that we don't display the value our function returns here, which is a subtle difference to what we did earlier, when we put our function call inside an `echo()` statement. However, the function is still executed, we just don't display the results it returns. This means it has no effect outside the function, unless we pass the value by reference.*

If we were to change the argument name in the function parameter and the variable within the function, and if we were to echo the contents of variable $FrenchMessage outside the function, it would have no value:

```php
<?php
$WelcomeMessage = "Hello world";
function translate_greeting($FrenchMessage)
{
    $FrenchMessage = "Bonjour Tout Le Monde";
    return $FrenchMessage;
}
translate_greeting();
echo $WelcomeMessage;
echo $FrenchMessage;
?>
```

This is because its lifetime terminates once the function returns a value. As we've already mentioned, the value that the function returns has no effect outside program.

## Using Global Variables Inside Functions

Conversely, if we were to display the contents of $WelcomeMessage inside our function it would display nothing because $WelcomeMessage doesn't exist inside the function:

```php
<?php
$WelcomeMessage = "Hello world";
function translate_greeting($FrenchMessage)
{
    echo $WelcomeMessage;
    $FrenchMessage = "Bonjour Tout Le Monde";
    return $FrenchMessage;
}
translate_greeting();
echo $WelcomeMessage;
echo $FrenchMessage;
?>
```

This makes sense – what happens if we have a local variable inside the function with the same name as a global variable outside the function? We have to have some way of identifying global variables because we need to ensure that it is the same variable, and doesn't just share the same name. There are two ways of doing this. The first is shown below:

```php
<?php
$WelcomeMessage = "Hello World";
function translate_greeting($FrenchMessage)
{
    global $WelcomeMessage;
    echo $WelcomeMessage;
    $FrenchMessage = "Bonjour Tout Le Monde";
    return;
}
translate_greeting();
echo $WelcomeMessage;
?>
```

In our function above, we have declared $WelcomeMessage to be a global variable. As we saw earlier, if we echoed $WelcomeMessage inside the function without declaring it global, it contained nothing because it was a local variable, and as such was undefined. Now, our echo() command displays "Hello World" as expected because the variable is global in scope.

Secondly, PHP can also achieve the same thing with the use of the $GLOBALS array. To display the contents of the global variable within the function using the $GLOBALS array we say the following:

```php
<?php
$WelcomeMessage = "Hello world";
function translate_greeting($FrenchMessage)
{
    echo $GLOBALS["WelcomeMessage"];
    $FrenchMessage = "Bonjour Tout Le Monde";
    return $FrenchMessage;
}
```

```
translate_greeting();
echo $WelcomeMessage;
echo $FrenchMessage;
?>
```

In both examples you'd see the message "Hello World" displayed twice. This is because we display it once inside the function and once outside it. Of course the variable $FrenchMessage still displays nothing, because we only echo it outside the function.

The global keyword is very simple to understand, but the $GLOBALS array is slightly less so. Let's take a closer look at how the $GLOBALS array works. It takes the following format:

```
$GLOBALS["VariableName"]
```

To reference it in any way, you place the variable name, minus the $ symbol inside quotation marks, and inside square brackets. You then prefix this with $GLOBALS in upper case to differentiate it from the local variable names. In fact it works in the same way as string indexed arrays, which we discussed in the last chapter.

## Getting Local Variables to Retain their Value

What happens when you call a function over and over again. We've defined the lifetime of a local variable beginning when the function is called, and ending when it's finished. There may be times though when you want the value of the variable to persist between function calls, so while it may not exist outside the function, when you call the function for a second time, it remembers a variable value from the first time. Imagine you're using a count of some sort that is set within the function. It won't be very good if it keeps on resetting each time you call the function.

```
function number_of_hits_on_web_site()
{
    return $number_of_people = $number_of_people+1;
}
```

Variables that persist between function calls are known as static variables. To make sure that your variable exists between calls of the function, you need to add the word static in front of it:

```
function number_of_hits_on_web_site()
{
    static $number_of_people = 0;
    return $number_of_people = $number_of_people+1;
}
```

This doesn't seem entirely logical. Surely, every time the function is called, the value is set to zero. The nature of the static keyword means that the line with the static definition on is only used the first time the function is called, and from then on this line is ignored.

If you displayed the value the function returns each time, it would increment by one:

```
echo(number_of_hits_on_web_site());    <-- would return 1
echo(number_of_hits_on_web_site());    <-- would return 2
echo(number_of_hits_on_web_site());    <-- would return 3
```

We've now looked at global, local, and static variables; let's recap on the difference between each one:

❑ Global variables have values that persist throughout the whole program, but to use them inside a function you have to prefix them with the keyword GLOBAL.

❑ Local variables have values that only exist inside of a function and for the duration of one function call.

❑ Static variables are local variables that persist in value, inside the function every time the function is called over and over again.

If you've got these points straight in your head, then it's time to do an example. We're going to do a simple example, where we create instances of each of these types of variables and display their contents on the web page as we go along, indicating when we're outside the function and when we're inside it.

## Try It Out – Using Scope

**1.** Open your web page editor and type in the following:

```
<HTML>
<HEAD></HEAD>
<BODY>
<BR>
<BR>
<FONT SIZE=-1>
<?php
$GlobalVariable = "Global";
function local()
{
    $LocalVariable="Local";
    static $StaticVariable=0;
    echo "<BR>The contents of GlobalVariable are " . $GLOBALS["GlobalVariable"];
    echo "<BR>The contents of LocalVariable are $LocalVariable";
    echo "<BR>The contents of StaticVariable are $StaticVariable";
    return $StaticVariable=$StaticVariable+1;
}
echo "<B>Calling Our function for the first time...</B>";
local();
echo "<BR><BR><B>Outside the function again...</B>";
echo "<BR>The contents of GlobalVariable are $GlobalVariable";
echo "<BR>The contents of LocalVariable are $LocalVariable";
echo "<BR>The contents of StaticVariable are $StaticVariable";
echo "<BR><BR><B>Calling Our function for the second time...</B>";
local();
echo "<BR><BR><B>Outside the function again...</B>";
echo "<BR>The contents of GlobalVariable are $GlobalVariable";
echo "<BR>The contents of LocalVariable are $LocalVariable";
echo "<BR>The contents of StaticVariable are $StaticVariable";
echo "<BR><BR><B>Calling Our function for the third time...</B>";
local();
echo "<BR><BR><B>Outside the function again...</B>";
echo "<BR>The contents of GlobalVariable are $GlobalVariable";
echo "<BR>The contents of LocalVariable are $LocalVariable";
echo "<BR>The contents of StaticVariable are $StaticVariable";
```

```
?>
</FONT>
</BODY>
</HTML>
```

**2.** Save this as `scope.php`.

**3.** Open up your browser and view `scope.php`:

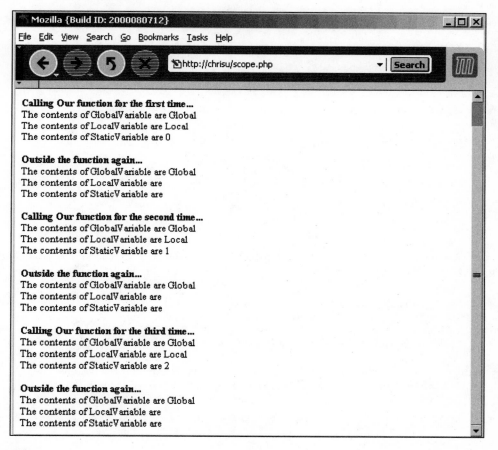

### How It Works

This program has no practical application, but given that variable scope is a difficult subject to grasp, we've used it to emphasize how the different types of variables work in PHP. The first line in our program creates and assigns `$GlobalVariable`:

```
$GlobalVariable = "Global";
```

We then defined our function local:

```
function local()
{
```

Inside it we create a local variable, called $LocalVariable, and a static variable called $StaticVariable:

```
$LocalVariable="Local";
static $StaticVariable=0;
```

The next three lines then display the contents of our global, local, and static variables within our function:

```
echo "<BR>The contents of GlobalVariable are " . $GLOBALS["GlobalVariable"];
echo "<BR>The contents of LocalVariable are $LocalVariable";
echo "<BR>The contents of StaticVariable are $StaticVariable";
```

Lastly, the return statement alters the contents of the static variable, incrementing it by 1:

```
return $StaticVariable=$StaticVariable+1;
}
```

Our program starts by calling our function local():

```
echo "<B>Calling Our function for the first time...</B>";
local();
```

We see the contents of our global, local, and static variables, which are "Global", "Local", and 0 inside the function. Once the function is completed, we display the contents of these variables outside the function:

```
echo "<BR><BR><B>Outside the function again...</B>";
echo "<BR>The contents of GlobalVariable are $GlobalVariable";
echo "<BR>The contents of LocalVariable are $LocalVariable";
echo "<BR>The contents of StaticVariable are $StaticVariable";
```

Outside the function, as we'd expect the local and static variables are empty and only $GlobalVariable contains anything. Next, we call our function for a second time:

```
echo "<BR><BR><B>Calling Our function for the second time...</B>";
local();
```

Once more $GlobalVariable is equal to "Global", $LocalVariable is redefined again and remains the same, but the contents of the $StaticVariable are different, because last time our function incremented them by 1. This time the number 1 is displayed. We go back outside the function and we can see yet again that only our $GlobalVariable has a value:

```
echo "<BR><BR><B>Outside the function again...</B>";
echo "<BR>The contents of GlobalVariable are $GlobalVariable";
echo "<BR>The contents of LocalVariable are $LocalVariable";
echo "<BR>The contents of StaticVariable are $StaticVariable";
```

Lastly, we call our function for a third time, and this time the only difference is that the static variable has added another 1 to its value:

```
echo "<BR><BR><B>Calling Our function for the third time...</B>";
local();
```

Outside the function as you've probably guessed, nothing has changed. Hopefully, this drives the point home, as we're not going to be discussing scope any further, and if you get unexpected values, you should be able to follow through and deduce why.

# Nesting

In the same way it's possible to nest one loop within another, or one `if` statement inside another, it's also possible to nest functions inside each other. However, nesting functions, while possible, isn't the most useful application of nesting as we'll see – so we'll only cover it briefly. If we take our tax rate function, we could nest it inside a pension calculating function that makes the necessary deductions from your salary, after the tax deductions:

```
function pension($Total)
{
   function tax($Salary)
   {
      return $Salary - (($Salary/100)*20);
   }
   $PostTax = tax($Total);
   return tax($Total)-(($PostTax/100)*3);
}

$Total = 2500;
echo (pension($Total));
```

Here the function `pension` is called, and in turn it creates a function `tax()`. What would happen if we did something like this:

```
function pension($Total)
{
   function tax($Salary)
   {
      return $Salary - (($Salary/100)*20);
   }
   $PostTax = tax($Total);
   return tax($Total)-(($PostTax/100)*3);
}

$Total = 2500;
echo (pension($Total));
echo (pension($Total));
```

Unfortunately, we would get an error message much like this:

Calling `pension()` twice means that we are asking PHP to define the `tax()` function twice. We will see a little later on in the chapter that we aren't allowed to do this. Instead, if we wanted to see `tax()` in action again, we could say something like this:

```
function pension($Total)
{
    function tax($Salary)
    {
        return $Salary - (($Salary/100)*20);
    }
    $PostTax = tax($Total);
    return tax($Total)-(($PostTax/100)*3);
}

$Total = 2500;
echo (pension($Total));
echo (tax($Total));
```

The output should look like this:

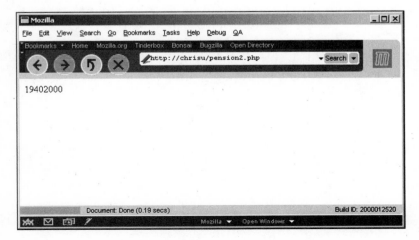

So, we can only call `pension()` once, otherwise we have multiple declarations of a function which causes an error. However, you're still able to call the two functions quite separately. This is quite confusing to follow, given the substitution of parameters, and actually offers no advantage over splitting the two functions up:

```
function tax (&$Salary)
{
    return $Salary = $Salary - (($Salary/100)*20);
}
function pension ($Salary)
{
    return $Salary - (($Salary/100)*3);
}

$Salary=2500;
echo (tax($Salary));
echo (pension($Salary));
```

Here you can see the two functions, one calculates the tax rate at twenty percent off your salary, and the other takes this value and lops three percent off the post-tax figure. Ultimately, both sets of functions will return the same value, so nesting offers no advantage, and separating out the functions makes them easier to read. However, there is a situation where nesting is sometimes useful – when a function calls itself.

# Recursion

A function calling itself is known as **recursion**. Recursion is traditionally a "thorny" topic in computer programming. The idea of a function calling itself sometimes sends people's heads spinning. Its main use is in reducing the amount of code needed in mathematical calculations. As with `While` loops, you must ensure that there is a value that is being tested at all times, and that this value changes with each iteration of the function, and that value moves closer to the condition each time to avoid an infinite loop.

Take a deep breath, we're going to have a quick look at an example of recursion now, and for brevity's sake we'll make it a small one. We're going to use recursion to find the factorial of a given number. Of course, you could do this with a loop, but this wouldn't require recursion. To find the factorial of a number, we use this equation:

$$n! = n * (n-1) * (n-2) \ldots (n-(n-2)) * 1$$

Obviously, if we are going to get our value from the user, we should check that they haven't entered something that will give us a trivial answer, like one or zero.

## Try It Out – Getting a Function to Call Itself (Recursion)

**1.** Start up your web page editor and type the following:

```
<HTML>
<HEAD></HEAD>
<BODY>
<FORM METHOD=GET ACTION="recursion.php">
I would like to know the factorial of
<INPUT NAME="Value" TYPE="Text">
```

```
<BR>
<BR>
<INPUT TYPE=SUBMIT>
</FORM>
</BODY>
</HTML>
```

**2.** Save this as `recursion.html`.

**3.** Now, open up a new file, and type in the following:

```
<?php
function recursion ($Value) {
  if ($Value <= 1)
   return 1;
  else
    return $Value*recursion($Value-1);
}
echo "The factorial of " . $Value . " is " . (recursion($Value));
?>
```

**4.** Save this as `recursion.php`

**5.** Open up `recursion.html` in your browser, and you will get something like this:

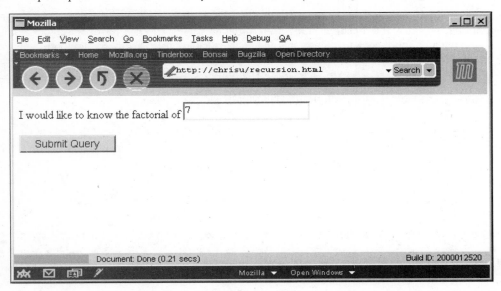

Of course, once you have chosen your value and pressed the submit button, our faithful recursive example will tell us that:

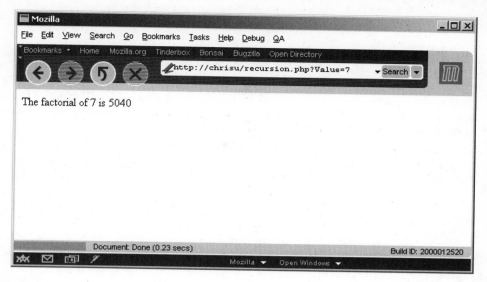

### How It Works

Recursion's primary use is to represent complicated mathematical formulae. Our example is relatively simple because a complicated example could take the rest of the chapter, if not the book. In this case, the recursion.html file is incidental to what we are really after here, and so we will discuss it no further. First, we declare our recursion function, and give it $Value as an argument:

```
<?php
function recursion ($Value) {
```

Then, we make sure that $Value has not been given as zero or one, if it has we return 1. We don't really need to calculate the factorial of one using a computer:

```
if ($Value <= 1)
   return 1;
```

If we are satisfied that we have been given a number greater than one, we execute the recursive part of our function. Like so:

```
else
    return $Value*recursion($Value-1);
```

Can you work out what is happening here? We are calling our recursion function from within itself, but with a decremented value. Lets go through it using some numbers – say we entered the value 3 (to make the math easy), this means we effectively have:

```
3 * recursion(2)
```

which, after another iteration becomes:

```
3 * 2 * recursion(1)
```

which again gives us:

```
3 * 2 * 1
```

The recursion ends when $Value gets to one, and then we return the value of our entire factorial calculation. Since recursion() eventually returns one (with no more recursion), we leave our function, and print out the answer with a simple message:

```
}
echo "The factorial of " . $Value . " is " . (recursion($Value));
?>
```

Of course, our program is incredibly easy to break, but we are just interested in understanding recursion for the moment, and this example is sufficient for that purpose.

# Include Files

Now we've covered the function statement, we'll look at another feature in PHP that allows you to include standalone segments of code or text at a specified point within a web page. Include files are a feature common to many server-side languages and technologies. An include file does exactly what it says on the tin, it includes a file, in another file. You can use includes files to include text, HTML code, or PHP script. The method for using include files in PHP is with the include statement. It takes the following format:

```
include("filename")
```

To include the file test.txt, you would type the following.

```
include("test.txt");
```

If the file test.txt contained the text "Hello", then this text would be included on the web page, as surely as if it had been part of the HTML. In fact if the text file looked like this:

```
I wandered lonely as a cloud
That floats on high o'er vales and hills,
When all at once I saw a crowd,
A host, of golden daffodils;
Beside the lake, beneath the trees,
Fluttering and dancing in the breeze.
```

This would be included in its entirety. You can also add variable names or concatenate them to the name of the file name, within the brackets, as long as it creates a legal file name:

```
$Name ="1";
include ("test" . $Name . ".txt");
```

The result of our concatenation is `test1.txt`, and if there is a file of that name, then it will be included – otherwise an error is generated. In fact there are generally five typical uses of include files:

❏ Include text files in the page

❏ Define variables and/or constants and details of certain error messages

❏ Insert the values of HTTP variables in the page

❏ Execute a separate PHP script

❏ Place commonly used functions that you need, but don't want to define in every page

This harks back to our touchstone of code reuse. Include files allow you to take a commonly used piece of text or code and insert it into your program at any point you need.

Include files are useful in that they can be added straight to a file, but you can create code that decides whether that file should be included or not. That's exactly what we're going to do in our next example.

## Try It Out – Conditional Includes

**1.** Start up your web page editor and type in the following words:

```
File One included
```

**2.** Save this as a text file and call it `file1.txt`.

**3.** Close it and create a new text file and type in the following:

```
File Two included
```

**4.** Save this as a text file and call it `file2.txt`.

**5.** Now close this and start yet another new file and type in the following:

```
<HTML>
<HEAD></HEAD>
<BODY>
<FORM METHOD=GET ACTION="condition.php">
What file do you wish to include?
<SELECT NAME="Choice">
<OPTION VALUE="1">File One</OPTION>
<OPTION VALUE="2">File Two</OPTION>
</SELECT>
<BR>
<BR>
<INPUT TYPE=Submit>
</FORM>
</BODY>
</HTML>
```

**6.** Save this as `condition.html` in the same place as the two text files.

**7.** One last time close down that file, create a new one and type in the following:

```
<HTML>
<HEAD></HEAD>
<BODY>
<?php
if ($Choice<>"")
{
include("file".$Choice.".txt");
}
?>
<BR>
Here is some text.
</BODY>
</HTML>
```

**8.** Save this as `condition.php` in the same location as you saved the last 3 files.

**9.** Open up `condition.html` in your browser and select a choice:

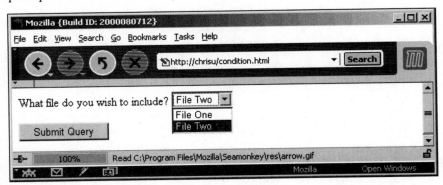

**10.** Click on Submit query and the contents of the file of your choice will have been added:

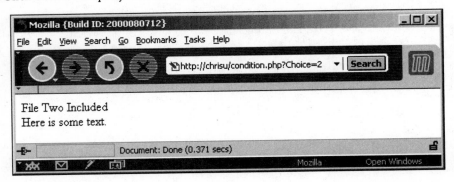

### How It Works

This is quite a clever little program. Our two text files are of no interest to us, they just provide example text. Our HTML program, takes the name of the file from the user:

```
<SELECT NAME="Choice">
<OPTION VALUE="1">File One</OPTION>
<OPTION VALUE="2">File Two</OPTION>
</SELECT>
```

However, it takes care to assign a numerical value, so our $Choice variable, taken from the NAME attribute, will either contain the value 1 or 2. Then we check to see if the user has selected one of the two options, and if they have we include the file, taking the contents of the $Choice variable and concatenating it to the words and .txt, to produce either the file name file1.txt or file2.txt:

```
if ($Choice<>"")
{
include("file".$Choice.".txt");
}
```

Depending on which choice the user made, the correct file is included.

> *Strictly speaking, the $Choice variable will always contain a value – if the user doesn't make a choice, then by default the <SELECT> list box will contain File One. However, it's good programming practice to make sure that if for some reason, no value is passed to $Choice that an error isn't generated.*

# Common Uses of Include Files

Typically a common set of variables will be declared in a file called something like common.inc (which is short for common include file). The things you will include will be things like the size of screen:

```
$edit_form_cols = 80;
$edit_form_rows = 25;
```

or the types of file extension:

```
$text_file_array = array("txt", "htm", "html", "php", "php3", "cfg",
                "inc", "ini", "js", "log", "pl", "doc");
```

These kinds of detail will never change between web pages, but still have to be defined somewhere. It makes sense to declare them in common.inc, and just include the file at the top of every HTML page that will need them.

> *Many web servers are not set up to parse .inc files; it's better to put includes in .php files so that their (potentially sensitive) contents are never visible unintentionally to the unwashed masses. Instead of common.inc, name the file common.php; nothing else need be changed. If you are using your own web server, then it's no big deal, but if you are installing PHP scripts onto shared servers at a hosting service then this is well worth taking account of.*

You can also declare functions, which will handle the HTML headers and footers. Instead of having to write header and footer information in every HTML page, like this:

```
<HTML>
<HEAD>
<TITLE>Car Application</TITLE>
<STYLE TYPE="text/css">
.style1 {color:black
      code here...
      }
</HEAD>
<BODY>
```

You can declare them in functions which add the HTML automatically and put this function in the include file:

```
<?php
function html_header() {
?>
   <HTML>
   <HEAD>
   <TITLE>Car Application</TITLE>
   <STYLE TYPE="text/css">
   .style1 {color:black
         code here...
            }
   </HEAD>
   <BODY>
<?php
}
?>
```

You then only have to include one line of code in your PHP files:

```
<?php
include("common.inc");
...rest of PHP code
?>
```

which will save you a lot of needless typing.

## Gotchas of Include Files

When PHP comes across an include file, the engine acts as if the script has been closed off (?>), the file included, and then the script opened again (<?php). So if we have something like this:

```
<?php
if ($Choice<>"")
{
include("file".$Choice.".txt");
```

PHP pretends it is seeing this:

```
<?php
if ($Choice<>"")
{
include("file".$Choice.".txt");
?>
```

It then inserts the text before re-opening the PHP brackets:

```
File One
<?php
```

This is great when using files that only contain HTML and text , but it does mean that you will have to delimit any PHP code inside include files with the opening `<?php` and closing `?>` PHP tags, in order for it to be treated like PHP code.

If you have an include file such as `common.inc` at the top of the page, and it calls another page that also includes `common.inc`, and your include file contains functions, then your code will generate an error. Any time you declare the same function twice within a page, it will cause an error. Here are some examples:

```
<?php
include("common.inc");
include("common.inc");
...rest of PHP code
```

While this would be rather obvious error to spot, it might not be if you include a file in `pageone.php`:

```
<?php
include("common.inc");
...some code...
call to pagetwo.php
```

and `pagetwo.php` starts like this:

```
<?php
if (!$COMMON_INCLUDED) include("common.inc");
...
```

Vigilance is required at all times. The solution to this problem is to declare a variable in every include file you create:

```
$COMMON_INCLUDED=1;
```

and then test for it at the beginning of the include, for example:

```
if (!$COMMON_INCLUDED) $COMMON_INCLUDED=1;
```

This brings us to the end of our tips on functions and include files.

# Summary

This chapter might have seemed quite brief in comparison to some of the earlier chapters, but the concepts introduced are no less important and we've taken a little longer over just this one feature as a result.

Functions are blocks of code that can be called up within your program and they are either defined automatically in PHP such as the array functions `sort()` and `ksort()`, which we saw in the last chapter, or can be created by the users themselves, as we demonstrated. They can be thought of as little black boxes which return a value if you feed them variables. Variables are passed to them via arguments defined at the beginning of the function. Unless you pass them by reference, the value a function returns doesn't have any effect on the variables outside it. You can then use the value the function returns to switch to different cases, and follow different courses of actions.

We saw that variables act differently inside functions because of something called scope. Variables with local scope only lasted while the function was in action, and would be terminated, unless you add the `static` keyword. Variables defined outside functions had to be used with the `global` keyword, or the `GLOBALS` array, inside functions in order to differentiate them.

We also looked at include files at the end of the chapter, and discussed how you can use them to modularize your code. This has been an important chapter and forms the close of our programming fundamentals section. In the next chapter we will see how you can go about debugging your PHP code.

# Handling and Avoiding Errors

Having spent the last few chapters covering programming fundamentals, we now have enough basic programming knowledge to be able to create our own standalone web applications. There is one thing though that we still haven't gone into, and we'll certainly need it to help create and maintain our PHP programs. It's no good being able to write these applications if you don't know how to spot, handle, and avoid bugs, and ultimately create bug-free software. Attaining this nirvana is harder than it may seem for we are inherently fallible and we all make mistakes occasionally! That's not to say it's impossible to write bug-free software; it's just very hard, and takes effort, practice, diligence and lots of experience.

We'll start this chapter by looking at how PHP handles errors, and then we'll break down the different types of errors that can occur in PHP. Good design principles are the first step – with good design we can ensure that we don't create nearly as many errors. If errors do occur, then identifying where they can occur is the next step to being able to handle them effectively. This in turn makes the process of debugging (the removal of errors in a program) much easier. Every programmer is familiar with the process of "debugging". You will usually encounter the need for debugging at the very point where you think that everything works. You've finished and tested your application and everything seems OK and you present it to the user, only for it to fall down on the first page.

The user can create some of these problems unexpectedly, so we will be looking at how to handle unforeseen conditions generated within a program gracefully. We shall be paying particular attention to the handling of errors created at run-time – bad (or missing!) user input, numeric conditions that may result in a division by zero, strange characters in the user input and so on, can all wreak havoc on the normal operational flow of a program. We will create a two-pronged attack, introducing some useful techniques for both coding and debugging, and applying them to our PHP environment. The main topics will be:

- ❑ Error handling for security and aesthetic purposes
- ❑ Syntax errors
- ❑ Logical errors
- ❑ Good coding practices
- ❑ Using regular expressions to filter user input
- ❑ Debugging

# Error Handling in PHP

There are many reasons why good error handling is essential. Let's start, with the first and foremost, security. Remember – if you're a programmer, your system (or site) security can be intimately tied to your *job security*, so this is doubly important!

PHP, unlike many other languages, is only used on the web. Therefore, it can't use the "standard out" and "standard error" streams in the same way as C, C++, Java, and other languages do, in order to separate error messages from ordinary output. Unlike CGI technology, PHP doesn't send error messages to the Web server's error log by default. Instead, PHP places error messages in the only place available to it, which is within its own HTML output to the user's browser! This can have several common negative effects.

## Insecure Information

The first such effect is the divulging of potentially sensitive file paths (among other such information) to the site's visitors. PHP error messages can be helpfully verbose, but this helpfulness becomes harmful when it tells users not only that a file handle cannot be opened, but also gives the exact path that the script was trying to open! In the wrong hands, this sort of information could be used to snoop about in your web site's data store.

## Unsightly Web Pages

The second such effect is one very commonly found on those unfortunate sites whose webmasters pay little or no heed to aesthetic concerns. Nonetheless, it can transform even the most powerful and beautiful PHP-powered Web site into a disorderly mess. This effect is simply stated – error messages are **ugly**, and tend to turn up exactly where you least want them. Nothing spells "amateur" quite like a giant:

 File not found: /var/www/mysite/important_file.php

message right in the middle of your page. By intelligently handling error conditions, your web sites can be kept free of unexpected blemishes.

## Invisible Error Messages

Since PHP can be made to output HTML code in any number of ways, the error messages it injects into its output might show up in a place in the code where they are invisible to browsers! For instance, an error message might show up inside an HTML comment, such as:

```
<!--
Comments, comments, comments.
ERROR MESSAGE
Comments, comments, comments.
-->
```

Perhaps the error would instead choose to hole-up with your dynamically generated JavaScript, having the likely side-effect of producing a JavaScript error:

```
<!--
<script language="JavaScript">
Code, code, code;
ERROR MESSAGE
Code, code, code;
</script>
-->
```

Or, even harder to find, an error message might show up inside an HTML tag, such as:

```
<table align="center" width="200" ERROR MESSAGE>
```

Browsers are very tolerant of incorrect HTML, and will try and display practically anything, so you might never notice the error message, but just the knock on effect that page doesn't quite look the way you intended it to. Proper error handling, which requires merely diligence and foresight, can help prevent this frustrating scenario.

# Error Types

We've noted that errors can arise in different places, but there are also several different types that may occur. This is important to realize, particularly given that some errors may not even generate an accompanying message at all. Debugging is a lot easier if you know where and what to look for. There are many types (and subtypes) of errors, but in PHP you can very broadly classify them into one of the following two types – syntax errors and logical errors.

# Syntax Errors

Syntax errors are generally more easily spotted as they're the ones that cause your program to go belly up. Computers are very precise machines, and the applications that run on them are just as picky. You and I can muddle up words in our sentences and still expect somebody else to make general sense of them. For example, I could say "good morning" to you at one o'clock in the afternoon, and you'd still know what I meant. However your PHP programs can be thrown out by the mildest of typos.

```
eco "Hello";
```

This would provoke a **parse error**, PHP failing completely to recognize that you merely missed an h out of the word echo. Another classic method of creating parse errors is by missing a semi-colon off the end of a statement:

```
echo "Hello"
echo "World";
```

Even though the error message generated would indicate that the error occurred on the second of the two lines, the message we get is still quite helpful:

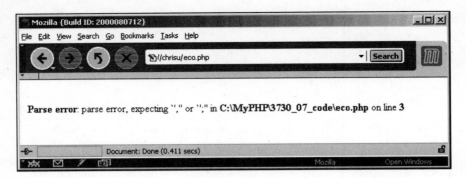

Another common error is to fail to create a loop structure correctly. For example, we could forget a closing brace from the end of a loop structure:

```php
<?php
for ($Loop = 0; $Loop <5; $Loop++)
{
        echo "Hello";
?>
```

If you fail to close a conditional structure with a closing brace, this will also cause problems:

```php
<?php
if ($Choice == "Yes")
{
     echo "Hello you are correct";
     echo "$Answer = ";
else
{
     echo "Unfortunately you didn't get it correct this time";
}
?>
```

The missing brace is in the middle of the above code snippet this time, but it should appear before the `else` statement. In fact, PHP will tell you very quickly about these types of errors when it encounters them. As you can imagine there are literally hundreds of different possible types of errors, so we can't go into them all here. Syntax errors are like abuses of the grammatical rules of language. If you wrote, "You was here on time", your old English tutor would have put a big red line under it. Writing a program is almost like writing an English essay, yet you *have* to get everything correct – one spelling mistake and everything will come tumbling down around your ears.

Ok, let's have a summary of a few very common causes of syntax errors.

## *Five Things That Might Cause a Syntax Error*

❑ **Typing Mistakes**

We've already mentioned it once, but let's say it again. Check your spelling.

❏ **Construct is not closed properly**

Most people take care to close loops and conditions, but it's still easy to be caught out when there are several combined. Look out for something like this:

```
for ($loop1 = 0; $loop1<10; $loop1++)
{
for ($loop2 = 2; $loop2<20;$loop2++)
{
for ($loop3 = 3; $loop2<30; $loop3++)
{
...Code here...
}
}
```

It's not always obvious if the loops are closed 10 pages of code later. However, indenting the code will certainly help, as well as making it easier to understand afterwards. Try formatting your loops this way:

```
for ($loop1 = 0; $loop1<10; $loop1++)
{
    for ($loop2 = 2; $loop2<20;$loop2++)
    {
        for ($loop3 = 3; $loop3<30; $loop3++)
        {
            ...Code here...
        }
    }
}
```

This time, it's obvious that we're missing a closing brace.

❏ **Missing a semi-colon from the end of a statement**

The semi-colon is vital in PHP – leave it off at your peril!

❏ **Getting the name of a function wrong**

It might only be a small misunderstanding, but trying to use some like `htmlspecialchar()` instead of `htmlspecialchars()` will generate a fatal error along the lines of

Fatal error: Call to undefined function: htmlspecialchar().

❏ **Not closing a string properly**

It seems obvious, but if you fail to add a closing set of quotation marks to your string such as:

```
echo "Hello world;
```

PHP will generate a parse error.

The one upside to all of this is that syntax errors are usually quite easy to spot. The parse errors in PHP will also give the accompanying line number of where the error was generated. Typically this line will be just before or after the error itself depending on how the erroneous code affects a function, set of braces, or such like. Also once you do spot them, they are almost all very easy to correct – unlike the next type of error we will look at.

# Logical Errors

The second type of error is harder to spot. To all intents and purposes your program is working and when you run it no parsing/syntax errors occur. You've checked and double-checked your code, cleared up any typos and obvious coding errors. Nevertheless, you run the program and it either starts returning data that can't possibly be correct, or doesn't return any data at all. In some cases it may not even return *any output* to the screen. At times your program works fine, but then you give it to the user and it suddenly breaks. All of this is usually down to mistakes being made in the **logic** of program.

There is further distinction to make here between the types of logical error. Some logical errors are errors that occur at runtime, and only under certain conditions. For example, the PHP code seems fine, and it will even be accepted and executed by the PHP engine, but errors will occur when you run the program, which will stop your program from completing – these are **runtime errors**. Runtime errors that stop your program from completing execution are termed **fatal**. Syntax errors are also invariably fatal, but runtime errors that stop your execution only under circumstances, aren't always fatal.

The second type of logical error doesn't actually cause your program to break by returning error messages, they run to completion but then just return incorrect information or no information at all. These are, for want of a better description, **unexpected output errors**. We'll start by looking at runtime errors first.

## Runtime Errors

There can be many reasons a program you're running doesn't get far as returning input or finishing execution. Typically, problems with file handling and databases can be two very common causes. However, as we've yet to discuss these topics, we won't cover these until the relevant chapter on that topic. Instead we'll look at two of the most common types of error that aren't caused by faulty access of objects or items outside PHP.

### Division By Zero Errors

First, a quick reminder – as most of us already know, computers can't divide by zero. In fact, no one can – it's impossible to represent an answer.

Division by zero is usually an unintentional mistake – you divide a variable by a positive number, but for some reason the variable is empty, so you inadvertently end up dividing your number by zero. Of course the computer will generate an error whenever this problem arises.

However the problem might not always be apparent. Consider a form in which you ask a user to enter a number of items for purchase. You also wish to give him/her a discount and calculate the requisite taxation. The user accidentally forgets to enter this number in the box and submits it to your server. Your program multiplies the number of items by the price and ends up with zero. This result could then be used as the basis for division later in the calculation, and we would end up with a division by zero error. However if the user had supplied a number other than zero then the program would have worked correctly.

Let's take a look at an example. In the construction of the twin Petronas towers in Malaysia, the crews working on the towers worked in an environment of "friendly competition", trying to see which tower would be completed first. Let's say that the project's Webmaster wrote a script for an internal web site documenting progress on each tower. Here is the script:

```php
<?php
//petronas.php
    $height_of_tower_a = 0;
    $height_of_tower_b = 12;

    if ($height_of_tower_a == $height_of_tower_b) {
       $towers_in_dead_heat = 1;
    } else {
       if ($height_of_tower_a > $height_of_tower_b) {
          $tallertowername = "Tower A";
          $shortertowername = "Tower B";
          $tallertowerheight = $height_of_tower_a;
          $shortertowerheight = $height_of_tower_b;
       } else {
          $tallertowername = "Tower B";
          $shortertowername = "Tower A";
          $tallertowerheight = $height_of_tower_b;
          $shortertowerheight = $height_of_tower_a;
       }
       $towers_in_dead_heat = 0;
    }

    if ($towers_in_dead_heat == 1) {
       echo("The two towers are <b>in a dead heat</b>!");
    } else {
    $taller_by_ratio = $tallertowerheight / $shortertowerheight;
    echo("At this moment, <b>${tallertowername}</b> is
          <b>${taller_by_ratio}</b> times taller
          than ${shortertowername}!");
    }
?>
```

However, when the script was first tested, it blew up. The script printed out something along the lines of:

**Warning**: Division by zero in **c:\inetpub\wwwroot\tower.php** on line 30
At this moment, Tower A is times taller than Tower B!

The root of the problem, as you've probably guessed, lies in the line reading:

```php
$taller_by_ratio = $tallertowerheight / $shortertowerheight;
```

When this first test was run, Tower B's height was set a non-zero value, and Tower A's height to 0. As a result, the computer tried to divide a non-zero number by 0. But *nothing* can divide a number by zero and get a numeric answer, and so the division failed, producing the error message.

The solution to the problem is simple – replace this code:

```
$taller_by_ratio = $tallertowerheight / $shortertowerheight;
echo ("At this moment, <b>${tallertowername}</b> is <b>${taller_by_ratio}</b>
        times taller than ${shortertowername}!");
```

with the following code.

```
if ($shortertowerheight == 0) {
    echo("At this moment, <b>${tallertowername}</b>
            has reached a height of   <b>${tallertowerheight}</b>,
            but ${shortertowername} hasn't even risen a foot!");
} else {
$taller_by_ratio = $tallertowerheight / $shortertowerheight;
    echo("At this moment, <b>${tallertowername}</b>
            is <b>${taller_by_ratio}</b> times taller than ${shortertowername}!");
}
```

This simple solution involves anticipating a possible division-by-zero error by checking the shortest tower height for a zero value • something that should be done **any** time two variables are divided. It lets us explain to the user why the sum can't be performed, rather than letting them work it out from PHP's terse warning.

Division by zero is not the only time that math functions can cause PHP to get into difficulties; there are other situations to watch out for – for example, trying to find the sqrt() (square root) of a negative number (that should be anticipated and handled in a similar way).

### Infinite Loops

We've already lectured you on the difficulties that can arise if you don't make sure your loops end, but given the potentially catastrophic web server killing implications it can have on Windows based platforms, it won't hurt to remind you again. One of the main problems with using while and do while is that if the condition that you set is never matched, then PHP will continually execute the loop and keep going around it a potentially infinite amount of times within, of course, the limits of the max_execution_time setting. If the max_execution_time setting is breached, then PHP will display a warning error. Consider the following, but **don't attempt to run it**:

```
$Counter=1;
$TestVariable = True;
While ($TestVariable)
{
      $Counter++;
}
```

We set two variables here, but the problem is that the $TestVariable is never altered anywhere within our loop. As a result, we might well be incrementing $Counter by one every time, but this has no effect on our $TestVariable. You shouldn't try and run this program, because on Windows this will hog resources as PHP tries to go through the loop fruitlessly and can end up using all your resources and tying up the whole machine.

If all infinite loops were as easy as that to spot, you wouldn't have a problem; however they're usually a bit more subtle, especially given the fact that they might only occur under certain circumstances:

```
$Counter=100;
Do
{
    $Counter = $Counter * $Variable;
    $Counter--;
} While ($Counter>0)
```

Depending on whatever value is in $Variable, this loop may or may not be an infinite loop. If the value in $Counter is always greater than or equal to 1, then it will be an infinite loop, if it reaches 0, then it won't be an infinite loop.

## Unexpected Output Errors

There are also many reasons why your program might fail to return the expected output. We've tried to generalize several common causes of this, and we will look at each one of them briefly. We can't, however, cover every situation; we can just give you clues on where to look.

### Errors In the Program Assumptions

I'd hazard that one of the most common types of logical error occurs when programmers make mistakes in their assumptions of their interpretation of the code, and program that error into their script. One recent example is the Mars probe lost by the US space program last year. The craft was apparently destroyed in the atmosphere of Mars because one portion of its navigation code had been written using metric units, and the other in Imperial. You can find more details of this at
http://mars.jpl.nasa.gov/msp98/news/mco990930.html

A second story (although whether it's unverifiable truth or merely urban myth is open to speculation) happened in the 1950s/60s within the U.S. nuclear defense system. A programmer calculated a number incorrectly – he or she managed to shift a decimal point one place to the left. The programmers assumed that they knew how to implement the missile trajectory calculation correctly. Unfortunately, the number in question corresponded to a flight trajectory angle in the algorithm that detected whether a nuclear missile attack had been launched. Once in operation the program detected an object corresponding to its calculations, and displayed that it was 99.9% certain that it was an incoming missile. It turned out that the rising moon had triggered the program!

The point of these stories is that while it may be impossible to detect these types of errors in the code before the situation actually arises, you should carefully think about what the program should do in the design phases and after that recheck the basic principles before you start coding.

### Functions with no Return Value

If you write a function and forget to put in the return statement, when you come to execute the function, you'll find that nothing is returned. In the following example, the code is all perfectly legal:

```
echo (tax(1600,25));
function tax ($Salary, $TaxRate)
{
    $Salary = $Salary - (($Salary/100)*$TaxRate);
}
```

However, you will see that we haven't returned a value. While the calculation within the function is performed, no value is ever returned, so if you echo the result of the function in any way, it will assume the result is 0, no matter what you might have intended.

**235**

## Arguments in the Wrong Order

Following on from the previous example that used functions, we come across another common problem. It is possible to get the arguments in the wrong order. Consider the previous example again, but with the return value correctly supplied:

```
echo (tax(1600,25));
function tax ($Salary, $TaxRate)
{
      return $Salary - (($Salary/100)*$TaxRate);
}
```

What happens if we get the main two arguments the wrong way around?

```
echo (tax(25,1600));
```

Well, not a lot (except that the result will be wrong). However, if you are supplying a string and a number, then you could quite easily end up with a zero for the numerical value, given that PHP will try and translate the string to a number. These types of errors can occur more easily in PHP than in other (more strictly typed) languages. You can just mess up all kinds of variable types and PHP will never let you know.

## Confusing the Assignment and Equality Operators

Anybody with a background in Visual Basic or Pascal is more than likely to fall foul of this one at some point. When creating an `if` structure, it's crucial to make sure that you use the equality operator `==`, and not the assignment operator `=`, otherwise things will probably not work as intended. Looking back at the towers example, if we omitted an equals sign from the following line (which should test for a zero value):

```
if ($shortertowerheight = 0) {
echo ("At this moment, <b>${tallertowername}</b> has ... risen a foot!");
```

We would end up setting `$shortertowerheight` to zero, thus completely altering the working of the example. The contents of the `if` block would never be executed for a start, since it tests on a value that's set permanently to zero, which is equivalent to a Boolean `False`, and because it is equal to the outcome of the assignment (which is 0). However, if the conditional evaluated to 1 or true, then the code would execute. The result of this conditional would be the intermediate value of the assignment operation, that is, 1 or true.

# Good Coding Practice

So, you've spotted your error. Now what are you going to do about it? The first advice we're going to offer is almost blindingly obvious. Don't write code with errors in it in the first place! This may seem easier said than done, but if you stick to some well-worn practices, that programmers from Roman times onwards have used, then you can vastly reduce the chances of introducing errors into your page.

These techniques are, without exception, simple to understand, easy to execute and yet a lot of programmers don't use them! "Why not?" you might be wondering. Well, because your average programmer is a busy person, who doesn't like anything that distracts from the actual task of programming. The main objections are usually that these techniques are time-consuming, they require some degree of forward planning and organization, and they don't guarantee that your code will be error free. Programmers might not couch their objections in these terms, but that's what it boils down to. Remember, nothing can guarantee that your code will be error free, and as doctors maintain, prevention is better than cure.

# Indent Your Code

We've said it before, and we'll say it again: indent your code! While it isn't necessary to ensure that your code works correctly, you can make your life so much easier by formatting and indenting your code as you write it. So for each loop structure or conditional structure, common convention is to indent the code with a tab or several spaces. An example snippet of code might look like this:

```
if ($Text == "right")
{
    $num = 7
    if ($Text2 == "right")
    {
        $num2 = 8;
    }
    else
    {
        $num2 = 0;
    }
}
```

In this case it makes it easier to see which bit of code the closing braces refer to. If a closing brace had been omitted, it would be much easier to spot with the code indented in this manner. When debugging, you would only need to glance at the code to spot, for example, code at the end of the structure that was still indented by several characters. You would know immediately that something had been left out.

Of course the flip side to this is that excessive indentation can make your code more difficult to read. One line might start outside of your viewing area to the left and another line might finish outside it to the right. In other words, you can't read the PHP script all at once without finding yourself constantly scrolling back and forth. To counteract this you can always reduce the amount you indent code to two or three characters per indent.

# Comment Your Code

This one is also very simple. You can't expect anyone else (even *yourself* just a few weeks down the line) to understand your code unless you comment it thoroughly. A comment is an annotation provided by the programmer in the course of the code to help explain what each section of code does. It needn't just be of use to the programmer who wrote it; the code may have to be maintained long after the programmer has left the company, or isn't in a position to be able to help. Whenever you write code for a commercial application, or just code that you want to be able to understand at a later date, you should comment it. Comments are helpful when planning the architecture – if you start with pseudo-code and move to PHP code, you can use the pseudo-code as your comments, adding no additional time and ensuring continuity between the modeling and coding stages. As with indenting, excessive commenting can make the code more difficult to read, so be sensible.

In PHP you can use the double forward slash to add a comment to the end of a line. Sensible places for comments are after variable or procedure declarations, to explain what each part does:

```
$Seconds=120;    //Number of Seconds before the nuclear reactor goes into meltdown
```

Comments are also useful after loops, to indicate what is being repeated, or after `else()` and `elseif()` to indicate what decision that branch of the code is taking:

```
if ($question == "Fax")  // If user selects fax then initiate fax confirmation
{
...code...
}
elseif ($question == "Email") // If user selects email start email confirmation
{
...more code...
}
else                     // don't send user confirmation
{
...yet more code...
}
```

You can also use the `/* */` combination to write comments that extend over several lines. This can be useful to add headings to the start of a section of code, or to write more lengthy explanations.

```
/*  +-------------------------------------------------+
    |                  USEFUL FUNCTIONS               |
    +-------------------------------------------------+  */

function myFunction($parameter) {

    /*
        myFunction is a useful function. It takes a single
        parameter as an argument, and does nothing at all with
        it. It doesn't return anything.
    */
}
```

As you can see, it's quite possible to spend a lot of time just laying out your code nicely. When you come back to try and adapt some code you wrote a year ago, though, you'll appreciate the difference it makes.

## Use Functions

We introduced functions in Chapter 6 and have already applied them to several of our examples. What you may not have realized is how useful they can be in optimizing your code. As you start writing more and more PHP code you'll find that you're using lots of similar routines in many of your pages, and possibly even several times in the same page. Instead of repeating this code, you can put it into a function and then just call this function when needed:

```
<?php
    // get the Form details

    ProcessFormDetails($Name, $Email);

    // some processing
```

```
    ProcessFormDetails($Name, $Email);

function ProcessFormDetails ($Name, $Email)
{
    // do some processing here
}
?>
```

Now the processing of the form details is only done in one place, within the function itself, and if anything is wrong you only need to look for errors in one place.

## Use Include Files

Using include files is just one step up from using functions, as it allows you to make your functions available to many PHP files. You'll see a really good example of this in the database chapters, where we have an include file, called common_db.inc, which contains functions that automatically create an HTML header and footer. This file can be included in any PHP script and lets you add header/footer as needed with only one command each – saving you having to type in <HTML><HEAD></HEAD> every time.

The one thing you have to watch out for, when using include files, is the possibility of changes affecting more than one PHP script. If you have taken out a set of routines and put them into an include file, and then made them available to other PHP developers in your organization, you must be careful not to suddenly change the functionality of those procedures. This could wreak havoc amongst other programs, so be careful when using this method in a shared development environment. To help safeguard against this, make sure you place comments in your include files that describe their purpose and intended output.

Also, as mentioned in Chapter 6, you must make sure that any functions you define in an include file, aren't defined twice, otherwise you will generate an error.

## Use Sensible Variable Names

Take a look at the following code:

```
<?php

    $a = 0;
    $b = 12;

    if ($a == $b) {
        $d = 1;
    } else {
        if ($a > $b) {
            $tn = "Tower A";
            $sn = "Tower B";
            $th = $a;
            $sh = $b;
        } else {
            $tn = "Tower B";
            $sn = "Tower A";
```

```
        $th = $b;
        $sh = $a;
    }
    $d = 0;
}


if ($d == 1) {
    echo("The two towers are <b>in a dead heat</b>!");
} else {
$r = $th / $sh;
echo("At this moment, <b>${tn}</b> is
        <b>${r}</b> times taller
        than ${sn}!");
    }
?>
```

The contents of the strings should be a giveaway that this is the twin towers example from earlier in the chapter, only the names of the variables have been changed. But if I wanted to come back and edit this code, I'd have a lot of trouble understanding what the variables represented. Does $a contain the name of tower A, or the height of tower A? Is $d true if the tower heights are Different, or in a Dead heat? This sort of confusion can easily lead to simple logic errors.

A rule of thumb is to give variables names that describe the piece of data they contain. $TallerTowerName is much more effective at communicating the value that I can expect to see on the screen if I echo the variable out to the browser. Once again, don't overdo this. Normally using more than two or three words is not recommended, for example $UsernameForLoginToDatabase might be perfect to understand, but it's a lot to type in and easier to make spelling errors on.

The only time single-letter variable names should really be used, is for holders of arbitrary data such as the counter in a for loop.

# Trying to Break Your Code

When you test your code, supply your programs with rogue values (massive numbers, or letters instead of numbers and such like) to see how your program reacts. You may not have intended your program to be abused in such a way but, when it's out in the real world, these are exactly the type of values that may get put into your program. If your program breaks under this sort of stress, then you'll have many perplexed and unhappy users.

In fact it's easier to assume that your code will break under rogue values and then code to try and prevent this. Think of the possible things that a user could do to either break your program or to let it accept invalid information or no information at all. For example, ages should be realistic values, addresses should contain states, zip codes and such like, and e-mail addresses should contain the ampersat (@) symbol. Your code should test for all these kind of things. Let's start by looking at how you can go about avoiding anomalous numerical values.

A good strategy for doing this is to break down all the possible values into three types:

❑   **Expected values** – these are values in the range that you ask for. If you asked for numbers between 1 and 10, these would be 2 through to 9.

❑ **Boundary condition values** – these are the values that lie at the boundaries of our range. If you asked for numbers between 1 and 10, then did you actually mean to include these values or not? Does your program deal with them correctly? You should test for them even if you didn't, and nearby values such as 0 and 11 as well.

❑ **Out-of-bounds values** – these are the values that fall anywhere outside the range. In our example, – 5, 0, and 999 would all be out of bounds values. But it doesn't stop there; this could equally apply to values of an unexpected type, such as a letter or date. For instance were you expecting one of these values: 0, –1, 0.9, –1E5, 10.1, 5.5, "dog", #5/9/58#, "true", "false", (empty), 4+4, 5/0, 9.9, 9.99, 9.999, 003, "three"? Will your program cope with all of these types?

Testing your code with the kind of values you'd expect your user to supply is an absolute must. If you ask a user to supply a number between 1 and 10, you must test your program using a large number of examples between one and ten. If the valid range is 1 to 10, you should always test boundary values such as 0 and 11 as well. And while, realistically, you couldn't test every possible out of bounds value that could be input, you do need to hypothesize a large possible range of values and different types. If your program doesn't break when the user inputs 29, that's all very well and good, but does it still work when the user enters "three", which would be a perfectly "correct" answer to the question in some user's minds?

# More Form Validation

Of course most of the errors will surface when requiring input from the user. The error-catching techniques outlined above are fairly cut-and-dried, but this sort of work can be exquisitely difficult. It is impossible to guess the strangest things users will expect your program to do.

## Thinking Like Your Users

The key here is not to think like an average user, but rather think like a complete stranger to computing. Your program will have to deal with every probability, and while the average user may act in just the way you envisage, it's often the complete novices to computing who end up breaking your application. While thinking like a computing novice can at times be quite tough for a seasoned "power user", programmer or administrator, if you can bugproof your applications against this kind of use, it will lead to a much smoother experience for your users. Every time you are creating a new page or script, think "how would Grandma (or Mom, or Dad, or Uncle Jimmy...) react to this?" This is especially evident when dealing with input from forms – the primary data-gathering tool used on web pages.

Every time you have an input field, think of the possible errors that a user might make in filling it out. These errors should be caught, and dealt with appropriately. Only after the entire form's input is free of errors should the user (and script) be allowed to continue.

The first, and most obvious possible mistake is not filling out the form element at all! Empty input should be noted, and the user forced to go back and try again until all required fields are filled out. I most often check for empty input by keeping a tally of empty fields, usually called $emptyfields, which I increment each time a required field is left blank. If the value of this variable is greater than zero by the time I'm done processing all of the form input, I force the user to go back and try again. A very simple implementation of this technique might look like this:

```
$emptyfields = 0;

if (!$form_field_one)    $emptyfields++;
```

```
if (!$form_field_three)   $emptyfields++;
if (!$form_field_four)    $emptyfields++;
if (!$form_field_five)    $emptyfields++;
if (!$form_field_eight)   $emptyfields++;

if ($emptyfields > 0) {

   DisplayForm();        // Display the form again; the user forgot
                         // at least one required field.
} else {

ProcessFormInput();      // Process the form input; all required
                         // fields were present.

}
```

There is truly no limit to the degree of detail you can enforce in this arena. If you're a perfectionist at heart, for instance, you could force users to re-enter the name of their hometown over and over until they bother to capitalize it. (Many users nowadays write in all lowercase, if not in all caps. It's certainly odd, but as a web programmer, it's a fact that you should be aware of.) However, this would be very bad practice and would severely antagonize your users, so be sensible about it. If it's something you could deal with in code, then don't get your users to do it.

If you're expecting neat, orderly, properly formatted data to start flowing into your database from your web site users, you are out of luck. You will likely get as much (or more) input like "nyc" (or even "ny") and "la" and "san fran" and "skenekdedy" as you will of the more technically correct "New York City", "Los Angeles", "San Francisco" or "Schenectady" sort. All of these things can be checked for, with varying degrees of success and by code of varying degrees of complexity.

The degree to which you screen user-input data for mistakes should vary based on how great your need for properly formatted data is. If the only people who will end up using the data being input are the users themselves (for instance, on a Web-based e-mail system), you'll likely have no incentive to care whether the user spells or capitalizes things properly. On the other hand, if you're trying to do serious demographic research with said data, you should definitely do everything within reason to try to keep the data pool clean.

## Protection From Mischievous or Malicious Users

Hacking is an unpleasant fact of life. While it's unlikely your early applications will have to do anything as grand as protect credit card details or keep database information secure, even on simple forms you'll probably be required to bugproof your applications against mischievous users. We saw an example of this in Chapter 4, where we performed form validation. The same goes for just about any form in this book.

If you were to correctly fill in the form, but used HTML tags along with the text input, then these tags would be displayed and interpreted by the browser as though they were actually part of the source code. Now, you can see that if someone supplied some malicious HTML, or worse still a script, they could get our program to execute it for them.

As we explained, PHP provides a function to stop this happening, called HTMLSpecialChars.

```
$String = HTMLSpecialChars("<B>This won't display the Bold tags </B>");
```

This function converts any HTML tags into the actual text we wish to display, and thus stops any HTML tags entered from being interpreted by the browser as HTML. It also stops any script that has been entered in the text box from being displayed by the browser. This doesn't stop hacking, but it goes a little way to prevent malicious use of your PHP scripts.

# Receiving Input from Users

Now it's time to move into some more coding examples – ones that are slightly more useful in the "real-world". **Regular expressions** can make your life so much easier when checking user input. They're rather complex, but very powerful, so we'll give a short explanation of them now.

# Regular Expressions

Regular expressions allow us look for patterns in our data. A regular expression, often known as a "regexp", is simply a sequence of characters that we can use to describe the form of a sub-string that we wish to find within a piece of data. PHP gives us a number of regexp functions, to which we can specify a regexp and a data string to match it against. Certain characters adopt special meanings in the context of a regexp, allowing us to make generalizations about the sub-strings we wish to find in the data. Some will find characters belonging to a specified group; others find characters repeated a certain number of times.

Regular expressions necessarily follow certain rules of syntax, which we'll briefly outline in this section.

> *Regular expressions are not limited to PHP – languages such as Perl and Python, along with UNIX utilities like* sed *and* egrep *use the same notation for finding patterns in text.*

# Patterns

So what constitutes a pattern? And how do you compare it against something? The simplest pattern is a word – a simple sequence of characters – and we may, for example, want to find out whether a certain string contains that word. We can do this with the techniques we have already seen – we just explode() the string into separate words, and then test to see if each word is the one we're looking for. Here's how we might do that:

```php
<?php
//explode_find.php
$words = "one, two, three, four, five, six";

$wordarray = explode(" ", $words);
foreach ($wordarray as $word) {
    if ($word == "six") echo "Found string 'six'";
}
?>
```

It works (to some extent), but it's messy, complicated, and worse still, the explode() function (which converts the single string of words into an array) actually **keeps** all the punctuation – the string 'one' won't be found in the above, whereas 'one,' would. This looks like a difficult problem, but it should be easy. This is how it looks using a regular expression:

```
<?php
//ereg_find.php
$words = "one, two, three, four, five, six";
if (ereg("one", $words)) echo "Found string 'one'";
?>
```

That's much simpler, and what's more, it produces the correct result! We've used the PHP function ereg(), just specifying the pattern we want to match (that's the actual regexp) and the string we want to match it against. It returns True if the pattern match was successful (in this case, on finding the character sequence 'one' in the string held by $words) and False if it wasn't.

We can also specify a third argument in ereg(): the name of an array, which is used to store successfully, matched expressions. We can modify the last example to make use of it like this:

```
<?php
//ereg_find2.php
$words = "one, two, three, four, five, six";
if (ereg("one", $words, $reg)) echo "Found string '$reg[0]'";
?>
```

Literal text is the simplest regular expression of all to look for, but we needn't look for just the one word – we could look for any particular phrase. However, we need to make sure that we match *all* the characters exactly – words (with correct capitalization), numbers, punctuation, and even whitespace:

```
<?php
//ereg_find3.php
$words = "It's life Jim, but not as we know it!";
if (ereg("jim but", $words, $reg)) echo "Found string '$reg[0]'";
?>
```

This string won't match, because it's not an exact match for capital "J" and the comma. Similarly, spaces inside the pattern are significant:

```
<?php
//ereg_find4.php
$words1 = "The dog is in the kennel...";
$words2 = "...but the sheepdog is in the field";
$regexp = " dog";
if (ereg($regexp, $words1, $reg)) echo "Found string '$reg[0]'";
if (ereg($regexp, $words2, $reg)) echo "Found string '$reg[0]'";
?>
```

This will only find the first dog, as both ereg() calls are specifically looking for a space followed by the three letters "d", "o", and "g".

# Special Characters

Of course, regular expressions can be more than just words and spaces. There are various ways to specify more advanced matches – where portions of the match are allowed to be one of a number of characters for instance, or where the match must occur at a certain position in the string. In a moment, we'll look at the special meanings given to certain characters called metacharacters, and we'll find out what sort of things we can express with them.

## Escaping Special Characters

At this stage though, we may want to literally match the characters themselves. As we've already seen, we can use a backslash to escape certain characters' special meanings. For example, to echo a double-quote character ", we have to use the escape sequence \ ".

> **These are the characters that are given special meaning within a regular expression, which you will need to backslash if you want to use literally:**
>
> . * ? + [ ] ( ) { } ^ $ | \
>
> **Any other characters automatically assume their literal meanings.**

For example, if you want to specifically match " . . . " in the samples of text above, you'd have to say:

```php
<?php
//ereg_find5.php
$words1 = "The dog is in the kennel...";
$regexp = "kennel\.\.\.";
if (ereg($regexp, $words1, $reg)) echo "Found string '$reg[0]'";
?>
```

If you used the regexp "kennel...", you'd find it still matched the test string, but would *also* match in the following case:

```php
<?php
//ereg_find6.php
$words1 = "The dog is in the kennel but the sheepdog is in the field.";
$regexp = "kennel...";
if (ereg($regexp, $words1, $reg)) echo "Found string '$reg[0]'";
?>
```

This will return the following:

Found string 'kennel bu'

So what's going on? This is actually our first encounter with a special character – this particular one, " . " will match against any single character (apart from a new line). We therefore get a match for "kennel" followed by the next three characters, a space, followed by a "b" and a "u".

## Shortcuts And Options

There are several options available to us for weeding out erroneous information, matching strings, and whatever else we may require. We'll take a brief look through them now.

## Character Classes – [xyz]

These signify that any one of a *set* of characters is acceptable; we put the acceptable characters inside square brackets. For example, the regexp "w[ao]nder" will match against both the words "wander" and "wonder".

Conversely, we can say that everything is acceptable **except** a given sequence of characters – we can "negate the character class". To do so, the character class should start with a ^. For example, the regexp "^1234567890" will match against anything that isn't a number.

If, like here, the characters we want to match form a sequence in the ASCII character set, we can use a hyphen to specify a range of characters, rather than spelling out the entire range. For instance, our last example can be rewritten as [^0-9]. Alternatively, a lower case letter can be matched with [a-z].

We can use one or more of these ranges alongside each other, so if you wanted to match a single hexadecimal digit, you could write [0-9A-F]. Note that the brackets contain the whole expression. If we used [0-9][A-F] instead, we'd match a digit *followed by* a letter from A to F.

Some character classes are going to come up again and again, like digits, letters, and various types of whitespace. There are some neat shortcuts for these – here are the most common ones, and what they represent:

| Shortcut | Expansion | Description |
|----------|-----------|-------------|
| \d | [0-9] | Digits 0 to 9 |
| \w | [0-9A-Za-z_] | A "word" character. |
| \s | [ \t\n\r] | A whitespace character. That is, a space, a tab, a newline or a return. |

Also the negative forms of the above:

| Shortcut | Expansion | Description |
|----------|-----------|-------------|
| \D | [^0-9] | Any non-digit |
| \W | [^0-9A-Za-z_] | A non-"word" character |
| \S | [^ \t\n\r] | A non-blank character |

## Anchors

So far, our patterns have all tried to find a match anywhere in the string. We can dictate where the match must occur – that is, we can say "these characters must match the beginning of the string" or "this text must be at the end of the string", by **anchoring** the match to either end.

The two anchors we have are ^, which appears at the beginning of the pattern, anchoring a match to the beginning of the string, and $ appearing at the end of the pattern, anchoring it to the end of the string. So, to see if a string ends with a full stop (and remember that the full stop is a special character) we could use a regexp like this: "\.$". Likewise, we can use "^I" tell us if we have a capital "I" at the beginning of the string.

### Word Boundaries

As we saw above, one problem we can have with trying to match against text is that words don't always sit neatly between two spaces. They may be followed or preceded by punctuation, or appear at the beginning or end of a string, or otherwise next to non-word characters. To help us properly search for words in such cases, we can use the special \b metacharacter. Like the anchors above, it doesn't actually match any character in particular – rather, it matches the point between something that isn't a word character (either \W, or one end of the string) and something that is – hence \b for boundary. For example, we could look for one-letter words using the regexp "\b\w\b".

### Alternatives

Instead of just giving a single series of acceptable characters, you may want to say "match *either* this *or* that". The "either-or" operator in a regular expression is just the same as the bitwise "or" operator: |. So to match either "yes" or "maybe" we'd just use the regexp "yes|maybe".

### Qualifiers

What if we want to match against a set of characters that may occur once, may occur more than once, or may even not occur at all? Call in the **qualifiers**!

The easiest of these is ?, which matches the immediately preceding character(s) or metacharacter(s) – if they either appear once, or not at all. It's a good way of saying that a particular character or group is optional. To match the word "he or she", you can therefore use "s?he". To make a series of characters (or metacharacters) optional, group them in parentheses: you can match either "man" or "woman" with the regexp "(wo)?man".

As well as matching something one or zero times, you can match something one or *more* times. We do this with the plus sign – to match an entire word without specifying how long it should be, you can use "\w+".

If, on the other hand, you have something which may occur any number of times but might not be there at all (that is, zero or one or many) you need what's called "Kleene's star" (the * quantifier). So, to find a capital letter after any (but possibly no) spaces at the start of the string, we could use "^\s*[A-Z]".

Let's review the three qualifiers:

| | |
|---|---|
| bea?t | Matches either "beat" or "bet" |
| bea+t | Matches "beat", "beaat", "beaaat"... |
| bea*t | Matches "bet", "beat", "beaat"... |

Novice programmers tend to go to town on combinations of dots and stars, and the results often surprise them – bear the following in mind:

> **A regular expression should seldom, if ever, start or finish with a starred character.**

You should also consider the fact that .* and .+ in the middle of a regular expression, will match as much of your string as they possibly can.

## Quantifiers

Now say we want to match against a specific *quantity* of characters – three digits in a row, for example. The metacharacters we use to handle such situation are called **quantifiers**.

If you want to be more precise about how many times a sequence of characters is repeated, you can specify maximum and minimum numbers of repeats in curly brackets: \s{2,3}" will match against "2 *or* 3 spaces".

Omitting either the maximum or the minimum signifies "or more" and "or fewer" respectively. For example, {2,} denotes "2 or more", while {,3} is "3 or fewer". In these cases, the same warnings apply as for the star operator.

Finally, we can specify exactly how many things are to be in a row by putting just that number inside the curly brackets. For example, "\b\w{5}\b" will match a five-letter word.

## Summary of Metacharacters

Here's a summary of the metacharacters we've seen:

| Metacharacter | Meaning |
|---|---|
| [abc] | any one of the characters a, b, or c |
| [^abc] | any one character other than a, b or c |
| [a-z] | any one ASCII character between a and z |
| \d \D | a digit; a non-digit |
| \w \W | a "word" character; a "non-word" character |
| \s \S | a whitespace character; a non-whitespace character |
| \b | the boundary between a \w character and a \W character |
| . | any character (apart from a new line) |
| (abc) | the phrase "abc" as a group |
| ? | preceding character or group may be present 0 or 1 times |
| + | preceding character or group is present 1 or more times |
| * | preceding character or group may be present 0 or more times |
| {x,y} | preceding character or group is present between $x$ and $y$ times |
| {,y} | preceding character or group is present at most $y$ times. |
| {x,} | preceding character or group is present at least $x$ times. |
| {x} | preceding character or group is present $x$ times. |
| ^ | the beginning of the string |
| $ | the end of the string |

### e-mail Address Checking

Ask a random user what their e-mail address is, and there is a sizable chance that you'll get an answer like "JoeSmith9467". In reality, their e-mail address is JoeSmith9467@somehost.com. However, since many ISPs don't require you to tack on the "@somehost.com" when mailing between other people with the same ISP, there are users out there on the Internet right now who think that they possess an e-mail address containing neither an at-sign (@ often known as an "ampersat") nor a domain name.

This is obviously not true, and the username alone is not much use to you if you want to e-mail them, unless you happen to have the same ISP. Obviously, if you were asking Joe Smith for his e-mail address in real life, you'd stop him and ask for the full address. But what if he was being asked to give his e-mail address to a web form? Obviously, it would be a good idea to have the form check the email to see if it's in the correct format.

One would think that the solution to this dilemma would be simple – if an e-mail address doesn't contain an at-sign, simply assume that it ends in "@somehost.com". Problem solved, right? Well, not necessarily – there still exists the possibility that a user will accidentally enter the wrong piece of data into a field where they are asked for their e-mail address. For all of these reasons, it is important to ensure that wherever a user is asked for an e-mail address, their input matches the pattern (something) at (something) dot (something), with no spaces or additional "@" signs among the various "something"s.

Here is a regexp pattern that codifies the above definition of a properly formatted e-mail address:

```
^[^@ ]+@[^@ ]+\.[^@ \.]+$
```

*Note that this procedure is a simple one and by no means foolproof. There are proper e-mail address / URL parsing procedures out there and they can be very complex and longwinded.*

The above expression may look strange, but most regexps do until you're used to them. If a string matches this particular regexp pattern, then it should be a valid e-mail address. The following table shows how the pattern breaks down:

| Symbols | Matches |
| --- | --- |
| ^ | The beginning of the string… |
| [^@ ] | …there is one character, which can be anything other than an ampersat or a space |
| + | …which is repeated one or more times. |
| @ | There is then an ampersat. |
| [^@ ] | Next, there is one character that can be anything other than an ampersat or a space |
| + | …which is repeated one or more times. |
| \. | There is then a period. (which must be escaped) |
| [^@ \.] | Next, there is one character that can be anything other than an ampersat, a space, or a period |
| + | …which is repeated one or more times. The last one must be followed immediately by… |
| $ | …the end of the string. |

Now let's use this regexp with `ereg()` to check for a correctly formatted e-mail address.

## Try It Out – Checking For Correctly Formatted e-Mail Addresses

**1.** Start your web page editor up and type in the following:

```
<HTML>
<HEAD></HEAD>
<BODY>
<?php
//email_check.php

function emailcheck($intext) {
    $theresults = ereg("^[^@ ]+@[^@ ]+\.[^@ \.]+$", $intext, $trashed);
    if ($theresults) { $isamatch = "Yes"; } else { $isamatch = "No"; }
    echo("E-mail address check for \"$intext\": $isamatch<br>\n");
}

emailcheck("ImaUser18523");
emailcheck("ImaUser18523@ola.com");
emailcheck("Bogus User@bigmailhost.com");
emailcheck("Bogus@User@2@bigmailhost.com");
emailcheck("joebeer62432@somehost.com");

?>
</BODY>
</HTML>
```

**2.** Save this as `email_check.php`.

**3.** When run, this script should output the following, indicating which of the test addresses used in the script are, and which are not, properly formatted e-mail addresses:

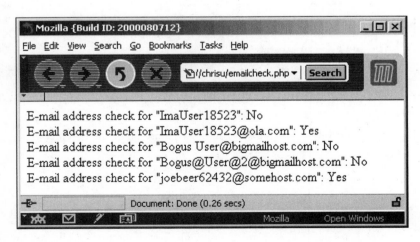

### How It Works

The "active ingredient" in this script is found in the very first line of `emailcheck()`, where `ereg()` is called with the aforementioned regexp pattern against the input address:

```
$theresults = ereg("^[^@ ]+@[^@ ]+\.[^@ \.]+$", $intext, $trashed);
```

If, after this line, `$theresults` is true, we know that our regexp pattern, which is designed to match any valid e-mail address, has been matched by the e-mail address given, and must be valid.

We just supply different fictitious e-mail addresses to our function to see if it works:

```
emailcheck("ImaUser18523");
emailcheck("ImaUser18523@ola.com");
emailcheck("Bogus User@bigmailhost.com");
emailcheck("Bogus@User@2@bigmailhost.com");
emailcheck("joebeer62432@somehost.com");
```

While this script can be used to ensure that the **format** of the address is valid, this doesn't necessarily guarantee that the address itself is any good at all. In fact, the regular expression we've used doesn't even guarantee a validly-formed address, since it allows characters after the @ sign which aren't, in fact, legal in a hostname ("*", for example). It also doesn't make any attempt to verify that the domain entered exists. "monkey@top.of.a.bananatree" validates as a properly-formed address. In other words, don't put this into your own applications as it stands, this is just to demonstrate the kind of things regexp can be used for.

### Checking the Format of Uniform Resource Locators Using Regexp

Another area of confusion for some novices is the concept of an "URL". Many users are unaware of the difference between a URL (such as http://www.myhostname.com/somedocument.html) and a domain name (like myhostname.com). What's worse, many users seem to think that the "www." is an automatic part of the beginning of **every** domain name, and some even go so far as to assume that all addresses end in ".com"!

The effects of these last two misconceptions can be seen in forms on domain registrar web sites around the globe, as they scramble to accommodate a world of misconceptions by making ".com", ".net", ".org", and the like available on a drop-down menu and displaying a prominent "www." before the field in which one enters one's requested domain name, thereby discouraging users from entering their "www." into the field itself.

The fact that the major browsers will happily accept a "URL" like "myhostname.com" (or sometimes even just 'myhostname') automatically inserting the necessary "http://" and ".com", doesn't help matters. The problem is that just like with e-mail addresses, today's users don't give a properly-formatted URL when asked for one.

Again, regexps to the rescue! This time, try this helpful (and highly aesthetically pleasing!) snippet:

```
^[a-zA-Z0-9]+://[^ ]+$
```

Similar to the key line in the last sample script, this expression can be used in a line like this:

```
$theresults = ereg("^[a-zA-Z0-9]+://[^ ]+$", $intext, $trashed);
```

In this example we'll be illustrating one way of checking URLs for correct formatting.

## Try It Out – Checking For Correctly Formatted URLs

**1.** Start your web page editor up and type in the following:

```
<HTML>
<HEAD></HEAD>
<BODY>
<?php
//urlcheck.php

function urlcheck($intext) {
    $theresults = ereg("^[a-zA-Z0-9]+://[^ ]+$", $intext, $trashed);
    if ($theresults) { $isamatch = "Yes"; } else { $isamatch = "No"; }
    print ("URL check for \"$intext\": $isamatch<br>\n");
}

# Main
urlcheck("www.whateverhost.com");
urlcheck("http://www.whateverhost.com/");
urlcheck("http://www.bogus host with spaces.com/");
urlcheck("http://www.abcd.cc/filenames should lack spaces.html");
urlcheck("http://www.abcd.cc/filenames%20should%20lack%20spaces.html");
urlcheck("ftp://ftp2.somegiantcompany.com/pub/largefiles/");
urlcheck("telnet://mytelnethost.org:8888");

?>
</BODY>
</HTML>
```

**2.** Save this as `urlcheck.php`.

**3.** When run, this script should output the following, indicating which of the test addresses used in the script are, and which are not, properly formatted URLs:

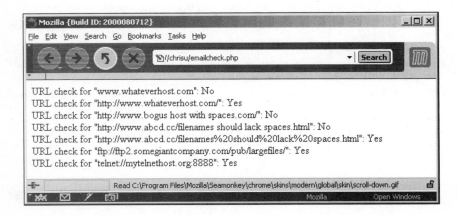

### How It Works:

Similar to `emailcheck.php`, this script is mostly powered by a single regular expression. Here's the first line of `urlcheck()`:

```
$theresults = ereg("^[a-zA-Z0-9]+://[^ ]+$", $intext, $trashed);
```

This checks the given URL against our regexp pattern, which is designed to match any valid URL. If `$theresults` is set to true, we know that the URL should be valid (or, at least, that our regexp pattern considers it valid!). Otherwise, we know that it should be invalid.

Our line of functions once again just supplies a list of test cases for the function:

```
urlcheck("www.whateverhost.com");
urlcheck("http://www.whateverhost.com/");
urlcheck("http://www.bogus host with spaces.com/");
urlcheck("http://www.abcd.cc/filenames should lack spaces.html");
urlcheck("http://www.abcd.cc/filenames%20should%20lack%20spaces.html");
urlcheck("ftp://ftp2.somegiantcompany.com/pub/largefiles/");
urlcheck("telnet://mytelnethost.org:8888");
```

Again, while this does checking for the above, the given regular expression allows some things through that wouldn't fly in a real system such as only checking for spaces following the "://", or the protocol ftphttptelnet://. If you're writing this kind of checking for your own system, then it's better to explicitly allow the things you want to accept, rather than trying to individually deny all the things that you don't want.

### File Path Parameters and Security

When scripting things in PHP, you will likely find that it would be simpler to merely store some or all of the data used by your script in ordinary text files, located in some directory on your web server's hard drive(s). Often there are situations where it would be convenient to specify which file is needed in the query string of an HTTP request. When allowing access to your system, it probably doesn't take very much from the user to browse your directory structure. If you're not careful though, this could become a tremendous security hole – users could request, to read "`../../../etc/passwd`" or the like, and thereby gain access to sensitive files on the server machine!

In this example, we'll stop users from going up the directory tree to more sensitive files, by removing potentially sensitive information from the file path.Again regexp comes to the rescue. This time though, it is the replacement functions like `ereg_replace()` that comes in handy. We can construct a function, `SanitizePath()`, which takes a file path and mangles it, if and only if, it is an attempt to jump "upwards" or "rootwards" in the directory tree by using "../", or by using a trailing slash ("/") or backslash ("\") (on UNIX systems, the trailing slashes are traditionally used where backslashes are used on UNIX systems, and colons are used on Mac OS systems.) Also, you need to remove any absolute paths, i.e. starting with "/" or [A-Z].

`SanitizePath()` is a simple function that prevents users from accessing any file further up in the directory tree than the directory the script is in. It will leave untouched only relative paths containing no "../" or "..\" patterns; all other sorts of path will be mangled into unusability, preventing users from ever accessing sensitive system files (or any files other than those in the script's directory, or its child directories for that matter). Let's get started.

## Try It Out – Preventing Users from Accessing Sensitive Files

**1.** Open your web page editor and type in the following:

```
<HTML>
<HEAD></HEAD>
<BODY>
<?
//sanitizepath.php

function SanitizePath($inpath) {
    $outpath = ereg_replace("\.[\.]+", "", $inpath);
    $outpath = ereg_replace("^[\/]+", "", $outpath);
    $outpath = ereg_replace("^[A-Za-z][:\|][\/]?", "", $outpath);
    return($outpath);
}

function SP($spinpath) { # A wrapper function used for display purposes.
    $spoutpath = SanitizePath($spinpath);
    print("Calling <b>SanitizePath()</b> on \"$spinpath\" yields
        \"$spoutpath\"<br>\n");
}

# Main
SP("/etc/passwd");
SP("myfilename.txt");
SP("mydir1/mydir2/mydir3/somefile.db");
SP("../../../../somefile.txt");
SP("............../........../mypath/sillyfile.txt");
SP("\windows\win.ini");
SP("C:\windows\system.ini");
SP("c|\windows\control.ini");
SP("C:/some/weird/path/filename.txt");
?>
</BODY>
</HTML>
```

**2.** Save this as `sanitizepath.php`.

**3.** When run, the program output should look like this:

As you can see, PHP can be used to filter out user input that is potentially dangerous as well as that which is simply incorrect.

### How It Works

The first line of `SanitizePath()` gets rid of ".." patterns (used to move up a level in the directory tree):

```
$outpath = ereg_replace("\.[\.]+", "", $inpath);
```

The second line eliminates trailing slashes or backslashes:

```
$outpath = ereg_replace("^[\/]+", "", $outpath);
```

The third line gets rid of DOS/Windows-style prefixes (for example "C:\"):

```
$outpath = ereg_replace("^[A-Za-z][:\|][\/]?", "", $outpath);
```

The fourth line returns the "sanitized" file path name:

```
return($outpath);
```

Our second function is for display purposes only. We pass the name of the file path, and then display the old and new paths within the function:

```
function SP($spinpath) { # A wrapper function used for display purposes.
    $spoutpath = SanitizePath($spinpath);
    print("Calling <b>SanitizePath()</b> on \"$spinpath\" yields
        \"$spoutpath\"<br>\n");
}
```

The rest of the code just provides some test cases for `SanitizePath()`:

```
SP("/etc/passwd");
SP("myfilename.txt");
SP("mydir1/mydir2/mydir3/somefile.db");
SP("../../../../somefile.txt");
SP("................/........./mypath/sillyfile.txt");
SP("\windows\win.ini");
SP("C:\windows\system.ini");
SP("c|\windows\control.ini");
SP("C:/some/weird/path/filename.txt");
```

# Debugging PHP Script

So you've done your best to make your code watertight; nevertheless, errors will always manage to seep through. So how do you go about removing the little blighters? One difficulty you might encounter when debugging is finding out exactly where the error is occurring. Remember the first PHP error we showed you? We tried to type the following:

```
   eco "Hello";
```

and ended up with a parse error. That's pretty easy to follow, but we've already mentioned that not all errors generate messages. Even if your error does generate a message, it is not always the line that is at fault that generates the error message (as in parse errors), it can easily be the line before or after it, or a line within a PHP programming structure that causes it. Let's look at some tips you can use to make your errors easier to find.

# Use echo()

This is one of the oldest methods of debugging, and involves putting in lots of trace statements that indicate where you are in a particular script. If you remember, echo() writes a line of text into the screen, so this will be seen as text when the page is viewed. For example, consider the following PHP script that expects some details from a form on the previous PHP page. You can start by echoing the details of variables you received or expected to receive from the form:

```php
<?php

  echo "Name is :$Name";
  echo "Email is :$Email";

  // do some complex processing with the form details

  // do more processing
?>
```

Let's suppose an error occurs in the "complex processing", and you have little idea what it is doing. Changing the script can help track down the problem:

```php
<?php

    echo "Name is :$Name";
    echo "Email is :$Email";
    echo "Debug: Now entering complex processing<BR>";

  // do some complex processing with the form details

  echo "Debug: Complex processing finished<BR>";

  // do more processing

  echo "<HR>More processing finished<BR>";
?>
```

Now, when you run this script you'll see the name and e-mail address displayed before the processing starts, and can tell you whether or not they are correct. If the last message does not appear, then you know that the error occurred before it got to this line.

Although a very simple idea it's extremely valuable, and is a technique I still use to debug complex PHP pages.

# Check the HTML Source

This second tip for debugging is just as simple as the first, but yet again can yield no end of hitherto "undetectable" errors. Occasionally, PHP will put the error messages in places where you don't want error messages, like the middle of some dynamically generated JavaScript, or inside an HTML tag. You can't read the error message on screen. The only way you'll come across this is to make sure you "view source" from the browser. For simple programs you could try submitting your code to the validation service at http://validator.w3.org.

Even if you don't always come across an error, the fact that the HTML source code doesn't end correctly with </BODY> or </HTML> tags might indicate that an error has occurred during the processing of the PHP script or HTML code and give you somewhere to start looking.

# Suppressing Error Messages

Not strictly a debugging tip, but sometimes you know about errors in your PHP script and you don't want to remove them at all, but ignore them or handle them separately. In this case there is a special notation that PHP uses; the @ notation when used with a function suppresses any mention of them. If you ran a function, such as our function `ProcessFormDetails`, with the @ symbol appended to it:

```
@ProcessFormDetails($Name, $Email);

function ProcessFormDetails ($Name, $Email)
{
    // do some processing here
}
```

then any errors within that function would not be returned. Of course, if the function has an error within it, it will still return a value zero. If the error is one that is fatal and would normally cause execution to halt, it will still stop the script, but it won't return any output. This might cause confusion, but this can still be a useful tool. You can then handle the error separately within your function and return a customized message to the user.

# Checking the Error Log

We mentioned very early in this chapter that PHP doesn't by default send error messages to the web server's error log. However, you might have taken this to infer that that PHP can log errors if you want it to, and you'd have been completely correct in this assumption. PHP can log to a file if you add the following directives to the php.ini file:

```
log_errors = On
error_log = /var/log/php.log
```

Secondly, there is also an `error_log` function within PHP that means that it's possible to have unexpected situations logged in the event that you haven't anticipated every possible situation and programmed a way to handle it. If you suppressed errors using the method mentioned previously, then you might also want to check any errors that occur.

The `error_log` function can take up to four arguments, but only two of them are actually compulsory. It has the following format:

```
error_log("Error Message", MessageType, "Destination", "Extra
Headers");
```

The error message is the actual error message received; the message type is the code signifying where you want this error message sent. There are four possible values:

- ❑    0      PHP error log
- ❑    1      e-mail address supplied in the third argument
- ❑    2      A PHP debugging connection – only when debugging has been enabled
- ❑    3      A destination log file, with the path specified in the third argument

The third argument takes either an email address or file path and the fourth argument can be used to send extra information in the form of email headers, when used with an e-mail address.

If you want further information about an error, such as when it actually occurred, then you can enable the error log or error log functions and check the information contained in the log.

## Doing the Hard Work Manually

Unfortunately, unlike some languages, PHP doesn't provide its own debuggers You'll probably have guessed from the above two examples, that the only way is to check the code by hand, line by line. There is unfortunately no easy way around this. Hopefully you can see that time spent designing, testing, and bugproofing your applications can save you a lot of time at the other end of the project, when you're about to deliver your software to the user.

# Summary

When it comes to error checking, the sky's the limit. You are constrained only by your available time and your coding skills. As has been demonstrated here, error checking is not only a way of avoiding unsightly and potentially security-damaging error messages – it is a way of ensuring that users give appropriate input whenever they are asked for it. The way in which you process that input is solely up to you. The "smarter" you make your script at recognizing and handling bad input, the better the source of data it is.

After reading this chapter, you should have a better understanding of the ways in which error handling can help make your site:

- ❑    More secure
- ❑    More reliable
- ❑    More aesthetically pleasing
- ❑    A better source of data

You should also be prepared to "role-play", to put yourself in the shoes of your users. Before you even submit your site to outside testing, you should go through the site, with a keen eye for detail, asking (as discussed in the chapter):

❑    How would my grandmother (or whoever) react to this?

❑    Where could users possibly submit incorrect data on any forms present, and how could you correct for it?

❑    How can I make my site clearer and less confusing to novice users?

❑    Is all sensitive data encapsulated and hidden out of the range of the overly inquisitive web visitor?

With a little planning (and, optionally, judicious use of regular expressions), error handling can make your site better in many ways. Just remember Murphy's Law: If something can go wrong, it will. With that in mind, try to one-up Murphy: Look for the places where things are most likely to go wrong, and modify your scripts accordingly. A little foresight now can save a tremendous amount of hassle later.

# Working With the Client

As the previous chapters have shown you, PHP offers a great number of advantages over plain old HTML for building web pages. One fundamental area that we've not yet looked at is **persistence** – the ability to retain information between two individual page requests from a browser.

Without any additional help, HTTP offers no mechanism for any data to be retained or processed between any two page loads – every page request is essentially a blank slate. To put it another way, HTTP is *stateless* – in other words, it cannot maintain a **state** or constant realm within which data can exist while the user interacts with the computer.

The ability to make data persist is by no means limited to PHP. We've already seen how it's possible to pass form data from one page to another without even straying beyond HTML. Nevertheless, that's rather a limited sort of persistence: once we leave the second page, the data's lost forever. Using PHP, we can explicitly tell the server to send back data in such a way that it won't be lost. As we'll see, there are several ways in which we can do this.

To truly take advantage of PHP's power, we require a good grasp of how PHP can be used to interact with the user and their browser, in order to overcome HTTP's inherent statelessness, and allow for the creation of truly interactive sites. This is the subject of this chapter. The topics we will cover include:

❑   HTML and HTTP, their limitations, and how PHP overcomes them

❑   Persistence of user data – preserving data we need between HTTP requests

❑   "Do It Yourself" persistence mechanisms

❑   The use of cookies

❑   PHP4's native sessions – a built-in mechanism for providing persistence

This chapter contains material that should be useful to virtually anyone new to the creation of medium- to large-scale interactive sites using PHP. It contains examples of a variety of tools you should have in your mental toolbox. The goal of this chapter is to teach you what you need to learn to create interactive sites which display persistence of user data – the holding of one or more variables between HTTP requests. It can be as simple as putting the current user's name at the top of each page they look at; the emphasis is on continuity of behavior.

# Making the Most of a Stateless Protocol

In the beginning, Tim Berners-Lee created HTTP, and what it did, it did well. The embryonic Web served an important role as a worldwide network of static content connected by hyperlinks. The key word here, however, is **static**. Despite the many advantages of a hypertext-based, platform-independent standard over earlier methods of disseminating documents, the content of the early Web essentially amounted to nothing more than a large pile of static documents. On today's Web, interactivity is the key, and technologies like PHP contribute towards creating this interactivity.

The reason that the early Web was static is simple: HTTP, or "HyperText Transfer Protocol", is a simple, stateless protocol, designed – as the name implies – merely for the transmission of hypertext. Surely no one in 1991 would have guessed that that very same hypertext – ordinary HTML code – would soon be used to deliver complex, interactive *applications* through the medium of HTTP!

Nevertheless, organizations (and ultimately even individuals) began demanding that their web servers support some sort of user-interaction, rather than simply serving up old-style static pages. After all, however useful a static online catalog may be, it's a lot more attractive to impatient customers and impulse-sale-savvy marketers alike, if users can actually **buy** products via the Web. What's more, if it can remember your preferences – for example, whether you prefer a graphics-heavy version of the site, or a cut down text-only version – you're more likely to come back again and again.

This doesn't only apply to commerce. Sites can remember the type of news that interests you, the level of moderated discussion threads you like to see, the region you requested a weather report for, and so on. They're all more likely to win a return visit by tailoring themselves to your particular tastes, and this depends on the ability to remember what you've done before – in other words a data persistence mechanism.

We're now going to take a quick overview of the ground covered in this chapter. Don't worry if everything doesn't click into place first time around – there's a lot to take in, and we'll look at it all in a lot more detail later on.

# Talking to the User – HTTP, HTML, PHP and Interactivity

When we talk about introducing interactivity, what we're ultimately trying to achieve is a better "data driven experience" for the user. To do this, we need to consider two things:

❑ How to dynamically change the web pages depending on the previous pages selected, or on other factors such as the time of day

❑ How to track what came before, so that users can tell a website something, and the website can respond to them individually, simultaneously, and perhaps anonymously. This can initiate a series of such user-website interactions, in which data is continually passed back and forth between the user and the website (in other words, data persistence).

A web server without support for any of the various technologies used to make web sites fully interactive – the most common are PHP, CGI and ASP – is a very simple beast indeed. For the most part, all it can do is receive a user request and respond immediately to it, with no thought involved: the name of the game here is **request-response**. As the figure opposite illustrates, a basic web server like this does no more than take a page request and grant it, then take another and grant it, then take a third and grant it, and so on. You might liken it to a fast-food restaurant where the staff don't have time to make small talk, and therefore won't recognize you from one visit to the next. Every request is completely separate from every other, likewise every response. No data is stored between requests, so very little interactivity is possible.

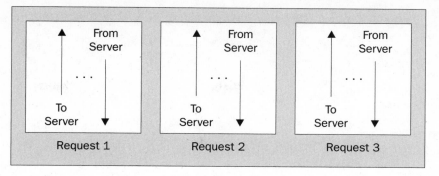

Request 1          Request 2          Request 3

That might be fine if all you want to do is serve up a fan page for your Great Aunt Millie, but if you want to create a dynamic web site – one that interacts with users, rather than merely proffering large amounts of static content – it's not good enough.

The problem boils down to HTTP's design. Since it wasn't designed with interactivity in mind, it's not well suited for that purpose – not on its own, that is. Interactive software generally works as depicted in the next figure; that is, with a continual interaction between user and program. Think of a more expensive restaurant, where the waiter not only takes your order but remembers which table to bring it to. (If you go back a few times, the staff may even get to know your regular order!) The user makes a selection, and the program responds; the user makes a mistake, and the program chastises them; the user types something in, and the program processes it appropriately; and so on.

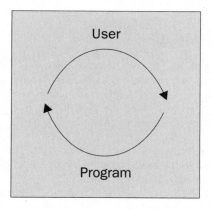

A basic web server isn't quite up to this task, so we add a little PHP magic. PHP and similar technologies are quite capable of storing data between user requests in a variety of ways, permitting interactivity and dynamic generation of pages to a degree impossible with plain old HTTP and HTML.

As we'll see in this chapter, PHP is able to bridge the gap between each request-response and the next, providing persistence of data – and hence true, prolonged interactivity. The next figure depicts this peculiar relationship between the HTTP request-response pairs and PHP (or CGI, ASP, or whatever).

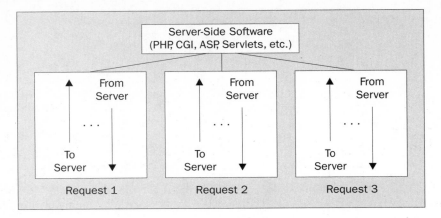

This process of continually updating the server with information, a key ingredient in most interactive sites, is necessary to maintain a **session**. This is how we refer to a series of interactions, beginning with the user accessing or logging on to a site, and ending with the user logging out or being timed out for inactivity.

The key to this process is usually a **cookie** (a small piece of data stored on the client's computer) or some sort of a variable that the client and server pass back and forth, often called a **session key**. These cookies and keys are used to help the server know which client it is interacting with for any given request. Just as a username identifies a user to a system, a session key (or an appropriate cookie) identifies a client to a web site.

## Native Sessions in PHP4

Way back when everyone was still using PHP3, user sessions would be managed by PHP code that had to be individually written by each site administrator. Tools created and distributed by free-software enthusiasts helped to lessen the programming load on each admin, but the point remained that if you wanted to do sessions with PHP3, you'd either have to "roll your own" session-handling routines, or try to understand a possibly cryptic solution created by others. PHP3, in short, had no **native** session handling.

That might have been fine if you had a lot of time on your hands, but most people wanted an easier solution. Fortunately PHP4 came to the rescue. Since the release of PHP 4.0, the core PHP language has included support for PHP's own native style of sessions.

Later on in this chapter, we'll take a proper look at PHP4's session support. However, before we do so, we're going to go through some of the main techniques that it uses "under the covers" to get around the problem of HTTP's inherent statelessness. By the time we actually get on to PHP4 sessions, you should have a good understanding of the concepts we've just introduced, the role that PHP actually provides, and how it performs that role.

# "Do It Yourself" Persistence

We're going to start off by looking at a number of ways in which you can make your data persist from one page request to the next. In many respects, this is a lot more flexible (not to mention educational) than using PHP4's sessions, which hide a lot of the implementation details from you. Sessions have their place, as we shall see later on, but they're sometimes too heavy-duty, or inappropriate for our purposes. Principally though, we're going to look at the following methods as a means to understanding how certain elements of session handling work.

# Hidden Form Fields Revisited

We've already seen how we can use form fields to pass data back from the client to the server. Hidden form fields are just like other form fields; only they are designed to lack any visible controls for the user. As they are merely part of an HTML document, they do not involve storing anything on the client's computer (as cookies do) **or** on the server's computer. Until you decide to commit the data stored in these variables to disk, the information stored in them exists solely in the memory occupied by the client's browser.

Hidden form fields are declared in forms. After all, they **are** form elements, just like the more familiar text, password, radio button and dropdown list box elements. We declare them like this:

```
<INPUT TYPE=HIDDEN NAME="myvar" VALUE="myvalue">
```

We saw in Chapter 3 that we can use them to store static data, which is made available to whichever script is called when the form is submitted. This is the first step on the way to creating multi-page forms, a common use for hidden form fields. Sometimes, for various reasons (often sheer aestheticism), it's preferable to break up a large form into several sections, which the user fills out sequentially, selecting Continue... or More... or Go on... to move from one to the next. These forms are very common in "Sign Up" or "Register" pages across the Web.

Say we have a sequence of three forms, each of which takes input from the user. When the user has filled in Form 1, they submit it, and their entries are passed on to the next form in the sequence. Form 2 will also have fields to be filled in, and has no problem passing *its* values on to Form 3. But how do we pass data from Form 1 to Form 3?

It's simple: we just define hidden fields in Form 2, and use the values passed by Form 1 to specify their values. The following example does exactly that.

## Try It Out – Persistence via Hidden Form Fields

This simple example uses three scripts to take food orders at "Charlie's Restaurant" and present an itemized bill. To keep it concise, we're only considering a single order for one entrée and one dessert, but it serves to illustrate the technique nevertheless.

**1.** Enter the following script and save it as `menu1.php`:

```
<HTML>
<HEAD><TITLE>Welcome to Charlie's</TITLE></HEAD>
<BODY>
<?php
```

```
$Entrees=array("Steak ($9)", "Pizza ($7)", "Pasta ($6)");

echo "<FORM METHOD=POST ACTION='menu2.php'>";
echo "Which of the following would you like as an entree?";
echo "<SELECT NAME='ListBox1'>";
echo "<OPTION SELECTED VALUE=''>Select...</OPTION>";
echo "<OPTION>$Entrees[0]</OPTION>";
echo "<OPTION>$Entrees[1]</OPTION>";
echo "<OPTION>$Entrees[2]</OPTION>";
echo "</SELECT><BR><BR>";
echo "<INPUT TYPE=SUBMIT>";
echo "</FORM>";
?>
</BODY>
</HTML>
```

**2.** Enter this script and save it as `menu2.php`:

```
<HTML>
<HEAD><TITLE>Welcome to Charlie's dessert selection</TITLE></HEAD>
<BODY>
<?php

$Desserts=array("Apple Pie ($3)","Pancakes ($3)","Ice Cream ($2)");

echo "<FORM METHOD=POST ACTION='bill.php'>";
echo "Which of the following would you like as a dessert?";
echo "<SELECT NAME='ListBox2'>";
echo "<OPTION SELECTED VALUE=''>Select...</OPTION>";
echo "<OPTION>$Desserts[0]</OPTION>";
echo "<OPTION>$Desserts[1]</OPTION>";
echo "<OPTION>$Desserts[2]</OPTION>";

echo "</SELECT><BR><BR>";
echo "<INPUT TYPE=HIDDEN NAME=Course1 VALUE='$ListBox1'>";
echo "<INPUT TYPE=SUBMIT>";
echo "</FORM>";
?>
</BODY>
</HTML>
```

**3.** Now save the following code as `bill.php`:

```
<HTML>
<HEAD><TITLE>Thank you for dining at Charlie's</TITLE></HEAD>
<BODY>
<?php
$total = 0;

echo "Your order was for the following:<BR><BR>";
echo "Entree: $Course1<BR>";
echo "Dessert: $ListBox2<BR><BR>";

foreach (array($Course1, $ListBox2) as $val) {
      if (ereg("[0-9]+", $val, $regs)) $total += $regs[0];}

echo "TOTAL BILL = $" . $total . "<BR>";
```

```
?>
</BODY>
</HTML>
```

**4.** Close the file and open up `menu1.php` in your browser:

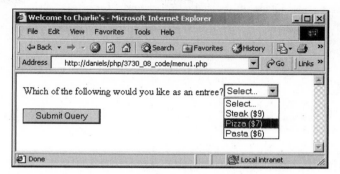

**5.** Choose an entree from the dropdown list box, and then click on **Submit Query**:

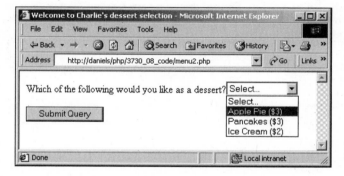

**6.** Select a dessert and submit your choice. You should see the bill for your meal:

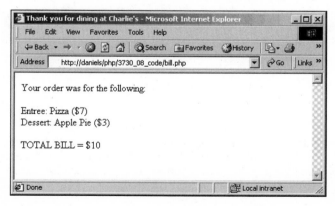

## How It Works

Okay, that's quite a lot of code to make a pretty small point. However, it's not that different from what we did with hidden form fields in Chapter 3. Let's strip it down and take a look at the crucial bits.

Our first script `menu1.php` barely even qualifies as a PHP script – it's only the fact that we've defined our selection of entrees in an array that stops us writing it as pure HTML. Nevertheless, PHP it is, and we use the array `$Entrees` to specify available options in a list box:

```
$Entrees=array("Steak ($9)", "Pizza ($7)", "Pasta ($6)");

echo "<FORM METHOD=POST ACTION='menu2.php'>";
echo "Which of the following would you like as an entree?";
echo "<SELECT NAME='ListBox1'>";
echo "<OPTION SELECTED VALUE=''>Select...</OPTION>";
echo "<OPTION>$Entrees[0]</OPTION>";
echo "<OPTION>$Entrees[1]</OPTION>";
echo "<OPTION>$Entrees[2]</OPTION>";
echo "</SELECT><BR><BR>";
echo "<INPUT TYPE=SUBMIT>";
echo "</FORM>";
```

When we click on the **Submit Query** button, the next script, `menu2.php`, is called, and our entree selection is passed on as the variable `$Listbox1`. Now for more of the same. We define an array of available desserts, and present each value as an option in a list box:

```
$Desserts=array("Apple Pie ($3)","Pancakes ($3)","Ice Cream ($2)");

echo "<FORM METHOD=POST ACTION='bill.php'>";
echo "Which of the following would you like as a dessert?";
echo "<SELECT NAME='ListBox2'>";
echo "<OPTION SELECTED VALUE=''>Select...</OPTION>";
echo "<OPTION>$Desserts[0]</OPTION>";
echo "<OPTION>$Desserts[1]</OPTION>";
echo "<OPTION>$Desserts[2]</OPTION>";
echo "</SELECT><BR><BR>";
```

Now, this is the crunch point. Before we specify a **Submit** button for the form, we add a hidden field called `Course1`, whose value is defined as `$Listbox1`. The `$Listbox1` variable still contains the entree selection from `menu1.php`, so by doing this we ensure that this value will persist through to the next script that we POST to:

```
echo "<INPUT TYPE=HIDDEN NAME=Course1 VALUE='$ListBox1'>";
echo "<INPUT TYPE=SUBMIT>";
echo "</FORM>";
```

Once more, the **Submit Query** button moves us on to the next script, in this case `bill.php`. This will list the dishes ordered in the previous scripts and give us the total cost of the food. Since `menu2.php` stored the choice of entrée in a hidden field called `Course1`, we can now get at it via the variable `$Course1`. The chosen dessert now occupies `$Listbox2`:

```
echo "Your order was for the following:<BR><BR>";
echo "Entree: $Course1<BR>";
echo "Dessert: $ListBox2<BR><BR>";
```

The final part of our example takes advantage of the fact that we've added prices to the end of the dish descriptions. We scan through the list (okay, there are only two entries here) extracting each dollar price with an ereg() pattern match, and (if there is one) adding it to $total. We finish off by echoing out the total bill:

```
foreach (array($Course1, $ListBox2) as $val) {
        if (ereg("[0-9]+", $val, $regs)) $total += $regs[0];}

echo "TOTAL BILL = $$total<BR>";
```

Don't be confused by the two $ signs in $$total; the first is displayed on the screen, and then PHP recognizes that what is left is $total, so it displays the contents of this variable – the total bill.

## A More Versatile Method

Hopefully you'll have got the last example to work without any hitches. Sure, it makes a point, but what about when "Charlie's" decides to expand beyond six dishes, two courses and one customer? Extending this example will not only involve adding extra scripts, but also adding new lines to each of the original ones.

We're now going to take a quick look at one way around this problem, using the associative array $HTTP_POST_VARS which we met in Chapter 5. At any given time, this array will contain a complete list of the variables passed to the current page by a POST type form. The elements of the array contain the values of the hidden variables; each value is indexed by the corresponding variable name. Therefore, the value for $number is placed in the element with index "number". By storing all the values which need to be made persistent in an array, we make it much easier to extend the pages as and when required.

Let's modify menu1.php so that the value we want to persist is posted as PERS_Entree:

```
...
echo "Which of the following would you like as an entree?";
echo "<SELECT NAME='PERS_Entree'>";
echo "<OPTION SELECTED VALUE=''>Select...</OPTION>";
echo "<OPTION>$Entrees[0]</OPTION>";
...
```

We then move on to menu2.php, and make two changes. The first is a similar change to above:

```
...
echo "Which of the following would you like as a dessert?";
echo "<SELECT NAME='PERS_Dessert'>";
echo "<OPTION SELECTED VALUE=''>Select...</OPTION>";
echo "<OPTION>$Desserts[0]</OPTION>";
...
```

For the second change we must also replace our definition of the hidden field `Course1` as follows:

```
...
echo "<OPTION>$Desserts[2]</OPTION>";

echo "</SELECT><BR><BR>";

if ($HTTP_POST_VARS) {
    while (list($lvar, $lvalue) = each($HTTP_POST_VARS)) {
        if (ereg ("^PERS_", $lvar, $throwaway) ) {
            echo "<INPUT TYPE=HIDDEN NAME='$lvar' VALUE='$lvalue'>\n";
        }
    }
}

echo "<INPUT TYPE=SUBMIT>";
echo "</FORM>";
...
```

So what's going on here then? These few lines of code pack in a lot of rather complex processing, but what they actually do is pretty straightforward. The `while` loop takes us through the contents of `$HTTP_POST_VARS`, two values at a time. Each pair of consecutive elements holds the name and value of a `POST` variable respectively, and these we store in `$lvar` and `$lvalue`.

We use `ereg()` to test whether the variable name stored in `$lvar` starts with the characters `"PERS_"`. If it does, we echo out a hidden field with *exactly the same* name and value attributes that we just read from `$HTTP_POST_VARS`. In this case, that's just going to be our `$PERS_Entree` field. So how do we benefit by doing it this way? Let's finish off the example and update `bill.php` before answering that – hopefully it will be obvious by the time we're done.

The changes we need to make here are similar to those above; we loop through the POST variables two at a time, testing whether each name begins with the letters `"PERS_"`. However, this time we don't need to create hidden form fields; we just have to echo out the name and value, so that each appears on the bill. (We'll leave it as an exercise for you to strip off the unwanted leading characters from the name.)

```
echo "Your order was for the following:<BR><BR>";

if ($HTTP_POST_VARS) {
    while (list($lvar, $lvalue) = each($HTTP_POST_VARS)) {
        if (ereg("^PERS_", $lvar, $throwaway) > 0) {
            echo "$lvar: $lvalue<BR>";
            if (ereg("[0-9]+", $lvalue, $regs)) $total += $regs[0];    }
    }
}

echo "TOTAL BILL = $$total<BR>";

?>
</BODY>
</HTML>
```

Apart from now using `$lvalue` to match on, the original `ereg()` call remains just the same, taking advantage of the `while` loop to step through each of the dishes ordered.

If you now call up `menu1.php` once again, and run these modified scripts, you should see exactly the same results as before (give or take the odd "PERS_" creeping in). Nevertheless, what we now have is a whole lot more useful than our original example. Why? Because now, any variable we post with a name like "PERS_#######" will **automatically** persist right through the chain, from start to finish.

No? Okay, you've caught me out; that last statement isn't strictly true. Not just yet anyway, as we've not done anything to allow for variables being posted to `menu1.php`. To make good on this, we just have to add a copy of the `while` loop from `menu2.php`. This is our automatic persistence mechanism, which you must now add to `menu1.php`:

```php
echo "</SELECT><BR><BR>";

if ($HTTP_POST_VARS) {
    while (list($lvar, $lvalue) = each($HTTP_POST_VARS)) {
        if (ereg("^PERS_", $lvar, $throwaway)) {
            echo "<INPUT TYPE=HIDDEN NAME='$lvar' VALUE='$lvalue'>\n";
        }
    }
}

echo "<INPUT TYPE=SUBMIT>";
```

To check it out, let's call `menu1.php` from a new script, called `waiter.php`. This can be used by the waiter (or waitress) to initiate the ordering process, and will add their name to your itemized bill. Note that we include our auto-persistence code in this script – we can't say for sure that we won't want to call *this* from elsewhere at some time in the future:

```php
<HTML>
<HEAD><TITLE>Register new customer order here</TITLE></HEAD>
<BODY>
<?php
//waiter.php

echo "<FORM METHOD=POST ACTION='menu1.php'>";
echo "Please enter your name:";
echo "<INPUT NAME='PERS_Waiter' TYPE='text'><BR><BR>";

if ($HTTP_POST_VARS) {
    while (list($lvar, $lvalue) = each($HTTP_POST_VARS)) {
        if (ereg("^PERS_", $lvar, $throwaway) > 0) {
            echo "<INPUT TYPE=HIDDEN NAME='$lvar' VALUE='$lvalue'>\n";
        }
    }
}

echo "<INPUT TYPE=SUBMIT>";
echo "</FORM>";
?>
</BODY>
</HTML>
```

Try running it, and you should end up with something like this:

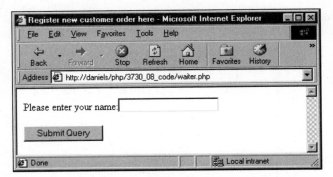

Enter a name – say "Chris" – in the text box, and once you've gone through the stages of selecting an entrée and dessert, that name will show up on the final bill:

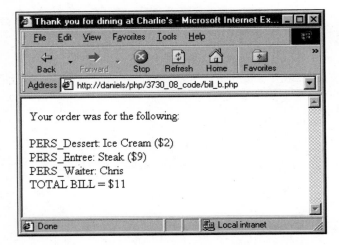

And that's all there is to it! Now that we've put this small but effective persistence mechanism into each of the scripts, we can add all the layers and functionality we like, secure in the knowledge that as long a variable's posted as a PERS_ field, it will persist for as long as the chain of forms continues unbroken.

Ah! This brings up an issue that we've so far taken for granted – what if we can't assume an unbroken chain of forms? There are actually two parts to this question, and the first is this: "What if we want data to persist, but aren't using forms?" We'll look at one available solution to this problem in the next section.

*The second part of the question presents us with a much bigger problem: getting data to persist even when the chain of page views is broken. We'll deal with that later on, when we introduce cookies.*

# Query Strings

Let's start this section by taking a proper look at our first problem: we want to make our data persist, but without using forms. Why would we want to limit ourselves like this, when forms offer us such a good way to do what we want? Well, we could give a number of reasons, but most would come back to the same basic issues:

❑ Forms are rather bulky creatures, both in terms of code size and screen presence.

❑ Different browsers will present forms in different ways, so it's quite difficult to ensure that your interface will work well for all potential users.

In more hands-on terms, if you want to give the user a lot of different options that they can simply click on, your interface isn't going to benefit from a forest of Submit buttons. If you want to present a single, consistent interface, that offers the user a lot of possible actions, it's often best to get back to basics and use hyperlinks. After all, that's what the Web has been built on; and even given the other options now available, simple is still best in many cases.

We've already seen how to use query strings to pass data from one page to another. The examples we'll see here won't be that much more sophisticated than those we saw in Chapter 3. However, by looking at them in the context of persistence of data, you'll hopefully gain some additional insights along the way. We shall also see some useful techniques that will benefit us later, when we look at more advanced examples.

As we know, passing query strings is pretty simple. If our earlier examples had used GET forms instead of POST, we would have seen all our persistent variables being passed in precisely this way:

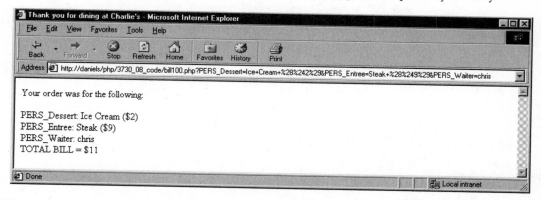

We simply add the variables' names and values onto the end of the URL, using ? to mark the start of the definitions, and & to delimit each of them. Of course, there are complications with this method of passing variables, especially from characters which need special URL encoding. For example, spaces are represented by +, while other characters have memorable names like %28, %29 and %24 (these represent the left and right parentheses and the dollar sign respectively).

Rather than trying to justify every possible reason for using query strings rather than forms to make data persist, we'll now look at a program which uses them in a context where forms simply wouldn't be practical. It should help you appreciate how they can offer us a similar level of functionality, but in a much more lightweight manner. Ladies and gentlemen, please take your seats – we're going to play a game.

## Try It Out – Using Query Strings to Play "Hangman"

This game should be familiar to you – it's a guessing game where the player picks letters, one at a time, to try and reveal a mystery word. Every time they select a letter that occurs in the word, all instances of that letter in the word are revealed. Whenever they pick a letter that isn't in the word, another line is drawn on a picture of a stick man hanging from gallows. Twelve lines make up the complete picture (OK; strictly speaking eleven lines and a circle), after which the player loses the game. If they manage to guess the word (or, by sheer chance, select all the right letters) before that, they win. What fun!

You may be surprised to discover that we're going to do all this in a single script – this is where our persistent variables come into play. We have one page, which we'll reload every time the user picks a letter. Obviously it will need to look slightly different each time it's loaded, but this will almost exclusively depend on which letters have been picked. By calling the script with a URL query string that contains all these letters, we can regenerate the page from scratch every time.

Enough of the talk – let's have a look at the code. We'll explain it in depth afterwards.

**1.** We start the script `hangman.php` by defining some essential variables.

```
<HTML>
<HEAD><TITLE>Hangman</TITLE></HEAD>
<BODY><DIV ALIGN = 'center'>

<?php
//hangman.php

$alphabet = array("A","B","C","D","E","F","G","H","I","J","K","L","M",
                  "N","O","P","Q","R","S","T","U","V","W","X","Y","Z");

$words = array("AARDVARK", "INDIGESTION", "CALCULATOR",
               "PERISTALSIS", "VERMILLION", "MNEMONIC");
$wrong = 0;

if (!isset($word_number)) { $word_number = rand(1,count($words)) - 1; }
```

**2.** We then loop through the letters in our mystery word, displaying any that have been guessed.

```
echo"<H1>";
$word = $words[$word_number];
$finished = 1;
for ($i=0; $i < strlen($word); $i++) {
  if (ereg($word[$i], $letters)) {
    echo $word[$i];
  }
  else {
    echo "_";
    $finished = 0;
  }
}
echo"</H1>";
```

**3.** If none of the letters remain to be guessed, the user has won the game.

```
if ($finished) {
  echo "<BR><BR>Congratulations! You win!<BR><BR>";
  echo "<A HREF=$PHP_SELF>Play again</A>";
```

**4.** If not, we build up a list of letters in `$links`. This is a mixture of selected letters (plain text, but formatted according to whether they show up in the mystery word) and unselected letters, which are hyperlinks.

```
    }
    else {
      foreach ($alphabet as $var) {
        if (ereg($var, $letters)) {
          if (ereg($var, $words[$word_number])) {
            $links .= "<B>$var</B>  ";
          } else {
            $links .= "$var  ";
            $wrong++;
          }
        }
        else {
          $links .= "<A HREF=\"$PHP_SELF?letters=$letters$var
                                      &word_number=$word_number\">
                  $var
                  </A>  ";
        }
      }
    }
```

**5.** We use the variable `$wrong` to count the number of wrong guesses. We show an appropriate picture of the hangman, finish if `$wrong` has reached twelve, and display the alphabetical links otherwise.

```
    echo "<BR><IMG SRC=\"./hangman$wrong.gif\"><BR>";

    if ($wrong == 12) {
      echo "<BR>HANGMAN!!<BR><BR>";
      echo "The word you were looking for was \"$word\"<BR><BR>";
      echo "<A HREF=$PHP_SELF>Play again</A>";
    } else {
      echo "Tries remaining = ".(12-$wrong)."<BR>";
      echo "<BR>Please pick a letter.<BR><BR>";
      echo $links;
    }
}
?>
</DIV></BODY>
</HTML>
```

**6.** Run the script, select a few letters, and you should see something rather like this:

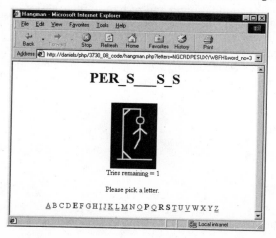

### How It Works

The power of this script lies in its ability to figure out the current state of play from nothing more than a list of letters, every time it runs. We therefore make things easy for ourselves, by giving it an array of letters to loop through. When we come to figure out what's what, we can simply look at each value in $alphabet and figure out its current status in light of the letters chosen and the actual mystery word.

```
$alphabet = array("A","B","C","D","E","F","G","H","I","J","K","L","M",
                  "N","O","P","Q","R","S","T","U","V","W","X","Y","Z");
```

That's what we come to next:

```
$words = array("AARDVARK", "INDIGESTION", "CALCULATOR",
               "PERISTALSIS", "VERMILLION", "MNEMONIC");
```

Yes, it's a bit of a cheat, hardwiring a rather limited vocabulary into the script like this. Couldn't we just let a user specify a word to use before the game starts – perhaps so that they can challenge a friend to figure out their own choice of mystery word?

The short answer is no. The trouble is this: we need the mystery word string data to persist from the first try of a game to the last – it wouldn't be much of a game if the word kept changing! Since we'd be using a query string to pass this data, it would be on display for all to see at *every* stage of the game. Likewise, it wouldn't be much of a challenge if the answer were staring you in the face from the very start.

> This is a significant and widely recognized drawback to the use of query strings. Any and all information you want to pass is on public display. However, this can also be an advantage. It means that people can save the query for later use, for example by "bookmarking" it. This means that the user can get straight back to a page of search results, for example, with a single click. They can also copy out the query from the address bar and send it to a friend via e-mail.

Our way around this problem is to define a vocabulary array, so that specified words can be identified by integer values. These values can be safely passed in the query string without needing even to hint at the actual word. (Of course with only six values, you won't be holding your breath very long – you'll probably spot the same words coming round and recognize their indices before even making a guess. We leave it up to you to find ways of expanding the program's vocabulary.)

The variable $wrong, which we'll use to count incorrect guesses, is set to zero, and if we've not chosen a word already (in other words we're starting a new game, with a plain and simple call to hangman.php), we pick an index $word_number to use. This will be used to specify one of the words in the array $words.

```
$wrong = 0;

if (!isset($word_number)) { $word_number = rand(1,count($words)) - 1; }
```

We now get ready to display each of the letters in the mystery word. We use Header 1 style to make it stand out, and put our mystery word into a handy variable called $word (really just for the sake of clarity). We then set a flag to tell us that we've finished finding letters in the word. Finished? But we've barely got started yet! That's quite true, and we'll see in a moment why we've done this.

```
echo"<H1>";
$word = $words[$word_number];
$finished = 1;
```

We use a `for` loop to look at each of the mystery letters in turn. We try and match each one against `$letters`, the string of letters selected by the player. If a match is found, the letter is displayed. If not, an underscore is used to mark the space, and `$finished` is set to `False`, indicating the game isn't over yet.

```
for ($i=0; $i < strlen($word); $i++) {
  if (ereg($word[$i], $letters)) {
    echo $word[$i];
  } else {
    echo "_";
    $finished = 0;
  }
}
echo"</H1>";
```

This is where the `$finished` flag earns its keep. We have set the `$finished` flag to `True` just before the loop. When we first loop through the mystery letters, we won't have anything to match against – consequently, we'll print a whole string of underscore characters, and along with each, we set the `$finished` flag to `False`. This way, `$finished` will only remain `True` at the end of the loop if *all* the mystery letters have been matched; that is, when the user has successfully guessed all the letters in the word.

If none of the letters remain to be guessed, the user's won the game.

```
if ($finished) {
  echo "<BR><BR>Congratulations! You win!<BR><BR>";
  echo "<A HREF=$PHP_SELF>Play again</A>";
```

Otherwise, we start building up an alphabetical list of letters in the variable `$links`. The letters in this list will either be: unformatted, indicating an unsuccessful guess; formatted in bold, indicating a successful guess; or **hyperlinked**, indicating that the letter hasn't been guessed yet.

For each letter in the alphabet (here's where that `$alphabet` array comes in handy) we use `ereg()` to test whether it's a letter that has been selected. In other words, does it match any of the characters in `$letters`?

```
} else {
  foreach ($alphabet as $var) {
    if (ereg($var, $letters)) {
```

If it does match, we perform a similar test to see whether the current letter actually occurs in the mystery word – was it a successful guess or an unsuccessful one? If it was successful, we format the letter in a `<B>` style and append it using `.=` to a variable called `$links`; otherwise, we append it without any formatting, and increment the `$wrong` count of wrong letter guesses:

```
if (ereg($var, $word)) {
  $links .= "<B>$var</B>  ";
```

```
      }
      else {
        $links .= "$var   ";
        $wrong++;
      }
```

If the current letter hasn't been selected, we echo it out as a hyperlink to $PHP_SELF. This global variable holds the name of the current script. This simply means that we've created a link back to hangman.php. We append (using .=) the current letter (held in $var) to the other guessed values stored in $letters, so that if the player follows this link, the appropriate letter registers as a guess on the new version of the page. We also specify word_number=$word_number, so that our mystery word selection persists to the new page:

```
    else {
      $links .= "<A HREF=\"$PHP_SELF?letters=$letters$var
                                 &word_number=$word_number\">
              $var
              </A>   ";
    }
  }
```

Now that we've looped through every letter in the alphabet, the variable $wrong contains an accurate count of wrong guesses. First, we use this variable to specify an image file to display.

```
    echo "<BR><IMG SRC=\"./hangman$wrong.gif\"><BR>";
```

If $wrong reaches twelve, we tell the player that they've lost, and display the mystery word.

```
    if ($wrong == 12) {
      echo "<BR>HANGMAN!!<BR><BR>";
      echo "The word you were looking for was \"$word\"<BR><BR>";
      echo "<A HREF=$PHP_SELF>Play again</A>";
```

Otherwise, we tell them how many tries they have left, and display the alphabetical links that we stored in $links.

```
    }
    else {
      echo "Tries remaining = ".(12-$wrong)."<BR>";
      echo "<BR>Please pick a letter.<BR><BR>";
      echo $links;
    }
  }
  ?>
  </DIV></BODY>
  </HTML>
```

## A Useful Way to Organize your Code

We've just seen how query strings can be used to make a single script modify its behavior from one call to the next. The hangman example demonstrates how easy it is to dynamically format the page contents according to a bare minimum of specified data. However, it's not just the formatting that we can modify with query strings – we can completely change a script's functionality.

One very convenient technique is to specify a variable (commonly called $action) in the query string, which we then use as the argument for a switch statement. Depending on the value assigned to $action, the script will follow one of several paths, which can be completely independent of one another.

Let's use our previous two examples to illustrate this point. We'll write a script that lets us choose which of the examples we want to run. If we don't specify an action (or specify an invalid action), it defaults to display a simple page giving us the valid options as hyperlinks.

```php
<?php
//selector.php
switch ($action)
{
    case "order_food":
        include "./waiter.php";
    break;
    case "play_hangman":
        include "./hangman.php";
    break;
    default:
        echo "Please choose what you'd like to do:<BR>";
        echo "<A HREF=$PHP_SELF?action=order_food>Order Food</A><BR>";
        echo "<A HREF=$PHP_SELF?action=play_hangman>Play Hangman</A>";
}
?>
```

We include the earlier scripts in this way simply to avoid having to specify them again from scratch. You can specify the contents of the case clauses in virtually any way you want – as we'll see in later chapters, it's often most useful to have each clause call a sequence of predefined functions.

Try it out, and you should see the following options:

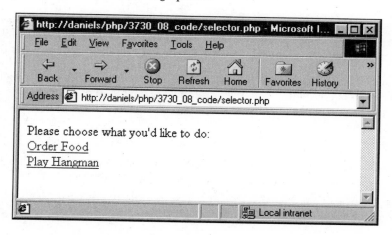

If we select the first option, we can run the sequence of food ordering scripts just as before. However, if we use this to execute the hangman game, we quickly run into trouble. The first screen appears as we'd expect, but as soon as we pick a letter, we're sent back to the selector screen. This underlines a very important point: in each case, the code we call is *part of* the selector program.

The food option has no problems, because the files we called from `waiter.php` were hard-coded into the original file; when we request `menu1.php`, it doesn't matter where we do it from. On the other hand, the hangman code makes extensive use of $PHP_SELF to call *itself*. If we run it from the selector though, $PHP_SELF naturally refers to `selector.php`. Note that we can get round this very simply, by adding `action=play_hangman` to each hyperlink in the hangman code.

You'll recall we ended the last section by raising an important issue; namely, how do we make data persist if we can't assume an unbroken chain of forms? We've covered one part of that question, by getting rid of any reliance on forms to do our dirty work. However, the other problem remains: so far all our persistence mechanisms have either relied on storing it in the pages themselves, or posting data to the server. However, although the server generates a response containing the data, it has no way to associate that data with any subsequent requests, making it useless thereafter.

We're now going to introduce a very convenient way around this problem: cookies.

# Cookies

So what *are* cookies? They're a quick (and some would say messy) method of storing, on the client's computer, small snippets of data that we want to persist between separate visits to a website. They aren't very powerful or reliable – you certainly wouldn't want to use them for permanent data storage, as the mere act of switching browsers will completely obliterate all your old cookies – but they can be very handy for a wide variety of things. Some of the most common examples of cookie use include things like:

❑ Storing a user's aesthetic preferences for a specific site.

❑ Storing a user key (or keys) that can be used to link users with their personal data – as used in countless "shopping basket" features, for example.

❑ Providing a semi-permanent "session key", allowing a user to remain "logged on" to a site until they explicitly ask to leave it or the browser is closed.

Cookies are best used for small, helpful but non-critical things. One of the best examples of cookie use is to store preferences describing how a user wants your site to appear. Although the ability to customize a site's color scheme is a nice perk for users, those who can't (or won't) use cookies won't be missing much.

Intended as innocuous "helpers" for web developers, cookies have built up a bad reputation in recent years. They are often overused (for example, to store large quantities of data which is really best kept on the server end) and sometimes even abused (to gather information on consumers without their knowledge, for instance). If used sparingly and responsibly though, cookies can be useful in a number of situations. They tend to be most useful:

❑ In situations where you know for a fact that all the visitors to your site will have cookie support enabled, for instance on corporate and educational intranets.

❑ To add "bells and whistles" to a site – features that add to a site's appeal but aren't required to make use of it.

## Messing Around With Cookies

Exact details of how cookies are implemented vary from browser to browser, but certain important points apply across the board, and these are as follows:

- A cookie is a short piece of data that can be used to store a variable's name and value, along with information on the site from which it came and an expiry time

- Cookies provide client-side storage, usually held in files on the client machine's hard drive

- Web sites can usually only modify their own cookies

- They can be accessed and (if the appropriate security criteria are met) altered at will by the web server from which they were originally sent.

When a client accesses a web site that uses cookies, the web server will tell the client (usually a web browser) to store away a given piece of data for later use. The client is then responsible for storing that data away. Cookie-supporting browsers accomplish this by storing the data in a file named after the site the cookie belongs to, in a directory they keep reserved for this purpose. On subsequent requests to that site, the client will send back a copy of that data – the data persists on the client side until a specified expiry period elapses, causing it to be removed from the system. This expiry period is set by the server when it tells the client to create the cookie, and is basically a number of seconds for which the client should keep the cookie. If the server tells the client to set an expiry period of zero seconds, this means the browser should only keep the cookie until the user quits the browser application.

Of course, since cookies are kept on the client side, they're not under the control of the server once they've been created. Users can elect to delete cookies themselves, often simply by clicking a button in their browser, or by deleting the browser's cookie files. They could also edit the contents of the files if the urge took them. Just because you wrote what's in the cookie, doesn't mean you should always expect the right data to come back!

Essentially, cookies are the server telling the client "here's something to remember; remind me of it when you come back next time" – "next time" could be anything from 'when you click on that link in two seconds from now "to" when you come back next week'. That's some serious persistence! It's a little like being at a conference, where delegates can be identified by their name badges for as long as they care to leave them on.

Web servers send clients cookies in HTTP headers, which are sent before any HTML text. Likewise, clients send back those cookies using HTTP headers. A client knows which cookies to share with a web site, based on the server and path the client is currently accessing. So, if you're accessing www.php.net, the browser doesn't send any cookies it received from www.wrox.com.

When a cookie is set, a server name and path name can optionally be set – this will limit access to the cookie to the specified server and/or path on that server. Clients use this information to determine whether or not they should send any given cookie. A cookie-enabled browser will generally send any and all cookies that it thinks applicable to a given site in the headers of any given access.

Before we go on to the sample code, though, let's finish with the basics – setting cookies, then retrieving them later. PHP, as a modern web scripting language, comes with full support, and setting cookie variables is as simple as making a call to setcookie(). As with header(), this must be called *before* any HTML is printed to the client's browser, as the cookies are set in the HTTP headers, which must be sent before any HTML.

`setcookie()` takes six parameters, of which the first three are by far the most important. These are, in order:

❑ A string to be used as the name of the variable.

❑ A string to be used as the value of the variable.

❑ A UNIX timestamp denoting the time at which the cookie will expire.

*A UNIX timestamp is simply a long integer that represents a time and date by counting seconds since midnight on 01/01/1970. We can get the current time in this form by using the function* `time()`. *If we want to set a cookie that would expire an hour from now, we could simply specify* `time()+3600` *for the third parameter.*

The remaining three parameters to `setcookie()` are less frequently used. They are:

❑ The path to whose files the cookie is relevant; the browser will not return cookies that are from inappropriate paths. For example, if you set this parameter to `/my/path/number/one` and accessed a page in `/my/path/number/two`, your browser wouldn't send the cookie. If you then went back to a page in `/my/path/number/one`, the browser would send the cookie.

❑ The domain to which the cookie applies; same rules applying as to the specified path above. This parameter may be useful if your web server hosts multiple domains.

❑ An integer called `secure` – set it to 1 if you only want your cookie to be sent when requesting an SSL-encrypted page. (The cookie won't be stored in an encrypted form on the client's hard drive – this merely ensures that it will be encrypted for transmission across the Internet.)

In the simplest possible situation, you might simply leave off these last three, so a typical call to `setcookie()` might look like this:

```
setcookie("fontprefs", "", time()+3600);
```

Accessing cookies is even simpler – there's nothing to call at all! Just as it does with POST variables, PHP automatically puts cookie information in the global domain, so it's as simple to use cookie values as it is to use any other variables. For example, a received cookie called `fontprefs` will automatically be available throughout the script as the global variable `$fontprefs`.

There are several ways to delete a cookie. Of course, if the client knows where to look on their machine, they can always edit or delete the files in which they're stored. However, it's sometimes useful to be able to get the server to delete (or "eat") a cookie, and if this is the case, there are two main options:

❑ Reset the cookie's expiry time to a time in the past, for example:
```
setcookie("num", "0", time()-9999);
```

❑ Reset the cookie, specifying only its name, for example:
```
setcookie("fontprefs");
```

## Try It Out – Using Cookies to Store User Preferences

We'll now look at a script that stores user-selected choices for font size and typeface in a cookie. On subsequent visits to the page, the cookie is examined, and the preferences stored in it remain in effect. Save the code as `cookie_test.php`.

**1.** Before doing anything else, we test for POST variables, and set cookie data accordingly.

```php
<?php
//cookie_test.php

if ($type_sel) setcookie ("font[type]", $type_sel, time()+3600);
if ($size_sel) setcookie ("font[size]", $size_sel, time()+3600);
```

**2.** We define some options for font size and typeface, and as it's now safe to add an HTML header, we do so:

```php
$type = array("arial", "helvetica", "sans-serif", "courier");
$size = array("1","2","3","4","5","6","7");

echo "<HTML><HEAD><TITLE>Cookie Test</TITLE></HEAD><BODY><DIV ALIGN = 'center'>";
```

**3.** The following form contains a pair of listboxes, which can be used to specify the user's preferences:

```php
echo "<FORM METHOD=POST>";
  echo "What font type would you like to use? ";
  echo "<SELECT NAME='type_sel'>";
    echo "<OPTION SELECTED VALUE=''>default</OPTION>";
    foreach ($type as $var) echo "<OPTION>$var</OPTION>";
  echo "</SELECT><BR><BR>";

  echo "What font size would you like to use? ";
  echo "<SELECT NAME='size_sel'>";
    echo "<OPTION SELECTED VALUE=''>default</OPTION>";
    foreach ($size as $var) echo "<OPTION>$var</OPTION>";
  echo "</SELECT><BR><BR>";

  echo "<INPUT TYPE=SUBMIT>";
echo "</FORM>";
```

**4.** Finally, we echo out some useful information, and format it using appropriate settings:

```php
echo "<B>Your cookies say:</B><BR>";
echo "<FONT ";
  if ($font[type]) echo "FACE=$font[type] ";
  if ($font[size]) echo "SIZE=$font[size] ";
echo ">";
  echo "\$font[type] = $font[type]<BR>";
  echo "\$font[size] = $font[size]<BR>";
echo "</FONT><BR>";

echo "<B>Your form variables say:</B><BR>";
echo "<FONT ";
  if ($type_sel) echo "FACE=$type_sel ";
  if ($size_sel) echo "SIZE=$size_sel ";
echo ">";
  echo "\$type_sel = $type_sel<BR>";
```

```
      echo "\$size_sel = $size_sel<BR>";
echo "</FONT>";

echo "</DIV></BODY></HTML>";

?>
```

### How It Works

The two lines currently of most interest to us also happen to be the first two functional lines in the script. Remember that the cookies are set in the HTTP headers, so we have to place these calls before outputting any HTML:

```
if ($type_sel) setcookie ("font[type]", $type_sel, time()+3600);
if ($size_sel) setcookie ("font[size]", $size_sel, time()+3600);
```

We test the variables $type_sel and $size_sel to find out whether there's anything to set. If these variables exist, it's because they have been posted by the user preferences form (which we'll take a look at below); they'll correspond to the typeface and font size preferences just submitted by the user. Note that by calling the cookies font[type] and font[size], we effectively define $font as an associative array. We won't be using this property, but it's quite useful to be aware of nevertheless.

We specify the expiry time for each cookie as one hour from the current system time, as returned by time().

We define a pair of arrays containing available font sizes and typefaces; the list boxes we subsequently put into the form use these arrays to specify all the possible options. When we Submit the form, the values chosen will be posted as variables $type_sel and $size_sel.

```
echo "<FORM METHOD=POST>";
  echo "What font type would you like to use? ";
  echo "<SELECT NAME='type_sel'>";
    echo "<OPTION SELECTED VALUE=''>default</OPTION>";
    foreach ($type as $var) echo "<OPTION>$var</OPTION>";
  echo "</SELECT><BR><BR>";

  echo "What font size would you like to use? ";
  echo "<SELECT NAME='size_sel'>";
    echo "<OPTION SELECTED VALUE=''>default</OPTION>";
    foreach ($size as $var) echo "<OPTION>$var</OPTION>";
  echo "</SELECT><BR><BR>";

  echo "<INPUT TYPE=SUBMIT>";
echo "</FORM>";
```

Finally, we echo out the cookies and the posted form variables to show how their values change as we make our selections. We format the variables displayed using their respective values.

```
echo "<B>Your cookies say:</B><BR>";
echo "<FONT ";
```

```
    if ($font[type]) echo "FACE=$font[type] ";
    if ($font[size]) echo "SIZE=$font[size] ";
  echo ">";
    echo "\$font[type] = $font[type]<BR>";
    echo "\$font[size] = $font[size]<BR>";
  echo "</FONT><BR>";

  echo "<B>Your form variables say:</B><BR>";
  echo "<FONT ";
    if ($type_sel) echo "FACE=$type_sel ";
    if ($size_sel) echo "SIZE=$size_sel ";
  echo ">";
    echo "\$type_sel = $type_sel<BR>";
    echo "\$size_sel = $size_sel<BR>";
  echo "</FONT>";
```

Nothing too tricky there – let's now have a look at what it does. When you run `cookie_test.php` for the first time, this is what you should see:

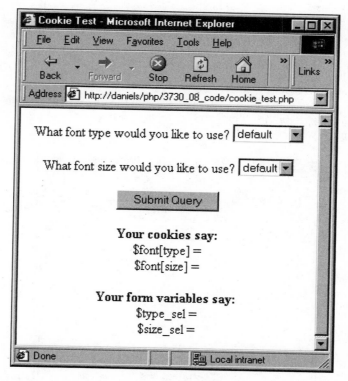

If you make a selection from each of the list boxes and click on the Submit Query button, you'll get something like the screenshot overleaf:

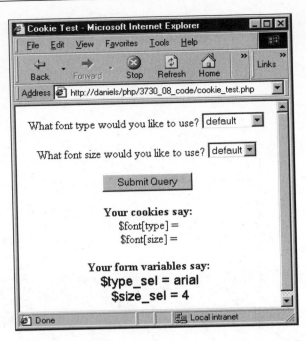

So what does this tell us? The form variables $type_sel and $size_sel have now been updated with the inputs selected in the previous form – in this case, with the typeface arial and font size 4. Note however that the cookies are both still empty. Don't worry though, they're present alright – all you need to do now is refresh the page:

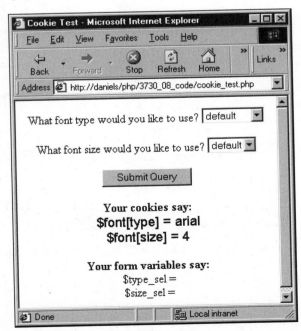

Now it's the form variables that are empty. This shouldn't come as much of a surprise, as we already know that these values won't persist without some sort of special intervention to make them do so. It's the cookies that are behaving rather unexpectedly here. Why couldn't we see them the first time round?

It's actually not that complicated – when the client initially submits their formatting choices, the form variables $type_sel and $size_sel are posted to the server. The server responds by preparing to execute cookie_test.php again. It sets up environment variables (which will include $type_sel and $size_sel) which it will use in the course of running the script. At this point in the proceedings, there are no cookies, so there's no way to define $font[type] and $font[size]. The only place the cookie data exists is in the HTTP header of the script that's about to be run.

When the script is run, this header information is sent to the client, which responds by extracting the cookies and putting them somewhere safe. This is too late, however, to have any effect on the output from the script, so we see no evidence of their existence.

Refreshing the view means that the client requests the cookie_test.php script again. This time though, the cookies exist on the client machine. The client will spot that it has a pair of cookies from that particular host, so they're sent along with the script request to the server. When the server prepares to execute the script again, it has cookies to draw on for additional data, and uses the values they specify for variables $font[type] and $font[size].

Now that the cookies have been stored on the client machine, they'll persist for another hour or so (barring accidents). Any time you care to revisit cookie_test.php during that period, you'll find the same cookie settings you left behind. In fact the same applies to any other scripts you run from the same host – if they use either of the variables $font[type] or $font[size] (that is, without having redefined them), these will automatically adopt the values that are recorded in the cookies.

Note that if we'd specified a specific domain or path when we created the cookies, we would have localized this effect to scripts executed from the specified locations.

# Sessions

We've now seen a number of different techniques that we can use to make data persist. Now that we've looked at what actually goes into a persistence mechanism, we are more able to appreciate what's going on when we talk about sessions.

We can define a **session** as a series of related interactions between a single client and the web server, which take place over an extended period of time. This could be a series of transactions that a user makes while updating their stock portfolio, or the set of requests that are made to check an e-mail account through a browser-based e-mail service. The session may consist of multiple requests to the same script, or of requests to a variety of different resources on the same web site.

Particularly when we want to work with sensitive (or bulky) information, it makes a lot of sense to submit it once and have it stored on the server. Rather than storing the actual data on the client machine, and have to pass it back and forth between the server and client each time, it's far more practical to keep the data on the server only, but give the client a "key" to allow it to uniquely identify itself, and consequently any server-side data associated with it. We call this key a "session identifier"; it uniquely associates a client with a session, and therefore with their data.

We've already seen how to establish a session of sorts – when we used cookies to make data persist on the client machine. As we pointed out at the time though, this isn't a terribly secure way to manage sessions. The metaphor we used before – of conference delegates and their persistent name badges – could be taken a step further. What if it wasn't just names, but credit card details that were shown on the badges; they surely wouldn't stay on many lapels for very long!

# PHP4 Sessions

Fortunately, PHP comes with its own session management system built in, so we don't need to worry too much about the precise implementation details. However, one detail needs to be introduced before we go any further. The **session identifier** (commonly known as **SID**) is a special variable that is specified as a reference number for any particular session. You can think of it as being like the reference number on an electric bill: you're given the number, the electric company files your details under that number, and hey presto: you no longer have to give them all your details every time you call up to complain about their outrageous charges.

When you start a PHP session, the server will assign it a SID. Any variables that you register as **session variables** (we'll see how to do this in a moment) will be stored **on the server** in a cookie-like file. (The name of this file will generally be the same as the value of the SID.) All the client has to do to access this data is to include the SID in their request to the server. They can use a hidden form field, a query string, a cookie, anything at all, as long as the SID makes it into the HTTP request. The server can then look up the appropriate session data and make it available for use in whatever script it then executes.

If you have cookie support enabled, even this is taken care of, as the session manager will automatically send the client a cookie for the SID value. If you can't (or don't want to) use cookies, the simplest thing to do is to add "SID" as a term in all query strings that point back to your web site.

PHP4 sessions handle this all very neatly; they're an excellent way to learn how to build interactive sites quickly, as they completely free you up from worrying about the nitty-gritty details of implementing persistence, and instead let you get on with the business of building your site. One particularly nice aspect is the knowledge that you have literally thousands of coders scrutinizing your persistence mechanism (as it's a part of PHP4 itself!) and ensuring that the underlying code works as well as possible. What's more, they're very well documented in the core PHP documentation, available at the official PHP web site (http://www.php.net/). So – it's easy, reliable, and almost universally available; but how exactly do we use it?

In most cases, using PHP4 sessions is as simple as telling PHP "I want variables X, Y and Z to remain persistent" and letting PHP do the dirty work. All that you, the coder, need to worry about is how to tell PHP to register a session variable – that is, make a given variable persistent – and then how to access those variables.

The function we use to register a persistent variable for use with PHP4 sessions is `session_register()`. Given the name (without the dollar sign) of a variable, it will make that variable and its contents persist for the duration of the current session. If there isn't currently a session defined, a new one will be created automatically.

Let's say you wanted to maintain persistent variables called `myvar1` and `myvar2`. You'd begin your PHP script thus:

```
<?php
session_register("myvar1");
session_register("myvar2");
?>
```

I *do*, by the way, mean **begin** – we must put this code at the *top* of the script. Behind the scenes, we're using cookies. Once again, in order not mess with HTTP headers, we must be sure to register all the session variables before any HTML headers are sent out. It's good practice to do so at the very top of a script, in a self-contained snippet of PHP, as we show here.

Once you've registered a variable, retrieving its contents is ridiculously simple – just access the session variable as if it were any other global variable! If we've used the code above to register variables $myvar1 and $myvar2, we can subsequently use them just like any other variables. The only difference is that they persist for as long as the session lasts – that is, the next time the page is called within the session, by the same user, they will contain the same values they had when the page finished executing last time.

> *In order to use PHP4 sessions with Windows, you may find you need to modify the variable* session.save_path *in your* php.ini *file, so that it refers to a valid Windows directory (*C:\WinNT\Temp *for example).*

## Try it Out – Counting Page Accesses

With that in mind, it's on to some more code. Let's examine a sample use for PHP sessions – counting the number of times a user has accessed pages on a website since the start of the current session. This task is easily accomplished using PHP4 sessions, with various counters (one for each page on the site) made persistent by registering them with session_register():

**1.** The four calls to session_register() at the top of the script comprise everything that needs to be done with regard to the session variables. The other code we see here is simply for aesthetic purposes – as the various "counters" will be printed out, it would be nice if they are set to "0" and not an empty string when they've not yet been incremented.

```
<?php
session_register("view1count");
session_register("view2count");
session_register("view3count");
session_register("view4count");
?>

<?php
//page_count.php

if (!$view1count) $view1count = 0;
if (!$view2count) $view2count = 0;
if (!$view3count) $view3count = 0;
if (!$view4count) $view4count = 0;
```

**2.** The rest of the script illustrates how to make hyperlinks that hand PHP what it needs to access your session data – namely, SID.

```
echo "<HTML><HEAD><TITLE>Web Page Hit Counter</TITLE></HEAD><BODY>";

if ($whichpage) {
  echo "<B>You are currently on page $whichpage.</B><BR><BR>\n";
  $GLOBALS["view${whichpage}count"]++;
}

for ($i = 1; $i <= 4; $i++) {

  if ($whichpage == $i) {
    echo "<B><A HREF=\"$PHP_SELF?".SID."&whichpage=$i\">Page $i</A></B>";
  } else {
    echo "<A HREF=\"$PHP_SELF?".SID."&whichpage=$i\">Page $i</A>";
  }
  echo ", which you have chosen ".$GLOBALS["view${i}count"]." times.<BR>\n";
}

echo "\n\n<BR><BR>\n\n";
echo "</BODY></HTML>";

?>
```

Run the script and change pages a few times; this is what you should see:

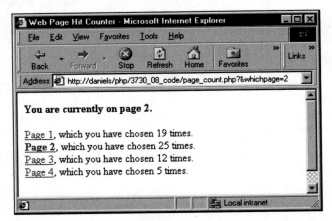

More to the point, if you now visit a bunch of other pages and then run the script again, you'll find that these numbers will have persisted. Only when you shut down the browser will the session end.

### How It Works

We start this simple program by using `session_register()` to register four session variables. We place them in a separate block of PHP code (starting with `<?php` and ending with `?>`) to make it clear that they sit before anything else, and don't fall foul of any HTML headers.

```
<?php
session_register("view1count");
session_register("view2count");
```

```
session_register("view3count");
session_register("view4count");
?>
```

We then begin the main block of PHP. If any of the view counts is undefined, we set it to zero, so that we can be sure that each contains a number that we can echo out later on.

```
<?php
//page_count.php
if (!$view1count) $view1count = 0;
if (!$view2count) $view2count = 0;
if (!$view3count) $view3count = 0;
if (!$view4count) $view4count = 0;
```

Once we've echoed out an HTML header, we test $whichpage (denoting which page we're currently on) to see if it's defined. If it is, we use its value to display an appropriate message and determine which page's view count variable we need to increment.

```
if ($whichpage) {
  echo "<B>You are currently on page $whichpage.</B><BR><BR>\n";
  $GLOBALS["view${whichpage}count"]++;
}
```

You may be wondering why we use the $GLOBALS array here, and exactly what we're doing. We're simply making use of the fact that $GLOBALS lets us refer to a global variable by specifying its name as a string argument. This, along with the fact that we can use braces { } to mark the limits of the variable name (in this case "whichpage"), means that if $whichpage has the value 1, we increment the variable $view1count; likewise if $whichpage is 2, we increment $view2count; and so on.

We now begin a for loop that cycles through each of the four pages we want to use. We display a link for each, along with a message that tells the user how many times that page has been visited during the current session. The link to the current page is displayed in bold type.

```
for ($i = 1; $i <= 4; $i++) {

  if ($whichpage == $i) {
    echo "<B><A HREF=\"$PHP_SELF?".SID."&whichpage=$i\">Page $i</A></B>";
  } else {
    echo "<A HREF=\"$PHP_SELF?".SID."&whichpage=$i\">Page $i</A>";
  }
  echo ", which you have chosen ".$GLOBALS["view${i}count"]." times.<BR>\n";
}
```

Each of the links specifies three things: the current script (as specified by $PHP_SELF), the current session (as identified by SID), and the page to which we want to link. (Ah! So that's where $whichpage comes from!) And that's it. All the session handling code we had to worry about was there in the first four lines. It could hardly be simpler!

# Summary

HTTP is a stateless protocol, so a web server doesn't automatically know how to associate data with a given request. There are two ways we can get around this:

❑ Send the data to the client, and make it send that data back alongside each request it makes.

❑ Get the client to identify itself every time it makes a request; then store and retrieve data relating to that client from some store on the server.

The client could provide the data we are referring to, by submitting forms, for example. Alternatively the server can generate it – for example, by recording requests the user has made. The source of the data is unimportant though. What we have to work out is how we are going to share this data between the different requests that the user makes. The most basic (though not necessarily the easiest) way to share session data is by using either **query strings** or **hidden form fields**. Both of these techniques write data into the HTML they send to the browser, in a way that forces the browser to include it with its next request – either as additional data alongside a form, or as parameters appended to the end of the URL.

There are several disadvantages to using query strings. For large amounts of session data, the URL can get lengthy and out of control. You may also run into some environment limitations as to how long your URL can be. Another problem with this is privacy related. Often, you may not want the actual data you are tracking to be visible. By sending it along with the URL, it is exposed to the user, anyone looking over the user's shoulder, as well as anyone who may happen to intercept the request or view it in the browser's history window. Nevertheless, query strings have a significant advantage over other options: since the data they're passing is included in the URL, they can be bookmarked, data and all, for future reference.

With hidden form fields, the same disadvantages apply as did with query strings; with a couple of exceptions. Since the values are stored as hidden form fields, an HTTP POST request eliminates *some* of the privacy problems as well as the environment limitations present when appending fields to an HTTP GET request. However, anybody who is sufficiently curious can discover exactly what data you are tracking about him or her by viewing the HTML source code. Remember also that HTML pages travel freely across the Internet on their way from the server to the client, leaving copies of themselves in cache servers over which neither you nor the client have any control. This can create security holes, particularly if the data tracked relates to user identification, so this technique, like the previous one, should be used with care.

The data can also be transferred using **cookies**, which are short text strings stored on the client machine and sent by the browser to the server along with subsequent requests. Cookies originate on the server, where they are sent as instructions in the header of the HTTP response. The instruction tells the browser to create a cookie with a given name, which has a given value. If the browser already has a cookie with that name, from that server, the value will be changed to the new one. The browser will then send the cookie back with any requests it subsequently makes to that same server. Cookies can have expiry dates set, after which the browser will stop sending the cookie.

The benefit of using cookies is that they are more intuitive than hiding data in a URL or a form. They don't involve us duping the browser into sending data back to us – the browser is participating deliberately in the process. There are still problems with using cookies though. Cookies can be used to track users over much longer periods of time than one short session – in fact, they can be used to track every request made to your site by a specific user. Some people worry that this means the administrators of web sites can gather too much information about which web pages they view, and so switch off the cookie function of their browsers. Older browsers may not even support cookies. If you rely solely on cookies to pass session data between requests, then your entire application could be rendered useless. It's therefore important to minimize the amount of data you store in cookies, and make sure your site will function acceptably without them.

With PHP though, we have another option. Using the session handling functions it provides, we can create **sessions** and use a session identifier, or SID, to associate HTTP requests with data stored on the server. By specifying the SID in subsequent requests, this data is made accessible to any scripts the user calls until we end the session.

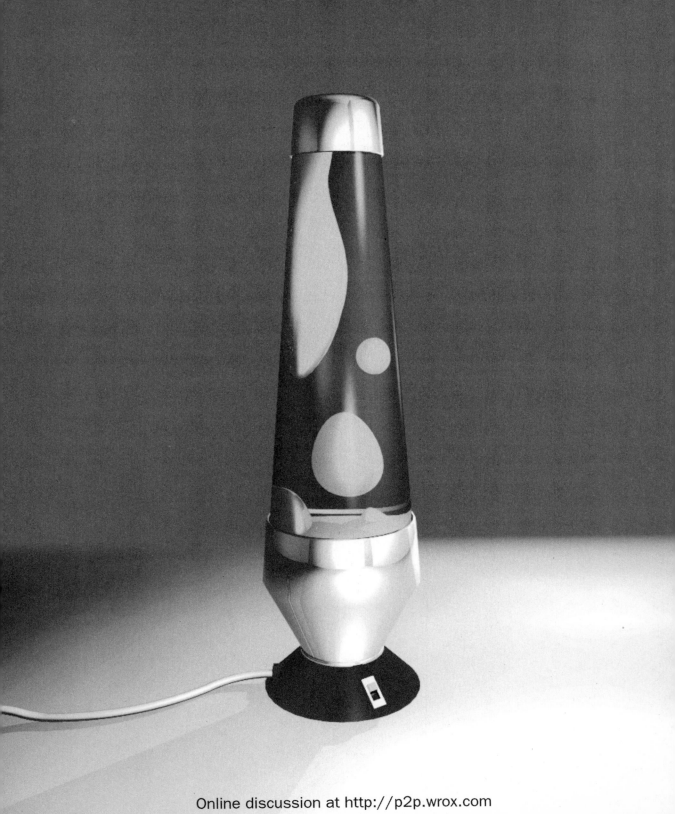

# Objects

We've now looked at quite a lot of ways of organizing our PHP code. We've used control structures to affect the flow of execution of our PHP pages. We've used forms, query strings and cookies to build applications that span across several pages. We've also used include files and functions to write reusable code. But sometimes, you may find yourself doing the same sort of thing over and over again. It isn't *exactly* the same thing, so you cannot simply include a common file full of functions and have the functionality repeat itself. You need something different, yet following some general principles. When you reach that point in your PHP experience, it's time to turn to objects.

Objects sound scary to many people, because they're associated with hardcore Computer Science. PHP is all about "lite" application development – it's a simple but powerful way for web developers to turn out decent applications without requiring a degree in Computer Science. But believe me, objects are a very simple and intuitive way to solve problems. Objects are in fact a *simplification*, and thinking about problems in terms of objects soon becomes very natural, as we shall see. Often the best way of visualizing a programming problem is through real world metaphors. Objects are a great way of actually programming the metaphor – they let you explain real world metaphors to the computer.

Objects help you separate the different logical components of your application, among other things. For example, you can separate those parts of code which actually write HTML to the browser (this is sometimes called **presentation logic**) from those parts which perform data manipulation and access (sometimes called **business logic**). They lead to cleaner design, better modularity and greater flexibility to change.

Another important reason to learn about objects is that sometimes other PHP programmers will use them, and you'll find yourself calling a function, and getting an object back in return. You'll need to understand some of the principles of PHP's object orientation to know what to do with it.

A few caveats are in order, though. PHP was not initially designed to be an object-oriented language (indeed, Rasmus Lerdorf, PHP's creator, often points out it was never intended to be a language at all), so there are many features that are not fully supported in the way that an OO programmer might expect. Nevertheless, as time goes on, PHP will very likely move towards better OO support. Object orientation is also a very transferable programming skill, and you'll find that using PHP objects gives you some preparation for moving to a fully object-oriented language, like Java or Python.

In this chapter, we will:

❑   Introduce the basic concepts of object-oriented programming

❑   Look at how we can manipulate objects in our code

❑   Find out how to define new classes of objects

❑   Examine how objects can facilitate code re-use

# Object-Oriented Terminology

Let's start by looking at some new words we're going to need to describe object-oriented programming concepts. In this section, we'll use code examples to illustrate language syntax points – but don't try to run these snippets, they're only intended to illustrate the concept, and won't work in isolation. Push your keyboard out of the way for a moment – we'll get onto some working examples in a minute.

It's very hard to define what an object is in isolation – it's easiest to introduce it together with another concept – that of a **class**. A class is a general definition for a group of "things". An object is an actual occurrence of a "thing". An object is also called an **instance** of a class. For example, *detective* is a class that makes deductions and solves crimes; *Sherlock Holmes* is an instance of the class *detective* – an object. *Hercule Poirot* is another instance of the same class. As you can see, we can have more than one object belonging to the same class. As an object-oriented PHP programmer, we can create objects belonging to a class we have defined and store them in variables. This is done using the keyword new.

```
$BelgianSleuth = new detective("Hercule Poirot");
$VictorianSleuth = new detective("Sherlock Holmes");
```

Just like other values in variables, these objects can be passed around in our code, for example as parameters for functions. This means, for example, that if we had defined a function which needed a detective in order to perform its task, we could hand it one of our two instances to work with:

```
$Baskerville = writeNovelAbout($VictorianSleuth);
$OrientExpress = writeNovelAbout($BelgianSleuth);
```

As you would expect, the output of this function can differ depending upon which detective the function is given. For example, we would expect the novel created to use the name of the detective we gave it, to refer to the main character. Well, when we created each instance of the detective class, we gave that instance a piece of information, in this case, the detective's name. If the class were designed to do so, that name would be stored as a piece of data inside each instance. How? Well, objects can hold pieces of data, which are known as **properties**, or occasionally **data members**. The class defines which properties instances of that class will have, but the actual data assigned to those properties belongs to the individual instances. So, if the detective class had a name property, which was set when we created the instances above, we could access it as follows:

```
echo $BelgianSleuth->name;          // echoes 'Hercule Poirot'
echo $VictorianSleuth->name;        // echoes 'Sherlock Holmes'
```

A class can define any number of properties. You can treat the properties of an instance of a class as ordinary PHP variables. The limitation is that the valid names for properties are defined in the object's class definition. So, if the detective class also had properties called address, prop and catchphrase, we could write the following code:

```
$VictorianSleuth->address = "221B Baker Street";
$VictorianSleuth->prop = "pipe";
$VictorianSleuth->catchphrase = "Elementary, my dear Watson";
```

Notice the (->) arrow which separates a property name from the object.

Now, unless detective also defined the existence of a property called musicalinstrument, the following code wouldn't work:

```
$VictorianSleuth->musicalinstrument = "violin";        // won't work
```

So, now when we pass $VictorianSleuth to the writeNovelAbout() function, the function has a lot more information to go on. It can write a novel, which not only uses Sherlock Holmes' name, but also refers to his home and his pipe, and uses his favorite phrase. If we wanted to, we could set different values for our $BelgianSleuth and obtain a completely different novel by passing him to the function instead.

But that hasn't really achieved anything that we couldn't have done with an associative array. However, objects can do more than simply contain data. A class also defines what the behavior of objects that belong to it will be. So, whether we were employing Sherlock Holmes or Hercule Poirot, we would expect them to be able to gather evidence, and to solve mysteries, for example. The fact that they can do this is part of their **class definition**. In programming terms, this means we can write the code necessary to perform these tasks only once, in the class definition, and it is available to be accessed wherever the objects end up. What's more, the code can make use of the object's properties. So, for example, if detective defined a method called solve() we could call it like this:

```
$VictorianSleuth->solve();
```

which might result in output text something like:

*Sherlock Holmes stroked his pipe thoughtfully. "Elementary, my dear Watson," he said.*

Whereas calling the function on our other instance ($BelgianSleuth->solve()), if we'd added a little information earlier, might give us:

*Hercule Poirot stroked his moustaches thoughtfully. "It is all thanks to my little gray cells," he said.*

# Using Pre-Defined Classes

Okay, enough theoretical examples, let's get onto some code which we can actually run. Let's start by just *using* an object before we look into how to define one of our own. There is a class called

`Calculator` defined in a file called `Calculator.inc` which you'll be able to download from the Wrox website at http://www.wrox.com/. Alternatively, you can type it in from the listing included later on in this chapter. Calculator objects mimic some of the functionality of a pocket calculator. Let's build a PHP page that uses one.

## Try it Out – The Calculator Class

**1.** If you want to create instances of the `Calculator` class in your programs, you first need to include this file in your program files with an `include` or the similar `require` command.

```php
<?php
    include("Calculator.inc");
?>
<HTML>
  <HEAD>
    <TITLE>Try it Out - The Calculator Class</TITLE>
  </HEAD>
  <BODY>
```

Now our program understands the classes defined in this file. In our case, there is only one class defined in `Calculator.inc`, and that happens to be the class `Calculator`.

**2.** We then need to create an instance of the class `Calculator`. Let's do this within the actual body.

```php
<?php
    $myCalculator = new Calculator();
```

As we said before, we simply use the keyword `new`, and we've created an object from a class. `Calculator` is the class, and `$myCalculator` now contains our object.

**3.** Now it's time to use our calculator to do some useful work. First we create two variables and announce their values.

```php
    ...
    $a = 20;
    $b = 4;
    echo("Our two numbers are $a and $b<br>\n");
```

**4.** Finally, we can call the object's methods. We're going to call four different methods, putting the returned value in a variable each time, then echoing it out to the screen.

```php
    $sum = $myCalculator->add($a, $b);
    echo("Their sum is $sum <br>\n" );

    $difference = $myCalculator->subtract($a, $b);
    echo("Their difference is $difference <br>\n");

    $product = $myCalculator->multiply($a, $b);
    echo("Their product is $product <br>\n");

    $quotient = $myCalculator->divide($a, $b);
    echo("Their quotient is $quotient <br>\n");
```

```
      ?>

   </body>
</html>
```

**5.** Now, ensure that you have the file `Calculator.inc` in the same directory before you run this example. You should see the following output:

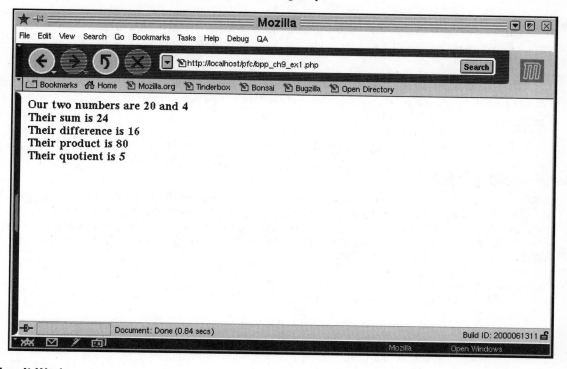

### How It Works

We first create an instance of the class "Calculator" and call it `$myCalculator`. Then we call some methods that have already been defined for the class, passing parameters to them and getting back a returned value each time. We prefix the function names with the variable holding the *instance* we have created, not the name of the class itself. Here, `$myCalculator` contains the instance, so we use its name, rather than the class name `Calculator`.

The way you call an object's methods is to first give the object's variable, then an arrow (`->`), then the name of the method. As you can see, this is a lot like calling an ordinary PHP function, if slightly more complex – a normal PHP function obviously only requires the name of the function.

So, how did I know that the class had methods called `add()`, `subtract()`, `multiply()`, and `divide()` that I could call? Unfortunately, there's no magic at work – I already knew what was in the class definition in the file `Calculator.inc`. Normally, I'd have had to refer to the documentation provided by the developer of the class to discover which methods exist. The set of methods and properties provided by a class is called the class's **interface**.

Say I made some alterations to the behavior of the Calculator class, perhaps to improve its performance or functionality. If the *interface* remained unchanged, you could download my updated `Calculator.inc` file, and your code would still work, but would benefit from the changes I had made. An interface consists of all of the methods (their names, accepted parameters, and return values) and properties that a class makes available to other programmers. Obviously, as well as documenting the names of these things, a developer should provide information on what behavior other programmers can expect from the class.

Having a well-defined interface makes it easy for other developers to use classes without worrying about what's inside. (In object-oriented terminology, this useful feature is known as "encapsulation", a fancy term for "ignorance is bliss". Encapsulation makes it possible to hide a lot of very complex logic behind some simple interfaces.)

In short, you can use classes to create objects for use in your programs without having to know how the class was written, or even how to write a class yourself. Just remember to call its defined functions using the object's name as a prefix, like this:

```
$myCalculator->add($value1, $value2);
```

## Why Use Objects?

A perceptive reader will point out that we have not obtained any benefit by using objects in the last example. The functionality could just as well have been achieved using regular functions called add(), subtract(), multiply() and divide(). We didn't need to define them as functions within a class. That's true enough, and the last example was admittedly too simple to illustrate the unique advantage of objects over mere collections of disjointed functions.

Let's now demonstrate how a class is superior to a collection of functions. We will use one function to store a value, and another function to retrieve it. Let's first do it the *non* object-oriented way.

```
<HTML>
  <BODY>
    <?php
      function setAValue()
      {
          $a = 5;
      }

      function getAValue()
      {
          return $a;
      }

      echo("About to set a value<BR>\n");
      setAValue();
      echo("The returned value is ".getAValue());
    ?>
  </BODY>
</HTML>
```

Here's what you get when you run this example:

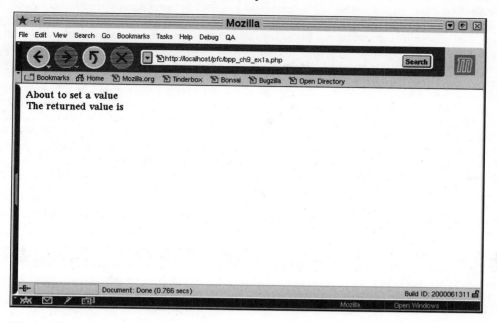

That's rather disappointing, isn't it? Well, it's only to be expected. We set a variable called $a to the value 5 inside a function. Then we used another function to retrieve the value of $a. Unfortunately, as we saw in Chapter 6 when we discussed variable scope, because PHP treats each function as a unit, the variable $a used in the function setAValue() is not the same as the variable of the same name in the function getAValue(). That's why we got back nothing. Is there a way to keep the value of $a visible between the two function calls, so that getAValue() sees the same value that setAValue() stored?

Well, we could use the global keyword, as we saw in Chapter 6.

```
<HTML>
  <BODY>
    <?php
      function setAValue()
      {
          global $a;
          $a = 5;
      }

      function getAValue()
      {
          global $a;
          return $a;
      }

      echo("About to set a value<BR>\n");
      setAValue();
      echo("The returned value is ".getAValue());
    ?>
  </BODY>
</HTML>
```

But what if we already had a variable we were using called $a? This is an easy way to create what are called **namespace conflicts** – different pieces of code trying to use the same name for different things. Imagine that those two functions had been written by one programmer, and we'd simply imported them using an include statement. We might not be aware that the person who wrote them had decided to use $a as a global variable, and decide to use the same name in our own code. This could be the basis for some very hard-to-track-down bugs.

So, a function acts like a container of some sort for variables. A variable used within a function retains its value throughout the function, but seems to disappear when the function exits. The main program itself is a separate container – variables created in the main program exist until it completes execution, and then disappear. We also saw, in Chapter 8, how PHP4's sessions allow us to make variables last as long as a user session. However, to solve our problem, what we need is a container that is larger than a function, a container that holds the functions as well as the variables they all refer to. That way, the variable can retain the value that one function put into it, even after that function exits, and it's available to another function that runs afterwards.

Now do you see what we're leading up to? That's right, object properties have precisely this characteristic. They exist inside a container, an object, and retain their value for as long as that object exists.

## Try it Out – Building a Simple Class

Let's try and do the same thing using a class. We will look in more detail at writing our own classes later on, but this is a sneak preview into the structure of a class. Notice that the class Store is like a container that holds both the variable $a and the two functions setAValue() and getAValue().

```
<HTML>
  <BODY>

    <?php
```

1. Here's where we start defining our class, surprisingly enough with the keyword class. Notice the braces { }, which show where the class definition starts and finishes.

```
    class Store
    {
```

2. $a is a property. It will be accessible to all of the methods in the class, so we'll use it to store the value between method calls. We use the keyword var to tell PHP it isn't just an ordinary variable, but a property. Here we refer to it as $a, although when it is accessed as a property, we omit the $.

```
      var $a;
```

3. This is the method that stores a value in $a. Notice that the way we define a method is simply as a function inside a class. Because this function will be called only as a method in the context of an instance of the class, when we're writing the code we don't know which instance the function will be referring to. So we use a special variable, $this, which contains the object on which the method is being called. So, when we call the setAValue() method on an instance of the Store class, that instance is copied into the $this variable, and this function is executed. Thus the property belonging to that instance will be set to 5.

```
        function setAValue()
        {
            $this->a = 5;
        }
```

**4.** This is the method that returns the value stored in $a. Again, we use $this to refer to the instance.

```
        function getAValue()
        {
            return $this->a;
        }
    }
```

We close the class definition after defining the second method.

**5.** Finally, here's where we use the class that we've defined.

```
        $myStore = new Store();
        echo("About to set a value<BR>\n");
        $myStore->setAValue();
        echo("The returned value is ".$myStore->getAValue());

    ?>

    </BODY>
</HTML>
```

Now here's what you get this time:

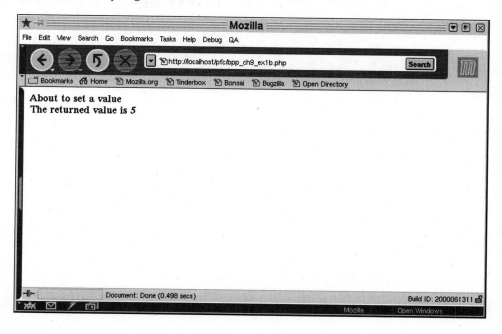

### How It Works

It works! We managed to store a value using one function, and to get it back through another. That's because the variable $a is not inside either function. It is outside both of them, but inside the class. So both the functions of the class can "see" the same variable. We can happily use $a as a variable in our own program, and there are no namespace conflicts.

Think of every object as containing both a set of data and a set of functions that define its behavior. These are the object's properties and methods. The data then remains intact across multiple invocations of the object's methods, so the methods can effectively share variables without the calling program having to store and pass them each time.

The example we've just created may seem overly trivial, but it's actually quite an important coding style. In object-oriented programming, it's common practice to have a pair of methods for every variable in the class, one to set its value and one to retrieve it. These are called **accessor methods**. We'll return to accessor methods again later, and explain why they're so useful.

# Giving the Calculator a Memory

Let's see how this concept has been used in our calculator. (We won't look inside the Calculator class just yet. We'll continue to treat it like a "black box" and see how it can be used. Later on, we'll write the class ourselves.) This time, we'll use some of the functions of the Calculator class that let us store a value inside the object and retrieve that value. This is similar to the *Min* (memory in) and *MR* (memory recall) buttons on your calculator. The corresponding methods in our Calculator class are setValue() and getValue(). Obviously again, if someone else had implemented the class for us, we'd have to discover these methods by reading the Calculator's documentation, or examining the class definition.

## Try it Out – Calculator Memory

**1.** First of all, let's include the Calculator.inc file again, and provide the standard HTML header.

```php
<?php
    include("Calculator.inc");
?>
<HTML>
  <HEAD>
    <TITLE>Try it Out - Calculator Memory</TITLE>
  </HEAD>
  <BODY>
    <?php
```

**2.** Create a value to store in memory.

```php
$valueToStore = 10;
echo("The value to be stored is $valueToStore<BR>\n");
```

**3.** Create an instance of the Calculator class.

```php
$myCalculator = new Calculator();
```

**4.** And finally call the object's functions to store and retrieve a value.

```
    $myCalculator->setValue($valueToStore);
    $restoredValue = $myCalculator->getValue();
    echo("The value returned is $restoredValue<BR>\n");
?>

</BODY>
</HTML>
```

**5.** When you run the example, this is the output you get:

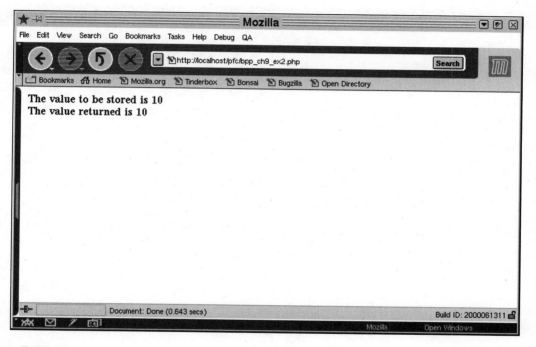

### How lit Works

You remember that methods that are used to store a value inside an object and retrieve such a value are called accessor functions, or simply accessors. Which are the accessor functions that we can see in the Calculator class? A little inspection will tell us that setValue() and getValue() are the most likely candidates. It's a naming convention, when you have a property called X, to define accessor functions called setX() and getX(). For this reason, accessor functions are also sometimes called **setters** and **getters**. As I said earlier, it's good practice to have accessor functions for all variables that a class contains. Why? Well, it comes down to what we were saying before about well-defined interfaces. I might decide later on that I want the value stored in the calculator's memory to be more persistent, and instead of just storing it in a variable in the object, store it in a file. If you had written your code to access the property directly, my changes would almost certainly mean your code would no longer work. But if you used the getter and setter methods, I'm free to change the calculator's behavior, so long as it still has the same interface.

In our example, we call the accessor function $myCalculator->setValue() (the "setter") and pass it the value stored in our local variable $valueToStore. The accessor function, unknown to us, squirrels away the value in a variable for later use. Sure enough, when we call the corresponding accessor function $myCalculator->getValue() (the "getter"), the value is returned. We can deduce that there is a variable inside the class Calculator (but outside all its functions) that is being used to store this value, although this needn't be the way it's implemented. From outside the object, we neither need to know nor care how it achieves its magic – the important thing is that it does it.

If we had another instance of the Calculator class in our program (for example, another object), we would find that the value stored in one object has no relationship at all with that stored in the other. The variables defined within a class are specific to an object. Each object has its own copy of such variables. An example will make this clearer.

## Try it Out – Two Calculators

Type in this program. It's very similar to the previous example.

```php
<?php
    include("Calculator.inc");
?>
<HTML>
  <HEAD>
  <TITLE>Try it Out - Two Calculators</TITLE>
  </HEAD>
  <BODY>
    <?php

    // Create two instances of the Calculator class

       $oneCalculator = new Calculator();
       $anotherCalculator = new Calculator();

    // Create values to store in memory.

       $value1 = 10;
       $value2 = 15;

       echo("The value to be stored in the first
             calculator is $value1<BR>\n");
       echo("The value to be stored in the second
             calculator is $value2<BR>\n");

    // Call the objects' accessor functions to store
    // and retrieve these values as before.

       $oneCalculator->setValue($value1);
       $anotherCalculator->setValue($value2);

       $restoredValue1 = $oneCalculator->getValue();
       $restoredValue2 = $anotherCalculator->getValue();
       echo("The value returned by the first
              calculator is $restoredValue1<BR>\n");
       echo("The value returned by the second
              calculator is $restoredValue2<BR>\n");
    ?>
  </BODY>
</HTML>
```

When you run the above program, this is what you should see:

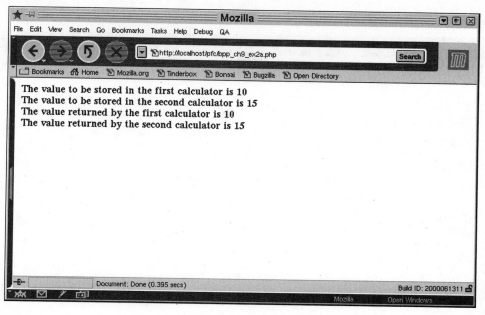

### How It Works

There are two objects in this example, $oneCalculator and $anotherCalculator. Even though they are both instances of the same class, each has a separate copy of the class's internal variables. So the value we store in the variable of one object is independent of the value we store in the other.

# Exploring Our Simple Class Further

We've seen how to instantiate an object from a class. We also know how to use accessor functions to store and retrieve values from an object. But there's a subtle point to be noted when passing values to PHP functions, whether they are regular functions or methods (which we've already seen are really just functions within classes).

## Passing By Value and By Reference

PHP normally passes variables "by value". In other words, PHP makes a copy of any variable that is an argument to a function, and passes only the copy to the function. So if the function modifies the value, the original variable is unaffected. Conversely, if the calling program changes a variable *after* passing it to a function, the function does not see the change. This has some advantages and disadvantages. On the one hand, the values seen by the calling program and the called function are insulated from each other. On the other, you may actually *want* the value passed to the function to change in lockstep with the value in your calling program. In that case, what do you do?

The answer to this has already been introduced in Chapter 6. You need to pass the variable "by reference". That way, there is only one copy of the variable, and both the calling program and the called function refer to the same copy. You recall the special PHP syntax that indicates when you are passing a variable "by reference". You simply prefix your variable with an ampersand (&) when passing it to the function. (Note: Those programmers familiar with the concept of pointers will understand what this is about. Others can simply remember that putting an ampersand before a variable name allows a function to see the variable itself and not a copy.)

## Try it Out – Passing By Value

Let's build a quick program using the calculator to see what we mean.

**1.** Let's start off with the usual header.

```php
<?php
    include("Calculator.inc");
?>

<HTML>
  <HEAD>
    <TITLE>Try it Out - Passing By Value</TITLE>
  </HEAD>
  <BODY>
    <?php
```

**2.** Now, let's create a value to store in memory.

```php
$valueToStore = 10;
echo("The value to be stored is $valueToStore<BR>\n");
```

**3.** Create an instance of the `Calculator` class again, as usual.

```php
$myCalculator = new Calculator();
```

**4.** Call the object's functions to store and retrieve the value as before.

```php
$myCalculator->setValue($valueToStore);
$restoredValue = $myCalculator->getValue();
echo("The value returned is $restoredValue<BR>\n");
```

**5.** Now, we modify the value we have in the variable we originally gave to the calculator.

```php
$valueToStore += 5;
echo("We have changed the value to $valueToStore<BR>\n");
```

**6.** It only remains to see whether the value in the calculator's memory has changed.

```php
$restoredValue = $myCalculator->getValue();
echo("The value returned is $restoredValue<BR>\n");
    ?>
  </BODY>
</HTML>
```

This is the output that you should see:

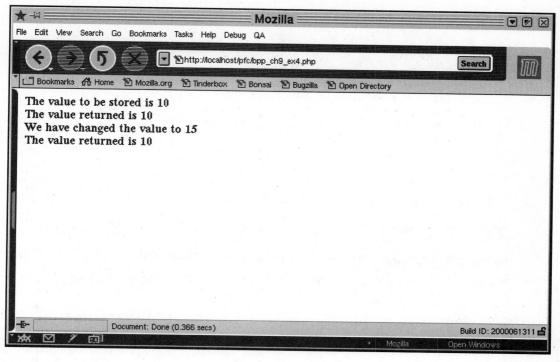

### How It Works

As you can see from the output, modifying a variable after passing it to an object's "set" accessor function does not affect the value now held within the object. A call to the "get" accessor function proves it. This is an example of a *pass by value*. The object has a separate copy of the data we originally gave it.

## Try it Out – Passing by Reference

Before we can see what it's like to pass a variable by reference, we should emphasize that it's not enough to pass the variable by reference in our program alone. The accessor functions we call should also pass the variable by reference; otherwise we are still left with the same situation. The object ends up storing a *copy* of the variable we pass, not the variable itself. We have another version of the Calculator class in the file Calculator2.inc, and this has a "setter" accessor function that passes by reference, too. We need to use this version of the Calculator class rather than the earlier one, if we are to get correct results. Now all we need to do is make these tiny changes to the previous example.

```php
<?php
    include("Calculator2.inc");
?>


<HTML>
  <HEAD>
    <TITLE>Try it Out - Passing By Reference</TITLE>
  </HEAD>
```

```
<BODY>
  <?php
    $valueToStore = 10;
    echo("The value to be stored is $valueToStore<BR>\n");
    $myCalculator = new Calculator();
    $myCalculator->setValue(&$valueToStore);
    $restoredValue = $myCalculator->getValue();
    echo("The value returned is $restoredValue<BR>\n");
    $valueToStore += 5;
    echo("We have changed the value to $valueToStore<BR>\n");
    $restoredValue = $myCalculator->getValue();
    echo("The value returned is $restoredValue<BR>\n");
  ?>
</BODY>
</HTML>
```

Take a look at the output this time.

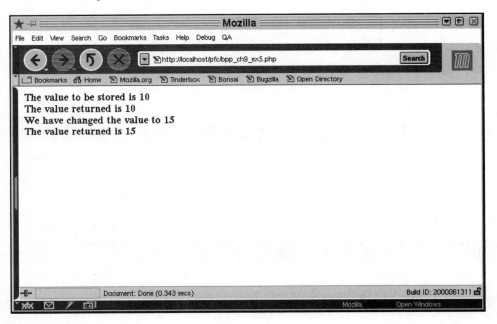

### How It Works

The "setter" accessor function in the later version of Calculator has the following form:

```
function setValue($passedValue)
{
    $this->storedValue = &$passedValue; // by reference
}
```

For purposes of comparison, the earlier version of `Calculator` had the function defined as follows:

```
function setValue( $passedValue )
{
    $this->storedValue = $passedValue; // by value
}
```

Now that the application and the class's accessor method are both passing by reference, it is exactly the same variable that is being referred to by both the calling program and the object. Hence any changes made by the calling program are immediately reflected in the object as well. (The reverse is also true. If the object makes a change to the internal variable, that change will be reflected in the calling program's variable as well.)

# Creating Classes of Our Own

It's been fairly smooth sailing so far, mainly because we haven't had to create classes of our own! But it's time to get around to this somewhat more challenging task now.

# Creating a Class From Scratch

Experienced designers will tell you that writing the programs for an object-oriented system isn't the hard part. The hard part is deciding just what the objects are in our system! In larger systems, some of the classes that need to be created don't directly correspond to anything tangible. But for our present purposes, we can stick to real, solid items like calculators. A calculator defines a definite set of "behaviors", so we can readily see that it is a candidate for a class.

### Inside the Calculator

Now let's actually examine the `Calculator` class we used earlier. The following code shows a version of the calculator class which could be used to execute the first of our examples from earlier in the chapter – it implements the `add()`, `subtract()`, `multiply()` and `divide()` methods.

```php
<?php
    class Calculator
    {
        function add( $number1, $number2 )
        {
            return $number1 + $number2;
        }

        function subtract( $number1, $number2 )
        {
            return $number1 - $number2;
        }

        function multiply( $number1, $number2 )
        {
            return $number1 * $number2;
        }
```

```
        function divide( $number1, $number2 )
        {
            return $number1 / $number2;
        }
    }
?>
```

Now, if you include this file in your program, or even simply paste in the class definition in place of the include statement, you should be able to run the first Calculator example we saw. The output of this is not reproduced here because it will be exactly the same as in that example!

It should be fairly obvious now how the class does its work. Each of the four functions in it (add(), subtract(), multiply() and divide()) takes two parameters and returns the result of a different calculation.

But we know that there's more to the Calculator class than this. We need to simulate the functioning of the *Min*, *M+* and *MR* buttons. Okay, so we never actually used the M+ button, but one of the benefits of developing a class is that you get to provide all the functionality you think might be needed. The ability to add a value to the stored value in memory might come in useful, so we provide it here.

We just need to add a few more function definitions to the class.

```php
<?php
class Calculator
{

    // Declare the internal variable
    var $storedValue;

    //Accessor functions
    //
    function setValue( $passedValue )
    {
        $this->storedValue = $passedValue;
    }
    function getValue()
    {
        return $this->storedValue;
    }
    function addValue( $passedValue )
    {
        $this->storedValue += $passedValue;
    }

    // Constructor function
    //
    function Calculator()
    {
        $this->storedValue = 0;
    }

    // Calculator functions as before
    //
    ...
}
?>
```

Now, with this version of the class you can even run the examples in this chapter that simulated the *Min* and *MR* buttons. Now you know about the addValue() method, you can write programs that use the *M+* button as well. Again, the output is not reproduced here because it is identical to what you would have got earlier.

## How Calculator Works

You can see that we have a local variable called $storedValue. This is declared just within the class, so it is clearly a variable that belongs to the class as a whole and not just to a function within the class. Also notice that the accessor functions all refer to this variable not simply as $storedValue but as $this->storedValue. *This is very important.* Whenever you refer to a variable belonging to the class within a function, you must make it clear what you mean using the $this keyword followed by the arrow sign and then the variable name.

Let's look at $this properly. It's just an object's way of saying "I" or "me". When you see the phrase $this->, it means the object is saying "my" or "mine". That's simple, so when you see the following two references to a variable called $thingummy within the function generalFunction(), you can readily tell the difference.

```
class SomethingOrOther
{
    var $thingummy;

    function generalFunction()
    {
        ...
        $thingummy = 5000;
        ...
        $this->thingummy = 0;
        ...
    }
}
```

That's right, the first reference is to a variable that's defined only within the function and is not known outside of it. It also ceases to exist once the function returns. The second is a variable declared within the *class*, so it remains persistent even across function invocations. The variable belongs to the class, not to any particular function.

So now, the only part of the class left unexplained is the Calculator() function. If a class contains a function with the same name as the class itself, it's called a "constructor". The constructor function is automatically called when a new instance of a class is created. It's a good idea to put code in the constructor that needs to be executed each time an object is created from a class definition. Initialization of class variables is the most common purpose for this type of code. As you can see, we are doing precisely this kind of initialization in the Calculator's constructor function. We're setting the class variable $this->storedValue to zero. There is nothing to stop you from writing classes whose constructors take parameters, which can be used to set certain initial values from the new instance's properties.

# Extending an Existing Class

We have actually covered a lot of ground here, and the concepts that we have explained take some digesting. However, there is a very important concept that needs to be discussed before we can claim to have done justice to object-oriented programming, and that is inheritance. Inheritance, like encapsulation, is a fundamental property of object-oriented systems. PHP supports inheritance like most other object-oriented languages, although in a limited way. The limitations generally make it a simpler job to write PHP object code, though, so it shouldn't cause us too much trouble.

What is inheritance? Sometimes, you find that you need to define a class with a certain set of "behaviors", but many of them are already defined in another class. You shouldn't have to rewrite all of that logic in your new class. You should be able to re-use what's already inside the existing class. It saves tons of effort. If done properly, inheritance is a good way to model how things actually work.

Inheriting from another class allows us to write a new class, but instead of coding its behavior in full, we can make use of existing functionality and merely enhance it. Let's say we want to model a scientific calculator with many complex mathematical functions. We already have a `Calculator` class that simulates a basic calculator. Since a scientific calculator can do all that a basic calculator can do *and more*, we can design it to simply inherit from the basic calculator class. We don't have to rewrite the functions of a basic calculator.

Let's say that our scientific calculator should be able to calculate the following functions in addition to whatever a basic calculator does: sine, cosine, logarithm and exponent (power).

## Try it Out – A Scientific Calculator

**1.** Type the following lines into a file (call it `ScientificCalculator.inc`).

```php
<?php
include("Calculator.inc");

class ScientificCalculator extends Calculator
{
    function getSine($value)
    {
        return sin($value);
    }
    function getCosine($value)
    {
        return cos($value);
    }
    function getLogarithm($value)
    {
        return log($value);
    }
    function getPower($value1, $value2)
    {
        return pow($value1, $value2);
    }
}
?>
```

This is our new class. Note that we have not bothered to redefine add(), subtract(), multiply() and divide(). They're already defined in the class Calculator, from which our new class ScientificCalculator inherits functionality. The keyword extends means "inherits from". Also note that we need to include the file in which the Calculator class is defined, otherwise PHP will complain that it doesn't know the class Calculator. Our calculator will also automatically have Calculator's memory.

**2.** Now we can use this class in a program. Type the following into another file:

```php
<?php
    include("ScientificCalculator.inc");
?>
<HTML>
  <HEAD>
    <TITLE>Try it Out - A Scientific Calculator</TITLE>
  </HEAD>
  <BODY>

    <?php
```

**3.** Create two variables and announce their values.

```php
$a = 20;
$b = 4;
echo("Our two numbers are $a and $b<BR>\n");
```

**4.** Create an instance of the ScientificCalculator class.

```php
$myCalculator = new ScientificCalculator();
```

**5.** Call the object's inherited functions.

```php
$sum = $myCalculator->add($a, $b);
echo("Their sum is $sum<BR>\n");

$difference = $myCalculator->subtract($a, $b);
echo("Their difference is $difference<BR>\n");

$product = $myCalculator->multiply($a, $b);
echo("Their product is $product<BR>\n");

$quotient = $myCalculator->divide($a, $b);
echo("Their quotient is $quotient<BR>\n");
```

**6.** Call the object's new functions.

```php
$sine = $myCalculator->getSine($a);
echo("The sine of $a is $sine<BR>\n");

$cosine = $myCalculator->getCosine($a);
echo("The cosine of $a is $cosine<BR>\n");
```

```
        $logarithm = $myCalculator->getLogarithm($a);
        echo("The natural logarithm of $a is $logarithm<BR>\n");

        $power = $myCalculator->getPower($a, $b);
        echo("$a raised to the power $b is $power<BR>\n");
    ?>

  </BODY>
</HTML>
```

**7.** And this is the output you should see:

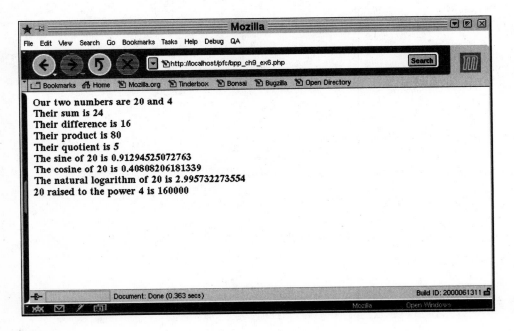

### How It Works

The beauty of this example is that inheritance is actually very simple to understand, though it's so powerful and cool. Once we create an instance of a class, we can not only invoke functions that are defined for the class, but also functions that are defined for classes that this class extends. This can go on up to any level. So we can have a class extending a "parent class", which in turn extends a "grandparent class", and so on ad infinitum. However, for practical reasons, you wouldn't let inheritance hierarchies get very "deep", because such systems get pretty hard to understand.

Why did we have to extend `Calculator` and create another class called `ScientificCalculator`? Why didn't we just put those extra functions into `Calculator` itself? We could certainly have done that, but it wouldn't have been clean design. As we encounter requirements for more and more specialized behavior, we would have to keep adding code in the parent class, and it would get more and more bloated with each addition. Every instance of the `Calculator` class would carry around more functionality than it strictly required. It would make our application code more bulky than it needed to be. The rule is, keep each class minimal in its functionality and provide specialized functions in inherited classes.

*In other object-oriented languages, there are other reasons for using inheritance, one of which is the ability of a subclass to "override" the functionality of a superclass by defining a function with the same name but with different logic. However, PHP does not support this, which is one of the reasons why it is not a "true" object-oriented language. If you're intrigued by the possibilities of object-oriented programming, your next stop after learning PHP4 should probably be to take a look at either Java or Python.*

And now, we can say with some satisfaction that we have covered object-orientation in PHP to a reasonable degree. You can now build web applications with chunks of logic encapsulated within classes.

# A Useful Object

Let's make a class that we might find useful in laying out our web pages. The class provides an easy way of inserting images and hyperlinks into our HTML. Let's think first about how we would go about designing such a class.

We're looking for a class that automatically echoes out strings in one of the following two formats:

```
<IMG SRC="someimage.gif" ALT="the image's title" WIDTH=x HEIGHT=y>
<A HREF="somedocument.html">the text of the hyperlink</A>
```

Immediately, we can see that they have a couple of things in common. They both contain a pointer to a document, and they both contain a piece of descriptive text – either the alternative text for the image, or the hyperlink text. The Image tag contains a couple of extra bits of data, which are actually optional, specifying the width and height of the image for display by the browser.

These attributes are all properties of the references, and are therefore candidates to be properties of our class.

So, what interface would we like to program for our class? It would be nice to simply specify the properties of the reference when we create it. We can do this with a constructor method. Then, whenever we want to echo out an HTML element for the reference, we should just have to call a method to print out the tag(s).

So, we want to be able to write code like this:

```
$logo = new Reference("logo.gif","Corporate Logo",150,100);
$catalog = new Reference("catalog/index.html","catalog");

...

$logo->insert();
echo "Please take a look at our online ".$catalog->insert();
```

Here, we're creating `Reference` objects, which store data about how we should display the company's logo, and where the catalog pages are. Then, in the body of the page, when we want to insert an `<IMG>` or `<A>` tag, we're calling a method on the `Reference` object to generate the HTML for us. As you can see, it keeps the page layout code very tidy indeed.

It would even be possible for the web site manager to create an include file containing object definitions for all of the most important image elements and hyperlink targets in the web site, and then, inserting the correct tag would simply be a case of the web page designers typing `<?php $logo->insert(); ?>` in amongst their HTML. Then if the logo changed size, or the `ALT` text needed altering, it could be done quickly and easily by altering the declaration in the include file, rather than altering hundreds of web pages.

So, having established a use case for the code, and described what we want the code to do, we can move on to actually designing our class.

## Try It Out – Building a Reference Class

Our class is going to be called `Reference`. Create a file called `Reference.inc`, and enter the code below.

**1.** First of all, we need to begin our class definition with our class's properties. We've got four, to accommodate the more demanding images. Obviously, for a simple hyperlink, the width and height won't be needed, but they do no harm just being there.

```php
<?php
   class Reference
   {
       var $document;
       var $title;
       var $imgwidth;
       var $imgheight;
```

`$document` will hold the path to the image or web page targeted by the link. `$title` will hold the text which will either fill the hyperlink, or constitute the image's `ALT` text. `$imgwidth` and `$imgheight` are self explanatory.

**2.** Next we build our constructor. It takes a minimum of two arguments – the target for the reference, and the descriptive text. It takes two optional arguments (made optional by making them default to zero), for the image width and height.

```php
       function Reference($target, $name, $width=0, $height=0)
       {
           $this->document = $target;
           $this->title = $name;
           $this->imgwidth = $width;
           $this->imgheight = $height;
       }
```

All the constructor does, is store all the values, which are passed to it in the appropriate variables.

**3.** Now, we need a way of telling whether the reference points to an image or a web page. We choose to implement a method on the reference object, `isImage()`, which returns `True` if the target is an image, and `False` if the target isn't.

```
function isImage()
{
    return(ereg("(\.jpeg$)|(\.gif$)|(\.jpg$)|(\.png$)",
            $this->document,$trash));
}
```

We use a regular expression that tests to see if the path to the document ends in some common file extensions for web images. If the regexp matches, it returns `True`, if not, it returns `False`.

**4.** Finally, the meat of the class is in the `insert()` method. We've decided to allow for the fact that sometimes people may want to add additional attributes to the generated HTML according to the location they're inserting the tag, such as ALIGN in IMG tags, or TARGET in A tags. Again, we allow for this using an optional parameter.

```
function insert($additionalAttributes="")
{
```

**5.** Next we check to see which type of tag we need to write out. We call the object's own `isImage()` method to check. If it's an image, we write out the element, including all the attributes we have data for, including any additional ones specified to the `insert()` method call.

```
if ($this->isImage())
{
    echo "<IMG SRC=\"".$this->document."\" ALT=\"".$this->title."\"";
    if ($this->imgwidth) echo " WIDTH=".$this->imgwidth;
    if ($this->imgheight) echo " HEIGHT=".$this->imgheight;
    if ($additionalAttributes) echo " $additionalAttributes";
    echo ">";
```

**6.** The last part of the method, and the end of the class, is the other half of the `if` statement – the half that writes out a hyperlink. It's workings are very similar to that of the image element writer.

```
} else {
    echo "<A HREF=\"".$this->document."\"";
    if ($additionalAttributes) echo " $additionalAttributes";
    echo ">".$this->title."</A>";
}
    }
}
?>
```

**7.** Now, let's make another file in the same folder called `definitions.inc`, and create some reference objects. First we need to include the `Reference.inc` file, then we can use the `new` command to make as many as our site demands.

```
<?php
    include "./Reference.inc";

// Images
    $logo=new Reference("logo.gif","Corporate Logo",150,100);
    $longline=new Reference("blackdot.gif",".","100%",1);
```

```
    $line=new Reference("blackdot.gif",".",200,1);

//Hyperlinks
    $Wrox=new Reference("http://www.wrox.com/","Wrox Press");
    $WroxConferences=new Reference("http://www.wroxconferences.com/",
                                   "Wrox Conferences");
?>
```

**8.** Finally, let's actually make a page that uses the objects defined in `definitions.inc`. Call this `testobjects.php`.

```
<?php include "./definitions.inc"; ?>

<HTML>
  <HEAD><TITLE>Try it Out - Building A Reference Class</TITLE></HEAD>
  <BODY>
    <?php $longline->insert(); ?><BR>
    <?php $logo->insert("ALIGN=\"RIGHT\""); ?>

    <H1>About Wrox</H1>
    <P><?php $line->insert(); ?></P>
    <BR CLEAR=BOTH>
    <P><?php $Wrox->insert(); ?> is a publisher of information
       for programmers. Its books cover a wide range of technologies,
       including PHP. <?php $WroxConferences->insert(); ?> has also
       been founded recently providing events for programmers around
       the world.</P>
    <?php $longline->insert(); ?>


  </BODY>
</HTML>
```

As you can see, in this final page, the amount of PHP code is minimal – and easily handled by a non-programmer who's been told what tags to add.

**9.** Finally, move all three files to the same directory on your web server, along with an image called `logo.gif` and one called `blackdot.gif` (there's one of each in the code download). You should see something like this:

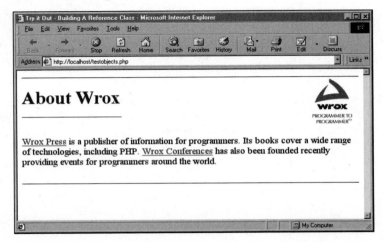

### How It Works

The look of the page – what we called presentation logic earlier in the chapter – is kept in the `testobjects.php` page. The web page designer makes use of a set of predefined objects set out by the site manager in `definitions.inc`, to enforce certain house styles, such as the size of logos. These objects make use of a class definition in a separate file, which is maintained by the site developer. Each of these three people can make independent changes to their part of the web page, provided they stick to certain well-defined interfaces.

This is a fairly trivial example, but you can imagine other object-oriented systems which can be used in a similar way to enforce consistency across a multi-developer web site.

# Summary

Are objects and classes really useful when building web applications? Or are they just a cool and glamorous way to do things that could be done much more simply using PHP's regular functions? This is a difficult question to answer because, frankly, those applications that are so complex that they *have* to be modelled using object-oriented techniques would probably benefit more from a full-fledged object-oriented system like Java or Python. PHP does not pretend to be a truly object-oriented system. It has limitations that make it less useful for really large and complex applications. Nevertheless, adding object-oriented skills to one's repertoire can certainly come in useful, even for a PHP developer.

We've covered a lot of new concepts in this chapter. We learnt that an identifiable set of properties and behaviors defines a class, and that instances, or occurrences of a class are called objects. Classes define local variables and functions. In order to facilitate encapsulation, local variables should be manipulated through accessor functions defined by the class. Constructor functions say what should happen every time a new instance of a class is created.

Classes can be extended by other classes. Behavior defined in a class is then available to the "subclass" as well. This is called inheritance.

Object-oriented features in PHP are not as sophisticated as those in other systems such as Java, but they are sufficiently advanced to be able to offer significant productivity advantages to developers who design their applications in an object-oriented way from the start. This chapter provided an introduction to those features. With practice and further reading, you should be able to build very sophisticated PHP-based applications indeed. Even if you never design a class, at least you won't have to run and hide when you're browsing the PHP function reference and the function you need returns an object.

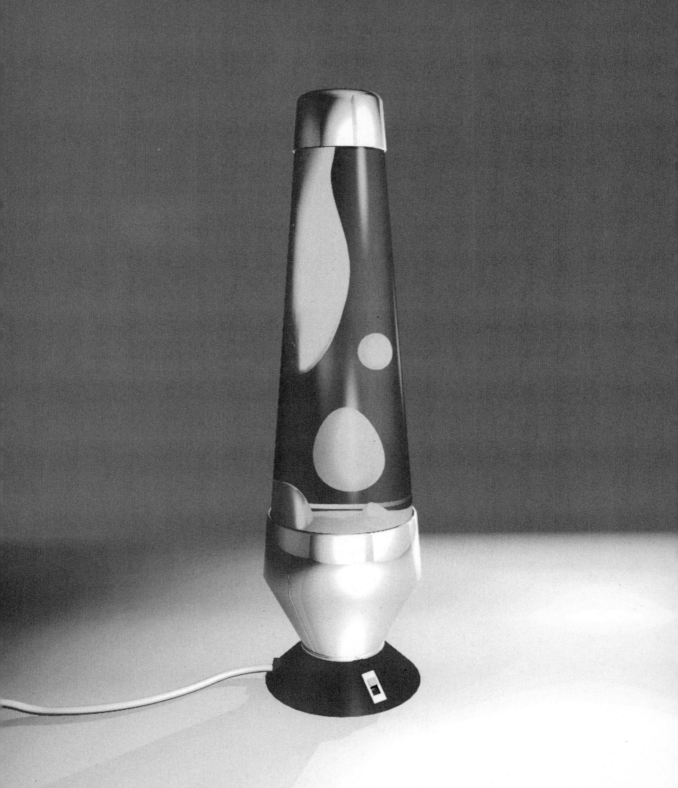

# File and Directory Handling

Every programmer must work with files and directories at some point. Your web applications will probably use files to store setup information for scripts, to store the data they read or write, or to save temporary data needed by the scripts between HTTP requests. For instance, even a simple hit counter needs a place to hold the number of accesses to the site on which it runs.

A **file** is nothing more than an ordered sequence of bytes stored on hard disk, floppy disk, CD-ROM or some other storage media. A **directory** is a special type of file that holds the names of other files and directories (sometimes denoted as subdirectories) and pointers to their storage area on the media. All you need to know in order to manipulate files and directories is how to connect your scripts to them.

This chapter will take you through the process of working with files and directories while providing a reference of essential PHP functions that can make the task easier. We'll cover:

- ❏ Opening and closing a file
- ❏ Reading from and writing to a file
- ❏ Deleting and renaming a file
- ❏ Navigating within a file
- ❏ Opening and closing a directory
- ❏ Reading directory entries
- ❏ Deleting and renaming a directory

We'll wrap things up by building a fully-fledged web text editor.

Before we start though, you should take note of a subtle difference between Linux and Windows when it comes to specifying directory paths. UNIX-based systems like Linux use forward slashes to delimit elements in a path, like this:

```
/home/dan/data/data.txt
```

Meanwhile, Windows uses backslashes:

```
C:\MyDocs\data\data.txt
```

Fortunately, PHP on Windows will automatically convert the former to the latter in most situations, so something like:

```
$fp = fopen("/data/data.txt", "r");
```

shouldn't cause you any problems, even if you *are* running the script on a Windows platform. However, there are some cases in which the path will be used directly (when you copy an uploaded file from the temporary directory to an archive directory, for example), in which case the backslashes will be necessary. Since PHP will interpret '\' as escaping the following character, the string will need to be specified like this:

```
"C:\\MyDocs\\data\\data.txt"
```

We'll show you an easy way of automatically converting forward slashes to backslashes in PHP later on.

# Working with Files

PHP provides two sets of file-related functions, distinguished by the different ways in which they handle files: some use a file handle, or a file pointer as it is commonly called; the others use filename strings directly. The same is true of PHP's directory-related functions, for that matter.

A **file handle** is nothing more than an integer value that will be used to identify the file you wish to work with until it is closed. If more than one file is opened, each file is identified by its own uniquely assigned handle. For example, the `fwrite()` function – used to write data out to a file – needs a file handle that points to the file it is to work with:

```
fwrite($fp, 'Hello world!');
```

On the other hand, the `file()` function – used to read data from a file – takes a string argument that holds the path to the file:

```
$lines = file('./data.txt');
```

Don't get overwhelmed by these new functions, we'll formally introduce them shortly.

> *Unless otherwise specified, all the functions mentioned in this chapter return* `True` *when a given operation is successful and* `False` *upon error.*

Let's begin with a simple script that works with a file.

# Opening and Closing Files

There are typically three steps involved in working with a file:

❑ Open the file you wish to work with by associating a file handle with it.

❑ Read from or write to the file using the file handle.

❑ Close the file using the file handle.

### fopen()

The first function we shall look at is `fopen()`. This is used to open a file, returning a file handle associated with the opened file. It can take either two or three arguments: `filename`, `mode`, and the optional `use_include_path`.

As well as using the file handle to refer to the file later, you can use it to detect if the file opened OK. If it did, the file handle will be a positive integer. If it failed, the file handle returned will be zero. Operations on files and directories are prone to errors, so you should always allow for things going wrong when using them. It's therefore good practice to use some form of error-checking procedure, so that if an error occurs (perhaps we don't have necessary privileges to access the file, or it doesn't even exist), our script will exit tidily, preferably with an appropriate error message. One way to do this is as follows: Because of the way PHP interprets integers in the context of Boolean operations, we can pretend (for the purposes of an `if()` statement) that the file pointer, which is actually an integer, has the value `True` if the operation succeeds, and `False` if it fails. This allows us to test to see if the file opened or not using a script like this:

```
$fp = fopen("./data.txt", "r");
if(!$fp) die ("Cannot open the file");
```

Alternatively, we can write it like this:

```
if(!($fp = fopen("./data.txt", "r"))) die ("Cannot open the file");
```

Don't get confused – we're not testing to see if `$fp` is equal to the result of the `fopen()` function call. That would use the `==` equality operator. As far as the `if` statement is concerned, the value it is testing is that returned by the `fopen()` command. We are simply using a shorthand trick to store it in `$fp` for later use. You can use either form, depending on what you're comfortable with.

So, let's look at how we use the `fopen()` function.

The first argument `filename` specifies the name of the file you wish to open, which can be just a filename, or a relative (`"./data.inc"` for example) or absolute (`"/myfiles/data.inc"`) path to a file. You can even specify a file on a remote host, opening it with an HTTP URL or via FTP:

```
if(!($fp = fopen("http://www.whatyoumaycallit.com/index.html", "r")))
        die ("Cannot open the file.");
```

```
if(!($fp = fopen("ftp://ftp.whatyoumaycallit.com/pub/index.txt", "r")))
        die ("Cannot open the file.");
```

Note that a remote file can only be opened for reading, so you can't modify or write to the file. We'll use this technique later on in the book in Chapter 15.

If you're not very familiar with command-line file operations on either UNIX or Windows, you might be a little confused by the relative path notation. From the perspective of a file, . refers to the directory the file is in, and .. refers to the immediate parent directory. So, ./data.txt points to a file called data.txt in the same directory as the script. ../data.txt points to a file called data.txt in the directory above that containing the script. ../../../data.txt backs us up the directory tree three levels before looking for data.txt. An absolute path is distinguished by the fact that it begins with a /, meaning the path is specified relative to the root of the filesystem, not to the location of the script.

We'll see what happens if we simply specify the filename as data.txt when we look at the use_include_path argument.

The mode argument specifies how the open file is to be used. You can open a file for reading, writing or appending to, with mode taking one of the following values:

| Value | Description |
| --- | --- |
| r | Open file for reading only. The file position indicator is placed at the beginning of the file. |
| r+ | Open file for reading and writing. The file position indicator is placed at the beginning of the file. |
| w | Open file for writing only. Any existing content will be lost; if the file does not exist, PHP will attempt to create it. |
| w+ | Open file for reading and writing. Any existing file content will be lost; if the file does not exist, PHP will attempt to create it. |
| a | Open file for appending only. Data is written to the end of an existing file; if the file does not exist, PHP will attempt to create it. |
| a+ | Open file for reading and appending. Data is written to the end of an existing file; if the file does not exist, PHP will attempt to create it. |

*The file position indicator is PHP's internal pointer that specifies the exact position in a file where the next operation should be performed.*

The mode argument can also take the value "b" to indicate that the opened file should be treated as a binary file. Although this is irrelevant for platforms such as Linux, which treat text and binary files identically, you may well find it useful if you're running on Windows.

If use_include_path is set to 1, and the filename isn't specified as a relative or absolute path, the function will search for the file specified by filename first in the script's own directory, and then in the directories defined by the variable include_path (set in the php.ini file).

The include path is especially useful if you want to specify a directory in which you put include files that are commonly accessed by your scripts. Let us suppose that include_path has been given the value /home/apache/inc in the php.ini file, and that we execute the following function call:

```
fopen("data.txt", "r", 1);
```

If this call now fails to find the file data.txt in the current directory, it will search in the directory /home/apache/inc.

### fclose()

Once you've finished working with a file, it needs to be closed – you can do this using fclose(), specifying the open file by using its associated file handle as a single argument, like this:

```
fclose ($fp)
```

Although PHP should close all open files automatically when your script terminates, it's still good practice to close files from within your script as soon as they're finished with, as this will free them up more quickly for use by other processes and scripts – or even by other requests to the same script.

# Reading and Writing to Files

Okay, so we've now seen how to open and close files, and know we can refer to them in the intervening period by using file handles. Let's take a look at some of the PHP functions we can use to read and write the data in one such file. We'll start with two quite simple ones, which we can use together to implement a basic working script.

### fread()

This function can be used to extract a character string from a file, and takes two arguments, a file handle fp and an integer length. It will read up to length bytes from the file referenced by fp and return them as string. For example, we can assume that we've just successfully opened a file with $fp = fopen("data.txt", "r"), and then say:

```
$data = fread($fp, 10);
```

This will read the first 10 bytes from data.txt and assign them to $data as characters in a string.

There are a couple of things to note at this stage:

- ❑ Say we now repeat this call to fread(); the first call will have left the file position indicator 10 bytes lower down the file. We therefore won't be reading the same data, rather the next 10 bytes in the file starting from where we left off last time.

- ❑ If there are less than 10 bytes left to read in the file, fread() will simply read and return as many as there are.

### fwrite()

In a similar fashion, we can use fwrite() to write data to a file. It requires two arguments, a file handle fp and a string string, and will write the contents of string to the file referenced by fp, returning the number of bytes written (or –1 on error). Assuming we've successfully opened a file with $fp = fopen("data.txt", "w"), we could say:

```
fwrite($fp, "ABCxyz");
```

This would write the character string `"ABCxyz"` to the beginning of the file `data.txt`. Having used write-only mode to open the file, we'll lose any prior contents (and even create the file if it didn't already exist); however, repeating this call will append the same 6 bytes to what we've just written, so that the file contains the characters `"ABCxyzABCxyz"`. Once again, it's the file position indicator in action.

If we specify an integer `length` as a third argument, it stops writing after `length` bytes (assuming this is reached before the end of `string`). We might have:

```php
fwrite($fp, "abcdefghij", 4);
```

This would write the first 4 bytes of `"abcdefghij"` (that is, `"abcd"`) to the file referenced by `$fp`. If `string` contained fewer than `length` bytes, it would be written to the file in full.

We now know enough to do something useful, so without further ado....

## Try It Out – A Simple Hit Counter

One very popular use for web scripts is the hit counter, which is used to show how many times a web page has been visited. It is therefore a useful way to find out how popular a web site is. Hit counters come in different forms, the simplest of which is a text counter. A simple script for a text-based counter is shown below.

```php
<?php
//hit_counter1.php
$counter_file = "./count.dat";
if(!($fp = fopen($counter_file, "r"))) die ("Cannot open $counter_file.");
$counter = (int) fread($fp, 20);
fclose($fp);

$counter++;

echo "You're visitor No. $counter.";

$fp = fopen($counter_file, "w");
fwrite($fp, $counter);
fclose($fp);
?>
```

Save this script as `hit_counter1.php` and give it a try. Here's a sample run:

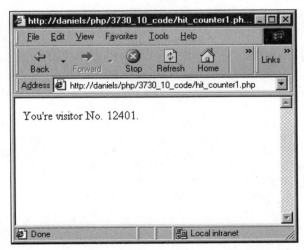

You'll see the counter incremented each time you reload the page.

> Note that the script assumes you already have a data file named `count.dat` in the current directory, that is, the directory from which you ran the script. If this file doesn't exist, an error occurs and the script aborts with an error message to that effect.
>
> You can make the file by saving a blank text file using a text editor, or by using the UNIX `touch` command:
>
> ```
> > touch count.dat
> ```

If you want to, you can specify a count number to start with inside the data file. If you're running the script on the Linux platform, make sure your web server has read and write permissions to this data file.

### How It Works

First of all, the file `count.dat` (in the current directory) is called by `fopen()` in read-only mode:

```
$counter_file = "./count.dat";
if(!($fp = fopen($counter_file, "r"))) die ("Cannot open $counter_file.");
```

We assign the file handle returned by `fopen()` to the variable `$fp`, which can be used from now on to refer to the open file. The function returns `False` upon error, so in the event that the specified file doesn't exist, or an error occurs while opening it, the script will `die` with an appropriate error message.

Next, the script uses the file handle to read the 'hit count' value from the open file. As you can see, the script calls `fread()` to read 20 bytes from the data file (enough to store at least half a million hits):

```
$counter = (int) fread($fp, 20);
```

Since `fread()` returns a string value, the last number of accesses read from the data file needs to be converted to an integer value, so we typecast it accordingly.

The `fclose()` function closes the file referenced by the file handle `$fp`, writing any unwritten data out to the file:

```
fclose($fp);
```

After closing the data file, the script increments the counter and tells the visitor how many times the page has been accessed:

```
$counter++;
echo "You're visitor No. $counter.";
```

If we were to stop here, the counter would never change, since the data file remains the same; we have yet to store the incremented counter in the data file. To do just that, we open the file once again by calling `fopen()`, but this time in write-only mode. Note that this mode overwrites the existing contents of the file.

```
    $fp = fopen($counter_file, "w");
    fwrite($fp, $counter);
    fclose($fp);
```

By calling `fwrite()` with the `$counter` variable as the second argument, we ensure that the exact length of the string is written to the data file, so the `length` argument is not required. Once again, we close the file with `fclose()` when we're finished with it.

You may decide to get creative and make a graphical counter. Used in conjunction with a set of images, the simple text counter script we've produced here can be modified to display graphics. For instance, if you have an image for each counter digit (`1.gif`, `2.gif`, `3.gif`, and so on), you could use each digit value to specify the image associated with the digit:

```php
<?php
//hit_counter2.php
$counter_file = "./count.dat";
$image_dir = "./images";
if(!($fp = fopen($counter_file, "r"))) die ("Cannot open $counter_file.");
$counter = (int) fread($fp, 20);
fclose($fp);

$counter++;

for($i=0; $i < strlen($counter); $i++) {
    $image_src = $image_dir . "/" . substr($counter, $i, 1) . ".gif";
    $image_tag_str .= "<IMG SRC=\"$image_src\" BORDER=\"0\">";
}

echo "You're visitor No. $image_tag_str.";

$fp = fopen($counter_file, "w");
fwrite($fp, $counter);
fclose($fp);
?>
```

We've simply added a `for` loop to step through possible values for the `$counter` variable, associating each digit value with a corresponding digit image. The loop tests to see if every digit has been processed by testing the length of the string held in the `$counter` variable.

Here's what it looks like when the script is run:

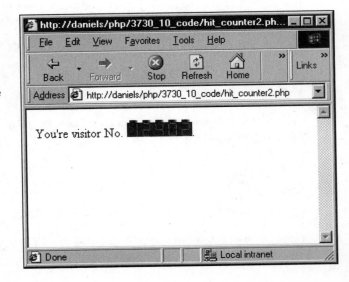

## Reading and Writing Characters in Files

Okay, so we can now write strings to a file and read them back again; all well and good. That's not the end of the story though.

Say we wanted to read the entire contents of a file, or perhaps analyze it one character at a time. We could do both of these using `fread()` without too much trouble, for example:

```
do {$one_char = fread($fp, 1); $counter .= $one_char; } while ($one_char);
```

However, PHP provides us with a set of functions that make this sort of thing much more straightforward.

### fgetc()

This function can be used to read from files one character at a time. `fgetc()` takes a single argument, a file handle `fp`, and returns just one character from the file it points to; it returns `False` when it reaches the end of the file. This is basically just the same as the `fread()` above:

```
$one_char = fgetc($fp)
```

is equivalent to saying:

```
$one_char = fread($fp,1)
```

So, what happens if we modify our original hit counter example to use `fgetc()`? We could have:

```php
<?php
//hit_counter3.php
$counter_file = "./count.dat";
if(!($fp = fopen($counter_file, "r"))) die ("Cannot open $counter_file.");

do {
    $one_char = fgetc($fp);
    $counter .= $one_char;
} while($one_char);
$counter = (int) $counter;
fclose($fp);

...
```

We use a `while` loop to read the entire contents of the data file, since `fgetc()` reads from the file one character at a time. We therefore need to know when to stop reading. Here, we've assigned the last-read character to a dummy variable, so that if it's `False` we can stop looping. However, there's a flaw. As soon as we read either `"0"` or `" "` from the file, our loop condition is going to fail and we won't read any more data. If we plan on attracting any more than 9 hits, this is going to be a big problem.

Fortunately, there's another way to do this.

### feof()

The `feof()` function serves a single, simple purpose: it returns `True` on reaching the **end** of a specified file (or if an error occurs) and returns `False` otherwise. It takes just one argument – the relevant file handle:

```
feof($fp)
```

We can therefore use its logical negative as the condition in our loop, to test whether the file position indicator has reached the end of the file:

```php
<?php
//hit_counter4.php
$counter_file = "./count.dat";
if(!($fp = fopen($counter_file, "r"))) die ("Cannot open $counter_file.");
while(!feof($fp)) $counter .= fgetc($fp);
$counter = (int) $counter;
fclose($fp);

$counter++;

echo "You're visitor No. $counter.";

$fp = fopen($counter_file, "w");
fwrite($fp, $counter);
fclose($fp);
?>
```

## fgets()

If we use `fgetc()` in this way to try and read a large file, it's going to take ages to run, as it will only read one character at a time. Fortunately though, PHP provides `fgets()` to help you read sets of characters. This function takes two arguments, `fp` and `length`, and returns a string of maximum length 'length – 1' bytes, as read from the file pointed to by `fp`. It will stop reading for any one of three reasons:

❑ the specified number of bytes has been read

❑ a new line is encountered

❑ the end of the file is reached

The difference between `fgets()` and `fread()` is that `fgets()` stops reading when it reaches end-of-line and reads up to `length - 1` bytes, whereas `fread()` reads past end-of-line and reads up to `length` bytes.

We can apply it to our hit counter like this:

```php
<?php
//hit_counter5.php
$counter_file = "./count.dat";
if(!($fp = fopen($counter_file, "r"))) die ("Cannot open $counter_file.");
$counter = (int) fgets($fp, 20);
fclose($fp);

...
```

Since the counter only needs one line from the data file, our call to `fgets()` will return the last counter value, as we want it to.

### *fputs()*

This is simply an alias for `fwrite()`, and the two are functionally identical.

## *Reading Entire Files*

We're now going to move to the opposite extreme, and look at functions we can use to access files' complete contents in one go.

### *file()*

This takes just one argument: a string containing the **name** of a file. For example:

```
file("/home/chris/myfile.txt")
```

will return the entire contents of `myfile.txt` (in the directory `/home/chris/`) as an array, using the newline character – CR LF on the Windows platform – to delimit elements. Note that the newline character is left attached at the end of each line stored in the array. This function doesn't require us to specify a file handle as it lets us refer to the filename explicitly; it automatically opens, reads, and closes the file once it's done.

Here's the `file()` version of our original hit counter:

```php
<?php
//hit_counter6.php
$counter_file = "./count.dat";
$lines = file($counter_file);
$counter = (int) $lines[0];

$counter++;

echo "You're visitor No. $counter.";

if(!($fp = fopen($counter_file, "w"))) die ("Cannot open $counter_file.");
fwrite($fp, $counter);
fclose($fp);
?>
```

The entire contents of the data file are read into the array `$lines` and only the first element of the array is extracted: the first line of the file.

We could actually do just the same using a mixture of `feof()` and `fgets()` like this:

```php
$fp = fopen ("./count.dat", "r");
while (!feof($fp)) $lines[] = fgets($fp, 1024);
fclose ($fp);
```

However, since the `file()` function will do all this for us, there's really no need.

As with `fopen()`, it can also fetch files on a remote host:

```php
$file_lines = file( "http://www.whatyoumaycallit.com/index.html" );
foreach($file_lines as $line) echo $line;
```

Although this function can be very useful for reading the entire contents of a file, you should exercise caution when using it – if it tries to read a very large file, it may end up consuming all the memory allocated to PHP; not a good move.

### fpassthru()

If all you want to do is read and print the entire file to the web browser, you can use the `fpassthru()` function. This takes a single argument, a file handle, which it uses to read the remaining data from a file (that is, from the current position until end-of-file). It then writes results to standard output.

Here's the corresponding version of the hit counter:

```php
<?php
//hit_counter7.php
$counter_file = "./count.dat";
if(!($fp = fopen($counter_file, "r"))) die ("Cannot open $counter_file.");
$counter = (int) fread($fp, 20);
fclose($fp);

$counter++;

if(!($fp = fopen($counter_file, "w"))) die ("Cannot open $counter_file.");
fwrite($fp, $counter);
fclose($fp);

if(!($fp = fopen($counter_file, "r"))) die ("Cannot open $counter_file.");
echo "You're visitor No. ";
fpassthru($fp);
?>
```

Note that only data from the *current* file position onwards is written. If you read a couple of lines from a file before calling `fpassthru()`, for example, it will only print the subsequent contents of the file. The file is closed when the function finishes reading, so there is no need to call `fclose()`. In fact, if you do, a warning will be displayed complaining the file pointer is not valid.

### readfile()

We can also print the contents of a file without even having to call `fopen()`, by using `readfile()`. This function takes a filename as its single argument, reads the whole file, and then writes it to standard output, returning the number of bytes read (or `False` upon error). We can apply it like this:

```php
<?php
//hit_counter8.php
$counter_file = "./count.dat";
if(!($fp = fopen($counter_file, "r"))) die ("Cannot open $counter_file.");
$counter = (int) fread($fp, 20);
fclose($fp);

$counter++;

if(!($fp = fopen($counter_file, "w"))) die ("Cannot open $counter_file.");
fwrite($fp, $counter);
fclose($fp);

echo "You're visitor No. ";
readfile($counter_file);
?>
```

Note that here, as in the previous script, all read and write operations on the data file take place *before* the incremented counter is echoed out.

## Random Access to File Data

As you may have realized, it would be rather more efficient if we opened the file for both read and write operations with a single `fopen()` call. However, using the functions we've met so far, we can only manipulate data sequentially, that is, in the same order that it is (or will be) arranged in the file. This puts a major limitation on what we can usefully achieve by doing it this way; once the file position indicator's passed a certain point in a file, we'd need to close and reopen the file before we could access data at that point. Unless our data access is terribly well organized in advance (not likely in real-life situations, where it's often impossible to predict what we might need to do), we'll end up opening our data file as many (if not more) times as before.

What we really need is some way to move the file position indicator around in the file without having to close and reopen it. We're now going to meet some functions that let us do just this.

### fseek()

PHP provides a number of functions that are specifically designed to let you read from or write to specific positions within a file.

Specifying a file handle `fp` and an integer `offset` as arguments, `fseek()` will move the file position indicator associated with `fp` to a position determined by `offset`; by default, this offset is measured in bytes from the beginning of the file. For example:

```
fseek($fp, 5);
$one_char = fgetc($fp);
```

This will place the file position indicator for the file associated with handle `$fp` just *after* the fifth byte in that file. The following call to `fgetc()` therefore returns the contents of the sixth byte.

A third optional argument, `whence`, can be specified with the following values, to calculate the relative offset as described:

❑   SEEK_SET – beginning of the file + `offset`

❑   SEEK_CUR – current position + `offset` (default)

❑   SEEK_END – end of the file + `offset`

Note that `fseek()` is rather unusual, as it's an integer PHP function that returns 0, not 1, upon success (it also returns –1 upon failure). Note that you can't use this function with files on remote hosts opened through either an HTTP URL or FTP.

### ftell()

This is another useful function, which takes a file handle and returns the current offset (in bytes) of the corresponding file position indicator. For example:

```
$fpi_offset = ftell($fp);
```

### *rewind()*

This does the equivalent of what a rewind button on your cassette player does – it takes a file handle and resets the corresponding file position indicator to the beginning of the file. We can say:

```
rewind($fp);
```

This is functionally equivalent to:

```
fseek($fp, 0);
```

As we saw earlier, the `fpassthru()` function outputs file data from the current file position onwards. Therefore, if you have already read data from a file, but want to echo its entire contents, you need to call `rewind()` first.

We can use `rewind()` to revise our counter script so that it only has to open the data file once, for both reading and writing:

```php
<?php
//hit_counter9.php
$counter_file = "./count.dat";
if(!($fp = fopen($counter_file, "r+"))) die ("Cannot open $counter_file.");
$counter = (int) fread($fp, 20);
$counter++;

echo "You're visitor No. $counter.";
rewind($fp);
fwrite($fp, $counter);
fclose($fp);
?>
```

As you see, the data file is only opened once, in 'read and write' mode. After reading the last access number from the file and displaying it, we rewind the file to reset the file position indicator.

## Try It Out – Navigating Within a File

Here's another example that uses these three navigating functions:

```php
<?php
//nav_file.php
$name_field_len = 15;
$country_code_field_len = 2;
$country_field_len = 20;
$email_field_len = 30;

if(!($fp = fopen("./address.dat", "r")))
    die ("Cannot open the address data file.");

do {
    $address = '';
    $field = fread($fp, $name_field_len);
    $address .= $field;
```

```
      $field = fread($fp, $country_code_field_len);
      $address .= $field;
      $field = fread($fp, $country_field_len);
      $address .= $field;
      $field = fread($fp, $email_field_len);
      $address .= $field;
      echo "$address<BR>";
   } while ($field);

   rewind($fp);

   echo "<BR>";

   fseek($fp, $name_field_len);

   do {
      $country_code = fread($fp, $country_code_field_len);
      fseek($fp, ftell($fp) + $country_field_len +
                              $email_field_len +
                              $name_field_len + 1);
      //NB: change '+1' to '+2' on Win32 platforms
      echo "$country_code<BR>";
   } while($country_code);

   fclose($fp);
?>
```

This script assumes you have an address book data file called `address.dat` in the current directory that looks like this:

```
Wankyu Choi     KRRepublic of Korea   wankyu@whatyoumaycallit.com
James Hetfield  USUnited States       james@headbangers.com
Nomura Sensei   JPJapan               nomura@nosuchsite.com
```

Here's the output from a test run:

```
Wankyu Choi KRRepublic of Korea wankyu@whatyoumaycallit.com
James Hetfield USUnited States james@headbangers.com
Nomura Sensei JPJapan nomura@nosuchsite.com


KR
US
JP
```

Records in this data file are separated by a newline character (CR LF for Windows platforms). Each field has a set length: 15 characters for the name field, 2 characters for the country code field, and so on.

### How It Works

We start by opening the file `address.dat` for reading in the current directory. First, we display all the records as they are. When `fread()` reaches end-of-file, `$field` is set to `False` and the first loop terminates:

```
if(!($fp = fopen("./address.dat", "r")))
                die ("Cannot open the address data file.");

do {
    $address = '';
    $field = fread($fp, $name_field_len);
    $address .= $field;
    $field = fread($fp, $country_code_field_len);
    $address .= $field;
    $field = fread($fp, $country_field_len);
    $address .= $field;
    $field = fread($fp, $email_field_len);
    $address .= $field;
    echo "$address<BR>";
} while ($field);
```

We then `rewind` the data file and move the file position indicator to the end of the first name field entry, so that we're ready to read and display the country code field values:

```
rewind($fp);
fseek($fp, $name_field_len);
```

We now initiate a `do...while` loop, within which we shall assign the country code data to a variable with `fread()`, move the file position indicator to the start of the next country code field, and finally output the country code that was just read. We start by assigning a value to `$country_code`:

```
do {
    $country_code = fread($fp, $country_code_field_len);
```

We determine the exact position of the next country code field as follows:

❑   get the current position of the file position indicator, as returned by `ftell($fp)`

❑   add to this the total length of the remaining fields and a trailing newline character

By using this as the second argument in a call to `fseek()`, we set the file position indicator to the appropriate point in the file:

```
fseek($fp, ftell($fp) + $country_field_len + $email_field_len +
                                    $name_field_len + 1);
```

Note that for Windows platforms, the length of a CR LF combination should be given as 2 instead of 1.

We echo the recorded value and close the loop, which cycles as long as `$country_code` is True:

```
    echo "$country_code<BR>";
} while($country_code);
```

Finally, we close the file with:

```
fclose($fp);
```

# Getting Information on Files

Earlier on, we demonstrated how we could run into problems if we ran the counter script and the file `count.dat` didn't exist, and so we made sure we performed some basic error checking when we opened the file. This is a very simple approach; if something does go wrong, the user won't necessarily know what the problem is.

We're now going to take a look at some of the functions PHP provides to let us access file information. For example, rather than just spewing out a standard error message when we fail to open a file, we can use `file_exists()` to discover whether the file exists. If it doesn't, we can infer that the current user is the first visitor to the site and create the data file. We can say:

```
file_exists("/home/chris/count.dat")
```

This will return `True` if `count.dat` exists in `/home/chris/`, and `False` otherwise. The error checking for our hit counter might now take this form:

```php
<?php
//hit_counter_10.php
$counter_file = "./count.dat";
if(file_exists($counter_file)) {
    if(!($fp = fopen($counter_file, "r+")))
                die("Cannot open $counter_file");
    $counter = (int) fread($fp, filesize($counter_file));
    $counter++;
    rewind($fp);
}
else {
    if(!($fp = fopen($counter_file, "w")))
                die("Cannot open $counter_file");
    $counter = 1;
}

echo "You're visitor No. $counter.";

fwrite($fp, $counter);
fclose($fp);
?>
```

This is just one of a number of functions that return useful information on a given file. In a similar fashion, we can use the `filesize()` function to determine exactly how many bytes should be read from the counter data file. Just as with `file_exists()`, this function takes a *filename string* argument directly instead of a file handle:

```
filesize("/home/chris/count.dat")
```

This will return the size of the specified file in bytes, or `False` upon error. We could therefore use `filesize()` in this example to determine how many bytes should be read from the data file to get the number of hits:

```
<?php
//hit_counter11.php
$counter_file = "./count.dat";
if(file_exists($counter_file)) {
    if(!($fp = fopen($counter_file, "r+")))
                    die("Cannot open $counter_file");
    $counter = (int) fread($fp, filesize($counter_file));
    $counter++;
    rewind($fp);
}

...
```

## Time-related Properties

As well as its contents, a file will have other properties that can provide useful information. These will principally depend on the operating system in which they are created and modified. On UNIX platforms such as Linux for example, properties will include creation date, modification date, last access date, and user permissions. With just a little extra code, we can make the hit counter show when the last access was made. The function `fileatime()` returns the **last access time** for a file in a UNIX timestamp format. Note that on Windows this will only return the *last modified date*.

> *A UNIX timestamp is a long integer whose value can be interpreted as the number of seconds between the UNIX Epoch (January 1 1970) and a specified time and date.*

PHP provides two other time-related file functions:

❑ `filectime()` returns the time at which the file was last **changed** as a UNIX timestamp; a file is considered changed if it is created, written, or its permissions have been changed.

❑ `filemtime()` returns the time at which the file was last **modified** as a UNIX timestamp; the file is considered modified if it is created or has its contents changed.

`getdate()` is another PHP function that can be very useful when working with timestamps.

### Try It Out – Displaying the Last Access Time to the Counter Data File

```
<?php
//last_counter_access.php
$counter_file = "./count.dat";
if(file_exists($counter_file)) {
    $date_str = getdate(fileatime($counter_file));
    $year = $date_str["year"];
    $mon = $date_str["mon"];
    $mday = $date_str["mday"];
    $hours = $date_str["hours"];
    $minutes = $date_str["minutes"];
    $seconds = $date_str["seconds"];

    $date_str = "$hours:$minutes:$seconds $mday/$mon/$year";

    if(!($fp = fopen($counter_file, "r+")))
                    die("Cannot open $counter_file");
```

```
    $counter = (int) fread($fp, filesize($counter_file));
    $counter++;

    echo "You're visitor No. $counter.";
    echo "The last access was made at $date_str";
    rewind($fp);
}
else {
    if(!($fp = fopen($counter_file, "w")))
                    die("Cannot open $counter_file");
    $counter = 1;
    echo "You're visitor No. $counter.";
}

fwrite($fp, $counter);
fclose($fp);

?>
```

### How It Works

If the specified count.dat file exists, the script gets the last access time for the data file as a UNIX timestamp. This is converted to an associative array containing date information with the getdate() function, values are extracted from the appropriate elements, arranged, and stored in a string variable:

```
$counter_file = "./count.dat";
if(file_exists($counter_file)) {
    $date_str = getdate(fileatime($counter_file));
    $year = $date_str["year"];
    $mon = $date_str["mon"];
    $mday = $date_str["mday"];
    $hours = $date_str["hours"];
    $minutes = $date_str["minutes"];
    $seconds = $date_str["seconds"];

    $date_str = "$hours:$minutes:$seconds $mday/$mon/$year";
```

When we create, write to, or read from a file, UNIX considers the file to have been accessed. For this reason, we've called fileatime() *before* reading from the data file. This is what we do next. Still conditional on the actual existence of the count.dat file, we open it – or die trying – read its entire contents into the variable $counter, increment that variable, and print it out along with our formatted date information. We then rewind() the file position indicator – so that we're ready to write the new count – and close the body of the if statement:

```
    if(!($fp = fopen($counter_file, "r+")))
                    die("Cannot open $counter_file");

    $counter = (int) fread($fp, filesize($counter_file));
    $counter++;

    echo "You're visitor No. $counter. "
    echo "The last access was made at $date_str";
    rewind($fp);
}
```

We now hit the `else` clause; if the file `count.dat` didn't already exist, we create it with `fopen()`, specifying write-only. We initialize the counter at 1 and incorporate it in a displayed message:

```
else {
    if(!($fp = fopen($counter_file, "w")))
                    die("Cannot open $counter_file");
    $counter = 1;
    echo "You're visitor No. $counter.";
}
```

Finally, we write the new counter value to the `count.dat` file, and close it with `fclose()`:

```
fwrite($fp, $counter);
fclose($fp);
```

## Ownership and Permissions

In a similar way, we can get information on file ownership and permissions. On a UNIX system like Linux, all files are associated with a specific user and a specific group of users, and assigned flags that determine who has permission to read, write, or execute their contents.

> *User groups are defined in UNIX so that permissions can be easily extended to a certain set of users without extending them to everyone on the system. For example, several users who are working on the same project might wish to share files with each other, but no one else.*

Each of these three permissions can be granted (or withheld):

❑   the file **owner** – by default, this will be the user whose account was used to create the file

❑   a **group** of users – by default, the group to which the owner belongs

❑   **all** users – everyone with an account on the system

Users and groups in UNIX are identified by ID numbers as well as names. If you want to get information on a user by his ID number, you can use the `posix_getpwuid()` function, which returns an associative array with the following references:

| | |
|---|---|
| name | the shell account username of the user. |
| passwd | the encrypted user password. |
| uid | the ID number of the user. |
| gid | the group ID of the user. |
| gecos | a comma separated list containing the user's full name, office phone, office number, and home phone number. On most systems, only the user's full name is available. |
| dir | the absolute path to the home directory of the user. |
| shell | the absolute path to the user's default shell. |

Another PHP function, `posix_getgrgid()`, returns an associative array on a *group* identified by a group ID. This will contain the following elements of the group structure:

| | |
|---|---|
| name | the name of the group |
| gid | the ID number of the group |
| members | the number of members belonging to the group |

We're now going to see three functions that we can use to get at this information from our PHP scripts. All take a single argument, a filename string, and return information as follows:

❑ `fileowner()` returns the user ID of the owner of the specified file

❑ `filegroup()` returns the group ID of the owner of the specified file

❑ `filetype()` returns the type of the specified file – possible values are `fifo`, `char`, `dir`, `block`, `link`, `file`, and `unknown`

For example, we can use `filetype()` to check whether a given filename is a file or a directory:

```php
<?php
//file_type.php
$filename = "./counter.php";

$filegroup = filegroup($filename);
$fileowner = fileowner($filename);
$filetype = filetype($filename);

if($filetype == 'dir') echo "$filename is a directory.";
else if($filetype == 'file') echo "$filename is a file.<BR>";
else echo "$filename is neither a directory nor a file.<BR>";

echo "It belongs to user no.$fileowner and group no.$filegroup.<BR>";

echo "<BR>The user $fileowner info<BR>";
$user_info_array = posix_getpwuid($fileowner);
foreach($user_info_array as $key => $val) echo "$key => $val<BR>";

echo "<BR>The group $filegroup info<BR>";
$group_info_array = posix_getgrgid($filegroup);
foreach($group_info_array as $key => $val) echo "$key => $val<BR>";
?>
```

Shown overleaf, is a sample run:

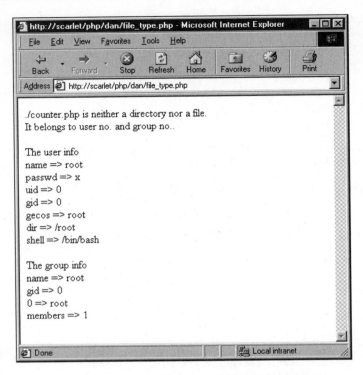

❑ is_dir() returns True if the given filename refers to a directory

❑ is_file() returns True if the given filename refers to a regular file

It's very simple to rewrite the script above so that it produces the same results using these functions:

```php
<?php
$filename = "./counter.php";
if(is_dir($filename)) echo "$filename is a directory.";
else if(is_file($filename)) echo "$filename is a file.";
else echo "$filename is neither a directory nor a file.";
?>
```

*As noted above, if you use fileatime() in Windows, it will return the last modified date; likewise, because Windows doesn't support file ownership, filegroup() and fileowner() will both return zero.*

## Try It Out – Getting More Information on a File

Here's a sample script that displays some properties on a given file:

```php
<?php
//file_info.php

function date_str($timestamp) {
```

```
        $date_str = getdate($timestamp);
        $year = $date_str["year"];
        $mon = $date_str["mon"];
        $mday = $date_str["mday"];
        $hours = $date_str["hours"];
        $minutes = $date_str["minutes"];
        $seconds = $date_str["seconds"];

        return "$hours:$minutes:$seconds $mday/$mon/$year";
    }

    function file_info($file) {
        global $WINDIR;

        $file_info_array["filesize"] =
                        number_format(filesize($file)) . " bytes.";
        $file_info_array["filectime"] = date_str(filectime($file));
        $file_info_array["filemtime"] = date_str(filemtime($file));

        if(!isset($WINDIR)) {
            $file_info_array["fileatime"] = date_str(fileatime($file));
            $file_info_array["filegroup"] = filegroup($file);
            $file_info_array["fileowner"] = fileowner($file);
        }
        $file_info_array["filetype"] = filetype($file);

        return $file_info_array;
    }

    $filename = "./count.dat";
    $file_info_array = file_info($filename);

    echo "<center>Stats for $filename</center>";
    foreach($file_info_array as $key=>$val) {
        echo ucfirst($key) . "=>". $val . "<br>";
    }
?>
```

### How It Works

Taking some lines of code from our last version of the hit counter, we put them in a complete function named date_str(), which returns a formatted date string:

```
function date_str($timestamp) {
    $date_str = getdate($timestamp);
    $year = $date_str["year"];
    $mon = $date_str["mon"];
    $mday = $date_str["mday"];
    $hours = $date_str["hours"];
    $minutes = $date_str["minutes"];
    $seconds = $date_str["seconds"];

    return "$hours:$minutes:$seconds $mday/$mon/$year";
}
```

The next `file_info()` function introduces a set of new file-related functions that return useful information on a given file:

```
function file_info($file) {
    global $HTTP_ENV_VARS;
    $file_info_array["filesize"] =
                    number_format(filesize($file)) . " bytes.";
    $file_info_array["filectime"] = date_str(filectime($file));
    $file_info_array["filemtime"] = date_str(filemtime($file));

    if(!isset($HTTP_ENV_VARS["windir"])) {
        $file_info_array["fileatime"] = date_str(fileatime($file));
        $file_info_array["filegroup"] = filegroup($file);
        $file_info_array["fileowner"] = fileowner($file);
    }

    $file_info_array["filetype"] = filetype($file);
    return $file_info_array;
}
```

Note that the environment variable `$WINDIR` is only set on the Windows platform, so we access it via `$HTTP_ENV_VARS` and use it as a flag to denote whether the script is being run on a Windows platform. If it is, we don't read the three fields that it doesn't support.

Finally, we specify a file, call our `file_info()` function and print out the contents of each element in the array it returns:

```
$filename = "./count.dat";
$file_info_array = file_info($filename);

echo "<center>Stats for $filename</center>";
foreach($file_info_array as $key=>$val) {
    echo ucfirst($key) . "=>". $val . "<br>";
}
```

This is what we see from a sample run with a Linux-based server:

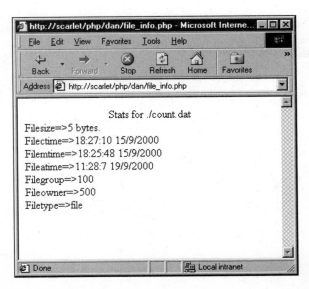

# Splitting the Name and Path from a File

It's often very useful to be able to separate a filename from its directory path; basename() does exactly this, taking a complete file path and returning just the filename. For example, the call:

```
$filename = basename("home/james/docs/index.html");
```

will assign "index.html" to $filename. You can specify a directory path, in which case the rightmost directory name is returned:

```
$dirname = basename("./docs");
```

This will assign the value "docs" to $dirname.

# Copying, Renaming and Deleting Files

PHP allows you to copy, rename, and delete files, as well as reading from them and writing to them. The functions we use to perform these operations are copy(), rename(), and unlink() respectively.

### copy()

The copy() function takes two string arguments referring to the source and destination files respectively. The following function call would copy the source file copyme.txt to the destination file copied.txt:

```
if(!copy("./copyme.txt", "copied.txt")) die("Can't copy the file copyme.txt to
copied.txt!");
```

### rename()

We can use this function to rename a file as follows:

```
if(!rename ("./address.dat", "address.backup"))
    die("Can't rename the file address.dat to address.backup!");
```

We can use these functions to upgrade the hit counter, so that it backs up its counter data after a given interval; that is, once an hour, once a day, once a week, and so on:

```
<?php
//hit_counter12.php
$counter_file = "./count.dat";
$counterbackup_file = "./count.backup";
$backup_interval = 24*60*60;

if(file_exists($counter_file)) {
    $date_str = getdate(filetime($counter_file));
    $year = $date_str["year"];
    $mon = $date_str["mon"];
    $mday = $date_str["mday"];
    $hours = $date_str["hours"];
```

```
    $minutes = $date_str["minutes"];
      $seconds = $date_str["seconds"];
    $date_str = "$hours:$minutes:$seconds $mday/$mon/$year";

      if((time() - fileatime($counterbackup_file)) >= $backup_interval) {
        @copy($counter_file, $counterbackup_file . time());
      }

    if(!($fp = fopen($counter_file, "r+")))
                    die("Cannot open $counter_file");
    $counter = (int) fread($fp, filesize($counter_file));
    $counter++;
    echo "You're visitor No. $counter. The
                    last access was made at $date_str";
    rewind($fp);
  }
  else {
    if(!($fp = fopen($counter_file, "w")))
                    die("Cannot open $counter_file");
    $counter = 1;
    echo "You're visitor No. $counter.";
  }

  fwrite($fp, $counter);
  fclose($fp);

  ?>
```

Here the $backup_interval variable is set in hours and subsequently multiplied by 3600 (one hour is 3600 seconds). Whenever the script is run, it checks the last access time for the counter data file. It also checks the current time by calling the time() function – this returns the current UNIX timestamp, that is, the current time in seconds since January 1st 1970 at 00:00:00.

If the last access time precedes the current time by more than $backup_interval seconds, the existing data file is backed up by using unlink() and copy() functions. We prevent old counter backup data from being deleted by appending the current time to the name of each file:

```
  @copy($counter_file, $counterbackup_file . time());
```

Note that we suppress any error messages the copy() function might churn out by putting the error suppressing operator @ before the function name.

### unlink()

This function takes a single string argument referring to the name of a file we want to delete. For example, if we wanted to say adios to the file trash.txt in the current directory, we should say:

```
  if(!unlink("./trash.txt")) die ("Can't delete the file trash.txt!");
```

Hang on just a minute – where did `unlink()` come from? Using the name `unlink()` for the 'delete file' function may seem quite odd, particularly if you don't have any experience with UNIX-like systems. Why don't we just call it `delete()`? Well, in a UNIX file system, there's a difference between the physical arrangement of files on a storage medium and the corresponding directory structure. It's perfectly possible, indeed common on UNIX, for different parts of a directory system to be stored on physically separate devices.

Files are stored in a specific location in the directory system by linking that point in the directory tree (called an **inode**) to the physical location where the file's data is stored. In UNIX, a file path is actually just a unique identifier for one of these inodes.

What's really odd about the UNIX system is that it's possible to link more than one point in the file system – more than one inode – to the same physical data, using what's called a **hard link** (see the manpage for the `ln` command for details). The data can be retrieved as long as there's at least one link to it. However, when you've destroyed *all* of the links, the data itself will be deleted. What we are actually doing when we use the command `unlink()` is destroying one of these links.

Since there will normally only be one link to a file's data, unlinking it will effectively delete the file. Consequently, if there's another link floating around the file system somewhere, the file won't actually be deleted. On Windows, it's not possible to link more than one point in the file system to the same data, so unlinking the file is equivalent to deleting it in all cases.

> **Many versions of PHP for Windows do not support the unlink() function at all.** Workarounds exist for this, but vary greatly according to which web server is being used. With Apache, for example, it's possible to pass a command like "del filename" direct to Windows, using a **system()** or **exec()** function call. If you've a combination such as this, you can therefore mimic **unlink()** with the following code:
>
> ```
> if(!isset($WINDIR)) {
>     $userfile = str_replace("/", "\\", $file);
>     exec("del $file");
>     if(file_exists("$file")) die("Can't delete the file $file.");
> }
> else if(!@unlink($file)) {
>     die("Can't delete the file $file.");
> }
> ```
>
> **Note that since del expects backslashes in the given path, we need to replace all the forward slashes in the path, which we do using str_replace().**

# Building a Text Editor

Now that we've gone through the basics of PHP's file handling capability, let's do something nice and practical. In this section, we'll see how to build a simple text file editor. It will take a filename as an argument, edit the file, and then save it. If it's not given a filename, the editor will create a new file.

First, let us imagine what the script would look like when finished. The picture in your mind eventually translates to the end-user interface. Since it's an editor, it would need a place where it stores text and lets the user manipulate it. We won't have to worry about implementing specific editing features like typing in characters, deleting them, moving the cursor, etc., since the HTML tag <TEXTAREA> can handle all the editing features we'll need. All we have to do is throw in a form that displays a scrolling text box, an edit field for typing in a file name, and a button to save the text.

Next, we need to decide how we'll alert the user upon errors, or get his confirmation about possibly disastrous actions such as overwriting an existing file. We'll be using some simple JavaScript tricks to achieve the goal. You can put a snippet of JavaScript into an HTML page by enclosing the code within the following tag combination:

```
<SCRIPT> JavaScript code goes here </SCRIPT>
```

For example, if you want to alert the user about an error, you can use the JavaScript's alert() method:

```
<SCRIPT> alert("Warning! An error occurred!"); </SCRIPT>
```

This will open up a small window displaying the specified error message. We can even tell the browser to return to the previous page upon error using the history.go(-1) method:

```
<SCRIPT>
alert("Warning! An error occurred! Let's get back to the previous page!");
history.go(-1);
</SCRIPT>
```

Getting confirmation from the user is just as easy. The confirm() method does the trick:

```
<SCRIPT>
result = confirm("Warning! Are you sure?");
if(!result) history.go(-1);
</SCRIPT>
```

The confirm() method returns the user's decision. If they press the YES button, True is returned and the specified action is executed. If they press CANCEL, False is assigned to the variable result, causing the browser to fall back to the previous page. We'll be using some of these tricks in the sample script. For now though, opposite is a sample run:

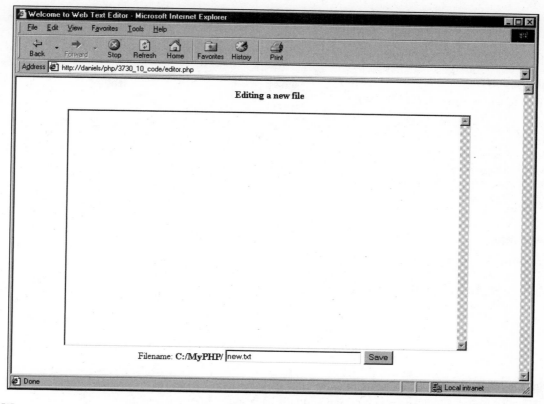

We start by putting global variables and commonly used functions in the `common.inc` include file. It's always good practice to put common elements that are shared and reusable by related scripts into a common include file.

## common.inc

First, the script needs to know the following information:

❑   the default directory path (outside which no user can access files)

```php
<?php
$default_dir = "./docs";
```

❑   the default filename for new files

```php
$default_filename = "new.txt";
```

❑   the size of the text area the editor will display

```php
$edit_form_cols = 80;
$edit_form_rows = 25;
```

We then define an array of filename extensions; we are going to interpret all files with these extensions as being plain text. If you want to add new extensions, just add them as elements here:

```
$text_file_array = array( "txt", "htm", "html", "php", "inc", "dat" );
```

We now define some functions that will simplify the process of making pages with HTML.

### html_header()

This function starts an HTML page:

```
function html_header() {
    ?>
    <HTML>
    <HEAD><TITLE>Welcome to Web Text Editor</TITLE></HEAD>
    <BODY>
    <?php
}
```

### html_footer()

This function ends an HTML page:

```
function html_footer() {
    ?>
    </BODY>
    </HTML>
    <?php
}
```

### error_message()

This function displays an error message and falls back to the previous page:

```
function error_message($msg) {
    html_header();
    echo "<SCRIPT>alert(\"$msg\"); history.go(-1)</SCRIPT>";
    html_footer();
    exit;
}
```

### date_str()

This is the same function we defined earlier in the chapter, and returns it a formatted date string:

```
function date_str($timestamp) {
    $date_str = getdate($timestamp);
    $year = $date_str["year"];
    $mon = $date_str["mon"];
    $mday = $date_str["mday"];
    $hours = $date_str["hours"];
    $minutes = $date_str["minutes"];
    $seconds = $date_str["seconds"];

    return "$hours:$minutes:$seconds $mday/$mon/$year";
}
```

### file_info()

This expands on the function we defined earlier, returning an associative array that contains various pieces of information relating to a given file:

```php
function file_info($file) {
    global $text_file_array, $WINDIR;

    $file_info_array["filesize"] =
                    number_format(filesize($file)) . " bytes.";

    $file_info_array["filectime"] = date_str(filectime($file));
    $file_info_array["filemtime"] = date_str(filemtime($file));
    if(!isset($WINDIR)) {
        $file_info_array["fileatime"] = date_str(fileatime($file));
        $file_info_array["filegroup"] = filegroup($file);
        $file_info_array["fileowner"] = fileowner($file);
    } else {
        $file_info_array["fileatime"] = "not available";
        $file_info_array["filegroup"] = "not available";
        $file_info_array["fileowner"] = "not available";
    }

    $extension = array_pop(explode(".", $file));

    if(in_array($extension, $text_file_array))
            $file_info_array["filetype"] = "text";
    else $file_info_array["filetype"] = "binary";

    return $file_info_array;
}

?>
```

Note how we extract the extension from a given file with explode(".", $file). This breaks up the filename using . as a delimiter, and returns the resulting pieces as an array. The last element of this array is extracted using the array_pop() function, and stored in $extension. We don't assume that the extension is the second element.

## editor.php

In the editor.php script, we begin by including the common.inc file:

```php
<?php
//editor.php
include "./common.inc";
```

### editor_form()

This function displays a form where the user can edit a file. It takes two arguments: the complete path to a file to edit, and an indicator whether it's a new file:

```php
function editor_form($dir, $filename, $is_new) {
    global $PHP_SELF, $edit_form_cols, $edit_form_rows;
```

Store the complete file path in the variable $filepath:

```
$filepath = "$dir/$filename";
```

If an existing filename is given, the function reads the entire file and joins every line into a single string $filebody, using the implode() function:

```
if(!$is_new) $filebody = implode("",file($filepath));
```

The file_info() function returns an array of useful information on a given file:

```
$file_info_array = file_info("$filepath");
```

The $editable flag is turned on first and gets turned off if a given file is not editable:

```
$editable = 1;
if($file_info_array["filetype"] != "text") {
    $filebody = $filepath . " is not a text file.
                    You had better not edit it.";
    $editable = 0;
}
```

If a given filename doesn't end with an editable extension, the editor refuses to load it and prompts a warning that the given file is not editable; otherwise it displays an editor form:

```
    if($editable) {
?>
```

If the file is editable, the function displays a form containing a scrolling text edit box:

```
<CENTER>
```

Note that we feed the $PHP_SELF variable to the form's action attribute, which ensures the form will always call the editor script even if we change its name:

```
<FORM NAME="edit_form" METHOD="POST" action="<?php echo $PHP_SELF ?>">
```

The script determines which course of action should be taken based on the value in the form's action hidden field:

```
<INPUT TYPE="HIDDEN" NAME="action" VALUE="save_file">
<INPUT TYPE="HIDDEN" NAME="dir" VALUE="<?php echo "$dir" ?>">
```

The form draws a text box based on the $edit_form_rows and $edit_form_cols variables:

```
<TEXTAREA ROWS="<?php echo $edit_form_rows ?>" NAME="filebody"
        COLS="<?php echo $edit_form_cols ?>" WRAP="soft">
<?php echo "$filebody"; ?>
</TEXTAREA><BR>
Filename: <?php echo "<STRONG>$dir/</STRONG>"; ?>
```

We also need a text edit field for the user to type in the name of a file when saving it:

```
<INPUT TYPE="TEXT" NAME="filename" VALUE="<?php echo $filename ?>"
                         SIZE="30">
<INPUT TYPE="SUBMIT" VALUE="Save" NAME="Submit">
</FORM>
</CENTER>

<?php
    }
```

If the file is not editable, display a warning message instead:

```
    else {
        echo "<CENTER><STRONG><FONT COLOR=\"RED\">
             $filebody</FONT></STRONG></CENTER>\n";
    }
}
```

### edit_new_form()

This displays a button giving the user an option to edit a new file:

```
function edit_new_form() {
    global $PHP_SELF, $default_dir, $dir;
?>

<CENTER><FORM METHOD="POST" ACTION="<?php echo $PHP_SELF ?>">
<INPUT TYPE="HIDDEN" NAME="action" VALUE="editor_page">
<INPUT TYPE="HIDDEN" NAME="dir" VALUE="<?php echo $dir ?>">
<INPUT TYPE="SUBMIT" VALUE="Edit New"></FORM></CENTER>

<?php
}
```

### save_file()

This function saves a given file:

```
function save_file() {
    global $filename, $filebody, $dir, $PHP_SELF;
```

If the file already exists, we prompt the user for confirmation of an "overwrite" operation using the JavaScript confirm() method. If the user clicks on the Cancel button or an error occurs while trying to open the file for writing, it falls back to the previous page:

```
    if(file_exists("$dir/$filename")) {
        echo "<SCRIPT>result =
            confirm(\"Overwrite '$dir/$filename'?\");
            if(!result) history.go(-1);</SCRIPT>";
    }
```

Then save the file as requested:

```
if($file = fopen("$dir/$filename", "w")) {
    fputs($file, $filebody);
    fclose($file);
}
```

Upon error, display an error message and move back to the previous page:

```
else {
    error_message("Can't save file $dir/$filename.");
}
```

This point will only be reached once the new file has been successfully written to the disk; whether or not the file existed before, we can now safely assume that it does. The final statement tells the browser to load the script with the given directory and filename:

```
    echo
"<SCRIPT>self.location.href='$PHP_SELF?dir=$dir&filename=$filename';</SCRIPT>";
}
```

### editor_page()

This is the main function for our text editor:

```
function editor_page() {
    global $dir, $filename, $default_filename;
```

The $is_new flag is turned off first and gets turned on if the name of a given file is empty, in which case, the default filename is assumed. You can run the editor script either with or without any filename argument. If you run it without giving any filename, the script will think you're editing a new file. If a filename is given like the following:

```
http://www.whatyoumaycallit.com/editor.php?filename=file.txt
```

The script will first test to see if that file exists. If it does, the script will load it into the editor form. We will introduce an easier way of loading existing files in the latter half of this chapter.

```
    $is_new = 0;

    if($filename == '') {
        $filename = $default_filename;
        $is_new = 1;
    }
```

If a given file is not to be found, the $is_new flag is turned on:

```
    if(!file_exists("$dir/$filename")) $is_new = 1;
```

If the script has loaded an existing file, a button will be displayed giving the user an option to edit a new one:

```
if(!$is_new) {
edit_new_form();
?>
```

A table of information on the file is also displayed:

```
<TABLE BORDER="1" WIDTH="100%">
<TR><TH WIDTH="100%" COLSPAN="2">
<CENTER><STRONG>Stats for <?php echo "$dir/$filename" ?>
</TD></TR>

<?php
$file_info_array = file_info("$dir/$filename");
```

The `foreach` loop steps through the `$file_info_array` assigning each key and its value to the `$key` and `$val` variables:

```
foreach($file_info_array as $key=>$val) {
```

The `ucfirst()` function capitalizes the first character of the string value in the `$key` variable:

```
        echo "<TR><TH WIDTH=\"30%\">". ucfirst($key) .
            "</TD><TD WIDTH=\"70%\">" . $val .
            "</TD></TR>\n";
    }
?>
</TABLE>
<?php
```

No information is displayed if the current file is a new one:

```
    } else {
        echo "<CENTER><STRONG>Editing a new file</STRONG></CENTER>\n";
    }
```

Note that the `editor_form()` function is called with the `$is_new` variable as the second argument. If the flag is turned off, the given file is opened and read into the editor form:

```
    editor_form($dir,$filename,$is_new);
}
```

Now we get to the main part of the script, where we choose which functions to call, based on the arguments specified in the URL that calls the script. First, we ensure that the specified directory `$dir` is defined and lives under our root directory `$default_dir`:

```
if(empty($dir) || !ereg($default_dir, $dir)) {
    $dir = $default_dir;
}
```

If $dir is empty or doesn't contain the default path $default_dir, it is set to the default path.

We now use the value of $action to determine which functions we want to call:

```php
switch ($action) {
    case "save_file":
        save_file();
        break;
    default:
        html_header();
        editor_page();
        html_footer();
        break;
}
?>
```

Now that we've covered how to deal with the members of the server file system family, let's move on to see the homes that house them.

# Working with Directories

PHP lets you manipulate directories in much the same way as files, providing a number of equivalent functions. As is the case with file functions, some directory functions use a directory handle, whereas others use a string containing the directory name you wish to work with. A **directory handle** is similar to a file handle – it's an integer value pointing to a directory, which can be obtained by specifying the directory in a call to the opendir() function:

```php
$dp = opendir ("/home/james/")
```

Upon error, this will return False. As you may have guessed, you can close a directory by specifying the appropriate handle to the function closedir():

```php
closedir($dp);
```

The readdir() function returns the next entry listed in the open directory. This list includes entries for . (used to specify the current directory) and .. (likewise, specifying the parent of the current directory). PHP maintains an internal pointer referring to the next entry in the list just as the file position indicator points to the position where next file operation should occur.

## Try It Out – Listing Directory Entries

We can now set up a loop to get all the entries from a specified directory:

```php
<?php
//dir_list.php
$default_dir = "./docs";
if(!($dp = opendir($default_dir))) die("Cannot open $default_dir.");
while($file = readdir($dp))
    if($file != '.' && $file != '..') echo "$file<br>";
closedir($dp);
?>
```

### How It Works

We first get a handle on the directory given, and then set up a loop that reads entries from that directory, and (as long as they're not "." or "..") prints them out. The loop is conditional on the return value of `readdir()`, which will be `False` when the list of entries is exhausted:

```php
while($file = readdir($dp))
    if($file != '.' && $file != '..') echo "$file<br>";
```

Finally, we close the directory with `closedir()`.

Note that the returned filenames are not sorted in any way. In order to sort them, we need to set up two loops, as illustrated below. First though, we read the entries into an array:

```php
<?php
$default_dir = "./docs";
if(!($dp = opendir($default_dir))) die("Cannot open $default_dir.");
while($file = readdir($dp)) $filenames[] = $file;
closedir($dp);
```

The `$filenames` array now contains every entry in the directory. Note that we didn't use any indexing number in the array, so PHP automatically takes care of the indexing.

Finally, we call `sort()` to arrange the array entries in ascending order, and display all except the current and parent directories:

```php
sort($filenames);

for($i=0; $i < count($filenames); $i++)
    if($filenames[$i] != '.' && $filenames[$i] != '..')
        echo $filenames[$i] . "<br>";
?>
```

## Other Directory Functions

Just as we saw with its file functions, PHP provides us with a range of ways to manipulate directories.

### rewinddir()

As is the case with files, if you want to move back to the first entry in a given directory while working with it, you need to reset PHP's internal pointer. To do so, just call `rewinddir()` – the directory counterpart to the `rewind()` function for files – specifying the relevant directory handle.

The rest of the directory handling functions take a path string directly instead of using a directory handle.

### chdir()

The `chdir()` function call changes PHP's current directory to the given directory:

```php
if(chdir("/home/apache/htdocs/htmls"))
echo "The current directory is /home/apache/htdocs/htmls.";
```

```
else
    echo "Cannot change the current directory to /home/apache/htdocs/htmls.";
```

### rmdir()

The `rmdir()` function **removes** a given directory. The directory must be empty, and you will need appropriate permissions to do so. For example:

```
rmdir("/tmp/rubbish/");
```

### mkdir()

The `mkdir()` function **creates** a directory as specified in its first argument. You can also specify a directory mode argument as a three digit octal number. The following code snippet first tests whether `/home/apache/htdocs/test` exists. If it does, it is removed, and the same directory is then recreated, with all permissions granted to all users:

```
$default_dir = "/home/apache/htdocs/test";
if(file_exists($default_dir)) rmdir($default_dir);
mkdir($default_dir, 0777);
```

### dirname()

The `dirname()` function returns the directory part of a given filename. For example:

```
$filepath = "/home/apache/htdocs/index.html";
$dirname = dirname($filepath);
$filename = basename($filepath);
```

The string `$dirname` will now contain `"/home/apache/htdocs"` and `$filename` will hold `index.html`.

### dir()

PHP offers an alternative object-oriented mechanism for working with directories: the `dir` object. In order to use this method, we need to instantiate the object first by calling the `dir()` constructor with the name of the directory we wish to work with as follows:

```
$dir = dir("/home/apache/htdocs");
```

The `dir` object provides two properties: handle and path. These refer to the directory handle and the path respectively:

```
echo $dir->handle; # echoes the directory handle
echo $dir->path; # echoes "/home/apache/htdocs"
```

You can use the handle property with other directory functions such as `readdir()`, `rewinddir()` and `closedir()`.

The `dir` object supports three methods: `read()`, `rewind()`, and `close()`. These are functionally equivalent to `readdir()`, `rewinddir()`, and `closedir()` respectively. We can rewrite the directory listing script by using the `dir` object:

```php
<?php
$default_dir = "/home/apache/htdocs";
$dir = dir($default_dir);

while($file = $dir->read()) if($file != '.' && $file != '..')
    echo $file . "<br>";
$dir->close();
?>
```

# Traversing a Directory Hierarchy

Now let's see how easily we can use recursive techniques in PHP to walk through a directory hierarchy. As we saw in Chapter 6, recursion is particularly useful when a script has to perform repetitive operations and iterate over a given set of data. Traversing a directory hierarchy is therefore a very good example. A directory may hold subdirectories as well as files. If you want to create a script that lists all the files and subdirectories under a given directory, you'd take the following steps:

**1.** Read the entries in the current directory.

**2.** If the next entry is a file, display its name. If the next entry is a subdirectory, display its name and go into it and return to step 1.

As you can see, step 2 repeats the whole process by itself when necessary – the recursion will continue until there are no more subdirectories left to traverse. Let's look at some code:

```php
<?php
//nav_dir.php
$default_dir = "/home/james";
```

The `traverse_dir()` function is based on the concept of recursion and traverses the whole directory hierarchy under a specified directory. First, the function echoes out which directory it is currently going through. Then, a call to `chdir()` ensures that the `$dir` directory string argument is equal to PHP's current working directory.

```php
function traverse_dir($dir) {
    echo "Traversing $dir....<BR>";
    chdir($dir);
    if(!($dp = opendir($dir))) die("Can't open $dir.");

    while($file = readdir($dp)) {
```

Recursion occurs when the next entry is a subdirectory. Note that we exclude both `.` and `..` from the returned entries. This is absolutely crucial for this example – if we didn't, they would throw the script into an infinite loop.

```php
        if(is_dir($file)) {
            if($file != '.' && $file != '..') {
                echo "/$file<BR>";
```

The `traverse_dir()` function calls itself to go further down the directory hierarchy, and the function changes the current working directory back to its original state:

```
                traverse_dir("$dir/$file");
                chdir($dir);
            }
        }
        else echo "$file<BR>";

    }

    closedir($dp);
}

traverse_dir($default_dir);

?>
```

Here's some sample output:

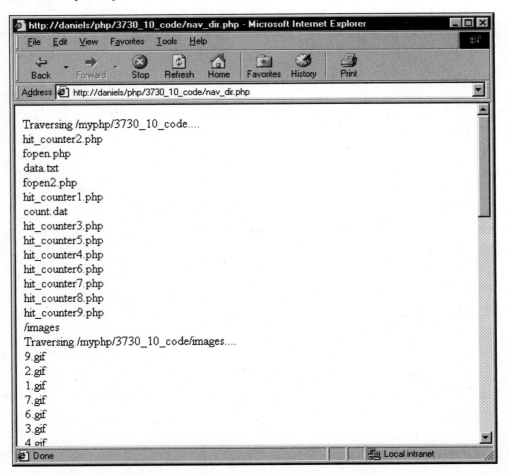

With the power of recursion as demonstrated in this sample script, you can create your own version of the `find` shell command.

# Creating a Directory Navigator

Now that we have the directory functions down, we're in a position to build a fairly powerful directory navigator, which we can use to scan the contents of existing directories and make new ones. We're going to include the `common.inc` file that we created earlier in the chapter, but with one minor addition. We need to add an array called `$img_file_array`, which holds extensions for image files that we want the script to display:

```
$edit_form_cols = 80;
$edit_form_rows = 25;

$text_file_array = array( "txt", "htm", "html", "php", "inc", "dat" );

$image_file_array =  array("gif", "jpeg", "jpg", "png");
```

## navigator.php

We start our navigator script by including this file:

```
<?php
//navigator.php
include "common.inc";
```

Next, we define some functions:

### mkdir_form()

The `mkdir_form()` function displays a form to create a new directory:

```
function mkdir_form() {
    global $PHP_SELF, $dir;
?>

<CENTER>
<FORM METHOD="POST"
    ACTION="<?php echo "$PHP_SELF?action=make_dir&dir=$dir"; ?>">
<INPUT TYPE="HIDDEN" NAME="action" VALUE="make_dir">
<INPUT TYPE="HIDDEN" NAME="dir" VALUE="<? echo $dir ?>">

<?php
echo "<STRONG>$dir</STRONG>"
?>

<BR>
<INPUT TYPE="TEXT" NAME="new_dir" SIZE="10">
<INPUT TYPE="SUBMIT" VALUE="Make Dir"  NAME="Submit">

</FORM>
</CENTER>
<?php
}
```

### make_dir()

The `make_dir()` function creates a given directory:

```
function make_dir() {
    global $dir, $new_dir;
    if(!@mkdir("$dir/$new_dir", 0700)) {
        error_message("Can't create the directory $dir/$new_dir.");
    }
    html_header();
    dir_page();
    html_footer();
}
```

### display()

The `display()` function prints out the contents of a given file in a new window. By comparing the file extension with elements in `$text_file_array` and `$image_file_array`, it determines the file type – either text, image, or (if neither of the above) binary:

```
function display() {
    global $filename, $dir, $text_file_array, $image_file_array;

    $extension = array_pop(explode(".", $filename));
```

Next, it calls the PHP `header()` function, to send an HTTP header string with an appropriate `Content-Type` header. The header string `Content-Type: text/html` tells the browser that the incoming contents are to be interpreted as HTML, whereas `Content-Type: image/gif` denotes a GIF image. (We'll look more closely at this header in Chapter 15 when we discuss e-mail handling in PHP.) It will refuse to display a binary file:

```
    if(in_array($extension, $text_file_array)) {
        readfile("$dir/$filename");
    }
    else if(in_array($extension, $image_file_array)) {
        echo "<IMG SRC=\"$dir/$filename\">";
    }
    else echo "Cannot be displayed. $dir/$filename has not been
        recognised as a text file, nor as a valid image file. ";
}
```

### dir_page()

This is our main function, being the one that scans the directory hierarchy, and lists directory entries, displaying them with a trailing slash. This is where the meat of the script lies:

```
function dir_page() {
    global $dir, $default_dir, $PHP_SELF, $default_filename;

    if($dir == '') {
        $dir = $default_dir;
    }
    $dp = opendir($dir);
```

```
?>
<TABLE BORDER="0" WIDTH="100%" CELLSPACING="0" CELLPADDING="0">
<?php
```

We set up two loops in order to sort the entries in a given directory: a `while` loop to read all the entries in the current working directory, and a `for` loop to display the entries once they're sorted:

```
while($file = readdir($dp)) $filenames[] = $file;

sort($filenames);

for($i = 0; $i < count($filenames); $i++)
{
    $file = $filenames[$i];
```

If the next entry is "`.`" (indicating the current directory), the function ignores it and continues the next loop cycle. However, if the current working directory *is* the default directory, both "`.`" and "`..`" are ignored:

```
if($dir == $default_dir && ($file == "." || $file == ".."))
        continue;
    if(is_dir("$dir/$file") && $file == ".")
        continue;
    if(is_dir("$dir/$file")) {
```

If the entry is "`..`" (indicating the parent directory), the function trims the name of the current directory from the `$dir` variable, to create a hyperlink pointing to the parent directory. Note that the function removes occurrences of the value in the `$dir` variable when creating a link using the `ereg_replace()` function we saw in Chapter 7:

```
if($file == ".."){
```

The `$current_dir` holds the rightmost directory name with the following `basename()` function call:

```
$current_dir = basename($dir);
```

If the `$dir` variable contains "`/home/apache/htdocs/images`" for example, `$current_dir` is assigned the value "`images`".

```
$parent_dir = ereg_replace("/$current_dir$","",$dir);
```

Following this line, the `$parent_dir` holds the value "`/home/apache/htdocs`" since the pattern `/$current_dir$` matches the trailing string "`/images`".

```
echo "<TR><TD WIDTH=\"100%\" NOWRAP>
    <A HREF=\"$PHP_SELF?dir=$parent_dir\">$file/
    </A></TD></TR>\n";
}
```

If the next entry is a subdirectory, the function creates a link pointing to it:

```
            else echo "<TR><TD WIDTH=\"100%\" NOWRAP>
                    <A HREF=\"$PHP_SELF?dir=$dir/$file\">
                        $file/</A></TD></TR>\n";
        }
```

If the next entry is a file, it creates a link to open a new browser that displays its contents:

```
            else echo "<TR><TD WIDTH=\"100%\" NOWRAP>
                    <A HREF=\"$PHP_SELF?action=display&dir=$dir&filename=$file\"
                        TARGET=\"_blank\">$file</A></TD></TR>\n";
        }
    ?>
    </TABLE>
    <?php
        mkdir_form();
    }
```

When we run the script, it first tests to see if the directory specified is above the default directory (for security reasons, the user should never be able to access files that aren't directly under the default directory). The `ereg()` pattern matching function we saw in Chapter 7 returns `False` if the `$dir` variable doesn't contain the value in `$default_dir`, in which case the `$dir` variable is assigned that value:

```
    if(empty($dir) || !ereg($default_dir, $dir)) {
        $dir = $default_dir;
    }
```

Finally, we call functions that correspond to the value in `$action`, defaulting to `dir_page()`:

```
    switch ($action) {
        case "make_dir":
            make_dir();
            break;
        case "display":
            display();
            break;
        default:
            html_header();
            dir_page();
            html_footer();
            break;
    }
    ?>
```

Here's a sample run:

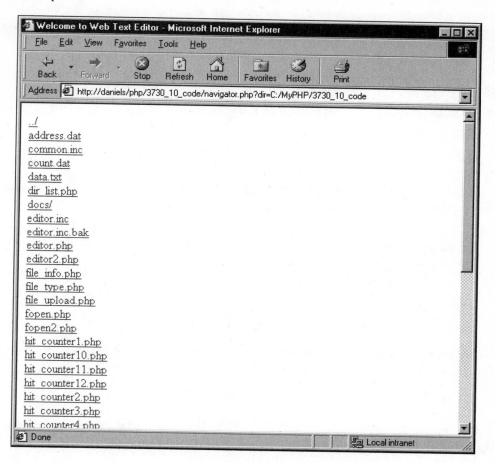

# Uploading Files

Wouldn't it be nice if we could upload files from a local machine to the server using the directory navigator we created above? PHP offers an easy way to put this sort of functionality into your applications. You can let users upload files with their browsers using an <INPUT> form tag of the type FILE. The <FORM> tag's ENCTYPE attribute, which is usually omitted when creating a normal form, also needs to be set to multipart/form-data.

Here's a sample upload form:

```
<FORM METHOD="POST" ENCTYPE="MULTIPART/FORM-DATA"
    ACTION="<?php echo "$PHP_SELF?action=upload_file&dir=$dir"; ?>">
  Local Filename <INPUT TYPE="FILE" NAME="userfile">
  <INPUT TYPE="SUBMIT" NAME="submit" VALUE="Upload">
</FORM>
```

**367**

The ACTION attribute of the form should point to a PHP script that will handle the uploaded file. You don't have to provide the second text input tag unless you want to let users choose a different filename with which the uploaded file will be stored on the server.

Once a file is uploaded, the following global variables become available for use:

| | |
|---|---|
| $userfile | the path to the uploaded file on the server |
| $userfile_name | the original path and the filename of the uploaded file |
| $userfile_size | the size of the uploaded file in bytes |
| $userfile_type | the type of the file (if the browser provides the information) |

Suppose a user has just uploaded a 20,000-byte zip file, C:\docs\projects.zip, using this form. These variables will now contain the following:

❑ $userfile – the path to the temporary directory (as set in php.ini) plus the temporary filename in the format "php-###" format (where "###" is a number which is automatically generated by PHP), for example, "/tmp/php-512"

❑ $userfile_name – "C:\docs\projects.zip"

❑ $userfile_size – 20000

❑ $userfile_type – "application/x-zip-compressed"

The uploaded file is saved in the temporary directory set in php.ini and destroyed at the end of the request. You will therefore need to copy it to somewhere else:

```
$archive_dir = "/home/apache/htdocs/archives";
$filename = basename($userfile_name);
if(!copy($userfile, "$archive_dir/$filename"))
      echo "Error: $filename cannot be copied.";
else echo "Successfully uploaded $filename.";
```

You may want to set a limit on the size of an uploaded file and check if the uploaded file is bigger than the limit by using the $userfile_size variable:

```
$archive_dir = "/home/apache/htdocs/archives";
$max_filesize = 200000;
$filename = basename($userfile_name);
if($userfile_size > $max_filesize)
    echo "Error: $filename is too big. " .
    number_format($max_filesize) . " bytes is the limit.";
else if(!copy($userfile, "$archive_dir/$filename"))
      echo "Error: $filename cannot be copied.";
else echo "Successfully uploaded $filename.";
```

You might also use a hidden field in the upload form to limit the size of the uploaded file:

```
<INPUT TYPE="HIDDEN" NAME="MAX_FILE_SIZE" VALUE="200000">
. . .
```

```
if($userfile_size > $MAX_FILE_SIZE)
   echo "Error: $filename is too big. " .
      number_format($MAX_FILE_SIZE) . " bytes is the limit.";
```

However, this means that anyone can edit the web page containing the upload form and increase the limit all they want. Setting the limit within the script is a much more secure method.

## Try it Out – File Uploading

Here's a complete example of how to implement the file-uploading feature:

```
<?
//file_upload.php
$archive_dir = "./docs";
function upload_form() {
   global $PHP_SELF;
?>
<FORM METHOD="POST" ENCTYPE="MULTIPART/FORM-DATA"
   ACTION="<? echo $PHP_SELF ?>">
   <INPUT TYPE="HIDDEN" NAME="action" VALUE="upload">
   Upload file!
   <INPUT TYPE="FILE" NAME="userfile">
   <INPUT TYPE="SUBMIT" NAME="SUBMIT" VALUE="upload">
</FORM>
<?
}

function upload_file() {
   global $userfile, $userfile_name, $userfile_size,
         $userfile_type, $archive_dir, $WINDIR;

   if(isset($WINDIR)) $userfile = str_replace("\\\\","\\", $userfile);

   $filename = basename($userfile_name);

   if($userfile_size <= 0) die ("$filename is empty.");

   if(!@copy($userfile, "$archive_dir/$filename"))
      die("Can't copy $userfile_name to $filename.");

   if(isset($WINDIR) && !@unlink($userfile))
      die ("Can't delete the file $userfile_name.");

   echo "$filename has been successfully uploaded.<BR>";
   echo "Filesize: " . number_format($userfile_size) . "<BR>";
   echo "Filetype: $userfile_type<BR>";
}
?>
<HTML>
<HEAD><TITLE>FILE UPLOAD</TITLE></HEAD>
<BODY>
<?
if($action == 'upload') upload_file();
```

```
   else upload_form();
?>
</BODY>
</HTML>
```

The upload form looks like this:

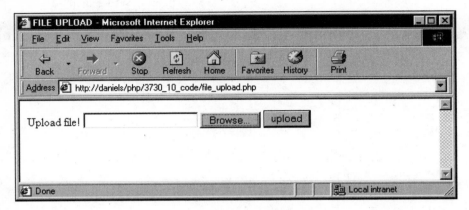

If a user uploads a file called x-wing.gif for example, he will see the following output:

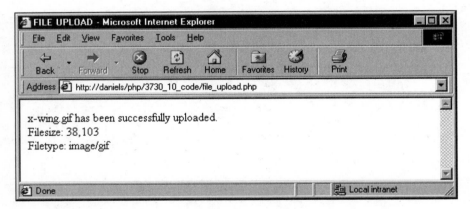

### How It Works

When a user uploads a file from his local machine, the script first tests the platform on which it is run. If it's the Windows platform, all occurrences of double forward slashes need to be reduced to single slashes:

```
   if(isset($WINDIR)) $userfile = str_replace("\\\\","\\", $userfile);
```

If the size of the file is less then 0, that means the user submitted the form without designating a file to be uploaded:

```
   if($userfile_size <= 0) die ("$filename is empty.");
```

If everything looks fine, the script copies the uploaded file to an archive directory and tests to see whether it's running on Windows. If not, we should be okay to use `unlink()` to delete the temporary file.

# Putting it All Together – A Web Text Editor

We wrap up this chapter by building a fully-fledged web text editor that combines the functionality of the text editor and directory navigator we made earlier, as well as the file uploading functionality covered in the previous section. The user will be able to upload files from his local machine to the server and edit them. You'll need to take the contents of our earlier scripts `navigator.php` and `editor.php`, strip away things like `include` and `switch` statements, and turn them into include files called `navigator.inc` and `editor.inc` respectively – all we really want from these files are the functions we define in them. That way, they lose all independent functionality, but we can still reuse their functions in a new script, which we'll call `webeditor.php`.

This script uses two frames: a `menu` frame on the left side that displays the directory navigator (by calling functions in `navigator.inc`) and a `main` frame on the right side that displays the editor form (by calling functions from `editor.inc`):

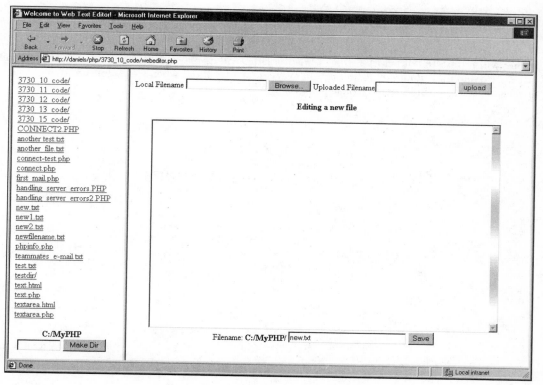

The functions contained in our two new include files will also need a little modification, since we now want them to communicate with one another. We'll start off by taking a look at `navigator.inc`.

## *navigator.inc*

In our original version of the navigator, a user would click on a directory link or file entry, and the script would either call itself with a new directory path or open a new window displaying the contents of the file. The following lines in the `dir_page()` function took care of this:

```
        echo "<TR><TD WIDTH=\"100%\" NOWRAP>
               <A HREF=\"$PHP_SELF?dir=$parent_dir\">$file/
               </A></TD></TR>\n";
      }

        else echo "<TR><TD WIDTH=\"100%\" NOWRAP>
               <A HREF=\"$PHP_SELF?dir=$dir/$file\">$file/
               </A></TD></TR>\n";
    }

else echo "<TR><TD WIDTH=\"100%\" NOWRAP>
          <A HREF=\"$PHP_SELF?action=display&
                         dir=$dir&filename=$file\"
           TARGET=\"_blank\">$file
          </A></TD></TR>\n";
    }
```

We now want to change these so that they call `dir_page` and `editor_page` actions respectively. The former will refresh the directory listing, while the latter will display the file contents. If we didn't specify these, we'd end up calling the default action every time – try it out when we're done, and you'll see that this has some rather unfortunate consequences.

This is what your new lines of code should look like:

```
        echo "<TR><TD WIDTH=\"100%\" NOWRAP>
               <A HREF=\"$PHP_SELF?action=dir_page&
                                    dir=$parent_dir\">$file/
               </A></TD></TR>\n";
      }

        else echo "<TR><TD WIDTH=\"100%\" NOWRAP>
               <A HREF=\"$PHP_SELF?action=dir_page&
                                    dir=$dir/$file\">$file/
               </A></TD></TR>\n";
    }

else echo "<TR><TD WIDTH=\"100%\" NOWRAP>
          <A HREF=\"$PHP_SELF?action=editor_page&
                         dir=$dir&filename=$file\"
           TARGET=\"main\">$file
          </A></TD></TR>\n";
    }
```

Note that in the last clause (which is used for file entries), the TARGET attribute is set to `main`. When we click on such a file link, and the `editor_page` function is called, it will therefore display the file contents in the `main` frame. If we didn't specify a TARGET attribute, it would just default to the current frame – that is, the `menu` frame – and overwrite our list of directory entries.

## editor.inc

If we use `editor.php` to edit a new text file and save it, the `save_file()` function will echo out the following snippet of JavaScript to refresh itself:

```
echo "<SCRIPT>self.location.href='$PHP_SELF?dir=$dir&
                                    filename=$filename';</SCRIPT>";
```

In our web editor application, the script will not only need to reload itself in the `main` frame, but also the directory listing in the `menu` frame, so that we maintain an up-to-date list of files. We therefore replace the line above with the following two:

```
echo "<SCRIPT>parent.menu.location.href='$PHP_SELF?action=dir_page\&
                                    dir=$dir';</SCRIPT>";

echo "<SCRIPT>self.location.href='$PHP_SELF?action=editor_page\&
                                    dir=$dir\&
                                    filename=$filename';</SCRIPT>";
```

## webeditor.php

First, we need to include the scripts we already have. By including `common.inc` first, we make sure that our earlier scripts both have access to its variables and functions:

```
<?php
include "./common.inc";
include "./editor.inc";
include "./navigator.inc";
```

### frame_page()

This creates a frame page containing two frames: `menu` where the navigator script appears, and `main` where the editor script resides:

```
function frame_page() {
    global $PHP_SELF, $dir;
?>
<HTML>
<HEAD><TITLE>Welcome to Web Text Editor!</TITLE></HEAD>
<FRAMESET COLS="200,*">
   <FRAME NAME="menu"
    SRC="<?php echo "$PHP_SELF?action=dir_page&dir=$dir"; ?>">
   <FRAME NAME="main"
    SRC="<?php echo "$PHP_SELF?action=editor_page&dir=$dir"; ?>">
   <NOFRAMES>
   <BODY TOPMARGIN="0" LEFTMARGIN="0">
   <P>This page uses frames, but your browser doesn't support them.</P>
   </BODY>
   </NOFRAMES>
</FRAMESET>
</HTML>
<?php
}
```

### upload_file_form()

This displays a file upload form. It's similar to the one we saw earlier but comes with an extra text edit field that allows the user to specify the filename to be used on the server:

```
function upload_file_form() {
   global $PHP_SELF, $dir;
?>
<FORM METHOD="POST" ENCTYPE="MULTIPART/FORM-DATA"
      ACTION="<?php echo $PHP_SELF ?>" TARGET="menu">
<INPUT TYPE="HIDDEN" NAME="action" VALUE="upload_file">
<INPUT TYPE="HIDDEN" NAME="dir" VALUE="<? echo $dir ?>">
   Local Filename <INPUT TYPE="FILE" NAME="userfile">
   Uploaded Filename<INPUT TYPE="TEXT" NAME="filename" LENGTH="20">
   <INPUT TYPE="SUBMIT" NAME="submit" VALUE="upload">
</FORM>
<?php
}
```

### upload_file()

This function handles an uploaded file. The only difference from the earlier file upload example is the $filename variable. If the $filename variable is set, that means the user wants to give the file a new name on the server:

```
function upload_file() {
   global $userfile, $userfile_name, $userfile_size, $userfile_type,
          $filename, $default_dir, $dir, $PHP_SELF, $WINDIR;
```

Note that we prevent the user from uploading files to a place above the default directory specified in the common.inc include file:

```
   if(empty($dir) || !ereg($default_dir, $dir)) {
      error_message("$dir/$filename is illegal directory.");
   }
```

If run on the Windows platform, replace double backslashes with single ones :

```
   if(!isset($WINDIR)) $userfile = str_replace("\\\\","\\", $userfile);
```

If the user didn't specify a filename to be used on the server, get the filename from the original path:

```
   if(empty($filename)) $filename = basename($userfile_name);

   if($userfile_size <= 0) {
      error_message("$filename is empty.");
   }
```

We test to see if the uploaded file already exists:

```
   if(file_exists("$dir/$filename")) {
      error_message("$filename already exists.");
   }
```

Copy the uploaded file from the temporary directory to the current working directory:

```
if(!@copy($userfile, "$dir/$filename")) {
   error_message("Can't copy $userfile_name to $filename.");
}
```

If we're not running on a Windows platform, we can unlink() the temporary file:

```
if(!isset($WINDIR) && !@unlink($userfile)) {
   error_message("Can't delete $userfile_name.");

}
```

If the uploaded file is a text file, we load it into the editor form on the main frame:

```
html_header();
$file_info_array = file_info("$dir/$filename");
if($file_info_array["filetype"] == 'text')
   echo "<SCRIPT>parent.main.location.href=
      '$PHP_SELF?action=editor_page&
      dir=$dir&filename=$filename';
      </SCRIPT>";
dir_page();
html_footer();
}
```

We prevent the user from going above the default directory:

```
if(empty($dir) || !ereg($default_dir, $dir)) {
   $dir = $default_dir;
}
```

We also prevent the user from editing the script itself:

```
if($filename == basename($PHP_SELF)) error_message("You can't edit me!");
```

Finally, we call functions that correspond to the value in the $action variable:

```
switch ($action) {
   case "editor_page":
      html_header();
      upload_file_form();
      editor_page();
      html_footer();
      break;
   case "dir_page":
      html_header();
      dir_page();
      html_footer();
      break;
   case "make_dir":
```

```
            make_dir();
            break;
      case "delete_dir":
          delete_dir();
          break;
      case "delete_file":
          delete_file();
          break;
      case "save_file":
          save_file();
          break;
      case "upload_file":
          upload_file();
          break;
      default:
          frame_page();
      break;
  }
?>
```

To test the script, set the $default_dir variable to any directory under your web document root and save the script as webeditor.php. Here's a sample run:

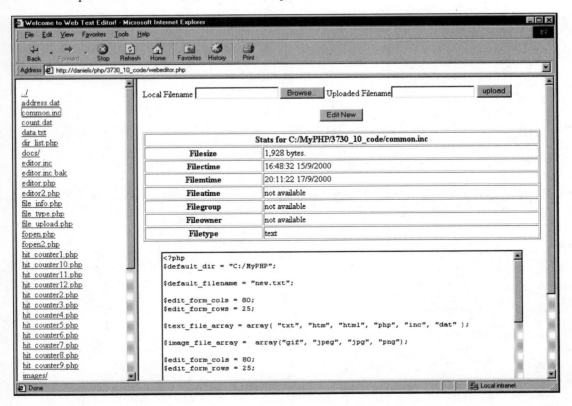

The script displays a directory listing on the left and an editor form on the right. You can load any file from the listing on the left frame while traversing the directory hierarchy. If you upload a file for editing, or delete an existing file or directory, the listing on the left will be updated automatically.

The script will come in handy when you want to edit HTML files on the fly, for example. However, if you try to edit any files that contain the tag `</TEXTAREA>`, you'll run into problems. The browser will interpret this as marking the end of the section of data which it's treating as plain text. Any markup or code that follows this will be parsed as normal, with highly unpredictable results.

To prevent this from happening, you can throw in an `ereg_replace()` function call to alias any such tags before loading a script into the editor form, and another to change them back before saving it. We'll leave this for you to try as an exercise.

# Resources

❑ PHP Homepage manual section on file systems:
http://www.php.net/manual/ref.filesystem.php

❑ PHP Homepage manual section on directories: http://www.php.net/manual/ref.dir.php

❑ *Professional PHP Programming* from Wrox Press

# Summary

In this chapter, we've learned how to work with files as well as how to read and write to them. We created a simple web text editor, and learned how to work with directories and created a directory navigator.

During the course of this chapter we covered most of the essential file/directory manipulating functions that PHP provides. Some used a file or directory handle – a pointer referring to an open file or directory – while others used string variables containing the name of a file or directory. To use functions requiring a handle, we went through the following process:

❑ Opened a file or directory to be used using `fopen()` or `opendir()`

❑ Worked with the open file or directory using the file manipulation functions `fread()`, `fgets()`, `fpassthru()` or `readdir()` (among others)

❑ Closed it using `fclose()` or `closedir()`

Finally, we created a fully-fledged web text editor that can scan through the directory hierarchy and manipulate entries in it.

We didn't cover some functions rarely used in web applications. For a full list of the file/directory functions, refer to the online PHP function list: http://www.php.net/manual/ref.filesystem.php.

# PHP Database Connectivity

Almost all useful applications need to be able to store and retrieve data. We have already discussed one way to manage data in the previous chapter – files. Although a file system can be used adequately for most applications, it has certain limits in terms of design, performance, and scalability. Another option is to use databases. This chapter is the first in a series of three that will teach you how to integrate databases with PHP. In this chapter we will:

❑　Discuss the advantages of databases over ordinary file systems.

❑　Explain what a relational database is, and introduce the concepts associated with it, such as normalization and indexing.

❑　Show you how to install a freely-available relational database management system, MySQL.

❑　Demonstrate some PHP functions that will allow you to connect to your database.

❑　Start getting to grips with using MySQL to retrieve and modify the contents of a database.

You'll find in no time that using databases from PHP couldn't be simpler!

## Databases

As a programmer, one of the first choices you'll have to make, when creating even the simplest application, is the correct **data storage model** to use – in other words, how is your application going to store (and access) data.

Choosing one particular data storage model over the others depends on the requirements of your application. If it only needs to get at small amounts of data, storing the data in a simple text file might suffice. As the amount of data increases though, you'll find yourself searching for a more efficient way to put away information. For example, it would be painfully inefficient (though not impossible) for a large commercial site such as Amazon to store all its transactions in plain text files: it would take ages for a user to order a single book.

Why? Well, a file system is a very primitive means of data storage because data is kept in *unstructured* chunks. For instance, when users request to enter a password-protected area, an Apache web server will (unless configured otherwise) authenticate them against a plain text file containing a complete list of user IDs and passwords. This isn't a problem when it's dealing with a small group of users, but if it has to validate hundreds of users at the same time, it must scan the text file one line at a time until it finds a matching user. One unlucky user would have to wait for Apache to find his details on the last line of the file before it let him enter the password-protected area!

A **database** is simply a collection of data which is organized in such a way that its contents can easily be accessed and manipulated. This organization means that they're almost invariably the most effective and viable way to store and manipulate large amounts of data.

A **database management system** (**DBMS**), or **database engine** as it is sometimes referred to, provides the software used to store, retrieve and modify data in a database. In this section we will study two aspects of DBMS design: data models, and database architectures. Looking at the former, we'll now take a look at how we can optimize database performance by choosing the right data model.

# Data Models

At its simplest, a database arranges data in **tables**, each divided into **rows** and **columns**. Each row of each table comprises a data **record**, which may contain several **fields** of information.

> **For all practical purposes, the term 'row' is synonymous with 'record', while 'column' is synonymous with 'field'. This is useful to bear in mind when visualizing tables.**

Suppose you wanted to log every user access to your site. The simplest (and most primitive) method of achieving this would be to create a single table that records both user information and log data. It might look something like this, consisting of five columns (or fields) and five rows (or records):

| User ID | User Name | User Country | Page | Last Access |
|---------|-----------|--------------|------|-------------|
| bundy | Wankyu Choi | Republic of Korea | `/index.html` | 2000-01-23 |
| sphinx | Yonsuk Song | Republic of Korea | `/info/contact.html` | 2000-06-20 |
| bundy | Wankyu Choi | Republic of Korea | `/php/index.php` | 2000-02-05 |
| john | John Smith | United Kingdom | `/quake/index.html` | 2000-04-21 |
| quake | Jonathan Carmack | United States | `/index.html` | 2000-06-21 |

## Normalization and Relational Databases

Take a closer look at the table above. The structure of the table is inefficient, because a visitor's information is recorded into the table *every* time he makes a visit. Because of this duplication, a lot of the data in the table is redundant.

Such redundancy is undesirable in a database. Why? Let's have an example. Say user "bundy" decided to move to the United States and change his User Name to Charlie Choi. In order to update the table, *every one* of his records would have to be modified to include his new name and country. This is on top of the fact that every copy of his details takes up precious space on our hard drive. Redundancy is terribly inefficient, potentially wasting a great deal of time and space.

The notion of database **normalization** was developed to reduce data redundancy as much as possible. Normalization is the process of breaking up the data into several tables, so as to minimize the number of times we have to repeat the same data. For example, we could split the table above into a user information table and an access log table:

| User ID | User Name | User Country |
| --- | --- | --- |
| bundy | Wankyu Choi | Republic of Korea |
| sphinx | Yonsuk Song | Republic of Korea |
| quake | Jonathan Carmack | United States |
| john | John Smith | United Kingdom |

| User ID | Page | Last Access |
| --- | --- | --- |
| bundy | `/index.html` | 2000-01-23 |
| bundy | `/php/index.php` | 2000-02-05 |
| john | `/quake/index.html` | 2000-04-21 |
| sphinx | `/info/contact.html` | 2000-06-20 |
| quake | `/index.html` | 2000-06-21 |

Notice how the original table splits naturally into these two new tables. This is because the original table provided data about two distinct things (or **entities**): users, and access logs. Each new table contains data concerning just one entity. The split into entity tables is an important part of the normalization process.

Having split our table up into entities, we can now take another step in the normalization process. Each entity must have (at least) one **unique** field – in other words no entries in the field are repeated. Because of the unique nature of this field, each entry in it uniquely identifies ("Ids") each record in the table. This is important, because the ID can then be used to refer to a specific record in the table. The field used to ID records is often known as the **primary key**. Note that only one primary key is permitted per table.

For example, in the user table we could use the User ID field as a primary key because it contains unique values. However, the User Name field also contains unique values. Which field should we pick to be the primary key? Well, there are other considerations. User names can often change – if a user gets married for instance. Also, users might withhold their names for security reasons, so the corresponding entries in the User Name field would be NULL. Since we don't expect IDs to be changed very often or withheld, it would seem best to use this field as the primary key in this case.

Let's review the benefits of normalization. Because we have moved the user information to one table and the access log entries to another, the process of modifying a user's details becomes much more simple – we only have to modify one record in the user table. You should note that since these tables are related (they both contain the field User ID, and the values in this field correspond between tables), the database is now termed **relational**. This means that we can **join** information from the related tables in order to find answers to complex **queries**, which otherwise couldn't be answered by either tables on its own.

For example: "What's the nationality of our resident Quake fan?" We know that it's "john" – that is, John Smith from the UK. This is illustrated in the figure below:

| ID | Name | Country |
|----|------|---------|
| bundy | Wankyu Choi | Republic of Korea |
| sphinx | Yonsuk Song | Republic of Korea |
| quake | Jonathan Carmack | United States |
| john | John Smith | United Kingdom |

User Table

| ID | Page | Last Access |
|----|------|-------------|
| bundy | /index.html | 2000-01-23 |
| bundy | /php/index.pho | 2000-02-05 |
| john | /quake/index.htm | 2000-04-21 |
| sphinx | /info/contact.html | 2000-06-20 |
| quake | /index.html | 2000-06-21 |

Access Log Table

To summarize the basic rules of normalization:

**1.** Eliminate redundant data in individual tables.

**2.** Create a separate entity table for each set of related data.

**3.** Specify a unique field on each table to act as the primary key.

Rule number three can be extended to use two or more fields as a primary key to further eliminate redundancy. For example, the user "bundy" might access the "/index.html" page many times. The only piece of information that needs to be changed in these access log records is his last access time to the page. Therefore, the User ID and Page fields could also be combined into a primary key to uniquely identify an access record.

Examples of so-called **Relational Database Management Systems** (**RDBMS**) include not only commercial products such as Microsoft SQL Server, Oracle, Informix, but also MySQL, which is freely available.

# Database Architecture

We've now seen how a relational database can give us an advantage over a non-relational database. Let's now examine another aspect of database design – the **architecture** of the database itself. There are two basic architectural models that can be applied to databases: standalone and client/server.

## Standalone Model

In a standalone database model, both the database and the database engine reside on the same machine in a local file system. Use is limited to a single concurrent user – *no two users can access the database at the same time*. The database is *not* networked, and is meant for use with applications which are distributed to single users: the database cannot be shared between different machines since each user would simply end up storing and manipulating their own data on their local machine. Good examples of standalone database engines include **dBase** and **DBM**. PHP provides connectivity to both of these.

## Client/Server Model

The client/server database model overcomes the limitations inherent in standalone database systems. Its concept is analogous to a restaurant, when a number of customers request service from a waiter. Depending on each of the services requested, the waiter might then have to ask a chef or bartender for help. Note that customers don't have to worry about how the service is actually provided, or how many people are involved in providing it. Also, the waiter is typically responsible for a number of customers at the same time. If he's efficient enough to satisfy them all, spending a reasonable amount of time per service request, none of them will feel that he's providing a poor service.

In the context of the client/server computing model, the **server** acts much like the waiter – it is responsible for responding to service requests made by a number of **client** programs at the same time, and then delivering the results to them as quickly as possible. This means that more than one user can access a client/server database system at the same time. When it is asked to perform a number of tasks concurrently by more than one user, the database engine gives them a share of its attention, in the same way as a CPU switches from one program to another so quickly that we get the feeling that all programs are being executed at the same time.

Although the client/server concept can also be employed by applications running on the same local machine, it is most suitable for a network. In a network, the client/server model helps programs scattered across different locations talk to each other. Lets have another example. When you order a book from Amazon, a client program – your web browser – forwards your request to a web server that resides at the Amazon site. Then the web server would probably forward your request to another of its own client programs, which in turn sends a request to a database server to store or update your transaction records in its database. The result is returned to the client program, which, in turn, tosses it back to the web server. Finally the server sends the results to the your web browser, which displays the transaction result for you. The web server at a high-profile web site like Amazon would have to handle multiple requests made by a number of web browsers at the same time.

We can now summarize the benefits of a relational database with client/server architecture (note that not all RDBMS support it):

❑ *Performance*: Database normalization increases performance dramatically.

❑ *Multi-user Environment*: The only limit on the number of concurrent users is imposed either by the type of license you purchase and/or your hardware performance.

❑ *Availability*: Based on a network, an RDBMS can fulfill requests "live", making up-to-date data available whenever required. In other words, you can access the database wherever and whenever you like.

❑ *Security*: In a multi-user environment, security comes on top of the administrator's worry list, thus controlling access to data through a well-organized security scheme is essential. MySQL, for example, does not allow direct access to any of its stored data, thereby making it very secure from the operating system level up. A user has to log on with his user ID and password to gain access to data stored in the database. A user without correct permissions is not allowed to perform unauthorized operations on the data, in much the same way as you can't modify other people's files without the proper permissions to do so on the Linux platform.

❑ *Reliability*: When it comes to software, the degree of reliability is generally measured by how often a product "dies" during service, requiring a restart. MySQL, for example, spawns child processes to handle concurrent requests. When a child process goes haywire and eventually dies, it seldom takes with it the database server as a whole, minimizing the impact on the integrity of the data stored in the database. Even recovering corrupted tables is often just a matter of running a recovery utility that comes with the server package (unless the tables are corrupted to the extent that they cannot be recovered by any means).

All in all, if you plan to develop mission-critical multi-user web applications, you should consider a networked RDBMS for your data storage backend.

One last point: client/server database management systems are often expensive and complex to set up and administer. However, a few are not, of which MySQL is one example. It's about time we took a closer look at it!

# Why MySQL?

MySQL is a freely available RDBMS, which fully joined the Open Source Community only recently, when it was released under the GNU Public License. Even before it went free, you didn't need a license unless you wanted to make money out of it, or run the server on the Windows platform (the Windows version of MySQL was shareware). Since you now don't have to pay a dime to use it, this alone makes MySQL a solid candidate for developing database applications. However, if the GPL worries you for any reason, or you need to incorporate MySQL into a commercial application, you can still buy a commercially licensed version from the developers at http://www.mysql.com.

In addition to its free availability, MySQL provides a whole lot of other features:

❑ *Open Source Software*: The MySQL package comes with the complete source code. This means that you may study the source code and modify it to suit your particular needs. Being open source has another important ramification: you can find a high degree of support from third parties.

❑ *SQL Support*: As the "SQL" in MySQL suggests, MySQL supports SQL (Structured Query Language), a standard high-level language used to make queries for data required from a database. Although the SQL syntax is slightly different from one RDMBS to another, the underlying concepts are much the same. MySQL uses its own set of SQL commands but the basic concept still survives.

❑ *Superb Performance and Reliability*: MySQL is remarkably fast and reliable even in a most demanding environment.

❑ *Ease of use*: MySQL is a relatively simple database management system in spite of its powerful features. In fact, MySQL's databases are nothing but a bunch of directories where database tables are kept in separate files. Removing a database or a database table is, in reality, simply deleting a directory or a file. MySQL is also easy to set up and manage. It comes with a complete suite of client/server applications plus a number of utilities that make the database administration easy.

❑ *Free Support*: You can get a certain degree of professional support from other users who use MySQL by various means: MySQL newsgroups; mailing lists; independent web sites that freely share their knowledge; among others. If you need a higher level of technical support, you can always ask for it from the developers at minimal cost.

❑ *Cross-platform*: MySQL can run on either the UNIX or Windows platforms.

# Installing MySQL

So you want to use MySQL as your RDBMS? Let's get it installed on your machine then.

## Installing On Windows

You can download a binary (pre-compiled) version of MySQL from the MySQL homepage at http://www.mysql.com. It should come to you as a zipped file, for example, `mysql-3.23.23-beta-win.zip`. If you unzip that, you'll find a file called `setup.exe`, which you should run. The standard installation wizard will run you through a couple of questions. The default values (a **Typical** install in `C:\MySQL`) will do fine.

Once the server and clients have installed, we'll need to get the server itself up and running. Windows 95 users should note that MySQL uses TCP/IP to talk to the client, so you'll need to install that from your Windows CD and download Winsock 2 from the Microsoft website. This will all be standard on any other version of Windows.

All the programs for MySQL are stored in the `bin` directory of your installation, typically `C:\mysql\bin`. Most of these programs (such as `mysql.exe`, `mysqladmin.exe` and `mysqld.exe`) are command-line tools, so you should never run them by double-clicking their icon. However, one very useful tool that comes with the standard Windows release of MySQL is the snappily titled `winmysqladmin.exe`, which provides us with a useful interface for controlling the MySQL server program. It's a graphical program, so we run it by double-clicking, as normal. The first time you run it, you'll be prompted to enter a username and password, which will generate a database user account for the administration tool to use. The administration tool will then try to start the MySQL server program, which, if the system has installed properly, should come up first time.

Once it's running, `winmysqladmin` hides itself in your system tray (at the right-hand end of your Start bar), where it is represented by a set of traffic signals, showing a green light when the server is running, and a red stop light when it isn't:

Right-clicking the icon brings up a menu, which allows you to start and stop the server, and show the `winmysqladmin` window, which in turn allows you to view and edit various parameters on the server.

Windows NT/2000 users also have the option of installing MySQL as a service, which means the MySQL server will run when your machine starts up. First though, you'll need to copy and rename `my-example.cnf` from `C:\MySQL` to `C:\my.cnf` (you will probably find that Windows hides the `.cnf` extensions of these files' names, rendering them as `my-example` and `my` respectively). This file holds global values for MySQL, which the service reads on startup. After that, it's simply a case of selecting the install the service option from winmysqladmin's menu. Note that you'll have to stop MySQL first if you have already run it as a standalone server, before you will be allowed to install the service.

Whichever method you choose to run MySQL, make sure that the green light is showing in your system tray before proceeding. The next step is detailed under the heading "Setting Up The Root Account".

## Installing On Linux

Linux users have the choice of installing MySQL from a package or compiling from source code. In either case, you can obtain the files you need from http://www.mysql.com/.

If you're after RPMs, then make sure you download the server, the client, the include files and libraries, and the client shared libraries, for the correct platform. You should end up with the following four files (the exact version number, and the platform, may vary):

- ❏   MySQL-3.23.23-1.i386.rpm
- ❏   MySQL-client-3.23.23-1.i386.rpm
- ❏   MySQL-devel-3.23.23-1.i386.rpm
- ❏   MySQL-shared-3.23.23-1.i386.rpm

If you're after the source, then you'll just need the tarball, mysql-3.23.23-beta.tar.gz.

### Installing MySQL using RPMs

We install RPMs using the following command:

```
> rpm -Uvh filename.rpm
```

If you install them in the order listed above, you should have no trouble.

When you install the first package, which contains the MySQL server, you'll see the following documentation appear on the screen:

```
PLEASE REMEMBER TO SET A PASSWORD FOR THE MySQL root USER !
This is done with:
/usr/bin/mysqladmin -u root password 'new-password'
See the manual for more instructions.

Please report any problems with the /usr/bin/mysqlbug script!

The latest information about MySQL is available on the web at http://www.mysql.com
Support MySQL by buying support/licenses at http://www.tcx.se/license.htmy.

Starting mysqld daemon with databases from /var/lib/mysql
```

However, the mysqladmin program is one of the client tools, so we'll have to wait until after installing the client package – we'll come to this step later. Note, though, that the RPM immediately starts up the MySQL server program, mysqld (for MySQL daemon). It also creates the startup and shutdown script /etc/rc.d/init.d/mysql, which will ensure that MySQL starts whenever your computer is booted, and shuts down conveniently whenever it is halted. You can use this script to start and stop mysqld, with the commands:

```
> /etc/rc.d/init.d/mysql start
> /etc/rc.d/init.d/mysql stop
```

Now install the `MySQL-client`, `MySQL-devel` and `MySQL-shared` packages, and we're done.

### Installing MySQL From Source

The installation procedure for the source code should be fairly simple.

```
> tar -zxvf mysql-3.22.32.tar.gz
> cd mysql-3.22.32
> ./configure --prefix=/usr
> make
```

If `make` fails it is often because of a lack of memory, even on fairly high-spec machines. In this case, try:

```
> rm -f config.cache
> make clean
> ./configure --prefix=/usr --with-low-memory
> make
```

Now we simply run:

```
> make install
> mysql_install_db
```

Now, we'll need to set up some scripts to start and stop the MySQL server, `mysqld`. A typical start-up script might read:

```
#!/bin/bash
/usr/bin/safe_mysqld &
```

And a script to shut the server down might be:

```
#!/bin/bash
kill `cat /usr/var/$HOSTNAME.pid`
```

You'll find these scripts in the source code download for this book from www.wrox.com. If you choose to set them up yourself, once you've created the files using your favorite text editor, you need to tell the system that they are executable scripts, which is done using the `chmod` command. If you had saved the startup script as `startmysqld`, for example, you would need to type:

```
> chmod ug+x startmysqld
```

## Setting Up The Root Account

Once the server and clients are installed, and the server's up and running, we can do the sensible thing and set the root password. On a Windows machine, bring up a DOS command prompt and navigate to your MySQL `bin` directory (typically, `C:\mysql\bin`) before typing this command:

```
> mysqladmin -uroot password elephant
```

Choose a much safer password than "elephant", obviously.

### Testing Our MySQL Server

With our setup complete, it just remains for us to test our MySQL installation with some or all of the following commands:

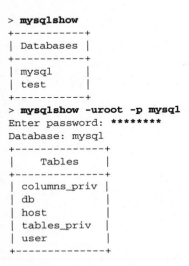

```
> mysqlshow
+-----------+
| Databases |
+-----------+
| mysql     |
| test      |
+-----------+
> mysqlshow -uroot -p mysql
Enter password: ********
Database: mysql
+--------------+
|    Tables    |
+--------------+
| columns_priv |
| db           |
| host         |
| tables_priv  |
| user         |
+--------------+
```

This should echo back to you the current MySQL configuration of databases. Now we move on to the next step in our quest to use MySQL: getting to grips with SQL.

# Introduction to SQL

**SQL**, or **Structured Query Language**, is the standard command set used to communicate with a relational database management system on any given platform. All tasks such as creating databases or tables, as well as saving, retrieving, deleting, and updating data from databases are done via SQL statements. Implementation of SQL features vary with RDBMS vendor, but since the basic concepts are identical, applying skills learned on one platform to another should be no more difficult than porting a computer program written for one platform to another using the same language. In this section we will closely examine some basic features of SQL: data types, indexes, keys, and queries.

### Data Types

When you create a database table, the type and size of each field must be defined. A field is similar to a PHP variable except that *you can store only the specified type and size of data in a given field*. Therefore, unlike PHP variables, you can't insert characters into an integer field, for example. The three usual sets of data types are supported in MySQL: numeric, date/time, and characters:

## Numeric Data Types

| Data Types | Description | Range/Format |
|---|---|---|
| INT | Normal-sized integer | $(-2^{31}$ to $2^{31}-1)$, or $(0$ to $2^{32}-1)$ if UNSIGNED |
| TINYINT | Very small integer | $(-2^7$ to $2^7-1)$, or $(0$ to $2^8-1)$ if UNSIGNED |
| SMALLINT | Small integer | $(-2^{15}$ to $2^{15}-1)$, or $(0$ to $2^8-1)$ if UNSIGNED |
| MEDIUMINT | Medium-sized integer | $(-2^{23}$ to $2^{23}-1)$, or $(0$ to $2^{24}-1)$ if UNSIGNED |
| BIGINT | Large integer | $(-2^{63}$ to $2^{63}-1)$, or $(0$ to $2^{64}-1)$ if UNSIGNED |
| FLOAT | Single-precision floating-point number | Minimum non-zero $\pm1.176\times10^{-38}$; maximum non-zero $\pm3.403\times10^{+38}$ |
| DOUBLE/REAL | Double-precision floating-point number | Minimum non-zero $\pm2.225\times10^{-308}$; maximum non-zero $\pm1.798\times10^{+308}$ |
| DECIMAL | Float stored as string | Maximum range same as DOUBLE |

## Date/Time Data Types

| Data Types | Description | Range/Format |
|---|---|---|
| DATE | A Date | YYYY-MM-DD format. Range 1000-01-01 to 9999-12-31 |
| DATETIME | A Date and Time | YYYY-MM-DD hh:mm:ss format. Range 1000-01-01 00:00:00 to 9999-12-31 23:59:59 |
| TIMESTAMP | A Timestamp | YYYYMMDDhhmmss format. Range 19700101000000 to sometime in 2037 |
| TIME | A Time | hh:mm:ss format. Range −838:59:59 to 838:59:59 |
| YEAR | A Year | YYYY format. Range 1900 to 2155 |

## Character Data Types

| Data Types | Description | Range/Format |
|---|---|---|
| CHAR | Fixed-length string | 0–255 characters |
| VARCHAR | Variable-length string | 0–255 characters |
| BLOB | Binary Large OBject | Binary data 0–65535 bytes long |
| TINYBLOB | Small BLOB value | Binary data 0–255 bytes long |
| MEDIUMBLOB | Medium-sized BLOB | Binary data 0–16777215 bytes long |
| LONGBLOB | Large BLOB value | Binary data 0–4294967295 bytes long |

*Table continued on following page*

| Data Types | Description | Range/Format |
|---|---|---|
| TEXT | Normal-sized text field | 0–65535 bytes |
| TINYTEXT | Small text field | 0–255 bytes |
| MEDIUMTEXT | Medium-sized text | 0–16777215 bytes |
| LONGTEXT | Large text field | 0–4294967295 bytes |
| ENUM | Enumeration | Column values are assigned one value from a set list |
| SET | Set value(s) | Column values are assigned zero or more values from a set list |

Note that the difference between a CHAR and VARCHAR type field is that the former stores a fixed-length value no matter how short it may be, whereas the latter stores exactly as many bytes as necessary to keep a given value. Suppose you insert the string "bundy" into the fields defined as char_field CHAR(10) and varchar_field(10), for example. They will store the same string slightly differently:

```
char_field: 'bundy     '// five blank spaces are right padded
varchar_field: 'bundy' // no space
```

It follows that declaring character fields as VARCHAR type will save you some disk space. However, don't get tempted to use VARCHAR type fields for storing every string, because this has drawbacks too. The MySQL server processes CHAR type fields much faster than VARCHAR type, for one thing, since their length is predetermined. If your strings don't vary in length much, you're better off using CHAR type fields. Moreover, when your strings are all the same length, VARCHAR will take up more disk space, because it has to store the length of each string in one additional byte.

A final note on VARCHAR/CHAR type fields: if your table has at least one VARCHAR field, all character fields are converted to VARCHAR type even if you define them otherwise.

## Indexes and Keys

Inexperienced database designers sometimes complain about their database engines being slow. This problem is often explained by the lack of an **index**. An index is a separate sorted list of a selected field (or fields) in a table. In order to explain why indexing a table has a dramatic effect on database performance, first consider a table without indexes. Such a table is basically the same as a plain text file if it's not indexed, since the database engine searches it sequentially. Rows in a relational database are not inserted in any particular order – the server inserts them in an arbitrary manner. In order to make sure it finds all entries matching the information we want, the engine must perform a full table scan, which is slow and inefficient, particularly if there are only a few matches.

Now consider an indexed table. Instead of moving straight to the table, the engine can scan the index for items that match our requirements. Since the index is a sorted list, this scan can be performed very quickly. The index guides the engine to the relevant matches on the database table, and a full table scan is not necessary.

So why not just sort the table itself? This might be practical if we knew there was only one field we might want to search on. However, this is rarely the case. Since it's not possible to sort a database by several fields at once, the best option is to use an index which is separate from the table.

Another question: what about the case of searching multiple tables at once? This is where we *really* benefit from an index. Searching for a possible match across joined databases *without* indexes is a terrible idea – the engine would have to check all possible combinations of rows in one table with another. For two tables each with 500 rows, this would be 500 times 500, or 250,000 combinations! Indexing however speeds searches up dramatically. The engine would check the index of the first table to find the position of matches to the first part of the query, and then it would use the index to the second table to find matches to the second part of the query. In other words we pull out the relevant records directly.

A **primary key** is a special index, which as we saw at the beginning of the chapter, is used to ID records and relate tables to one another, giving us the relational database model. Each related table must have one (and only one) primary key.

One last point: indexes and primary keys can be derived from combinations of fields (note that for a key formed in this way, the combination of items from each field should still be unique).

Since an index brings about a significant boost in performance, we could create as many indexes as possible for maximum performance gain, right? Not always. An index is a sure-fire way to increase the speed of searching and retrieving data from a database, but sacrifices performance when saving or updating records, and also increases the size of a table. Why? When you insert a record into an indexed table, the database engine has to record its position in the corresponding index table. Do the math!

What's more, if you have more than one index on a table, multiple write operations have to be performed on the index table too. So when creating indexes on a table, don't create more than you need: try to limit indexed columns to those that will be searched or sorted frequently. If required, you can create additional indexes on a table to increase performance when you need them.

## Queries

**SQL statements** or **commands** are used to construct queries – the question your application asks to a database engine, which, in turn, returns the records that meet the criteria specified in the query. Queries return an *array* of records that meet the specified conditions, and contain information from selected fields. Why did we emphasize the word "array", you ask? PHP, and other languages that support database connectivity for that matter, can treat the returned array as a normal array variable. We'll get back to this topic later; for now, bear it in mind. The returned array of records, called the **result set**, is the database engine's answer to your query. If you ask the engine to retrieve the records containing "John" as the first name, for example, it will return the records conforming to the query. If none are found, NULL is returned. We will look more closely at NULL in a moment.

Some SQL commands are literally "commands" that tell the database engine to do something instead of asking for an answer: "Delete those rows of information that contain John as the first name!" SQL commands of this type don't return a result set.

### NULL

Consider the following scenarios:

❑ A class takes a spelling test at school, but the teacher has yet to mark the test sheets and fill the results into a database table. It would be unfair of the teacher to fill default values into the results column before the sheets have been marked, because a default score is irrelevant in this context. What can we place in the column to signify that we are awaiting data?

❑ You want to construct a database table which contains information about endangered bird species. One of the fields provides the fastest recorded flight speed for each bird in the table. You begin to create records for endangered penguins, and then you remember that they can't fly! What do we place in the flight speed column to indicate that the field is not applicable to penguins?

In both of these cases data is missing from a table. The only difference is that, for the first case, this situation is temporary because the teacher will soon add the missing test results to the table, whereas in the second case the values for the flight speed of penguins is impossible to obtain. Therefore we need a way to represent missing data in fields.

In a MySQL table, a NULL entry represents a missing value. NULL doesn't belong to any particular data type, but it can replace any value. Since it is not a data type or value, but it can be a field entry, the concept of a NULL is often difficult to grasp for experienced programmers and beginners alike. Programmers often have a mistaken idea of NULL. For example, a common mistake is to think of NULL as zero, which is wrong because zero is a value; NULL is not. Strings filled with one or more blank spaces, and strings of zero length, may also be mistaken for NULL. This is a mistake because string is a data type, but NULL isn't. NULL is nothing, no data type, no value.

So what happens if the result set from one of your queries contains a NULL, and this result set is then used in your program in subsequent calculations? The rule of thumb for math with NULL is that they propagate. Any arithmetic operation involving a NULL will return NULL. This makes sense: how can we provide a result, when all the data needed to perform the calculation is not present? This also applies to dividing a NULL value by zero; NULL will be returned.

### Query Commands

MySQL queries issued to manipulate data in a table can be constructed using the following main commands:

❑ SELECT: used to **retrieve** data from a database

❑ DELETE: used to **delete** data from a database

❑ INSERT: used to **insert** data into a database

❑ REPLACE: used to **replace** data in a database. If the same record exists in a table, the command overwrites the record with the new data.

❑ UPDATE: used to **update** data in a table.

The rest of the command set involves creating or modifying the database structures, rather than the data stored in it:

❑ CREATE: used to **create** a database, table or index.

❑ ALTER: used to **modify** the structure of a table.

❑ DROP: used to **wipe out** a database or table.

The typical form of a MySQL SELECT query, which retrieves records from a table, looks like this:

```
mysql> SELECT last_name, first_name FROM user WHERE first_name =
'John';
```

The first thing to note is that each query is terminated with a semicolon, just as a PHP statement is. A query statement may expand to multiple lines. The following query is essentially the same as the above:

```
mysql> SELECT last_name, first_name
    -> FROM user
    -> WHERE first_name = 'John'
```

Take a closer look at the FROM, WHERE, and ORDER BY **clauses** in the query. The query returns any record *from* the user table *where* the value of the first_name field is "John". Here's a sample of the output:

```
Simpleton John
Smith John
Thomas John
```

Now lets have some fun with MySQL!

# A Quick Play with MySQL

Let's now see how we can work with the MySQL server using the mysql client program. On the way, we will get a taste for MySQL query commands, and play around with user privileges.

## Running the mysql Client

Fire up the mysql client by issuing the following command at your command prompt:

> **mysql -uUSER -pPASSWORD -hHOST**

Replace the USER, PASSWORD and HOST arguments to reflect your personal settings. For example, if your database username and password are "phpuser" and "phppass" and you're connecting to the host "db.whatever.com", the command would look like this:

> **mysql -uphpuser -pphppass -hdb.whatever.com**

All the arguments are optional. If missing, the following values will be assumed for them:

| | |
|---|---|
| -u | your shell account username |
| -p | no password |
| -h | localhost |

The mysql client now connects to the database server running on the specified HOST with the given user ID/password combination. You may also specify a database to use by providing its name at the end of the above command.

You should see a response similar to the following:

```
Welcome to the MySQL monitor.  Commands end with ; or \g.
Your MySQL connection id is 10 to server version: 3.22.32

Type 'help' for help.

mysql>
```

If the `mysql` client complains it can't connect to the specified server, check to see if the provided arguments are correct.

# Selecting a Database to Use

To see the list of databases available, use the `SHOW DATABASES` command:

```
mysql> SHOW DATABASES;
+---------------+
| Database      |
+---------------+
| mysql         |
| test          |
+---------------+
2 rows in set (0.00 sec)
```

The `mysql` client reports that two databases, named `mysql` and `test` respectively, are currently available in the system, as well as displaying the number of rows returned (2) and the time the server took to execute the query (0.00 seconds to two decimal places).

To select a database, utilize the `USE databasename` syntax:

```
mysql> USE mysql;
Database changed
```

Note that on the Windows platform, MySQL keywords, like `USE`, and arguments, such as `mysql` here, are not case-sensitive. However, on the Linux/UNIX platforms the arguments *are* case-sensitive: "Mysql", "MYSQL", and "mysql" are all different database names. Field names are also case-insensitive, so "USERID", "Userid", and "userid" all refer to the same field, but we recommend that you stick to lower case letters when specifying field names for the sake of readability.

# Taking a Peek at Data in a Database

Now the MySQL server is ready to work with the database `mysql`. To see the list of available tables in a database, use the `SHOW TABLES` command:

```
mysql> SHOW TABLES;
+-----------------+
| Tables in mysql |
```

```
+-----------------+
| columns_priv    |
| db              |
| func            |
| host            |
| tables_priv     |
| user            |
+-----------------+
6 rows in set (0.00 sec)
```

The above command will list the privilege tables MySQL uses to authenticate database users. Let's view how the user table is structured. Use the DESCRIBE command, or DESC for short:

```
mysql> DESC user;
+-----------------+---------------+------+-----+---------+-------+
| Field           | Type          | Null | Key | Default | Extra |
+-----------------+---------------+------+-----+---------+-------+
| Host            | char(60)      |      | PRI |         |       |
| User            | char(16)      |      | PRI |         |       |
| Password        | char(16)      |      |     |         |       |
| Select_priv     | enum('N','Y') |      |     | N       |       |
| Insert_priv     | enum('N','Y') |      |     | N       |       |
| Update_priv     | enum('N','Y') |      |     | N       |       |
| Delete_priv     | enum('N','Y') |      |     | N       |       |
| Create_priv     | enum('N','Y') |      |     | N       |       |
| Drop_priv       | enum('N','Y') |      |     | N       |       |
| Reload_priv     | enum('N','Y') |      |     | N       |       |
| Shutdown_priv   | enum('N','Y') |      |     | N       |       |
| Process_priv    | enum('N','Y') |      |     | N       |       |
| File_priv       | enum('N','Y') |      |     | N       |       |
| Grant_priv      | enum('N','Y') |      |     | N       |       |
| References_priv | enum('N','Y') |      |     | N       |       |
| Index_priv      | enum('N','Y') |      |     | N       |       |
| Alter_priv      | enum('N','Y') |      |     | N       |       |
+-----------------+---------------+------+-----+---------+-------+
17 rows in set (0.00 sec)
```

This command describes the user table's structure. For example, you can see the Host field can hold up to 60 characters and is defined as a primary key. Note that the User field is also defined as a primary key. It doesn't mean that the Host and User fields are both primary keys (you should remember that this is forbidden). Instead, the combination of the Host and User fields works as a sole primary key in "Host-User" format. For example, if user john at localhost has been given the server access privileges, localhost-john becomes the primary key value for his record. Another user at localhost whose name is also "john" cannot be inserted as a record in this table. However, "john" at "whatever.com" can.

All the fields in the user table except the Host, User, Password, are declared as ENUM('N', 'Y'). This means that only one from the specified set of values (either N or Y in this case) can be used in each field. Note that N is the default value when no value is provided.

We can see who's given access privileges at the local machine, by issuing the following SELECT query:

```
mysql> SELECT User FROM user WHERE Host='localhost';
+----------+
| User     |
+----------+
| root     |
+----------+
1 row in set (0.00 sec)
```

Note how we have narrowed the scope of the retrieved records, by using a WHERE clause. This works much the same as PHP's if statement, except that the former uses a single equal sign (=) whereas the latter uses two (==) to test for equality.

If you wanted the server to retrieve all fields available instead of a few specified ones, you could use the * wildcard. For example:

```
mysql> SELECT * FROM tablename;
```

This command would retrieve all of the records from tablename.

## Manipulating Data in a Database

Now let's create a new database user, by *inserting* a new record into the user table using the INSERT command:

```
mysql> INSERT INTO user VALUES(
    -> 'localhost',
    -> 'phpuser',
    -> Password('phppass'),
    -> 'N', 'N', 'N', 'N', 'N', 'N', 'N',
    -> 'N', 'N', 'N', 'N', 'N', 'N', 'N');
Query OK, 1 row affected (0.00 sec)
```

This INSERT query creates a record for the user phpuser, using the password phppass, in the user table, and specifies no access privileges. Note that string values are all placed between quotes – we'll discuss this issue in greater detail later on. As you can see, the mysql client reports that the query was successfully executed, and that one row of data has been inserted as requested.

MySQL saves database user passwords after encrypting them. It uses its own password encryption scheme (which is different to that of Linux), so you should use MySQL's built in password() function to encrypt your password.

What if we change our minds, and want to give user phpuser (who presently has no access privileges at all) the server administration privileges, Reload_priv and Shutdown_priv? You could *update* the user table to reflect your whimsical decision using an UPDATE query, like this:

```
mysql> UPDATE user SET Reload_priv='Y', Shutdown_priv='Y'
    -> WHERE User='phpuser';
Query OK, 1 row affected (0.00 sec)
Rows matched: 1  Changed: 1  Warnings: 0
```

The `mysql` client reports that only one row matched the condition set in the query and that it has been successfully updated. User `phpuser` now has server administration privileges only: `phpuser` is only allowed to reload or shutdown the server.

The `WHERE` clause is optional, and when omitted, the `UPDATE` query changes all the records in a given table with the new values provided. Warning: make sure you don't change records by accident. A nightmare can sometimes turn into reality if you're not careful: you might change 10,000 user records to have the same password with a careless `UPDATE` query, for example. Even worse, you might unwittingly *delete* all the records in a table, with a `DELETE` query such as:

```
mysql> DELETE FROM test;
Query OK, 0 rows affected (0.00 sec)
```

Here all of the records in the table `test` have been deleted. Don't be fooled by the `mysql` client reporting that no row is affected by this query. Following the query, the server has no way of knowing how many rows are affected (deleted) since they're gone forever after the query. Note the syntax of this `DELETE` command; in the example above it contained no clauses, but (thankfully) you may specify which records are to be deleted with a `WHERE` clause:

```
DELETE FROM tablename WHERE condition(s);
```

Now we change our minds again and want to give user `phpuser` all of the server administration privileges. What do we do? We can make either another `UPDATE` query, or `REPLACE` the whole record. The syntax is pretty simple:

```
mysql> REPLACE INTO user VALUES(
    -> 'localhost', 'phpuser', Password('phppass'),
    -> 'Y', 'Y', 'Y', 'Y', 'Y', 'Y', 'Y',
    -> 'Y', 'Y', 'Y', 'Y', 'Y', 'Y', 'Y');
Query OK, 1 row affected (0.00 sec)
```

So `REPLACE` overwrites an old record with a new one. Note that the new record and the old record must have the same value in a field designated as a key (or the combined key formed by the `Host` and `User` fields in this case). The difference between the `UPDATE` and `REPLACE` commands is that `UPDATE` replaces only the selected set of fields in a record, while `REPLACE` replaces the whole record with the given values.

Finally, in order to activate the newly created account `phpuser`, you need to **flush** privileges, reloading the privilege information from the table. The server normally only reads the access privilege information once, when it's loaded.

```
> mysqladmin -uUSER -pPASSWORD -hHOST flush-privileges
```

Alternately you can issue the `FLUSH PRIVILEGES` command to reflect the change in the `mysql` client program:

```
mysql> FLUSH PRIVILEGES;
```

# Using GRANT and REVOKE commands

Previously we created a new user by manipulating the MySQL grant tables directly. We can achieve the same goal more simply using the GRANT command. Let's see how.

## *GRANT*

The simplest form of the GRANT command looks like this:

```
mysql> GRANT ALL PRIVILEGES ON *.* TO
    -> phpuser@localhost IDENTIFIED BY 'phppass';
```

The above command gives every access privilege, on every database in the system, to the user phpuser at localhost if he logs on to the server using the password phppass. Note that the user and host arguments are *not* given in quotes.

If we wanted to let him access the tables in the test database only, we would have used the following command:

```
mysql> GRANT ALL PRIVILEGES ON test.*
    -> TO phpuser@localhost IDENTIFIED BY 'phppass';
```

Here, test.* denotes all tables in test. In a similar way, to grant access to only the sample table in test, we can use:

```
mysql> GRANT ALL PRIVILEGES ON test.sample
    -> TO phpuser@localhost IDENTIFIED BY 'phppass';
```

By replacing the ALL PRIVILEGES keyword with a selection of query types, a set of access privileges can be granted as shown below:

```
mysql> GRANT SELECT,INSERT,UPDATE ON test.*
    -> TO phpuser@% IDENTIFIED BY 'phppass';
```

With the above command, the user phpuser can issue only SELECT, INSERT, UPDATE queries to any of the tables in the database test. A DELETE query won't be allowed, for example. Wildcards like * are extremely useful. For example, by replacing localhost with the % wild card, we can allow the user phpuser to access the specified tables from any server.

You can also specify the host with a partial domain name: if you used "phpuser@%.whatever.com" for instance, only users with the user ID phpuser connecting from the domain "whatever.com" would be granted access to the server.

You can split hairs even further, by specifying fields to which the user can have access:

```
mysql> GRANT SELECT (User, Host) ON mysql.user
    -> TO phpuser@localhost IDENTIFIED BY 'phppass';
```

Here the user phpuser can only issue SELECT queries on the User and Host fields in the user table.

You can use the WITH GRANT OPTION clause to give the specified user the ability to grant other users any privileges he has at the specified privilege level:

```
mysql> GRANT ALL PRIVILEGES ON test.*
    -> TO phpuser@localhost IDENTIFIED BY 'phppass' WITH GRANT OPTION;
```

The above command is equivalent to creating another superuser, called phpuser. You should be careful with the WITH GRANT OPTION clause: two users with different privileges can easily team up and extend their privileges by exchanging them!

### REVOKE

The REVOKE command removes access privileges from a user. If you want to revoke *all* privileges given to user phpuser, for example, issue the following command:

```
mysql> REVOKE ALL PRIVILEGES ON *.* FROM phpuser;
```

Multiple usernames can be specified by separating them with a comma:

```
mysql> REVOKE ALL PRIVILEGES ON *.*
    -> FROM phpuser@localhost, phpuser2, phpuser3;
```

Note that all specified users must exist, and possess the specified privileges, in order for the above command to work.

The following command revokes only the SELECT privilege from the user phpuser:

```
mysql> REVOKE SELECT ON *.* FROM phpuser;
```

Again, we can split hairs by specifying field names:

```
mysql> REVOKE SELECT (User, Host) ON mysql.user FROM phpuser;
```

Note that if you modify the grant tables using GRANT or REVOKE commands, the changes take effect immediately. You don't have to flush privileges, or reload the server.

# Summing Up

We skimmed through some of the core SQL queries in this section. If you didn't understand any of them, don't worry. The material in this chapter is intended to give you a good feel for how relational databases and SQL work. You'll learn more about them as you read through the following chapters.

In the next section we will (at last!) use PHP. At the start of the chapter, we noted that PHP supports a number of popular database engines: Microsoft SQL Server, Informix, PostgreSQL, and, of course, MySQL, to name but a few. Let's now move on to see how PHP allows you to connect to a MySQL server in your scripts.

# PHP MySQL Connectivity

In order to work with a MySQL server (or any other RDBMS) in PHP you must use the following steps:

1.  Open a connection to the server.

2.  Work with databases in the server.

3.  Close the connection.

Does this list sound familiar? You followed similar steps when working with files and directories in the preceding chapter. No big deal!

## Basic Connection Functions

Let's begin this section by familiarizing ourselves with some basic PHP functions we can use to work with MySQL.

### mysql_connect()

PHP provides the `mysql_connect()` function to create a connection to a MySQL server. It takes three string arguments: the hostname; the database username; and the database user password. The function returns a **link identifier** when it successfully connects to the specified MySQL server (or NULL upon error):

```
$link_id = mysql_connect("localhost", "phpuser", "phppass");
```

The link identifier works much the same as a file or directory handle: we will use the link identifier later on, to issue queries. All of the arguments are optional, and when none are provided, "localhost", the web-server owner's username, and an empty password are all assumed.

### mysql_close()

As in the case of working with files, the link to the MySQL server is closed when the script is terminated. If you want to close the connection earlier than this, you can use the `mysql_close()` function, with the link identifier as its argument:

```
mysql_close($link_id);
```

The `mysql_close()` function returns `true` on success and `false` upon error. If the link identifier is omitted, the previously opened link is used (if not specified otherwise, all `mysql_*` functions which take an optional link ID argument assume the previously-opened link in its absence).

### mysql_list_dbs()

This function is PHP's equivalent to MySQL's SHOW DATABASES command. Its only argument is the (optional) link identifier. It returns a pointer (`$result below`) to the array containing the names of available databases:

```
$result = mysql_list_dbs($link_id);
```

### mysql_select_db()

This function is used to select a database, returning `True` on success and `False` upon error. It takes the name of the database as an argument, although a link identifier argument is optional. An example:

```
mysql_select_db("mysql", $link_id);
```

If no connection has been made before calling the `mysql_select_db()` function, it attempts to establish a link before selecting the specified database.

Let's take a moment to illustrate how we can connect to the local MySQL server with the account we created earlier, using PHP:

```
$link_id = mysql_connect("localhost", "phpuser", "phppass");
if(mysql_select_db("mysql", $link_id) echo "Connected to the localhost.";
else die ("Connection failed.");
```

This code establishes a connection to the local MySQL server, and selects the `mysql` access privilege database. If the connection fails, an error message is displayed.

### mysql_list_tables()

This function is equivalent to MySQL's `SHOW TABLES` command. The database name and the optional link identifier are taken as arguments. A pointer is returned, to the array containing the names of available tables associated with the database:

```
$result = mysql_list_tables("mysql", $link_id);
```

### mysql_num_rows()

We can find the number of rows in a result set returned by a given query by calling this function. The `mysql_num_rows()` function takes the result set pointer as an argument.

```
$num_rows = mysql_num_rows($result);
```

Use it on result sets returned by `SELECT` queries, and other functions which retrieve rows.

### mysql_affected_rows()

In order to get the number of rows *affected* by `INSERT`, `UPDATE`, or `DELETE` commands, you need to use the `mysql_affected_rows()` function instead of `mysql_num_rows()`. It takes an optional link ID argument:

```
$num_rows = mysql_affected_rows($link_id);
```

Recall from earlier in the chapter that a `DELETE` query with no `WHERE` clause wipes out all the records in a given table and causes the `mysql_affected_rows()` function call to return zero.

You should also note that the return value of `mysql_num_rows()` and `mysql_affected_rows()` is the actual count of rows selected/affected, whereas the return value from `mysql_list_dbs()` and `mysq_list_tables()` is a pointer to a result set.

### mysql_fetch_row()

To retrieve the rows of records returned from the server, the `mysql_fetch_row()` function is used. It takes a result set pointer returned from a previous query, and returns an array corresponding to the fetched row (or `false` if there are no more rows left):

```
$fetched_row = mysql_fetch_row($result_set);
```

PHP maintains an internal pointer to the row returned from a previous query. Each subsequent call to the `mysql_fetch_row()` function moves this pointer to the next row available. When the pointer moves past the result set array boundary, the `mysql_fetch_row()` function returns `False`.

## Try It Out – Connecting to a MySQL Server in PHP

Here's a sample script which uses the functions introduced above to list the databases and tables available to the MySQL user `phpuser`:

```php
<?php
//list_db.php

$link_id = mysql_connect("localhost", "phpuser", "phppass");
$result = mysql_list_dbs($link_id);
$num_rows = mysql_num_rows($result);

while($db_data = mysql_fetch_row($result)) {
        echo $db_data[0]. "<BR>";
        $result2 = mysql_list_tables($db_data[0]);
        $num_rows2 = mysql_num_rows($result2);
        while($table_data = mysql_fetch_row($result2)) echo "--" .
$table_data[0]. "<BR>";
        echo "==> $num_rows2 table(s) in " . $db_data[0] . "<P>";
}
?>
```

The above script lists all databases available and tables in each of them. Here's a sample run.

```
mysql
--columns_priv
--db
--func
--host
--tables_priv
--user
==> 6 table(s) in mysql
test_db
--sample_table1
--sample_table2
==> 2 table(s) in test_db
```

### How It Works

The script first makes a connection to the server with the given set of values: `localhost`, `phpuser`, and `phppass`. Replace the values here with the appropriate ones for you, if you wish to use your own username and password instead of those we gave to the user we created earlier.

Note that the link identifier returned by the `mysql_connect()` function is used by the `mysql_list_dbs()` function call. In fact, we don't need to pass the link identifier to the latter function anyway, since it would assume the last opened link in the absence of the link argument – as demonstrated in the `mysql_list_tables()` function call:

```
$result = mysql_list_dbs($link_id);
$result2 = mysql_list_tables($db_data[0]);
```

One of the common mistakes you can make is overwriting the result pointer when you issue another query while stepping through the result set returned from a previous query. Just as you can open multiple files with different file handles, you should maintain multiple result sets by assigning unique pointers to each set.

A while loop in the script cycles through the result set returned by the `mysql_list_dbs()` function call. Another while loop is set up to look into every element in the result set returned by the `mysql_list_tables()` function call. Both loops are terminated when there are no more rows left in the result sets because `$db_data` and `$table_data` are False when the `mysql_fetch_row()` function is done fetching the returned rows.

Also note that each of the arrays returned by `mysql_list_dbs()` or `mysql_list_tables()` contain only one element; the name of a database `$db_data[0]`, and that of a table `$table_data[0]`, respectively. If you wanted to retrieve more than one field from a table, you can refer to each one by a corresponding array index:

```
$result_set = mysql_fetch_row($result);
$first_column = $result_set[0];
$second_column = $result_set[1];
$third_column = $result_set[2];
```

Note that we have not used the `mysql_close()` function; it is seldom used in real-life applications unless you need to close the connection for some reason before your applications end. PHP automatically closes the open connection before your script ends.

We will be looking further into how MySQL and PHP can work in tandem in the following chapters.

## Handling Server Errors

Now let's try something rather dumb: take the last script, change the database username to `no_such_user`, and see what happens. You'll see a bunch of warnings thrown out (unless you've set the error reporting level in the `php.ini` configuration file to suppress them):

```
Warning: MySQL Connection Failed: Access denied for user: 'no_such_user@localhost'
(Using password: YES) in /home/apache/htdocs/ db_connect.php on line 3

Warning: Supplied argument is not a valid MySQL-Link resource in
/home/apache/htdocs/ db_connect.php on line 5
```

```
Warning: Supplied argument is not a valid MySQL result resource in
/home/apache/htdocs/ db_connect.php on line 6

Warning: Supplied argument is not a valid MySQL result resource in
/home/apache/htdocs/ db_connect.php on line 8
```

Why do we get such uninformative warnings? It's simple – the script we just created isn't smart enough to say what went wrong upon error; it just knows that it tried to access some MySQL resources but failed. PHP is generating the warnings, but the errors are on the database server.

So how do we catch server errors and determine what went wrong? PHP provides a couple of functions that do just that, returning values from the server's own error-handler. If a MySQL server encounters an error while executing a specified task, it returns the text and number of the error message. You can get at these values using the PHP functions `mysql_errno()` and `mysql_error()`.

The `mysql_errno()` function returns the error number and `mysql_error()` the error text from the previous MySQL operation. They both take an optional link identifier argument (defaulting to the previously-opened link):

```
$MYSQL_ERRNO = mysql_errno($link_id);
$MYSQL_ERROR = mysql_error($link_id);
```

These functions assume the connection to the server has already been made, so if you call them to see what went wrong when a connection has failed, no error will be reported since no opened link is available. As we've seen though, we can still use the `die()` function to exit with a message that the connection attempt has failed:

```
if(!mysql_connect("localhost", "no_such_user", "phppass"))
                                        die("Connection failed!");
```

The only problem with this approach is that PHP still churns out its own warning messages when the connection attempt fails. To prevent warnings and/or error messages we either precede the function call with the error message suppressing operator '@', or use the `error_reporting()` function.

As we saw in Chapter 7, we can use the `error_reporting()` function call to set the level of error reporting that PHP applies while executing subsequent code. By specifying `error_reporting(0)`, we can ensure that no PHP error/warning messages will be invoked. This is what we'll do in the following example.

*It's not a good idea to set the level to produce warnings in production environment since they might scare away your users. Set it to a higher level only when you are debugging your applications. Refer back to Chapter 7 for more information.*

## Try It Out – Handling Server Errors

We're now going to define a couple of functions that we'll find very useful in later sections. We shall therefore place them in a separate file, `common_db.inc`, which we can include in later examples, and expand as necessary. Note in particular the function `db_connect()`, which is dedicated to making connections to the MySQL server. We'll be using it a lot!

```php
<?php
//common_db.inc
$dbhost = 'localhost';
$dbusername = 'phpuser';
$dbuserpassword = 'phppass';
$default_dbname = 'mysql';

$MYSQL_ERRNO = '';
$MYSQL_ERROR = '';

function db_connect() ?>{
   global $dbhost, $dbusername, $dbuserpassword, $default_dbname;
   global $MYSQL_ERRNO, $MYSQL_ERROR;

   $link_id = mysql_connect($dbhost, $dbusername, $dbuserpassword);
   if(!$link_id) {
      $MYSQL_ERRNO = 0;
      $MYSQL_ERROR = "Connection failed to the host $dbhost.";
      return 0;
   }
   else if(empty($dbname) && !mysql_select_db($default_dbname)) {
      $MYSQL_ERRNO = mysql_errno();
      $MYSQL_ERROR = mysql_error();
      return 0;
   }
   else return $link_id;
}

function sql_error() {
   global $MYSQL_ERRNO, $MYSQL_ERROR;

   if(empty($MYSQL_ERROR)) {
      $MYSQL_ERRNO = mysql_errno();
      $MYSQL_ERROR = mysql_error();
   }
   return "$MYSQL_ERRNO: $MYSQL_ERROR";
}
```

Now try the following script with an incorrect username/password combination or non-existent database names:

```php
<?php
//db_connect.php
include "common_db.inc";
error_reporting(0);

$link_id = db_connect();
if(!$link_id) die(sql_error());
else echo "Successfully made a connection to $dbhost.<BR>";
?>
```

Try the script using an invalid username or password, and you should see the following error message:

```
0: Connection failed to the host localhost.
```

If $default_dbname is empty, you'll get:

```
1046: No Database Selected
```

If it's set to a non-existent database name (no_such_db for example) you'll see:

```
1049: Unknown database 'no_such_db'
```

## How It Works

Once we've included our variable and function definitions, we specify error_reporting(0) to prevent PHP from displaying any error/warning messages.

> *Note that we could also have suppressed error messages by prefixing the following* mysql_connect() *and* mysql_select_db() *function calls with an @ symbol.*

If the database connection is made successfully, db_connect() returns a link identifier. Otherwise it sets global variables $MYSQL_ERRNO and $MYSQL_ERROR accordingly, and returns zero to indicate an error. Consequently, the script dies:

```
if(!$link_id) die(sql_error());
```

Rather than directly specifying an error message, we've called sql_error() to produce one for us:

```
function sql_error() {
    global $MYSQL_ERRNO, $MYSQL_ERROR;

    if(empty($MYSQL_ERROR)) {
        $MYSQL_ERRNO = mysql_errno();
        $MYSQL_ERROR = mysql_error();
    }
    return "$MYSQL_ERRNO: $MYSQL_ERROR";
}
```

Basically all this function does is return a character string containing the error number and error message, separated by a colon. However, this is going to be quite useful to us in future, in situations where we can't assume that the returned variables have been defined. For example, we might want to call sql_error() following a database query error; the trouble is that $MYSQL_ERRNO and $MYSQL_ERROR would not have been defined. To make this function useful in such an event (as well as the failed connection we're anticipating), we check the $MYSQL_ERROR global variable's value. If it's empty, we call mysql_errno() and mysql_error() again and assign values to both.

Note that after a successful connection, db_connect() attempts to select the default database, which we've set in the $default_dbname global variable. We can improve db_connect() by having it take an optional argument $dbname, so that it selects whichever database is specified in the argument:

```
function db_connect($dbname='') {
    global $dbhost, $dbusername, $dbuserpassword, $default_dbname;
    global $MYSQL_ERRNO, $MYSQL_ERROR;

    $link_id = mysql_connect($dbhost, $dbusername, $dbuserpassword);
    if(!$link_id) {
        $MYSQL_ERRNO = 0;
        $MYSQL_ERROR = "Connection failed to the host $dbhost.";
        return 0;
    }
    else if(empty($dbname) && !mysql_select_db($default_dbname)) {
        $MYSQL_ERRNO = mysql_errno();
        $MYSQL_ERROR = mysql_error();
        return 0;
    }
    else if(!empty($dbname) && !mysql_select_db($dbname)) {
        $MYSQL_ERRNO = mysql_errno();
        $MYSQL_ERROR = mysql_error();
        return 0;
    }
    else return $link_id;
}
```

We can now call it like this:

```
$link_id = db_connect("sample_db");
```

and the connection held by `$link_id` will automatically use the database `sample_db`. If we don't specify an argument, it defaults to the database specified by `$default_dbname`.

# Creating Databases and Tables from MySQL

Creating a database from MySQL is very simple indeed. To create a database called `sample_db`, you just have to say:

```
mysql> CREATE DATABASE sample_db;
Query OK, 1 row affected (0.05sec)
mysql>
```

Removing it is just as simple:

```
mysql> DROP DATABASE sample_db;
Query OK, 0 rows affected (0.00sec)
mysql>
```

Note that the number of rows it counts as having been affected doesn't include the ones it's removed. You could have just deleted thousands of data entries, but from the information presented here, you'd have no way of knowing! This is all the more reason to use **extreme caution** – this small, harmless looking command will totally *wipe out* the specified database and all the tables in it, and won't even *hint* at what it's done, let alone ask you for confirmation. You have been warned!

> Assuming you just got rid of your `sample_db` database, `CREATE` it again. We're going to be using it rather a lot in the next couple of chapters, and the rest of the examples in this chapter will take us through the steps we need to set it up.

Creating a database table is a little more complicated. Let's say we want to create a table called `user`. We start off with the obvious syntax:

```
mysql> CREATE TABLE user;
ERROR 1113: A table must have at least 1 column
mysql>
```

Okay, we're going to need a little more than that. While a database can quite happily exist without any tables living under its roof, tables are rather more fussy. We shall have to give it some structure.

We do this by following our table name with a bracketed list of field descriptors, each one in the form:

```
fieldname TYPE(length)
```

We could therefore create a very simple two-field table with:

```
mysql> CREATE TABLE test_table ( name CHAR(40), number INT);
Query OK, 0 rows affected (0.06sec)
mysql>
```

We've already had a look at the various types of variable supported by MySQL. We also have the option of specifying attributes for each of the fields – to do so, we simply append them to the descriptor. They can consist of any combination of the following:

| Attributes | Description |
| --- | --- |
| BINARY | Makes the field's value case-sensitive. Only works with CHAR and VARCHAR type fields. |
| NULL or NOT NULL | NOT NULL fields cannot take a NULL value. |
| | Fields that are declared NULL will store a specified default value whenever a NULL value is given. If there is no default value provided, they simply store NULL. |
| | If unspecified, NULL is assumed. |
| DEFAULT *default_value* | Specifies the default value to store when NULL is given. |
| AUTO_INCREMENT | When a NULL value is placed in an AUTO_INCREMENT field, the field value is set to one greater than its current maximum value in that table. AUTO_INCREMENT only works with unique, integer type fields. |
| | There can be only one AUTO_INCREMENT field per table. |

Once we've listed all those we need, we can specify selected fields as holding indexes, primary keys and unique values. Let's have a quick recap and see what each of these entails:

- ❏ KEY/INDEX – these are synonymous keywords and both specify fields that are to be used as indexes. The specified field entries are copied to a separate index table, where they're listed against pointers to the corresponding entries in the original table. They're then sorted, producing an index much the same as you'd find in the back of a book. If we specify multiple fields ("field1", "field2", ...) for our index, the index will be sorted first on "field1", and then any duplicate values in "field1" will be sorted on "field2", and so on.

- ❏ UNIQUE – the value of each entry in a UNIQUE field must be unique among all other entries in the same field. That is, if one record's entry in the field contains the value "10", it's guaranteed that no other entry in that field will have the same value. As mentioned, uniqueness is a requirement for AUTO_INCREMENT fields.

- ❏ PRIMARY KEY – you can specify exactly one field in any given table as a PRIMARY KEY; it will then be used as an index of unique values. Consequently, each entry can be used in other tables as a unique reference to the record it belongs to – it's essentially the glue that holds a relational database together. In order to use a field as a primary key, it must be declared as NOT NULL. Once again, if you pass more than one field name when defining a primary key, the specified field names are combined to create a primary key.

In the course of the next couple of chapters, we're going to be seeing a lot of examples based around a homemade relational database comprising two tables. The first is called user, and this will serve as a record of all users registered on an imaginary web server. The other, access_log, will contain relative paths to the web pages each user accesses, plus counters measuring how many times they visit each page. We'll house both these tables in our sample_db database.

Our first table, user, is structured as follows:

| Field | Type | Null | Attributes |
|-------|------|------|------------|
| usernumber | mediumint(10) | no | AUTO_INCREMENT |
| userid | varchar(8) | no | BINARY |
| userpassword | varchar(20) | no | BINARY |
| username | varchar(30) | no | none |
| usercountry | varchar(40) | no | none |
| useremail | varchar(50) | no | none |
| userprofile | text | no | none |
| registerdate | date | no | none |
| lastaccesstime | timestamp(14) | yes | none |

The usernumber field has an AUTO_INCREMENT attribute. Therefore the field will be automatically incremented (that is, its value increased by 1) whenever a new record is inserted with a NULL value in the first field. For example, when a new user registers and his record is added to the user table, the user number assigned will be one more than the largest that's already in the table. We will also declare this field as UNIQUE, ensuring that no two rows can have the same value.

The fields `userid` and `userpassword` are both variable-length strings (lengths specified as 8 and 20 characters respectively). They are declared as `BINARY`, and are therefore case-sensitive. By default, character fields are case-insensitive.

The `registerdate` field holds the date on which the user registered as a member, while the `lastaccesstime` field contains the date and time they last accessed the site.

The `userid` field is defined as a primary key and will be used to establish a relationship with the `access_log` table, which also has a `userid` field.

The fields declared `NOT NULL` cannot contain `NULL` values and must be given a value when a new record is inserted unless you specified a default value for the field. The `lastaccesstime` field is the only one that is allowed to take a `NULL` value. In fact, a `TIMESTAMP` type field can always take a `NULL` value since it stores the current system time in "YYYYMMDDhhmmss" format when a new record is inserted, or an existing record is updated, unless it is explicitly given a date and time to store.

| Field | Type | Null | Attributes |
| --- | --- | --- | --- |
| page | varchar(250) | no | none |
| userid | varchar(8) | no | BINARY |
| visitcount | mediumint(5) | no | none |
| accessdate | timestamp(14) | yes | none |

Recall that the `access_log` table has the same `userid` field as the `user` table. The `userid` field serves as the key to define a relationship between the two tables.

Now that we defined the structures of the tables we need, let's create them and their home, the `sample_db` database.

---

In case you're dreading the prospect of typing in the following twelve-line SQL statement (because you don't want to have to retype the whole thing when it doesn't work first time), we suggest a couple of options:

If you're running PHP from UNIX, use the **edit** command from the **mysql** command line, which calls the text editor of your choice (this command doesn't work on Windows). This is held in the **$EDITOR** environment variable, and is typically the **vi** editor.

```
mysql> edit
```

If you make a typo, just reissue the edit command again. Your editor would still have what you previously typed in.

Note that the previous command is remembered by the **mysql** client program. You can go back a single line by pressing the up arrow key.

You can save your lines of SQL in a text file and feed it to the **mysql** client as shown below:

```
> mysql -uphpuser -pphppass -hlocalhost < query.sql
```

The following CREATE TABLE command creates the user table in the sample_db database:

```
mysql> CREATE TABLE user (
    ->     usernumber MEDIUMINT(10) DEFAULT '0' NOT NULL AUTO_INCREMENT,
    ->     userid VARCHAR(8) BINARY NOT NULL,
    ->     userpassword VARCHAR(20) BINARY NOT NULL,
    ->     username VARCHAR(30) NOT NULL,
    ->     usercountry VARCHAR(50) NOT NULL,
    ->     useremail VARCHAR(50) NOT NULL,
    ->     userprofile TEXT NOT NULL,
    ->     registerdate DATE DEFAULT '0000-00-00' NOT NULL,
    ->     lastaccesstime TIMESTAMP(14),
    ->     PRIMARY KEY (userid),
    ->     UNIQUE usernumber (usernumber)
    -> );
Query OK, 0 rows affected (0.00 sec)
mysql>
```

The following CREATE TABLE command creates the access_log table:

```
mysql> CREATE TABLE access_log (
    ->     page VARCHAR(250) NOT NULL,
    ->     userid VARCHAR(8) BINARY NOT NULL,
    ->     visitcount MEDIUMINT(5) DEFAULT '0' NOT NULL,
    ->     accessdate TIMESTAMP(14),
    ->     PRIMARY KEY (userid, page),
    -> );
Query OK, 0 rows affected (0.00 sec)
mysql>
```

The userid in the access_log table is neither declared as a primary key nor a unique value, since a user can access multiple web pages, and each visited web page constitutes a record in the table. Instead, the combination of userid and page is defined as the primary key.

# Creating the Sample Database and Tables with PHP

If all has gone to plan, you should now be the proud owner of a couple of tables, user and access_log. All well and good, but aren't we getting away from the main topic a little? The fact is, it's just as easy to generate these tables from our PHP scripts. Let's see how we might create the same database and tables using PHP instead of the mysql client.

First, we need a way to issue queries to the MySQL server from within PHP. For precisely this purpose, we have the mysql_query() function. This takes a query string as its first argument, and makes that query on the currently selected database, using the link identifier specified as the second argument. (As usual, you can omit the identifier, in which case the last opened link is assumed.) If no link is currently open, it attempts to establish a connection first.

> Note that you should not use semicolons to terminate query strings when using them as arguments to PHP functions.

If the given query is successfully executed, `mysql_query()` returns a non-zero value pointing to the returned result set, or `False` upon error. The following call is equivalent to having made the query `SHOW DATABASES` in the `mysql` client:

```
$link_id = db_connect();
$result = mysql_query("SHOW DATABASES", $link_id);
while($query_data = mysql_fetch_row($result)) {
echo $query_data[0],"<P>";
}
```

This will pass the expected list of databases to a table, returning a pointer to that table. We then just fetch each row and echo it out. It should look like this:

```
mysql
sample_db
test
```

Note that `$link_id` could have been omitted from the code snippet above, as the `mysql_query()` function would have defaulted to the last opened connection.

If you want to specify the name of the database to issue a query on, you can use the PHP function `mysql_db_query()` like this:

```
$result = mysql_db_query("sample_db", "SHOW TABLES");
```

This call will return the list of tables available in the `sample_db` database – even if we haven't used `mysql_select_db()` to select it explicitly.

We can also use `mysql_query()` to create and drop databases:

```
$result = mysql_query("CREATE DATABASE dummy_db");
$result = mysql_query("DROP DATABASE dummy_db");
```

However, PHP provides us with an alternative – a pair of functions specifically designed for creating and dropping databases: `mysql_create_db()` and `mysql_drop_db()`. These both take the name of a database to be created or dropped as the first argument, followed by an optional link identifier. Both functions return `True` if a database is successfully created/dropped and `False` upon error. For example:

```
$link_id = db_connect();
if(!mysql_create_db("dummy_db", $link_id)) die(sql_error());
                    echo "Successfully created the database dummy_db.";
if(!mysql_drop_db("dummy_db", $link_id)) die(sql_error());
                    echo "Successfully dropped the database dummy_db.";
```

## Try It Out – Creating Databases and Tables

The following script is an alternative to our earlier exploits at the command line: first, it creates the `sample_db` database; then it defines the tables `user` and `access_log` as specified above.

```php
<?php
//create_db.php
include "./common_db.inc";

$dbname = "sample_db";
$user_tablename = 'user';
$user_table_def = "usernumber MEDIUMINT(10) DEFAULT '0' NOT NULL AUTO_INCREMENT,";
$user_table_def .= "userid VARCHAR(8) BINARY NOT NULL,";
$user_table_def .= "userpassword VARCHAR(20) BINARY NOT NULL,";
$user_table_def .= "username VARCHAR(30) NOT NULL,";
$user_table_def .= "usercountry VARCHAR(50) NOT NULL,";
$user_table_def .= "useremail VARCHAR(50) NOT NULL,";
$user_table_def .= "userprofile TEXT NOT NULL,";
$user_table_def .= "registerdate DATE DEFAULT '0000-00-00' NOT NULL,";
$user_table_def .= "lastaccesstime TIMESTAMP(14),";
$user_table_def .= "PRIMARY KEY (userid),";
$user_table_def .= "UNIQUE usernumber (usernumber)";

$access_log_tablename = "access_log";
$access_log_table_def = "page VARCHAR(250) NOT NULL,";
$access_log_table_def .= "userid VARCHAR(8) BINARY NOT NULL,";
$access_log_table_def .= "visitcount MEDIUMINT(5) DEFAULT '0' NOT NULL,";
$access_log_table_def .= "accessdate TIMESTAMP(14),KEY page (page),";
$access_log_table_def .= "PRIMARY KEY (userid, page)";

$link_id = db_connect();
if(!$link_id) die(sql_error());

if(!mysql_query("CREATE DATABASE $dbname")) die(sql_error());

echo "Successfully created the $dbname database.<BR>";

if(!mysql_select_db($dbname)) die(sql_error());

if(!mysql_query("CREATE TABLE $user_tablename ($user_table_def)"))
                                            die(sql_error());

if(!mysql_query("CREATE TABLE $access_log_tablename ($access_log_table_def)"))
die(sql_error());

echo "Successfully created the $user_tablename and $access_log_tablename tables.";

?>
```

### How It Works

Our script is very straightforward. We begin by including `common_db.inc`, giving us use of the functions `db_connect()` and `sql_error()`, which we defined earlier:

```php
<?php
//create_db.php
include "./common_db.inc";
```

We then define the variables that describe our two tables. This is where all the hard work pays off – we just have to specify the same field descriptors as we did at the command line:

```
$dbname = "sample_db";
$user_tablename = "user";
$user_table_def = "usernumber MEDIUMINT(10) DEFAULT '0' NOT NULL AUTO_INCREMENT,";
$user_table_def .= "userid VARCHAR(8) BINARY NOT NULL,";
$user_table_def .= "userpassword VARCHAR(20) BINARY NOT NULL,";
$user_table_def .= "username VARCHAR(30) NOT NULL,";
$user_table_def .= "usercountry VARCHAR(50) NOT NULL,";
$user_table_def .= "useremail VARCHAR(50) NOT NULL,";
$user_table_def .= "userprofile TEXT NOT NULL,";
$user_table_def .= "registerdate DATE DEFAULT '0000-00-00' NOT NULL,";
$user_table_def .= "lastaccesstime TIMESTAMP(14),";
$user_table_def .= "PRIMARY KEY (userid),";
$user_table_def .= "UNIQUE usernumber (usernumber)";

$access_log_tablename = "access_log";
$access_log_table_def = "page VARCHAR(250) NOT NULL,";
$access_log_table_def .= "userid VARCHAR(8) BINARY NOT NULL,";
$access_log_table_def .= "visitcount MEDIUMINT(5) DEFAULT '0' NOT NULL,";
$access_log_table_def .= "accessdate TIMESTAMP(14),KEY page (page),";
$access_log_table_def .= "PRIMARY KEY (userid, page)";
```

We connect to the server...

```
$link_id = db_connect();
if(!$link_id) die(sql_error());
```

...create the `sample_db` database...

```
if(!mysql_query("CREATE DATABASE $dbname")) die(sql_error());
echo "Successfully created the $dbname database.<BR>";
```

....and select it with `mysql_select_db()`:

```
if(!mysql_select_db($dbname)) die(sql_error());
```

Subsequent calls to `mysql_query()` create the `user` and `access_log` tables. If an error occurs during a query, the error number and text are displayed by calling the `sql_error()` function.

```
if(!mysql_query("CREATE TABLE $user_tablename ($user_table_def)"))
                                                    die(sql_error());

if(!mysql_query("CREATE TABLE $access_log_tablename ($access_log_table_def)"))
                                                    die(sql_error());
```

If we make it through to the end of the script, we confirm a successful run:

```
echo "Successfully created tables $user_tablename and $access_log_tablename.";
?>
```

Recall that the `sql_error()` function calls the `mysql_errno()` and `mysql_error()` functions if the $MYSQL_ERRNO variable is empty:

```
if(empty($MYSQL_ERRNO)) {
     $MYSQL_ERRNO = mysql_errno();
     $MYSQL_ERROR = mysql_error();
}
```

This ensures that the function will return the error number and text even when a database connection is successfully made but a subsequent query fails.

# Altering Tables

So you've created a database, and populated it with carefully constructed tables. You've used it for a while and not had too much trouble – it's not perfect, but it does the job. Then out of the blue, you realize one day that your precious little database isn't all it's cracked up to be. You've caught on to the fact that your tables are badly designed. You've found some new data that doesn't quite fit the format you expected. Any number of things can make you sit up and realize that you need to modify the tables in your database.

MySQL provides the ALTER TABLE command to do just that. With this command, you can:

❑ **add** and **delete** fields or indexes (ADD and DROP)

❑ **change** the definition of existing fields (ALTER, CHANGE and MODIFY)

❑ **rename** fields (CHANGE) or even the table itself (RENAME AS)

For example, if you wanted to change the name of the table test to "tested", you could issue the following command:

```
mysql> ALTER TABLE test RENAME AS tested;
Query OK, 0 rows affected (0.02 sec)
```

Note that the AS keyword is optional – this will work just as well:

```
mysql> ALTER TABLE test RENAME tested;
Query OK, 0 rows affected (0.02 sec)
```

Let's add a new ENUM field to our user table. We'll call it sex, and it can be used to indicate whether a user is male or female:

```
mysql> ALTER TABLE user ADD sex ENUM('M', 'F') DEFAULT 'M';
Query OK, 0 rows affected (0.24 sec)
Records: 0  Duplicates: 0  Warnings: 0

mysql> DESC user;
+----------------+----------------+------+-----+---------+----------------+
| Field          | Type           | Null | Key | Default | Extra          |
+----------------+----------------+------+-----+---------+----------------+
| ...            |                |      |     |         |                |
| lastaccesstime | timestamp(14)  | YES  |     | NULL    |                |
| sex            | enum('M','F')  | YES  |     | M       |                |
+----------------+----------------+------+-----+---------+----------------+
10 rows in set (0.00 sec)
```

Note that the new field has been added as the last field in the table. You can insert a new field in the middle of a table by means of the keyword AFTER. Let's drop the field, so that we can insert it again:

```
mysql> ALTER TABLE user DROP sex;
Query OK, 0 rows affected (0.08 sec)
Records: 0  Duplicates: 0  Warnings: 0
```

Say we wanted the sex field to come right after the username field. We could say:

```
mysql> ALTER TABLE user ADD sex ENUM('M', 'F') DEFAULT 'M' AFTER username;
Query OK, 0 rows affected (0.00 sec)
Records: 0  Duplicates: 0  Warnings: 0

mysql> desc user;
+----------------+-----------------+------+-----+------------+----------------+
| Field          | Type            | Null | Key | Default    | Extra          |
+----------------+-----------------+------+-----+------------+----------------+
| username       | varchar(30)     |      |     |            |                |
| sex            | enum('M','F')   | YES  |     | M          |                |
+----------------+-----------------+------+-----+------------+----------------+
10 rows in set (0.00 sec)
```

Note that to place a new field at the start of the field list, you'd have to use the FIRST keyword instead, since there would be no preceding field.

Suppose we're running a site aimed at female visitors. We should probably change the default value of the sex field to "F" instead of 'M':

```
mysql> ALTER TABLE user ALTER sex SET DEFAULT 'F';
Query OK, 0 rows affected (0.01 sec)
Records: 0  Duplicates: 0  Warnings: 0
```

In order to change the whole definition of a field, use the MODIFY keyword:

```
mysql> ALTER TABLE user MODIFY userprofile VARCHAR(250) NOT NULL
    -> DEFAULT 'No Comment';
Query OK, 0 rows affected (0.01 sec)
Records: 0  Duplicates: 0  Warnings: 0
```

To change the field's name as well as its definition, you can use the CHANGE keyword:

```
mysql> ALTER TABLE user CHANGE usercountry nationality VARCHAR(50) NOT NULL;
Query OK, 0 rows affected (0.01 sec)
Records: 0  Duplicates: 0  Warnings: 0
```

Adding or dropping indexes or primary keys is just as easy:

```
mysql> ALTER TABLE user ADD INDEX (registerdate);
Query OK, 0 rows affected (0.08 sec)
Records: 0  Duplicates: 0  Warnings: 0
```

```
mysql> ALTER TABLE user DROP INDEX registerdate;
Query OK, 0 rows affected (0.09 sec)
Records: 0  Duplicates: 0  Warnings: 0
```

Experiment a little with the ALTER TABLE command, and you'll soon master it. As an exercise, change back the structure of the user table.

Altering table structures in PHP is as simple as issuing any other query using the mysql_query() function. Assuming we're connected to our sample_db database, the following line is all it takes to drop the index registerdate:

```
mysql_query("ALTER TABLE user DROP INDEX registerdate");
```

# Inserting Data Into a Table

It's time to insert some data into the tables we created. We're not going to introduce data insertion using PHP until the next chapter, where we deal with it in great detail.

Unsurprisingly, we use the SQL command INSERT to insert new records into a table. Try this:

```
mysql> INSERT INTO access_log VALUES('/update.html', 'bundy', 0, NULL);
Query OK, 1 row affected (0.00 sec)

mysql> SELECT * FROM access_log WHERE userid = 'bundy';
+-------------+--------+------------+----------------+
| page        | userid | visitcount | accessdate     |
+-------------+--------+------------+----------------+
|/update.html | bundy  |          0 | 20000804153559 |
+-------------+--------+------------+----------------+
1 row in set (0.00 sec)
```

Note that if you're inserting a string value, you have to specify it in quotes.

If you wanted to carry on using this syntax, you'd need to specify all the values to be inserted into every corresponding field in a table. Note that we gave NULL as a value for the accessdate field, which is of type TIMESTAMP. If you give it a NULL value, it saves the current system time in the format "YYYYMMDDhhmmss". You also provide a NULL or 0 value to an integer type field with an AUTO_INCREMENT attribute.

If you want to insert values into only a subset of the fields in a table, you use a slightly different syntax. We might say:

```
mysql> INSERT INTO access_log (page, userid, visitcount)
    -> VALUES('/update.html', 'bundy', 1);
Query OK, 1 row affected (0.00 sec)
```

Assuming this query is successful, the specified fields are given the values listed, while the rest are assigned default values. For example, accessdate is a timestamp field, so its default is the current system time – just what we want:

```
mysql> SELECT * FROM access_log WHERE userid = 'bundy';
+------------+--------+------------+----------------+
| page       | userid | visitcount | accessdate     |
+------------+--------+------------+----------------+
| /update.html| bundy  |          1 | 20000804153559 |
+------------+--------+------------+----------------+
1 row in set (0.00 sec)
```

## Escaping Quotes

When you insert a string value into a character or text type fields, you need to make sure no unescaped single quotes are inserted, otherwise you're bound to see an error:

```
mysql> INSERT INTO user (userprofile)
    -> VALUES('I'm a PHP developer.');
    '>
    '>
    '> ';
ERROR 1064: You have an error in your SQL syntax near 'm a PHP developer.');
 at line 1
```

Even if you issue the above query terminating it with a semicolon, the `mysql` client insists on getting more of it because the MySQL server expects another single quote to pair off the last one. This is why there is a quote mark before the prompt. When we do supply one more single quote to satisfy the server's expectation, it generates an error. The solution? You can either escape the inside single quote:

```
mysql> INSERT INTO user (userprofile) VALUES('I\'m a PHP developer.');
```

or use double quotes to surround the string value:

```
mysql> INSERT INTO user (userprofile) VALUES("I'm a PHP developer.");
```

Remember that a backslash (which is used to denote a directory in a path on the DOS/Windows platform, for example) also needs to be escaped. In this case, use a double backslash:

```
mysql> INSERT INTO user (userprofile) VALUES("C:\\Program Files\\PHP");
```

If you try to insert a new record that contains the same value for a primary or unique key of an existing record, an error occurs:

```
mysql> INSERT INTO user (userid, userprofile)
    -> VALUES('bundy', 'I\'m a PHP developer.');
ERROR 1062: Duplicate entry 'bundy' for key 1
```

The MySQL server complains that you are trying to insert a duplicate record that contains the same value for a primary key, `userid`. User `bundy` already exists in the table. Since the `userid` field is defined as a primary key, no duplicate entries are allowed.

However, you might want to insert a new record overwriting the existing one. Say you inserted wrong values for a user record and rather than deleting the record and inserting it again, you wanted to replace it with a new correct one. In this case, you'd use the REPLACE command. The only difference between the INSERT and REPLACE is this: if the primary key for the new record duplicates an existing one, REPLACE will overwrite the existing record, whereas INSERT won't, as we've seen.

```
mysql> REPLACE INTO user (userid, userprofile)
    -> VALUES('bundy', 'I\'m a PHP developer.');
Query OK, 1 row affected (0.00 sec)
```

## Populating our Database Tables

Now we're all set to put some records into our tables. For example, you can use the following INSERT command to insert the record for the user "bundy":

```
mysql> INSERT INTO user VALUES(
    -> NULL,
    -> 'bundy',
    -> password('12345'),
    -> 'Wankyu Choi',
    -> 'Republic of Korea',
    -> 'wankyu@neoqst.com',
    -> 'A PHP Developer.',
    -> '1999-01-01',
    -> '20000825140152');
```

Note that we use the function password() to encrypt the password '12345'. This is a MySQL server function, and we'll learn more about these in the next chapter.

*Normally, we'd use the* curdate() *server function to fill in* registerdate *and give* lastaccesstime *a NULL value. However, for the sake of creating a reasonable set of records with different sets of values we're inserting values directly.*

Also note that we give a NULL value to the usernumber field – you'll remember that since it's an AUTO_INCREMENT field, this will automatically add one to the number assigned to each new user.

| user number | userid | user name | user country | user email | user profile |
|---|---|---|---|---|---|
| 1 | bundy | Wankyu Choi | Republic of Korea | wankyu@neoqst.com | A PHP Developer. |
| 2 | judy | Yonsuk Song | Republic of Korea | yonsuk@neoqst.com | Just another Internet user:-) |
| 3 | phantom | Julia Ann | United States | julia@whatyoumaycallit.com | Care for a dance? |
| 4 | davidme | Dave Mercer | South Africa | davidme@wrox.com | It works! |
| 5 | daniels | Dan Squires | United Kingdom | daniels@wrox.com | Editor |
| 6 | jamesh | James Hart | United Kingdom | jamesh@wrox.com | T.A. |

Likewise, the following command will insert an access log record for user "metal" in the `access_log` table:

```
mysql> INSERT INTO access_log VALUES(
    -> '/headbangers/index.html',
    -> 'bundy',
    -> 9,
    -> '19990921123155');
```

Again, the `accessdate` field would normally be assigned a NULL value. The `access_log` table should contain records that look like the following:

| page | userid | visitcount |
|------|--------|------------|
| /headbangers/index.html | bundy | 9 |
| /index.html | judy | 2 |
| /index.html | phantom | 8 |
| /php/myscript.php | phantom | 5 |
| /php/myscript.php | davidme | 1 |
| /who.html | bundy | 6 |

> **Don't worry – you don't have to type these all in by hand if you don't want to. The file `pop_table.sql`, available for download from http://www.wrox.com, contains all the SQL code necessary to populate the tables as described.**

Congratulations – you now have a database, populated and ready for use!

# Resources

MySQL Homepage: http://www.mysql.com

MySQL Online Reference: http://www.mysql.com/documentation

# Summary

We began this chapter by tackling the issue of data storage models. We looked at why databases are the most viable option for mass data storage and gave a brief overview of the benefits of Relational Database Management Systems (RDMBS), encompassing issues such as performance, availability, and security.

We also pointed out why we chose MySQL, a freely available RDMBS, as a solid candidate for many of your database needs, helped you install it on your server, and walked through the basics of SQL, the Structured Query Language on which MySQL is based.

We had a brief play with the `mysql` client, and got familiar with some of the core SQL queries: SELECT, INSERT, REPLACE, DELETE, and UPDATE. We also toyed around with MySQL access privileges.

We devised a script that used PHP functions to connect us to a MySQL server and let us take a peek at the data in its databases. We looked at a number of ways to handle errors that occur on the MySQL server, and how we can pass useful error messages back to the user. The three essential steps of working with a MySQL server were noted as follows:

- Open a connection to the server
- Work with databases in the server
- Close the connection

We then went on to look at creating and modifying tables using SQL statements, looking at some of the core MySQL commands in more depth:

- SELECT command to retrieve data from a table
- INSERT command to insert new data into a table
- REPLACE command to replace existing data in a table

Finally, we populated our sample database tables with data, ready for use in the following chapters.

# Retrieving Data from MySQL Using PHP

This chapter is going to focus on the different ways we can use PHP scripts to get at the data stored in a MySQL database. We'll start off by looking at PHP's data retrieval functions, and then take a close look at how to construct SQL SELECT statements so that they access the data you want, arranged in the way you want. We'll learn how to limit the number of results returned, and how to order and group them, using clauses that make sophisticated queries possible.

We'll wrap up the chapter by building a "user record" viewer script, which will enable us to navigate around the database tables we developed in the last chapter.

## Retrieving Data Using PHP

The last chapter took us through the basic steps involved in setting up a MySQL database, connecting to it, defining databases and tables, and then filling them up with data. We also had a taste of the many ways it's possible to interact with the database, via a select few PHP functions and whole host of SQL commands. By now, you're probably getting quite comfortable with PHP's mysql_query() function, which lets us use SQL statements to query the database, almost as if we were typing them straight into the client.

If we use SELECT statements with mysql_query(), the result set (as we'd expect to see displayed on the mysql command line) is passed into result memory, and a **result identifier** is returned. We'll normally store this in a variable called $result, and use it to specify our result set in subsequent function calls.

We've already seen how mysql_fetch_row() returns a single row of data from a result set. Our simple example in the last chapter used a while loop to step through each row of a result set for the SHOW DATABASES statement. Here's a slightly more advanced version:

```php
<?php
//show_more_db.php
include "./common_db.inc";

$link_id = db_connect('sample_db');
```

```
$result = mysql_query("SELECT * FROM user", $link_id);

while($query_data = mysql_fetch_row($result)) {
echo "'",$query_data[1],"' is also known as ",$query_data[3],"<P>";
}
?>
```

It should return the following:

```
'bundy' is also known as Wankyu Choi
'judy' is also known as Yonsuk Song
'phantom' is also known as Julia Ann
'davidme' is also known as Dave Mercer
'daniels' is also known as Dan Squier
'jamesh' is also known as James Hart
```

We start out by connecting to the server with db_connect (which is included in common_db.inc), specifying that we want to use the sample_db database. We query the database with the SQL statement "SELECT * FROM user", whose result set will be the entire contents of the user table.

The variable $result stores the returned result identifier, with which we specify the result set when calling mysql_fetch_row(). This in turn fetches the first row of results, from which we echo the second and fourth fields (userid and username respectively). The internal pointer then moves to the next row, and the while loop cycles until all the rows in the table have been fetched.

Note that we can achieve the same result more efficiently by saying:

```
$result = mysql_query("SELECT userid, username FROM user", $link_id);

while($query_data = mysql_fetch_row($result)) {
echo "'",$query_data[0],"' is also known as ",$query_data[1],"<P>";
}
```

By extracting only the fields we're interested in, we save both time and memory.

PHP has two more functions that we can use to fetch data with: mysql_fetch_array() and mysql_fetch_object(). Both basically work the same as mysql_fetch_row(), the only difference being their return types. This is best illustrated by showing how our last example would look if we'd used either of the other functions to fetch values from the result set.

mysql_fetch_array() returns a single **associative array** from a result set, storing each entry in the record against the respective field name. We'd therefore say:

```
while($query_data = mysql_fetch_array($result)) {
echo "'",$query_data["userid"],"' is also known as ",
        $query_data["username"],"<P>";
}
```

mysql_fetch_object() returns a single **object** from a result set, storing each entry as a property of that object. The properties are named according to the field name, so we might say:

```
   while($query_data = mysql_fetch_object($result)) {
   echo "'",$query_data->userid,"' is also known as ",
         $query_data->username,"<P>";
   }
```

These two functions are particularly useful in situations where you might need to alter the structure of the database tables. Unless you change the names of the fields, you don't have to worry about the order in which they appear in the table, since you can fetch the field value by specifying its name and not its index number. Although they're both slightly slower than `mysql_fetch_row()` they do have the added benefit of making your scripts more readable – further down a long stretch of code, you might get confused as to which field was being referred to if you were just specifying indices.

There's one more function that deserves a mention at this point: `mysql_result()` returns the value of a specified field in a specified row. It takes the usual result indicator, plus a row number and field name as its arguments. We could rewrite our example like this:

```
$result = mysql_query("SELECT * FROM user", $link_id);
```

```
for($i =0; $i < mysql_num_rows($result); $i++){
echo "'", mysql_result($result, $i, "userid"),"' is also known as ",
         mysql_result($result, $i, "username"),"<P>";
}
```

Now though, we also have the option to do it backwards!

```
$result = mysql_query("SELECT * FROM user", $link_id);
```

```
for($i = mysql_num_rows($result)-1; $i >=0; $i--){
echo "'", mysql_result($result, $i, "userid"),"' is also known as ",
         mysql_result($result, $i, "username"),"<P>";
}
```

You should now see:

```
'jamesh' is also known as James Hart
'daniels' is also known as Dan Squier
'davidme' is also known as Dave Mercer
'phantom' is also known as Julia Ann
'judy' is also known as Yonsuk Song
'bundy' is also known as Wankyu Choi
```

The field name argument can also be written as an integer indicating the field's offset:

```
echo "'", mysql_result($result, $i, 1),"' is also known as ",
         mysql_result($result, $i, 3),"<P>";
```

> For the reasons mentioned above, it's probably wiser to stick to using field names, unless you have good reason to do otherwise. Moreover, if you have the option, we recommend using one of the previously mentioned functions rather than `mysql_result()`, since they are much faster.

Another way to jump straight to a specific row of data is to use the `mysql_data_seek()` function. It works in a similar way to the `fseek()` function, which we used in Chapter 10 to navigate within a file stream. It takes as arguments a result indicator and an integer that indicates the position in the result set to move to. As you might expect, the function returns `True` on success and `False` if you move past the array boundary.

```php
<?php
//show_seek_db.php
include "./common_db.inc";

$link_id = db_connect('sample_db');
$result = mysql_query("SELECT * FROM user", $link_id);

for($i = mysql_num_rows($result)-1; $i >=0; $i--){

mysql_data_seek($result, $i);
$query_data = mysql_fetch_array($result);

echo "'", $query_data["userid"], "' is also known as ",
        $query_data["username"], "<P>";
}
?>
```

We've now seen a number of different ways to access result sets from our PHP scripts. With these techniques under your belt, you should be able to deal with quite a broad range of situations, and show the data you want, presented the way you want it. However, this is only half the story.

We've already noted how we can improve the efficiency of our scripts by keeping the result sets small. We did this by specifying the fields we wanted to view in the original `SELECT` statement:

```php
$result = mysql_query("SELECT userid, username FROM user", $link_id);
```

What's more, we had to go to some trouble to show the results in reverse order – what if we wanted them displayed alphabetically? The mind boggles! We're going to save ourselves a whole lot of bother if we can **arrange** the data that gets put into the result set. For that reason, we're now going to get back to some pure MySQL, and take a look at what's possible with the `SELECT` command.

# SQL Statements for Retrieving Data

Fire up the `mysql` client again: we're going to have a closer look at the `SELECT` command. Remember that everything we cover here is totally applicable to the PHP examples above – the table you see at the command line is simply a representation of the result set your PHP script will ultimately have to deal with.

## Server Functions

We'll begin by going back to basics, issuing `SELECT` queries that don't require a database table at all. MySQL has a lot of very useful built-in server functions. Want to know what time it is? Don't have a watch? Let's ask the server:

```
mysql> SELECT now();
+---------------------+
| now()               |
+---------------------+
| 2000-08-03 16:56:03 |
+---------------------+
1 row in set (0.00 sec)
```

The now() function returns the current time of the system on which the server is running. You can retrieve the current date and time separately using the curdate() and curtime() functions:

```
mysql> SELECT curdate(), curtime();
+------------+-----------+
| curdate()  | curtime() |
+------------+-----------+
| 2000-08-03 | 16:57:19  |
+------------+-----------+
1 row in set (0.00 sec)
```

Many of MySQL's built-in functions are very similar to PHP's in both appearance and functionality. However, there are certain subtle differences. For example, MySQL's substring() function works much the same as PHP's substr(), but the former returns a substring counting from 1 whereas the latter counts from 0:

```
mysql> SELECT substring('test',1,1);
+-----------------------+
| substring('test',1,1) |
+-----------------------+
| t                     |
+-----------------------+
1 row in set (0.00 sec)
```

The equivalent call to PHP's substr() function would be:

```
$substring = substr('test', 0, 1);
```

# Retrieving Fields

We've already seen how to retrieve data from a database table. Say we want to look at the contents of the field userid in table user. We just say:

```
mysql> SELECT userid FROM user;
+----------+
| userid   |
+----------+
| bundy    |
| judy     |
| phantom  |
| davidme  |
| daniels  |
| jamesh   |
+----------+
6 rows in set (0.05 sec)
```

We can see that 6 user records exist in the user table. Note that neither field names nor table names contain any spaces; they must be typed as one word, just as variables in PHP are.

We can retrieve multiple fields by separating them with commas:

```
mysql> SELECT userid, username FROM user;
+---------+--------------+
| userid  | username     |
+---------+--------------+
| bundy   | Wankyu Choi  |
| judy    | Yonsuk Song  |
| phantom | Julia Ann    |
| davidme | Dave Mercer  |
| daniels | Dan Squier   |
| jamesh  | James Hart   |
+---------+--------------+
6 rows in set (0.00 sec)
```

Or we can look at all the fields in the table by specifying '*':

```
mysql> SELECT * FROM access_log;
+-------------------------+---------+------------+----------------+
| page                    | userid  | visitcount | accessdate     |
+-------------------------+---------+------------+----------------+
| /headbangers/index.html | bundy   |          9 | 20000913165329 |
| /index.html             | judy    |          2 | 20000913165350 |
| /index.html             | phantom |          8 | 20000913165409 |
| /php/myscript.php        | phantom |          5 | 20000713220144 |
| /php/myscript.php        | davidme |          1 | 20000826071502 |
| /who.html               | bundy   |          6 | 19991123172000 |
+-------------------------+---------+------------+----------------+
6 rows in set (0.00 sec)
```

This is equivalent to specifying every field in the table. However, when writing applications, it's worth avoiding this notation, even when you want to get all the fields from a table. If you later alter the structure of the table by adding new fields, or changing the order they are arranged in, your applications might find the resultset they retrieve is not the one they were expecting, with unpredictable results.

## Limiting the Number of Results Returned

We can narrow the scope of retrieved data by using LIMIT and WHERE clauses. Perhaps you want the MySQL server to retrieve just a few rows of records rather than spewing them all out. You can tell it to do this using a LIMIT clause. Say we want to fetch the first 2 rows of data matched, counting from record 0. We could say:

```
mysql> SELECT userid, username FROM user LIMIT 0, 2;
+---------+--------------+
| userid  | username     |
+---------+--------------+
| bundy   | Wankyu Choi  |
| judy    | Yonsuk Song  |
+---------+--------------+
2 rows in set (0.00 sec)
```

If the starting point is not specified, zero is assumed, so the following query achieves the same goal:

```
mysql> SELECT userid, username FROM user LIMIT 2;
```

A WHERE clause is used to selectively retrieve rows of data according to specified conditions. Say we only want to consider users who live in the United Kingdom. We could say:

```
mysql> SELECT userid, username FROM user
    -> WHERE usercountry = 'United Kingdom';
+---------+-------------+
| userid  | username    |
+---------+-------------+
| daniels | Dan Squier  |
| jamesh  | James Hart  |
+---------+-------------+
2 rows in set (0.00 sec)
```

Notice that we use an equals sign to see who comes from the United Kingdom. Apart from the equality operator, which is equivalent to PHP's ==, logical operators in WHERE clauses look much the same as those in PHP:

| Logical Operator | Description |
|---|---|
| = | equal to |
| != or <> | not equal to |
| < | less than |
| > | greater than |
| <= | less than or equal to |
| >= | greater than or equal to |

> One notable exception is this: NULL values cannot be compared using = or != operators. You need to use IS NULL and IS NOT NULL respectively.

We can narrow the scope of returned rows even further by adding a LIMIT clause to a WHERE clause. Say we wanted just the first user from the United Kingdom:

```
mysql> SELECT userid, username FROM user
    -> WHERE usercountry = 'United Kingdom' LIMIT 1;
+---------+-------------+
| userid  | username    |
+---------+-------------+
| daniels | Dan Squier  |
+---------+-------------+
1 row in set (0.00 sec)
```

Note that the LIMIT clause always comes at the end of the query.

Multiple conditions can be specified using the logical operators AND and OR:

```
mysql> SELECT usernumber, userid, usercountry FROM user
    -> WHERE usercountry = 'United Kingdom'
    -> OR usercountry = 'Republic of Korea'
    -> AND usernumber < 5;
+------------+--------+-------------------+
| usernumber | userid | usercountry       |
+------------+--------+-------------------+
|          1 | bundy  | Republic of Korea |
|          2 | judy   | Republic of Korea |
|          5 | daniels| United Kingdom    |
|          6 | jamesh | United Kingdom    |
+------------+--------+-------------------+
4 rows in set (0.05 sec)
```

Wait a minute; something's wrong here. We only wanted to list rows of data whose usernumber field values are less than 5, but last user's usernumber is 6. Why is this? It's very simple – the AND operator has only been applied to the usercountry='Republic of Korea' condition. When the server retrieves users from the United Kingdom, it doesn't get as far as the last condition, so the trailing AND operator is useless. In order to group conditions and force the precedence of these comparisons, you simply use parentheses as you would in PHP:

```
mysql> SELECT usernumber, userid, usercountry FROM user
    -> WHERE (usercountry = 'United Kingdom'
    -> OR usercountry='Republic of Korea')
    -> AND usernumber <5;
+------------+--------+-------------------+
| usernumber | userid | usercountry       |
+------------+--------+-------------------+
|          1 | bundy  | Republic of Korea |
|          2 | judy   | Republic of Korea |
+------------+--------+-------------------+
2 rows in set (0.00 sec)
```

## Ordering the Results

If you need the retrieved rows of data to be sorted on a particular field, you can add an ORDER BY clause:

```
mysql> SELECT usernumber, userid, usercountry FROM user
    -> WHERE usernumber < 5 ORDER BY userid;
+------------+---------+-------------------+
| usernumber | userid  | usercountry       |
+------------+---------+-------------------+
|          1 | bundy   | Republic of Korea |
|          4 | davidme | South Africa      |
|          2 | judy    | Republic of Korea |
|          3 | phantom | United States     |
+------------+---------+-------------------+
4 rows in set (0.00 sec)
```

*Note that when sorting character fields, MySQL will order them according to ASCII value, so that upper case letters will all be placed before any lower case letters.*

An ORDER BY clause sorts retrieved values in ascending order by default. Therefore, in the ORDER BY clause above, the values are first sorted in ascending order by "usercountry", and then values which have the same value of "usercountry" are sorted in ascending order by 'userid'

In order to sort the values in descending order, the DESC keyword is used:

```
mysql> SELECT userid FROM user ORDER BY userid DESC;
+---------+
| userid  |
+---------+
| phantom |
| judy    |
| jamesh  |
| davidme |
| daniels |
| bundy   |
+---------+
6 rows in set (0.00 sec)
```

You can sort the retrieved rows on multiple fields by separating the field names with commas. This will sort by usercountry (in ascending order) and username (in descending order):

```
mysql> SELECT userid, username, usercountry FROM user
    -> WHERE usercountry = 'United Kingdom'
    -> OR usercountry = 'Republic of Korea'
    -> ORDER BY usercountry, userid DESC;
+---------+-------------+-------------------+
| userid  | username    | usercountry       |
+---------+-------------+-------------------+
| judy    | Yonsuk Song | Republic of Korea |
| bundy   | Wankyu Choi | Republic of Korea |
| jamesh  | James Hart  | United Kingdom    |
| daniels | Dan Squier  | United Kingdom    |
+---------+-------------+-------------------+
4 rows in set (0.00 sec)
```

> Remember that the effect of an ORDER BY clause may also depend on the character set you specified when you compiled the MySQL package.

## Pattern Matching

With the LIKE or NOT LIKE operators, you can specify patterns to match against, using the following special characters:

❏   % matches any possible string, including empty ones (like * in shell or DOS commands)

❏   _ matches any single character (like ? in shell or DOS commands)

To match all useremail fields ending with "wrox.com", we could say:

```
mysql> SELECT userid, username, usercountry FROM user
    -> WHERE useremail LIKE '%wrox.com'
    -> ORDER BY username;
+---------+-------------+----------------+
| userid  | username    | usercountry    |
+---------+-------------+----------------+
| daniels | Dan Squier  | United Kingdom |
| davidme | Dave Mercer | South Africa   |
| jamesh  | James Hart  | United Kingdom |
+---------+-------------+----------------+
3 rows in set (0.05 sec)
```

*Note that values in TEXT type fields are case-insensitive. If you want them to be compared case-sensitively, you need to use a BLOB type instead.*

The following pattern matches the userid "judy" but not "bundy", as two "_" wild cards will only match against exactly two characters. If we were to add one more "_" wildcard to the query, "bundy" would be returned instead of "judy":

```
mysql> SELECT userid FROM user WHERE userid LIKE '__dy';
+--------+
| userid |
+--------+
| judy   |
+--------+
1 row in set (0.00 sec)
```

The NOT LIKE operator does precisely the opposite. Here we're selecting any userids that don't end in the letters "dy":

```
mysql> SELECT userid FROM user
    -> WHERE userid NOT LIKE '%dy';
+---------+
| userid  |
+---------+
| daniels |
| davidme |
| jamesh  |
| phantom |
+---------+
4 rows in set (0.00 sec)
```

# Getting Summaries

Now let's look at how a MySQL server reports summaries on data in a table. MySQL has a number of **aggregate** functions that summarize the results of a query instead of retrieving rows:

❑   sum() reports the total of a given field.

❑   max() reports the largest number in the given field.

❑ min() reports the smallest number in the given field.

❑ avg() reports the average of the given field.

❑ count() reports the number of rows returned.

For instance, you can retrieve both the minimum and maximum values on integer fields by using the min() and max() server functions:

```
mysql> SELECT min(usernumber), max(usernumber) FROM user;
+-----------------+-----------------+
| min(usernumber) | max(usernumber) |
+-----------------+-----------------+
|               1 |               6 |
+-----------------+-----------------+
1 row in set (0.00 sec)
```

The number of rows returned can be obtained by using count(). You can apply it in two ways:

❑ count(*fieldname*) only counts rows where the value of the specified field isn't NULL

❑ count(*) counts every row in the result set

The following query uses count(*) to show the number of users registered before the year 2000:

```
mysql> SELECT count(*) FROM user WHERE registerdate < '2000-01-01';
+----------+
| count(*) |
+----------+
|        4 |
+----------+
1 row in set (0.00 sec)
```

# More Complex Retrievals

Say we want a list of the countries from which our users come. A simple list of usercountry fields would give you this information, but would probably contain a lot of duplicate entries. What you really want is a list of *distinct* values. It'll therefore come as no surprise to find that SQL offers us the keyword DISTINCT to specify such a list. We can use it like this:

```
mysql> SELECT DISTINCT usercountry FROM user ORDER BY usercountry;
+-------------------+
| usercountry       |
+-------------------+
| Republic of Korea |
| South Africa      |
| United Kingdom    |
| United States     |
+-------------------+
4 rows in set (0.06 sec)
```

We may want to apply aggregate functions (`min()`, `max()`, `count()` etc.) to specific groups of records, rather than the database as a whole. For example, we might want to count how many of our users come from each country – we can group the rows returned by means of a GROUP BY clause:

```
mysql> SELECT usercountry, count(*) FROM user GROUP BY usercountry
    -> ORDER BY usercountry DESC;
+-------------------+----------+
| usercountry       | count(*) |
+-------------------+----------+
| Republic of Korea |        2 |
| South Africa      |        1 |
| United Kingdom    |        2 |
| United States     |        1 |
+-------------------+----------+
4 rows in set (0.00 sec)
```

Note that if you mix field names and aggregate functions in a single query without using a GROUP BY clause, you're bound to see an error:

```
mysql> SELECT usercountry, count(*) FROM user ORDER BY usercountry;
ERROR 1140: Mixing of GROUP columns (MIN(),MAX(),COUNT()...) with no GROUP columns
is illegal if there is no GROUP BY clause
```

Remember that an ORDER BY clause will come at the end of a query (unless we LIMIT the query). A GROUP BY clause should immediately precede it.

Now let's say we want to sort our last table by the values in the second column – that is, sort its rows by the user counts returned against each country. We can't refer to `count(*)` in an ORDER BY clause, so what do we do? MySQL provides us with a solution: **aliases**.

An alias is effectively just a new name for an expression, a field, or even a table. When we specify a field (or expression) in the SELECT statement, we can append a term like "AS alias_name" to it. For example:

```
mysql> SELECT usercountry, count(*) AS num_users FROM user
    -> GROUP BY usercountry;
+-------------------+-----------+
| usercountry       | num_users |
+-------------------+-----------+
| Republic of Korea |         2 |
| South Africa      |         1 |
| United Kingdom    |         2 |
| United States     |         1 |
+-------------------+-----------+
4 rows in set (0.05 sec)
```

The results of `count(*)` now show up in the result set as a field called num_users. What's more though, we can treat alias_name just as though it were a normal field, so we can use this in an ORDER BY clause:

```
mysql> SELECT usercountry, count(*) AS num_users FROM user
    -> GROUP BY usercountry ORDER BY num_users;
```

```
+-------------------+-----------+
| usercountry       | num_users |
+-------------------+-----------+
| United States     |         1 |
| South Africa      |         1 |
| Republic of Korea |         2 |
| United Kingdom    |         2 |
+-------------------+-----------+
4 rows in set (0.06 sec)
```

What about listing the countries from which we have more than one user? You might think of saying this:

```
mysql> SELECT usercountry, count(*) AS num_users FROM user
    -> WHERE num_users > 1 GROUP BY usercountry;
ERROR 1054: Unknown column 'num_users' in 'where clause'
```

We have a problem – num_users can't be defined until we've specified how to group the records, but we need to specify the WHERE clause before the GROUP BY clause, otherwise we'll just see a syntax error. The solution is to use a HAVING clause. We use it in just the same way as WHERE, except that we place it immediately *after* the GROUP BY clause. The server executes the query as it did before, but before returning the result set, it filters out the results that don't meet the specified condition:

```
mysql> SELECT usercountry, count(*) AS num_users FROM user
    -> GROUP BY usercountry HAVING num_users > 1;
+-------------------+-----------+
| usercountry       | num_users |
+-------------------+-----------+
| Republic of Korea |         2 |
| United Kingdom    |         2 |
+-------------------+-----------+
2 rows in set (0.05 sec)
```

## Retrieving Fields from More Than One Table

Say we want to pull data from both of our tables; we just specify them both in the FROM clause:

```
mysql> SELECT username, page FROM user, access_log;
+-------------+---------------------------+
| username    | page                      |
+-------------+---------------------------+
| Wankyu Choi | /headbangers/index.html   |
| Yonsuk Song | /headbangers/index.html   |
| Julia Ann   | /headbangers/index.html   |
| ...         | ...                       |
| Dave Mercer | /who.html                 |
| Dan Squier  | /who.html                 |
| James Hart  | /who.html                 |
+-------------+---------------------------+
36 rows in set (0.05 sec)
```

We've not defined a relationship between the two fields, so this returns every possible combination of values. However, you'll note that the MySQL server *is* smart enough to know which field belongs to which table. What if we used a field name that we've used in both tables?

```
mysql> SELECT userid, page from user, access_log;
ERROR 1052: Column: 'userid' in field list is ambiguous
```

Well, the error message says it all. Our use of the `userid` field is ambiguous, because we could be specifying either of two separate fields. We know that they refer to the same data, but as far as the server is concerned, the fields are completely independent of one another.

We can resolve the ambiguity by explicitly specifying which table we want to take the field values from, using the following notation:

```
mysql> SELECT user.userid, page FROM user, access_log;
+---------+------------------------+
| userid  | page                   |
+---------+------------------------+
| bundy   | /headbangers/index.html |
| daniels | /headbangers/index.html |
| davidme | /headbangers/index.html |
| jamesh  | /headbangers/index.html |
| ...     | ...                    |
| judy    | /who.html              |
| phantom | /who.html              |
+---------+------------------------+
36 rows in set (0.06 sec)
```

Every entry in the `access_log` table should correspond to one in the `user` table – that's the way our database is designed to work. It makes sense really: we're only logging page accesses for registered users, so anyone showing up in the access log must be a registered user. In this case, the `userid` field is common to both tables. Say we want to look at who's been viewing which pages. Now that we can make a distinction between the two fields called `userid`, we can equate them in a `WHERE` clause, and narrow down the result set as required:

```
mysql> SELECT user.userid, page FROM user, access_log
    -> WHERE user.userid = access_log.userid;
+---------+------------------------+
| userid  | page                   |
+---------+------------------------+
| bundy   | /headbangers/index.html |
| judy    | /index.html            |
| phantom | /index.html            |
| phantom | /php/myscript.php       |
| davidme | /php/myscript.php       |
| bundy   | /who.html              |
+---------+------------------------+
6 rows in set (0.05 sec)
```

We've just witnessed the power of Relational Databases. The connection we've just made to relate data records in multiple tables is called a **join** – you're producing a result set by joining the records from one table to those in another. In our last query, the `userid` field served as a **key** to join the `user` and `access_log` tables: that is, we used `userid` to establish explicit relationships between the records in the two tables. Keys are essential in join operations since they are related across tables, removing the need for database designers having to repeat that data in every table.

There are many more advanced join operations than the one we've seen here. However, this one will be more than adequate for most situations. You may want to read some more advanced MySQL references for further information on more complex queries and join operations. However, one rule of thumb applies no matter what level you're aiming for in building your SQL muscle: practice makes perfect. Use your `mysql` client to experiment with queries with a variety of field types – ultimately, that's the only way to really appreciate the possibilities and intricacies of the SQL syntax.

# Putting It All Together

We shall now build a user record viewer, `userviewer.php`, which is going to use the tables from our `sample_db` database. It will perform the following functions:

❑   Connect to the database `sample_db` that holds the `user` and `access_log` tables.

❑   Display a list of registered users and navigation links, giving the administrator the option to move back and forth.

❑   Display field name links that can be toggled to sort the list of users either in ascending or descending order on the specified field.

❑   For each user display a link to a new window that presents more detailed information on that user and their access log records.

Here's the code in all its glory. Once again, we're putting global variables and commonly used functions into the include file `common_db.inc`. We assume the existence of database `sample_db` and tables `user` and `access_log`, and that data is present in both these tables.

## common_db.inc

Here's what we should have in the file `common_db.inc`. Note that for the sake of brevity we've not shown the code for functions `db_connect()` and `sql_error()`. These should be exactly as specified in the last chapter.

### Global Variables

You should change these variables to reflect your settings:

```php
<?php
$dbhost = 'localhost';
$dbusername = 'phpuser';
$dbuserpassword = 'phppass';
$default_dbname = 'sample_db';
```

We specify defaults for the sort order (ascending), field on which to sort ('usernumber') and number of records to be displayed per page (5):

```php
$default_sort_order = 'ASC';
$default_order_by = 'usernumber';
$records_per_page = 5;
```

We specify the names of the user and access log tables:

```
$user_tablename = 'user';
$access_log_tablename = 'access_log';
```

holders for MySQL error numbers and error text:

```
$MYSQL_ERRNO = '';
$MYSQL_ERROR = '';
```

and the size of the new browser window:

```
$new_win_width = 600;
$new_win_height = 400;
```

### html_header()

The `html_header()` function starts an HTML page and defines a JavaScript function `open_window()` that we can call to open a new window when displaying a user's record:

```
function html_header() {
    global $new_win_width, $new_win_height;
    ?>
    <HTML>
    <HEAD>
    <SCRIPT LANGUAGE="JavaScript" TYPE="text/javascript">
    <!--
    function open_window(url) {
        var NEW_WIN = null;
        NEW_WIN = window.open ("", "RecordViewer",
                            "toolbar=no,width="+
                            <?php echo $new_win_width ?>+
                            ",height="+<?php echo $new_win_height?>+
                            ",directories=no,status=no,
                            scrollbars=yes,resize=no,menubar=no");
        NEW_WIN.location.href = url;
    }
    //-->
    </SCRIPT>
    <TITLE>User Record Viewer</TITLE>
    </HEAD>
    <BODY>
    <?php
}
```

### html_footer()

The `html_footer()` function ends an HTML page:

```
function html_footer() {
    ?>
    </BODY>
    </HTML>
```

```php
<?php
}

function db_connect($dbname='') {
    ...
}

function sql_error() {
    ...
}
```

### error_message()

The `error_message()` function reports errors using the JavaScript `alert()` method:

```php
function error_message($msg) {
    html_header();
    echo "<SCRIPT>alert(\"Error: $msg\");history.go(-1)</SCRIPT>";
    html_footer();
    exit;
}
?>
```

## userviewer.php

As we've established, the `userviewer.php` script makes use of the include file `common_db.inc`. We include the file from the current directory for the sake of simplicity. However, in practice it's never a good idea to include your database username and password in web scripts – you should ideally put them in a separate file and place it beyond the web document root.

```php
<?php
include "./common_db.inc";
```

### list_records()

This function displays a list of registered users, along with navigation links and a record viewer link that calls the `view_record()` function. We start by connecting to the default database, and fetching the total number of registered users. If there aren't any, we display an error message to that effect.

```php
function list_records() {
    global $default_dbname, $user_tablename;
    global $default_sort_order, $default_order_by, $records_per_page;
    global $sort_order, $order_by, $cur_page;
    global $PHP_SELF;

    $link_id = db_connect($default_dbname);
    if(!$link_id) error_message(sql_error());

    $query = "SELECT count(*) FROM $user_tablename";

    $result = mysql_query($query);
    if(!$result) error_message(sql_error());
```

```
        $query_data = mysql_fetch_row($result);
        $total_num_user = $query_data[0];
        if(!$total_num_user) error_message('No User Found!');
```

The $cur_page global variable – denoting the current page number – holds the key to the list navigation. If more than one page of data is returned in the list, we chop it up into multiple pages. The page length is determined by the global variable $records_per_page. The total number of pages is therefore obtained by dividing the total number of users ($total_num_user) by the length of a page ($records_per_user) and rounding up the resulting value with the ceil() function.

We increment the page number before it's echoed out, since the $cur_page global variable counts from zero, whereas the page numbering that we display should start at 1:

```
        $page_num = $cur_page + 1;

        $total_num_page = $last_page_num
                        = ceil($total_num_user/$records_per_page);

        html_header();

        echo "<CENTER><H3>$total_num_user users found. Displaying the page
                        $page_num out of $last_page_num.</H3></CENTER>\n";

        if(empty($order_by)) {
           $order_by_str = "ORDER BY $default_order_by";
           $order_by = $default_order_by;
        }
        else $order_by_str = "ORDER BY $order_by";
```

The list of users is presented in ascending order by default. The $sort_order and $order_by global variables determine in which order and on which field the list is going to be sorted, and they default to the $default_sort_order and $default_order_by global variable values.

The sort order can be toggled by clicking on field names in the header cell of the list table. This feature is implemented by giving the opposite sort order value to the $sort_order variable before echoing it out in HTML anchors:

```
        if(empty($sort_order)) {
           $sort_order_str = $org_sort_order = $default_sort_order;
           $sort_order = 'DESC';
        }
        else {
           $sort_order_str = $org_sort_order = $sort_order;
           if($sort_order == 'DESC') $sort_order = 'ASC';
           else $sort_order = 'DESC';
        }

        if(empty($cur_page)) {
           $cur_page = 0;
        }
```

We build a `LIMIT` clause in `$limit_str` using variables `$cur_page` and `$records_per_page` to calculate start and end pointers:

```
$limit_str = "LIMIT ". $cur_page * $records_per_page .
                          ", $records_per_page";
```

The finalized query is constructed by putting the `$order_by_str`, `$sort_order_str` and `$limit_str` strings together:

```
$query = "SELECT usernumber, userid, username FROM $user_tablename
                         $order_by_str $sort_order_str $limit_str";

$result = mysql_query($query);
if(!$result) error_message(sql_error());
?>
```

We now create a table to hold the list:

```
<DIV ALIGN="CENTER">
<TABLE BORDER="1" WIDTH="90%" CELLPADDING="2">
    <TR>
        <TH WIDTH="25%" NOWRAP>
            <A HREF="<?php echo "$PHP_SELF?action=list_records&
                                 sort_order=$sort_order&
                                 order_by=usernumber"; ?>">
            User Number
            </A>
        </TH>
        <TH WIDTH="25%" NOWRAP>
            <A HREF="<?php echo "$PHP_SELF?action=list_records&
                                 sort_order=$sort_order&
                                 order_by=userid"; ?>">
            User ID
            </A>
        </TH>
        <TH WIDTH="25%" NOWRAP>
            <A HREF="<?php echo "$PHP_SELF?action=list_records&
                                 sort_order=$sort_order&
                                 order_by=username"; ?>">
            User Name
            </A>
        </TH>
        <TH WIDTH="25%" NOWRAP>Action</TH>
    </TR>
<?php
```

A `while` loop steps through the result set, constructing each row in the table:

```
while($query_data = mysql_fetch_array($result)) {
    $usernumber = $query_data["usernumber"];
    $userid = $query_data["userid"];
    $username = $query_data["username"];
```

```
        echo "<TR>\n";
        echo "<TD WIDTH=\"25%\" ALIGN=\"CENTER\">$usernumber</TD>\n";
        echo "<TD WIDTH=\"25%\" ALIGN=\"CENTER\">$userid</TD>\n";
        echo "<TD WIDTH=\"25%\" ALIGN=\"CENTER\">$username</TD>\n";
        echo "<TD WIDTH=\"25%\" ALIGN=\"CENTER\">
             <A HREF=\"javascript:open_window('$PHP_SELF?action=view_record&
             userid=$userid');\">View Record</A></TD>\n";
        echo "</TR>\n";
    }
?>
</TABLE>
</DIV>
<?php
    echo "<BR>\n";
    echo "<STRONG><CENTER>";
```

We build navigation links based on the current page number and the total number of pages. Since the $cur_page variable starts counting from zero, we use another variable, $page_num, to maintain the current page number. If the current page number is greater than 1, that means we need [Top] and [Prev] links to let us jump to the first page and previous page respectively:

```
    if($page_num > 1) {
        $prev_page = $cur_page - 1;

        echo "<A HREF=\"$PHP_SELF?action=list_records&
                         sort_order=$org_sort_order&
                         order_by=$order_by&cur_page=0\">[Top]</A>";

        echo "<A HREF=\"$PHP_SELF?action=list_records&
                         sort_order=$org_sort_order&
                         order_by=$order_by&
                         cur_page=$prev_page\">[Prev]</A> ";
    }
```

Likewise, [Next] and [Bottom] links are displayed if the current page number is smaller than the total number of pages:

```
    if($page_num <  $total_num_page) {
        $next_page = $cur_page + 1;
        $last_page = $total_num_page - 1;

        echo "<A HREF=\"$PHP_SELF?action=list_records&
                         sort_order=$org_sort_order&
                         order_by=$order_by&
                         cur_page=$next_page\">[Next]</A> ";

        echo "<A HREF=\"$PHP_SELF?action=list_records&
                         sort_order=$org_sort_order&
                         order_by=$order_by&
                         cur_page=$last_page\">[Bottom]</A>";
    }
```

```
        echo "</STRONG></CENTER>";
        html_footer();
}
```

### view_record()

The `view_record()` function displays detailed information on a given user and his access log data. When clicked on, a **View Record** link opens up a new browser window to display the specified user's information, by calling the JavaScript function `open_window()` which in turn calls the script with the `$action` variable set to invoke the `view_record()` function.

We start by fetching the entire record of the specified user (from the `user` table), along with his access log records (from the `access_log` table). If no access has been made to any of the web pages that are currently set up to be logged, a message to that effect is displayed and the script terminates:

```
function view_record() {
    global $default_dbname, $user_tablename, $access_log_tablename;
    global $userid;
    global $PHP_SELF;

    if(empty($userid)) error_message('Empty User ID!');

    $link_id = db_connect($default_dbname);

    if(!$link_id) error_message(sql_error());

    $query = "SELECT usernumber, userid, username,
                    usercountry, useremail, userprofile,
                    registerdate, lastaccesstime FROM $user_tablename
                    WHERE userid = '$userid'";
    $result = mysql_query($query);

    if(!$result) error_message(sql_error());

    $query_data = mysql_fetch_array($result);
    $usernumber = $query_data["usernumber"];
    $userid = $query_data["userid"];
    $username = $query_data["username"];
    $usercountry = $query_data["usercountry"];
    $useremail = $query_data["useremail"];
    $userprofile = $query_data["userprofile"];
    $registerdate = $query_data["registerdate"];
```

In order to get a formatted date string, we make use of PHP's `substr()` function. We'll meet a MySQL server function in the next chapter that does the trick in one go.

```
$lastaccesstime = substr($query_data["lastaccesstime"], 0, 4) . '-' .
        substr($query_data["lastaccesstime"], 4, 2) . '-' .
        substr($query_data["lastaccesstime"], 6, 2) . ' ' .
        substr($query_data["lastaccesstime"], 8, 2) . ':' .
        substr($query_data["lastaccesstime"], 10, 2) . ':' .
        substr($query_data["lastaccesstime"], 12, 2);
```

We display a table of information pertaining to the selected user:

```
    html_header();
    echo "<CENTER><H3>
          Record for User No.$usernumber - $userid($username)
          </H3></CENTER>";


?>
<DIV ALIGN="CENTER">
<TABLE BORDER="1" WIDTH="90%" CELLPADDING="2">
   <TR>
      <TH WIDTH="40%">Country</TH>
      <TD WIDTH="60%"><?php echo $usercountry ?></TD>
   </TR>
   <TR>
      <TH WIDTH="40%">Email</TH>
      <TD WIDTH="60%"><?php echo "<A HREF=\"mailto:$useremail\">$useremail</A>";
?></TD>
   </TR>
   <TR>
      <TH WIDTH="40%">Profile</TH>
      <TD WIDTH="60%"><?php echo $userprofile ?></TD>
   </TR>
   <TR>
      <TH WIDTH="40%">Register Date</TH>
      <TD WIDTH="60%"><?php echo $registerdate ?></TD>
   </TR>
   <TR>
      <TH WIDTH="40%">Last Access Time</TH>
      <TD WIDTH="60%"><?php echo $lastaccesstime ?></TD>
   </TR>
</TABLE>
</DIV>
<?php
    echo "<HR SIZE=\"2\" WIDTH=\"90%\">\n";
```

We then display a second table, listing the user's access log records:

```
    $query = "SELECT page, visitcount, accessdate FROM $access_log_tablename
              WHERE userid = '$userid'";

    $result = mysql_query($query);
    if(!$result) error_message(sql_error());
```

The `mysql_num_rows()` function returns 0 when no record has been found in the `access_log` table containing the specified user's access data:

```
    if(!mysql_num_rows($result))
        echo "<CENTER>No access log record for $userid ($username).</CENTER>";
    else {
        echo "<CENTER>Access log record(s) for $userid ($username).</CENTER>";
?>
<DIV ALIGN="CENTER">
```

```
<TABLE BORDER="1" WIDTH="90%" CELLPADDING="2">
   <TR>
      <TH WIDTH="40%" NOWRAP>Web Page</TH>
      <TH WIDTH="20%" NOWRAP>Visit Counts</TH>
      <TH WIDTH="40%" NOWRAP>Last Access Time</TH>
   </TR>
<?php
      while($query_data = mysql_fetch_array($result)) {
         $page = $query_data["page"];
         $visitcount = $query_data["visitcount"];
         $accessdate = substr($query_data["accessdate"], 0, 4) . '-' .
                 substr($query_data["accessdate"], 4, 2) . '-' .
                 substr($query_data["accessdate"], 6, 2) . ' ' .
                 substr($query_data["accessdate"], 8, 2) . ':' .
                 substr($query_data["accessdate"], 10, 2) . ':' .
                 substr($query_data["accessdate"], 12, 2);

         echo "<TR>\n";
         echo "<TD WIDTH=\"40%\">$page</TD>\n";
         echo "<TD WIDTH=\"20%\" ALIGN=\"CENTER\">$visitcount</TD>\n";
         echo "<TD WIDTH=\"40%\" ALIGN=\"CENTER\">$accessdate</TD>\n";
         echo "</TR>\n";
      }
?>
   </TR>
</TABLE>
</DIV>
<?php

   }

   html_footer();
}
```

### Choosing an Action to Take

The last section of `userviewer.php` is the one that's initially run when we execute the script. Depending on the value of the variable $action, it calls one or other of the main functions defined above. We therefore build dual functionality into one script:

```
switch($action) {
   case "view_record":
      view_record();
   break;
   default:
      list_records();
   break;
}
?>
```

# Using the User Viewer

Now that we're done, here are some screenshots of a sample run:

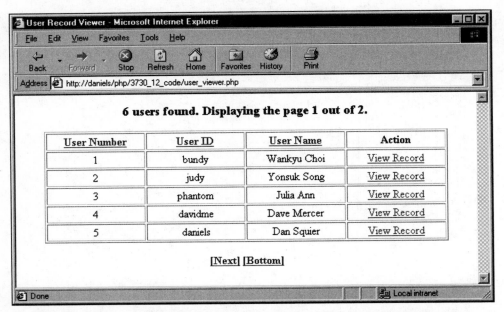

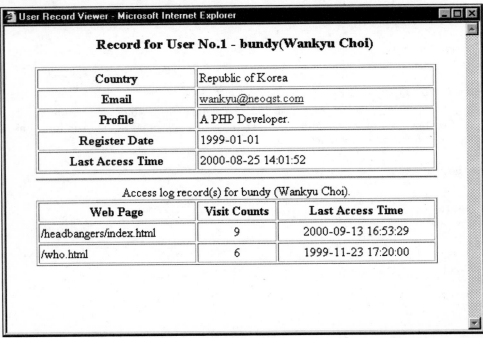

# Resources

MySQL Online Reference: http://www.mysql.com/documentation

MySQL-related PHP Function List: http://www.php.net/manual/ref.mysql.php

# Summary

In this chapter, we looked at ways of retrieving data from a database. We've used the following core MySQL command extensively:

❑   SELECT command to retrieve data from a table

We also learned that a number of clauses are often utilized to construct a query in order to narrow the scope of the retrieved results, order them or group them:

❑   LIMIT clause to limit the number of results returned

❑   WHERE clause to specify conditions of retrieval

❑   ORDER BY clause to order the returned results

❑   GROUP BY clause to group the returned results

Aliases and simple join operations were also introduced to retrieve data from multiple tables. Along the way, we met built-in MySQL server functions, and MySQL-related PHP functions to work with data in a database.

We wrapped up this chapter by creating a user record viewer that can divide the list of user records into a number of pages and gives an option to navigate through them. The script also enabled us to view a specific user's personal data and access log information.

We will further the discussion of database management in the following chapter: inserting, deleting, and updating database records using PHP.

# Manipulating Data in MySQL Using PHP

This chapter concludes our three-part series of adventures into the world of MySQL and PHP MySQL connectivity. In this chapter, we'll be learning how to manipulate MySQL database records within PHP:

- ❑  Inserting new records into a database table using PHP
- ❑  Deleting existing records from a database table
- ❑  Updating existing records in a database table

To demonstrate these PHP functionalities, we'll be creating user registration and access logger scripts. And we'll finish by upgrading the user record viewer we built in the previous chapter to allow us to manipulate user records.

## Inserting Records Using PHP

We saw how we can insert data into a table using the `mysql` client in the previous chapter. Recall that the following query inserted a record for the user "bundy":

```
mysql> INSERT INTO user VALUES(
    -> NULL, 'bundy', password('12345'),
    -> 'Wankyu Choi', 'Republic of Korea', 'wankyu@neoqst.com',
    -> 'A PHP Developer.', '1999-01-01', '20000825140152');
```

and that we can achieve the same goal using PHP:

```
$result = mysql_query("INSERT INTO user VALUES( ... )");
```

Normally, we'll use PHP variables to insert values into a table instead of specifying them directly in a query:

```
$query = "INSERT INTO user VALUES(NULL, '$userid',
                         password('$userpassword'),
                    '$username', '$usercountry', '$useremail',
                    '$userprofile', curdate(), NULL)";
$result = mysql_query($query);
```

Recall that the usernumber field is of AUTO_INCREMENT type – we specify it as NULL so that each new record we add has a usernumber value that's one greater than the last.

It's sometimes quite useful to get at the resulting value; for example, you might want to show a new user their user number on registration. The auto-incremented number generated by the last INSERT query can be obtained using mysql_insert_id().

### mysql_insert_id()

This function returns the auto-incremented value that was generated by the last INSERT query. If you want to let our hypothetical user know his automatically generated user number when he registers as a member of your site, you might use the following snippet of code:

```
$link_id = db_connect('sample_db');
$result = mysql_query("INSERT INTO user (userid)
                      VALUES('sphinx')");
$usernumber = mysql_insert_id($link_id);
echo "Thank you. Your usernumber is $usernumber.";
```

## Special Characters

As we saw in Chapter 11, it's essential to escape every single quote contained in a string value before inserting it into a database table. Otherwise, it will cause an error. Back then, we wanted to enter the string "I'm a PHP developer." into the TEXT type userprofile field. This particular string works nicely in MySQL as well as PHP because it's surrounded by double quotes. If we were to use single quotes to surround the string, we'd need to escape the quote mark contained within it:

❑    "I'm a PHP developer." works.

❑    'I\'m a PHP developer.' also works.

❑    'I'm a PHP developer.' doesn't work.

But why bother to make the distinction? Surely the best thing to do is to escape all instances of both sorts of quote marks – after all, in PHP, escaped quotes work in both single and double quoted string values. The problem is this: it depends what program you're using it in. If we backslashed the single quote in our first case above, we'd have this:

"I\'m a PHP developer."

If we used PHP to echo this out, we'd get the whole string, backslash and all, which is not what we want. With this problem in mind, PHP provides us with a pair of very useful functions.

### addslashes() and stripslashes()

These two functions are very closely related – the former, `addslashes()`, takes a string argument, prefixes every character that should be escaped in database queries with a backslash, and then returns the modified string. The latter, `stripslashes()`, complements it by stripping off these backslashes.

The following lines of code show how we might use these functions to insert a record into the `user` table, having escaped the values as required:

```
$link_id = db_connect('sample_db');
$userprofile = addslashes($userprofile);
$query = "INSERT INTO user (userprofile) VALUES('$userprofile')";
mysql_query($query, $link_id);
$userprofile = stripslashes($userprofile);
```

We assume that `$userprofile` initially contains the following:

I'm a PHP developer.

We pass it through `addslashes()`, after which it contains this:

I\'m a PHP developer.

It's therefore safe to pass it to the SQL statement. When we come to read the value out of the database again, it'll be just as we want it – the server will return the quote character, and not the escape sequence. However, if we want to use the variable `$userprofile` in subsequent code, we don't want extraneous backslashes messing up our beautifully formatted text. That's where `stripslashes()` comes in; we use it to tidy the string up.

### htmlspecialchars()

Escaped quotes are by no means the end of the story as far as special characters are concerned. As we know, certain characters have special significance in HTML – for example, < denotes the start of a tag. If this was contained in a user-entered string which was then presented in an HTML page, it would inevitably throw the browser (or the HTML parser program at least) into a hundred kinds of bother. The parser would assume that everything following it (until a > character was reached) referred to a tag. Suffice to say, it's very unlikely that it would!

In order to avoid this character looking like the start of a tag, we can represent it in the form of an **HTML entity**, which looks like this:

```
&lt;
```

The PHP function `htmlspecialchars()` – which you may remember we saw very briefly, way back in Chapter 4 – takes care of translating HTML special characters like this into their entity form, so you've no need to worry about translating them by yourself. Just as with the slash adding/stripping functions we saw above, `htmlspecialchars()` takes a string argument, changes all instances of special characters to corresponding safe forms (entity form in this case) and returns the modified string:

```
$userprofile = htmlspecialchars($userprofile);
```

The following characters are translated:

| Special Character | HTML Entity |
|---|---|
| & (ampersand) | &amp; |
| " (double quote) | &quot; |
| < (less than) | &lt; |
| > (greater than) | &gt; |

Now that we've seen some of the subtleties involved in PHP data insertion, let's move on to look at how we can update or delete existing data.

# Updating and Deleting Records in Tables

Let's say one of your registered users asked you to change his name complaining that it contains a typo. Instead of replacing a whole record for that user with a new value for the username field, you'd probably just want to change his name in the existing record. As we've seen, this is where the UPDATE command comes into play. We'd use a statement like this:

```
UPDATE user SET username = 'Dan Squier'
          WHERE username = 'Dan Squires'
```

This will change all instances (just the one, in this case) of the value 'Dan Squires' in the username field to 'Dan Squier'.

If you want to throw away an existing record from a table, use the DELETE command:

```
DELETE FROM access_log WHERE page = 'who.html'
```

This would delete any record with `page = 'who.html'`.

> **Warning! It cannot be overemphasized that you should be very careful when issuing UPDATE or DELETE queries – in the absence of a WHERE clause, they will update/delete *all* the records in the specified table.**

The following UPDATE query is an example of what you should take care **not** to do. It will update every record in the user table in such a way that any user can log on to your site using the password 'comeonin':

```
UPDATE user SET userpassword = password('comeonin')
```

Worse still, the following query **empties** the user table:

```
DELETE FROM user
```

Even an experienced database manager can make this kind of blunder – it just takes a bit of carelessness or the accidental dropping of a cigarette lighter onto the *Enter* key while typing in a query. The best course of action is this:

> Always double check when making **UPDATE** or **DELETE** queries.

Suppose you want to delete all access log records from the year 1999 because they're no longer needed. You'd probably use a query that looks like this:

```
mysql> DELETE FROM access_log WHERE accessdate LIKE '1999%';
```

A user might want to change his password from time to time. The following query changes his password to 'guessit':

```
mysql> UPDATE user SET userpassword = password('guessit')
    -> WHERE userid = 'bundy';
Query OK, 1 row affected (0.00 sec)
Rows matched: 1  Changed: 1  Warnings: 0
```

Note that the server reports that one record matched the specified condition and has therefore been changed. If the server finds no matching record, no update operation is performed:

```
mysql> UPDATE user SET userpassword = password('guessit')
    -> WHERE userid = 'bundy2';
Query OK, 0 rows affected (0.00 sec)
Rows matched: 0  Changed: 0  Warnings: 0
```

You can utilize existing values to update a record. For example, the visitcount field keeps track of how many times a specific user has visited a certain web page. If the user visits that page again, you'll need some way to increment its value. You might do this by fetching the current value from the access_log table, incrementing it and putting it back again. However, you can make the job a lot simpler by simply using the existing value in your UPDATE query.

The following query does exactly what we want – it increments the visitcount field for user judy on the /index.html page:

```
mysql> UPDATE access_log SET visitcount = visitcount + 1
    -> WHERE user_id = 'judy' AND page = '/index.html';
Query OK, 1 row affected (0.00 sec)
Rows matched: 1  Changed: 1  Warnings: 0
```

*Note that we'll need to update the* lastaccesstime *field separately. We'll see more on this later on in the chapter.*

String values can be modified in a similar way:

```
mysql> UPDATE user SET userid = concat(userid, '_1');
Query OK, 1 row affected (0.00 sec)
Rows matched: 6  Changed: 6  Warnings: 0
```

This query uses the MySQL server function to join strings, appending the string "_1" to every userid field value. The user ID bundy, for example, becomes bundy_1. This method comes in handy when a new user requests a user ID that is already in use, and you want to suggest an alternative.

*Note that if you were to use SET userid = userid + '_1', it would set the userid to 0, rather than bundy_1.*

Multiple assignments involving the same field are also possible:

```
mysql> UPDATE access_log
    -> SET visitcount = visitcount + 1, visitcount = visitcount * 2;
Query OK, 6 rows affected (0.00 sec)
Rows matched: 6  Changed: 6  Warnings: 0
```

Assignments are evaluated from left to right, so the second assignment will use the incremented visitcount value from the first assignment. That is, it will increment and *then* double each and every value in the visitcount field.

### mysql_affected_rows()

By now you're probably used to seeing a query report at the MySQL command line. If we use a DELETE or UPDATE query, the server will automatically tell us how many rows have been affected, as well us telling us how long it took to execute the query, counts for rows matched and changed, and any warnings produced.

We can get at the first of these from our PHP scripts by using the function mysql_affected_rows(). This takes an optional link identifier and returns the number of rows affected by the previous DELETE or UPDATE query. The following code submits a DELETE query, and returns the number of rows deleted as a consequence:

```
$link_id = db_connect("sample_db");
mysql_query("DELETE FROM user
             WHERE lastaccesstime < '20000101000000'");
$num_rows = mysql_affected_rows($link_id);
echo "$num_rows user(s) have been deleted.";
```

Supposing five of our users haven't visited the site since the beginning of year 2000, the code snippet would echo:

```
5 users have been deleted.
```

Note that if you were to delete *all* the records in a table, mysql_affected_rows() will return 0.

# Working with Date and Time Type Fields

Arguably, of all the MySQL data types, the trickiest to handle properly are date and time types. In order to work with them comfortably, you'll need a lot of practice. These fields store date and time values in the following format:

| Data Type | Data Format |
|-----------|-------------|
| DATE | 2000-01-01 |
| TIME | 12:00:00 |
| DATETIME | 2000-01-01 12:00:00 |
| TIMESTAMP | 20000101120000 |
| YEAR | 2000 |

If you attempt to insert illegally formatted date and/or time values into fields with these data types, the relevant entry will be filled with 0's. For example, inserting the string "bundy" into a DATE field will result in the value "0000-00-00" being saved in the field:

```
mysql> INSERT INTO user (userid, registerdate)
    -> VALUES('bundy', 'bundy');
Query OK, 1 row affected (0.00 sec)

mysql> SELECT registerdate FROM user WHERE userid='bundy';
+--------------+
| registerdate |
+--------------+
| 0000-00-00   |
+--------------+
1 row in set (0.00 sec)
```

The MySQL server provides a set of built-in date- and time-related functions that can help you to ensure that you insert correct values. We've already seen the now() function, which returns the current date and time in DATETIME format:

```
mysql> select now();
+---------------------+
| now()               |
+---------------------+
| 2000-08-04 19:30:15 |
+---------------------+
1 row in set (0.00 sec)
```

and also the curdate() and curtime() functions, which return the same as separate DATE and TIME type values:

```
mysql> select curdate(), curtime();
+------------+-----------+
| curdate()  | curtime() |
+------------+-----------+
| 2000-08-04 | 19:31:33  |
+------------+-----------+
1 row in set (0.00 sec)
```

To work with a TIMESTAMP field, you can either specify the date and time to insert in a string of 14 digits, or specify NULL to store the current system date and time in the same format. To properly update the access log (completing the example we began above), we'd therefore say:

```
mysql> UPDATE access_log
    -> SET visitcount = visitcount + 1, lastaccesstime = NULL
    -> WHERE user_id = 'judy' AND page = '/index.html';
Query OK, 1 row affected (0.00 sec)
Rows matched: 1  Changed: 1  Warnings: 0
```

The date_format() server function returns a formatted date and time value. It takes a DATE or DATETIME type argument, followed by a formatting string argument:

```
mysql> SELECT date_format(lastaccesstime, '%M %e, %Y') FROM user
    -> WHERE userid = 'bundy';
+------------------------------------------+
| date_format(lastaccesstime, '%M %e, %Y') |
+------------------------------------------+
| August 4, 2000                           |
+------------------------------------------+
1 row in set (0.00 sec)
```

We can use the following specifiers to construct the formatting string:

| Specifier | Description |
|-----------|-------------|
| %s | Second in 2-digit numeric form (00,01...) |
| %i | Minute in 2-digit numeric form (00,01...) |
| %H | Hour in 2-digit 24-hour numeric form (00,01...) |
| %h | Hour in 2-digit 12-hour numeric form (00,01...) |
| %T | Time in 24-hour form (hh:mm:ss) |
| %r | Time in 12-hour form (hh:mm:ss AM|PM) |
| %W | Weekday name (Monday, Tuesday, Wednesday...) |
| %a | Abridged weekday name (Mon, Tue, Wed...) |
| %d | Day of the month in 2-digit numeric form (01,02,03...) |
| %e | Day of the month in numeric form (1,2,3...) |
| %D | Day of the month with an ordinal suffix (1st, 2nd, 3rd...) |
| %M | Name of the month (January, February...) |
| %b | Abridged name of the month (Jan, Feb...) |
| %Y | Year in 4-digit numeric form |
| %y | Year in 2-digit numeric form |

In the view_record() function of the user record viewer script that we created in the last chapter, we formatted the lastaccesstime field value with the following lines of code:

```
$lastaccesstime = substr($query_data["lastaccesstime"], 0, 4) . '-' .
substr($query_data["lastaccesstime"], 4, 2) . '-' .
substr($query_data["lastaccesstime"], 6, 2) . ' ' .
substr($query_data["lastaccesstime"], 8, 2) . ':' .
substr($query_data["lastaccesstime"], 10, 2) . ':' .
substr($query_data["lastaccesstime"], 12, 2);
```

which produced the date and time in this format:

```
2000-08-04 19:33:42
```

We can now achieve the same goal with a single query:

```
mysql> SELECT date_format(lastaccesstime, '%Y-%m-%d %H:%i:%s')
    -> FROM user WHERE userid='bundy';
+---------------------------------------------------+
| date_format(lastaccesstime, '%Y-%m-%d %H:%i:%s')  |
+---------------------------------------------------+
| 2000-08-04 19:33:42                               |
+---------------------------------------------------+
1 row in set (0.00 sec)
```

If you want to know the weekday name of the date when a user registered, you can make the following query using the dayname() server function that returns the weekday name of a given date value:

```
mysql> SELECT registerdate, dayname(registerdate) FROM user
    -> WHERE userid='bundy';
+--------------+-----------------------+
| registerdate | dayname(registerdate) |
+--------------+-----------------------+
| 2000-08-04   | Friday                |
+--------------+-----------------------+
1 row in set (0.00 sec)
```

The to_days() server function calculates the total number of days from a given DATE or DATETIME.

```
mysql> SELECT to_days(registerdate) FROM user
    -> WHERE userid='bundy';
+-----------------------+
| to_days(registerdate) |
+-----------------------+
|                730701 |
+-----------------------+
1 row in set (0.00 sec)
```

Suppose you want to know how many days have passed since a user has made his last visit to your site:

```
mysql> SELECT userid, to_days(now()) - to_days(lastaccesstime)
    -> FROM user GROUP BY userid LIMIT 5;
+-----------+-----------------------------------------+
| userid    | to_days(now()) - to_days(lastaccesstime) |
+-----------+-----------------------------------------+
| Gibemall  |                                     471 |
| Mobster   |                                       1 |
| aria      |                                       1 |
| bundy     |                                       1 |
| cutie     |                                       1 |
+-----------+-----------------------------------------+
5 rows in set (0.00 sec)
```

You can see that the user "Gibemall" has not been to your site for more than a year. It's probably quite safe to consider him gone forever! If you want to delete users who haven't visited your site for more than 100 days, you might issue the following query:

```
mysql> DELETE FROM user
    -> WHERE to_days(now()) - to_days(lastaccesstime) > 100;
Query OK, 5 rows affected (0.00 sec)
```

This is just a taster of the many date- and time-related server functions MySQL provides. Refer to the MySQL online reference manual for more information.

# Getting Information on Database Tables

Retrieving database table information from PHP is just as easy as retrieving data from them. Suppose we want use PHP to look at the structure of a database table – we'd use the following functions.

### mysql_list_fields()

This is the first function you'll want to call to get information on table fields. It takes three arguments (a database name, a table name, and an optional link identifier) and returns a result pointer. This pointer refers to **a list of all the fields** in the specified table of the specified database. For example, if we wanted to get a pointer to a list of all the fields in the user table in our sample_db database, we could use:

```
$result = mysql_list_fields("sample_db", "user");
```

The $result variable now holds a pointer to a list of fields in the user table.

### mysql_num_fields()

This takes a result pointer (as returned by the previous function) and returns **the total number of fields** from the result set it points to. If we wanted to get the number of fields in the user table, we'd just pop the pointer $result that we obtained above into the mysql_num_fields() function:

```
$number_of_fields = mysql_num_fields($result);
```

Hey presto! The variable $number_of_fields contains (surprise) the number of fields in the user table.

### msyql_field_name(), mysql_field_len() and mysql_field_type()

These functions return properties of a field. All of them take both a result pointer and a field index as arguments, which specify the table and field (counting fields from zero) respectively. As you may have already guessed, the functions return **field name**, **field length** and **field type**. For example, to get the length of the username field in the user table, we would first note that username is the fourth field in the table, and it therefore has a field index of 3 (indexes start at zero). So, to retrieve the length of this field we could use:

```
$username_length = mysql_field_len($result, 3);
```

Since we defined username as having a length of 30 characters, $username_length should contain 30. We won't give examples for the other functions because they work much the same.

### mysql_field_flags()

This function takes a result set pointer and a field index, and returns a string containing the **attribute** for the given field. Attributes of a field include NULL or NOT NULL, PRIMARY KEY, UNIQUE, and so on. We can place the attributes of the username field (from the user table) into the variable $attributes using the following code:

```
$attributes = mysql_field_flags($result, 3);
```

The only attribute of the username field is that it is NOT NULL, so this is the value of $attributes.

### Try It Out – Getting Information on Fields

Let's take a look at these functions in action. The following script returns the name, length and type of each field defined in the user table:

```php
<?php
//metadata.php
include "./common_db.inc";
$link_id = db_connect();
$result = mysql_list_fields("sample_db", "user", $link_id);

for($i=0; $i < mysql_num_fields($result); $i++ ) {
    echo mysql_field_name($result,$i );
    echo "(" .  mysql_field_len($result, $i) . ")";
    echo " - " . mysql_field_type($result, $i) . "<BR>";
}
?>
```

Shown overleaf is the output you should see:

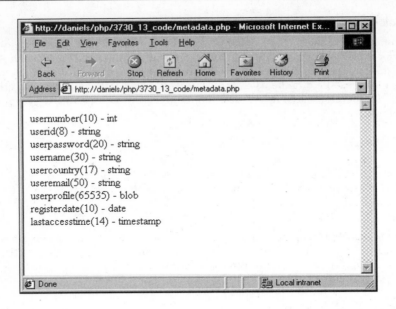

```
usernumber(10) - int
userid(8) - string
userpassword(20) - string
username(30) - string
usercountry(17) - string
useremail(50) - string
userprofile(65535) - blob
registerdate(10) - date
lastaccesstime(14) - timestamp
```

### How It Works

We start, as usual, by including our database functions in `common_db.inc`, and then connect to the server using `db_connect()`:

```
include "./common_db.inc";
$link_id = db_connect();
```

We now call the `mysql_list_fields()` function, specifying the database, table and connection that we want to use (`sample_db`, `user` and `$link_id` respectively):

```
$result = mysql_list_fields("sample_db", "user", $link_id);
```

This returns a pointer to a result set that lists all fields in the `user` table. We store this in the variable `$result`, and use it with `mysql_num_fields()` to find out how many fields the table contains. This sets the upper limit of a `for...next` loop:

```
for($i=0; $i < mysql_num_fields($result); $i++ ) {
```

Using the loop index to specify which field to work with, we call the functions `mysql_field_name()`, `mysql_field_len()` and `mysql_field_type()` which return the name, length and type of the fields available:

```
echo mysql_field_name($result,$i );
echo "(" .  mysql_field_len($result, $i) . ")";
echo " - " . mysql_field_type($result, $i) . "<BR>";
```

Note that some of the field types returned are ambiguous: for example, CHAR and VARCHAR are both returned as `string`, while TEXT is returned as BLOB. To get exact field types (as they are defined in a MySQL table) involves a bit more work. That's where the `mysql_field_flags()` function comes in.

We can easily modify the code to show field attributes. Here's the revised code:

```
$link_id = db_connect();
$result = mysql_list_fields("sample_db", "user", $link_id);

for($i=0; $i < mysql_num_fields($result); $i++ ) {
   echo mysql_field_name($result,$i );
   echo "(" .  mysql_field_len($result, $i) . ")";
   echo " - " . mysql_field_type($result, $i);
   echo " " . mysql_field_flags($result, $i) . "<BR>";
}
```

and here's a sample run:

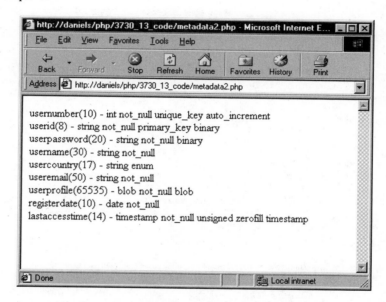

Finally, let's have a quick look at a single function that can be used to get all the information on a table's fields in one go.

### mysql_fetch_field()

If we pass this function a result set pointer and a field index (again, counting fields from zero), it returns an *object* whose properties include the name of the field and the name of the table it belongs to, along with its length, attributes and other details as used above. Properties of the returned object include:

| Property | Description |
|---|---|
| blob | True if the field is a BLOB |
| max_length | The maximum length of the field |

*Table continued on following page*

| Property | Description |
|---|---|
| multiple_key | True if the field is a key but not unique |
| name | The field name |
| not_null | True if the field cannot be NULL |
| numeric | True if the field is numeric |
| primary_key | True if the field is a primary key |
| table | The name of the table to which the field belongs |
| type | The field type |
| unique_key | True if the field is a unique key |
| unsigned | True if the field is unsigned |
| zerofill | True if the field is zero-filled – a zerofill attribute is used to force a number to be a certain width by padding it with leading zeros |

We can use this function to produce a similar result to the previous example.

```php
<?php
//metadata3.php
include "./common_db.inc";
$link_id = db_connect();
$result = mysql_list_fields("sample_db", "user", $link_id);

for($i=0; $i < mysql_num_fields($result); $i++ ) {
    $field_info_object = mysql_fetch_field($result, $i);

    echo $field_info_object->name . "(" .
        $field_info_object->max_length . ")";

    echo " - " . $field_info_object->type;

    if($field_info_object->not_null) echo " not_null ";
    else " null ";

    if($field_info_object->primary_key) echo " primary_key ";
    else if($field_info_object->multiple_key) echo " key ";
    else if($field_info_object->unique_key) echo " unique ";

    if($field_info_object->unsigned) echo " unsigned ";

    if($field_info_object->zerofill) echo " zero-filled ";

    echo "<BR>";
}
?>
```

The top figure on the opposite page is a sample run:

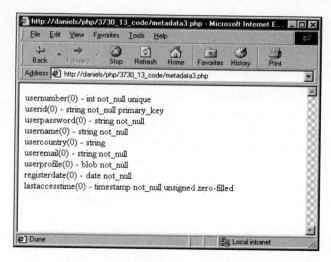

This works much the same as the last script, but something looks amiss – the length of each field is reported as 0 bytes. Unfortunately, while it's very versatile, the `mysql_fetch_field()` function contains a small bug that causes its `max_length` property to always contain 0 – no matter what size the specified field is defined with.

At time of writing, the latest version of PHP is 4.02 – we can but hope this bug is crushed in the next release. Until then, we just revert to using `mysql_field_len()` for this particular information:

```
$field_info_object = mysql_fetch_field($result, $i);

echo $field_info_object->name . "(" .
    mysql_field_len($result, $i) . ")";

echo " - " . $field_info_object->type;
```

Now the script reports the correct size of each field:

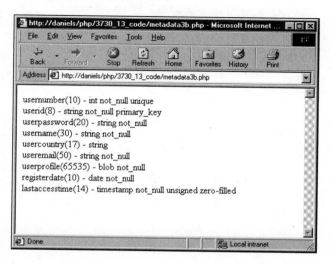

The ability to access metadata on database tables is essential to any general-purpose database management application, which will not know anything beforehand about the table structures it has to work with. In order to handle tables correctly every time, it will therefore have to rely heavily on functions such as those we've just seen.

## ENUM Options and Field Defaults

We've already encountered ENUM type fields, when we briefly included the field sex in our table of users in Chapter 11. The field could take either one of two values: 'M' or 'F'. For the sake of a nice substantial demonstration, we're now going to modify the usercountry field so that it also limits entries to specific, preset values.

We originally defined the field type for usercountry as VARCHAR(50) NOT NULL. We shall now assume that all future users will come from one of the four countries that already occur as entries in the field, and redefine the field like this:

```
mysql> ALTER TABLE user MODIFY usercountry
    -> ENUM('Republic of Korea','United States',
    -> 'United Kingdom','South Africa') DEFAULT 'Republic of Korea';
Query OK, 6 rows affected (0.01 sec)
Records: 0  Duplicates: 0  Warnings: 0
```

*If you've added your own records to the table, you'll probably want to modify these values to match your own. All being well, the values that were previously contained in this field will remain intact.*

Pop quiz! Which of the PHP functions will give you the default value of a table field? Which tell us the options that are available in ENUM type fields? The answer to both these questions is "none". At time of writing, there's no such function in PHP. Nevertheless, it would be very handy if we could use a predefined function to construct a dropdown menu for an ENUM type field, for example.

Well, here's a workaround for the first problem, which you've probably spotted already: we just need to use mysql_query() to issue the following query:

```
mysql> SHOW COLUMNS FROM access_log LIKE 'visitcount';
+------------+--------------+------+-----+---------+-------+
| Field      | Type         | Null | Key | Default | Extra |
+------------+--------------+------+-----+---------+-------+
| visitcount | mediumint(5) |      |     | 0       |       |
+------------+--------------+------+-----+---------+-------+
1 row in set (0.02 sec)
```

We can see that the visitcount field's default value is 0. Retrieving it with your PHP script is a snap:

```
$query = "SHOW COLUMNS FROM access_log LIKE 'visitcount'";
$result = mysql_query($query);
$query_data = mysql_fetch_array($result);

$default_value = $query_data["Default"];
```

The $default_value variable will now contain the default value for the specified field visitcount.

Getting a list of options available in an ENUM type field is a little more complicated. If we issue the following query:

```
mysql> SHOW COLUMNS FROM user LIKE 'usercountry';
+-------------+-------------------------------+------+-----+-------------------+
| Field       | Type                          | Null | Key | Default           |
+-------------+-------------------------------+------+-----+-------------------+
| usercountry | enum('Republic of Korea',     |      |     |                   |
|             |        'United States',       |      |     |                   |
|             |        'United Kingdom',      |      |     |                   |
|             |        'South Africa')        | YES  |     | Republic of Korea |
+-------------+-------------------------------+------+-----+-------------------+
1 row in set (0.05 sec)
```

We can see that the Type information actually contains the values we want. Extracting them is a little tricky, but not too hard once you know how. The following script will do just this, ultimately producing an array whose elements contain each option. The last element of the array will hold the default value from the set.

## Try It Out - Getting ENUM Options

```php
<?php
//enum_options.php
include "./common_db.inc";
$link_id = db_connect();
mysql_select_db("sample_db");

$query = "SHOW COLUMNS FROM user LIKE 'usercountry'";
$result = mysql_query($query);
$query_data = mysql_fetch_array($result);

if(eregi("('.*')", $query_data["Type"], $match)) {
    $enum_str = ereg_replace("'", "", $match[1]);
    $enum_options = explode(',', $enum_str);
}

array_push($enum_options, $query_data["Default"]);

echo "ENUM options with the default value:<BR>";
foreach($enum_options as $value) echo "-$value<BR>";

echo "<P>";

array_pop($enum_options);

echo "ENUM options without the default value:<BR>";
foreach($enum_options as $value) echo "-$value<BR>";
?>
```

Here's how it should look:

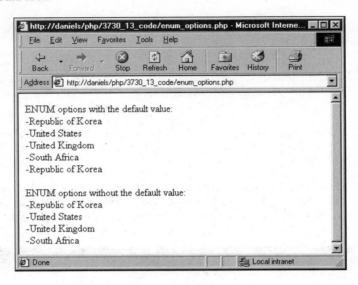

### How It Works

We start by issuing a SQL query – this finds the record containing the definition of the field `usercountry`. We fetch this data in the form of an associative array called `$query_data`:

```
$query = "SHOW COLUMNS FROM user LIKE 'usercountry'";
$result = mysql_query($query);
$query_data = mysql_fetch_array($result);
```

Field definition entries for `Type` and `Default` can now be accessed as array entries `$query_data["Type"]` and `$query_data["Default"]` respectively. The former should now contain a string that looks like this:

```
enum('Republic of Korea', 'United States', 'United Kingdom', 'South Africa')
```

In order to extract the option strings, we must eliminate the preceding string "enum", braces and enclosing single quotes. We start off by using `eregi()` with the regular expression `('.*')` to match everything inside the brackets:

```
eregi("('.*')", $query_data["Type"], $match)
```

The third argument is an array that holds matches for the given pattern – its second element, `$match[1]`, therefore contains the string we want:

```
'Republic of Korea','United States','United Kingdom','South Africa'
```

Assuming this goes to plan, we then strip off single quotes by calling the `eregi_replace()` function, and place the modified string in `$enum_str`:

```
$enum_str = eregi_replace("'", "", $match[1]);
```

which should look like this:

```
Republic of Korea, United States, United Kingdom, South Africa
```

Then we explode() the $enum_str variable, so that its comma-separated values can be put into the array $enum_options. This array will now contain each option from the ENUM field as a separate element:

```
$enum_options = explode(',', $enum_str);
```

Finally, we insert the Default value as the last element of $enum_options, using the array_push() function:

```
array_push($enum_options, $query_data["Default"]);
```

The rest of the script simply steps through the elements in $enum_options and echoes them out, first with the default value, then without:

```
echo "ENUM options with the default value:<BR>";
foreach($enum_options as $value) echo "-$value<BR>";

echo "<P>";

array_pop($enum_options);

echo "ENUM options without the default value:<BR>";
foreach($enum_options as $value) echo "-$value<BR>";
```

We can take the above example and put it into a function that returns an array containing each option from a specified ENUM field. Add the following code to the end of the common include file common_db.inc:

```
function enum_options($field, $link_id) {
    $query = "SHOW COLUMNS FROM user LIKE '$field'";
    $result = mysql_query($query, $link_id);
    $query_data = mysql_fetch_array($result);

    if(eregi("('.*')", $query_data["Type"], $match)) {
        $enum_str = ereg_replace("'", "", $match[1]);
        $enum_options = explode(',', $enum_str);
        return $enum_options;
    } else return 0;
}
```

You can test it with the following script:

```
<?php
//test_enum.php
```

```
include "./common_db.inc";
$link_id = db_connect();
mysql_select_db("sample_db");

$array = enum_options('usercountry', $link_id);
foreach($array as $var) echo $var,"<P>";
?>
```

# Creating a User Registration Script

It's now time to start welcoming users to our system. If you plan on building a web site that requires user membership, you'll probably want to provide some means for new users to register. A common-or-garden registration script will step through the following procedures:

**1.** Display a "Terms Of Use" page – a user will be obliged to agree with these terms if they want to register as a member.

**2.** Present one or more registration forms requesting necessary information.

**3.** Create the user's account – create a new record in the `user` table and insert relevant information (as specified in step 2).

**4.** Let the user know that their membership account has been created.

**5.** Send a confirmation e-mail to the user's address (as specified in step 2).

*We won't be implementing the first step here – it's really just a matter of how you grant access to the actual registration form. Likewise, we're not covering the last step, as we've not yet looked at e-mail. Nevertheless, it's worth bearing in mind – an e-mail to the user is an ideal place to confirm secure information such as the user's password selection. You might like to add this functionality yourself after we cover e-mail in Chapter 15.*

## register.php

Creating a new user account involves a process of creating a primary key in a user table which will be used all across the tables recording the user's activities at your site: an access log table, an invoice table, a newsletter mailing list table, and whatnot. The account is also used for authenticating the user when he attempts to enter a password-protected area of your site. Therefore, an account is comprised of a user ID and a password.

Nothing stops you from saving user passwords as plain text for all to see. But we will be encrypting passwords for better security.

Here's the source code of the user registration script, `register.php`. We'll explain it as we go along.

### Global Variables

We start by including the `common_db.inc` file, connecting to the database and finding out which countries we can present as options:

```php
<?php
//register.php
include "./common_db.inc";

$link_id = db_connect();
mysql_select_db("sample_db");
$country_array = enum_options('usercountry', $link_id);
mysql_close($link_id);
```

The array `$country_array` now holds all the countries the user can choose from.

### in_use()

This function queries the MySQL server as to whether the typed in `userid` is already in use, and returns 1 if it is:

```php
function in_use($userid) {
   global $user_tablename;

   $query = "SELECT userid FROM $user_tablename WHERE userid = '$userid'";
   $result = mysql_query($query);
   if(!mysql_num_rows($result)) return 0;
   else return 1;
}
```

### register_form()

This function displays the form into which a user types in their membership details:

```php
function register_form() {
  global $userid, $username, $usercountry, $useremail, $userprofile,
$country_array;
  global $PHP_SELF;
?>
<CENTER><H3>Create your account!</H3></CENTER>
<FORM METHOD="POST" ACTION="<?php echo $PHP_SELF ?>">
<INPUT TYPE="HIDDEN" NAME="action" VALUE="register">
  <DIV ALIGN="CENTER"><CENTER><TABLE BORDER="1" WIDTH="90%">
    <TR>
      <TH WIDTH="30%" NOWRAP>Desired ID</TH>
      <TD WIDTH="70%"><INPUT TYPE="TEXT" NAME="userid"
                            VALUE="<?php echo $userid ?>"
                            SIZE="8" MAXLENGTH="8"></TD>
    </TR>
    <TR>
      <TH WIDTH="30%" NOWRAP>Desired Password</TH>
      <TD WIDTH="70%"><INPUT TYPE="PASSWORD"
                            NAME="userpassword" SIZE="15"></TD>
    </TR>
    <TR>
      <TH WIDTH="30%" NOWRAP>Retype Password</TH>
      <TD WIDTH="70%"><INPUT TYPE="PASSWORD"
                            NAME="userpassword2" SIZE="15"></TD>
    </TR>
```

```
    <TR>
      <TH WIDTH="30%" NOWRAP>Full Name</TH>
      <TD WIDTH="70%"><INPUT TYPE="TEXT" NAME="username"
                          VALUE="<?php echo $username ?>" SIZE="20"></TD>
    </TR>
    <TR>
      <TH WIDTH="30%" NOWRAP>Country</TH>
      <TD WIDTH="70%"><SELECT NAME="usercountry" SIZE="1">
<?php
```

Note that we present two password fields rather than one – because we specify TYPE = "PASSWORD", the value entered will be masked by asterisks, so that not even the user can see what they're typing in. In case they mistype it, we give them a chance to enter it twice. Later on, we'll check that the two values match.

The usercountry dropdown menu is constructed on the fly from the values held in the $country_array variable:

```
    for($i=0; $i < count($country_array); $i++) {
      if(!isset($usercountry) && $i == 0) {
        echo "<OPTION SELECTED VALUE=\"". $country_array[$i] .
             "\">" . $country_array[$i] . "</OPTION>\n";
      }
      else if($usercountry == $country_array[$i]) {
        echo "<OPTION SELECTED VALUE=\"". $country_array[$i] . "\">" .
                                 $country_array[$i] . "</OPTION>\n";
      }
      else {
        echo "<OPTION VALUE=\"". $country_array[$i] . "\">" .
                                 $country_array[$i] . "</OPTION>\n";
      }
    }
?>
      </SELECT></TD>
    </TR>
    <TR>
      <TH WIDTH="30%" NOWRAP>Email</TH>
      <TD WIDTH="70%"><INPUT TYPE="TEXT" NAME="useremail" SIZE="20"
                          VALUE="<?php echo $useremail ?>"></TD>
    </TR>
    <TR>
      <TH WIDTH="30%" NOWRAP>Profile</TH>
      <TD WIDTH="70%"><TEXTAREA ROWS="5" COLS="40"
                          NAME="userprofile"></TEXTAREA></TD>
    </TR>
    <TR>
      <TH WIDTH="30%" COLSPAN="2" NOWRAP>
        <INPUT TYPE="SUBMIT" VALUE="Submit">
        <INPUT TYPE="RESET" VALUE="Reset"></TH>
    </TR>
  </TABLE>
  </CENTER></DIV>
</FORM>
<?php
}
```

### create_account()

This function inserts the new record into the `user` table:

```
function create_account() {
    global $userid, $username, $userpassword, $userpassword2,
        $usercountry, $useremail, $userprofile;
    global $default_dbname, $user_tablename;
```

The user-submitted values are verified, to check that they've been entered correctly:

```
if(empty($userid)) error_message("Enter your desired ID!");
if(empty($userpassword)) error_message("Enter your desired password!");
if(strlen($userpassword) < 4 ) error_message("Password too short!");
if(empty($userpassword2))
                error_message("Retype your password for verification!");
if(empty($username)) error_message("Enter your full name!");
if(empty($useremail)) error_message("Enter your email address!");
if(empty($userprofile)) $userprofile = "No Comment.";

if($userpassword != $userpassword2)
    error_message("Your desired password and retyped password mismatch!");

$link_id = db_connect($default_dbname);

if(in_use($userid))
        error_message("$userid is in use. Please choose a different ID.");
```

When we query to insert a new user's details, we pass NULL to fields `usernumber` and `lastaccesstime` (auto-incrementing one, and timestamping the other), and use the `curdate()` server function to store the current system date in the `registerdate` field. We also use the `password()` server function to encrypt the user-specified password:

```
$query = "INSERT INTO user VALUES(NULL, '$userid',
                            password('$userpassword'), '$username',
                            '$usercountry', '$useremail',
                            '$userprofile', curdate(), NULL)";
$result = mysql_query($query);
if(!$result) error_message(sql_error());
```

We report the newly incremented user number using `mysql_insert_id()`:

```
$usernumber = mysql_insert_id($link_id);
html_header();
?>
```

Finally, we display a table showing the user their membership information:

```
<CENTER><H3>
<?php echo $username ?>, thank you for registering with us!
</H3></CENTER>
```

**471**

```
<DIV ALIGN="CENTER"><CENTER><TABLE BORDER="1" WIDTH="90%">
  <TR>
    <TH WIDTH="30%" NOWRAP>User Number</TH>
    <TD WIDTH="70%"><?php echo $usernumber ?></TD>
  </TR>
  <TR>
    <TH WIDTH="30%" NOWRAP>Desired ID</TH>
    <TD WIDTH="70%"><?php echo $userid ?></TD>
  </TR>
  <TR>
    <TH WIDTH="30%" NOWRAP>Desired Password</TH>
    <TD WIDTH="70%"><?php echo $userpassword ?></TD>
  </TR>
  <TR>
    <TH WIDTH="30%" NOWRAP>Full Name</TH>
    <TD WIDTH="70%"><?php echo $username ?></TD>
  </TR>
  <TR>
    <TH WIDTH="30%" NOWRAP>Country</TH>
    <TD WIDTH="70%"><?php echo $usercountry ?></TD>
  </TR>
  <TR>
    <TH WIDTH="30%" NOWRAP>Email</TH>
    <TD WIDTH="70%"><?php echo $useremail ?></TD>
  </TR>
  <TR>
    <TH WIDTH="30%" NOWRAP>Profile</TH>
    <TD WIDTH="70%"><?php echo htmlspecialchars($userprofile) ?></TD>
  </TR>
</TABLE>
</CENTER></DIV>
<?php
    html_footer();
}
```

### Choosing Actions to Take

Finally, we use $action to specify the appropriate functions to call:

```
switch($action) {
    case "register":
        create_account();
    break;
    default:
        html_header();
        register_form();
        html_footer();
    break;
}
?>
```

Let's see how that looks in action. First, register_form() displays a form into which the user can enter their details:

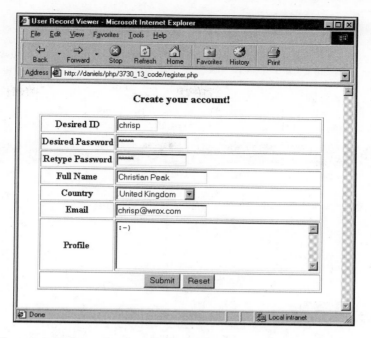

As the last step, the script displays a thank you note plus a table showing the information that the user entered and was used to create his account. Here's the resulting page of creating an account for the user 'chrisp':

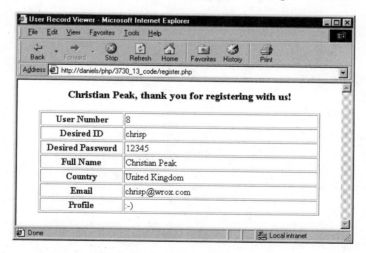

You should note that it's not a good idea to display a user's password like this. As mentioned earlier, a relatively secure way to confirm this information is to include it in an e-mail sent to the user's specified account. However, since we're not developing that functionality here, this is a compromise we'll have to put up with.

Now let's move on to see how we can record users' accesses to your site.

# Creating an Access Logger Script

In order to track users' activities, we need to know who has made a request for what: that is, we require users to log in to the site. Without a login process, there's no way for us to identify anyone requesting a web page.

The most convenient way of authenticating users is to specify a unique ID and associated password for each one. When they log in, all we need to do is to check the values they submit against the ones we have stored (and in the case of the password, encrypted). Let's see how this can be done.

## Try It Out – User Authentication

The following script makes a query to the table user for user authentication:

```php
<?php
//auth_user.php
include "./common_db.inc";
$register_script = "./register.php";

function auth_user($userid, $userpassword) {
    global $default_dbname, $user_tablename;

    $link_id = db_connect($default_dbname);
    $query = "SELECT username FROM $user_tablename
                        WHERE userid = '$userid'
                        AND userpassword = password('$userpassword')";
    $result = mysql_query($query);
    if(!mysql_num_rows($result)) return 0;
    else {
        $query_data = mysql_fetch_row($result);
        return $query_data[0];
    }
}

function login_form() {
    global $PHP_SELF;
?>
<HTML>
<HEAD>
<TITLE>Login</TITLE>
</HEAD>
<BODY>
<FORM METHOD="POST" ACTION="<? echo $PHP_SELF ?>">
    <DIV ALIGN="CENTER"><CENTER>
        <H3>Please log in to access the page you requested.</H3>
        <TABLE BORDER="1" WIDTH="200" CELLPADDING="2">
            <TR>
                <TH WIDTH="18%" ALIGN="RIGHT" NOWRAP>ID</TH>
                <TD WIDTH="82%" NOWRAP>
                    <INPUT TYPE="TEXT" NAME="userid" SIZE="8">
                </TD>
            </TR>
            <TR>
                <TH WIDTH="18%" ALIGN="RIGHT" NOWRAP>Password</TH>
                <TD WIDTH="82%" NOWRAP>
                    <INPUT TYPE="PASSWORD" NAME="userpassword" SIZE="8">
                </TD>
            </TR>
```

```
            <TR>
                <TD WIDTH="100%" COLSPAN="2" ALIGN="CENTER" NOWRAP>
                    <INPUT TYPE="SUBMIT" VALUE="LOGIN" NAME="Submit">
                </TD>
            </TR>
        </TABLE>
        </CENTER></DIV>
</FORM>
</BODY>
</HTML>
<?
}

session_start();
if(!isset($userid)) {
    login_form();
    exit;
}
else {
    session_register("userid", "userpassword");
    $username = auth_user($userid, $userpassword);
    if(!$username) {
        session_unregister("userid");
        session_unregister("userpassword");
        echo "Authorization failed. " .
            "You must enter a valid userid and password combo. " .
            "Click on the following link to try again.<BR>\n";
        echo "<A HREF=\"$PHP_SELF\">Login</A><BR>";
        echo "If you're not a member yet, click " .
            "on the following link to register.<BR>\n";
        echo "<A HREF=\"$register_script\">Membership</A>";
        exit;
    }
    else echo "Welcome, $username!";
}
?>
```

This is how the interface should look:

Once you've successfully logged in, you'll be greeted by name:

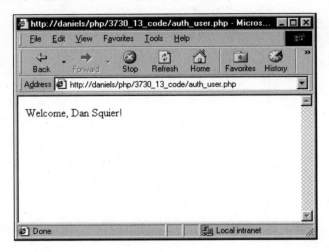

### How It Works

We start by including `common_db.inc` and specifying a link to the registration page:

```
$register_script="./register.php";
```

Next we define the functions `auth_user()` and `login_form()` – more on these in a moment – but the main story begins with a `session_start()` call. We're going to store the user-entered values for ID and password as session variables, thereby saving them from having to re-enter the values every time they access a new page.

If `$userid` has not been defined, we call the `login_form()` function, which displays (surprise, surprise!) a login form, into which the user can enter ID and password:

```
session_start();
if(!isset($userid)) {
    login_form();
    exit;
```

If `$userid` is defined (as will be the case if the script has been called from the login form), we register the user-provided values `userid` and `userpassword` as session variables for later use, and use them as arguments to call our `auth_user()` function:

```
} else {
    session_register("userid", "userpassword");
    $username = auth_user($userid, $userpassword);
```

The value returned by `auth_user()` will either be:

❑ the user's name as stored in the user table – this is only returned if the submitted ID/password values correspond to those stored in a specific record in the table.

❑    0 – if no match is found, the function returns `False`.

We store this value in `$username`, and use it to determine a response:

```
if(!$username) {
    session_unregister("userid");
    session_unregister("userpassword");
    echo "Authorization failed. " .
        "You must enter a valid userid and password combo. " .
        "Click on the following link to try again.<BR>\n";
    echo "<A HREF=\"$PHP_SELF\">Login</A><BR>";
    echo "If you're not a member yet, click " .
        "on the following link to register.<BR>\n";
    echo "<A HREF=\"$register_script\">Membership</A>";
    exit;
}
else echo "Welcome, $username!";
}
```

If authentication fails, we unregister the session variables. We can therefore be sure that `login_form()` is called whenever an unauthenticated user tries to access a password protected area.

The real meat of the script lies in our `auth_user()` function, which takes `$userid` and `$userpassword` as arguments, and validates them against the values stored in the `user` table:

```
function auth_user($userid, $userpassword) {
    global $default_dbname, $user_tablename;

    $link_id = db_connect($default_dbname);
```

Once we've connected to the database, we query for a record whose `userid` and `password` entries correspond to the user-provided arguments, and `SELECT` the username value for that record:

```
$query = "SELECT username FROM $user_tablename
                    WHERE userid = '$userid'
                    AND userpassword = password('$userpassword')";
$result = mysql_query($query);
```

If no records match both criteria, we return `False`; otherwise we fetch and return the `username` value:

```
if(!mysql_num_rows($result)) return 0;
else {
    $query_data = mysql_fetch_row($result);
    return $query_data[0];
}
}
```

Note that we encrypt `$userpassword` *before* comparing it with the value in the `user` table. We therefore compare two encrypted values, which will have been derived by exactly the same process, and will therefore be identical.

## access_logger.php

We can develop our last script so that it authenticates users and logs their visits to web pages. We'll call this modified version access_logger.php. We're going to log user accesses by automatically attaching access_logger.php to the beginning of all our web pages. We can do this very simply, by setting auto_prepend_file in the php.ini configuration file so that it specifies the absolute location of the script. For example:

```
auto_prepend_file  = /home/james/access_logger.php
```

Another option would be to include the logging script at the top of each of the web pages we wanted to password-protect. Note that we'd need to be sure to include it at the **top** of the page, that is, before sending out any HTML tags or text, otherwise the header() function wouldn't work.

Assuming we use the blanket approach and set auto_prepend_file, we're going to be attaching the access logging script to every .php page on the server. What if we want to exclude certain files and directories from our authentication process? We can do this by listing them respectively in a pair of arrays. When a user tries to access a web page, our access logging script can check the page's name and path against the arrays' contents, and only demand authentication if there's no match.

### Try It Out – Logging User Accesses

Here's the complete source code for the access logger script. Note that login_form() is exactly as defined in user_auth.php:

```php
<?php
//access_logger.php
include "./common_db.inc";
$exclude_dirs = array('/', '/info', '/contact');
$exclude_files = array('index.html', 'info.html', 'index.php');
$user_tablename = 'user';
$access_log_tablename = 'access_log';

function login_form() { ... }

function do_authentication() {
    global $PHP_AUTH_USER, $PHP_AUTH_PW, $PHP_SELF;
    global $userid, $userpassword, $register_script;
    global $default_dbname, $user_tablename, $access_log_tablename;
    global $MYSQL_ERROR, $MYSQL_ERRNO;

    if(!isset($userid)) {
        login_form();
        exit;
    }
    else session_register("userid", "userpassword");

    $link_id = db_connect($default_dbname);
    $query = "SELECT username FROM $user_tablename
                WHERE userid = '$userid'
                AND userpassword = password('$userpassword')";
    $result = mysql_query($query);
```

```php
        if(!mysql_num_rows($result)) {
            session_unregister("userid");
            session_unregister("userpassword");
            echo "Authorization failed. " .
               "You must enter a valid userid and password combo. " .
               "Click on the following link to try again.<BR>\n";
            echo "<A HREF=\"$PHP_SELF\">Login</A><BR>";
            echo "If you're not a member yet, click on the " .
               "following link to register.<BR>\n";
            echo "<A HREF=\"$register_script\">Membership</A>";
            exit;
        }
        else {
            $query = "UPDATE $user_tablename SET lastaccesstime = NULL
                        WHERE userid = '$userid'";
            $result = mysql_query($query);

            $num_rows = mysql_affected_rows($link_id);
            if($num_rows != 1) die(sql_error());

            $query = "SELECT userid FROM $access_log_tablename
                            WHERE page = '$PHP_SELF'
                            AND userid = '$userid'";
            $result = mysql_query($query);

            if(!mysql_num_rows($result))
               $query = "INSERT INTO $access_log_tablename
                            VALUES ('$PHP_SELF', '$PHP_AUTH_USER', 1, NULL)";
            else $query = "UPDATE $access_log_tablename
                        SET visitcount = visitcount + 1, accessdate = NULL
                        WHERE page = '$PHP_SELF' AND userid = '$userid'";

            mysql_query($query);

            $num_rows = mysql_affected_rows($link_id);
            if($num_rows != 1) die(sql_error());
        }
    }

$filepath = dirname($PHP_SELF);
$filename = basename($PHP_SELF);

if($filepath == '') $filepath = '/';

$auth_done = 0;

for($j=0; $j < count($exclude_dirs); $j++) {
    if($exclude_dirs[$j] == $filepath) break;
    else {
        for($i=0; $i< count($exclude_files); $i++) {
            if($exclude_files[$i] == $filename) break;
            else {
                session_start();
```

```
            do_authentication();
            $auth_done = 1;
            break;
        }
    }
  }
  if($auth_done) break;
}
?>
```

If you try running just this script, you'll just see a blank page in your browser. However, if you then take a look at the contents of the `access_log` table, you'll see that your activity has been logged:

```
mysql> SELECT * FROM access_log;
+------------------------------+---------+------------+----------------+
| page                         | userid  | visitcount | accessdate     |
+------------------------------+---------+------------+----------------+
| /headbangers/index.html      | bundy   |          9 | 20000913165329 |
| /index.html                  | judy    |          2 | 20000913165350 |
| /index.html                  | phantom |          8 | 20000913165409 |
| /php/myscript.php            | phantom |          5 | 20000713220144 |
| /php/myscript.php            | davidme |          1 | 20000826071502 |
| /who.html                    | bundy   |          6 | 19991123172000 |
| /php/access_logger.php       | daniels |          1 | 20000919171422 |
+------------------------------+---------+------------+----------------+
7 rows in set (0.05 sec)
```

### How It Works

We start off by including the `common_db.inc` file, and defining our exclusion arrays and table names:

```php
<?php
include "./common_db.inc";
$exclude_dirs = array('/', '/info', '/contact');
$exclude_files = array('index.html', 'info.html', 'index.php');
$user_tablename = 'user';
$access_log_tablename = 'access_log';
```

We begin the main part of the script by extracting the path and name of the current web page from the global variable $PHP_SELF. After checking the path and filename of the current page against the elements in the $exclude_dirs and $exclude_files arrays, the script determines whether to do authentication or not:

```php
$filepath = dirname($PHP_SELF);
$filename = basename($PHP_SELF);

if($filepath == '') $filepath = '/';
```

When given a "root" directory "/", `dirname()` returns nothing at all, in which case we need to assign the value explicitly. The $auth_done variable is now used to break out of both inner and outer `for` loops when the authentication is complete:

```
$auth_done = 0;

for($j=0; $j < count($exclude_dirs); $j++) {
    if($exclude_dirs[$j] == $filepath) break;
    else {
        for($i=0; $i< count($exclude_files); $i++) {
            if($exclude_files[$i] == $filename) break;
            else {
                session_start();
                do_authentication();
                $auth_done = 1;
                break;
            }
        }
    }
    if($auth_done) break;
}
```

The script begins by checking the path and name of the current web page against every element in the $exclude_dirs and $exclude_files arrays to see whether it is to be exempted from authentication. If authentication is needed, it calls the do_authentication() function, which should mostly be familiar to you from the earlier user_auth.php script.

Note that we pulled the session_start() function out of the do_authentication() function since the $userid variable should be fetched from the global namespace. On the other hand, we've squeezed auth_user() into do_authentication() for the sake of efficiency.

The do_authentication() function starts by updating the lastaccesstime field to reflect the current system date and time when the script is called:

```
$query = "UPDATE $user_tablename SET lastaccesstime = NULL
                                WHERE userid = '$PHP_AUTH_USER'";
$result = mysql_query($query);
```

If an error occurs, it echoes out a message to that effect and dies:

```
$num_rows = mysql_affected_rows($link_id);
if($num_rows != 1) die(sql_error());
```

*Remember that the mysql_affected_rows() function should only return 1 or 0 since user IDs are supposed to be unique in the user table.*

Next, it queries the access_log table to see if a record already exists containing the path of the current web page and the user ID. If it does, the function increments its visitcount field and updates its acccessdate field to the current system date and time. Otherwise, it inserts a new record:

```
$query = "SELECT userid FROM $access_log_tablename WHERE page = '$PHP_SELF' AND
userid = '$userid'";
$result = mysql_query($query);
```

```
if(!mysql_num_rows($result)) $query = "INSERT INTO $access_log_tablename VALUES
('$PHP_SELF', '$PHP_AUTH_USER', 1, NULL)";
else $query = "UPDATE access_log SET visitcount = visitcount + 1, accessdate =
NULL WHERE page = '$PHP_SELF' AND userid = '$userid'";

mysql_query($query);
```

Again, it checks whether just a single record has been updated or inserted:

```
$num_rows = mysql_affected_rows($link_id);
if($num_rows != 1) die(sql_error());
```

Once a user has been authenticated, the `$userid` session variable is assumed to be holding the correct `userid` for the current client making requests for your resources. We can therefore record any accesses he makes to our web pages in the `access_log` table.

# Creating a User Manager

At last we can put all our examples together, and upgrade our user record viewer (as built in the previous chapter) so that it can manipulate data in the related tables. Using the following script, which we'll call `userman.php`, you can edit and delete user records and/or corresponding access log records. We start as we did with `register.php`, by fetching ENUM options on the `usercountry` field:

```
<?php
//userman.php
include "./common_db.inc";

$link_id = db_connect();
mysql_select_db("sample_db");
$country_array = enum_options('usercountry', $link_id);
mysql_close($link_id);
```

### user_message()

This will report the result of a given operation. If fed an optional URL argument, it will load the specified page:

```
function user_message($msg, $url='') {
  html_header();

  if(empty($url))
      echo "<SCRIPT>alert(\"$msg\");history.go(-1)</SCRIPT>";
  else echo "<SCRIPT>alert(\"$msg\");self.location.href='$url'</SCRIPT>";

  html_footer();
  exit;
}
```

### list_records()

The revised `list_records()` function adds an option to delete a chosen record. The rest of the function is all the same as in the previous version:

```
function list_records() {
...
      echo "<TD WIDTH=\"25%\" ALIGN=\"CENTER\">
            <A HREF=\"javascript:open_window('$PHP_SELF?action=view_record&
                                           userid=$userid');\">
            View</A>
            <A HREF=\"$PHP_SELF?action=delete_record&userid=$userid\"
               onClick=\"return confirm('Are you sure?');\">
            Delete</A>
            </TD>\n";
      echo "</TR>\n";
...
}
```

### delete_record()

This function deletes a given user's record from the `user` table, along with corresponding records in the `access_log` table:

```
function delete_record() {
  global $default_dbname, $user_tablename, $access_log_tablename;
  global $userid;

  if(empty($userid)) error_message('Empty User ID!');

  $link_id = db_connect($default_dbname);
  if(!$link_id) error_message(sql_error());

  $query = "DELETE FROM $user_tablename WHERE userid = '$userid'";
  $result = mysql_query($query);
  if(!$result) error_message(sql_error());

  $num_rows = mysql_affected_rows($link_id);
  if($num_rows != 1) error_message("No such user: $userid");

  $query = "DELETE FROM $access_log_tablename WHERE userid = '$userid'";
  $result = mysql_query($query);

  user_message("All records regarding $userid have been trashed!");
}
```

### edit_record()

This function updates a given user's record in the `user` table. If a `userid` is changed, it also updates the related records in the `access_log` table to reflect that change:

```
function edit_record() {
  global $default_dbname, $user_tablename, $access_log_tablename;
```

```
        global $userid, $new_userid, $userid, $username, $userpassword,
               $usercountry, $useremail, $userprofile, $registerdate,
               $lastaccesstime;

        if(empty($userid)) error_message('Empty User ID!');

        $link_id = db_connect($default_dbname);
        if(!$link_id) error_message(sql_error());

        $field_str = '';
```

Yes, the userid field itself can be changed. From a database manager's point of view though, it's generally unacceptable for a user to change his userid, since it acts like his social security number: that is, both *unique and unchangeable*. Nevertheless, if a user were to *insist* on changing his userid, every record in every related table, no matter how many there were, would also have to be changed. You'd otherwise end up with a bunch of useless, orphan records that have lost their owner.

```
        if($userid != $new_userid) $field_str = " userid = '$new_userid', ";
```

Unless the $userpassword variable is empty, the userpassword field is updated:

```
        if(!empty($userpassword)) {
          $field_str .= " userpassword = password('$userpassword') ";
        }
```

By checking like this, we prevent an administrator from accidentally putting empty values into the userpassword field. We then update the other fields and check that everything's gone to plan:

```
        $field_str .= " username = '$username', ";
        $field_str .= " usercountry = '$usercountry', ";
        $field_str .= " useremail = '$useremail', ";
        $field_str .= " userprofile = '$userprofile', ";
        $field_str .= " registerdate = '$registerdate', ";
        $field_str .= " lastaccesstime = '$lastaccesstime' ";

        $query = "UPDATE $user_tablename SET $field_str WHERE userid = '$userid'";

        $result = mysql_query($query);
        if(!$result) error_message(sql_error());

        $num_rows = mysql_affected_rows($link_id);
        if(!$num_rows) error_message("Nothing changed!");
```

If the userid field is to be changed, the function changes all the related records in the access_log table too and refreshes the view:

```
        if($userid != $new_userid) {
          $query = "UPDATE $access_log_tablename SET userid = '$new_userid'
                                              WHERE userid = '$userid'";
          $result = mysql_query($query);
          if(!$result) error_message(sql_error());
```

```
          user_message("All records regarding $userid have been changed!",
                       "$PHP_SELF?action=view_record&userid=$new_userid");
        }
        else {
          user_message("All records regarding $userid have been changed!");
        }
      }
```

Note that *if* the userid field has been changed, we call user_message() with the second URL argument specifying userid=$new_userid. Since the existing userid has been changed, falling back to the script with the old userid value would produce an unexpected result: an edit form for a non-existent user.

### edit_log_record()

The edit_log_record() function updates a given user's access records in the access_log table:

```
function edit_log_record() {
  global $default_dbname, $access_log_tablename;
  global $userid, $org_page, $new_page, $visitcount, $accessdate;

  if(empty($userid)) error_message('Empty User ID!');

  $link_id = db_connect($default_dbname);
  if(!$link_id) error_message(sql_error());

  $field_str = '';

  $field_str .= " page = '$new_page', ";
  $field_str .= " visitcount = $visitcount, ";
  $field_str .= " accessdate = '$accessdate' ";
```

This function works in a similar way to edit_record(). However, one major difference is that this function uses both userid *and* page fields to select relevant access log records. Also note that we preserve the existing value of the page field in the $org_page variable. This is just in case the administrator changes its value in an edit form:

```
  $query = "UPDATE $access_log_tablename SET $field_str
                                          WHERE userid = '$userid'
                                          AND page = '$org_page'";
  $result = mysql_query($query);
  if(!$result) error_message(sql_error());
```

If no record has been updated, that means the administrator has pressed the Submit button without changing anything in the corresponding edit form.

The mysql_affected_rows() function returns 0 because the previous UPDATE operation resulted in no changed rows. An UPDATE command does nothing if the new record has the same values as the ones in the existing record:

```
  $num_rows = mysql_affected_rows($link_id);
```

```
    if(!$num_rows) error_message("Nothing changed!");

    user_message("All records regarding $userid have been changed!");
  }
```

### view_record()

The revised `view_record()` function lets the administrator edit user records:

```
function view_record() {
  global $default_dbname, $user_tablename, $access_log_tablename;
  global $country_array, $userid;
  global $PHP_SELF;

  if(empty($userid)) error_message('Empty User ID!');

  $link_id = db_connect($default_dbname);

  if(!$link_id) error_message(sql_error());
```

Take a close look at how the `view_record()` function retrieves formatted date strings from the `user` and `access_log` tables:

```
$query = "SELECT usernumber, userid, username, usercountry,
                 useremail, userprofile, registerdate,
                 date_format(registerdate, '%M, %e, %Y')
                   as formatted_registerdate,
                 lastaccesstime, date_format(lastaccesstime, '%M, %e, %Y')
                   as formatted_lastaccesstime
                 FROM $user_tablename WHERE userid = '$userid'";
$result = mysql_query($query);

if(!$result) error_message(sql_error());

$query_data = mysql_fetch_array($result);
$usernumber = $query_data["usernumber"];
$userid = $query_data["userid"];
$username = $query_data["username"];
$usercountry = $query_data["usercountry"];
$useremail = $query_data["useremail"];
$userprofile = $query_data["userprofile"];
```

As you can see, we issue the queries using aliases for additional date values. You can access these virtual field values by using the aliases as a reference just like you do the preceding date fields with their names:

```
$registerdate = $query_data["registerdate"];
$formatted_registerdate = $query_data["formatted_registerdate"];
$lastaccesstime = $query_data["lastaccesstime"];
$formatted_lastaccesstime = $query_data["formatted_lastaccesstime"];

html_header();
```

```
    echo "<CENTER><H3>
        Record for User No.$usernumber - $userid($username)
        </H3></CENTER>";
?>
```

Finally, the function displays a number of forms from which the administrator can edit the user's record and his access log data:

```
<FORM METHOD="POST" ACTION="<?php echo $PHP_SELF ?>">
<INPUT TYPE="HIDDEN" NAME="action" VALUE="edit_record">
<INPUT TYPE="HIDDEN" NAME="userid" VALUE="<? echo $userid ?>">
<DIV ALIGN="CENTER"><CENTER>
<TABLE BORDER="1" WIDTH="90%" CELLPADDING="2">
    <TR>
        <TH WIDTH="30%" NOWRAP>User ID</TH>
```

Note the hidden field `new_userid` is being used in case an administrator changes the `userid` of a given user:

```
        <TD WIDTH="70%">
        <INPUT TYPE="TEXT" NAME="new_userid"
                        VALUE="<?php echo $userid ?>"
                        SIZE="8" MAXLENGTH="8"></TD>
    </TR>
    <TR>
        <TH WIDTH="30%" NOWRAP>User Password</TH>
```

We're not echoing out the encrypted password since it's of no use:

```
        <TD WIDTH="70%"><INPUT TYPE="TEXT" NAME="userpassword" SIZE="15"></TD>
    </TR>
    <TR>
        <TH WIDTH="30%" NOWRAP>Full Name</TH>
        <TD WIDTH="70%"><INPUT TYPE="TEXT" NAME="username"
                        VALUE="<?php echo $username ?>" SIZE="20"></TD>
    </TR>
    <TR>
        <TH WIDTH="30%" NOWRAP>Country</TH>
        <TD WIDTH="70%"><SELECT NAME="usercountry" SIZE="1">
<?php
```

We use the `$country_array` variable to construct a droplist of countries:

```
    for($i=0; $i < count($country_array); $i++) {
        if(!isset($usercountry) && $i == 0) {
            echo "<OPTION SELECTED VALUE=\"". $country_array[$i] . "\">" .
                                    $country_array[$i] . "</OPTION>\n";
        }
        else if($usercountry == $country_array[$i]) {
            echo "<OPTION SELECTED VALUE=\"". $country_array[$i] . "\">" .
                                    $country_array[$i] . "</OPTION>\n";
        }
```

```
        else {
          echo "<OPTION VALUE=\"". $country_array[$i] . "\">" .
                                  $country_array[$i] . "</OPTION>\n";
        }
      }
    ?>
        </SELECT></TD>
      </TR>
      <TR>
        <TH WIDTH="30%" NOWRAP>Email</TH>
        <TD WIDTH="70%"><INPUT TYPE="TEXT" NAME="useremail" SIZE="20"
                              VALUE="<?php echo $useremail ?>"></TD>
      </TR>
      <TR>
        <TH WIDTH="30%" NOWRAP>Profile</TH>
```

The `htmlspecialchars()` function ensures that any HTML special characters in the `$userprofile` variable are echoed as HTML entities, and can't do any damage to the surrounding markup:

```
        <TD WIDTH="70%">
          <TEXTAREA ROWS="5" COLS="40" NAME="userprofile">
            <?php echo htmlspecialchars($userprofile) ?>
          </TEXTAREA>
        </TD>
      </TR>
      <TR>
        <TH WIDTH="30%" NOWRAP>Register Date</TH>
        <TD WIDTH="70%">
          <INPUT TYPE="TEXT" NAME="registerdate" SIZE="10" MAXLENGTH="10"
                            VALUE="<?php echo $registerdate ?>">
          <?php echo $formatted_registerdate?>
        </TD>
      </TR>
      <TR>
        <TH WIDTH="30%" NOWRAP>Last Access Time</TH>
        <TD WIDTH="70%">
          <INPUT TYPE="TEXT" NAME="lastaccesstime" SIZE="14" MAXLENGTH="14"
                  VALUE="<?php echo $lastaccesstime ?>">
          <?php echo $formatted_lastaccesstime ?>
        </TD>
      </TR>
      <TR>
        <TH WIDTH="100%" COLSPAN="2" NOWRAP>
          <INPUT TYPE="SUBMIT" VALUE="Change User Record">
          <INPUT TYPE="RESET" VALUE="Reset">
        </TH>
      </TR>
    </TABLE>
    </CENTER></DIV>
  </FORM>
  <?php
    echo "<HR SIZE=\"2\" WIDTH=\"90%\">\n";
```

Each access log record is presented in a separate form:

```
    $query = "SELECT page, visitcount, accessdate,
             date_format(accessdate, '%M, %e, %Y') as formatted_accessdate
             FROM $access_log_tablename WHERE userid = '$userid'";
    $result = mysql_query($query);

    if(!$result) error_message(sql_error());
    if(!mysql_num_rows($result))
      echo "<CENTER>No access log record for $userid ($username).</CENTER>";
    else {
      echo "<CENTER>Access log record(s) for $userid ($username).</CENTER>";
?>
<DIV ALIGN="CENTER"><CENTER>
<TABLE BORDER="1" WIDTH="90%" CELLPADDING="2">
  <TR>
    <TH WIDTH="20%" NOWRAP>Page</TH>
    <TH WIDTH="20%" NOWRAP>Hits</TH>
    <TH WIDTH="30%" NOWRAP>Last Access</TH>
    <TH WIDTH="30%" NOWRAP>Action</TH>
  </TR>
<?php
```

Note how we access virtual fields by using aliases:

```
    while($query_data = mysql_fetch_array($result)) {
      $page = $query_data["page"];
      $visitcount = $query_data["visitcount"];
      $accessdate = $query_data["accessdate"];
      $formatted_accessdate = $query_data["formatted_accessdate"];

      echo "<FORM METHOD=\"POST\" ACTION=\$PHP_SELF\">";
      echo "<INPUT TYPE=\"HIDDEN\" NAME=\"action\"
                                VALUE=\"edit_log_record\">";
      echo "<INPUT TYPE=\"HIDDEN\" NAME=\"userid\" VALUE=\"$userid\">";
      echo "<INPUT TYPE=\"HIDDEN\" NAME=\"org_page\" VALUE=\"$page\">";
      echo "<TR>\n";
      echo "<TD WIDTH=\"20%\"><INPUT TYPE=\"TEXT\"
             NAME=\"new_page\" SIZE=\"30\" VALUE=\"$page\"></TD>\n";
      echo "<TD WIDTH=\"20%\" ALIGN=\"CENTER\">
             <INPUT TYPE=\"TEXT\" NAME=\"visitcount\" SIZE=\"3\"
                                VALUE=\"$visitcount\"></TD>\n";
      echo "<TD WIDTH=\"30%\" ALIGN=\"CENTER\">
             <INPUT TYPE=\"TEXT\" NAME=\"accessdate\" SIZE=\"14\"
                    MAXLENGTH=\"14\" VALUE=\"$accessdate\">
          <BR>$formatted_accessdate</TD>\n";
      echo "<TD WIDTH=\"30%\" ALIGN=\"CENTER\">
             <INPUT TYPE=\"SUBMIT\" VALUE=\"Change\">
             <INPUT TYPE=\"RESET\" VALUE=\"Reset\"></TD>\n";
      echo "</TR>\n";
      echo "</FORM>\n";
    }
?>
```

```
   </TR>
</TABLE>
</CENTER></DIV>
<?php
  }
  html_footer();
}
```

## Choosing an Action to Take

Finally, we use $action to specify which functions to call:

```
switch($action) {
  case "edit_record":
    edit_record();
  break;
  case "edit_log_record":
    edit_log_record();
  break;

  case "delete_record":
    delete_record();
  break;
  case "view_record":
    view_record();
  break;
  default:
    list_records();
  break;

}

?>
```

The first screen you will see from running the script looks like this:

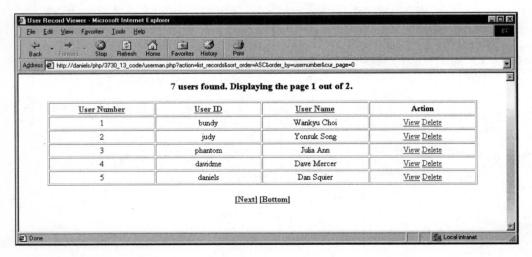

When you click on a View link, it will open up a new window displaying the records of the user associated with the link:

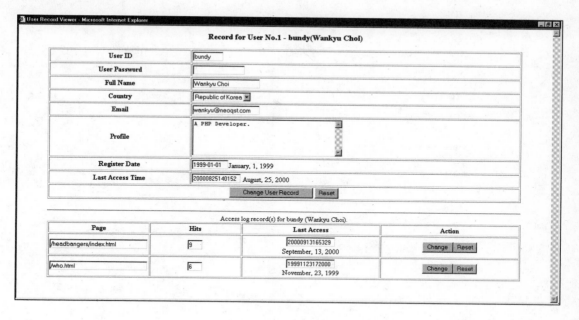

# Resources

MySQL Online References: http://www.mysql.com/documentation

MySQL-related PHP Function List: http://www.php.net/manual/ref.mysql.php

# Summary

In this chapter, we walked you through the process of manipulating existing data in database tables.

Along the way, we built a user registration script and an access logger script that can be used together to track user accesses to your web site. While working on these scripts, we also showed you how easily user authentication can be done in PHP using its session management feature.

We concluded the three part series of MySQL saga with a user manager script. With MySQL as the backend for your data storage, the extent to which you can develop high performance applications is restricted only by your imagination: let your imagination fly!

# 14

# XML

In this chapter, we're going to complete a brief introduction to XML and the ways that we can use PHP4 to interact with it. This is not going to be an in-depth treatment, as XML is a large topic that can get fairly complicated. However, by the end you'll be able to use PHP4 to perform a useful task – taking data from an XML file and displaying it dynamically on a web page.

There are very few requirements for the exercises that we're going to go through. Basically, as long as you have a network connection and a properly configured PHP4 environment, you're ready to go. As far as Linux users are concerned, "properly configured" means that your PHP4 binary was configured at compile time with:

`#  ./configure --with-xml`

This will compile in the XML support, which is included by default with the PHP4 distribution.

*The included functionality comes from James Clark's **expat** parser. More information on this widely used piece of software can be found at* http://www.jclark.com.

To begin with, let's start by talking about XML.


## What is XML?

Depending on whom you are talking to, the question "What is XML?" can get many different answers. These may vary from things like "XML is a flat-file format" to "XML is the saving grace of both the Internet and mankind itself". About the only things everyone will agree on are that XML is an Internet buzzword, and that there are a lot of resources being put into its development.

XML stands for e**X**tensible **M**arkup **L**anguage, and it is a subset of SGML (the **S**tandard **G**eneralized **M**arkup **L**anguage.) Since you're already familiar with HTML, you already know something about markup languages. Basically, you have information of some sort, and you put bracketed <tags> around this information in a file. Then, another application such as a web browser or a parser will look at this file and know how to interpret the data in a useful way. In this sense, XML files are no different from the HTML files that we all know and love.

So what's the big deal then? The difference is this: with an HTML file the available tags and their attributes are defined in a reference specification. This means that you are handed a set of tags and attributes to use, and you go from there to create web pages. This is very good for displaying information in web browsers. For example, if I wanted to show people my name, I might create an HTML document like this one:

```
<HTML>
<HEAD>
<TITLE>My Name</TITLE>
</HEAD>
<BODY>
<P>Chris Lea</P>
</BODY>
</HTML>
```

Using this document, anybody with a web browser would be able to see my name with ease (although they wouldn't necessarily know what they were looking at.)

Unfortunately, HTML is limited beyond this kind of browser-based application. With an XML file, you can define the tags and attributes yourself in ways that are well suited to the types of information you are trying to transmit or record. As a result, you can have a document, which is *self-descriptive* in the sense that the tags clearly indicate the kinds of data that lies between them. Also, you can structure your data so that it forms a convenient and logical tree structure. Using my name again for an example, I might make an XML file like this:

```
<?xml version="1.0"?>
<name>
  <first>Chris</first>
  <last>Lea</last>
</name>
```

The beauty here is that anyone can clearly see what kind of information I'm trying to get across, since the tags do such a good job of describing the data they contain. Also, the data is arranged in a nice tree-style fashion for me, as shown in the diagram below.

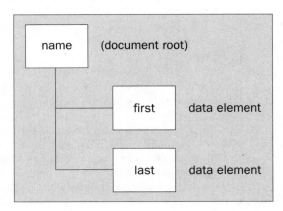

Using an XML parser, I can easily access the data in a structured way.

Going one step further with XML, you can describe your data format and tags to other people, so that they can use your format and be guaranteed that they are getting the right kinds of data. We'll learn more about this later in the DTDs section.

All of this forces us to examine an important question – why do we care about all of this? How are these XML files going to help?

To begin with, XML files are generally easy to read. Granted, you'll usually be looking at the data through the eyes of a parser program, but it's always nice to be able to see what's going on for yourself. Second, at their core, XML documents are flat text files. This means that it's simple to transfer them around the Internet. Third, because we can define and read rules that describe document structure, we can guarantee that we're using the same data format as other people we're interacting with. This allows developers (such as you) to write powerful applications that can be deployed in many different circumstances. Finally, because XML files are not specific to the web, you can use the data in many different kinds of applications. In this chapter, we're going to put data onto web pages. However, you could also put that data into a database, create formatted PDF files, or any number of other potential tasks.

Of course, there is a great deal more to say about the nature of XML than is outlined here. If you wish to investigate, an excellent resource is *Beginning XML (ISBN 1861003412)*, from Wrox Press.

# XML Document Structure

Before we jump in and create our first XML file, we should talk for a minute about the structural requirements for these documents. As we noted, XML files are collections of tags and data. These collections are called elements of the document.

> *An element consists of a start tag and a corresponding end tag, as well as everything that lies between the two.*

Now, looking at our name example, it's obvious that the lines:

```
<first>Chris</first>
<last>Lea</first>
```

are elements. However, we should also note that everything between the <name> and </name> tags is also considered an element. As we noted, XML documents form a tree structure, so it's perfectly legitimate for elements to nest.

There are two ways to transmit data within a given element. The first is through the character data, which is inserted between the start and end tags. The second is through the use of tag attributes, which look very similar to HTML. They are nothing more than name/value pairs, which are attached to a start tag. The following two files convey the same data; the first uses standard elements, and the second uses an attribute:

```
<?xml version="1.0"?>
<name>
  <first>Rich</first>
  <last>Fremont</last>
  <nickname>Vinnie</nickname>
</name>

<?xml version="1.0"?>
<name nickname="Vinnie">
  <first>Rich</first>
  <last>Fremont</last>
</name>
```

The choice to use attributes vs. elements is generally driven by personal preference. In some cases, it may make more sense to use one or the other to attain a consistent structure for your documents.

# Well-Formed XML

Unlike some HTML that you may be accustomed to seeing, all XML documents must be *well-formed,* as described by the XML 1.0 specification. Naturally, the precise definition of well-formed is somewhat complicated, but for beginning purposes there are basically four rules to keep in mind:

- ❑ Tags must be nested properly.
- ❑ All start-tags must have end-tags.
- ❑ You must use quotation marks correctly for tag attributes.
- ❑ You must be careful using certain characters ('&' and '<' specifically) in your data.

Let's examine each of these, taking examples from HTML.

First, there's tag nesting. On web pages, you may sometimes see HTML that looks like this:

```
<FONT FACE="verdana"><B>I love penguins.</FONT></B>
```

In this case, the tags are not properly nested since the </B> tag should be inside of the </FONT> tag. The proper code would be the following:

```
<FONT FACE="verdana"><B>I love penguins.</B></FONT>
```

All tags within XML documents must nest properly, and not overlap as they do in the first example here. If the tags do not nest correctly, the parser will not be able to parse the document.

The second rule to keep in mind is the need for every opening tag to have an appropriate end tag. In HTML, coders are often sloppy with their <p> tags. They will put one at the beginning of a paragraph, but won't close the paragraph with the </p> tag as they should. Again, this is a sin in the XML world. The following file is invalid:

```
<?xml version="1.0"?>
<name>
```

```
    <first>Chris
    <last>Lea</last>
</name>
```

because the:

```
</first>
```

tag is not present to close out the first name. There is something that appears to be an exception to this rule (although it's not). It exists in the case that there's no data between a specific start and end tag. If you have such a case, which would look like this:

```
<emptytag></emptytag>
```

then it is acceptable shorthand notation to simply type:

```
<emptytag/>
```

This may look like a standalone tag, but keep in mind that it is exactly equivalent to the fully expanded version. You may ask why you would ever have need for a completely empty tag. The answer is that you can still pass information to the parser with tag attributes. For example:

```
<emptytag name="somevalue"/>
```

is a legitimate way to get somevalue to the parser.

The third rule is an easy one. When you have tag attributes, you have to make sure that you use either single (') or double (") quotes consistently in tag attributes. The following two examples are both correct:

```
<name nickname="Vinnie">
<name nickname='Vinnie'>
```

whereas these examples aren't:

```
<name nickname=Vinnie>
<name nickname="Vinnie'>
```

The first example highlights a potential bad habit you may have from HTML coding. Many browsers will still interpret a name/value attribute even if you leave out these quotes. However, you can't do this in an XML document. Also, looking at the second bad example, you have to be consistent with your use of either single or double quotes. This should be easy, since you can't do this in HTML either, and probably don't have any bad habits as a result.

You must be careful not to use single quotes inside of a single-quote delimited attribute. It's the same story for double quotes inside a double-quote delimited attribute. If you do, the parser will think the attribute has ended too soon, and won't be able to finish getting through the document. As an example, the following line wouldn't be interpreted correctly:

```
<bar name='Linda's Bar and Grill'>
```

To get it right, you would use:

```
<bar name="Linda's Bar and Grill">
```

Finally, you need to be wary when the characters '<' or '&' are between two tags as data, since the parser interprets these specially. If you use the corresponding HTML character code values, which are &lt, and &amp respectively, then your data will be handled correctly.

## Try It Out - Our First XML Document

Now that we're armed with our new-found XML knowledge, let's create our first useful and well-formed document. I'm a big fan of J.R.R.Tolkien's book *The Lord of the Rings,* so we'll create a file to represent characters from the associated books. Create a new file called lotr.xml and put the following into it:

```xml
<?xml version="1.0"?>
<lotr_characters>
  <person alignment="good">
    <name>Gandalf</name>
    <race>Maia</race>
    <home/>
  </person>
  <person alignment="evil">
    <name>Melkor</name>
    <race>Valar</race>
    <home>Angband</home>
  </person>
  <person alignment="good">
    <name>Aragorn</name>
    <race>Human</race>
    <home>Gondor</home>
  </person>
</lotr_characters>
```

Let's see what we are looking at here. This file describes three different characters from the books. Each person element has an attribute, which tells us whether they are good or evil. Then, there are three elements that tell us the character's name, race, and home. Note that the Gandalf character's "home" tag is empty, because he doesn't really have a home. Keep in mind that this line could have been written:

```
<home></home>
```

and it would have meant exactly the same thing.

It would be nice if we had some way (other than human inspection) to make sure that this file was well-formed. Fortunately, IE 5 (and higher) has some good facilities for looking at raw XML data. Open up your lotr.xml file with this browser. Your screen should look like the screenshot opposite:

```
http://www.chrislea.com/xml/chapter/lotr.xml - Microsoft Interne...

File   Edit   View   Favorites   Tools   Help

  ↵           →          ⊗         ↻         🏠         🔍
 Back      Forward      Stop     Refresh     Home      Search

Address  http://www.chrislea.com/xml/chapter/lotr.xml          Go    Links

    <?xml version="1.0" ?>
  - <lotr_characters>
    - <person alignment="good">
        <name>Gandalf</name>
        <race>Maia</race>
        <home />
      </person>
    - <person alignment="evil">
        <name>Melkor</name>
        <race>Valar</race>
        <home>Angband</home>
      </person>
    - <person alignment="good">
        <name>Aragorn</name>
        <race>Human</race>
        <home>Gondor</home>
      </person>
    </lotr_characters>

Done                                        Internet
```

We know that the document was well-formed, because IE was able to display it without choking. Just for fun, modify the file in such a way as to break its well-formedness. For example, you could remove an end tag. Now look at it again in IE 5. You'll see an error message, because it's a requirement that XML documents always be well-formed. This may seem like a fairly extreme requirement, but it's ultimately one of the things, helps guarantee that XML can be used consistently for data exchange.

# DTDs

At this point, we know how to make well-formed XML documents, and we can look at them in the IE 5 web browser. Unfortunately, well-formed is only half of what we need to get a really good piece of data written. The other important issue is making sure that the data we have is complete. When we're looking at a particular document, we need a way to ascertain which tags are required, what kinds of data they should hold, what order they should come in, and which tags are not allowed. Fortunately, the XML specification provides us with a good mechanism for doing all of these things. It's called the **D**ocument **T**ype **D**efinition or **DTD**.

A DTD is a set of rules that may be included in the document itself or may be linked to externally. It defines a structure that the document in question should make use of, so that we can be sure we're looking at all the information we're supposed to. If a document conforms to all the rules in its DTD, and it's also *well-formed*, then it's said to be *valid*. Valid XML documents are the most useful kind because we know that the parser can read them, and we know that they contain all of the information they're supposed to.

So let's see what a DTD would look like for our "Lord of the Rings" example. The easiest way to gain some insight is to dissect an existing file. Here's a version of our old file with a DTD added to it. You should save this as `lotr_with_dtd.xml` on your machine, since we'll use it in the next section:

```
<?xml version="1.0" encoding="UTF-8" standalone="yes"?>
<!DOCTYPE lotr_characters [
  <!ELEMENT person (name, race, home)>
  <!ATTLIST person alignment (good | evil) #REQUIRED>
  <!ELEMENT name (#PCDATA)>
  <!ELEMENT race (#PCDATA)>
  <!ELEMENT home (#PCDATA)>
]>
<lotr_characters>
  <person alignment="good">
    <name>Gandalf</name>
    <race>Maia</race>
    <home/>
  </person>
  <person alignment="evil">
    <name>Melkor</name>
    <race>Valar</race>
    <home>Angband</home>
  </person>
  <person alignment="good">
    <name>Aragorn</name>
    <race>Human</race>
    <home>Gondor</home>
  </person>
</lotr_characters>
```

So what does all of this mean? The general format of a DTD looks like this:

```
<!DOCTYPE rootElementName [
...<insert declarations here>...
]>
```

where `rootElementName` is the root element of your XML document. Correspondingly, the first line of this DTD reads:

```
<!DOCTYPE lotr_characters [
```

there are some declarations in the middle, and it ends with:

```
]>
```

Next, we see:

```
<!ELEMENT person (name, race, home)>
```

This seemingly simple declaration says three things about the <person> tag. First, it says that it only holds other elements, so we can't have any text data standing by itself between the person tags. Second, it says that there must be exactly one <name>, <race>, and <home> tag within each person. Finally, it says that those three tags must appear in the order specified in this list.

Moving on, we see:

```
<!ATTLIST person alignment (good | evil) #REQUIRED>.
```

As you may have guessed from the name, an `ATTLIST` declaration describes what the attributes for a tag are allowed to be. In this case, it says that the person tag may have one "alignment" attribute, the possible values for this attribute are "good" and "evil," and that this is a required attribute. This makes sense, since all the characters in the book worth talking about are either good or evil, so they should always have an alignment with respect to this.

The last three lines are all basically the same. They indicate that the name, race, and home tags contain data of type `PCDATA`. This is a fancy expression for **P**arsed **C**haracter **DATA**, which is another fancy expression for plain text. So, we are allowed to have text data in these three elements, but no other kinds of data are allowed.

Now, this is by no means intended to be a full or even modest discussion about what DTDs are, what they can do, and the syntax employed to write one. The important thing to keep in mind is that a DTD lets you define the things that are allowed to be in your XML document.

Another important note is that although this example has the DTD embedded into the document, it's possible (and in fact very common) to link to an external DTD stored on your file system or on a server computer. This is important, because it allows you to share DTDs with other people who will be using a particular document structure. In this way, you can be assured that everyone's documents will follow the same patterns, and it will be easier to write applications that can parse information from a variety of sources. We'll see an example of this at the end of the chapter when we parse an RSS (**R**ich **S**ite **S**ummary) file to attain headlines and put them on a web page.

# Event Driven Parsing

Now we're almost ready to parse our first document and do something with the data. Before we start, it makes sense to talk briefly about how PHP4 actually parses XML documents.

There are several different ways of accessing your XML data, and they depend on the parsing model that you're making use of. One of these is called SAX, which stands for the **S**imple **A**PI for **XML**. It was originally developed in Java and is described as an "event driven" parsing model. What this means is that, as the parser reads through the document, it sends signals out when certain events occur. For example, when the parser gets to the beginning of a new element (an event) it sends out a **signal**, along with some data, that is specific to the event in question. When our application receives this signal, a special function known as a **callback function** is executed automatically. We program these callback functions ourselves, so that they can handle the data that gets transferred over however we choose. This is known as a "signal/callback framework" and it is used in many different types of programming.

Don't be concerned if this all seems a little confusing right now. In just a moment, we'll start looking at some concrete examples with real code. This will help to shed some light on the nuances of things like events and callbacks.

The advantage of this type of model is that we don't have to read in the entire XML file before we can start using the data that's in it. For small files like our examples in this chapter, reading in the whole file wouldn't be a problem. However, in more complicated situations such as data sharing between businesses, the XML files can be very large and complicated. As the tree structure for a document gets deeper, the amount of work the computer has to do to organize the information increases greatly. As a result, there would be substantial overhead involved with parsing through the whole file before we were allowed access to the data.

We mention SAX, which is a Java-based API, because it's the most popular event-driven API that is currently being widely employed. Due to its ease of use, it's not surprising that the PHP4 API for XML looks strikingly similar to SAX. It's also event driven, and has very similar functions for assigning callbacks to the events produced by the parser. You can find out more about it at http://www.megginson.com/SAX.

# Parsing the Example File

There are basically five functions from the PHP4 API that we'll use to parse our example file. They are:

| Function: | Description: |
|---|---|
| `int xml_parser_create()` | Creates an XML Parser referenced by `int`. This will return false if the parser is not created. |
| `int xml_set_element_handler (`<br>`        int parser,`<br>`        string startElementHandler,`<br>`        string endElementHandler`<br>`)` | Sets up the callback functions for the "begin element" and "end element" events. The functions are referenced by the strings `startElementHandler` and `endElementHandler`. Returns `true` if the functions are set successfully, `False` otherwise. |
| `int xml_set_character_data_handler (`<br>`        int parser,`<br>`        string characterDataHandler`<br>`)` | Sets up the callback function to handle character data between elements. This function is referenced by the string `characterDataHandler`. Returns `True` if the function is set successfully, `False` otherwise. |
| `int xml_parse (int parser,`<br>`            string data`<br>`            [,int isFinal]`<br>`)` | Starts parsing the information represented by *data*. The `isFinal` argument is an optional argument that may be used to tell the parser when to quit. Returns `True` as long as the data is parsed successfully. |
| `string xml_parser_free (int parser)` | Frees the memory used by `parser`. Returns `True` if the memory is freed successfully, `False` otherwise. |

Now, we need to look at those three callbacks that were mentioned in conjunction with `xml_set_element_handler` and `xml_set_character_data_handler`. You can define your own callbacks to handle the data as you see fit, but they are required to accept certain argument lists. We say that callbacks have some degree of pre-definition, especially with regards to the arguments that they take.

The function for `startElementHandler` must have the following format:

```
startElementHandler ( int parser , string name , array attribs )
```

Here, `parser` is the pointer to the XML parser that you got from `xml_parser_create()`. The string name is the **case folded** (we'll explain this term in a moment) name of the element, which you've just started parsing. Finally, `attribs` is an associative array in which the keys are the case-folded names of the attributes for this element, and the array values are the corresponding attribute values. In a typical `startElementHandler` type function, you'll want to collect information about any attributes for the element, and you'll also want to set variables which tell other functions what the current tag being processed is.

> *Case folded is a fancy way of saying "uppercase", meaning that any element name or attribute name will be converted to all uppercase characters for use in processing. It's possible to turn this feature off, but that's unnecessary for our application here.*

Moving on, the function for `endElementHandler` needs the following arguments:

```
endElementHandler ( int parser , string name )
```

As before, `parser` is the pointer to your XML parser, and `name` is the name of the element which you've just finished examining. Usually, you will want to clean up any variables that you set in the `startElementHandler` with this function.

Finally, there's the `characterDataHandler` function, which looks like this:

```
characterDataHandler ( int parser , string data )
```

The `parser` is our familiar XML parser pointer, as before. The `data` string is all the character data within the current element. So typically in this function, you'll want to check on the current state of the parser (probably using the variables you set in `startElementHandler`) and put `data` into some container for later use in the application.

## Try It Out - Parsing the lotr_with_dtd.xml File

So now we've covered all of the event-driven functions that we're going to need for our first application – it's time to dive in. The first thing to do is create a new file called `lotr_parsed.php` in the same directory on your web server as the `lotr_with_dtd.xml` file. The first piece of code you'll want is something to open up the data file. First we'll open the XML file:

```php
<?php
if( ! ($fp = fopen( "./lotr_with_dtd.xml" , "r" )) )
  die("Couldn't open xml file!");
```

Next, we'll need to define a few global variables that we'll use to keep track of the parser as it goes through the application:

```
$person_counter = 0;
```

This will be used to store the data about our characters:

```
  $person_data = array();
```

Finally, this will be needed to tell the character data handler what to do:

```
  $xml_current_tag_state = '';
```

Now for the bulk of the work, which is defining the callback functions. One important note is that all of your callback functions must be defined on the page before they are applied to the XML parser. The first one is the callback that handles the start element signal:

```
function startElementHandler( $parser, $element_name, $element_attribs )
{
  global $person_counter;
  global $person_data;
  global $xml_current_tag_state;
```

If we're starting on a person tag, get the alignment from the attribute, otherwise set the tag state to the name of the current tag:

```
  if( $element_name == "PERSON" )
  {
    $person_data[$person_counter]["alignment"] = $element_attribs["ALIGNMENT"];
  }
  else
  {
    $xml_current_tag_state = $element_name;
  }
}
```

Let's see what's happening here. First, we declare our global variables. Then, we check to see if we're looking at a PERSON element. Note that we look for the element name in uppercase, since case folding is on. We know two things about the <person> tag. First, it doesn't contain any character data. Second, it does contain one attribute for the person's alignment (good or evil). So, if we've just started a person element, then we need to grab the information from that attribute and store it in our global associative array person_data. If we're not starting a person element, then we know we must be looking at one of the other tags, which contain character data. So in this case, we make a note of which tag we're looking at in our xml_current_tag_state variable. That way, we can do something useful with the character data when we define the character data handler.

Next, we'll define what happens when we finish with an element.

This is the "end element" callback function; this is what will execute when the parser gets to the end of an element:

```
function endElementHandler( $parser, $element_name )
{
  global $person_counter;
  global $person_data;
  global $xml_current_tag_state;
```

The tag state should always be empty if we've just finished an element:

```
$xml_current_tag_state = '';
```

If we've just finished processing a person element, increment the counter:

```
    if( $element_name == "PERSON" )
    {
      $person_counter++;
    }
  }
```

At the end of a given element, it doesn't make any sense to have xml_current_tag_state defined since we're between tags. Therefore, we clear this variable of any value it might have had. Also, if we've just finished a person element, then we need to increment our variable person_counter so that we'll know which person we're collecting data about.

Finally, we have to define the character data handler, so that we can do something with the data we haven't collected so far:

```
function characterDataHandler( $parser , $data )
{
  global $person_counter;
  global $person_data;
  global $xml_current_tag_state;
```

If this is empty, just return:

```
  if( $xml_current_tag_state == '' )
    return;
```

Check the tag state, and put data into the proper place in the associative array:

```
    if( $xml_current_tag_state == "NAME" ) {
      $person_data[$person_counter]["name"] = $data;
    }
    if( $xml_current_tag_state == "RACE" ) {
      $person_data[$person_counter]["race"] = $data;
    }
    if( $xml_current_tag_state == "HOME" ) {
      $person_data[$person_counter]["home"] = $data;
    }
  }
```

If, for whatever reason, the xml_current_tag_state isn't set, then we don't need to do anything, so we just return. If it is set, then we look at the value of xml_current_tag_state to see which element we have character data from. Then, we put that data into an appropriate place in our global associative person_data array for use later in the application.

We're almost there. In fact, all of the hard work has been done. We've defined all of the callback functions that we need to use, so all that's left is to actually parse the data with an XML parser. To do this, we will create a parser, assign the callbacks to it, and parse through our data file. The code that accomplishes these tasks is:

```
if( !($xml_parser = xml_parser_create()) )
  die("Couldn't create XML parser!");

xml_set_element_handler($xml_parser, "startElementHandler", "endElementHandler");
xml_set_character_data_handler($xml_parser, "characterDataHandler");
```

Finally, we'll parse the file. This will put the useful data into our global associative array for use on the page:

```
while( $data = fread($fp, 4096) )
{
  if( !xml_parse($xml_parser, $data, feof($fp)) )
  {
    break; // get out of while loop if we're done with the file
  }
}
```

Be sure to free the parser!

```
xml_parser_free($xml_parser);?>
```

Of course, like all good programmers, we remembered to free the memory for our parser when we were done with it.

Believe it or not, all of the real work has been done now. We've accomplished the goal of parsing our XML file, and putting the data we need into a convenient array so that we can get at it easily. All that's left is some simple display code to see our results:

```
<!DOCTYPE HTML PUBLIC "-//IETF//DTD HTML//EN">
<HTML>
<HEAD>
  <TITLE>Parsing the Sample XML File</TITLE>
</HEAD>

<BODY BGCOLOR="#ffffff">

<?php
```

We have all of our data in the array $person_data, so we can easily display it by looping through:

```
for( $i=0 ; $i < $person_counter ; ++$i )
{
```

Let's make the name of good characters blue, and the names of evil characters red:

```
    $font_color = $person_data[$i]["alignment"] == "good" ? "#0000ff" : "#ff0000";

    echo "<FONT SIZE=\"+1\" color=\"$font_color\">" .
            $person_data[$i]["name"] . "</FONT><BR>\n";
    echo "Race:   " . $person_data[$i]["race"] . "<BR>\n";
    echo "Home:   " . $person_data[$i]["home"] . "<BR>\n";
    echo "<BR>\n";
}

?>

</BODY>
</HTML>
```

As you can see, in this example I've changed the color that is used to print out each person's name depending on whether or not they are good or evil. The result should look a lot like this:

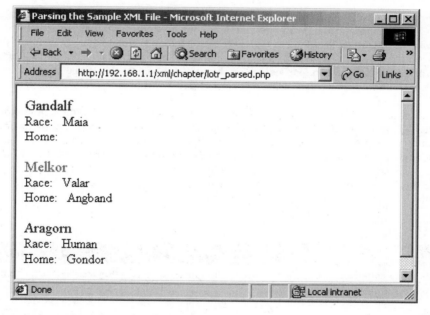

As an exercise, you could modify this file so that the printout is a nicely formatted table. Another good exercise would be to check for data items that are missing (such as Gandalf's home) and have conditional logic that would print "Unknown" when this was the case.

We've covered a great deal in this section. First, we talked about what event-driven parsing was. Next, we looked at the functions we needed from PHP4's XML API. Finally, we wrote a small application that parsed an XML file we had locally, and displayed the data in a web browser. Excellent job!

In the next section, we're going to parse another XML file and get the data to a web browser. However, this time, we won't be using a file that we created ourselves. In fact, it's not even going to be residing on our local file system! Fortunately for us, this seemingly complicated activity is aided greatly by PHP4's built-in functionality.

# Parsing an External File

One of the much-touted benefits of XML is that is enables people to exchange data across the Internet easily. For example, a common application is to take a file from a server other than your own and look at the data it contains. We're going to do exactly this in our example here. Specifically, we're going to look at the headlines file from the popular free software site http://www.freshmeat.net. You can view this file right away by pointing a browser at http://www.freshmeat.net/backend/fm.rdf.

If you look at this file, you'll note that the first four lines read:

```
<?xml version="1.0"?>
<!DOCTYPE rss PUBLIC "-//Netscape Communications//DTD RSS 0.91//EN"
"http://my.netscape.com/publish/formats/rss-0.91.dtd">
<rss version="0.91">
```

This is not the same kind of DOCTYPE declaration that we used before! However, you'll recall that it's possible to link to a DTD which is not embedded in your XML file, and that's exactly what is happening here. In fact, this document is linking to the DTD for RSS files, which was developed by Netscape. It's quickly becoming a de facto standard for exchanging headline-style data for web sites. This illustrates the power of linking to standardized external DTDs. Everyone who uses this format is guaranteed to have compatible data, and many sites are using this kind of document to grab and display various headlines.

Let's look at the fm.rdf (RDF stands for **R**esource **D**escription **F**ramework) file a little more. You'll note that there are several different container tags ("container tag" just means a tag that holds only other tags). These include <channel>, <image>, and <item>. Upon inspection, we can see that if what we want is software announcement headlines, and the corresponding links and descriptions, then all we're interested in is the <item> tags. We'll have to be sure to set up our callback functions to notice when we're in an item tag, and not to do any processing when we're outside one. Let's get started.

The first problem is: "How do we get the file since it's on another server?" Fortunately, PHP4 is really smart, and makes this task easy for us.

## Try It Out – Parsing the fm.rdf File

Create a new file called parse_freshmeat.php somewhere on your web server. The beginning code to open up the remote file looks like this:

```php
<?php
if( ! ($fp = fopen("http://freshmeat.net/backend/fm.rdf" , "r" )) )
    die("Couldn't open xml file!");
```

As you can see, PHP4's ability to open files over HTTP (and FTP, for that matter) makes this a simple task. Now, as before, we'll want to define a few global variables. First, we'll need this variable to keep track of which item we're looking at in the XML file:

```php
$item_counter = 0;
```

This variable will be used to indicate whether or not we're in an item tag:

```php
$in_item_tag = 0;
```

This will be used to let the character data handler decide what to do with its data-based, on the tag it's looking at:

```
$fm_current_tag_state = '';
```

This is our associative array, which will hold the data we grab from the file:

```
$fm_headline_data = array();
```

There's one more global variable here than there was in the case of our simple example before. This is because we need an extra piece of information to keep track of whether or not we're inside an <item> tag.

Now that we've got the global variables set up, let's go on to the start element callback function:

```
function startElementHandler( $parser, $element_name, $element_attribs )
{
  global $item_counter;
  global $in_item_tag;
  global $fm_current_tag_state;
  global $fm_headline_data;
```

The next line is *very* important – we need to know if we're in an item tag:

```
  if( $element_name == "ITEM" )
  {
    $in_item_tag = 1;
  }
```

If we're in an item tag, then we need to set the tag state for the character data handler. If we're not in an item tag, then the tag state should be empty, since we don't care what the data is:

```
  if( $in_item_tag == 1 )
  {
    $fm_current_tag_state = $element_name;
  }
  else
  {
    $fm_current_tag_state = '';
  }
}
```

Does this look familiar? It certainly should, since it is very similar to what we did before. Specifically, we look in this function to ascertain the state of the parser, and set the global variables $in_item_tag and $fm_current_tag_state accordingly. Since the elements in the file we're interested in don't contain any attributes, we don't need to do anything with the $element_attribs variable which gets passed to the function.

Now, we'll put together our end element handler:

```
function endElementHandler( $parser, $element_name )
{
  global $item_counter;
  global $in_item_tag;
  global $fm_current_tag_state;
  global $fm_headline_data;
```

Once again, we clear out the tag state, since we've just finished an element:

```
$fm_current_tag_state = '';
```

If we've just finished with an item tag, then we increment the item counter and set $in_item_tag to zero:

```
  if( $element_name == "ITEM" )
  {
    $item_counter++;
    $in_item_tag = 0;
  }
}
```

It's important to note that we set $in_item_tag back to zero if we've just finished looking at an <item> tag. This will ensure that we're only grabbing the data we're really interested in.

Last, but not least, we'll define our workhorse characterDataHandler callback:

```
function characterDataHandler( $parser , $data )
{
  global $item_counter;
  global $in_item_tag;
  global $fm_current_tag_state;
  global $fm_headline_data;
```

If we're not in an item tag, or if the tag state is empty, then just return:

```
  if( $fm_current_tag_state == '' || $in_item_tag == 0 )
    return;
```

Check the tag state, and put data into the proper place in the associative array:

```
  if( $fm_current_tag_state == "TITLE" ) {
    $fm_headline_data[$item_counter]["title"] = $data;
  }
  if( $fm_current_tag_state == "LINK" ) {
    $fm_headline_data[$item_counter]["link"] = $data;
  }
  if( $fm_current_tag_state == "DESCRIPTION" ) {
    $fm_headline_data[$item_counter]["description"] = $data;
  }
}
```

As you can see, we simply check on the current state of the parser and act accordingly. If we're not in an <item> tag, or if the current state isn't set, then we just return, since we don't need to do anything with the data. If we are in an <item> tag, then we check the current state to see which element we're looking at. We store the data from the different elements in the associative array for use later.

So, now we've defined all the parsing logic, and we are again ready to parse the file. Now, we'll create the parser and assign the handlers to it:

```
if( !($xml_parser = xml_parser_create()) )
  die("Couldn't create XML parser!");

xml_set_element_handler($xml_parser, "startElementHandler", "endElementHandler");
xml_set_character_data_handler( $xml_parser , "characterDataHandler" );
```

Finally, we'll parse the file. This will put the useful data into our global associative array for use on the page:

```
while( $data = fread($fp, 4096) )
{
  if( !xml_parse($xml_parser, $data, feof($fp)) )
  {
    break; // get out of while loop if we're done with the file
  }
}
```

Be sure to free the parser:

```
xml_parser_free($xml_parser);
?>
```

Assuming that all this executes without a hitch, we'll have all the data from the file stored neatly in an array. Some simple display logic will then put it onto a web page for us:

```
<HTML>
<HEAD>
<TITLE>Parsing the Freshmeat RDF File</TITLE>
</HEAD>

<BODY BGCOLOR="#ffffff">

<H3>Freshmeat Headlines</H3>
<BR>
<?php

for( $i=0 ; $i < $item_counter ; ++$i )
{
  printf("<A HREF=\"%s\">%s</a> - %s<br>\n" , $fm_headline_data[$i]["link"] ,
                                              $fm_headline_data[$i]["title"] ,
                                              $fm_headline_data[$i]["description"]
);
}

?>

</BODY>
</HTML>
```

This will generate a simple page that displays the current items from Freshmeat's homepage, complete with links and descriptions. Of course, as an exercise, you may beautify it as you see fit. The previous example will look something like this, except that yours will reflect the current Freshmeat headlines:

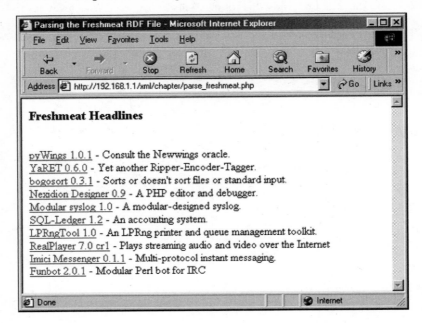

# Summary

We've covered quite a lot in this chapter, especially in light of the fact that XML is a very broad topic. To begin with, we discussed what XML documents are and why they are both important and useful for network data transfer. Then, we examined the document structure for **well-formed** XML files, and talked about the rules you need to adhere to so that your documents can be parsed properly. We also touched on DTDs and how they are used to ensure that files are **valid**. Along the way, we created a valid XML document from scratch, and we then parsed this file and displayed the data in a web browser. Finally, we got our hands on a remote XML file that was located on a different server on the Internet. Again, we used PHP4's XML parsing routines to get the data from this file into a useful form on a web page. Congratulations!

In closing, there are two points I should bring up. The first is that we have only just barely scratched the surface of the XML format. In fact, there are major pieces of the XML specification such as **XSLT**, **XPath**, and **namespaces** that we didn't mention at all. If you are going to be engaging in serious XML-related projects, then you really should acquire a book devoted to this topic to get a broader view of all the features and issues that you'll be dealing with.

The second point is that we have not covered the entire API that PHP4 has for dealing with XML. There are several more functions for things like different event handlers and error reporting, which weren't needed for the examples we tackled. However, with your current understanding of how PHP4 deals with XML, you should have little trouble investigating the rest of the functionality if you are so inclined. As always, the complete reference can be found at the PHP web site (http://www.php.net/manual/).

# 15

# E-Mail Handling

In the last few years, e-mail has become one of the most widely used communication tools in the world, and is now a standard for many businesses. Consequently, as a web programmer, you'll have to build some sort of e-mail functionality into virtually all of your applications.

A shopping cart application, for example, will often use e-mail to send confirmation to a shopper after they place an order. Another confirmation may be sent once the ordered items have been shipped. The shopper might also want to subscribe to a newsletter to get the latest news on new products. Since e-mail is a highly cost-effective way to reach a large target audience, increasing sales and improving customer service, mass-mailing functionality is essential in such an application. Without the help of mailing list management applications, a site owner would have to hire a number of employees devoted to these tedious bits of work.

In this chapter, we'll explore PHP's e-mail capability and go over some of the rules for creating PHP e-mail scripts. Along the way, we'll also learn how to attach files to an e-mail. Finally, we'll build a complete e-mail script that can handle both individual e-mails and newsletter mailing lists.

## Sending E-mails in PHP

Here's some good news: the only function you need to learn about to send an e-mail within PHP is `mail()`. Isn't it painfully simple? The `mail()` function takes three essential arguments:

- ❑ the e-mail address of the intended recipient
- ❑ the subject of the e-mail
- ❑ the body of the e-mail

> *Both subject and body can be empty strings; that is, you can send an empty e-mail without a subject or body, with no ill effects.*

You can also specify an optional fourth argument; a string containing any additional headers. We'll look into this header argument shortly since it holds the key to many of the mysteries of e-mail.

Here's a catch, though. For the `mail()` function to work properly, you'll need to have specified a working local mail server in the `php.ini` file. There should already be a section looking something like this:

```
[mail function]
SMTP = localhost                                              ;for win32 only
sendmail_from = me@localhost.com                              ;for win32 only
;sendmail_path =                   ;for unix only, may supply arguments as well
                    (Defaults to local sendmail program - default is sendmail -t)
```

If you specify a remote SMTP outgoing server to relay your e-mail messages (which you can only do if you're running PHP on Windows), the server must be configured to allow relays; otherwise your e-mail messages will get bounced. These days, most mail servers will not allow relays, in order to block malicious spammers from using them as relay servers – so it's unlikely you'll be able to use your ISP's SMTP server, for example. If you're running a recent version of the IIS server on Windows NT, `localhost` should work since it comes with a built-in mail server. Refer to the online help for information on configuring it correctly.

On UNIX systems, PHP relies on the almost ubiquitous Sendmail program, or a compatible mail agent. Sendmail will be installed by default on almost any free UNIX (such as Linux or the BSD variants), and should be available even on commercial UNIXes. Sendmail is a simple program which handles the details of actually sending e-mail to the recipient's e-mail server, absolving PHP of the responsibility for knowing anything other than to tell Sendmail what it needs to do.

The `mail()` function itself is nothing but a wrapper that tosses the mail message over to the local mail system (Sendmail, or a nearby SMTP server). If there isn't one there to respond to the function, it's doomed to failure. Even if you have a working mail system, that doesn't mean the `mail()` function will always work. The function returns `True` when it successfully passes the given mail message to the local mail system. It doesn't care whether the message has actually been sent. Unfortunately, the command doesn't return `False` on failure – it just doesn't return at all, freezing execution of the script, and meaning the browser simply doesn't receive a response.

Now we're ready to look at a very simple script that sends an e-mail to someone. We'll put the text we want to send into three variables, and then pass them into the `mail()` function:

```php
<?php
//first_mail.php
$mail_to ="nobody@whatyoumaycallit.com";
$mail_subject = "Hi there!";
$mail_body = "We'll have a meeting next Wednesday.\n";
$mail_body .= "7 P.M. in Judy's Office.\n";
$mail_body .= "Oh, BYOB!\n";

if(mail($mail_to, $mail_subject, $mail_body))
          echo "Successfully sent the e-mail \"$mail_subject\" to $mail_to.";
else echo "Failed to send the e-mail \"$mail_subject\".";
?>
```

Note that it calls the `mail` function without the optional fourth argument. This is the simplest way of sending an e-mail to someone under PHP.

Say you want to send an e-mail to more than one person – you just need to pass `mail()` a list of addresses. Entries must be separated by commas, and not semicolons (as used in many e-mail clients). Suppose you have a text file holding dozens of your teammates' e-mail addresses, each separated by newlines, and want to send a copy of an e-mail to each one of them. Here's one way to do it:

```php
<?php
//mass_mail.php
$team_mates = "./teammates_email.txt";
$emails = file($team_mates);

for($i=0; $i < count($emails); $i++) $emails[$i] = trim($emails[$i]);
$recipients = implode(",", $emails);

$mail_subject = "Hi there!";
$mail_body = "We'll have a meeting next Wednesday.\n";
$mail_body .= "7 P.M. in Judy's Office.\n";
$mail_body .= "Oh, BYOB!\n";

mail($recipients, $mail_subject, $mail_body);
echo "Successfully sent the e-mail \"$mail_subject\" to $recipients.";
?>
```

First, we open the text file containing the teammates' e-mail addresses by calling the `file()` function (as introduced in Chapter 10). Recall that `file()` reads the entire contents of the specified file into an array, with a newline character on the end of each line. We therefore trim all whitespace (including the newlines) by placing the `trim()` function in a `for` loop that cycles through the `$emails` array. Next, the script calls the `implode()` function to join every element in the `$emails` array with a comma. Finally, the `mail()` function sends the e-mail to everyone in the e-mail file.

> While this is a very simple example, it's also a powerful bulk-mailer that can easily be used as a spam mailer (in other words, to send unsolicited e-mail to a large number of recipients). Spamming is considered illegal in many parts of the world, and is certainly not a desirable activity, wasting Internet bandwidth, and the time and download costs of the recipients. You should be careful not to use this kind of script to send unsolicited e-mails to those who don't want them.

That's practically all there is to it. However, what if you want to specify who it was that sent the e-mail? Perhaps you want the recipient(s) to reply to a designated e-mail address which is different from that of the sender, to redirect responses to other departments in your company, for example? What if you want to send copies of the e-mail to others?

To answer these and other questions, we'll need to get an overview of the essential structure of an e-mail. Get a scalpel – it's time for dissection.

# Anatomy of an E-Mail

An e-mail message is actually nothing more than a plain text file, consisting of a number of headers and a message body. A typical e-mail message looks like this (refer to the RFC 822 at http://www.rfc.net/ for further information):

```
From orders@never_sell_anything.com Sun Jul 16 01:18:01 2000
Return-Path: <orders@never_sell_anything.com>
Received: (from nobody@localhost)
        by mail.never_sell_anything.com (8.9.3/8.9.3) id BAA06100;
        Sun, 16 Jul 2000 01:18:01 +0900
Date: Sun, 16 Jul 2000 01:18:01 +0900
Message-Id: <200007151618.BAA06100@mail.never_sell_anything.com>
To: deadbeat@never_buy_anything.com
Subject: Your order!
From: orders@never_sell_anything.com
Reply-to: service@never_sell_anything.com
Cc: service@never_sell_anything.com

Order Number: #ZILLION-1
Your order information appears below.  If you need to get in touch with us about
your order, just reply to this message.

Blah Blah Blah...
```

An e-mail message consists of a set of newline-separated headers followed by two more newlines and the message body.

Strictly speaking, header fields must be separated by a carriage return/line feed (CR LF) pair. Although this is the standard newline character \n for Windows platforms, you will need to exercise care with respect to UNIX systems, which use LF alone as a newline; where stated explicitly, use the combination \r\n.

A **header field** either represents an instruction to an e-mail program or summarizes the nature and structure of an e-mail message. The second half of this chapter goes into greater detail about the latter set, but for now let's focus on the former. As you can see, each header consists of a title, followed by a colon and some whitespace, and then some information. Note also that although it looks like a header, the Order Number line on the e-mail above comes after the two newlines which separate the headers from the message body, so will be treated as part of the message.

The header fields you will most commonly encounter include:

| | |
|---|---|
| To: | A comma-separated list of e-mail recipients. |
| From: | The sender's e-mail address. |
| Reply-to: | The e-mail address to which replies should be sent. |
| Cc: | Carbon Copy – A comma-separated list of additional recipients. |
| Subject: | The message's subject |

There's one more common header that won't appear on incoming e-mails. If it does, something must have gone seriously wrong, since it's specifically intended not to appear in the headers. Bcc, short for *Blind Carbon Copy*, is used to send copies of an e-mail to people who don't want their addresses to appear in other recipients' headers. In other words, nobody else getting the e-mail would know that these people had been sent the same message.

Note also that a lot of the headers on the e-mail example shown aren't set by the person or program which sends the e-mail – they're set by the servers it passes through. Timestamps, information about the hosts it has been handled by, and automatically generated ID numbers are all added by servers.

Extra headers can be added to an e-mail message by passing the optional fourth parameter to mail(). For example, if you wanted to set From and Reply-to header fields to an e-mail address other than your own, you would use the following mail() function call:

```
mail("someone@a.com","Hi there!","Hello!",
                "From: spammer@b.com\r\nReply-to: spammer2@b.com");
```

Note again that multiple headers need to be separated by a CR LF combo. The above mail() function call will send an e-mail to someone@a.com; as far as the recipient is concerned though, it has been sent by spammer@b.com, and his replies would be sent to spammer2@b.com.

You can specify Cc and Bcc fields much the same way:

```
mail("someone@a.com","Hi there!","Hello!",
                "From: spammer@b.com\r\nReply-to: spammer2@b.com\r\n
                Cc: someoneelse@a.com\r\nBcc: mole@a.com");
```

This will send a total of three copies of the mail. Once we've done this:

❑   someone@a.com can see that someoneelse@a.com was also sent a copy.

❑   someoneelse@a.com can see that someone@a.com was sent the original.

❑   mole@a.com can see that both of the above were sent copies of the mail.

Note that *neither* of the first two would know that mole@a.com had also been sent a copy.

Now that we've seen the mail() function in action, let's try something a little more ambitious and write a custom e-mail function.

## Try It Out – A Simple E-Mailer

We're now going to create a web interface from which you can edit each of the header fields we've examined and send a customized e-mail. Our script will make use of seven custom functions and a global variable $action, which when specified tells the script which action should be taken. This format should be pretty familiar by now.

**1.**   We start by defining mailer_header(), which simply starts an HTML page:

```php
<?php
//simple_mailer.php

function mailer_header()
{
?>
<HTML>
<HEAD><TITLE>E-mailer</TITLE></HEAD>
<BODY>
<?php
}
```

**2.** Next, to end an HTML page, we have `mailer_footer()`:

```php
function mailer_footer()
{
?>
</BODY>
</HTML>
<?php
}
```

**3.** We define `error_message()` to report errors using the JavaScript `alert()` method:

```php
function error_message($msg)
{
   mailer_header();
   echo "<SCRIPT>alert(\"Error: $msg\");history.go(-1)</SCRIPT>";
   mailer_footer();
   exit;
}
```

**4.** Similarly, we have `user_message()` to report the result of an action, once again using the JavaScript `alert()` method:

```php
function user_message($msg)
{
   mailer_header();
   echo "<SCRIPT>alert(\"$msg\");history.go(-1)</SCRIPT>";
   mailer_footer();
   exit;
}
```

**5.** The main web interface for sending e-mail is displayed by `mail_form()`:

```php
function mail_form()
{
   global $PHP_SELF;
?>
<FORM METHOD="POST" ENCTYPE="MULTIPART/FORM-DATA"
      ACTION="<?php echo $PHP_SELF ?>">
<INPUT TYPE="hidden" NAME="action" VALUE="send_mail">
```

```
<DIV ALIGN="CENTER ">
<TABLE CELLSPACING="2" CELLPADDING="5" WIDTH="90%" BORDER="1">
   <TR>
      <TH ALIGN="CENTER" WIDTH="30%">To</TH>
      <TD WIDTH="70%"><INPUT NAME="mail_to" SIZE="20"></TD>
   </TR>
   <TR>
      <TH ALIGN="CENTER" WIDTH="30%">Cc</TH>
      <TD WIDTH="70%"><INPUT NAME="mail_cc" SIZE="20"></TD>
   </TR>
   <TR>
      <TH ALIGN="CENTER" WIDTH="30%">Bcc</TH>
      <TD WIDTH="70%"><INPUT NAME="mail_bcc" SIZE="20"></TD>
   </TR>
   <TR>
      <TH ALIGN="CENTER" WIDTH="30%">From</TH>
      <TD WIDTH="70%"><INPUT SIZE="20" NAME="mail_from"></TD>
   </TR>
   <TR>
      <TH ALIGN="CENTER" WIDTH="30%">Reply-To</TH>
      <TD WIDTH="70%"><INPUT SIZE="20" NAME="mail_reply_to"></TD>
   </TR>
   <TR>
      <TH ALIGN="CENTER" WIDTH="30%">Subject</TH>
      <TD WIDTH="70%"><INPUT SIZE="40" NAME="mail_subject"></TD>
   </TR>
   <TR>
      <TH ALIGN="CENTER" WIDTH="30%">Body</TH>
      <TD WIDTH="70%"><TEXTAREA NAME="mail_body" ROWS="16"
         COLS="70"></TEXTAREA></TD>
   </TR>
   <TR>
      <TH WIDTH="100%" COLSPAN="2" ALIGN="CENTER">
         <INPUT TYPE="SUBMIT" VALUE="Send" NAME="SUBMIT">
         <INPUT TYPE="RESET" VALUE="Reset" NAME="RESET">
      </TH>
   </TR>
</TABLE>
</DIV>
</FORM>
<?php
}
```

**6.** In send_mail(), we define a wrapper function that calls my_mail() and reports the result:

```
function send_mail()
{
   global $mail_to, $mail_cc, $mail_bcc, $mail_from, $mail_reply_to;
   global $mail_body, $mail_subject;

   $mail_parts["mail_to"] = $mail_to;
   $mail_parts["mail_from"] = $mail_from;
   $mail_parts["mail_reply_to"] = $mail_reply_to;
   $mail_parts["mail_cc"] = $mail_cc;
   $mail_parts["mail_bcc"] = $mail_bcc;
   $mail_parts["mail_subject"] = trim($mail_subject);
```

```
    $mail_parts["mail_body"] = $mail_body;

    if(my_mail($mail_parts))
        user_message("Successfully sent an e-mail titled '$mail_subject'.");

    else error_message("An unknown error occurred while attempting to
                                send an e-mail titled '$mail_subject'.");
}
```

**7.** We shall use `my_mail()` to actually send the user-defined e-mail:

```
function my_mail($mail_parts)
{
    $mail_to = $mail_parts["mail_to"];
    $mail_from = $mail_parts["mail_from"];
    $mail_reply_to = $mail_parts["mail_reply_to"];
    $mail_cc = $mail_parts["mail_cc"];
    $mail_bcc = $mail_parts["mail_bcc"];
    $mail_subject = $mail_parts["mail_subject"];
    $mail_body = $mail_parts["mail_body"];

    if(empty($mail_to)) error_message("Empty to field!");
    if(empty($mail_subject)) error_message("Empty subject!");
    if(empty($mail_body)) error_message("Empty body! ");

    $mail_to = str_replace(";", ",", $mail_to);

    $mail_headers = '';

    if(!empty($mail_from)) $mail_headers .= "From: $mail_from\n";
    if(!empty($mail_reply_to)) $mail_headers .= "Reply-to: $mail_reply_to\n";
    if(!empty($mail_cc))
            $mail_headers .= "Cc: " . str_replace(";", ",", $mail_cc) . "\n";
    if(!empty($mail_bcc))
            $mail_headers .= "Bcc: " . str_replace(";", ",", $mail_bcc) . "\n";

    $mail_subject = stripslashes($mail_subject);
    $mail_body = stripslashes($mail_body);

    return mail($mail_to,$mail_subject,$mail_body,$mail_headers);
}
```

**8.** Finally, we have a switch block that uses our global variable `$action` to determine which functions to call. If `$action` is unspecified, we default to the `mail_form()` function:

```
switch ($action)
{
    case "send_mail":
        mailer_header();
        send_mail();
        mailer_footer();
        break;
    case "mail_form":
```

```
        mailer_header();
        mail_form();
        mailer_footer();
        break;
    default:
        mailer_header();
        mail_form();
        mailer_footer();
        break;
    }
?>
```

**9.** Save the finished script as `simple_mailer.php` and put it in the appropriate directory.

**10.** Here's a sample run of the script. The `mail_form()` function displays a web-style user interface for sending an e-mail:

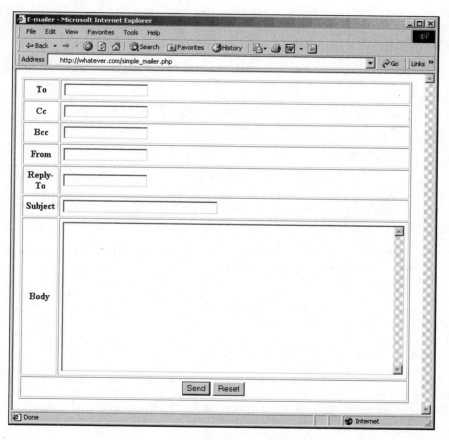

### How It Works

Since the others are fairly self-explanatory, we're just going to take a look at the key function: my_mail(). This function takes an associative array that holds header field information, along with e-mail subject and body contents.

First, it tests to see whether the variables $mail_to, $mail_subject, and $mail_body are empty. If any of them are, it calls error_message() to warn the user accordingly:

```
if(empty($mail_to)) error_message("Empty to field!");
if(empty($mail_subject)) error_message("Empty subject!");
if(empty($mail_body)) error_message("Empty body!");
```

If you want the script to be able to send an empty e-mail, remove the last two statements that test the $mail_subject and $mail_body variables.

Next, it initializes the $mail_headers variable to an empty string:

```
$mail_headers = '';
```

Variables $mail_from, $mail_reply_to, $mail_cc, and $mail_bcc are tested for contents. As long as they're not empty, they are added to the $mail_headers variable with a trailing CR LF:

```
if(!empty($mail_from)) $mail_headers .= "From: $mail_from\r\n";
if(!empty($mail_reply_to)) $mail_headers .= "Reply-to: $mail_reply_to\r\n";
if(!empty($mail_cc))
        $mail_headers .= "Cc: " . str_replace(";", ",", $mail_cc) . "\r\n";
if(!empty($mail_bcc))
        $mail_headers .= "Bcc: " . str_replace(";", ",", $mail_bcc) . "\r\n";
```

Note that the function uses str_replace() to replace any occurrence of a semicolon with a comma, just in case the user has separated multiple recipients with a semicolon.

Finally, the function strips any slashes that may have been applied to the message's subject and body, and calls the mail() function to actually send the e-mail:

```
$mail_subject = stripslashes(trim($mail_subject));
$mail_body = stripslashes($mail_body);
return mail($mail_to,$mail_subject,$mail_body,$mail_headers);
```

Note that we also trim() the mail subject, in order to remove any trailing whitespace.

If you want to strip out any HTML or PHP tags that have sneaked their way into the subject or body, you can use the strip_tags() function to root them out. This function also ensures that only text is used in the mail message. We could replace the second line above with:

```
$mail_body = strip_tags(stripslashes($mail_body));
```

Since my_mail() is called by the wrapper function send_mail(), it returns the return value from the mail() function, thereby indicating whether the e-mail was submitted successfully.

Remember though – even if the `mail()` function returns `True`, it doesn't guarantee that the e-mail has been successfully delivered to the recipient(s), only that it has been successfully submitted to the local mail system.

Now, it's time to look a little further into the anatomy of an e-mail. Sharpen up that scalpel!

# Handling Attachments

The e-mail script we made in the previous section is good enough for most web applications in need of e-mail functionality, but it lacks a couple of important features of modern e-mail software: MIME handling and attachments. **MIME**, Multipurpose Internet Mail Extensions, is a specification for enhancing the capabilities of standard e-mail. It provides a simple but standardized way to represent and encode a wide variety of media types for transmission via e-mail. In plain English: you can send more than just plain text in a MIME e-mail.

Using the MIME standards, an e-mail can contain the following:

❑   Text messages in the US-ASCII character set.

❑   Character sets other than US-ASCII.

❑   Non-textual media including image, audio, and video

❑   Binary files

❑   Messages of unlimited length

For example, if you're living in a country where 8-bit multi-byte characters are used in computing, our original script will be unusable for most situations, since it supports only 7-bit ASCII characters, which can only encode the basic characters of standard English. MIME, on the other hand, gives you a lot more control over how the message should be interpreted.

At first glance, attaching files can seem like a daunting task. However, it's not as overwhelming as it may appear. An attachment is nothing more than specially encoded text data. When you attach a file to your e-mail message, all you have to do is encode the file into mail-friendly text and specify for the recipient which encoding method was used to pack the data into the mail body, so they know how to extract it.

## Anatomy of E-Mail Revisited

We saw before what goes into a regular e-mail; here's what a MIME e-mail looks like:

```
From orders@never_sell_anything.com Sun Jul 16 01:18:01 2000
Return-Path: <orders@never_sell_anything.com>
Received: (from nobody@localhost)
        by mail.never_sell_anything.com (8.9.3/8.9.3) id BAA06100;
        Sun, 16 Jul 2000 01:18:01 +0900
Date: Sun, 16 Jul 2000 01:18:01 +0900
Message-Id: <200007151618.BAA06100@mail.never_sell_anything.com>
To: deadbeat@never_buy_anything.com
Subject: Your order!
From: orders@never_sell_anything.com
```

```
Reply-to: service@never_sell_anything.com
Cc: service@never_sell_anything.com
MIME-Version: 1.0
Content-type: multipart/mixed;boundary="01fedcb871d3f012e43680250ba5ca3f"

This is a multi-part message in MIME format.

--01fedcb871d3f012e43680250ba5ca3f
Content-type:text/plain;charset=us-ascii
Content-transfer-encoding:7bit

Order Number: #ZILLION-1
Your order information is attached as a file below.  If you need to get in touch
with us about your order, just reply to this message.

Blah Blah Blah...
--01fedcb871d3f012e43680250ba5ca3f
Content-type:application/octet-stream;name=order.dat
Content-transfer-encoding:base64
```

cmVtIC0gQnkgV2luZG93cyA5OCBOZXR3b3JrIC0gQzpcV0lORE9XU1xuZXQgQgc3RhcnQQNC1NFVCBC
..............
YXRyb3hcdXRpbFxwWYmV4dC5leGUNCg0K

```
--01fedcb871d3f012e43680250ba5ca3f--
```

## Content-type

To use a different character set or data format, you must explicitly specify the character set and data format using the `Content-type` header field. In other words, if the `Content-type` header field is omitted, a local e-mail program will generally assume the following:

```
Content-type: text/plain; charset=us-ascii
```

What if you want to send an HTML e-mail using a richer character set than US-ASCII, say, a Korean character set? The following `Content-type` header explicitly specifies the message contains an HTML text file using a Korean character set:

```
Content-type: text/html; charset=euc-kr
```

As you have probably noticed, some header fields may be fed more than one item of information. The additional information assigned to a header field is called a **parameter** and is separated by a semicolon, as in the above example.

The `Content-type` header field is used to specify the **type** and **subtype** of data in the body of a message, and to specify the encoding of such data. Possible types include text, image, audio, video, multipart, application, and many more. A media type of `image/gif`, for example, indicates that the message body contains a GIF image.

Since no default value for a subtype is presumed, subtypes cannot be omitted; that is, either `text` or `video` alone has no significance. They should be explicitly specified as `text/html` and `video/mpeg`, for example.

Unrecognized types should be treated as `application/octet-stream` to denote that the message body contains binary data. An octet stream is simply a way of saying that the data is a stream of eight-bit numbers, or octets. In other words, the characters should not be interpreted as characters, but as binary numbers. The receiving e-mail program will deal with this by offering to save the data to a file.

If a message contains a known application type, such as `application/msword` for example, the e-mail program will call the corresponding application program to deal with the data.

## Content-transfer-encoding

Many content types that could usefully be transmitted by e-mail are naturally represented as 8-bit character or binary data. Such data, however, cannot be transported over certain transport protocols, such as SMTP, which restricts e-mail messages to 7-bit US-ASCII data with lines no longer than 1000 characters. MIME provides a mechanism for overcoming this limitation: the `Content-transfer-encoding` header field. This is used to specify an **encoding transformation** that has been applied to the message body; this will convert the native format to a protocol-friendly one, and once it's been received, a reciprocal transformation will convert it back.

The `Content-transfer-encoding` field's value is a single token specifying the type of encoding; usually `7bit`, `8bit`, `binary`, `quoted-printable`, or `base64`. An encoding type of `7bit` requires that the message body be already in a 7-bit mail-ready representation. This is the default value, so in the absence of the field, `Content-transfer-encoding: 7bit` is assumed.

An `8bit` encoding type is usually required for transmitting e-mails using 8-bit multi-byte characters. For example, most Asian languages (and a number of European ones) store characters in 8-bit format.

```
Content-type: text/plain; charset=euc-kr
Content-transfer-encoding: 8bit
```

The above headers will transmit an e-mail message using a Korean character set in 8-bit data format.

The `quoted-printable` and `base64` encoding types transform data into 7-bit format, making it quite safe to carry over restricted transports. However, the former doesn't work reliably with some mail transports, leaving `base64` as sole candidate for the most reliable encoding type for transferring non-textual data. Note that both `quoted-printable` and `base64` encoded data must be represented in lines of no more than 76 characters.

## MIME-Version

We won't explore every nook and cranny of the MIME specifications here, leaving the full discussion to more advanced books. However, there's one more header field that needs a mention: although it's the last one we cover here, the `MIME-Version` field must be placed before any of the others.

It declares that a message is conformant with MIME specifications, and allows e-mail programs to distinguish MIME messages from those generated by older (or non-conformant) software, which are presumed to lack such a field. Messages composed in accordance with the MIME standards must include this header field with the following verbatim text:

```
MIME-Version: 1.0
```

## *Multiple Mail Components*

To incorporate non-textual data into an e-mail, the `Content-type` header field value should be a **multipart** media type. This allows one or more different sets of data to be combined in a single message body. The multipart media type also supports a number of subtypes, of which we'll be using `mixed` for attaching generic mixed sets of data to an e-mail.

The multipart media type messages must contain one or more body parts, each beginning with a header area followed by a blank line, and a body area. No header fields are actually required in body parts. A body part that starts with a blank line is assumed to be using default values. Therefore, the absence of a `Content-type` header indicates that the corresponding body has a `Content-type` of `text/plain;charset=us-ascii`.

The `Content-type` header field for multipart e-mail messages requires one parameter, `boundary`:

```
Content-type: multipart/mixed; boundary="123456789"
```

The body parts must be preceded by **boundary delimiter lines**, each one containing two hyphen characters, `--`, followed by the boundary parameter value from the `Content-type` header field (in this example, `12345678`) and a CR LF character to terminate the line:

```
--12345678
```

The boundary delimiter line is considered terminated by a CR LF character and the header fields for the next part, or by two CRLF characters – in which case there are no header fields for the next part.

Boundary delimiters must be no longer than 70 characters, not counting the two leading hyphens.

The boundary delimiter line following the last body part is distinguished by a pair of hyphens that follow the boundary parameter value, and this indicates that no further body parts will follow:

```
--123456789--
```

Since it is used specifically to identify separate body parts, the boundary delimiter mustn't appear inside any of the encapsulated parts. It's therefore crucial that your e-mail script uses a unique boundary parameter value that will never occur in the enclosed body. For example, the following will work just fine until you find the characters `--12345678` in the body of plain text:

```
MIME-Version: 1.0
Content-type: multipart/mixed; boundary="123456789"

This is a multi-part message in MIME format.

--12345678
Content-type:text/plain;charset=us-ascii
Content-transfer-encoding:7bit

Order Number
--12345678
```

```
Your order information is attached as a file below.  If you need to get in touch
with us about your order, just reply to this message.

Blah Blah Blah...
--12345678
Content-type:application/octet-stream;name=order.dat
Content-transfer-encoding:base64

cmVtIC0gQnkgV21uZG93cyA5OCBOZXR3b3JrIC0gQzpcV01ORE9XU1xuZXQQgc3RhcnQNC1NFVCBC
...............
YXRyb3hcdXRpbFxYWmV4dC51eGUNCg0K

--12345678--
```

For this reason a real e-mail message with a MIME-conformant attachment was shown at the beginning of this section. Take another look at it, and you'll see the boundary parameter made up of 32 hexadecimal digits (that is, characters 0-9 and a-f):

```
Content-type: multipart/mixed;boundary="01fedcb871d3f012e43680250ba5ca3f"
```

This is the result of representing a 128-bit value in hex, one very effective way to minimize the risk of in-body occurrences. Select a new 128-bit number at random, and the odds of it appearing in the e-mail are practically non-existant.

# Attaching Files to E-Mail

Now the fun begins. Suppose you want to attach a word document "project.doc" in the current directory to an e-mail. Assuming you've already defined values $mail_to, $mail_subject, $mail_body as you would for a simple e-mail, you must then take the following steps:

**11.** Set up the MIME headers.

Use a multiple function call to ensure that a unique boundary delimiter is created:

```
$mail_boundary = md5(uniqid(time()));
```

The time() function returns the current time in a UNIX timestamp format (don't worry – it's a UNIX format, but it works just the same on Windows), which is used as a seed for the uniqid() function to produce a unique identifier.

In turn, the outermost function, md5(), generates a 32-character boundary delimiter to ensure that no repeated IDs will be generated. The md5() function is based on an algorithm that takes a string of arbitrary length and uses it to generate a scrambled key. Since there are $2^{128}$ possible key values (that's of the order of 340 billion billion billion billion), it is almost impossible to produce two keys with the same value – using md5(), we therefore ensure that the possibility of generating duplicate ID's is almost nil.

This is important because it's possible that someone might want to attach a copy of an e-mail to another e-mail – and if the MIME boundaries were the same, the MIME separation at the receiving end would get confused.

The `MIME-Version` header field must come before any other MIME headers:

```
$mail_headers = "MIME-Version: 1.0\r\n";
```

Set the `Content-type` header field to `multipart/mixed` indicating that one or more different sets of data are encapsulated in the message and assign the `$mail_boundary` variable to the boundary parameter:

```
$mail_headers .= "Content-type: multipart/mixed;boundary=\"$mail_boundary \"";
```

Following two sets of CR LF characters, insert a message for display by older e-mail clients which are non-conformant with the MIME specifications:

```
$mail_headers .= "\r\n\r\n";
$mail_headers .= "This is a multi-part message in MIME format.";
```

Insert another two CR LF sets again to indicate the end of the header part of the message:

```
$mail_headers .= "\r\n\r\n";
```

**12.** Open up the file you want to attach to the e-mail.

```
$userfile = "./projects.doc";
$fp = fopen($userfile, "r");
$file = fread($fp, filesize($userfile));
```

**13.** Encode the file contents as a single long string, `$file`, and split it up into sets of 76 characters, which you'll recall is the maximum length allowed for lines of encoded data.

PHP provides two functions that can be used together to achieve this goal:

| | |
|---|---|
| `base64_encode(data)` | This takes data in the form of a string, and returns the same data having encoded in the `base64` encoding type. |
| `chunk_split(data, length, delimiter)` | This splits a given string of data into smaller chunks by inserting the string `delimiter` after every `length` characters. These parameters default to '76' and 'CR LF ' respectively if the last two parameters are omitted. |

We therefore say:

```
$file = chunk_split(base64_encode($file));
```

**14.** Set up the message body, enclosed by copies of the unique boundary delimiter created in Step 1:

```
$mail_body = "--$mail_boundary\n";
$mail_body.= "Content-type: text/plain; charset=euc-kr\r\n";
$mail_body .= "Content-transfer-encoding: 8bit\r\n\r\n";
$mail_body .= " Here goes the project document.\r\n";
```

```
$mail_body .= "--$mail_boundary\r\n";
$filename = basename($userfile);
```

Set the `Content-type` header field to the file's media type, and assign the filename extracted from the `$userfile` variable to the additional parameter "name". In this case, we're going to open a Microsoft Word document (`application/msword`), so we put:

```
$mail_body .= "Content-type: application/msword; name=$filename\r\n";
```

Specify that base64 content transfer encoding has been applied:

```
$mail_body .= "Content-transfer-encoding:base64\r\n\r\n";
```

**15.** Attach the base64-encoded string from the file content:

```
$mail_body .= $file. "\r\n\r\n";
```

**16.** Terminate the message using the closing boundary delimiter with trailing two hyphens indicating there's no more data:

```
$mail_body .= " --$mail_boundary--";
```

**17.** Finally, send the e-mail message:

```
mail($mail_to, $mail_subject, $mail_body, $mail_headers);
```

The resulting e-mail will look something like the following:

```
From whatyoumaycallit  Sun Aug 13 16:59:02 2000
Return-Path: <info@whatyoumaycallit.com>
Received: (from nobody@localhost)
        by mail.whatyoumaycallit.com (8.9.3/8.9.3) id QAA10075;
        Sun, 13 Aug 2000 16:59:02 +0900
Date: Sun, 13 Aug 2000 16:59:02 +0900
Message-Id: <200008130759.QAA10075@mail.whatyoumaycallit.com>
To: john@nosuchsite.com
Subject: A MIME mail!
From: jill@whatyoumaycallit.com
Reply-to: jill@whatyoumaycallit.com
Cc: doe@nosuchsite.com
MIME-Version: 1.0
Content-type: multipart/mixed;boundary="8a4ce7464a3b5ae557974aa7ad70279c"

This is a multi-part message in MIME format.

--8a4ce7464a3b5ae557974aa7ad70279c
Content-type:text/plain;charset=euc-kr
Content-transfer-encoding:8bit

Here goes the body.
```

```
--8a4ce7464a3b5ae557974aa7ad70279c
Content-type:application/octet-stream;name=Autoexec.bat
Content-transfer-encoding:base64

cmVtIC0gQnkgV21uZG93cyA5OCBOZXR3b3JrIC0gQzpcV01ORE9XU1xuZXXQgc3RhcnQQNC1NFVCBC
...
YXRyb3hcdXRpbFxWYmV4dC51eGUNCg0K

--8a4ce7464a3b5ae557974aa7ad70279c--
```

With that and the previous sections under your belt, you should now know enough to be able to modify the simple e-mail script we made in the first half of this chapter so that it can handle MIME headers and attachments. So without further ado...

## Try It Out – An Advanced E-Mailer

Let's copy our first, simple e-mail example and rename it adv_mail.php. We now need to add extra input fields to the user form:

❏ mail_type – specifies whether the message contains a text/plain or text/html media type, defaulting to the former. The latter enables you to send an HTML e-mail. If a file is attached to the e-mail, it will also default to text/plain regardless of the user's choice.

❏ mail_encoding – specifies whether the message contains 7bit or 8bit data, defaulting to the former.

❏ mail_charset – specifies the character set used in the message, defaulting to US-ASCII. This and EUC-KR (Korean) character sets are provided as options, but you can add more character sets to suit your needs. A list of registered character sets can be found at ftp://ftp.isi.edu/in-notes/iana/assignments/character-sets. For more information, refer to RFC 2278 at http://www.rfc.net.

❏ userfile – enables the user to upload a file from the local machine and attach it to an e-mail.

We modify our original function as follows:

```
function mail_form() {
    global $PHP_SELF;
?>
<FORM METHOD="POST" ENCTYPE="MULTIPART/FORM-DATA" ACTION="<?php echo $PHP_SELF
?>">
<INPUT TYPE="HIDDEN" NAME="action" VALUE="send_mail">
<DIV ALIGN="CENTER ">
<TABLE CELLSPACING="2" CELLPADDING="5" WIDTH="90%" BORDER="1">
    ...
    <TR>
        <TH ALIGN="CENTER" WIDTH="30%">Reply-to</TH>
        <TD WIDTH="70%"><INPUT SIZE="20" NAME="mail_reply_to"></TD>
    </TR>
    <TR>
        <TH ALIGN="CENTER" WIDTH="30%">Attachment</TH>
        <TD WIDTH="70%"><INPUT TYPE="FILE" NAME="userfile"></TD>
    </TR>
    <TR>
```

```
        <TH ALIGN="CENTER" WIDTH="30%">Type</TH>
        <TD WIDTH="70%">
        <INPUT TYPE="RADIO" VALUE="text" NAME="mail_type" CHECKED>TEXT
        <INPUT TYPE="RADIO" VALUE="html" NAME="mail_type">HTML</TD>
    </TR>
    <TR>
        <TH ALIGN="CENTER" WIDTH="30%">Encoding</TH>
        <TD WIDTH="70%">
        <INPUT TYPE="RADIO" VALUE="7bit" NAME="mail_encoding" CHECKED>7BIT
        <INPUT TYPE="RADIO" VALUE="8bit" NAME="mail_encoding">8BIT</TD>
    </TR>
    <TR>
        <TH ALIGN="CENTER" WIDTH="30%">Character Set</TH>
        <TD WIDTH="70%">
        <INPUT TYPE="RADIO" VALUE="us-ascii" NAME="mail_charset" CHECKED>US-ASCII
        <INPUT TYPE="RADIO" VALUE="euc-kr" NAME="mail_charset">EUC-KR</TD>
    </TR>
    <TR>
        <TH ALIGN="CENTER" WIDTH="30%">Subject</TH>
        <TD WIDTH="70%"><INPUT SIZE="40" NAME="mail_subject"></TD>
    </TR>
    ...
</TABLE>
</DIV>
</FORM>
<?php
}
```

The user interface should now look something like this:

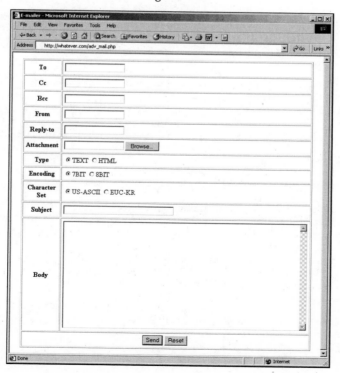

Here's the new, improved version of my_mail():

```
function my_mail($mail_parts) {

    $mail_to = $mail_parts["mail_to"];
    ...
    $mail_body = $mail_parts["mail_body"];
```

Our first change is to fetch the extra values stored in the $mail_parts associative array:

```
    $mail_type = $mail_parts["mail_type"];
    $mail_charset = $mail_parts["mail_charset"];
    $mail_encoding = $mail_parts["mail_encoding"];

    $userfile = $mail_parts["userfile"];
    $userfile_type = $mail_parts["userfile_type"];
    $userfile_name = $mail_parts["userfile_name"];
    $userfile_size = $mail_parts["userfile_size"];

    if(empty($mail_to)) error_message("Empty to field!");
    if(empty($mail_subject)) error_message("Empty subject!");
    if(empty($mail_body)) error_message("Empty body!");
    ...
```

We then add MIME-specific headers and content, according to the options specified on the form:

```
    ...
    $mail_subject = stripslashes($mail_subject);
    $mail_body = stripslashes($mail_body);

    if($userfile_size > 0)
    {
        $mail_boundary = md5(uniqid(time()));
        $mail_headers .= "MIME-Version: 1.0\r\n";
        $mail_headers .= "Content-type: multipart/mixed;
                                    boundary=\"$mail_boundary\"\r\n\r\n";
        $mail_headers .= "This is a multi-part message in MIME format.\r\n\r\n";

        $fp = fopen($userfile, "r");
        $file = fread($fp, filesize($userfile));
        $file = chunk_split(base64_encode($file));

        $new_mail_body = "--$mail_boundary\r\n";
        $new_mail_body .= "Content-type:text/plain;charset=$mail_charset\r\n";
        $new_mail_body .= "Content-transfer-encoding:$mail_encoding\r\n\r\n";
        $new_mail_body .= "$mail_body\r\n";
        $new_mail_body .= "--$mail_boundary\r\n";
        if(!empty($userfile_type)) $mime_type = $userfile_type;
        else $mime_type = "application/octet-stream";

        $new_mail_body .= "Content-type:$mime_type;name=$userfile_name\r\n";
        $new_mail_body .= "Content-transfer-encoding:base64\r\n\r\n";
        $new_mail_body .= $file . "\r\n\r\n";
        $new_mail_body .= "--$mail_boundary--";
        $mail_body = $new_mail_body;
    }
```

```
        else if($mail_type == 'html')
        {
            $mail_headers .= "Content-type: text/html; charset=$mail_charset\r\n";
            $mail_headers .= "Content-transfer-encoding:$mail_encoding\r\n\r\n";
        }
        else
        {
            $mail_headers .= "Content-type: text/plain; charset=$mail_charset\r\n";
            $mail_headers .= "Content-transfer-encoding:$mail_encoding\r\n\r\n";
        }
```

```
    return mail($mail_to,$mail_subject,$mail_body,$mail_headers);
}
```

Note that $userfile, $userfile_type, $userfile_name, and $userfile_size only become available when the user uploads a local file to the server. The send_mail() wrapper function should also be modified to pass these values over to the my_mail() function:

```
function send_mail() {
...
```

```
global $userfile, $userfile_type, $userfile_name, $userfile_size;
global $mail_type, $mail_charset, $mail_encoding;

$mail_parts["mail_type"] = $mail_type;
$mail_parts["mail_charset"] = $mail_charset;
$mail_parts["mail_encoding"] = $mail_encoding;

$mail_parts["userfile"] = $userfile;
$mail_parts["userfile_type"] = $userfile_type;
$mail_parts["userfile_name"] = $userfile_name;
$mail_parts["userfile_size"] = $userfile_size;
...
}
```

### How It Works

After setting up variables and the usual message headers in my_mail(), we test the variable $userfile_size as follows:

❑   If $userfile_size is greater than zero, this indicates that the user has uploaded a local file to the server. The function then sets up additional MIME headers and prepares the file for attachment, following the steps we illustrated in the previous section:

```
if($userfile_size > 0)
{
    $mail_boundary = md5(uniqid(time()));
    $mail_headers .= "MIME-Version: 1.0\r\n";
    $mail_headers .= "Content-type: multipart/mixed;
                                boundary=\"$mail_boundary\"\r\n\r\n";
    $mail_headers .= "This is a multi-part message in MIME format.\r\n\r\n";

    $fp = fopen($userfile, "r");
    $file = fread($fp, filesize($userfile));
    $file = chunk_split(base64_encode($file));
```

```
$new_mail_body = "--$mail_boundary\r\n";
$new_mail_body .= "Content-type:text/plain;charset=$mail_charset\r\n";
$new_mail_body .= "Content-transfer-encoding:$mail_encoding\r\n\r\n";
$new_mail_body .= "$mail_body\r\n";
$new_mail_body .= "--$mail_boundary\r\n";
```

If $userfile_type is not set (leaving the function unable to determine the media type of the file uploaded) the default media type application/octet-stream is assigned:

```
if(!empty($userfile_type)) $mime_type = $userfile_type;
else $mime_type = "application/octet-stream";

$new_mail_body .= "Content-type:$mime_type;name=$userfile_name\r\n";
$new_mail_body .= "Content-transfer-encoding:base64\r\n\r\n";
$new_mail_body .= $file . "\r\n\r\n";
$new_mail_body .= "--$mail_boundary--";
$mail_body = $new_mail_body;
}
```

❑  If $userfile_size is not greater than zero, the user didn't upload a local file to the server. We therefore check the $mail_type variable to set the Content-type header field accordingly. The charset parameter and Content-transfer-encoding header fields are assigned according to the contents of $mail_encoding and $mail_charset variables respectively:

```
else if($mail_type == 'html')
{
    $mail_headers .= "Content-type: text/html; charset=$mail_charset\r\n";
    $mail_headers .= "Content-transfer-encoding:$mail_encoding\r\n\r\n";
}
else
{
    $mail_headers .= "Content-type: text/plain; charset=$mail_charset\r\n";
    $mail_headers .= "Content-transfer-encoding:$mail_encoding\r\n\r\n";
}
```

Finally, we send the e-mail and return to the calling function:

```
return mail($mail_to, $mail_subject, $new_mail_body, $mail_headers);
```

# A Newsletter Mailing List Manager

We're now going to go one step further, and create a script that not only covers all we've done in previous examples, but also incorporates mass-mailing functionality. The newsletter mailing list manager we're going to build has the following features:

❑  It can send both regular and MIME e-mail to individuals.

❑  It can create a newsletter mailing list, which users can both subscribe to and unsubscribe from.

❑  It can display a list of subscribers to a newsletter, and let the administrator remove any of them.

❏ It can send a newsletter to each of its subscribers in a separate, user-specified format: text, HTML, zip, or Microsoft Word document.

Users can subscribe to (or unsubscribe from) a newsletter by means of a subscription script. Given the user's e-mail address, this little script will show whether that user is currently subscribed to any of the available newsletters. It will also give them the option of ending any of these subscriptions or starting a new one.

> *The administration and user scripts both rely on MySQL for their back ends. You may want to refer back to Chapters 11 through 13 for further information on MySQL.*

Our scripts will use two tables – the structure of the first is defined as follows:

```
# Table structure for table 'newsletters'
CREATE TABLE newsletters (
    newsletter_id smallint(3) DEFAULT '0' NOT NULL auto_increment,
    newsletter_name varchar(100) NOT NULL,
    newsletter_info varchar(200) NOT NULL,
    PRIMARY KEY (newsletter_id),
    UNIQUE newsletter_name (newsletter_name)
);
```

The `newsletters` table holds information on currently available newsletters:

❏ `newsletter_id` is an `auto_increment` type field that serves as a key, uniquely identifying each newsletter.

❏ `newsletter_name` holds the name of the newsletter.

❏ `newsletter_info` holds information about the newsletter for display to users.

The second – the `subscribers` table – is defined like this:

```
# Table structure for table 'subscribers'
CREATE TABLE subscribers (
    newsletter_id tinyint(3) DEFAULT '0' NOT NULL,
    email varchar(50) NOT NULL,
    type enum('text','html','zip','word') DEFAULT 'text' NOT NULL,
    PRIMARY KEY (newsletter_id, email)
);
```

It shouldn't come as any surprise to learn that we're going to use this table to hold information relating to current subscribers to the newsletters:

❏ `newsletter_id` serves as a key, establishing a relationship between this and the previous table.

❏ `email` holds the subscriber's e-mail addresses.

❏ `type` holds the subscriber's choice of newsletter format – it uses the enumeration data type, allowing only the values `text`, `html`, `zip` and `word`, and defaults to `text` if given a non-member value.

❑     `newsletter_id` and `email` fields are *combined* to create the primary key – this is so that each user can subscribe to as many newsletters as they like, but not to the same newsletter twice.

Now we have the tables we need, it's time to get back to some PHP!

### common_mail.inc

Before we start work on our pair of scripts, we're going to put together an include file `common_mail.inc` that defines common global variables and functions that will be used by both administration and user scripts. Most of this will be familiar from our earlier adventures with database techniques.

First it sets the information you need to connect to a MySQL server and the names of the newsletter table and subscribers table that hold the information on available newsletters and their subscribers respectively. The `$newsletter_mailer` variable is used in `From:` and `Reply-To:` headers.

```php
<?php
//common_mail.inc
$dbhost = "localhost";
$dbname = "sample_db";
$dbusername = "phpuser";
$dbuserpassword = "phppass";

$newsletters_table = "newsletters";
$subscribers_table = "subscribers";

$newsletter_mailer = "NewsMailer<newsmailer@b.com>";

function db_connect()
{
    global $dbhost, $dbname, $dbusername, $dbuserpassword;
    if(!@mysql_connect($dbhost, $dbusername, $dbuserpassword))
        error_message("DB Connection failed!");
    if(!@mysql_select_db($dbname)) error_message("Error selecting $dbname!");
}
```

The function `db_connect()` connects to a MySQL server as specified. Note that MySQL error reporting is suppressed by placing the character @ at the start of `mysql_connect()` and `mysql_select_db()` function calls. Errors are reported by the custom function `error_message()`.

```php
function mailer_header()
{
?>
<HTML>
<HEAD><TITLE>Mailer</TITLE></HEAD>
<BODY>
<?php
}

function mailer_footer()
{
?>
</BODY>
```

```
</HTML>
<?php
}

function error_message($msg)
{
   mailer_header();
   echo "<SCRIPT>alert(\"Error: $msg\");history.go(-1)</SCRIPT>";
   mailer_footer();
   exit;
}

function user_message($msg)
{
   mailer_header();
   echo "<SCRIPT>alert(\"$msg\");history.go(-1)</SCRIPT>";
   mailer_footer();
   exit;
}
```

The final three functions are taken directly from our previous script adv_mail.php.

```
function mail_form() { ... }

function send_mail() { ... }

function my_mail($mail_parts) { ... }

?>
```

### newsletter.php

Now let's examine our user script, newsletter.php. When a user runs this script, they receive a text edit field asking for an e-mail address:

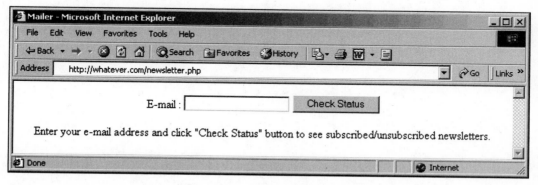

Once the user has given their e-mail address and clicked the Check Status button, the next screen displays their subscription status:

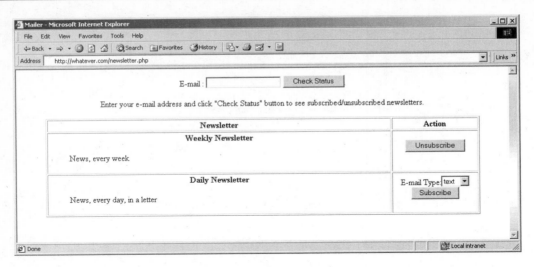

As you can see, the user is subscribed to Weekly Newsletter and has yet to subscribe to Daily Newsletter. They now have the opportunity either to unsubscribe from the former or subscribe to the latter. If they decide to subscribe to Daily Newsletter, they can specify a preferred delivery format, choosing either text, HTML, zip, or word. Whenever a user subscribes or unsubscribes, an e-mail is sent to them in confirmation.

Here's the complete source code of `newsletter.php`:

**1.** First, we need to make the common include file available to the script:

```php
<?php
//newsletter.php
include "./common_mail.inc";
```

**2.** We then define `check_status_form()` – this displays the form into which the user enters their e-mail address:

```php
function check_status_form()
{
    global $PHP_SELF;
?>
<FORM METHOD="POST" ACTION="<?php echo $PHP_SELF ?>">
<INPUT TYPE="HIDDEN" NAME="action" VALUE="check_status">
    <DIV ALIGN="CENTER"><P>
    E-mail :
    <INPUT TYPE="TEXT" NAME="user_email" SIZE="20">
    <INPUT TYPE="submit" VALUE="Check Status" NAME="Submit"><P>
    Enter your e-mail address and click &quot;Check Status&quot; button to see
    subscribed/unsubscribed newsletters.
    </DIV>
</FORM>
<?php
}
```

**3.** The `check_status()` function lists currently available newsletters, placing a `subscribe` or `unsubscribe` button next to each, according to the user's subscription status:

```
function check_status()
{
    global $PHP_SELF, $user_email, $newsletters_table,
                    $subscribers_table, $user_msg;

    check_status_form();
    db_connect();
```

We fetch all the records from the newsletter table:

```
    $result = mysql_query("SELECT newsletter_id, newsletter_name,
                            newsletter_info FROM $newsletters_table");

    if(!$result) error_message("Error fetching data from $newsletters_table");
?>
    <DIV ALIGN="CENTER"><CENTER>

    <TABLE BORDER="1" WIDTH="90%">
        <TR>
            <TH WIDTH="70%" NOWRAP>Newsletter</TH>
            <TH WIDTH="30%" NOWRAP>Action</TH>
        </TR>
```

We step through the result set and get the user's subscription status on each newsletter with a second query on the `subscribers` table:

```
<?php
    while($query_data = mysql_fetch_row($result)) {
        $newsletter_id = $query_data[0];
        $newsletter_name = stripslashes($query_data[1]);
        $newsletter_info = stripslashes($query_data[2]);

        $result2 = mysql_query("SELECT email FROM $subscribers_table
                                    WHERE email = '$user_email'
                                    AND newsletter_id=$newsletter_id");
        if(!$result2)
            error_message("Error fetching data from $subscribers_table");

        if(!mysql_num_rows($result2)) $action = 'subscribe';
        else $action = 'unsubscribe';
?>
    <TR>
        <TD WIDTH="80%"><?php echo "<CENTER><STRONG>$newsletter_name</STRONG>
        </CENTER><BR><BLOCKQUOTE>$newsletter_info</BLOCKQUOTE>"; ?>
        </TD><TD WIDTH="20%" ALIGN="CENTER">
        <FORM METHOD="POST" ACTION="<?php echo $PHP_SELF ?>">
        <INPUT TYPE="HIDDEN" NAME="action" VALUE="<?php echo $action ?>">
        <INPUT TYPE="HIDDEN" NAME="user_email"
                            VALUE="<?php echo $user_email ?>">
        <INPUT TYPE="HIDDEN" NAME="newsletter_id"
                            VALUE="<?php echo $newsletter_id ?>">
<?php
```

If the user is unsubscribed to any newsletter, we show a dropdown menu to let them select their desired file format, along with a **Subscribe** button:

```php
    if($action == 'subscribe') {
?>
        E-mail Type:<SELECT NAME="email_type" SIZE="1">
        <OPTION SELECTED VALUE="text">text</OPTION>
        <OPTION VALUE="html">html</OPTION>
        <OPTION VALUE="zip">zip</OPTION>
        <OPTION VALUE="word">word</OPTION>
        </SELECT><BR>
<?php
    }
?>
        <INPUT TYPE="submit" VALUE="<?php echo ucfirst($action); ?>" NAME="Submit">
    </FORM>
    </TD>
    </TR>
<?php
    }
?>
    </TABLE>
    </CENTER></DIV>
<?php
}
```

**4.** The function `subscribe()` inserts a user record into the `subscribers` table and sends a confirmation e-mail to the user:

```php
function subscribe()
{
    global $user_email, $newsletter_id, $email_type, $newsletters_table,
                        $subscribers_table, $user_msg, $newsletter_mailer;
    db_connect();
    $result = mysql_query("INSERT INTO $subscribers_table
                    VALUES($newsletter_id, '$user_email', '$email_type')");

    if(!$result) error_message("Error inserting values into $subscriber_table");

    $result = mysql_query("SELECT newsletter_name FROM $newsletters_table
                                    WHERE newsletter_id = $newsletter_id");

    if(!$result) error_message("Error fetching data from $newsletters_table");

    $query_data = mysql_fetch_row($result);
    $newsletter_name = $query_data[0];

    $mail_subject = $user_msg;
    $mail_body = "Thank you for subscribing to $newsletter_name.";
    $mail_header = "From: $newsletter_mailer\r\n";

    mail($user_email,$mail_subject,$mail_body,$mail_header);

    user_message("Successfully subscribed to $newsletter_name.");
}
```

**5.** The function `unsubscribe()` deletes a user record from the `subscribers` table and sends a confirmation e-mail to the user:

```
function unsubscribe()
{
    global $user_email, $newsletter_id, $newsletters_table,
                    $subscribers_table, $newsletter_mailer, $user_msg;
    db_connect();

    $result = mysql_query("DELETE FROM $subscribers_table
                        WHERE email = '$user_email'
                        AND newsletter_id = $newsletter_id");
```

Note that if we don't set the second condition in the WHERE clause (using the `newsletter_id` field), all records referring to the current user will be deleted.

```
    if(!$result) error_message("Error deleting from $newsletter");

    $result = mysql_query("SELECT newsletter_name FROM $newsletters_table
                        WHERE newsletter_id = $newsletter_id");

    if(!$result) error_message("Error fetching data out of $newsletter");
    $query_data = mysql_fetch_row($result);
    $newsletter_name = $query_data[0];

    $mail_subject = $user_msg;
    $mail_body = "We're sorry to see you go.";
    $mail_header = "From: $newsletter_mailer\r\n";

    if(!mail($user_email, $mail_subject, $mail_body, $mail_header))
                    error_message("Error sending a confirmation e-mail!");

    user_message("Successfully unsubscribed to $newsletter_name.");
}
```

**6.** We call functions that correspond to the value set in `$action`:

```
switch ($action)
{
    case "check_status":
        mailer_header();
        check_status();
        mailer_footer();
        break;
    case "subscribe":
        mailer_header();
        subscribe();
        mailer_footer();
        break;
    case "unsubscribe":
        mailer_header();
        unsubscribe();
        mailer_footer();
        break;
    default:
```

```
        mailer_header();
        check_status_form();
        mailer_footer();
        break;
    }
?>
```

Overall, the script is fairly straightforward. The two complementary functions – `subscribe()` and `unsubscribe()` – do all of the dirty work. Each selects the `newsletter_name` field from the `newsletters` (to get the name of the newsletter a user is subscribing or unsubscribing to), and sends the user an e-mail confirming that their request to subscribe/unsubscribe has been granted.

### admin_mailer.php

With the `my_mail()` function in our bag of tricks already, the administration script is no more difficult to write than the user script. Our `admin_mailer.php` script defines a number of new functions:

**1.** Our first, `admin_menu_form()`, displays two dropdown menus, letting us specify a newsletter and an action respectively:

```
<?php
//admin_mailer.php
include "./common_mail.inc";

function admin_menu_form() {
    global $PHP_SELF, $newsletters_table;
    db_connect();

    $result = mysql_query("SELECT newsletter_id, newsletter_name
                                        FROM $newsletters_table");

    if(!$result) error_message("Error fetching data from $newsletters_table");
?>
<CENTER><H3>Welcome to Newsmailer!</H3></CENTER>
<CENTER>
<FORM METHOD="POST" ACTION="<?php echo $PHP_SELF ?>">
<INPUT TYPE="HIDDEN" NAME="action" VALUE="mail_menu">
<SELECT NAME="newsletter_id" SIZE="1">
<OPTION SELECTED VALUE="!">Select a newsletter</OPTION>
<?php
    while($query_data = mysql_fetch_row($result)) {
        $newsletter_id = stripslashes($query_data[0]);
        $newsletter_name = $query_data[1];
        echo "<OPTION VALUE=\"$newsletter_id\">$newsletter_name</OPTION>";
        }
?>

    </SELECT> <SELECT NAME="option" SIZE="1">
    <OPTION SELECTED VALUE="send_email">Send an e-mail</OPTION>
    <OPTION VALUE="send_newsletter">Send a newsletter</OPTION>
    <OPTION VALUE="create">Create a newsletter</OPTION>
    <OPTION VALUE="view">View subscribers</OPTION>
    </SELECT><INPUT TYPE="submit" VALUE="Go!" NAME="Submit">
```

```
    </FORM>
    </CENTER>
    <?php
    }
```

**2.** We then have `newsletter_mail_form()`, an abridged version of `mail_form()`. The only difference is that we leave out certain header fields that aren't necessary for sending a newsletter. The screenshot overleaf shows what it looks like:

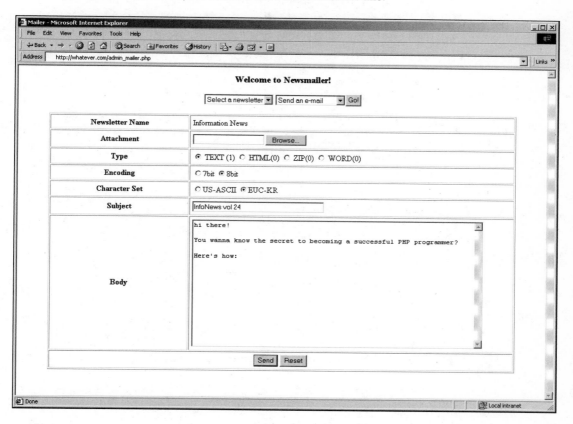

**3.** We're now going to define a short function `format_count()` to query the `subscribers` table for how many users subscribing to the current newsletter (as specified by `$newsletter_id`) wish to receive it in a specific format:

```
function format_count($format){
    global $newsletter_id;
    $result = mysql_query("SELECT email FROM $subscribers_table
                                    WHERE newsletter_id = $newsletter_id
                                    AND type = $format");

    if(!$result) error_message("Error fetching data from $subscribers_table");
    $query_data = mysql_fetch_row($result);
```

```
        return mysql_num_rows($result);
}
```

**4.** Note that `admin_menu_form()` is called **before** we create the mail form. We do this in case the administrator changes his mind and wants to follow another course of action:

```
function newsletter_mail_form() {
    global $PHP_SELF, $newsletter_id, $subscribers_table, $newsletters_table;

    admin_menu_form();
```

We get the name of the newsletter:

```
$result = mysql_query("SELECT newsletter_name FROM $newsletters_table
                                WHERE newsletter_id = $newsletter_id");

if(!$result) error_message("Error fetching data from $newsletters_table");
$query_data = mysql_fetch_row($result);
$newsletter_name = $query_data[0];
```

We use the `format_count()` function to get subscriber numbers for each format:

```
    $text_total = format_count('text');
    $html_total = format_count('html');
    $zip_total = format_count('zip');
    $word_total = format_count('html');
```

We then display our slimmed-down mail form:

```
?>
<FORM METHOD="POST" ENCTYPE="MULTIPART/FORM-DATA" ACTION="<?php echo $PHP_SELF
?>">
<INPUT TYPE="HIDDEN" NAME="action" VALUE="send_newsletter">
<INPUT TYPE="HIDDEN" NAME="newsletter_id" VALUE="<?php echo $newsletter_id ?>">
<DIV ALIGN="CENTER"><CENTER>
<TABLE CELLSPACING="2" CELLPADDING="5" WIDTH="90%" BORDER="1">
    <TR>
        <TH ALIGN="CENTER" WIDTH="30%">Newsletter Name</TH>
        <TD WIDTH="70%"><?php echo $newsletter_name ?>
        <INPUT TYPE="HIDDEN" VALUE="<?php echo $newsletter_id ?>"
                        NAME="newsletter_id">
        </TD>
    </TR>
    <TR>
        <TH ALIGN="CENTER" WIDTH="30%">Attachement</TH>
        <TD WIDTH="70%">
        <INPUT TYPE="file" NAME="userfile">
        </td>
    </TR>
    <TR>
        <TH ALIGN="CENTER" WIDTH="30%">Type</TH>
        <TD WIDTH="70%">
        <INPUT TYPE="RADIO" VALUE="text" NAME="mail_type" checked>
                            TEXT <?php echo "($text_total)"; ?>
```

```
            <INPUT TYPE="RADIO" VALUE="html" NAME="mail_type">
                              HTML<?php echo "($html_total)"; ?>
            <INPUT TYPE="RADIO" VALUE="zip"  NAME="mail_type">
                              ZIP<?php echo "($zip_total)"; ?>
            <INPUT TYPE="RADIO" VALUE="word" NAME="mail_type">
                              WORD<?php echo "($word_total)"; ?>
        </TD>
    </TR>
    <TR>
        <TH ALIGN="CENTER" WIDTH="30%">Encoding</TH>
        <TD WIDTH="70%">
        <INPUT TYPE="RADIO" VALUE="7bit" NAME="mail_encoding" checked>7bit
        <INPUT TYPE="RADIO" VALUE="8bit" NAME="mail_encoding">8bit
        </TD>
    </TR>
    <TR>
        <TH ALIGN="CENTER" WIDTH="30%">Character Set</TH>
        <TD WIDTH="70%">
        <INPUT TYPE="RADIO" VALUE="us-ascii" NAME="mail_charset" CHECKED>US-ASCII
        <INPUT TYPE="RADIO" VALUE="euc-kr" NAME="mail_charset">EUC-KR
        </TD>
    </TR>
    <TR>
        <TH ALIGN="CENTER" WIDTH="30%">Subject</TH>
        <TD WIDTH="70%"><INPUT SIZE="40" NAME="mail_subject">
        </TD>
    </TR>
    <TR>
        <TH ALIGN="CENTER" WIDTH="30%">Body</TH>
        <TD WIDTH="70%"><TEXTAREA NAME="mail_body" ROWS="16" COLS="70"></TEXTAREA>
        </TD>
    </TR>
    <TR>
        <TH WIDTH="30%" COLSPAN="2" ALIGN="CENTER">
        <INPUT TYPE="submit" VALUE="Send" NAME="submit">
        <INPUT TYPE="reset" VALUE="Reset" NAME="reset">
        </TH>
    </TR>
</TABLE>
</CENTER></DIV>
</FORM>
<?php
}
```

**5.** The function `create_newsletter_form()` displays a form that gives us options to create a new newsletter. Overleaf is a sample:

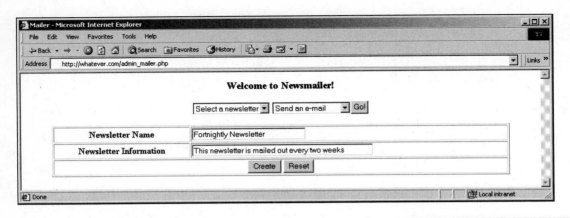

```php
function create_newsletter_form() {
   global $PHP_SELF;

   admin_menu_form();
?>
<FORM METHOD="POST" ACTION="<?php echo $PHP_SELF ?>">
<INPUT TYPE="HIDDEN" NAME="action" VALUE="create_newsletter">
<DIV ALIGN="CENTER"><CENTER><TABLE BORDER="1" WIDTH="90%">
   <TR>
      <TH WIDTH="30%">Newsletter Name</TH>
      <TD WIDTH="70%"><INPUT TYPE="TEXT" NAME="newsletter_name" size="30">
      </TD>
   </TR>
   <TR>
      <TH WIDTH="30%">Newsletter Information</TH>
      <TD WIDTH="70%"><INPUT TYPE="TEXT" NAME="newsletter_info" size="50">
      </TD>
   </TR>
   <TR>
      <TH WIDTH="30%" COLSPAN="2"><DIV ALIGN="CENTER"><CENTER>
      <INPUT TYPE="submit" VALUE="Create" NAME="Submit">
      <INPUT TYPE="reset" VALUE="Reset" NAME="reset">
      </TH>
   </TR>
</TABLE>
</CENTER></DIV>
</FORM>
<?php
}
```

6. According to the value of the $option variable (passed from the Action dropdown menu) mail_menu() either calls a corresponding function or displays a second form to be filled in:

```php
function mail_menu() {
   global $PHP_SELF, $newsletters_table, $subscribers_table, $option;

   switch($option) {
      case "create":
```

```
            create_newsletter_form();
            break;
        case "view":
            view_subscribers();
            break;
        case "send_newsletter":
            newsletter_mail_form();
            break;
        case "send_email":
            mail_form();
            break;
    }
}
```

**7.** `view_subscribers()` displays a list of subscribers to a selected newsletter, giving the administrator the option to remove any of them. The screenshot below shows how it looks:

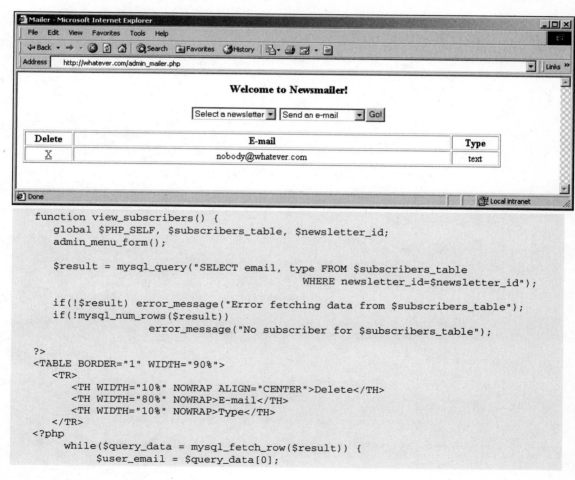

```
function view_subscribers() {
    global $PHP_SELF, $subscribers_table, $newsletter_id;
    admin_menu_form();

    $result = mysql_query("SELECT email, type FROM $subscribers_table
                                    WHERE newsletter_id=$newsletter_id");

    if(!$result) error_message("Error fetching data from $subscribers_table");
    if(!mysql_num_rows($result))
                error_message("No subscriber for $subscribers_table");

?>
<TABLE BORDER="1" WIDTH="90%">
    <TR>
        <TH WIDTH="10%" NOWRAP ALIGN="CENTER">Delete</TH>
        <TH WIDTH="80%" NOWRAP>E-mail</TH>
        <TH WIDTH="10%" NOWRAP>Type</TH>
    </TR>
<?php
    while($query_data = mysql_fetch_row($result)) {
        $user_email = $query_data[0];
```

```
            $email_type = $query_data[1];
?>
    <TR>
        <TD WIDTH="10%" ALIGN="CENTER" NOWRAP>
            <A HREF="<?php echo "$PHP_SELF?action=unsubscribe&
                                    user_email=$user_email&
                                    newsletter_id=$newsletter_id"; ?>"
                onClick="return confirm('Are you sure?');">X</A>
        </TD>

        <TD WIDTH="80%" ALIGN="CENTER" NOWRAP><?php echo $user_email ?></TD>
        <TD WIDTH="10%" ALIGN="CENTER" NOWRAP><?php echo $email_type ?></TD>
    </TR>
<?php
    }
?>
</TABLE>
<?php
}
```

**8.** unsubscribe() simply removes a selected subscription:

```
function unsubscribe() {
    global $user_email, $newsletter_id, $subscribers_table;
    db_connect();

    $result = mysql_query("DELETE FROM $subscribers_table
                                    WHERE email='$user_email'
                                    AND newsletter_id=$newsletter_id");
    if(!$result) error_message("Error deleting from $subscribers_table");

    view_subscribers();
}
```

**9.** create_newsletter() adds a newly-created newsletter's properties to the newsletters table:

```
function create_newsletter() {
    global $newsletter_name, $newsletter_info, $newsletters_table;

    if($newsletter_name == '') error_message("Empty Newsletter Name!");
    if($newsletter_info == '') error_message("Empty Newsletter Information!");

    $newsletter_name = addslashes($newsletter_name);
    $newsletter_info = addslashes($newsletter_info);

    db_connect();

    $result = mysql_query("INSERT INTO $newsletters_table values(NULL,
                                '$newsletter_name', '$newsletter_info')");

    if(!$result) error_message("Error creating $newsletter_name!");

    user_message("Successfully created newsletter titled '$newsletter_name'.");
}
```

**10.** The `send_newsletter()` function works in much the same way as the `send_mail()` wrapper function, which calls `my_mail()` to actually send an e-mail. `send_newsletter()` sets the `From` and `Reply-To` header fields to the global variable `$newsletter_mailer` and uses a `while` loop to step through each e-mail address in the given newsletter table:

```
function send_newsletter() {
    global $mail_to, $mail_from, $mail_reply_to, $mail_body, $mail_subject;
    global $userfile, $userfile_type, $userfile_name, $userfile_size;
    global $mail_type, $mail_charset, $mail_encoding, $newsletter_id,
           $subscribers_table, $newsletters_table, $newsletter_mailer;

    $mail_parts["mail_subject"] = $mail_subject;
    $mail_parts["mail_body"] = $mail_body;

    $mail_parts["mail_type"] = $mail_type;
    $mail_parts["mail_charset"] = $mail_charset;
    $mail_parts["mail_encoding"] = $mail_encoding;

    $mail_parts["userfile"] = $userfile;
    $mail_parts["userfile_type"] = $userfile_type;
    $mail_parts["userfile_name"] = $userfile_name;
    $mail_parts["userfile_size"] = $userfile_size;

    admin_menu_form();

    $result = mysql_query("SELECT newsletter_name FROM $newsletters_table
                                      WHERE newsletter_id = $newsletter_id");

    if(!$result) error_message("Error fetching data from $newsletters_table");
    $query_data = mysql_fetch_row($result);
    $newsletter_name = $query_data[0];

    $result = mysql_query("SELECT email FROM $subscribers_table
                                      WHERE type='$mail_type'
                                      AND newsletter_id=$newsletter_id");

    if(!mysql_num_rows($result))
                        error_message("No subscribers to $newsletter_name
                                             for the mail type: $mail_type");

    $mail_parts["mail_reply_to"] = $mail_parts["mail_from"] = $newsletter_mailer;

    $num_email=0;
    while($query_data = mysql_fetch_row($result)) {
        $mail_parts["mail_to"] = $query_data[0];
        if(!my_mail($mail_parts))
              error_message("An error occurred while attempting to send the
                                  $newsletter_name to " . $mail_parts["mail_to"]);
        $num_email++;
    }

user_message("Successfully sent the $newsletter_name titled '$mail_subject'.");
}
```

**11.** Finally, we use the `$action` variable to switch between the different sets of functions we must call to perform different tasks:

```
switch ($action) {
    case "send_mail":
        mailer_header();
        send_mail();
        mailer_footer();
        break;
    case "mail_form":
        mailer_header();
        mail_form();
        mailer_footer();
        break;
    case "mail_menu":
        mailer_header();
        mail_menu();
        mailer_footer();
        break;
    case "create_newsletter":
        mailer_header();
        create_newsletter();
        mailer_footer();
        break;
    case "send_newsletter":
        mailer_header();
        send_newsletter();
        mailer_footer();
        break;
    case "unsubscribe":
        mailer_header();
        unsubscribe();
        mailer_footer();
        break;
    default:
        mailer_header();
        admin_menu_form();
        mailer_footer();
        break;
}
?>
```

# Resources

The user-annotated "Online PHP Reference" for the mail() function:

❏   http://www.php.net/manual/function.mail.php

For information on Internet Mail:

❏   RFC 822 – http://www.rfc.net

Multipurpose Internet Mail Extensions:

❑ RFCs 2045-2049 – http://www.rfc.net

and Charsets:

❑ RFC 2278 – http://www.rfc.net

❑ List of Registered Charsets – ftp://ftp.isi.edu/in-notes/iana/assignments/character-sets

For more details of the MIME Mail Class implementation, you may wish to refer to:

❑ *Professional PHP Programming* from Wrox Press (*ISBN 1-861002-96-3*)

# Summary

We've learned in this chapter how to send both regular and sophisticated e-mails with PHP. We introduced you to the mail() function that lies at the heart of PHP's e-mail capability.

```
mail (mail_to, mail_subject, mail_body [, additional_headers])
```

Along the way, we created a useful custom e-mail function my_mail() that can handle MIME headers and file attachment. We learned how MIME headers are used to enhance the capabilities of standard e-mail by providing a simple but standardized way to represent and encode a wide variety of media types for transmission via e-mail: unlimited length of textual and non-textual data in various character sets.

Finally, we built a newsletter mailing list manager that incorporates all of the skills discussed in this chapter.

# 16

# Generating Graphics

By now you will have a very good understanding not only of how PHP works but the flexibility and wide range of platforms and programming applications that you can interact with in PHP. You can confidently connect to databases and create textual output for the person browsing your web site to view, but sooner or later you are going to need to output that information in a graphical format. Sure you could fire up a graphics program and create a few good looking graphics for your site, but what about when your graphic is directly related to the data in your database?

PHP contains a range of functions that allow you to open, manipulate and output graphics to the web browser. During this chapter we will explore how these functions work and how we can apply them to display our data.

By the end of the chapter we will not only have seen how to create images on the fly, but will have built a practical application using these methods and concepts.

## Laying a Foundation

As with all things in life, we have to learn to walk before we can run – before we can jump in and start producing the goods, we have a few basics to get through.

PHP uses the gd graphics library for all but its most basic image functions. Provided you have a recent version of the library, you can create and manipulate images in a number of different formats; the two most noteworthy are JPEG and PNG. These are both compressed file formats, which means that they use mathematical algorithms to reduce the amount of data required to completely describe the image. They therefore play a very important role in keeping your file sizes small and download times short!

It's important to be able to recognize where you should use each format – they use quite different compression techniques, and most images will be better suited to one or the other.

The JPEG format uses **lossy** compression. What this means is that some of the data in the original image is lost during compression. The format is designed to work best with images like photographs (that's where the "P" in "JPEG" comes from), where there's a lot of subtle shading and not too much fine detail. It's the format to use when a slight loss in quality won't be too apparent to the viewer.

The PNG format on the other hand is compressed in a **lossless** fashion. It works best with images that contain lines and large blocks of color, cartoons for example. When the image is uncompressed, it will contain all of its original information. This means that sharp edges and straight lines (which suffer under JPEG compression) will be reproduced faithfully.

*Early versions of gd (and thus PHP) contained support for **GIF** files, which are similar in many respects to PNG. However, Unisys holds a patent on the LZW compression algorithm used to create fully compressed GIFs, and consequently GIF support has been completely replaced by that for PNG files since gd version 1.6. All is far from lost though, as JPEG and the excellent PNG image encoding formats should be sufficient for all your graphics needs.*

Before we even look at the technicalities of creating the image, let's go through the steps involved in getting PHP to create an image and display it in the browser:

This is effectively just a section of memory in which we define an image before outputting it to the browser or to disk.

1.  Create an **image canvas** for PHP to work on – this is simply a reserved portion of server memory, onto which the script will "draw" (that is, write data) before outputting it to the browser or disk as an image.

2.  Draw the picture on the image canvas.

3.  Send the image to the browser.

4.  Clean up memory by throwing away the image canvas.

# Creating an Image

As mentioned above, the first thing we need to do is create a blank image canvas for PHP to work on – a call to the `ImageCreate()` function does just this. The only two things we need to tell it are the width and height of the image we wish to create. `ImageCreate()` will then return an identifier that identifies that blank image in memory. All the subsequent image functions we use will have to refer to the image in memory by means of this identifier.

*This identifier is similar to a file handle or database link ID, as we've used in recent chapters, but refers to the location of our image canvas in memory rather than an open file on the disk or an active database connection.*

```
$image = ImageCreate(200,150);
```

We've now defined `$image` as the identifier referring to the new, blank canvas (200 pixels wide by 150 pixels high) that `ImageCreate()` has just created for us. Now that this 200 x 150 pixel image is in memory we can start drawing on it. First though, we need to know what color we'll be drawing in.

## Setting up Colors

Before we can tell PHP that we want to use a certain color on our canvas, we have to create that color. We do this in a similar fashion to that of creating the image canvas:

```
$gray = ImageColorAllocate($image,204,204,204);
$blue = ImageColorAllocate($image,0,0,255);
```

We've used the function `ImageColorAllocate()` to define two colors for our image: a gray and a blue. Each color is assigned a unique identifier and tied to an existing image canvas. As you can see, this function requires 4 pieces of information:

❑ The first is the identifier of the image canvas with which this color will be used. This is the same identifier that we saw returned to us earlier from the `ImageCreate()` function.

❑ The second, third and fourth things we need to tell `ImageColorAllocate()` are the respective values of red, green and blue components for that color, which must lie between 0 and 255.

*Computers make up color by mixing different quantities of Red, Green and Blue. This is what is known as **RGB** mode color. Each of red, green and blue can range from 0 to 255. Setting each of red, green and blue to 0 will give us black (total absence of color), a value of 255 for all three will give us white. If we want to stick to **web-safe** colors, then we have to limit our values of red, green and blue to multiples of 51. That gives us 6 possible values for each of red, green and blue, for a total of 216 colors.*

`$gray` and `$blue` are now two new identifiers to the colors gray and blue. We created the former by specifying equal values of each color. Note that 204 was not a number we pulled from the hat, but a multiple of 51, and we've therefore defined a web-safe color. We defined `$blue` by telling `ImageColorAllocate()` that the red component was 0, the green component was 0 and that the blue component was 255.

## The Image Coordinate System

While we're dealing with theory here, we may as well take a look at how the image coordinate system works. It may sound like a mouthful but it's simply a way for us to precisely describe points in the image.

If you're familiar with creating graphs, you'll probably be used to the x and y values radiating outwards from the bottom left hand corner. In PHP, all coordinates radiate outwards from the **top** left-hand corner of the image, as the image below shows:

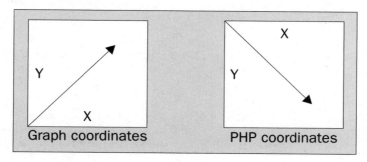

Graph coordinates　　　PHP coordinates

With this in mind, let's take a look at how our blank $image is laid out:

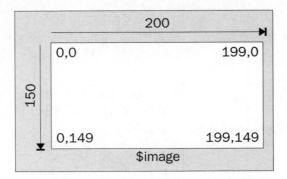

The x-y coordinates for the top left corner of $image are 0,0. This will be true for every image that you create. The x-coordinates extend to the right for 200 pixels and y-coordinates extend down for 150 pixels, so the bottom right-hand corner of the image has x-y coordinates of 199,149.

# Drawing on our Image

Now that we've seen how the coordinate system works and have two colors to draw with, we can start making pictures. But what about allocating a background color for our image? ImageCreate() didn't have an argument that allowed us to specify the background color of the image.

As it happens, we don't need to tell the image what its background color is explicitly; the first color we allocate to the image automatically becomes the background color. Looking back at the code that we've covered so far:

```
$image = ImageCreate(200,150);
$gray = ImageColorAllocate($image,204,204,204);
$blue = ImageColorAllocate($image,0,0,255);
```

we see that the first color allocated was $gray. Our background color for $image will therefore automatically be gray. We will use our pure blue $blue to draw the shapes on our image.

## Lines

To draw a line, we use the ImageLine() function, using the following format:

```
ImageLine($image, 10,10, 150,30, $blue);
```

As usual, the first thing we have to tell the function is the identifier of the image canvas we're working on. The next two arguments are the x and y coordinates of the start of the line, while the two after that are coordinates for the end of the line. The final argument is the identifier for the color in which we'll be drawing the line.

The example above draws a line that starts 10 pixels from the left and 10 pixels from the top of the image, and ends at x = 150, y = 30. The layout of the resulting image is shown in the diagram below:

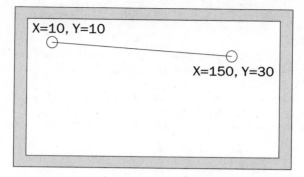

Once the line has been drawn onto the image canvas, we need to either save the canvas to disk or send it to the browser. We're going to do the latter, using a function. This only requires one piece of information: the identifier of the image canvas that we want to output:

```
ImageJPEG($image);
```

If we want to save the image to disk, we can specify a second argument, containing the filename we want to use:

```
ImageJPEG($image, "image.jpg");
```

If we're saving the image as a disk file, we can also specify a third argument. This must be an integer value between −1 and 100, which specifies the quality of the resulting JPEG image.

A value of 0 will generate a small file but consequently a very low quality image. On the other hand, a value of 100 will give you high quality but a larger file. The images below should gives you some idea of the trade-offs you'll be looking at:

*Line quality = -1*

*Line quality = 20*

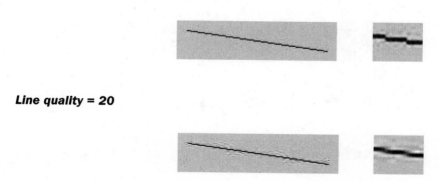

*Line quality = 100*

A value of −1 tells the `ImageJPEG()` function that it should use default quality, which should be very close to optimal – in practice this is equivalent to a setting of around 70.

Something else that we need to bear in mind at this point is the `Header()` function. Whenever we send non-HTML data to the browser, we should let it know what it is, so that it can be properly processed. We use this function at the top of our example to produce a page header, and let the browser know what sort of file to expect:

```
Header("Content-type: image/jpeg");
```

Finally, we need to call the `ImageDestroy()` function with the image identifier. It will be no surprise to you that this function destroys the image canvas, freeing up the server memory it occupied.

Let's take a look at our complete code at this point:

```php
<?php
//draw1.php
Header("Content-type: image/jpeg");
$image = ImageCreate(200,150);
$gray = ImageColorAllocate($image,204,204,204);
$blue = ImageColorAllocate($image,0,0,255);
ImageLine($image,10,10,150,30,$blue);
ImageJPEG($image);
ImageDestroy($image);
?>
```

Which gives us:

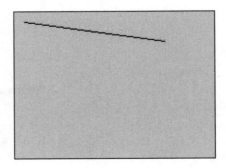

## Circles

To create an arc, circle or ellipse in PHP, we use a function called `ImageArc()` with the following syntax:

```
ImageArc(image_id, x, y, width, height, start, end, color_id);
```

As you can see this function takes quite a few arguments. The first is, as usual, the image identifier. Next are our x and y coordinates, and in this case they specify the center point of our arc. The width and height are the width and height of the circle or ellipse from which we take the arc.

Note we don't use a radius, as this would limit us to using a perfect arc or circle. The option to have different height and width means that we can use this function to create ellipses. A circle is simply an ellipse whose height and width are equal.

Start and end points for the arc are measured clockwise in degrees from the right-hand horizontal radius (that is, three o'clock):

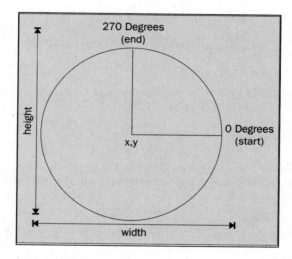

The slanted line we created earlier had one end at the position x = 150, y = 30. We're now going to create a circle that's 70 pixels across, the top of which touches this end of that line. The x value for the center of our circle will therefore be 150 again, but the y value must be greater than that of the line end by 35 (that is, half the width of the circle – remember we're dealing with a **width** of 70, not a radius).

The y value for the end of the line is 30, the circle center must have y = 65. Since we are going to create a full circle, we must draw our arc through a complete 360 degrees: start = 0 and end = 360. We'll draw the circle in blue as well.

Our code now looks like this:

```php
<?php
//draw2.php
Header("Content-type: image/jpeg");
$image = ImageCreate(200,150);
$gray = ImageColorAllocate($image,204,204,204);
$blue = ImageColorAllocate($image,0,0,255);
ImageLine($image,10,10,150,30,$blue);
ImageArc($image,150,65,70,70,0,360,$blue);
ImageJPEG($image);
ImageDestroy($image);
?>
```

and produces this:

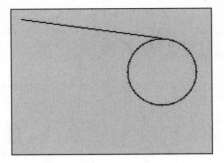

## *Rectangles*

If you've picked up on any of the trends in this chapter, you'll have guessed by now that the function to create a rectangle in PHP is ImageRectangle():

```
ImageRectangle(image_id, x1, y1, x2, y2, color_id);
```

The arguments correspond to the image identifier, the x and y coordinates of the top left-hand corner of the rectangle, the x and y coordinates of the bottom right-hand corner of the rectangle, and the identifier for the color we want it drawn in.

Pretty straightforward, right? Here's the code, which now adds a box whose top right-hand corner is at x = 150, y = 65, the same as the center of the circle.

```php
<?php
//draw3.php
Header("Content-type: image/jpeg");
$image = ImageCreate(200,150);
$gray = ImageColorAllocate($image,204,204,204);
$blue = ImageColorAllocate($image,0,0,255);
ImageLine($image,10,10,150,30,$blue);
```

```
ImageArc($image,150,65,70,70,0,360,$blue);
ImageRectangle($image,10,65,150,140,$blue);
ImageJPEG($image);
ImageDestroy($image);
?>
```

This now returns the following image:

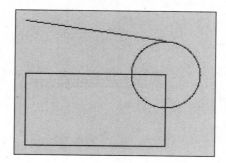

# Putting it all Together

So far we've covered creating an image, outputting it to the browser and cleaning up after ourselves. Between creating the image and outputting it we also covered creating lines, circles and rectangles on our image.

PHP currently has no function that allows us to create a rectangle with rounded corners. In order to recap what we covered so far, we're going to create a function that does just that. We'll be able to pass this function the same information that you would pass to ImageRectangle(), but with an extra argument telling it the radius of the arc that we want to use for the corner. Our prototype will therefore be:

```
udImageRoundRect($image, $x1, $y1, $x2, $y2, $arcradius, $color)
```

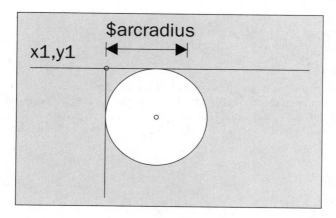

We'll never use $x1$, $y1$, $x2$, or $y2$ as actual points in any of the plots, but we will use them to work out where our arcs must be centered, as well as where our lines must start and end. In the image above, we know that ($x1$, $y1$) is where our rectangle would have started if it didn't have a rounded corner. We can work out where the center of the arc must be by adding $arcradius to each of $x1$ and $y1$. Remember that we will only be adding to both x and y values in the top left-hand corner of the rectangle. In other corners we will have to subtract $arcradius from one or both of the values.

Let's dive into the code and take a look. We're going to define our function in an include file called roundrect.inc:

```php
<?php
//roundrect.inc
function udImageRoundRect($image,$x1,$y1,$x2,$y2,$arcradius,$color) {

  $arcwidth = ($arcradius*2);

  // top left hand corner
  ImageArc($image, $x1+$arcradius, $y1+$arcradius,
                   $arcwidth,      $arcwidth,
                   180,            270,
              $color);
```

The first thing we do is to double $arcradius, giving us the **width** of the arc; we can pass this directly to ImageArc().

The next line draws the top left-hand corner arc. The center of the arc is at:

❑  x = $x1 + $arcradius (just to the right of the corner of the rectangle),

❑  y = $y1 + $arcradius (just down from the same corner).

The width and height of the arc are both equal to $arcwidth, since we want the corner to be rounded, not ellipsoid. We start the arc at 180° (9 o'clock) and end at 270° (12 o'clock) – a 90° arc. As we move around the corners our degrees will shift by 90° each time.

```php
      // top right hand corner
      ImageArc($image, $x2-$arcradius, $y1+$arcradius,
                       $arcwidth,      $arcwidth,
                       270,            360,              $color);
```

Now that we're at the top right-hand corner we must use the $x2 value and this time subtract $arcradius – the center of the arc will be to the left of the rectangle corner. We are still working with $y1 and since it's at the same horizontal level, we still use $y1 + $arcradius. As you can see in the diagram opposite, we also need to shift each of our degrees clockwise by 90 degrees.

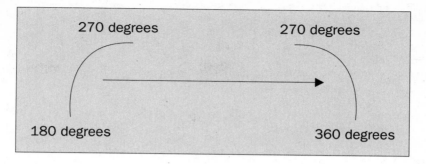

Each of the bottom corners work in exactly the same way; you just have to remember whether to add or subtract, and which x and y values you should be working with:

```
// bottom right hand corner
  ImageArc($image, $x2-$arcradius, $y2-$arcradius,
                   $arcwidth,       $arcwidth,
                   0,               90,             $color);

  // bottom left hand corner
  ImageArc($image, $x1+$arcradius, $y2-$arcradius,
                   $arcwidth,       $arcwidth,
                   90,              180,            $color);
```

The last part of our script draws in the connecting lines between the rounded corners. Now if we were going to draw in our top line as if we weren't using rounded corners, we would simply use ($x1, $y1) as our first coordinate and ($x2, $y1) as our second coordinate. Since we have to take the corners into account, we must adjust some of these coordinates by $arcradius:

```
    // top line
    ImageLine($image, $x1+$arcradius, $y1,
                      $x2-$arcradius, $y1, $color);
    // right line
    ImageLine($image, $x2, $y1+$arcradius,
                      $x2, $y2-$arcradius, $color);

    // bottom line
    ImageLine($image, $x1+$arcradius, $y2,
                      $x2-$arcradius, $y2, $color);
    // left line
    ImageLine($image, $x1, $y1+$arcradius,
                      $x1, $y2-$arcradius, $color);
}
?>
```

And that's it for `roundrect.inc`. We can now write a PHP script like this:

```
<?php
//roundrect.php
Header("Content-type: image/jpeg");
include "roundrect.inc";
```

```
$image = ImageCreate(200,150);
$gray = ImageColorAllocate($image,204,204,204);
$blue = ImageColorAllocate($image,0,0,255);
udImageRoundRect($image,10,10,190,140,30,$blue);
ImageJPEG($image);
ImageDestroy($image);
?>
```

The first line includes the `roundrect.inc` file created above, so we have access to our new user-defined function `udImageRoundRect()`:

```
udImageRoundRect($image,10,10,190,140,30,$blue);
```

We start the rectangle at (10,10) and end it at (190,140); 10 pixels clear of each edge of the image. The radius of our corner arcs will be 30 pixels. If we run the script we get an image like this:

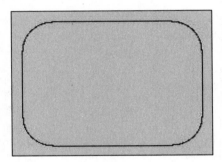

# Practical Application

It's all very well being able to draw images on the fly, but it's all very superficial. Thousands of web sites provide copies of the same bland information and links to the same articles/jokes/urban legends. What makes a web site truly stand out is when you offer something unique and dynamic – something that the people browsing your site can't easily do for themselves or get somewhere else.

What we're going to do for the rest of this chapter is look at how we can take content from a database – content that only you or your client will have – and present it in a way that is clever, useful and appealing for the person browsing your web site. What we're going to build is an **interactive map**. By the end of the chapter, we'll have created an application that lets us query a database, and will display a diagram based on the criteria that we have entered.

# Interactive Maps

Most of you have had to deal with a map or layout diagram at some time or another. How have you managed to find the road or city that you were looking for? Look it up in an index at the back of the map and then scour the reference it gives you for the one tiny piece of information that you are looking for. What if we could take all of that data, and move it into a database. The index then acts as a search function for our database and the results are highlighted on our map using the graphics techniques that you already know.

The example that we are going to create is a layout diagram for a local shopping mall. Browsers will be able to search for the position of shops by name or single keyword search.

*Apart from file format issues, map data can use any number of coordinate systems, ranging from familiar degrees, minutes and seconds to projections like the Universal Transverse Mercator. Each coordinate system would require a different method to reference it to your image map, a topic that's considerably beyond the scope of this book.*

We'll be using an existing layout of the shopping mall; from this it will be easy to work out x and y coordinates for the shops, as they will all be based within this one existing image.

When we store the information in our database, we should not only store the coordinate information, but also any extra metadata that we could use to enhance our map. Remember that anybody can get a layout map of an area and hunt their way through it – what is going to add value to our diagram is the fact that we will have **data associated** with the layout information.

## Getting Started

We don't want to have to draw our layout diagram from scratch every single time. PHP has a function that allows us to create an image from an already existing file. What I've done is created the basic outline of the shops in our mall and shown them below. To begin with our mall only has a ground floor. Most malls have some sort of shop naming convention and that is what we have added in the diagrams. The images that we work with in our code will look exactly like these but without the shop names. The shop names will be stored in our database and written onto the diagram by our code.

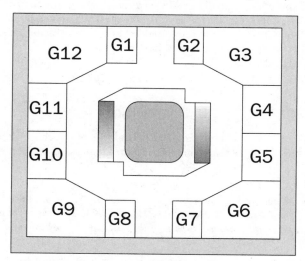

The dark gray blob in the middle represents some foliage, while the rectangles on either side are for up and down escalators. (The owners intend to expand the mall in the future, so we make provision for the escalators now.)

## *Creating the database*

We're going to store all our data in a MySQL database called `mapping` and use our old friend `phpuser` (with password phppass) to access this new database:

```
mysql> create database mapping;
```

Let's take a look at the layout of our database and the information we'll be storing in it. Below is the rest of our SQL script to create the database:

```
use mapping;
CREATE TABLE mall (
  m_id int(11) DEFAULT '0' NOT NULL AUTO_INCREMENT,
  m_floor char(1) NOT NULL,
  m_shop varchar(64) NOT NULL,
  m_name varchar(64) NOT NULL,
  m_phone varchar(64),
  m_area varchar(128) NOT NULL,
  m_center varchar(64) NOT NULL,
  m_desc varchar(128),
  PRIMARY KEY (m_id)
);
```

We have a field called `m_id` that is the primary key of my table. Because our mall may have more than one level in the future we are storing the level that the shop is on in the `m_floor` field. Later when we add more floors to our mall this field will be important. `m_shop` stores the shop name as it is known in the mall layout – this is something like G4 or M8 – we saw these in the figure above. `m_name` is the name of the shop that the proprietor has given it, `m_phone` is the shop's phone number. `m_area` is the important one here as this holds a comma separated list of the coordinates of each of the corners of the shop's outline. A typical coordinate list will look like this:

```
500,350,500,500,0,500,0,350,100,350,150,400,350,400,400,350
```

and consist of alternating x and y coordinates.

The next field `m_center` is an (x, y) coordinate of the middle of the shop. In order to fill shapes with color we'll have to start filling from somewhere inside the shape, and this center point will be the place where we start.

> *Possibly a better way to approach this would be to have the script work out the center point itself, saving us the need to store it in the database; however, in order to keep the script as simple as possible and concentrate on the graphical aspects of the script, we'll store the center point for now.*

The last field `m_desc` contains a comma-separated list of keywords describing each shop. This is so that the person browsing through the mall will be able to search for the products or services that they want.

## *Adding data*

Here's a SQL script to populate our mall table with its data.

```
INSERT INTO mall VALUES (1,'G','G1','Fast Snax',
        '555-7089','150,0,150,100,200,100,200,0','175,50',
        'food,sweets,soda,drinks,chips,cola,pies,fast food,candy');
INSERT INTO mall VALUES (2,'G','G2','ACME Newsagent',
        '555-6843','300,0,300,100,350,100,350,0','325,50',
        'newspapers,magazines,paper,stationary,newsagents,periodicals');
INSERT INTO mall VALUES (3,'G','G3','Fashion Warehouse',
        '555-7521','350,0,350,100,400,150,500,150,500,0','425,65',
        'clothes,clothing,shoes,pants,suits,dresses');
INSERT INTO mall VALUES (4,'G','G4','CD&#059; R Us',
        '555-0459','400,150,400,250,500,250,500,150','450,200',
        'cds,dvds,music,tapes,videos,rock,pop');
INSERT INTO mall VALUES (5,'G','G5','Garden Bounty Florists',
        '555-9561','400,250,400,350,500,350,500,250','450,300',
        'gardening,flowers,florists,arrangements,floral');
INSERT INTO mall VALUES (6,'G','G6','National Bank',
        '555-3675','400,350,350,400,350,500,500,500,500,350','425,440',
        'money,banks,banking,cheques,deposit,withdrawal,cash,atm');
INSERT INTO mall VALUES (7,'G','G7','Sweetime',
        '555-7659','300,400,300,500,350,500,350,400','325,450',
        'candy,sweets,candy floss,cola,sodas,drinks,chips,crisps');
INSERT INTO mall VALUES (8,'G','G8','The Classics',
        '555-4395','150,400,150,500,200,500,200,400','175,450',
        'cds,dvds,music,jazz,classics');
INSERT INTO mall VALUES (9,'G','G9','The Computer Matrix',
        '555-7001','100,350,150,400,150,500,0,500,0,350','65,435',
        'pc,computers,components,software,hardware,books,cds');
INSERT INTO mall VALUES (10,'G','G10','Bibliophile',
        '555-3752','100,250,100,350,0,350,0,250','50,300',
        'books,magazines,periodicals,reading');
INSERT INTO mall VALUES (11,'G','G11','Well Heeled',
        '555-2564','0,150,100,150,100,250,0,250','50,200',
        'shoes,trainers,boots,heels');
INSERT INTO mall VALUES (12,'G','G12','The Great Outdoors',
        '555-7269','0,0,0,150,100,150,150,100,150,0','65,70',
        'hiking,camping,rafting');
```

We can save it as `map_data.sql` and import it into our mapping database:

```
> mysql -u phpuser -pphppass mapping < map_data.sql
```

## Testing our data

The coordinates for the outline of the shops are now all stored in our database. In order to test that everything is working correctly we are going to write a script to create an image of our mall.

### Try It Out - Drawing The Mall

```php
<?php
//drawmall.php
include "./common_db.inc";

Header("Content-type: image/png");
```

```
$image = ImageCreate(501,501);
$white = ImageColorAllocate($image,255,255,255);
$black = ImageColorAllocate($image,0,0,0);

$link_id = db_connect('mapping');

$query = "SELECT m_area FROM mall";
$mallResult = mysql_query($query,$link_id);

while ($mallRow = mysql_fetch_array($mallResult)) {
    $area = explode(",", $mallRow[0]);
    for ($i=0; $i < count($area)-2; $i=$i+2) {
        ImageLine($image,$area[$i],$area[$i+1],$area[$i+2],$area[$i+3],$black);
    }
    ImageLine($image,$area[count($area)-2],
                     $area[count($area)-1], $area[0], $area[1], $black);
}

for ($i=0; $i<count($area)-2; $i=$i+2) {
    ImageLine($image,$area[$i], $area[$i+1], $area[$i+2], $area[$i+3],
$black);
}
ImageLine($image, $area[count($area)-2],
                  $area[count($area)-1], $area[0], $area[1], $black);
    ImagePNG($image);
    ImageDestroy($image);
    mysql_free_result($mallResult);
?>
```

When you run this script, you should see the image below:

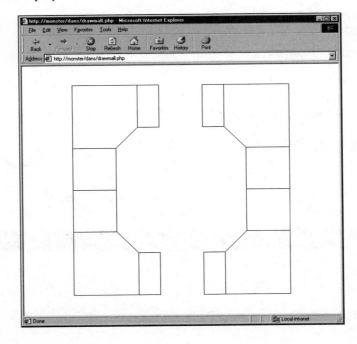

### How It Works

After including the include file `common_db.inc`, we start by creating our blank image canvas and allocating 2 colors to the image:

```
Header("Content-type: image/png");
$image = ImageCreate(501,501);
$white = ImageColorAllocate($image,255,255,255);
$black = ImageColorAllocate($image,0,0,0);
```

We then connect to the MySQL server on the local machine using the `db_connect()` function that we defined back in Chapter 11. We set up and execute a SQL query to return all of the `m_area` fields:

```
$link_id = db_connect('mapping');
$query = "SELECT m_area FROM mall";
$mallResult = mysql_query($query, $link_id);
```

We then loop around through the rows that our query returned. The important bits to do with graphics start now.

The first thing we have to do is to grab that comma-separated list of x-y coordinates and turn it into something that we can easily use. The simplest way to do that is to use the `explode()` function to break up the list (or in this case `$mallRow[0]`) on commas. We therefore define `$area` as an array of all of our x and y coordinates:

```
while ($mallRow = mysql_fetch_array($mallResult)) {
    $area = explode(",", $mallRow[0]);
    for ($i=0; $i < count($area)-2; $i=$i+2) {
        ImageLine($image,$area[$i],$area[$i+1],$area[$i+2],$area[$i+3],$black);
    }
    ImageLine($image,$area[count($area)-2],
                    $area[count($area)-1], $area[0], $area[1], $black);
}
```

The `for()` statement that we now use may look a little bit strange:

```
for ($i=0; $i < count($area)-2; $i=$i+2) {
    ImageLine($image,$area[$i], $area[$i+1], $area[$i+2], $area[$i+3],
    $black);
}
```

What we're doing here is looping around from 0 while `$i` is less than the count of `$area` minus 2, each time incrementing `$i` by 2. The trick to understanding this is that we have an array of alternating x and y coordinates, so we have to use the coordinates in pairs in order to make any sense of them. If `$mallRow[0]` was:

```
150,0,150,100,200,100,200,0
```

then `$area` would be an array of elements, so the first element `$area[0]` would be 150, while the last one `$area[7]` would be 0.

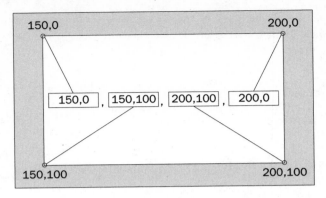

Each pair of elements represents a coordinate set, and our first line should be drawn from the first set to the second. Likewise, the second line will be from the second set to the third and the third line from the third set to the fourth set. The last line is drawn between the last set of coordinates and the first; this completes the shape.

The first time we get into the loop, $i equals 0, so looking at the code that draws the lines:

```
ImageLine($image, $area[$i], $area[$i+1], $area[$i+2], $area[$i+3],
$black);
```

Our first coordinate set corresponds to the first two elements of the array [$i] and [$i+1]. The second set corresponds to [$i+2] and [$i+3]. The variable $i then has 2 added to its value, and the next pair of coordinates are linked.

The diagram below shows how the loop progresses in steps of 2. The square bracketing on the right (around groups of four elements from $area) show the coordinates that will be used to draw the line in each loop. Remember that our loop is set to continue while $i is less than count($area) −2. Since there are 8 values in the array, it will stop on reaching $i = 6:

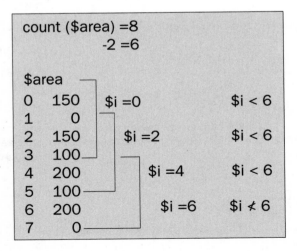

This has only drawn 3 lines for us and the shape will need 4, so once we have dropped out of the bottom of the loop we draw a line from the last pair of elements to the first pair:

```
ImageLine($image, $area[count($area)-2],
                   $area[count($area)-1],
                   $area[0], $area[1], $black);
```

The last thing we need to do then is output the graphic and clean up memory:

```
ImagePNG($image);
ImageDestroy($image);
mysql_free_result($mallResult);
?>
```

# Building a Framework

Before we can start writing the actual scripts we need to create a framework for them to work in. We are going to use a frameset of two frames alongside one another. The left-hand frame is a sidebar, while the right-hand frame will be where all of our scripts run. Here is index.html:

```
<HEAD><TITLE>Our Interactive Mall</TITLE></HEAD>
<FRAMESET COLS="170,*">
    <FRAME NAME="sidebar" SRC="menu.html" FRAMEBORDER="No" BORDER=0 NORESIZE>
    <FRAME NAME="mall" SRC="blank.html" FRAMEBORDER="No" BORDER=0 NORESIZE>
</FRAMESET>
```

To begin with, the right-hand frame will be blank, so here is blank.html:

```
<html>
<body>
</body>
</html>
```

and menu.html, our sidebar:

```
<HTML>
<BODY>
Enter an item to search for...
<FORM NAME="search" ACTION="mall.php" TARGET="mall">
<INPUT TYPE="text" NAME="criteria" SIZE="20">
<BR>
<INPUT TYPE="submit" VALUE="Search">
</FORM>
</BODY>
</HTML>
```

Our form has an action of mall.php and a text box called criteria. The target of the form is the right-hand frame, in which we want our results displayed. Here's the script that will do that job:

```
<?php
//mall.php
include "./common_db.inc";
```

```
if ($criteria!="") {
    $link_id = db_connect('mapping');
    $query = "SELECT m_name FROM mall WHERE m_desc LIKE '%".$criteria."%'";
    $mallResult = mysql_query($query, $link_id);

    if (mysql_num_rows($mallResult) > 0) {
        while ($mallRow = mysql_fetch_array($mallResult)) {
            echo $mallRow[0]."<BR>";
        }
    }
}
?>
```

Fire up the `index.html` file we created earlier, enter `shoes` in the text box and click on **Submit**. You should see the following results:

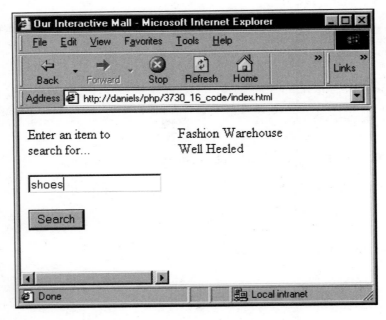

## *Drawing the Layout*

As we said earlier, we ultimately want our results displayed in a diagram, so let's modify `mall.php` to display the information graphically.

```
<?php
//mall2.php
include "./common_db.inc";

if ($criteria!="") {
    $link_id = db_connect('mapping');
    $query = "SELECT m_id FROM mall WHERE m_desc LIKE '%".$criteria."%'";
    $mallResult = mysql_query($query,$link_id);
```

```php
        if (mysql_num_rows($mallResult) > 0) {
            $stores = array();
            while ($mallRow = mysql_fetch_array($mallResult)) {
                $stores[count($stores)] = $mallRow[0];
            }
            mysql_free_result($mallResult);
            $show = implode(",",$stores);
            echo "<IMG SRC=\"showmall.php?show=".urlencode($show)."\">";
        } else {
            echo "no shops found";
        }
    }
?>
```

All the image creation tasks are farmed out to a new script, showmall.php:

```php
<?php
//showmall.php
include "./common_db.inc"

Header("Content-type: image/png");
if ($show!="") {
    $image = ImageCreateFromPNG("groundfloor.png");
    $shops = explode(",", urldecode($show));

    $link_id = db_connect('mapping');

    $gray = ImageColorAllocate($image, 204, 204, 204);
    for ($x=0; $x<count($shops); $x++) {
        $query = "SELECT m_center FROM mall WHERE m_id=".$shops[$x];
        $mallResult = mysql_query($query, $link_id);
        $mallRow = mysql_fetch_array($mallResult);
        $center = explode(",", $mallRow[0]);
        ImageFill($image, $center[0], $center[1], $gray);
    }
} else {
    $image = ImageCreate(100,50);
    $white = ImageColorAllocate($image, 255, 255, 255);
    $black = ImageColorAllocate($image, 0, 0, 0);
    ImageString($image, 5, 1, 1, "Error", $black);
}
ImagePNG($image);
ImageDestroy($image);
?>
```

If we perform the same search again, the result should look more like the figure shown overleaf.

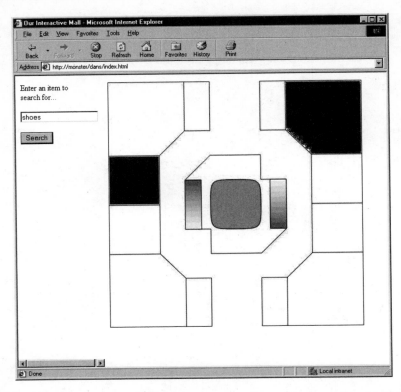

Our two PHP scripts `mall.php` and `showmall.php` work together to create the finished result you see above. The former handles the criteria we've passed from our `menu` form in the sidebar. It builds an HTML `IMG` tag, whose `SRC` attribute will specify the `showmall.php` script; it's this that actually draws the image.

The first thing we do in `mall.php` is to test that the user has entered something in the text box:

```php
<?php
//mall2.php
include "./common_db.inc";

if ($criteria!="") {
```

We then connect to database `mapping` and make a SQL query based on the user-entered value of `$criteria`. If any results are returned, we can process them:

```php
$link_id = db_connect('mapping');
$query = "SELECT m_id FROM mall WHERE m_desc LIKE '%".$criteria."%'";
$mallResult = mysql_query($query,$link_id);
if (mysql_num_rows($mallResult) > 0) {
```

We need to communicate these results to `showmall.php`, so we pass through a comma-separated list of the shops that need to be highlighted.

The `$stores` array will store all the shops that match our query. As we loop through each of the rows, we add the current shop to the end of the `$stores` array.

```
$stores = array();
while ($mallRow = mysql_fetch_array($mallResult)) {
    $stores[count($stores)] = $mallRow[0];
}
```

Once done looping through our rows we can free the memory associated with the result. We now have almost everything that we need to build the `img` tag that we'll use to display the mall. Our shops are currently stored in the `$stores` array, but we actually need them in a comma-separated list. We therefore use `implode()` to join all the elements in our array into a single string, separated by the specified delimiter `','`. We also use `urlencode()` to URL encode `$show`, so as to escape the commas.

```
mysql_free_result($mallResult);
$show = implode(",",$stores);
echo "<IMG SRC=\"showmall.php?show=".urlencode($show)."\">";
```

If we haven't found any records, then we let the user know:

```
} else {
    echo "no shops found";
}
}
?>
```

When we searched on "shoes" earlier we were returned the two shops that had the word "shoes" in the keyword field: "Fashion Warehouse" and "Well Heeled" – shops 3 and 11. If we look at the source of `mall.php` after it has been processed the following is the `img` tag in the page:

```
<IMG SRC="showmall.php?show=3%2C11"">
```

In `showmall.php` we first test to see that the `$show` variable contains something that we can use.

```
Header("Content-type: image/png");
if ($show!="") {
```

We then create the image in memory from the existing `groundfloor.jpg`. Because we want to start our image from an already existing image, we use the `ImageCreateFromPNG()` function to create the image canvas. This function reads an image file off disk and uses that image file as the basis for our image canvas in memory:

```
$image = ImageCreateFromPNG("groundfloor.png");
```

We then create an array called `$shops` by splitting up `$show` by commas using the `explode()` function. We also need to URL decode `$show` to unescape the commas. We then loop through the `$shops` array, and for each element in the array, perform a SQL query to grab the center point of the shop, and fill the appropriate area with a new color to highlight it.

```
$shops = explode(",", urldecode($show));
```

```
$link_id = db_connect('mapping');

$gray = ImageColorAllocate($image, 204, 204, 204);
for ($x=0; $x<count($shops); $x++) {
    $query = "SELECT m_center FROM mall WHERE m_id=".$shops[$x];
    $mallResult = mysql_query($query, $link_id);
    $mallRow = mysql_fetch_array($mallResult);
```

Once we have our array in $mallRow we can use the explode() function again to split up the x and y coordinates from our m_center field. We then use the ImageFill() function to fill each shop area with the light gray color that we allocated earlier. The ImageFill() function takes the following syntax:

```
ImageFill(image identifier, x, y, color identifier);
```

and flood-fills your image outwards from the coordinates you specify. It only affects pixels that are exactly the same color as the specified origin. If the pixel at position (x, y) was white (as it will be in our image) it fills in all white pixels surrounding that point.

```
    $center = explode(",", $mallRow[0]);
    ImageFill($image, $center[0], $center[1], $gray);
}
```

If $show is empty, we create a new blank image and use the function ImageString() to write the text string error onto it:

```
} else {
    $image = ImageCreate(100, 50);
    $white = ImageColorAllocate($image, 255, 255, 255);
    $black = ImageColorAllocate($image, 0, 0, 0);
    ImageString($image, 5, 1, 1, "Error", $black);
}
ImagePNG($image);
ImageDestroy($image);
?>
```

The syntax for ImageString() is:

```
ImageString(image_id, font, x, y, text, color_id);
```

The only arguments we haven't seen before are text and font. The former is just the text string that you want to write onto the image. The latter is an integer between 1 and 5, specifying one of the system's built-in fonts. If you don't enter anything in the text box, you'll therefore see the figure opposite:

## Further Interactivity

What we have so far is a searchable database whose results can be displayed graphically. However, suppose we want to make the map more interactive and let the user click on the shop to get more information? What we need is an **imagemap**, a piece of HTML that defines regions within an image so that different actions can be taken when the user clicks on different parts of the image.

All the information that we need to create an imagemap is already stored in our database: m_area contains coordinates for each corner of a shop, while m_name contains the name of the shop.

If we were building an imagemap by hand for our image above, we would first open the map tag and give it a name:

```
<MAP NAME="mall">
```

We'd then create an AREA entry for each of the areas we wanted to make clickable:

```
<AREA ALT='Fashion Warehouse' SHAPE='poly'
    COORDS='350,0,350,100,400,150,500,150,500,0' HREF='malldetail.php?id=3'>
```

The ALT attribute of an IMG element is principally there for the sake of users with browsers that don't display images – in such a browser, the ALT text is used instead in place of the image. We are going to use the ALT text for something different. In recent versions of Internet Explorer and Netscape (since version 4 of each, in fact) the ALT text appears as a tool tip whenever the mouse pointer hovers over the image. We are going to use this feature to display a tool tip containing the shop name.

*Note that IE4 and above support the TITLE attribute, which has the same effect, but can be used in any tag.*

The shape attribute in the tag gives the shape of the area. Currently supported shapes are poly, rect and circle. The poly shape expects to find coordinates for the corners of the shape in coordinate pairs in the COORDS attribute, which is exactly what we have stored in our database. The last attribute we specify is HREF, which as usual specifies the URL to be followed when that particular area is clicked. We mark the end of the imagemap element with </MAP>.

We still need to link the image to our imagemap, and we do that with the USEMAP attribute in the IMG tag.

```
<IMG SRC="showmall.php?show=3,11" USEMAP="#mall" BORDER=0>
```

The hash symbol # specifies that the imagemap is inside the current document, while BORDER=0 prevents us getting an ugly blue block around our image now that it's clickable.

## Try It Out - Generating an Imagemap from the Database

Our imagemap is pretty useless unless we can create it on the fly, so let's change our mall.php script to create an imagemap for our mall diagram:

```php
<?php
//mall3.php
include "./common_db.inc";
if ($criteria!="") {
    $link_id = db_connect('mapping');

    $query = "SELECT m_id, m_center, m_name, m_area FROM mall
             WHERE m_desc LIKE '%".$criteria."%'";
    $mallResult = mysql_query($query,$link_id);

    if (mysql_num_rows($mallResult) > 0) {
        $stores = array();
        $mapstring = "";

        while ($mallRow = mysql_fetch_array($mallResult)) {
            $stores[count($stores)] = $mallRow[0];
            $mapstring .= "<AREA ALT=\"".$mallRow[2].
                      "\" SHAPE=\"poly\" COORDS=\"".$mallRow[3].
                      "\" HREF=\"malldetail.php?id=".$mallRow[0]."\">\n";
        }

        mysql_free_result($mallResult);
        $show = implode(",", $stores);
        echo "<IMG SRC=\"showmall.php?show=".urlencode($show).
            "\" USEMAP=\"#mall\" BORDER=0>";
    } else {
        echo "no shops found";
    }
}
?>
<P>
<MAP NAME="mall">
<?php echo $mapstring ?>
</MAP>
```

### How It Works

The first thing we do is to alter our SQL query to include the extra data m_center, m_name, and m_area, which we'll need to build the imagemap:

```
$query = "SELECT m_id, m_center, m_name, m_area FROM mall
        WHERE m_desc LIKE '%".$criteria."%'";
```

We then declare a variable called $mapstring which will contain the meat of the imagemap definition:

```
$mapstring = "";
```

We already have a loop that runs through our selected records and builds up a string to pass to the image-drawing script showmall.php. We can therefore use this to build our imagemap as well. We can't yet output the imagemap to the browser, as we're still inside the IMG element, so sending any spurious text will break our image.

So, while we're inside the loop, we add code to build up $mapstring, using the same format as we would if building the imagemap manually. We define links to a new script, called malldetail.php, which we'll build in the next section; this will display details of the selected shop.

```
$mapstring .= "<AREA TITLE=\"".$mallRow[2].
            "\" SHAPE=\"poly\" COORDS=\"".$mallRow[3].
            "\" HREF=\"malldetail.php?id=".$mallRow[0]."\">\n";
```

When we come to write out the IMG element, we need to add in the USEMAP attribute as well as the BORDER attribute:

```
echo "<IMG SRC=\"showmall.php?show=".urlencode($show).
        "\" USEMAP=\"#mall\" BORDER=0>";
```

After we have written out the IMG tag we can create the imagemap:

```
<P>
<MAP NAME="mall">
<?php echo $mapstring ?>
</MAP>
```

## Showing the Shop Detail

We're now going to develop the script malldetail.php, which will display details of the specific shop that the user clicked on. The first thing it has to do is a database lookup for the shop information. It will then display a thumbnail of the mall layout with just the current shop highlighted.

In order to display a thumbnail of the image, we're going to use a function called ImageCopyResized(). This lets us copy a section of a source image, resize it, and paste it into a new image. The function works with two images: a source image and a destination image. It uses the following syntax:

```
ImageCopyResized(destination image,
                 source image,
```

```
                destination x, destination y,
                source x, source y,
                destination width, destination height,
                source width, source height);
```

For each image, we specify x and y coordinates, as well as a width and a height. An area `width` wide and `height` high, the top-left hand corner of which lives at (x, y) is copied from the source image, scaled to the correct `width` and `height` (as specified for the destination image) and placed into the destination image at the specified (x, y) position. The diagram below illustrates the process:

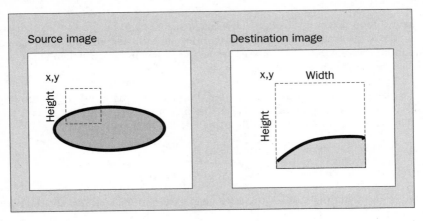

Since `showmall.php` already has all the code we need to display our mall, we'll just modify it to be able to display a thumbnail of our image instead of the full thing.

## Try It Out - Resizing Images

The first thing we need to do is to create our script `malldetail.php`:

```php
<?php
//malldetail.php
include "./common_db.inc";

$link_id = db_connect('mapping');
$query = "SELECT * FROM mall WHERE m_id=".$id;
$mallResult = mysql_query($query,$link_id) or die($query);
$mallRow = mysql_fetch_array($mallResult);
?>
<HTML>
  <HEAD><TITLE><?php echo $mallRow[1]; ?></TITLE></HEAD>
  <BODY>
    <H3><?php echo $mallRow[3]; ?></H3>
    <TABLE BORDER=0 WIDTH=500>
      <TR>
        <TD VALIGN="TOP" WIDTH=100>
          <IMG SRC="showmall.php?show=<?php echo $mallRow[0]; ?>&
                          thumbnail=on" WIDTH=100 HEIGHT=100>
```

```
           <TD VALIGN="TOP">
           <TABLE BORDER=0 WIDTH=300>
             <TR>
               <TD><b>Shop Number:</b><br> <?php echo $mallRow[2]; ?></TD>
               <TD><b>Phone Number:</b><br> <?php echo $mallRow[4]; ?></TD>
             </TR>
             <TR>
               <TD COLSPAN=2><b>Keywords:</b><br>
                 <?php echo $mallRow[7]; ?>
               </TD>
             </TR>
           </TABLE>
         </TR>
       </TABLE>
       <A HREF="javascript:history.back()">Return</A>
     </BODY>
   </HTML>
```

We then have to modify our `showmall.php` script to handle thumbnails:

```php
<?php
//showmall2.php
include "./common_db.inc";

Header("Content-type: image/png");
if ($show!="") {
    $image = ImageCreateFromPNG("groundfloor.png");
    $shops = explode(",", urldecode($show));

    $link_id = db_connect('mapping');

    $gray = ImageColorAllocate($image,204,204,204);
    for ($x=0;$x<count($shops);$x++) {
        $query = "SELECT m_area,m_center FROM mall WHERE m_id=".$shops[$x];
        $mallResult = mysql_query($query,$link_id);
        $mallRow = mysql_fetch_array($mallResult);
        $center = explode(",",$mallRow[1]);
        ImageFill($image,$center[0],$center[1],$gray);
    }
} else {
    $image = ImageCreate(100,50);
    $white = ImageColorAllocate($image,255,255,255);
    $black = ImageColorAllocate($image,0,0,0);
    ImageString($image,5,1,1,"Error",$black);
}
if ($thumbnail=="on") {
    $thumb = ImageCreate(100,100);
    ImageCopyResized($thumb,$image,0,0,0,0,100,100,500,500);
    ImagePNG($thumb);
} else {
    ImagePNG($image);
}
ImageDestroy($image);
?>
```

When we run our script we should this sort of result:

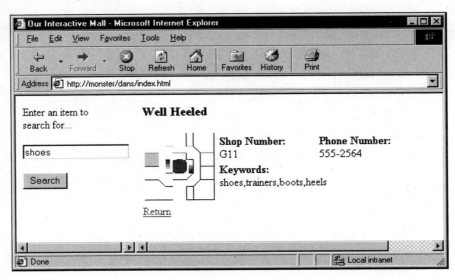

## How It Works

`Malldetail.php` writes out an HTML file that contains the information about the shop, as well as a thumbnail image of the mall layout. This is the line that creates the image:

```
<IMG SRC="showmall.php?show=<?php echo $mallRow[0]; ?>&thumbnail=on"
    WIDTH=100 HEIGHT=100>
```

This is almost exactly as we've seen before; the only difference is that the script has the extra argument of `thumbnail=on`. In `showmall.php` we now check whether to output a thumbnail or the full size image. All we need to change is the line:

```
ImagePNG($image);
```

We check for the value of `$thumbnail`, and if it's 'on' we resize the mall plan from its original dimensions of 500x500 to a more compact 100x100:

```
if ($thumbnail=="on") {
    $thumb = ImageCreate(100,100);
    ImageCopyResized($thumb,$image,0,0,0,0,100,100,500,500);
    ImagePNG($thumb);
} else {
    ImagePNG($image);
}
```

If the `$thumbnail` variable isn't set (or is set to anything other than "on") we display the image as normal.

# Advanced Graphics Manipulation

Now that we understand the basics of image functions and how we can apply them, let's take a look at some of the more advanced functions, the concepts behind them and their application.

## A Stylized Map

For this example we're going to dynamically create a stylized map. The map of the area itself will already exist and we will use this as a starting point. We shall then create a series of separate images, each containing an icon that represents an attraction on our map. We can then combine the images to create a composite map, with icons highlighting any of the tourist attractions.

The code that we use in this example will not be database driven, but will have the coordinates hard-coded into the script. You can easily combine the techniques we use here with the techniques we covered in the previous example if you wish to make a dynamic version of this map.

Here's the map that we'll be dropping our icons onto:

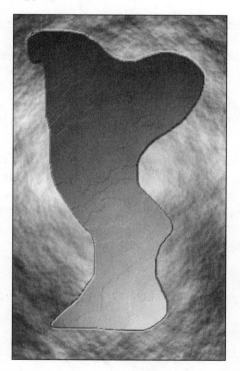

On top of this image we want to draw what appears to be a pin stuck into the map:

We'll call these files `island.jpg` and `pin.jpg` respectively.

Copies of these files are included in the code download for this book, available from http://www.wrox.com. Alternatively, you can use your own images and modify the following code accordingly.

We simply open up both of our image files and use `ImageCopyResized()` to copy the pin into the map image, and place it where we want:

```php
<?php
//map.php
Header("Content-type: image/jpeg");

$image = ImageCreateFromJPEG("island.jpg");
$icon = ImageCreateFromJPEG("pin.jpg");
$width = ImageSX($icon);
$height = ImageSY($icon);

ImageCopyResized($image,$icon,174,200,0,0,$width,$height,$width,$height);
ImageJPEG($image);
ImageDestroy($image);

?>
```

> *Note that we use three JPEG-specific functions here that are completely equivalent to the corresponding PNG functions we've used above. Only the names have been changed.*

Two more functions that we haven't seen before, `ImageSX()` and `ImageSY()` return the width and height of the specified image respectively. We then use these values as width and height values for source and destination images in `ImageCopyResized()`.

You'll notice straight away that there's a problem with the figure, as shown below. The white background of our pin image has been copied through as well as the pin itself, and has obscured part of the map.

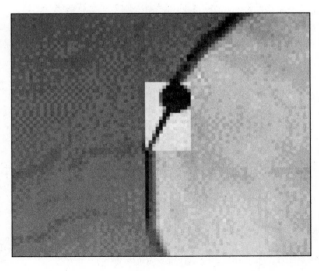

What we need to be able to do is to specify certain areas or colors of the image as being transparent. The function ImageColorTransparent() does just that, and takes 2 arguments: an image identifier and a color identifier. The specified color is then marked as transparent. However, there's a problem – in this case, we know that we want white to be the transparent color, and we know how to create white with ImageColorAllocate(); but what if the background was purple? How would we know exactly what values to use when defining $purple?

It's actually quite simple: we use the ImageColorAt() function, which returns an image identifier for the color of a specific pixel in a specified image. ImageColorAt() requires an image identifier and x and y image coordinates for the pixel to use. We then use the returned color identifier to specify a transparent color in ImageColorTransparent():

```php
<?php
//map.php
Header("Content-type: image/jpeg");

$image = ImageCreateFromJPEG("island.jpg");
$icon = ImageCreateFromJPEG("pin.jpg");
$trans = ImageColorAt($icon, 0, 0);
ImageColorTransparent($icon, $trans);
$width = ImageSX($icon);
$height = ImageSY($icon);

ImageCopyResized($image,$icon,174,200,0,0,$width,$height,$width,$height);
ImageJPEG($image);
ImageDestroy($image);

?>
```

Below is a portion of the result, which hasn't given us the results we expected:

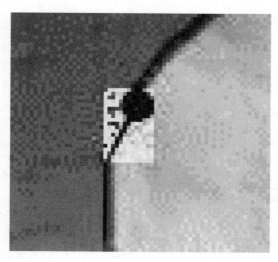

Only some parts of the white have been made transparent. If you open up pin.jpg and zoom in on a portion of the white part of the image, you'll notice that the white is not actually pure white, but a mixture of very light colors with subtle variations in their RGB values.

The following piece of code uses a new function, ImageColorsForIndex() that returns to us an associative array of the red, green and blue components of a specified color. We can use this to highlight what our eyes can't necessarily detect:

```php
<?php
//color_table.php
$image = ImageCreateFromJPEG("pin.jpg");
echo "<table border=1>\n";
for ($y=0;$y<4;$y++) {
    echo "<tr>\n";
    for ($x=0;$x<4;$x++) {
        $temp = ImageColorAt($image,$x,$y);
        $colorarray = ImageColorsForIndex($image,$temp);
        echo "<td>";
        echo "<font color=red>".$colorarray["red"]."</font><br>\n";
        echo "<font color=green>".$colorarray["green"]."</font><br>\n";
        echo "<font color=blue>".$colorarray["blue"]."</font><br>\n";
        echo "</td>\n";
    }
}
echo "</table>\n";
ImageDestroy($image);
?>
```

This script creates a 4x4 table containing the RGB components of the corresponding 4pixel x 4pixel area in the top left-hand corner of our image. The resultant output:

| 252 | 252 | 252 | 252 |
|-----|-----|-----|-----|
| 250 | 254 | 254 | 254 |
| 252 | 252 | 252 | 252 |
| 252 | 252 | 252 | 252 |
| 254 | 254 | 250 | 254 |
| 252 | 252 | 252 | 252 |
| 252 | 252 | 252 | 252 |
| 254 | 250 | 250 | 254 |
| 252 | 252 | 252 | 252 |
| 252 | 252 | 244 | 252 |
| 254 | 254 | 254 | 254 |
| 252 | 252 | 252 | 244 |

highlights the subtle differences between the pixels. In our previous example we were marking the very top left-hand pixel at 0,0 as the transparent color. In the 16 pixels we've chosen, only 3 others have the same RGB values as the top left-hand one.

One of the options that we have open to us to remedy this situation is to save the JPEG at a very high quality; hopefully this will minimize color variation through the image. Another option is to use an **indexed color image**. An indexed color image is commonly used for putting images on the web or for multimedia output, and has 256 or fewer colors.

One of the nicest features of an indexed color image is the ability to drop the number of colors in the image. This not only reduces the file size but (crucially for us) eliminates the variations in color that have so far foiled our attempts at making the area around our pin transparent.

`pin.png` is simply a copy of `pin.jpg` in PNG format. It was converted by a graphics program and the number of colors in the image was reduced to 10. The only alterations we need to make are to modify the line that opens `pin.jpg` so that it opens `pin.png` instead, and exchange the function `ImageCreateFromJPEG()` for `ImageCreateFromPNG()`:

```
$image = ImageCreateFromPNG("pin.png");
```

The result is immediately apparent:

## Palette Limitations

This is far better, but although the horrible white block has been removed from around the pin you may notice that the head of the pin is the wrong color. This is due to the relatively small number of colors available in the color table. As pixels are copied from one image to another, we can't use the same color indexes between images. Images may have different color tables and the color that we see on the screen for the index in the source image is not always the same color in the corresponding color index in the destination image.

For this reason when we use the `ImageCopyResized()` function a number of things happen in the background. The first thing that happens is the `ImageColorExact()` function is used to try and find an exact RGB color match in the destination image. If no match is found, `ImageColorAllocate()` is used to try and allocate the color for the destination image. If this also fails the `ImageColorClosest()` function is used to find the closest approximate color in the destination image.

Because our pin head is not appearing in the red that we would expect, we can assume that the `ImageCopyResized()` function has had to use the closest color that it could find. So why can it not allocate a nice, bright red in the destination image?

If we turn to the documentation for the `gd` libraries themselves, we find that `gdImageColorAllocate` (as it's called in the library) will fail if all 256 colors have already been allocated.

The following piece of code uses the `ImageColorsTotal()` function to display the number of colors in a given image's palette:

```php
<?php
//color_count.php
$image = ImageCreateFromJPEG("island.jpg");
echo ImageColorsTotal($image);
ImageDestroy($image);
?>
```

This will return a value of 256, explaining why `ImageColorAllocate()` fails and resorts to the closest available color. The JPEG format itself is not restricted to 256 colors, but the current version of the `gd` libraries only supports this many colors in a single image palette.

We saw earlier that with an indexed color image we could specify the number of colors in its palette. If we were to save our image of the island as a PNG file with 128 colors, we would have 128 colors available, and therefore not impact as heavily on the quality of the image:

```php
<?php
//map2.php
Header("Content-type: image/png");
$image = ImageCreateFromPNG("island.png");
$icon = ImageCreateFromPNG("pin.png");
$trans = ImageColorAt($icon,0,0);
ImageColorTransparent($icon,$trans);
$width = ImageSX($icon);
$height = ImageSY($icon);
ImageCopyResized($image,$icon,174,200,0,0,$width,$height,$width,$height);
ImagePNG($image);
ImageDestroy($image);
?>
```

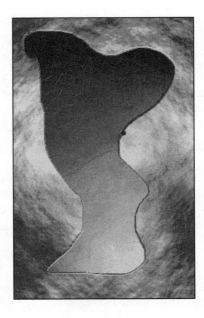

# Summary

During the course of this chapter we looked at how to create, open, manipulate and output images with PHP. This can enable you to add a new dimension to the scripts and web pages that you are already creating.

We have seen how these tools can be used in a practical and meaningful way to add value to the content in a web site. Now, not only can it have good looking graphics, but those graphics can engage visitors to your site by making them relate directly to a topic that interests them.

We have looked at some background information on graphics, and seen a little of their internal workings. Insight like this is essential if you want to really understand what's happening when you use the PHP's image functions.

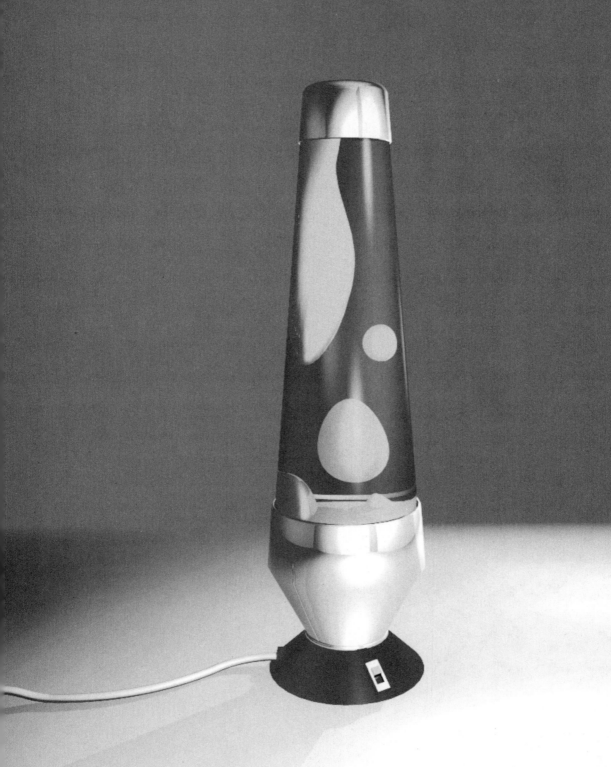

# 17

# Case Study
# A URL Directory Manager

For the first half of this book, we concentrated on teaching you the fundamentals of programming in PHP. We've covered basic programming concepts step-by-step, throwing in relatively simple examples of PHP code along the way, to reinforce your knowledge. This approach is fine to a degree, but it doesn't give you the bigger picture. Imagine that you had never seen a car. Even if you understood how every car part functions, it would be difficult to imagine how they could all be fitted together to form a car, and how useful a car could be. It's much the same with code; we can learn all the basics we want, but until we use them to build a useful PHP application, we will never appreciate the full power of PHP.

With this in mind, for the latter half of this book, we've built on the basics, and begun to find more exciting ways to use PHP: to generate graphics; to send e-mail applications; to interact both with XML and, especially, MySQL databases.

In this chapter we will use our knowledge of PHP/MySQL interactivity to build the most complex PHP application that you will encounter in this book. Along the way we will highlight the need for good planning and design of the application before we implement the code, and the importance of extensive testing of the finished application.

## Introducing the URL Directory Manager

So what are we going to build? We are going to construct a **URL directory** – a database containing many of web page links and descriptions, like Yahoo – and its associated **management system**.

Okay, so what can it do? Well, we've already mentioned a similarity to the Yahoo search engine. Like Yahoo, our application will allow us to navigate intuitively through a mass of URLs and when we find a URL that sounds interesting, our application will take us to the appropriate page. The application will enable directory users to:

❑ Search for URLs by category (for any URLs relating to "Eagles", say, as long as there is such a category in the directory)

❑ Search for URL descriptions which contain a keyword

❑ Submit new URLs to the directory

❑ Delete out-of-date URLs

❑ Modify URLs which are already in the directory

❑ Retrieve the most recent URLs to be added to the directory, and the most popular URLs

Surely we can't build something so complex after just 16 chapters of PHP? We can, and in this chapter we'll see how. We'll deal with all of the important stuff associated with building a large application:

❑ Designing the application

❑ Implementing the code

❑ Testing the application

So now we've got your interest, let's take a look at the design of the application.

# Designing the Directory Manager

The first and most important stage of creating any large application is design. If you jump right into writing code, without considering the most efficient design for your application, you will almost always end up with a poor application. The end product may be very inefficient, or it might not work properly. The code may also be badly structured, making it difficult to debug. These problems may result in you scrapping the application and starting again, wasting time (and probably money).

Depending on the scale of the project on hand, you may have to spend weeks, or even months, on initial designs. But you don't have to follow the traditional approach of drawing a bunch of flow charts using diagrams though. Just grab a piece of paper and jot down anything useful that comes to your mind about the requirements for your application, and how your application might fulfil these requirements.

Let's now illustrate this point by taking a look at the design considerations for our directory management application.

## User Requirements

Let's start with a handy hint. We recommend that, when creating a site, you get ideas from other sites that use applications similar to the one you need. For example, Yahoo is a similar kind of application to the one we want to build – a URL directory. It divides up URLs on the basis of web page content into subject categories. Each of these categories contains a set of subcategories. The subcategories contain subsubcategories, and so on, forming a *category hierarchy* or *tree*. Such a system makes browsing for URLs relating to a particular topic a breeze.

So we'll take a similar approach, and also allow users to post a new URL anywhere within the tree – even in the middle of the category hierarchy – just like in Yahoo. We shall also allow the same URL to be posted more than once throughout the tree, although obviously we won't allow two of the same URLs to inhabit the same place in the tree.

> The terminology 'category', 'subcategory', 'subsubcategory', and so on, is pretty
> clumsy, so from now on we'll refer to any point within the tree as a category. Finally,
> the category which spawns all the other categories will be known as the *root*.

## Users vs Administrators

So we want to build an application where users provide URLs for our directory tree. But what do we do
about links that are out-of-date, or need to be modified in other ways? We could let any user access the
URL database and modify URLs, but this is inviting trouble; a devious user could mess up URL data or
even wipe the whole directory!

We can partially solve this problem by asking for proof that the user who wants to alter a URL record
submitted the URL in the first place. In other words, we want to incorporate user *authentication*. Users
will be only allowed to alter URL data which they orginally submitted.

However, this still leaves the problem of how to handle out-of-date links. We don't want to allow users
to be able to delete links which are out-of-date, because we would be giving our devious user another
chance to delete lots of perfectly good URLs and mess up our directory.

What we really need is an *administrator* (also known as a *superuser*) who can check whether a link really
is broken or not, and modify URL data which needs fixing. Essentially, the administrator would act as
the directory caretaker. Note that to fulfill this role, administrators also require access privileges which
allow them to modify any URL data present in the directory.

This distinction between users and administrators impacts upon the design of our script, because
administrators have different requirements from the application than users. For example, there are
actions, such as deleting URLs, that only administrators should be able to perform. We must build our
directory manager in such a way that it prohibits users from being able to delete URLs. Therefore we
must first consider the requirements of both users and administrators:

**Users should be able to:**

❑ Navigate through a category tree of URLs

❑ Look for relevant URLs by performing a keyword search

❑ Add new URLs and update them if necessary

❑ See the number of hits, and the most recent access times to URLs

❑ Browse the most visited URLs, and newly added URLs, by category

**Administrators should also be able to:**

❑ Organize the categories hierarchically, by adding, deleting, and modifying them

❑ Review, and subsequently approve/reject, user submissions

❑ Modify or delete user submissions

❑ Notify users (via e-mail) when they make URL submissions, and also when their submissions
have been approved

We won't automatically list submitted URLs: administrators will review them, and then decide whether to approve them. A user will get notified via e-mail when he makes a contribution, and if his contribution is approved.

Note that in order to display the most-visited URLs, and the recently-added ones, we also need a way to keep track of when, and how often, users visit each URL. We'll look more closely at this later.

### User Authentication

The directory management system we'll build is free for all: anyone can contribute a URL. However, we can't allow ordinary users to mess with information that doesn't belong to them, which means some kind of authentication is required.

We'll use an e-mail and password pair to identify the owner of a submitted URL. Since an e-mail address should be unique for every user, this seems a reasonable way of authenticating users.

# User Interface

User interface design is another important area of application design. The user interface allows a user to "talk" to an application. One way to do this is using web browser forms: the user submits data to the form, and the data is sent to the application for processing. Then the application often returns new data which is printed out by the user's browser. Yahoo is one such example; we can submit a keyword into a search form, and get a list of related URLs back. Other interactive sites like this are often full of flashy graphics and designs, to attract our attention.

You might prefer these web sites that have the "looks". However, elegant layouts with fancy graphics often translate to slow interpretation by web browsers. Repeat visitors tend to prefer faster performance than cool looks. Again, look at Yahoo. Yahoo's success partly stems from its simplicity. Remember: users come to your site to get information, not to be overawed by site design. Therefore, we will keep our application "bare". (Anyway, a professional web designer might come in later and give it a better look!)

One rule of thumb for budding "application developers": when you create a user interface, make it as compact as possible. In other words, refrain from using more HTML tags than necessary just for the application's layout. That way, any web designer can take your application as a building block, and easily plug it into another web page.

Now, let's move on to actually creating the application. First, we need to determine how the data should be managed.

# Data Storage

Our first major technical consideration when designing this directory management application is: how are we going to save, and retrieve, URL-related data? In other words, which data storage model should we use: a file system, or a database?

Choosing a relational database over a file system seems the best option here. As we discussed in Chapter 11, the file system has inherent limits in terms of performance and scalability, and should therefore be avoided when you build applications like the URL directory manager, which uses lots of stored data.

For instance, using a relational database for data storage means that a query or two will suffice when you perform a URL search of the database for information. With the file system, however, you might have to perform a series of file operations to produce even a simple search result.

We're going to use the free relational database MySQL as for data storage. We covered MySQL and relational databases extensively in Chapters 11.

> If you skipped or skimmed through these chapters, we strongly recommend you read and understand them before continuing. The rest of the chapter assumes a strong understanding of MySQL and relational databases.

## Connecting to the Database

We've assumed so far that we are going to use a PHP "front end" to connect to a MySQL database. We've justified our choice of MySQL for the database, so we should really justify our choice of PHP as well. Ignore the fact that you're learning PHP – in the real world we have a range of different languages to choose from that can be used to connect to databases: CGI languages including Perl; embeddable scripting languages such as ASP; mod_perl and PHP; and commercial products. However, we shall ignore commercial products due to their cost and licensing requirements. Let's consider the other options.

Perl is an excellent general-purpose language, which could work with MySQL if we installed a database interface package which provides connectivity. But Perl is not suitable for web applications that have to deal with heavy traffic. Perl does come in an Apache module, mod_perl, but this is not yet optimized for high-volume web applications.

ASP also offers database connectivity (through ODBC) but we could only use it with Internet Information Server.

PHP is highly optimized for web applications development, and we can get immediate help from the PHP community through discussion forums, IRC channels, and mailing lists. PHP also ensures cost-effective and high-performance applications, since we can embed it into the Apache web server as a module. Plus, PHP is extremely easy to understand and use, and so we can get scripts up and running quickly.

So it seems that PHP was probably the best choice anyway. Phew!

## Database Schema

Since we have decided to use a relational database, the next step is to design the database *schema* – in other words we need to consider the type of data our database will be handling. This will enable us to construct a suitable database table to hold the URL data. A set of records for a particular URL should include the following:

❑   URL (the URL itself, for example: http://www.php.net)

❑   URL Title (for example: 'PHP Home Page')

❑   URL Description (for example: 'The site you can't miss if you're interested in PHP: PHP Home Page!')

## Chapter 17

- ❑ In addition, we need to store the following items of URL information:
- ❑ Register Date: The submission date of a URL (for example: August 7, 2000)
- ❑ Approval Flag: Indicates if a URL submission has been approved for listing
- ❑ Hit counter for URL
- ❑ Last access time for URL

The submission date will be used to determine which URLs have been recently added. We also need to store the following items, which will enable us to identify the user who submitted the URL:

E-mail Address: The e-mail address of the user posting a URL

Password: The user's password

Finally, we are going to group the URLs into categories, so will also need to store some information about the categories themselves:

- ❑ Category: The name of the category (for example "Eagles")
- ❑ Number of Items: The number of URLs present in the category

Now, we could create a database table containing a field for each of these items of information. However, this would be inefficient as the table would contain information about two entities: URLs and categories. As we saw in Chapter 11, relational databases work best when each table contains information on one entity only. Therefore we will create two tables: one to hold URL information, and the other for category data.

### URL Integer Identifiers

Are we done? Not yet. We need to choose primary keys for the URL and category tables, which we can use to uniquely identify records.

The URL string could serve as a primary key in the URL table. However, for improved database performance, we should assign a unique integer to each URL, the **URL ID**, to use as a primary key: integers are indexed and retrieved more quickly and efficiently than strings. Plus, we can ensure that each new URL record added to the database has a unique integer identifier, by giving the ID field in the URL table an AUTO_INCREMENT attribute. So we have another field to add to the URL table:

- ❑ URL ID: A unique URL indentifier.

### Defining the Category Tree

We must also decide how to uniquely identify category records. Again, we would like to avoid using unwieldy category name strings. We *could* use an integer identifier field, as for URLs, and use the AUTO_INCREMENT attribute to make sure that each category record is unique.

However, if we review the fields present in the category table, we can see that we have overlooked something. There is presently no way to find the *relationship* between different categories in the directory tree. For example; how do we know if the category "Eagles" is actually a subcategory of the category "Birds"?

You might wonder why this is important. Well, consider what happens when we want to navigate through the categories in the directory tree, to find a URL related to, say, wild eagles. Without defining the relationship between categories, the best that the directory can do is to present us with a list of *all* the categories in the directory, because it doesn't know how they are organized. We would have to search through all the categories until we find "Eagles". This is not what we want! We would like to navigate more intuitively than this, progressing through categories: subcategories, and so on, until we find the category that we want.

Therefore, we need to find a way to define the tree structure of the directory. Let's use an analogy. If we look at a file system, it contains directories, which in turn may hold files and subdirectories. Between a directory and its subdirectories a parent-child relationship exists. The same parent-child relationship exists in our directory: each category may contain URLs and may spawn a family of other categories.

One way to define this kinship would be to give each category a **local** ID number, and a **category** ID number. The local ID tells us about the parent-child relationship of the category; for example, if the category "Eagles" is the second child of "Birds", then the local ID of "Eagles" would be 002.

The category ID is simply a concatenation of the local ID, the parent's local ID, the grandparent's local ID, and so on, until we reach the category before the root. For example, imagine "Eagles" is the fifth child of "Birds", which in turn is the third child of "Wildlife". Assume that there are no categories (except for the root) above "Wildlife". Let's give the "Eagles", "Birds", and "Wildlife" categories local ID numbers of 002, 003 and 001 respectively. Then the category ID for "Birds" should be 001003 ("Birds" has a parent but no grandparent, so a concatenation of its parent's local ID 001 with its own local ID 003 gives 001003). Similarly, the category ID for "Eagles" should be 001003002, because "Eagles" has a parent and a grandparent, and a concatenation of all their local IDs is 001003002. This is illustrated in the figure below:

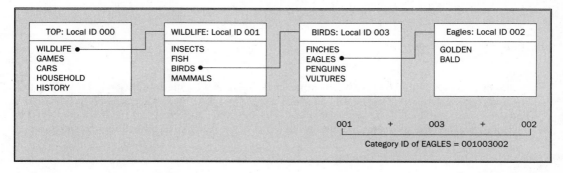

Since we know each category must have a unique category ID, we will use it as the primary key in the category table.

❑    Category ID: A unique category identifier

Note that to create the category ID for "Eagles" we concatenated 001 to 003 and to 002. We can't concatenate integers, only strings, so in our table we shall store the category ID as a variable length string. It might seem strange that we are storing integers as strings, but actually it's pretty useful. For example, it is much easier to extract the string "003" from "001003002", than to extract the integer 003 from 001003002.

The root is given the special local ID "000". But it's not stored in the table, since URLs should not be posted at the root.

## Database Tables

Now that we know our data schema, we can create some database tables for our directory. In a relational database, each table should list data only about a single entity, and complex queries can be answered by joining related tables. We need at least two tables, for storing URL information, and for maintaining a hierarchical list of categories. The relationship between the two tables is established by the category ID, because each URL must belong to a particular category. We'll call these tables php_directory and php_category respectively. Let's look now at the structures of these two tables. You can create them both, using the MySQL CREATE TABLE command described in Chapter 12, or you can download the SQL commands to do this from the Wrox web site: www.wrox.com. Place the tables in the sample_db database which you created for the examples in Chapters 11–13.

Here's the php_directory table structure as listed by the MySQL client:

```
mysql> DESC php_directory;
+----------------+--------------------+------+-----+---------+----------------+
| Field          | Type               | Null | Key | Default | Extra          |
+----------------+--------------------+------+-----+---------+----------------+
| url_id         | int(10)            |      | PRI | 0       | auto_increment |
| category_id    | varchar(15)        |      |     |         |                |
| title          | varchar(150)       |      |     |         |                |
| url            | varchar(150)       |      | MUL |         |                |
| description    | text               |      |     | NULL    |                |
| registerdate   | date               | YES  |     | NULL    |                |
| hit            | int(5)             |      |     | 0       |                |
| lastaccesstime | timestamp(14)      | YES  |     | NULL    |                |
| password       | varchar(20) binary | YES  |     | NULL    |                |
| e-mail         | varchar(100)       |      |     |         |                |
| approved       | char(1)            |      |     | 0       |                |
+----------------+--------------------+------+-----+---------+----------------+
11 rows in set (0.00 sec)
```

The names of the fields should be pretty self-explanatory. approved is the submission approval flag to which we alluded earlier. Note that the lastaccesstime field is defined as a timestamp type field: it gets updated every time the URL record is accessed. The url and category_id fields are combined (MUL) into a unique index, which allows for multiple submissions of the same URL under different categories.

Heres the php_category table structure:

```
mysql> DESC php_category;
+-------------+--------------+------+-----+---------+-------+
| Field       | Type         | Null | Key | Default | Extra |
+-------------+--------------+------+-----+---------+-------+
| category    | varchar(30)  |      |     |         |       |
| category_id | varchar(15)  |      | PRI |         |       |
| num_item    | int(5)       |      |     | 0       |       |
+-------------+--------------+------+-----+---------+-------+
3 rows in set (0.00 sec)
```

The num_item field in the php_category table keeps track of the number of records a particular category holds in the php_directory table. The rest of the fields are self-explanatory.

We have now built the database 'back end' for our URL directory, and devised a list of features that the directory should have. We know what we want our code to do. In a moment we shall begin to plan how our PHP script should be laid out. But first, a word or two about the limitations of PHP.

# Other Design Considerations

PHP can do a lot. But there are things it can't do. Even when you decide to use PHP as your web script language, you might need to get help from other languages for implementing features PHP can't help you with. Suppose you wanted your script to open up a new window whenever a user clicks on a link. Or, you might want to check to see if a user enters a valid value into a form field even before the form has been submitted. PHP can't help you with this, although JavaScript could.

We will demonstrate how you can incorporate lines of JavaScript code into PHP scripts as we develop the directory manager application.

# Code Layout

In this section we will plan how the PHP code should be laid out. In Chapter 6 we saw how it is often useful to modularize code, particularly when it makes that code clearer, more concise, and reusable. This approach makes code easier to read and debug. We are now going to consider how to "modularize" our application, first into scripts, and then into individual functions.

## Security Issues

Take another look at the list of requirements for the application. We have features that are used by both users and administrators, and other features that are used by either users or administrators. This means that we have a security issue: we must not allow users access to features which only administrators should use (URL record deletion, for instance). We could put all our functions into a single script, and ask for administrator authentication as we run the script. But it isn't very secure to include administrative code in a file which users can access by their web browsers.

A more secure system is to place administrative code in a separate script, which only administrators have access to. We then place functions used by both administrators and ordinary directory users into a common file. Finally, we have a separate script which calls those functions available to the user. The user and administrator scripts both have access to the functions in the common file.

The application will therefore be divided up into three scripts:

| | |
|---|---|
| php_directory.inc | the file where "common" code resides |
| php_directory.php | the file where user code resides |
| dir_manager.php | the file where administration code resides |

We will put all the scripts into the same directory for the sake of simplicity. However, it is not recommended in any way, for obvious security reasons. You need to store the administrator script in a password-protected directory to which no unauthorized user has access.

### Administrator Authentication

This modular approach, however, highlights another problem which didn't surface when we were designing the application – how do we determine if the current user is an administrator?

We *could* use a special e-mail account and password combination, only known by administrators, for authentication. Then we would propagate a flag variable through the URL indicating that the current user is an administrator. However, this is not only cumbersome, but could create a security hole in your application if a user ever finds out your authentication scheme.

We will take a different approach, which is simple but efficient: since administrators will be using their own script, we can use the name of the script to authenticate them. For example, the following line of PHP code, taken from the directory script we shall see later, marks the current user as administrator:

```
if(basename($PHP_SELF) == $admin_script) $admin = 1;
```

The `$admin_script` variable holds the name of the script used by administrators – `dir_manager.php` here. The `basename()` function returns the filename part of a given filepath. So this code checks the name of the user's script, and if it matches `$admin_script`, the administrator flag variable `$admin` is switched on.

So what happens if a devious user looks through the `php_directory.php` and `php_directory.inc` scripts, spots that the `$admin` flag is used to indicate an administrator, and switches the flag on? Actually, the user still can't use any administrator functions, because they are defined in the `dir_manager.php` script, which should be hidden in a password-protected directory.

## Directory Functions

So we know that there will be three PHP scripts associated with our URL directory manager. Now we need to consider the type of functions we need to create, and which of the scripts each function should be located in.

### Types of Functionality

We need three types of functionality. The first is a set of functions that displays data on the user's browser. For example, we need a function that will print out the category tree, and another that will list URLs in a particular category.

The second type of function provides the user with an interface, which can be used to send or retrieve data within the database. This interface is invariably an HTML form of some kind. Here we have functions which produce forms to submit a new URL, or modify existing URL data, or perform a keyword search.

The third set of functions could be termed "utility" functions. These are the functions that interact with the database. For example, we need functions to connect to the database, to add categories and URLs, and to retrieve URL records.

Let's now consider the content of each script in turn.

## The User Script – php_directory.php

Since all of the functions available to the user should also available to the adminstrator too, we don't need to hide any functions in the user script `php_directory.php`. Instead we will use this script to hold the "engine" of the directory, where the user selects which course of action to take (submit a URL, select a category, go to a URL, and so on).

## The Common Script – php_directory.inc

The common file `php_directory.inc` should contain all of the functionality available to all directory users. Display functions in this script should:

- ❑ Start and end an HTML page
- ❑ List categories and URL data in the browser window
- ❑ List recently-submitted URLs and the most popular URLs
- ❑ Inform the user when an action is successful

We also need functions which produce HTML forms for:

- ❑ Submitting a URL
- ❑ Modifying URL data
- ❑ Performing a keyword search of URL data

Finally, we need utility functions to carry out the following actions:

- ❑ Connect to the database
- ❑ Retrieve information about URLs and categories
- ❑ Add URL records to the database
- ❑ Modify URL records in the database
- ❑ Handle errors

Note the presence of error-handling functions. We saw in Chapter 7, how important it is to build in error handling to our applications, so that we can easily locate the source of errors, should they occur.

## The Administrator Script – dir_manager.php

All the extra functions that administrators need to manage the directory are located in `dir_manager.php`. These will include the display functions needed to:

- ❑ List categories for editing
- ❑ List recently-submitted URLs
- ❑ Display a set of links useful to administrators

The script also needs some functions that produce HTML forms. These forms should enable the administrator to:

❑    Add or modify categories

❑    Edit, approve or delete newly-submitted URLs

Administrative utility functions should take care of the following activities:

❑    Adding new categories to the database

❑    Modifying existing categories

❑    Deleting categories and URL records

❑    Editing newly-submitted URLs

❑    Checking for inconsistencies between database tables and correcting them

The last feature is needed to account for errors which sometimes occur when attempting database queries. The result of the error may be a discrepancy between data in both tables.

Now that we've dealt with the broad structure of the code let's take a detailed look at each of our three scripts.

# Code Implementation

At last, it's time to do some coding. We'll start by looking at the function code common to both users and administrators. We'll then look at the user script, and finish off with the administrative code. The URL directory manager code is substantially longer than any other PHP code that you have encountered so far in this book, so we'll take it slowly, with plenty of explanation along the way.

## Common Code – php_directory.inc

We will put common functions used by both users and administrators into this include file php_directory.inc. However, the first step is to define some global variables, which will be useful later.

The first global variables we define are associated with MySQL database connection. These variables will be familiar to those of you who have tried the examples in Chapters 11 – 13:

```php
<?php
$dbhost = 'localhost';            // database server
$dbusername = 'phpuser';          // username
$dbuserpassword = 'phppass';      // user password
$default_dbname = 'sample_db';    // default database

$directory_tablename = 'php_directory';    // URL table
$category_tablename = 'php_category';      // Category table

$link_id = 0;
```

If you did try the examples, then you should have a database user record for user "phpuser", and also a database called "sample_db". If not, you should change the values of the first three variables to reflect your settings, and change the name of the default database to the one containing tables "php_directory" and "php_category", which we created earlier.

The next two variables simply contain the names of the database tables associated with the URL directory. By using these variables throughout the script instead of the actual table names, we are ensuring that if we change the table names in the future, we won't have to go back through the script, changing all the old table names to the new ones. We only need to change the table names once, here.

The $link_id is the database connection link identifier, described in Chapter 11.

The next global variables govern properties of certain fields in the database tables:

```
$category_id_length = 3;
$root_category_id = '000';
$max_desc_length = 250;
```

The $category_id_length variable dictates the length of the local ID string used to construct category IDs. As we have already seen, the root category of the tree has the special local ID "000". The $max_desc_length variable limits the length of the URL description submitted by users – 250 characters at most here.

Next up, we have some variables which influence the browser window and its contents:

```
$new_window_width = 600;
$new_window_height = 500;
$welcome_message = "Welcome to PHP Directory!";
$records_per_page = 3;
$num_top_sites = 5;
$num_new_sites = 5;
```

The $new_window_width and $new_window_height variables hold the size information of new windows containing forms.

The string in the $welcome_message variable is displayed when the current category ID is either at the root or empty – indicating the user is at the root, or is viewing the category tree. The $records_per_page variable controls the number of URLs listed per page, while the $num_top_sites and $num_new_sites variables are used to limit the number of URLs returned when creating the lists of the most popular and recently-added URLs respectively.

The next three variables are used for administrative purposes:

```
$admin_script = 'dir_manager.php';
$send_mail = False;
$dirmaster_email = "dirmaster<phpdir@phpdirectory.com>";
```

The $admin_script variable is set to the name of the PHP script run by administrators, and is used to turn on the $admin flag, indicating that the current user is an administrator. The next two variables are concerned with e-mails to and from the server. The $send_mail flag variable should only be turned on if the server is configured to send and receive mail. The 'From' and 'Reply-To' header fields in the e-mails sent by the application contain the e-mail address defined in the $dirmaster_e-mail variable.

In addition, we'll be using two global variables to detect what went wrong upon error while trying to talk to the server:

```
$MYSQL_ERRNO = '';
$MYSQL_ERROR = '';
```

The $MYSQL_ERRNO and $MYSQL_ERROR variables capture the error number and error text returned by the server on error.

Now, let's define some functions common to both the user and administrator scripts. Note how the global variables defined above are used in these functions.

## directory_header()

Our application often needs to open and close browser windows. We will use the directory_header() and directory_footer() functions to start and end HTML pages respectively. These simple functions contain mostly HTML, and hardly any PHP code, so we won't take much time out to explain how they work.

```
function directory_header() {
    global $new_window_width, $new_window_height;
?>
<HTML>
<HEAD>
<SCRIPT LANGUAGE="JavaScript" TYPE="text/javascript">
<!--
function open_window(url) {
    var NEW_WIN = null;

    NEW_WIN =  window.open ("", "RecordViewer", "toolbar=no,width="+<?php echo
$new_window_width ?>+",height="+<?php echo $new_window_height
?>+",directories=no,status=no,scrollbars=yes,resize=no,menubar=no");
    NEW_WIN.location.href = url;
}
//-->
</SCRIPT>
<TITLE>PHP Directory</TITLE>
</HEAD>
<BODY>
<?php
}
```

The directory_header() function contains a JavaScript function definition. This function is called open_window(), which (unsurprisingly) opens a new window with a given URL. Note how the directory_header() function makes use of the $new_window_width and $new_window_height global variables we defined earlier.

## directory_footer()

The directory_footer() function is the simplest function in the application, basically comprising of two closing HTML tags:

```
function directory_footer() {
?>
</BODY>
</HTML>
<?php
}
```

## db_connect()

The db_connect() function should be familiar to those who have tried the examples in Chapters 11 through 13. The function attempts a connection to the MySQL server. On error it displays an error code and message. We won't take much time to explain it because it is covered in some depth in Chapter 11.

```
function db_connect($dbname='') {
    global $dbhost, $dbusername, $dbuserpassword, $default_dbname;
    global $MYSQL_ERRNO, $MYSQL_ERROR;

    $link_id = @mysql_connect($dbhost, $dbusername, $dbuserpassword);
    if(!$link_id) {
        $MYSQL_ERRNO = 0;
        $MYSQL_ERROR = "Connection failed to the host $dbhost.";
        return 0;
    }
    else if(empty($dbname) && !@mysql_select_db($default_dbname)) {
        $MYSQL_ERRNO = mysql_errno();
        $MYSQL_ERROR = mysql_error();
        return 0;
    }
    else if(!empty($dbname) && !@mysql_select_db($dbname)) {
        $MYSQL_ERRNO = mysql_errno();
        $MYSQL_ERROR = mysql_error();
        return 0;
    }
    else return $link_id;
}
```

Note that we have prefixed the mysql_connect() and mysql_select_db() functions here with @ to suppress error messages. The function returns a connection link identifier, $link_id, that will be used to issue subsequent queries.

## sql_error()

At the start of the script, we introduced the $MYSQL_ERRNO and $MYSQL_ERROR variables. These hold the error number and text when something goes wrong while trying to make a connection to the server or issuing a query. All you have to do upon such error is to take a peek into these variables.

The sql_error() function constructs a string containing the error code and message, should an error occur while connecting to (or querying) the database server:

```
function sql_error() {
    global $MYSQL_ERRNO, $MYSQL_ERROR;
```

The first step is to fill the error variables with values if they are empty. We retrieve the relevant MySQL error code and message using the mysql_errno() and mysql_error() functions respectively. Without the optional link identifier ($link_id) argument, both of these functions will return the errors associated with the last opened link.:

```
    if(empty($MYSQL_ERROR)) {
        $MYSQL_ERRNO = mysql_errno();
        $MYSQL_ERROR = mysql_error();
    }
```

The next line just returns a string containing the error code and message, separated by a colon:

```
    return "$MYSQL_ERRNO: $MYSQL_ERROR";
}
```

## error_message()

The `error_message()` function alerts users to an error which occurred while attempting to perform a given operation, by displaying an error message. The message $msg is supplied as an argument to the function:

```
function error_message($msg) {
    directory_header();
    echo "<SCRIPT>alert(\"Error: $msg\");history.go(-1)</SCRIPT>";
    directory_footer();
    exit;

}
```

The `directory_header()` and `directory_footer()` functions are used to invoke a new window to display the error message in. When the user clicks the **OK** button in the window, the browser is returned to the previous page using JavaScript's `history` object: `history.go(-1)` causes the browser to go back to the previous page.

We can combine these two functions to find out what went wrong upon database error, as the following line of code shows:

```
error_message(sql_error());
```

The `sql_error()` function constructs the error message and `error_message()` displays it. It's as simple as that.

## user_message()

We'll also need a way to display confirmation messages to the user. The `user_message()` function confirms that an action was completed by echoing out a confirmation message $msg on a new page:

```
function user_message($msg, $url='') {
    directory_header();
    if(empty($url)) echo "<SCRIPT>alert(\"$msg\");history.go(-1)</SCRIPT>";
    else echo "<SCRIPT>alert(\"$msg\");self.location.href='$url'</SCRIPT>";

    directory_footer();
    exit;

}
```

You should note the use of the `directory_header()` and `directory_footer()` functions to create a new window to place the message in. The $url argument to `user_message()`, when given, is used to determine which page the script needs to fall back to.

## get_category_info()

It is often useful to create functions which return information about data, but not the actual data itself. Information about data is known as *meta data*. The get_category_info() function returns an associative array of meta data about a specific category, called $category_info_array. The array contains the following items:

| | |
|---|---|
| "category" | The name of the category. |
| "num_item" | The number of URLs the category holds. |
| "num_child" | The number of children the category has. |
| "next_id" | Next possible name of a child. For example, if the category ID "003001" already had two children, the next child ID would be "003001003". |
| "depth" | The 'generation' that the category belongs to. For example, the root category is 1st generation. The categories immediately below the root are second generation. Children of these top-most categories are 3rd generation, and so on. So category ID "003001003" would be 4th generation, and this array element would contain 4. |
| "fullname" | The expanded family name of the category. To use an example from earlier in the chapter, if "Eagles" is the child of "Birds", which is the child of "Wildlife", the expanded family name would be "Wildlife->Birds->Eagles". |
| "href_fullname" | The hyperlinked expanded family name of the category. This is the family name made into a hypertext HTML link. For example, the "Eagles" hyperlinked family name would be: "<A HREF=\"url_to_jump_to_Wildlife\">Wildlife</A>-><A HREF=\" url_to_jump_to_Birds \">Birds</A>-><A HREF=\" url_to_jump_to_Eagles\">Eagles</A>" |

OK, let's now look at the function.

**1.** Define function, declare global variables, and check connection to database.

As usual, the function definition is followed by some global variable declarations. Note that the function requires a category ID argument:

```
function get_category_info($category_id) {
    global $default_dbname, $category_tablename, $root_category_id,
$category_id_length, $welcome_message, $PHP_SELF;
    global $link_id;
```

The function first checks to see if a database link has been established; if not, it calls the db_connect() function which will do the job. Actually, you will find this initial check in every function which accesses the MySQL database:

```
    if(!$link_id) $link_id = db_connect($default_dbname);
```

**2.** Retrieve metadata for the root category.

The next step is to fill `category_info_array()` with values for the category in question. However, we must first check to see if the category is root, because this is a special case:

```
if($category_id == $root_category_id) {
    $category_info_array["category"] = "Top";
    $category_info_array["num_item"] = 0;
```

The root's official name is "Top", and since no URL records may be posted at the root, the `num_item` element of the array must contain zero. These values are pushed into the array.

We must now search the database to find more root meta data. We construct a query string which will retrieve both the ID of the root's 'youngest' child (the child with the largest local ID), and the total number of children of the root:

```
$query = "SELECT max(category_id), count(*) FROM $category_tablename WHERE
length(category_id) = $category_id_length";
```

Then we feed the query string into `mysql_query()` to perform the search, printing out an error message if an error occurs (in which case `$result` is zero):

```
$result = mysql_query($query);
if(!$result) echo sql_error();
```

Next we extract the meta data for each category. The function `mysql_fetch_row()` is used to pass the meta data one category at a time to the `$query_data` array:

```
$query_data = mysql_fetch_row($result);
$sibling_id = $query_data[0];
$num_child = $query_data[1];
```

Then we move values for the ID of the root's youngest child, and the number of children of the root, into the `$sibling_id` and `$num_child` variables respectively. What we want to do now is move values from these variables into the appropriate elements of `$category_info_array`. We can now transfer the number of children of the root into the appropriate element of `$category_info_array`:

```
$category_info_array["num_child"] = $num_child;
```

The next element we would like to fill in `$category_info_array` is next_id. We already know the ID of the root's youngest child, `$sibling_id`, and so the next child will have an ID one greater than `$sibling_id`. First we check to see if the root has any children; if not, we know the next child should be ID "001":

```
if(!$sibling_id) $next_category_id = '001';
```

If the root does have children, then we have a trickier task to get the value of next_id. If we simply add the integer 1 to the string value of `$sibling_id`, then an implicit type conversion of the string will occur and the answer will be an integer. For example, 1 + "003" = 4. This is a problem, because we want a string answer – an ID, and because we want an ID we also want it to be three characters long.

Let's see the way we get around this problem. First, we first measure the length of the $sibling_id string, using the strlen() function:

```
else {
    $sibling_length = strlen($sibling_id);
```

Then we add 1 to $sibling_id, which yields the integer value of next_id. We store this in $next_category_id:

```
$next_category_id = $sibling_id + 1;
```

Before we change $next_category_id to a string, we create a string of zeros which we will use to pad out $next_category_id until it is the same length as $sibling_id:

```
for($i = strlen($next_category_id); $i < $sibling_length; $i++) $left_pad
.= '0';
```

The last step is to concatenate the string of zeros with $next_category_id. Concatenation forces an implicit type conversion (to a string) upon $next_category_id. We end up with a string of the same length as $sibling_id:

```
$next_category_id = $left_pad . $next_category_id;
}
```

Now that we have the value that we need for $category_info_array["next_id"] stored in $next_category_id, we can fill up the rest of $category_info_array:

```
$category_info_array["next_id"] = $next_category_id;
$category_info_array["depth"] = 1;
$category_info_array["href_fullname"] = $welcome_message;
$category_info_array["fullname"] = $welcome_message;
}
```

Note that on the root category page, we don't get a clickable category title. Instead, a directory welcome message ("Welcome to PHP Directory!") is displayed. Therefore, we fill the welcome message into the final two elements of $category_info_array.

**3.** Now retrieve metadata for other categories. Start by querying the database.

So we have dealt with retrieving meta data for the root category. Now let's have a look at how the process differs when we deal with any other category:

```
else {
```

As before, we need to search the database to retrieve the meta data. So we build a query string that will retrieve the name of a category and the number of items it holds, given the category's ID:

```
$query = "SELECT category, num_item FROM $category_tablename WHERE
category_id = '$category_id'";
```

```
$result = mysql_query($query);
if(!$result) echo sql_error();
```

Again, we feed the query string to `mysql_query()` and check for errors. We follow this by extracting meta data for each category, one at a time, using `mysql_fetch_array()` to fill the `$query_data` array:

```
$query_data = mysql_fetch_array($result);
$category_info_array["category"] = $query_data["category"];
$category_info_array["num_item"] = $query_data["num_item"];
```

The meta data in `$query_data` (category name and number of URLs) is then passed on to `$category_info_array`.

Remember the query string we used before, to extract the youngest child and the number of children for the root? The following query string is the equivalent for *any* category:

```
$query = "SELECT max(category_id), count(*) FROM $category_tablename WHERE
(length(category_id) = length('$category_id') + $category_id_length) AND
category_id LIKE '$category_id%'";
```

This differs from the query we used for the root, because we have a more complex WHERE clause and an extra AND clause. The WHERE clause contains:

```
length(category_id) = length('$category_id') + $category_id_length
```

This restricts the search to the children of the category specified by `category_id`. The AND contains:

```
category_id LIKE '$category_id%'
```

This restricts the search to the category in question, plus all of the categories that it spawns, down to the bottom of the directory tree. Next we carry out the query, and check for error:

```
$result = mysql_query($query);
if(!$result) echo sql_error();
```

We've seen the next step before as well. We transfer the meta data retrieved for each category to an array, and then to appropriate variables:

```
$query_data = mysql_fetch_row($result);
$sibling_id = $query_data[0];
$num_child = $query_data[1];
```

The next section of code should look familiar too. We add the number of children to the `$category_info_array`, and then use the ID of the youngest child to derive `$next_category_id`. This will contain the value we need to feed into `$category_info_array["next_id"]`:

```
$category_info_array["num_child"] = $num_child;
```

```
if(!$sibling_id) $next_category_id = $category_id . '001';
else {
    $sibling_length = strlen($sibling_id);
    $next_category_id = $sibling_id + 1;
    for($i = strlen($next_category_id); $i < $sibling_length; $i++)
        $left_pad .= '0';
    $next_category_id = $left_pad . $next_category_id;
}

$category_info_array["next_id"] = $next_category_id;
```

The next step is to derive the depth of the category within the category tree. We can do this by working out how many generations from root the category is. We do this by measuring the length of the category ID string, and then dividing this by the length of a local ID ($category_id_length). For example "003001002" is nine characters long, and each local ID is three characters long. Nine divided by three equals three, so this is a third-generation category. However, since root is defined as having a category depth of one, the depth of any category is the generation plus one. So the category with ID "003001002" has a depth of four.

The following definition of category depth in PHP code is much more concise! We feed the resulting value into $category_info_array:

```
$category_info_array["depth"] = (strlen($category_id) / $category_id_length)
+ 1;
```

The last step is to work out the expanded family name of the category. This is actually pretty tricky. First we need to chop up the category ID into its constituent local IDs (for example "002003006" will be chopped into "002", "003" and "006"). We will then use these local IDs to retrieve the category names that we need to construct the family name.

**4.** Retrieve the extended family name of a category.

The first step is to set up a for loop to derive the names of the categories needed for the extended family name:

```
$j = 0;
for($i=0; $i < strlen($category_id); $i += $category_id_length) {
```

Note that we have set up two loop counters, $i and $j. We'll see why in a moment. Also note that the loop is a bit unusual because the loop counter $i starts at zero but increments by the value of $category_id_length every loop. Again, the reason for this will become clear soon. The next step is to extract a substring from category ID using the substr() function:

```
$parent_id .= substr($category_id,$i,$category_id_length);
```

Let's look more closely at what's happening here. We are feeding three arguments to the substr() function. The first is the string to extract from. The second is a number which indicates how many characters in from the start of the string we should begin the extraction (the 'offset'). The last argument is a number, the length of the string that we want to extract.

Let's have an example. Say we wanted to extract the string "daft" from another string "adaftexample", which is stored in the variable $example. Then because "daft" is offset by one character from the start of "adaftexample", and "daft" is four characters long, we would use substr($example,1,4) to extract "daft".

Okay, now return to the function. The previous line of code extracts a substring which is $category_id_length long from $category_id. We noted before that $i begins at zero and is incremented by the value of $category_id_length with every loop. This means that the offset for the extraction must be a multiple of $category_id_length (or zero) too. Are you getting the picture? Since $category_id_length defines the length of a local ID, *the substr() function extracts one of the local IDs from the category ID string.*

But we haven't finished yet. Note that the previous line of code contains the .= operator, not the = operator. Why? Well, consider what happens each time we go around a loop. At the start of the first for loop, parent_id is empty. It is then filled with the first local ID from the category ID string. When we reach the substr() function again in the second loop, the function returns the second local ID from the category ID string to parent_id. However, the presence of the .= operator means that this local ID string does not replace the first ID string still present in $parent_id. Instead, the two local IDs are concatenated and placed in $parent_id. We'll use an example to illustrate this. Say that the category ID was "002003006". Then the value of $parent_id at this point in each loop would be:

❑   First loop: "002"

❑   Second loop: "002003"

❑   Third loop: "002003006"

In other words, during the first loop, $parent_id contains the category ID of the grandparent of the category. During the second loop it contains the category ID of the category's parent. During the last loop it contains the category ID.

That was a lot of explanation for one line of code. But understanding this line is crucial to understanding the rest of the loop. The next step is to build up the query string that will retrieve the name of the category defined by $parent_id:

```
$query = "SELECT category FROM $category_tablename
                         WHERE category_id = '$parent_id'";
$result = mysql_query($query);
$query_data = mysql_fetch_row($result);
```

Then we feed the query to mysql_query() as usual, and check for errors. With each loop we construct a string containing a hypertext link to the category defined by $parent_id:

```
$parent_href_array[$j] = "<A
HREF=\"$PHP_SELF?action=show_list&category_id=$parent_id\">" . $query_data[0]
."</A>";
```

These hypertext links are placed in an array. We feed the names of all the categories present in the family name into another array:

```
$parent_array[$j] = $query_data[0];
$j++;
}
```

The loop counter $j records which iteration we're on, so that each name and hyperlink is placed in the correct elements of the arrays. The final step is to create the extended family name string, and the hyperlinked family name string, by combining (imploding) the elements of each array. We also add the "->" string between each category name to show the hierarchy. Then we place the strings in the correct elements of $category_info_array:

```
        $category_info_array["href_fullname"] = implode("->", $parent_href_array);
        $category_info_array["fullname"] = implode("->", $parent_array);
    }

    return $category_info_array;
}
```

This get_category_info() function is pretty intricate. Most of the other functions are rather straightforward.

## get_url_info()

We store data about two entities in this directory: categories and URLs. The get_category_info() function returns information on a given category. We'll also need a function that returns information on a given URL. The get_url_info() function returns an associative array with information on a given URL:

```
function get_url_info($url_id) {
    global $link_id, $default_dbname, $directory_tablename;

    if(!$link_id) $link_id = db_connect($default_dbname);
```

As usual, we need to check if a database connection is open. We then issue the following single query to get all the necessary information on a given URL:

```
$query = "SELECT url_id, category_id, title, url, description,
                registerdate, date_format(registerdate, '%M, %e, %Y') as
                formatted_registerdate, hit, lastaccesstime,
                date_format(lastaccesstime, '%M, %e, %Y %r') as
                formatted_lastaccesstime, password, email, approved FROM
                $directory_tablename WHERE url_id = '$url_id'";
```

Note that aliases are used here to get formatted date and time strings from a URL record. We can access the field values using the aliases:

```
$formatted_registerdate = $query_data["formatted_registerdate"];
$formatted_lastaccesstime = $query_data["formatted_lastaccesstime"];
```

We feed the query into mysql_query() which performs the search, and then check for errors:

```
$result = mysql_query($query);
if(!$result) echo sql_error();
```

Then we simply return the URL data to the function which called get_url_info():

```
        return mysql_fetch_array($result);
    }
```

And that's it. Obviously this function is much simpler than `get_category_info()`.

## search_form()

Search engines make the job of searching for useful URLs in a directory a piece of cake. This function produces an HTML form which enables the user to search for keywords. The search can be performed directory-wide. It can also be confined to a specific category, if the category ID is provided as an argument to the function:

```
function search_form($category_id) {
    global $root_category_id, $PHP_SELF;

    if(!isset($category_id)) $category_id = $root_category_id;
```

If the `$category_id` argument is not given, we default to the root category ID, enabling a directory-wide search operation. The function then displays a search form:

```
?>
<CENTER>
<FORM METHOD="POST" ACTION="<?php echo $PHP_SELF ?>">
<INPUT TYPE="HIDDEN" NAME="action" VALUE="show_list">
```

The `search_form()` function is called by the `show_list()` function, as we'll see shortly. We insert a `search_on` hidden field into the form, which indicates whether we are performing a keyword search or not. When the **Submit** button is pressed, `search_on=1` will be passed to the `show_list()` function. This will cause `show_list()` to go into search mode, retrieving search results and displaying them in the browser window:

```
<INPUT TYPE="HIDDEN" NAME="search_on" VALUE="1">
```

Next we create a text box where the user can enter keywords. The keywords will be passed to `show_list()` in the `$keywords` variable:

```
    Search: <INPUT TYPE="TEXT" NAME="keywords" SIZE="20"><SELECT
NAME="search_category" SIZE="1">
```

We also produce a dropdown list, giving the user an option to do a search either on the current category or the whole directory. The type of search chosen will be passed via the `$search_type` variable to `show_list()`, and the present category will be passed via `$search_category`.

```
        <OPTION SELECTED VALUE="<?php echo $category_id ?>">Current Category</OPTION>
        <OPTION VALUE="<?php echo $root_category_id ?>">All Categories</OPTION>
    </SELECT><INPUT TYPE="RADIO" VALUE="OR" NAME="search_type" CHECKED>OR <INPUT
TYPE="RADIO"  VALUE="AND" NAME="search_type">AND <INPUT TYPE="SUBMIT"
VALUE="Search">
    </FORM>
```

```
</CENTER>
<?php
}
```

## show_list()

Now we come to the function where the real action takes place: the show_list() function. It displays a list of the subcategories under a given category, and the URLs belonging to it (if any).

Here's the main page of the application that the show_list() function displays:

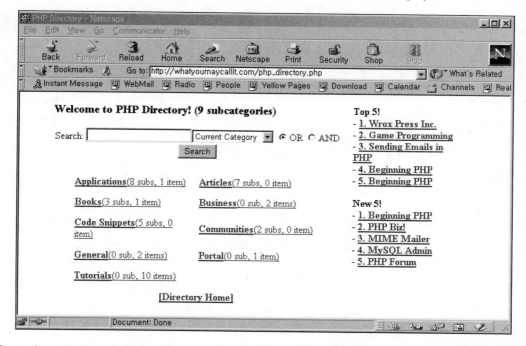

Every directory page is laid out in a simple table. Each category page, for example, is divided into two columns: the lists of categories and/or URLs (if any) on the left, the most-visited and recently-added URLs on the right. At the top of the left column is a keyword search form. Navigation links are displayed at the bottom of the left column. The screenshot above displays the contents of the root category. The root contains no URLs, only top-most categories.

The next screenshot shows the Applications category page, just below the root. You can see it holds eight subcategories and a single URL. The "Top 5" and "New 5" listings in the right column are restricted to URLs in the current category. This feature is implemented by using the list_sites() function we'll meet shortly.

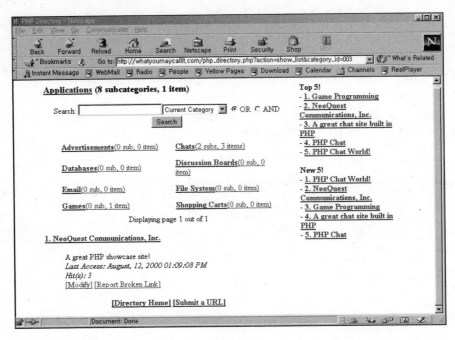

When a user clicks on the [Report Broken Link] link, a local e-mail client application is run with the information needed to report a broken link.

An administrator can view the same page in administration mode, as shown in the following screenshot:

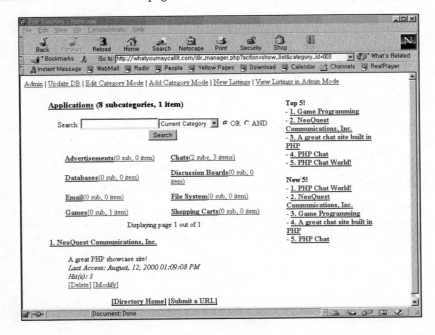

Note that administrators see a [Delete] link instead of [Report Broken Link]. An administrator can delete a URL by clicking on this link.

Let's list the function bit by bit.

**1.** We start by including some global variables for use in the function, and checking that we have a connection to the database established:

```
function show_list() {
    global $default_dbname, $directory_tablename, $category_tablename,
           $records_per_page, $root_category_id, $category_id_length,
           $welcome_message, $dirmaster_email;
    global $PHP_SELF, $link_id, $category_id, $admin_script, $cur_page,
           $search_on, $keywords, $search_type, $search_category;
```

The function needs to determine whether the current user is an administrator, in which case it can step into adminstration mode by switching the $admin flag variable on:

```
if(basename($PHP_SELF) == $admin_script) $admin = 1;
```

As we mentioned earlier, basename($PHP_SELF) returns the filename of the script currently running, which will be dir_manager.php if an administrator is using the directory. If this is the case, the if statement will return true, and the $admin flag will be switched on.

Next the function checks to see if a database connection has been made. If not ($link_id is empty), it attempts to establish a connection to it using the db_connect() function:

```
if(!$link_id) $link_id = db_connect($default_dbname);
```

**2.** The next step is to extract information about the current category.

First we introduce a flag variable called $submittable, and switch it on:

```
$submittable = 1;
```

This flag will indicate whether users are allowed to submit a new URL under the current category (we mustn't allow users to post URLs under the root category, or when no category is selected).

First we check to see if there is no current directory (the user is viewing the category tree), or if the user is at the root category. Assuming that one of these conditions applies, the get_category_info() function places information about the root category into the array $category_info_array:

```
if(empty($category_id) || $category_id==$root_category_id) {
    $category_info_array = get_category_info($root_category_id);
    $submittable = 0;
}
```

Because we don't want users submitting URLs at the root, or while they are viewing the tree, note that we switch the $submittable flag off.

**619**

Assuming that the category is not root, and the user is not viewing the directory tree, we introduce another variable $parent_category_id which will contain the ID of the current category. Again, we use the get_category_info() function to get information from the database about the current category. Then we extract useful items from $category_info_array:

```
else {
    $parent_category_id = $category_id;
    $category_info_array = get_category_info($category_id);
    $category_fullname = $category_info_array["fullname"];
    $num_item = $category_info_array["num_item"];
}
```

The next few lines consist of extracting more category data from $category_info_array:

```
$category_href_fullname = $category_info_array["href_fullname"];
$category_depth = $category_info_array["depth"];
$num_child = $category_info_array["num_child"];
?>
```

**3.** Next we display the clickable full name of the category, the number of subcategories it spawns, and the number of URL items it contains, (for example, Applications (8 Subcategories, 1 Item).

The first step is to set up the browser display. We want to create two columns in the window; the left column will display info about the current category, and a keyword search form. The right column will display the most popular URLs and recently submitted URLs. We will sort out the items which need to be displayed in the left column first, and leave the right column until later:

```
<CENTER>
<TABLE BORDER="0" WIDTH="90%" CELLSPACING="5" CELLPADDING="5">
  <TR>
    <TD WIDTH="70%" VALIGN="TOP">
```

In order to display grammatically correct category information, we now test to see how many children and URLs the current category holds, and selects whether it needs the string "category", or "categories":

```
<?php
    if($num_child <= 1) $num_child_str = "$num_child subcategory";
    else $num_child_str = "$num_child subcategories";
    if($num_item <= 1) $num_item_str = "$num_item item";
    else $num_item_str = "$num_item items";
```

Next, the function displays the 'clickable' full name of the current category and the number of subcategories it spawns. If the current category is not root ($submittable contains 1), we also display the number of URL items the category contains:

```
    if($submittable) echo "<H3>$category_href_fullname ($num_child_str,
$num_item_str)</H3>\n";
    else echo "<H3>$category_href_fullname ($num_child_str)</H3>\n";
```

Note that because we display the clickable full name of the category, it allows users to easily jump to the category's parent, grandparent, and so on.

**4.** The search form is displayed immediately after the category name.

To display the form we call the `search_form()` function:

```
search_form($category_id);
```

**5.** Now it's time to fetch information from the database on the current category's children, and for each child, display its name, number of children, and number of URLs.

The children of the current category are returned by the following MySQL query, which we encountered before, when examining the `get_category_info()` function:

```
$query = "SELECT category, category_id FROM $category_tablename WHERE
(length(category_id) = $category_depth * $category_id_length) AND category_id LIKE
'$category_id%' ORDER BY category";
$result = mysql_query($query);
```

The names and IDs of the children are now stored in `$result`. We must also take into account the possibility of an error occurring during the query, so if no data is returned by the query we jump to the error-handling function `sql_error()`:

```
if(!$result) echo sql_error();
```

If we do get data back from the query, the next step is to set up a table on the page and display the names of the children in the category:

```
if(mysql_num_rows($result) > 0) {
    ?>
```

We set up a table:

```
<CENTER>
<TABLE BORDER="0" WIDTH="90%" CELLPADDING="5" CELLSPACING="5">
<?php
```

and then prepare a loop to read in the data for each child one at a time and display the child's name, number of children, and the number of URL items it contains. Essentially, we are repeating steps 2 and 3, but using the current category's children instead of the category itself.

```
$i = 1;
while($query_data = mysql_fetch_array($result)) {
```

The `while` loop iterates through the result set until `mysql_fetch_array($result)` doesn't return any more data to place in `$query_data`, indicating that there are no more results. We also set up a loop counter variable, `$i`. The next step is to extract the child's name and ID:

```
$my_category = $query_data["category"];
$my_category_id = $query_data["category_id"];
```

Note how we create new variables to store the child's name and ID so that we don't mix them up with the current category's name and ID. Then the data for each child is retrieved by using the `get_category_info()` function again:

```
$category_info_array = get_category_info($my_category_id);
$num_child = $category_info_array["num_child"];
$num_item = $category_info_array["num_item"];
```

Again we extract the items of data we need (number of children and URLs) from the result set. As before, the function builds (grammatically correct) messages stating the number of subcategories and URLs returned:

```
if($num_child <= 1) $num_child_str = "$num_child sub";
else $num_child_str = "$num_child subs";
if($num_item <= 1) $num_item_str = "$num_item item";
else $num_item_str = "$num_item items";
```

We will display two children on every row of the table. The next line adds another row to the table if it is needed. Remember that `$i` is the counter variable, so every time `$i` is odd we need to start a new row of the table. The line after makes sure that each child takes up only half the table row:

```
if(($i % 2)) echo "<TR>\n";
echo "<TD WIDTH=\"50%\">\n";
```

Next we display the (clickable) child's name:

```
echo "<A HREF=\"$PHP_SELF?action=show_list&
                        category_id=$my_category_id\">
        <STRONG>$my_category</STRONG>
        ($num_child_str, $num_item_str)</A>\n";
echo "</TD>\n";
```

The next line ends a row when necessary. After that, all we have left to do in the loop is to increment the counter:

```
        if(!($i % 2)) echo "</TR>\n";
        $i++;
    }
```

The next few lines of code account for the fact that the category may have an odd number of children. In this case we will have an unfilled cell at the end of the table, which we need to fill with a non-breaking space:

```
if(!($i % 2)) {
    echo "<TD WIDTH=\"50%\"> </TD>\n" ;
    echo "</TR>";
}
```

The final step is to close the remaining HTML tags:

```
    ?>
    </TABLE>
    </CENTER>
    <?php
}
```

**6.** Now let's see how the function incorporates a keyword search feature. The first step is to build a query string. This will contain the instructions needed by the `mysql_query()` function to search the MySQL database for keywords.

The `search_form()` function we saw earlier passes the following three variables about the URL to the `show_list()` function (in addition to the `$search_on` flag):

❑ `$keywords`: List of the keywords entered by the user, each one separated by a blank space.

❑ `$search_category`: ID of the category under which the `show_list()` function should perform the search operation. If the ID is `"000"` or no ID is given (indicating the root of the category hierarchy), a directory-wide search is performed.

❑ `$search_type`: Search operator (either AND or OR). OR is default.

The `$search_on` global variable is also turned on whenever the user submits the keyword search form.

To perform a keyword search, we need to construct an appropriate query string to pass to the `mysql_query()` function. The first step is to initialize two string variables that we will use in the query string. The first variable will eventually contain the keywords, and the second will tell the database which category or categories to search through:

```
    $keyword_str = '';
    $category_str = "category_id = '$category_id'";
```

Next we check to see if we need to do a search:

```
    if($search_on && !empty($keywords)) {
```

When the `$search_on` flag is on, and search keywords are present, we search down the category tree beginning with the current category. To achieve this, we modify the `$category_str` variable to include the `"LIKE '$search_category%'"` string. The effect of this is will be to make the database search all the category's children, grandchildren, and so on, until it reaches the bottom of the tree.

However, if the `$search_category` variable was empty, an error would occur because of a trailing AND operator in the final query string:

```
    ... WHERE category_id = AND approved = 1 ... ; (Error)
```

Therefore, when `$search_category` is empty or contains the root "000", the `$category_str` variable is set to 1 (or "true") in the WHERE clause instead:

```
    ... WHERE 1 AND approved = 1 ... ; (For searching the whole directory)
```

**623**

Here's the code which does the job, producing the category clause for the final query string:

```
if($search_category == $root_category_id) $category_str = '1';
else $category_str = "category_id LIKE '$search_category%'";
```

The trickiest part of implementing a search feature is dealing with multiple keywords, because we need to construct a query string which accounts for this. We also need to search through both URL descriptions and URL titles. Let's see how to construct a multiple keyword string that we can use in a database query.

First, we create the query string to search through URL descriptions. We split up all of the keywords and place each one into an array element using the explode() function. The delimiter we use to split up the keywords is a single space. Then we prepend every keyword with the string "description LIKE '%". Next we add the string "%'" onto the end of every keyword. Finally, we concatenate these keyword strings together using the implode() function, placing either "AND" or "OR" between each string, depending upon which of these is specified in $search_type. Here's the code to do this:

```
$keywords_array = explode(" ", $keywords);
$temp_str = "description LIKE '%";
$keyword_str = implode("%' $search_type $temp_str", $keywords_array);
$keyword_str_desc = $temp_str . $keyword_str . "%'";
```

For example, if a user typed in "PHP book" in the keyword form field, the above lines of code will produce either of the following series of LIKE clauses, depending on the $search_type variable selected (AND or OR):

```
description LIKE '%PHP%' AND description LIKE '%book%'
description LIKE '%PHP%' OR description LIKE '%book%'
```

Now we go through the same process to get the query string to search through URL titles:

```
$temp_str = "title LIKE '%";
$keyword_str = implode("%' $search_type $temp_str", $keywords_array);
$keyword_str_title = $temp_str . $keyword_str . "%'";
```

Then we combine these two query strings with an OR logical operator, prepend the result with "AND" and place the resulting keyword clause string in $keyword_str:

```
$keyword_str = "AND (($keyword_str_title) OR ($keyword_str_desc))";
}
```

The next step is to build an initial query string, ready to send to the mysql_query() function, which will be used to check how many 'hits' we will get from the final query. Therefore we incorporate a call to the MySQL server count() function into the query string, which will count up the number of query matches the search generates:

```
$query = "SELECT count(*) FROM $directory_tablename WHERE $category_str AND
approved = 1 $keyword_str";
```

Note how we will only include approved URLs in the search results.

**7.** Next step is to try an initial keyword search to find out how many hits we can expect, and display the result on the browser.

We feed the query string $query into the mysql_query() function. If it doesn't return any results, then we display an error message:

```
$result = mysql_query($query);
if(!$result) echo error_message(sql_error());
```

Next we extract data from $result, and use it to check the total number of hits returned ($total_num):

```
$query_data = mysql_fetch_row($result);
$total_num = $query_data[0];
```

We will use this information to construct another clause for the final query string. If the list of all URLs returned will not fit onto a single page, the URLs will be presented one page at a time. The number of URLs displayed per page is dictated by the value of the $records_per_page global variable. Therefore, we can construct a LIMIT clause string $limit_str, to insert into the final query string, so that we retrieve only the page of URL results we want:

```
$limit_str = "LIMIT " . $cur_page * $records_per_page . ", $records_per_page";
```

Here $cur_page is the current page of search results, starting from zero. Although $cur_page is useful for the LIMIT clause, it would also be convenient if we had another page index variable, which starts from page 1 instead:

```
$page_num = $cur_page + 1;
```

We also need to find the total number of pages $total_num_page of search results and the last page number $last_page_num. Since these values should be the same, we can define simultaneously. The value of both variables is easily found. We first divide the total number of hits by the number of records per page. We account for a fractional number of pages by feeding the answer into the ceil() function, which rounds up fractions to the next highest integer. The result is the number of pages we need:

```
$total_num_page = $last_page_num = ceil($total_num/$records_per_page);
```

We must also account for a zero result for $total_num_page; for navigation's sake we need the total number of pages to be at least one:

```
if(!$total_num_page) $total_num_page++;
```

Next step is to display the number of hits on the browser. We construct a string to echo out first, such as "8 URLs found.". Then we echo out this string, along with "– Keyword(s):", and follow this with the keywords chosen by the user:

```
        if($total_num <= 1 ) $found_str = "$total_num URL found.";
        else $found_str = "$total_num URLs found.";
        if($search_on) echo "<H3>$found_str - Keyword(s): $keywords</H3><P>\n";
```

So, if the user chose "search" and as a search keyword, the search might return:

**2 URLs found. Keyword(s): search**

Next we indicate which page of search results we are going to display (assuming we got any hits):

```
        if($total_num > 0) echo "<CENTER>Displaying page $page_num out of
    $last_page_num</CENTER><P>\n";
```

So if there is one page of hits, we get the message:

**Displaying page 1 out of 1**

**8.** Now we construct the final query string and perform the full keyword search, retrieving the URL data for each hit.

First we construct the final query string. It is built by combining the `$category_str`, `$keywords_str` and `$limit_str` terms:

```
    $query = "SELECT url_id, category_id, title, url, description,
                    date_format(registerdate, '%M, %e, %Y') as
                    formatted_registerdate, hit,
                    date_format(lastaccesstime, '%M, %e, %Y %r') as
                    formatted_lastaccesstime, hit FROM $directory_tablename
                    WHERE $category_str AND approved = 1 $keyword_str
                    ORDER BY registerdate DESC $limit_str";
```

For each hit, the query will retrieve the URL, URL ID, URL title, URL description, the number of URL accesses, the URL submission date, the last time it was accessed, and the ID of the category that the URL is posted in. The MySQL server function `date_format()` returns a formatted date and time value from a given date or datetime argument. We use it here to format the submission date and last access time, and then we create the aliases `formatted_registerdate` and `formatted_lastaccesstime` for these formatted values. Note that we will order the URL results by submission date, with the most recent first.

As before, we feed the query string into `mysql_query()` to perform the database search, and throw out an error message if `$result` doesn't contain any results:

```
    $result = mysql_query($query);
    if(!$result) echo sql_error();
```

**9.** Display a page of hits from the search.

A `while` loop is used to display the page of URLs. First we initialize a loop counter variable:

```
    $i = 1;
```

The while loop is pretty straightforward; we retrieve one URL record at a time using mysql_fetch_array($result) and read it into $query_data. Then we start by extracting values one item at a time from $query_data and placing them into appropriate variables:

```
while($query_data = mysql_fetch_array($result)) {
    $url_id = $query_data["url_id"];
    $formatted_registerdate = $query_data["formatted_registerdate"];
    $formatted_lastaccesstime = $query_data["formatted_lastaccesstime"];
    $url = "http://" . $query_data["url"];
    $title = $query_data["title"];
    $description = $query_data["description"];
    $hit = $query_data["hit"];
```

The next line displays the clickable title of the URL, along with the hit number:

```
echo "<STRONG>
        <A HREF=\"$PHP_SELF?action=go_url&url=$url&url_id=$url_id\">".
        ($i+($cur_page * $records_per_page)).".".$title
        </A></STRONG>\n";
```

Note that clicking on the title will eventually redirect the program to the go_url() function, which will take us to the URL. Having displayed the title, we now display an indented paragraph of URL information (URL description, last access time, and number of accesses) just beneath it:

```
echo "<BLOCKQUOTE>\n";
echo $description;
echo "<BR>\n";
echo "<EM>Last Access: $formatted_lastaccesstime</EM><BR>\n";
echo "<EM>Hit(s): " . number_format($hit) . "</EM><BR>\n";
```

The <BLOCKQUOTE> tag indents the displayed data. Note that it is always a good practice to present information in as readable a format as possible. The number_format() function formats numbers into a presentable format (for example, it changes 1794523 to the easier-to-read form 1,794,532), so we use it here to format the number of accesses, which is a potentially large number.

Let's see an example of a search result. In the screenshot overleaf, results of a keyword search for "search" are shown:

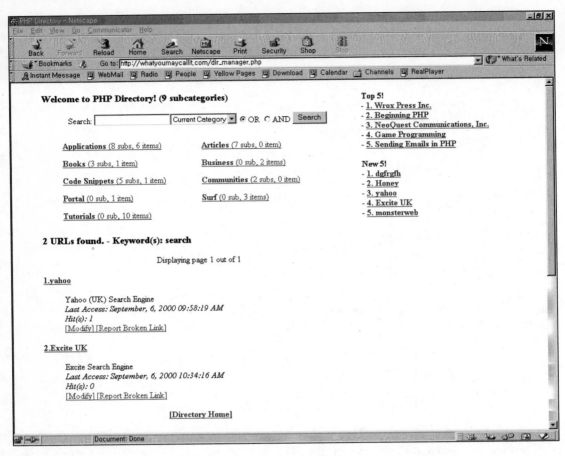

What we do next depends on whether the user is an administrator. If this is true, the $admin flag is on, so the function displays the clickable [Delete] link:

```
if($admin) echo "<A HREF=\"$PHP_SELF?action=delete_url&url_id=$url_id&
                                    category_id=$category_id&url=$url&
                                    title=$title&cur_page=$cur_page\"
                 OnClick=\"return confirm('Are you sure?');\">
                 [Delete]
                 </A>\n";
```

Note how we use the JavaScript's confirm() method to make the administrator confirm that he wants to delete the URL. Clicking on this hyperlink will eventually send the program to the delete_url() function, which will delete the URL.

Next, we display a clickable [Modify] link, whether the user is an administrator or not. Clicking on this link invokes a JavaScript function which opens a new window, and sends the program to the modify_url_form() function. This function produces a form which can be used to modify the data associated with this URL:

```
echo "<A HREF=\"javascript:open_window('$PHP_SELF?
                action=modify_url_form&url_id=$url_id&
                category_id=$category_id&cur_page=$cur_page');\">
        [Modify]
        </A>\n";
```

If the user is not an administrator, we also provide a clickable [Report Broken Link] link so that the user can inform the administrator that the URL link is broken:

```
if(!$admin) echo "<A HREF=\"mailto:$dirmaster_email?
                    subject=PHPDirectory]SiteMissing&
                    body=url_id:$url_id($url)\">
            [Report Broken Link]
            </A>\n";
```

Note that clicking on the link will create an e-mail to send to the administrator: in the subject field of the mail will be the message **PHPDirectory-SiteMissing**; the content of the e-mail will be the URL ID and the broken URL of the site (for example url_id:40(http://www.brokensite.com).

Next we increment the loop counter and end the loop:

```
echo "</BLOCKQUOTE>\n";

$i++;
}
```

**10.** Now we provide navigation links for jumping between pages of keyword search hits.

If the function is in the search mode, it needs to propagate search-related variables via the URL. So we need to create a string, $search_str, which contains these variables, and which we can propagate via the URL:

```
if($search_on) $search_str =
        "&search_on=1&search_type=$search_type&keywords=$keywords
        &search_category=$search_category";

echo "<CENTER>";
```

Without the addition of the above lines of code, the next call to the show_list() function after a search operation will pull it out of the search mode: if multiple pages of hits were returned from a search, clicking on the [Next] link, for example, would lead the user to an unexpected page.

If the number of pages of hits $page_num is greater than one, we provide the [Top] and [Prev] navigation links that help jump to the first page and previous page respectively.

```
if($page_num > 1) {
    $prev_page = $cur_page - 1;
```

We have created a variable, $prev_page, to hold the previous page number. Next we create clickable links to the first page of hits, and the previous page of hits: [Top] and [Prev] respectively:

```
        echo "<A HREF=\"$PHP_SELF?action=show_list&category_id=$category_id
                           &cur_page=0$search_str\">[Top]</A>";
        echo "<A HREF=\"$PHP_SELF?action=show_list&category_id=$category_id
                           &cur_page=$prev_page$search_str\">[Prev]</A> ";
    }
```

Note that clicking on both links will call the show_list() function again, to perform another query and obtain another page of hits. State information (current page of hits, keywords, categories to search, and so on) is propagated through the URL.

The clickable [Next] and [Bottom] links are also displayed if the current page number is smaller than the total number of pages. These links take the user to the next page, or the last page of hits respectively:

```
    if($page_num < $total_num_page) {
        $next_page = $cur_page + 1;
        $last_page = $total_num_page - 1;
        echo "<A HREF=\"$PHP_SELF?action=show_list&category_id=$category_id
                          &cur_page=$next_page$search_str\">[Next]</A> ";
        echo "<A HREF=\"$PHP_SELF?action=show_list&category_id=$category_id
                          &cur_page=$last_page$search_str\">[Bottom]</A>";
    }
```

Again we create variables ($next_page and $last_page) which we use to pass state information, via the URL. As before, clicking on the links will route us back to the start of the show_list() function.

The final clickable links displayed on the browser are the [Directory Home] and [Submit a URL] links. Before we display them we place a bit of space between these links and the previous ones by starting a new paragraph, using the <P> HTML tag. Then we display [Directory Home], which takes the user to the root page, where the top-most categories are displayed:

```
    echo "</CENTER>";
    echo "<P><STRONG><CENTER><A HREF=\"$PHP_SELF?action=show_list\">
                           [Directory Home]</A> \n";
```

Provided the current category is not root (so $submittable is not zero), we also display the clickable link which allows users to submit URLs to the category. Clicking on the link will send the program to add_url_form(), which produces the submission form:

```
    if($submittable) echo "<A HREF=\"javascript:open_window('$PHP_SELF?
                   action=add_url_form&category_id=$category_id');\">
                           [Submit a URL]</A>\n";
    echo "</CENTER></STRONG>";
?>
</TD>
```

**11.** Finally, we fill the most popular URLs and the recently-added URLs into the right column of the browser window.

We noted at the beginning of the function that the show_list() function uses a table to lay out the contents of the web page it displays. Category and search information go into the left column. The right column lists both the most-visited and recently-added URLs; these are displayed by calling the list_sites() function which we will examine next:

```
            <TD WIDTH="30%" VALIGN="TOP">
            <?php
               list_sites('top', $category_id); echo "<P>";
               list_sites('new', $category_id);
            ?>
            </TD>
         </TR>
      </TABLE>
   </CENTER>
   <?php
   }
```

Well done! We've reached the end of a pretty involved function. The others in `php_directory.inc` are straightforward compared with `show_list()`.

## add_url_form()

Under any category except root, the user may click the [Submit a URL] link to submit a new URL. This link opens up a new window that displays a URL submission form:

As shown in the screenshot below, the form is smart enough to know under which category a user is trying to add a URL (the "Applications" category in the figure). Note that the E-mail and Password fields are required for authentication.

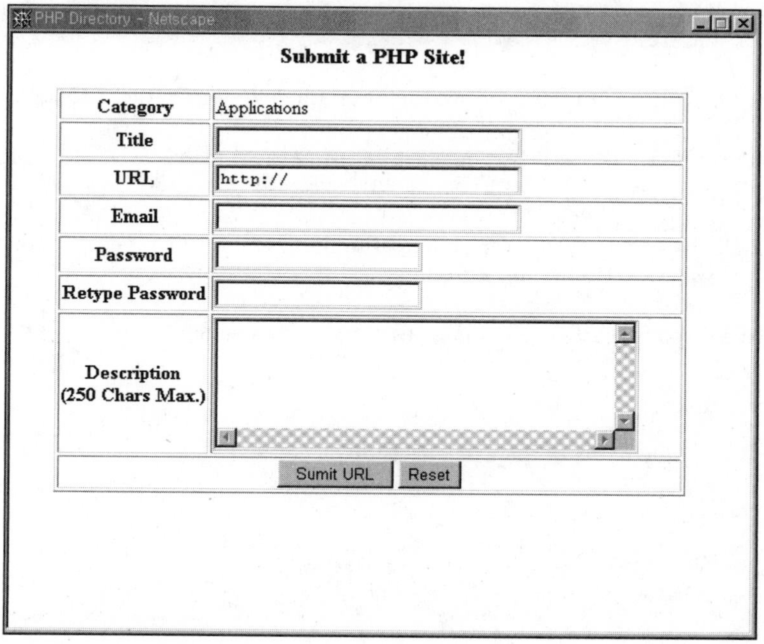

The `add_url_form()` function displays a form, enabling users to submit URLs:

```
function add_url_form() {
   global $PHP_SELF, $max_desc_length, $category_id;
```

```
$category_info_array = get_category_info($category_id);
```

**1.** Retrieve category meta data.

Following the function definition and global variable declarations, the first thing the function does is to retrieve meta data for the current category, using the `get_category_info()` function. This meta data is passed to an array, `$category_info_array`. The next step is to retrieve the expanded family name of the category:

```
$category_fullname = $category_info_array["fullname"];
```

The expanded family name lists the names of the category, its parent, its grandparent, and so on until root. The example "Eagles" category that we used earlier might have an expanded family name of "Wildlife->Birds->Eagles" for instance (note the separation names using "->").

**2.** Build the form. Start with the title and hidden form fields.

Now we start to build the form. We call `directory_header()`, which opens a new window, and display the title "Submit a PHP Site!" at the top of the new window:

```
    directory_header();
?>
<CENTER><H3>Submit a PHP Site!</H3></CENTER>
```

When we submit the contents of the window, the program will jump to the `add_url()` function:

```
<FORM METHOD="POST" ACTION="<?php echo $PHP_SELF ?>">
<INPUT TYPE="HIDDEN" NAME="action" VALUE="add_url">
```

We need to pass the `$category_id` variable over to the `add_url()` function to let it know under which category we want the URL to be stored:

```
<INPUT TYPE="HIDDEN" NAME="category_id" VALUE="<? echo $category_id ?>">
```

**3.** Add form fields.

Next the expanded family name of the category is displayed:

```
<CENTER><TABLE BORDER="1" WIDTH="90%">
  <TR>
    <TH WIDTH="20%" NOWRAP>Category</TH>
    <TD WIDTH="80%"><?php echo $category_fullname ?></TD>
  </TR>
```

Now we add three text form fields (`Title`, `URL`, and `E-mail`):

```
    <TR>
      <TH WIDTH="20%" NOWRAP>Title</TH>
```

```
      <TD WIDTH="80%"><INPUT TYPE="TEXT" NAME="title"
                            SIZE="30" MAXLENGTH="150"></TD>
  </TR>
  <TR>
    <TH WIDTH="20%" NOWRAP>URL</TH>
    <TD WIDTH="80%"><INPUT TYPE="TEXT" NAME="url" VALUE="http://"
                            SIZE="30" MAXLENGTH="150"></TD>
  </TR>
  <TR>
    <TH WIDTH="20%" NOWRAP>Email</TH>
    <TD WIDTH="80%"><INPUT TYPE="TEXT" NAME="email"
                            SIZE="30" MAXLENGTH="150"></TD>
  </TR>
```

Two password fields (one for confirmation):

```
  <TR>
    <TH WIDTH="20%" NOWRAP>Password</TH>
    <TD WIDTH="80%"><INPUT TYPE="PASSWORD" NAME="password"
                            SIZE="20" MAXLENGTH="20"></TD>
  </TR>
  <TR>
    <TH WIDTH="20%" NOWRAP>Retype Password</TH>
    <TD WIDTH="80%"><INPUT TYPE="PASSWORD" NAME="password2"
                            SIZE="20" MAXLENGTH="20"></TD>
  </TR>
```

And finally a five-line text field in which the user can place the URL description (limited to the length set in the $max_desc_length global variable):

```
  <TR>
    <TH WIDTH="20%" NOWRAP>Description<BR>
    (<?php echo $max_desc_length; ?> Chars Max.)
    </TH>
    <TD WIDTH="80%">
      <TEXTAREA NAME="description" ROWS="5"COLS="40"></TEXTAREA>
    </TD>
  </TR>
  <TR>
```

**4.** Add buttons.

We add **Submit** and **Reset** Buttons:

```
    <TH WIDTH="100%" NOWRAP COLSPAN="2">
    <INPUT TYPE="SUBMIT" VALUE="Submit URL" NAME="Submit">
    <INPUT TYPE="RESET" VALUE="Reset"></TH>
  </TR>
 </TABLE>
 </CENTER>
</FORM>
<?php
```

**633**

Finally, we call the `directory_footer()` function to end the HTML page:

```
    directory_footer();
}
```

## add_url()

The `add_url_form()` function works in tandem with the `add_url()` function. The `add_url()` function inserts the submitted data into the database:

```
function add_url() {
    global $default_dbname, $directory_tablename,
            $category_tablename, $max_desc_length, $PHP_SELF;
    global $category_id, $title, $url, $description,
            $email, $password, $password2, $email, $admin_script;
    global $dirmaster_email, $link_id, $send_mail;
```

We begin with the function definition and global variable declarations as usual. We have seen the next line before, at the start of the chapter; it switches the administration flag `$admin` on if the function is called by an administrator:

```
    if(basename($PHP_SELF) == $admin_script) $admin = 1;
```

**1.** Format the URL string, and test for empty form fields and illegal characters.

Next we use the `eregi_replace()` function to remove the string "http://" from the submitted URL string, and any trailing forward slashes at the end of the URL too:

```
    $url = eregi_replace('http://', "", $url);
    $url = eregi_replace("/$", "", $url);
```

The next step is to test the values of the form fields which should not be empty, and to warn the user if any of them is missing content:

```
    if(empty($title))
        error_message("Please enter the title!");
    if(empty($url))
        error_message("Please enter the URL!");
    if(empty($email))
        error_message("Please enter your email address!");
    if(empty($password))
        error_message("Please enter a password for later modification!");
    if(empty($password2))
        error_message("Please retype the password!");
    if($password != $password2)
        error_message("Desired password and retyped password mismatch!");
    if(empty($email))
        error_message("Please enter your email!");
    if(empty($description))
        error_message("Please enter the description!");
```

If something is wrong with the submission, the error_message() function displays an error message and throws the user back to the form. The entered password is checked by forcing the user to retype it in another form field; note that both these passwords must be identical for the password to be accepted.

The description field cannot accommodate more than the preset length of characters, so we must check for overflow:

```
if(strlen($description) > $max_desc_length)
    error_message("Description too long! $max_desc_length chars max!");
```

We also check fields for illegal characters (such as quotes or apostrophes), which then have escape characters (back slashes) added to them using the addslashes() function:

```
$title = addslashes($title);
$description = addslashes($description);
```

Then we encrypt the user's password for better security using the crypt() function:

```
$password = crypt($password, '.v');
```

The second argument to the encryption function is the salt ".v", which controls the type of encryption used.

**2.** Is the new URL a duplicate?

Before inserting a new record into the database, we must first check to see that it's not a duplicate record. To do this we must search the database, looking for a URL in the current category which has the same URL string as the one we want to add.

We first check to see that a database connection is established; if not we use db_connect() to connect. Then we construct a query string which we can give to mysql_query() so that it will search for our URL string:

```
if(.$link_id) $link_id = db_connect($default_dbname);
$query = "SELECT url FROM $directory_tablename
          WHERE url = '$url' AND category_id = '$category_id'";
$result = mysql_query($query);
if(!$result) error_message(sql_error());
```

As usual, we have checked the results of the search to see if there has been an error. If there are any URL records retrieved, we display an error message telling the user that the URL is already present in this category, and send the user back to the previous page, using our error_message() function:

```
if(mysql_num_rows($result) != 0)
    error_message("$url already exists in the directory!");
```

Provided that the URL is not already present in the category, we can continue. The $approved flag is turned off by default:

```
$approved = 0;
```

**3.** Approve URL if user is administrator.

If the current user is an administrator, however, the submitted record is immediately approved. We perform a query which updates the database table `php_category`, so that the "number of URL items" entry for the current category is incremented by one:

```
if($admin) {
    $query = "UPDATE $category_tablename SET num_item = num_item + 1
            WHERE category_id = '$category_id'";
    $result = mysql_query($query);
    if(!$result) error_message(sql_error());
```

We also indicate that the URL should be added to this category in the directory by switching on the `$approved` flag:

```
    $approved = 1;
}
```

**4.** Insert URL data into URL table, and send confirmation e-mail to user.

Next we insert the URL data into the database. Note that the `$approved` flag will only be on if an administrator has submitted the URL:

```
$query = "INSERT INTO $directory_tablename
                VALUES(NULL, '$category_id', '$title', '$url',
                        '$description', curdate(), 0, NULL,
                        '$password', '$email', $approved)";
$result = mysql_query($query);
if(!$result) error_message(sql_error());
```

If the server is configured to send e-mail (`$send_mail` is true), the function now uses the `mail()` function to send a notification e-mail to the user. The users e-mail address is in the `$e-mail` variable:

```
if($send_mail){
    $mail_subject = "PHP Directory>> Thank you for your listing.";
    $mail_body = "Thank you for sharing your resources with us.\n";
    $mail_body = "Your contribution will be listed after
                                review in a day or two.\n\n";
    $mail_body .= "Title: $title\n";
    $mail_body .= "URL: $url\n";
    $mail_body .= "Description: $description";
    mail($email, $mail_subject, $mail_body, "From: $dirmaster_email\nReply-to:
$dirmaster_email");
}
```

Note that the "From" and "Reply to mail" e-mail header fields are set to the e-mail address held by the `$dirmaster_e-mail` variable.

Finally, the function checks to see whether the record has actually been inserted by calling the `mysql_affected_rows()` function, which returns the number of rows affected by the previous DELETE or UPDATE query:

```
$num_rows = mysql_affected_rows($link_id);
```

The returned value should be 1 in this case. If it isn't we know something's wrong and we display an error message:

```
if($num_rows != 1) error_message(sql_error());
```

Otherwise, we display a confirmation that the URL was successfully submitted:

```
    else echo "<SCRIPT>
            alert(\"$title($url) has been successfully submitted!\");
            opener.location.href='$PHP_SELF?action=show_list&
                                    category_id=$category_id';
            self.close();
            </SCRIPT>";
}
```

The function ends with a JavaScript code snippet that causes the browser to refresh the parent window with a given URL, and closes the current window.

## modify_url_form()

A user can modify URL listings which were originally submitted by him. If the user clicks on the [Modify] link under any URL on any category page, a new window opens up. This form allows the user to modify the URL title, the URL, and the URL description as shown in the screenshot below. However, any changes made will only be executed if the user can prove that he submitted the form originally. This is achieved by supplying the correct e-mail/password combination.

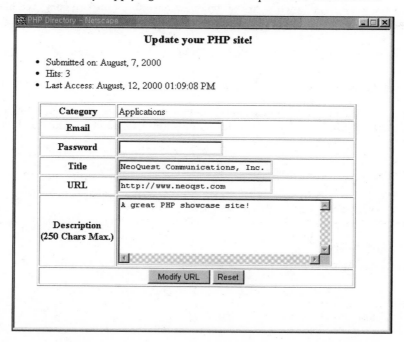

Modifying a URL is a similar process to adding a new URL, except that modification involves fetching an existing record and displaying it as a user form. Therefore the functions `modify_url_form()` and `modify_url()` are very similar to `add_url_form()` and `add_url()` respectively. Let's take a look at `modify_url_form()`, which displays the modification form:

```
function modify_url_form() {
    global $PHP_SELF, $max_desc_length, $url_id,
           $category_id, $admin_script, $cur_page;
```

Ignoring the function definition, and the global variable declarations, the first step is to open a new HTML page in a new window using `directory_header()`:

```
    directory_header();
```

Next we switch the `$admin` flag on if an administrator is using the directory:

```
    if(basename($PHP_SELF) == $admin_script) $admin = 1;
```

**1.** Retrieve URL data.

We now use our `get_url_info()` function to retrieve data for the URL in question from the database. This data is transferred to an array, `$url_info_array`:

```
    $url_info_array = get_url_info($url_id);
```

Next we retrieve the ID of the category that the URL is posted in, and then use this as the argument to our `get_category_info()` function to retrieve meta data about the category. We place this meta data in another array, `$category_info_array()`:

```
    $category_info_array = get_category_info($url_info_array["category_id"]);
```

**2.** Build the form. Start with the title and hidden form fields.

The next step is to add text and form fields to the editing form. We start by displaying a title, "Update your PHP site!". Then we display some URL statistics: submission date, number of hits, and date of last access:

```
?>
<CENTER><H3>Update your PHP site!</H3></CENTER>
<UL>
<LI>Submitted on: <?php echo $url_info_array["formatted_registerdate"] ?></LI>
<LI>Hits: <?php echo $url_info_array["hit"] ?></LI>
<LI>Last Access: <?php echo $url_info_array["formatted_lastaccesstime"] ?></LI>
</UL>
```

Next we create some hidden fields to pass to the `modify_url()` function on submission of the form:

```
<FORM METHOD="POST" ACTION="<?php echo $PHP_SELF ?>">
<INPUT TYPE="HIDDEN" NAME="action" VALUE="modify_url">
<INPUT TYPE="HIDDEN" NAME="url_id" VALUE="<? echo $url_id ?>">
<INPUT TYPE="HIDDEN" NAME="category_id" VALUE="<? echo $category_id ?>">
```

**3.** Add form fields.

The next block of code is essentially the same section of code that creates the form fields in `add_url_form()`. However, we only need one password field here, and we must also fill the fields in the editing form with the URL data stored in the array `$url_info_array`. First we create the Category (name) form field, and fill it with the expanded family name of the category that the URL is posted to:

```
<CENTER><TABLE BORDER="1" WIDTH="90%">
  <TR>
     <TH WIDTH="20%" NOWRAP>Category</TH>
     <TD WIDTH="80%"><?php echo $category_info_array["fullname"] ?></TD>
  </TR>
<?php
```

Next we include e-mail and password form fields, unless the user is an administrator. Administrators are allowed to modify any records:

```
   if(!$admin) {
?>
  <TR>
     <TH WIDTH="20%" NOWRAP>Email</TH>
     <TD WIDTH="80%"><INPUT TYPE="TEXT" NAME="email"
                          SIZE="30" MAXLENGTH="150"></TD>
  </TR>
  <TR>
     <TH WIDTH="20%" NOWRAP>Password</TH>
     <TD WIDTH="80%"><INPUT TYPE="PASSWORD" NAME="password"
                          SIZE="20" MAXLENGTH="20"></TD>
  </TR>
<?php
   }
?>
```

Then we add a URL title form field, and a URL form field, and fill them with the current values for the URL:

```
<TR>
   <TH WIDTH="20%" NOWRAP>Title</TH>
   <TD WIDTH="80%"><INPUT TYPE="TEXT" NAME="title"
                        VALUE="<?php echo $url_info_array["title"] ?>"
                        SIZE="30" MAXLENGTH="150"></TD>
</TR>
<TR>
   <TH WIDTH="20%" NOWRAP>URL</TH>
   <TD WIDTH="80%"><INPUT TYPE="TEXT" NAME="url"
                     VALUE="<?php echo "http://".$url_info_array["url"];?>"
                     SIZE="30" MAXLENGTH="150"></TD>
</TR>
<TR>
```

The final form field to add holds the current URL description:

```
        <TH WIDTH="20%" NOWRAP>Description<BR>
        (<?php echo $max_desc_length ?> Chars Max.)
        </TH>
        <TD WIDTH="80%"><TEXTAREA NAME="description" ROWS="5" COLS="40">
        <?php echo $url_info_array["description"] ?>
        </TEXTAREA></TD>
    </TR>
    <TR>
```

The final step is to add a button to submit the form called **Modify URL**, and another to reset the fields to their original values:

```
        <TH WIDTH="100%" NOWRAP COLSPAN="2">
        <INPUT TYPE="SUBMIT" VALUE="Modify URL" NAME="Submit">
        <INPUT TYPE="RESET" VALUE="Reset"></TH>
    </TR>
    </TABLE>
    </CENTER>
</FORM>
<?php
    directory_footer();
}
```

## modify_url()

In the function `modify_url()`, the current user is authenticated against the e-mail and password pair stored with the URL information. If the `$admin` flag is set, this authentication is not necessary. Provided that the user is authenticated, the modifications made to the URL record via the edit form will be mirrored in the database. The user is informed when the database record has been successfully modified:

```
function modify_url() {
    global $default_dbname, $directory_tablename,
            $max_desc_length, $PHP_SELF, $cur_page;
    global $title, $url, $description, $category_id,
            $url_id, $email, $password, $admin_script;
    global $link_id;
```

Again, we shall skip over the function definition and global variable declarations. We start by checking to see whether the user is an administrator:

```
    if(basename($PHP_SELF) == $admin_script) $admin = 1;
```

As in the `add_url()` function, we need to format the URL string input by the user. We remove "http://" and any trailing forward slash from the URL using the `eregi_replace()` function:

```
    $url = eregi_replace('http://', "", $url);
    $url = eregi_replace("/$", "", $url);
```

Again we reach a section of code similar to that found in `add_url()`. This code block checks that all of the form fields contain data, and displays an error message if they don't:

```
    if(!$admin && empty($email))
        error_message("Please enter your email address!");
    if(!$admin && empty($password))
        error_message("Please enter the password you used when posting your url!");
    if(empty($title)) error_message("Please enter the title!");
    if(empty($url)) error_message("Please enter the URL!");
    if(empty($description)) error_message("Please enter the description!");

    if(strlen($description) > $max_desc_length)
        error_message("Description too long! $max_desc_length chars max!");
```

The last check was to see if the URL description overflowed the maximum length defined in the $max_desc_length variable. Note that the user is thrown back to the previous page on error.

Next we obtain data from the database about the URL, by calling our get_url_info() function. The data retrieved is placed in $url_info_array:

```
    $url_info_array = get_url_info($url_id);
```

We retrieve from the array the user password associated with this URL, encrypt it using crypt(), and then check it against the encrypted version of the password provided by the user. We also retrieve the e-mail address associated with the URL, and check this against the address entered by the user. If either e-mails or passwords don't match, we display an error message, and launch the user back to the previous page. Of course, we only need to do all this if the user is not an administrator:

```
    if(!$admin && (($url_info_array["password"] != crypt($password, '.v'))
        || ($url_info_array["email"] != $email)))
        error_message("You don't have permission to modify this URL!");
```

Assuming that the user has been authenticated, now we must check fields for illegal characters. Any found have escape characters (backslashes) added to them using the addslashes() function:

```
    $title = addslashes($title);
    $description = addslashes($description);
```

Next we make sure that we have a database connection, and then we perform an UPDATE query which updates the URL record in the database with the data from the form:

```
    if(!$link_id) $link_id = db_connect($default_dbname);

    $query = "UPDATE $directory_tablename
            SET title='$title', url='$url', description='$description'
            WHERE url_id='$url_id'";
    $result = mysql_query($query);
    if(!$result) error_message(sql_error());
```

As always, we check whether any errors have occured during the query. The last step is to check that one record has been modified using the mysql_affected_rows() function. If this is not the case, we generate an error message, and send the user back to the previous page. If it is the case, we display a confirmation message to the user:

```
        $num_rows = mysql_affected_rows($link_id);
        if($num_rows != 1) error_message(sql_error());
        else echo
            "<SCRIPT>alert(\"$title($url) has been successfully modified!\");
```

As with add_url(), the function ends with a JavaScript code snippet that causes the browser to refresh the parent window with a given URL, and closes the current window:

```
        opener.location.href='$PHP_SELF?
        action=show_list&category_id=$category_id&cur_page=$cur_page';
        self.close();</SCRIPT>";

    }
```

## go_url()

This function is pretty straightforward; it redirects the user's browser to a new URL from the directory, and increments the "Number of Hits" field in the URL's record by one:

```
    function go_url()
    {
        global $default_dbname, $directory_tablename;
        global $url_id, $url;
```

First we check that the global variables $url_id and $url contain values:

```
        if(isset($url_id) && isset($url)) {
```

Next we establish a connection to the database, unless we already have one:

```
            if(!$link_id) $link_id = db_connect($default_dbname);
```

Then we perform a query to increment the value of the hit field by one for this URL. As usual, we check afterwards for a query error:

```
            $result = mysql_query("UPDATE $directory_tablename
                                 SET hit = hit + 1 WHERE url_id=$url_id");
            if(!$result) error_message(sql_error());
```

The last step is to call the header() function, which sends the string provided between the parentheses as an HTTP header:

```
            header("Location: $url");
```

In other words, this function call redirects the browser to the URL given in $url. Then we exit the script:

```
            exit;
        }
    }
```

## list_sites()

The `list_sites()` function displays a list of either the most-visited or the most recently-added URLs, depending on the `$mode` argument supplied to it. If the `$category_id` argument is passed as well, only those URLs belonging to the category defined by `$category_id` are included in the list.

We start with the function definition, and a list of global variables to be included in the function:

```
function list_sites($mode='top', $category_id='') {
    global $directory_tablename, $root_category_id, $PHP_SELF,
                                $num_top_sites, $num_new_sites;
```

Next we check to see if we have already established a database connection. If not, `$link_id` will be empty, and the program will use the `db_connect()` function to establish a new link:

```
if(!$link_id) $link_id = db_connect($default_dbname);
```

The `list_sites()` function will either display the list of most popular sites (if `$mode=="top"`) or a list of the most-recently added URLs (if `$mode= ="new"`). To extract URL data for either list requires a database query, so we need to construct a query string to feed into the `mysql_query()` function. This function will perform the database search.

The contents of the query string should depend upon which list is required. For the most popular sites, the list should have the most popular site at the top, so we will need an "ORDER BY hit DESC" clause in our query string:

```
if($mode=='top') {
    $order_by_str = 'ORDER BY hit DESC';
    $limit_str = "LIMIT $num_top_sites";
}
```

On the other hand, our recently-submitted URL list should have the most recently-submitted URL at the top of the list, so we need to sort by the `registerdate` field. Therefore, we need an "ORDER BY registerdate DESC" clause in the query string:

```
else {
    $order_by_str = 'ORDER BY registerdate DESC';
    $limit_str = "LIMIT $num_new_sites";
}
```

Note that in both cases we have also built a LIMIT clause, which will limit the number of entries in each list to the number specified in the `$num_top_sites` or `$num_new_sites` global variables.

Now we define a category string `$category_str` for use in the query, which will specify the category or categories to search. As in step 6 of the `show_list()` function, if the query needs to cover all categories in the URL directory, we fill `$category_str` with "1" so that the query does not produce an error:

```
if($category_id == $root_category_id) $category_str = '1';
else $category_str = "category_id LIKE '$category_id%'";
```

Otherwise, we build up a clause which selects only a portion of the category tree. We now add the clauses that we have constructed so far to the main SELECT query string $query:

```
$query = "SELECT url_id, title, url FROM $directory_tablename WHERE
$category_str AND approved = 1 $order_by_str $limit_str";
```

Then we feed the query to mysql_query() so that it will search the database, displaying an error message if no query results are returned:

```
$result = mysql_query($query);
if(!$result) echo sql_error();
```

Next, provided we have search results:

```
if(mysql_num_rows($result) > 0) {
```

we display the title for the list that we are about to display:

```
    if($mode=='top') echo "<STRONG>Top $num_top_sites!</STRONG><BR>";
    else if($mode=='new') echo "<STRONG>New $num_new_sites!</STRONG><BR>";
}
```

The final step is to use a while loop to display the title of each URL found in the search. We initialize a loop counter $i, and at the start of each loop use the mysql_fetch_array() function to retrieve a URL data record. This data is transferred to the array $query_data:

```
$i = 1;
while($query_data = mysql_fetch_array($result)) {
```

Next we extract the URL ID, the URL, and the URL title:

```
    $url_id = $query_data["url_id"];
    $url = "http://" . $query_data["url"];
    $title = $query_data["title"];
```

Then we display the clickable URL title, and a number showing the position of the URL on the list. When the title is clicked, the user is taken to the go_url() function, which jumps to the URL:

```
        echo "<STRONG> - <A HREF=\"$PHP_SELF?action=go_url&
                                url=$url&url_id=$url_id\">
                        $i. $title</A></STRONG><BR>\n";
```

Finally, we increment the loop counter, ready for the next loop:

```
        $i++;
    }
}
?>
```

Now let's move on to the user code.

# User Code – php_directory.php

Since all the functions that users make use of are shared with administrators, in the php_directory.inc file, there's not much left to cover in the user script. The script uses an include() call to include all the functions in php_directory.inc. Aside from these functions, the script consists of a switch statement which is used to redirect the flow of the program.

One feature of our script is that we must always be aware of the next required action; in other words we need to keep track of the *state* of the program. For instance, if we use a function which invokes a form, when we submit the form, how does the program know which function it is supposed to jump to next?

Since many of the functions open up new windows containing forms, or move the browser to a new URL, keeping track of the state information can be quite difficult. We achieve it in this script by propagating a special variable through hidden form fields, and by tagging the value of the variable onto the end of URLs. This special variable, $action, contains a string which defines the next course of action.

Usually what happens is that an action is performed (for example, the user submits a form), and this php_directory.php script is then called. During the call, the $action variable is also passed, and it is then used in the following switch statement to control the next course of action (specifically which function to call next):

```php
<?php
include ("./php_directory.inc");

switch($action) {
    case "add_url_form":
        add_url_form();
    break;
    case "add_url":
        add_url();
    break;
    case "modify_url_form":
        modify_url_form();
    break;
    case "modify_url":
        modify_url();
    break;
    case "go_url":
        go_url();
    break;
    default:
        directory_header();
        show_list();
        directory_footer();
    break;

}
?>
```

Make sure that you put the common file into a safe place. We're including the file from the current directory for the sake of simplicity. Putting it beyond the web document root is a good idea. At least hide it in a password-protected web directory.

# Administration Code – dir_manager.php

The administration script also uses a switch statement similar to the one in `php_directory.php`. However it also defines 12 functions used solely by administrators. We'll see what the functions do first.

Now let's look at the code. First, we need to include the common file which contains the functions used by all users:

```php
<?php
include "./php_directory.inc";
```

## list_categories()

The `list_categories()` function illustrates the current category tree, as shown in the following figure:

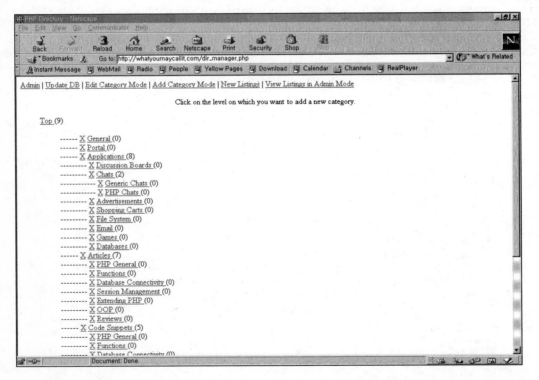

On this page, an administrator can add, delete or modify categories by clicking on the [Add Category Mode] or [Edit Category Mode] links at the top of the page.

Although at first it looks rather complex, the function is pretty easy to understand:

```php
function list_categories() {
    global $default_dbname, $directory_tablename, $category_tablename,
                                                   $PHP_SELF;
    global $link_id, $mode, $root_category_id, $category_id_length;
```

As usual we'll jump staight to the meat of the function. First we ensure that we have a database connection:

```
if(!$link_id) $link_id = db_connect($default_dbname);
```

That done, we check the value of the $mode variable, which is another state variable like $action, except that it stores which administration mode we are in:

```
if(!isset($mode)) $mode = 'add_category';
```

We put the page into the "Add Category" mode by default.

**1.** Retrieve categories for list.

Next we perform a query to retrieve the number of top most categories: the children of the root:

```
$query = "SELECT count(*) FROM $category_tablename
          WHERE length(category_id) = $category_id_length";
$result = mysql_query($query);
if(!$result) die(sql_error());
```

We mustn't forget to check for query errors. Then we move the results into an array, $query_data. The first element of this array is the number of top-most categories:

```
$query_data = mysql_fetch_row($result);
$top_level_total = $query_data[0];
```

The following query retrieves all the categories in the directory in order of category ID:

```
$query = "SELECT category_id FROM $category_tablename
          ORDER BY category_id";
$result = mysql_query($query);
if(!$result) die(sql_error());
```

**2.** Add administration links to window.

We now use the directory_header() function to open a new window, and the top_menu() function (which we'll meet later) to display a set of links for the administrator in the window:

```
directory_header();
top_menu();
```

These links are [Admin], [Update DB], [Edit Category Mode], [Add Category Mode], [New Listings], and [View Listings in Admin Mode]. We'll come back to these later.

Next we retrieve meta data for the root category using get_category_info(), and place it into $category_info_array:

```
$category_info_array = get_category_info($root_category_id);
```

Depending upon the value of the $mode flag (either "add_category" or "modify_category"), categories can be added, edited, or deleted. First, if we are in adding categories mode, we display a message to the administrator instructing him to "Click on the level on which you want to add a category.":

**3.** Deal with the root category.

```
if($mode == 'add_category') {
        echo "<CENTER>
                Click on the level on which you want to add a new category.
                </CENTER><P>";
        echo "<BLOCKQUOTE>\n";
```

The next line of code displays the hyperlinked name of the root ("Top"), and then its number of children. When clicked, the link redirects the program to add_category_form(), which displays a form. The form enables users to add another child below the root:

```
        echo "<A HREF=\"javascript:open_window('$PHP_SELF?
                action=add_category_form&parent=$root_category_id')\">" .
$category_info_array["category"] ." </A>(" . $category_info_array["num_child"] .
")";
        }
```

The $parent variable is passed on to the form to let it know under which category (the root) a new category will be created.

If we are in editing categories mode, we do almost the same thing, except that the hyperlinked name "Top", when clicked, displays a form which shows users the ID and name of the root, as well as the number of URLs posted to it (zero). Note that even the administrator cannot modify the name of the root, because it does not have a record in the database.

```
else {
        echo "<CENTER>Click on the category you want to edit.</CENTER><P>";
        echo "<BLOCKQUOTE>\n";
        echo "<A HREF=\"javascript:open_window('$PHP_SELF?
                action=edit_category_form&category_id=$root_category_id')\">" .
$category_info_array["category"] ." </A>(" . $category_info_array["num_child"] .
")";
    }
    echo "<BR>\n";
    echo "<BLOCKQUOTE>\n";
```

The next step is to list hyperlinked names for all the categories, in category ID order. We set up a while loop; each iteration of the loop processes the data of one of the root's children. The first step is to retrieve the meta data for a category.

```
    while($query_data = mysql_fetch_array($result)) {
```

Then we retrieve the category ID from the array, and use this as the argument in a call to our get_category_info() function. This returns meta data for the category in question:

```
        $category_id = $query_data[0];
        $category_info_array = get_category_info($category_id);
        for($i=0; $i < $category_info_array["depth"]; $i++) echo "---";
```

**4.** Display category list.

Next we display a hyperlinked "X", which on clicking deletes the category. We use the JavaScript `confirm()` method to bring up a window which asks for confirmation of the delete first though:

```
    echo " <A HREF=\"$PHP_SELF?
        action=delete_category&category_id=$category_id&mode=$mode\"
        OnClick=\"return confirm('Are you sure? It holds " .
        $category_info_array["num_child"] . " subcategories and " .
        $category_info_array["num_item"] . " items.');\">X</A> \n";
```

The confirmation window displays the number of children in the category and also the number of URLs there. If we are in the adding categories mode, we display a hyperlinked category name. When the name is clicked, the JavaScript function `open_window()` is called to open a new window. Then the `add_category_form()` function is called to display an "Add Category" form in the window:

```
    if($mode == 'add_category')
        echo "<A HREF=\"javascript:open_window('$PHP_SELF?
            action=add_category_form&parent=$category_id')\">" .
$category_info_array["category"] ." </A>(" . $category_info_array["num_child"] .
")";
```

If we are in editing categories mode, we do the same thing, except that the hyperlinked categories name links to an "Edit Category" form instead:

```
    else echo "<A HREF=\"javascript:open_window('$PHP_SELF?
        action=edit_category_form&category_id=$category_id')\">" .
$category_info_array["category"] ." </A>(" . $category_info_array["num_child"] .
")";
```

Finally, we close HTML tags and close the HTML page using the `directory_footer()` function:

```
    echo "<BR>\n";

  }
  echo "</BLOCKQUOTE>\n";
  echo "</BLOCKQUOTE>\n";
  directory_footer();
}
```

## add_category_form()

The `add_category_form()` function creates an input form by which a user can pass on the necessary information for creating a new category. This information is then passed to the `add_category()` function, which actually adds the category to the directory:

```
function add_category_form() {
    global $default_dbname, $directory_tablename, $category_tablename,
                                                        $PHP_SELF;

    global $link_id, $parent;
```

The $parent global variable holds the ID of the parent of the new category to be added. We use it as an argument to the get_category_info() function, which then retrieves meta data about the parent category. We place this meta data into an array, and then retrieve the expanded family name of the parent category from it, along with the category ID of the new category:

```
$category_info_array = get_category_info($parent);
$category_id = $category_info_array["next_id"];
$category_fullname = $category_info_array["fullname"];
```

The next step is to create the "Add Category" form. We start a new HTML page in a new window by calling the directory_header() function:

```
directory_header();
```

Then we add a title to the new page, and create hidden fields. The field "action" is used to hold state information; it is given the value "add_category" here, which indicates that the program should jump to the add_category() function after the form has been submitted. We also store the category ID of the category to add in a hidden field:

```
?>
<CENTER><H3>Adding a New Category:
            <?php echo $category_fullname ?></H3></CENTER>
<FORM METHOD="POST" ACTION="<?php echo $PHP_SELF ?>">
<INPUT TYPE="HIDDEN" NAME="action" VALUE="add_category">
<INPUT TYPE="HIDDEN" NAME="category_id" VALUE="<? echo $category_id ?>">
  <CENTER><TABLE BORDER="1" WIDTH="90%">
    <TR>
```

The next step is to add some form fields: Category ID, and Category Name. Note that we fill the ID field with the new category's ID:

```
    <TH WIDTH="30%" NOWRAP>Category ID</TH>
    <TD WIDTH="70%"><?php echo $category_id ?></TD>
  </TR>
  <TR>
    <TH WIDTH="30%" NOWRAP>Category Name</TH>
    <TD WIDTH="70%"><INPUT TYPE="TEXT" NAME="category" SIZE="20"></TD>
  </TR>
  <TR>
```

We add a couple of buttons: "Submit" and "Reset", which do what they say:

```
    <TH WIDTH="100%" COLSPAN="2" NOWRAP>
    <INPUT TYPE="SUBMIT" VALUE="Submit">
    <INPUT TYPE="RESET" VALUE="Reset"></TH>
```

```
        </TR>
      </TABLE>
    </CENTER>
  </FORM>
```

Finally we call the `directory_footer()` function to end the HTML page:

```php
<?php
  directory_footer();
}
```

## add_category()

The `add_category()` function inserts the submitted category data into the `php_category` table. It's a pretty simple utility function. Let's take a look:

```php
function add_category() {
    global $default_dbname, $directory_tablename, $category_tablename,
                                                    $PHP_SELF;
    global $link_id, $category_id, $category;
```

We can't add a category if we don't have a name for it, so we check that `$category` contains the new category's name before proceeding any further:

```php
    if(empty($category)) error_message("Enter the category name!");
```

Provided we've got a name for the category, we then check that we have a connection to the database, and perform a query to insert the category's name and ID into the `php_category` table. The `hit` field for the new category is also initialized (set to zero). In other words, we create a new record in the table for the new category:

```php
    if(!$link_id) $link_id = db_connect($default_dbname);

    $query = "INSERT INTO $category_tablename
                VALUES('$category', '$category_id', 0)";
    $result = mysql_query($query);
```

We mustn't forget to check for any query errors:

```php
    if(!$result) error_message(sql_error());
```

The final step is to open a new HTML page in a new window using `directory_header()`, and then we display a message to the user saying that the category was successfully added. Finally we use the `directory_footer()` function to end the HTML page:

```php
    directory_header();
    echo "<SCRIPT>alert(\"$category was successfully added!\");
          opener.location.href='$PHP_SELF'; self.close();</SCRIPT>";
    directory_footer();
}
```

## edit_category_form()

The `edit_category_form()` function allows an administrator to change the name of a category via a form. The actual editing is performed by the `edit_category()` function, which is called on submission of the editing form. Let's take a look at `edit_category_form()` first:

```
function edit_category_form() {
    global $default_dbname, $directory_tablename, $category_tablename,
                                                    $PHP_SELF;

    global $link_id, $category_id;
```

We start by retrieving meta data on the category we want to edit. To do this we call the `get_category_info()` function; we then feed the meta data into `$category_info_array`:

```
    $category_info_array = get_category_info($category_id);
```

Next we create the edit form. We call the directory header to start a new HTML page in a new window:

```
    directory_header();
```

The page is given the title "Editing the Category:" followed by the expandable family name of the category:

```
    ?>
    <CENTER><H3>Editing the Category:
            <?php echo $category_info_array["fullname"] ?>
            </H3></CENTER>
```

As usual, we use hidden form fields to pass state information (via `$action`) and the category ID:

```
<FORM METHOD="POST" ACTION="<?php echo $PHP_SELF ?>">
<INPUT TYPE="HIDDEN" NAME="action" VALUE="edit_category">
<INPUT TYPE="HIDDEN" NAME="category_id" VALUE="<? echo $category_id ?>">
```

Then we add some form fields: Category ID, Category Name, and Resources (in other words, the number of URLs posted to the category). We fill the ID and Resources fields with the corresponding meta data, by retrieving it from `$category_info_array`:

```
    <CENTER><TABLE BORDER="1" WIDTH="90%">
      <TR>
        <TH WIDTH="30%" NOWRAP>Category ID</TH>
        <TD WIDTH="70%"><?php echo $category_id ?></TD>
      </TR>
      <TR>
        <TH WIDTH="30%" NOWRAP>Category Name</TH>
        <TD WIDTH="70%">
        <INPUT TYPE="TEXT" NAME="category" VALUE=
        "<?php echo $category_info_array["category"] ?>"
        SIZE="20"></TD>
      </TR>
      <TR>
        <TH WIDTH="30%" NOWRAP>Resources</TH>
        <TD WIDTH="70%"><?php echo $category_info_array["num_item"] ?></TD>
      </TR>
      <TR>
```

As usual we add "Submit" and "Reset" buttons:

```
        <TH WIDTH="100%" COLSPAN="2" NOWRAP><INPUT TYPE="SUBMIT" VALUE="Submit">
    <INPUT TYPE="RESET" VALUE="Reset"></TH>
      </TR>
    </TABLE>
    </CENTER>
  </FORM>
```

The last step is to call the `directory_footer()` function to end the HTML page:

```
<?php
    directory_footer();
}
```

## edit_category()

The actual update operation is performed by the `edit_category()` function. It's actually pretty similar to `add_category()`, except that we perform an UPDATE query instead of an INSERT. Take a look:

```
function edit_category() {
    global $default_dbname, $directory_tablename, $category_tablename,
                                                        $PHP_SELF;
    global $link_id, $category_id, $category;
```

Ignoring the preliminaries (function definition and global variable declarations), we first check that we have been supplied with the category name form field (stored in `$category`), otherwise we display an error message and knock the user back to the previous page:

```
    if(empty($category)) error_message("Enter the category name!");
```

Assuming we've got a name for the category, we then make sure that we have a connection to the database, and then perform a query to update the category's name in the `php_category` table. We follow this by checking for any query errors:

```
    if(!$link_id) $link_id = db_connect($default_dbname);

    $query = "UPDATE $category_tablename SET category = '$category'
            WHERE category_id = '$category_id'";
    $result = mysql_query($query);
    if(!$result) error_message(sql_error());
```

We now use the `mysql_affected_rows()` function to check that a modification was made to the category record; if not we display an error message and launch the user back to the previous page:

```
    if(!mysql_affected_rows($link_id)) error_message("Nothing changed!");
```

Note that the MySQL server does nothing if no record needs to be changed by the UPDATE operation – the `mysql_affected_rows()` function call will return 0, meaning that the administrator submitted the form without changing anything.

We finish by opening a new window, and displaying an update confirmation message in it:

**653**

```
    directory_header();

    echo "<SCRIPT>alert(\"$category was successfully updated!\");
 opener.location.href='$PHP_SELF?mode=edit_category'; self.close();</SCRIPT>";

    directory_footer();
 }
```

## delete_category()

The delete_category() function trashes a given category. If the category has subcategories or URLs, all of theae are also wiped out:

```
function delete_category() {
    global $default_dbname, $directory_tablename, $category_tablename,
                                                    $PHP_SELF;

    global $link_id, $category_id, $mode;
```

The first step is to check that the ID of the category to check has been supplied: if it is present in $category_id, then we follow this with another check to see if we have a database connection. If not, we open one:

```
    if(empty($category_id)) error_message("Empty Category ID!");
    if(!$link_id) $link_id = db_connect($default_dbname);
```

Next we perform two DELETE queries. The first removes the category, and any categories that it spawns, from the database:

```
    $query = "DELETE FROM $category_tablename WHERE category_id
                                    LIKE '$category_id%'";
    $result = mysql_query($query);
    if(!$result) error_message(sql_error());
    $del_subs = mysql_affected_rows($link_id) - 1;
```

The second removes any URLs from the php_directory table which are posted under the just-deleted categories:

```
    $query = "DELETE FROM $directory_tablename WHERE category_id
                                    LIKE '$category_id%'";
    $result = mysql_query($query);
    if(!$result) error_message(sql_error());
    $del_items = mysql_affected_rows($link_id);
```

After both queries, we check for query errors, and check that how many items have been deleted using the mysql_affected_rows() function. The variable $del_subs contains the number of categories spawned by the deleted category, which were also deleted by the query. The number of deleted URLs is held in $del_items.

The function now reports how many spawned categories and/or URLs have been deleted, and refreshes the browser to reflect the change. (Note that simply going back to the previous page by calling JavaScript's history() method won't give the administrator the changed page. We need to explicitly call the script again.):

```
echo "<SCRIPT>alert(\"1 category, $del_subs subcategories,
                    and $del_items items were deleted!\");
self.location.href='$PHP_SELF?mode=$mode';</SCRIPT>";
}
```

## update_db()

The update_db() function corrects any inconsistencies found between the two tables. Since the total number of URLs in each category is stored in the php_category table, inconsistencies might be found if an error occurs during a DELETE, UPDATE, or INSERT operation. The function repairs them:

```
function update_db() {
    global $default_dbname, $directory_tablename, $category_tablename,
                                                        $PHP_SELF;
    global $link_id, $category_id, $mode;
```

The first step is to display a new window and start a new HTML page in it using our directory header() function:

```
directory_header();
```

**1.** Retrieve data from category table.

Next, we make sure that we have established a connection to the database...

```
if(!$link_id) $link_id = db_connect($default_dbname);
```

... and then we carry out a SELECT query which retrieves all the data from the php_category table:

```
$query = "SELECT category, category_id, num_item
            FROM $category_tablename";
$result = mysql_query($query);
if(!$result) error_message(sql_error());
```

The $num_revs variable holds the number of inconsistencies that have been repaired. We set its initial value to zero:

```
$num_revs = 0;
```

Then we retrieve meta data from each category record one record at a time (using a while loop and the mysql_fetch_row() function), and pass it to the $query_data array:

```
while($query_data = mysql_fetch_row($result)) {
    $category = $query_data[0];
    $category_id = $query_data[1];
    $num_item = $query_data[2];
```

From the $query_data array we retrieve the category name, category ID, and the number of URLs posted to the category. We save the number of URLs found posted to this category in the variable $num_items. Bear in mind that this is the result from searching the category table.

**2.** Retrieve data from URL table

Now we want to do the same URL count as before, but in the `php_directory` table instead. So we use the same category name and ID in another SELECT query, which counts how many (approved) URL records that are posted to this category in the URL table:

```
$query = "SELECT count(*) FROM $directory_tablename
          WHERE category_id = '$category_id' AND approved = 1";
$result2 = mysql_query($query);
$query_data2 = mysql_fetch_row($result2);
$total = $query_data2[0];
if(!$result2) error_message(sql_error());
```

As usual, we perform a check of the results from the query to see if there has been an error. We also use `mysql_fetch_row()` again, in order to extract the number of URL records which exist for the specified category ID in the URL table. We place this number in the `$total` variable.

**3.** Compare tables and correct inconsistencies.

Then we compare the number of URLs found in the first query, with the number found in the second query. Since the first query searched through the category table, and the second through the URL table, we are effectively comparing table content:

```
if($num_item != $total) {
```

If there is a difference between the two tables, we perform another query to update the category table:

```
$query = "UPDATE $category_tablename SET num_item = $total
          WHERE category_id = '$category_id'";
$result2 = mysql_query($query);
if(!$result2) die(sql_error());
```

We follow this by displaying a message to the user, stating that an update has been made. Then we increment the counter that keeps track of the number of database inconsistencies:

```
        echo "Number of resources in <STRONG>\"$category\"</STRONG> mismatch ->
revised: $total resources.<BR>\n";
        $num_revs++;
    }
}
```

With each row of the table, we check to see whether the `num_item` field contains the same number of URLs as returned from MySQL's `count(*)` aggregate function. If not, the row is updated to correct the inconsistency.

When all the records have been searched, we report how many inconsistencies have been found to the user:

```
if(!$num_revs) echo "No inconsistency found.<BR>\n";
else if($num_revs) echo "$num_revs inconsistency has been corrected.<BR>\n";
else echo "$num_revs inconsistencies have been corrected.<BR>\n";
```

Then we display "Done" and close the HTML page using `directory_footer()`:

```
    echo "Done.\n";
    directory_footer();
}
```

## view_new()

An administrator can view the list of recently-added URLs by calling the `view_new()` function.

Clicking on the [New Listings] link displays details of URLs that have been recently added, but have yet to be approved for listing. An example is shown in the screenshot:

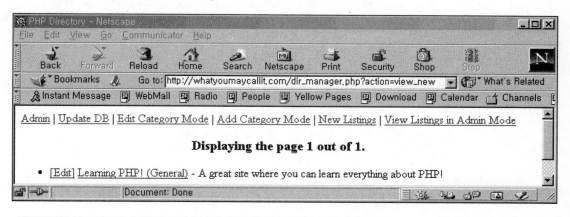

```
function view_new() {
    global $default_dbname, $directory_tablename, $category_tablename,
                          $records_per_page, $PHP_SELF, $link_id;
    global $cur_page;

    if(!$link_id) $link_id = db_connect($default_dbname);
```

**1.** How many new URLs have been submitted?

After first checking that we have a database connection, we use the following initial query to return the number of recently-added URLs. The records for these URLs will have a value of 0 for the `approved` field, since they are yet to be approved:

```
$query = "SELECT count(*) FROM $directory_tablename
                        WHERE approved != 1";
$result = mysql_query($query);
if(!$result) echo error_message(sql_error());
```

We now use the `mysql_fetch_row()` function to extract the number of URLs returned by the query:

```
$query_data = mysql_fetch_row($result);
$total_num = $query_data[0];
```

If the $total_num variable is zero, we have no new listings:

```
if(!$total_num) echo error_message("No new listing!");
```

We might have to split the list of URLs into pages, if there are too many returned by the query to display on one page. Therefore, we need to construct a LIMIT clause string to place in in our final query string. (The final query will retrieve the URL records for the yet-to-be approved URLs):

```
$limit_str = "LIMIT " . $cur_page * $records_per_page . ",
                                       $records_per_page";
```

This LIMIT clause will retrieve a given number of URLs at a time; the number retrieved is stored in the $records_per_page variable. The $cur_page variable stores the index of the page of URLs that are currently displayed upon the browser.

**2.** Retrieve URL data.

The next step is to perform the final query, which will return the records of the URLs which are yet to be approved:

```
$query = "SELECT url_id, url, title, description, category_id
          FROM $directory_tablename
          WHERE approved = 0
          ORDER BY registerdate $limit_str";
$result = mysql_query($query);
if(!$result) echo error_message(sql_error());
```

Actually, this function employs the same method of navigating through multiple pages as the show_list() function in php_directory.inc. To implement the navigation, we first define a page-number variable $page_num which starts at 1 (unlike $cur_page which starts at zero):

```
$page_num = $cur_page + 1;
```

Then we derive the total number of whole pages that we will need to display all the URLs, and the last page number. We store these values in $total_num_page and $last_page_num respectively:

```
$total_num_page = floor($total_num/$records_per_page);
$last_page_num = $total_num_page + 1;
```

**3.** List newly-submitted URLs.

Next we open a new page and place administration links at the top of it, using the top_menu() function:

```
directory_header();
top_menu();
```

We display the page number and the total number of pages:

```
        echo "<CENTER><H3>Displaying the page $page_num out of
$last_page_num.</H3></CENTER>";
```

Now, the function retrieves data for every submitted URL. We use a `while` loop combined with the `mysql_fetch_array()` function to retrieve one URL record at a time:

```
    echo "<UL>\n";
    while($query_data = mysql_fetch_array($result)) {
```

Note how we have placed the data for each record into an array. We now move values from the array into specific variables:

```
        $url_id = $query_data["url_id"];
        $url = "http://" . $query_data["url"];
        $title = $query_data["title"];
        $description = $query_data["description"];
        $category_id = $query_data["category_id"];
```

We then use `get_category_info()` to retrieve meta data about the category that the URL has been posted to, and then extract the expanded family name of the category:

```
        $category_info_array = get_category_info($category_id);
        $category_fullname = $category_info_array["fullname"];
        echo "<LI>\n";
```

We also add a hyperlink with the name "Edit", which, when clicked brings up a form to edit the URL's records:

```
        echo "<A HREF=\"javascript:open_window('$PHP_SELF?
                     action=edit_new_form&url_id=$url_id
                     &category_id=$category_id');\">[Edit]</A> \n";
```

By the side of this link we display a hyperlink containing the URL string, the URL title, and the expanded family name. On clicking, the link takes the user to the URL. Next to this link we display the URL description:

```
        echo "<A HREF=\"$url\" TARGET=\"_BLANK\">
                     $title ($category_fullname)</A> - $description\n";
        echo "</LI>";
    }
    echo "</UL>\n";
    echo "<BR>\n";
```

The final step is to display the hyperlinked navigation links [Top], [Prev], [Next], and [Bottom]. Clicking on any of them will knock the program back to the start of the `view_new()` function. We keep the function informed of the current page number between function calls by passing the `$cur_page` variable via the URL:

```
    echo "<STRONG><CENTER>";

    if($cur_page > 0)
        echo "<A HREF=\"$PHP_SELF?action=view_new&cur_page=0\">[Top]</A>";
    if($cur_page != 0) {
        $prev_page = $cur_page - 1;
        echo "<A HREF=\"$PHP_SELF?action=view_new
                               &cur_page=$prev_page\">[Prev]</A> ";
    }

    if($cur_page <  $total_num_page) {
        $next_page = $cur_page + 1;
        echo "<A HREF=\"$PHP_SELF?action=view_new&cur_page=$next_page\">[Next]</A>
";
    }

    if($cur_page != $total_num_page) echo "<A
HREF=\"$PHP_SELF?action=view_new&cur_page=$total_num_page\">[Bottom]</A>";

    echo "</CENTER></STRONG>";
```

The last step is to end the HTML page:

```
    directory_footer();
}
```

## edit_new_form()

While checking through the list of the newly-added URLs, an administrator can either delete, approve or edit a new submission, by calling the edit_new_form() function. This function displays an editing form that contains the submitted details of the URL. It calls the edit_new() function, which actually performs the deletion or approval:

```
function edit_new_form() {
    global $PHP_SELF, $max_desc_length, $url_id, $category_id;

    directory_header();
```

First, we open a new page with the directory_header() function. Then we retrieve the data associated with the URL by calling the get_url_info() function:

```
    $url_info_array = get_url_info($url_id);
```

The URL data is placed in an array. We now want to get meta data about the category that the URL is posted to, so we extract the category ID from $url_info_array, and use our get_category_info() function to retrieve the meta data:

```
    $category_info_array = get_category_info($url_info_array["category_id"]);
```

We provide a title for our editing form, and display the submission date:

```
?>
<CENTER><H3>Editing a new listing.</H3></CENTER>
<UL>
<LI>Submitted on:
<?php echo $url_info_array["formatted_registerdate"] ?></LI>
</UL>
```

Next we add some hidden fields to the form, which will enable us to pass state information after the form is submitted:

```
<FORM METHOD="POST" ACTION="<?php echo $PHP_SELF ?>">
<INPUT TYPE="HIDDEN" NAME="action" VALUE="edit_new">
<INPUT TYPE="HIDDEN" NAME="url_id" VALUE="<? echo $url_id ?>">
<INPUT TYPE="HIDDEN" NAME="category_id" VALUE="<? echo $category_id ?>">
```

We add five form fields: Category, E-mail, Title, URL, and Description, and fill the fields with the values from the URL record. Note that only three of the fields can be edited: Title, URL and Description:

```
    <CENTER><TABLE BORDER="1" WIDTH="90%">
    <TR>
      <TH WIDTH="20%" NOWRAP>Category</TH>
      <TD WIDTH="80%"><?php echo $category_info_array["fullname"] ?></TD>
    </TR>
    <TR>
      <TH WIDTH="20%" NOWRAP>Email</TH>
      <TD WIDTH="80%"><?php echo $url_info_array["email"] ?>
      <INPUT TYPE="HIDDEN" NAME="email"
       VALUE="<?php echo $url_info_array["email"] ?>"></TD>
    </TR>
    <TR>
      <TH WIDTH="20%" NOWRAP>Title</TH>
      <TD WIDTH="80%"><INPUT TYPE="TEXT" NAME="title" VALUE="<?php echo
$url_info_array["title"] ?>" SIZE="30" MAXLENGTH="150"></TD>
    </TR>
    <TR>
      <TH WIDTH="20%" NOWRAP>URL</TH>
      <TD WIDTH="80%"><INPUT TYPE="TEXT" NAME="url" VALUE="<?php echo "http://" .
$url_info_array["url"]; ?>" SIZE="30" MAXLENGTH="150"></TD>
    </TR>
    <TR>
      <TH WIDTH="20%" NOWRAP>Description<BR>(<?php echo $max_desc_length ?> Chars
Max.)</TH>
      <TD WIDTH="80%"><TEXTAREA NAME="description" ROWS="5" COLS="40"><?php echo
$url_info_array["description"] ?></TEXTAREA></TD>
    </TR>
    <TR>
```

Note that we tell the user how long the description can be. Next we add radio buttons, which allow the user to select whether the URL record is approved or trashed. The value of "option" is passed to the edit_new() function on form submission, and it signifies whether the record should be approved or not:

```
    <TH WIDTH="20%" NOWRAP>Action</TH>
    <TD WIDTH="80%">
    <INPUT TYPE="RADIO" VALUE="approve" NAME="option" CHECKED>
    Approve <INPUT TYPE="RADIO" VALUE="delete" NAME="option">
```

```
            Delete</TD>
      </TR>
      <TR>
```

Finally, we add the requisite "Submit" and "Reset" buttons, and end the HTML page using the `directory_footer()` function:

```
        <TH WIDTH="100%" NOWRAP COLSPAN="2">
        <INPUT TYPE="SUBMIT" VALUE="Edit URL" NAME="Submit">
        <INPUT TYPE="RESET" VALUE="Reset"></TH>
      </TR>
    </TABLE>
    </CENTER>
  </FORM>
  <?php
    directory_footer();
  }
```

## edit_new()

The `edit_new()` function discards the given URL if the `$option` flag is "delete"; otherwise it sets the `approved` field value to 1, indicating that the submission has been approved for listing:

```
function edit_new() {
    global $default_dbname, $directory_tablename,
           $category_tablename, $max_desc_length;
    global $title, $url, $description, $category_id,
           $url_id, $email, $option;
    global $dirmaster_email, $link_id, $send_mail;
```

First, the function makes sure that the submitted URL doesn't start with "http://" or end with "/" by calling the `eregi_replace()` PHP function, which removes them:

```
    $url = eregi_replace('http://', "", $url);
    $url = eregi_replace("/$", "", $url);
```

Next we check to see if all fields contain values:

```
    if(empty($title)) error_message("Please enter the title!");
    if(empty($url)) error_message("Please enter the URL!");
    if(empty($description)) error_message("Please enter the description!");
```

Next we check to see that a database link has been established, so that we can perform a database query:

```
    if(!$link_id) $link_id = db_connect($default_dbname);
```

If the administrator chose to delete the submission, we perform a query that deletes the URL record from the database:

```
    if($option == 'delete') {
        $query = "DELETE FROM $directory_tablename
```

```
                        WHERE url_id = '$url_id'";
        $result = mysql_query($query);
        if(!$result) error_message(sql_error());
```

We make sure that just one record in the database has been modified, by calling the `mysql_affected_rows()` function:

```
        $num_rows = mysql_affected_rows($link_id);
        if($num_rows != 1) error_message(sql_error());
```

Now we tell the administrator that the record has been deleted, and refresh the window to reflect the change in the submitted URLs list:

```
        else
          echo "<SCRIPT>alert(\"$title($url) has been successfully deleted!\");
                                      opener.location.href='$PHP_SELF?
                                action=view_new'; self.close();</SCRIPT>";
    }
```

Now we have approved URL submissions to deal with. First, we check the length of the URL description, in case it is too long. We must also check the title and description for problematic characters (such as quotes and apostrophes) and escape them using the `addslashes()` function:

```
    else {
        if(strlen($description) > $max_desc_length)
            error_message("Description too long! $max_desc_length chars max!");

        $title = addslashes($title);
        $description = addslashes($description);
```

It's time to perform the queries to insert the new URL record. We need more than one because we must update both the category table and the URL table. We'll start by updating the category table; this involves incrementing the number of hits in the relevant category (the one that the approved URL is posted in):

```
        $query = "UPDATE $category_tablename
                    SET num_item = num_item + 1
                    WHERE category_id = '$category_id'";
        $result = mysql_query($query);
        if(!$result) error_message(sql_error());
```

Then we update the URL table to include the new record:

```
        $query = "UPDATE $directory_tablename SET title='$title', url='$url',
    description='$description', approved = 1 WHERE url_id='$url_id'";
        $result = mysql_query($query);
        if(!$result) error_message(sql_error());
```

Provided that the server is configured to send e-mail, the function sends a confirmation e-mail to the user once his submission has been approved:

```
        if($send_mail){
            $mail_subject =
                        "PHP Directory>> Your contribution has been listed.";
            $mail_body = "Thank you for sharing your resources with us.\n";
            $mail_body = "Your contribution has been listed. Thank you.\n\n";
            $mail_body .= "Title: $title\n";
            $mail_body .= "URL: $url\n";
            $mail_body .= "Description: $description";
            mail($email, $mail_subject, $mail_body,
                "From: $dirmaster_email\nReply-to: $dirmaster_email");
        }
```

We must check that our query entered a new record. We use the `mysql_affected_rows()` function to make sure there is one (and one only) affected record:

```
        $num_rows = mysql_affected_rows($link_id);
        if($num_rows != 1) error_message(sql_error());
```

The last step is to display a message to the administrator, saying that the URL has been approved:

```
        else
        echo "<SCRIPT>alert(\"$title($url) has been successfully approved!\");
                                            self.close();</SCRIPT>";
    }
}
```

## delete_url()

The `delete_url()` function – as the name implies – deletes a URL. The function is called by clicking the "X" hyperlink, which is displayed next to the category name when an administrator is viewing the category list. These hyperlinks are created by the `show_list()` function when the `$admin` flag is on (in other words an administrator is using the script):

```
function delete_url() {
    global $default_dbname, $directory_tablename,
            $category_tablename, $category_id, $url_id, $url, $title;
    global $PHP_SELF, $link_id;

    if(!$link_id) $link_id = db_connect($default_dbname);
```

We ensure that a database connection has been established, and then perform an UPDATE query. This query searches for the `hit` field of the category that the URL belongs to, and decrements this field by one in anticipation of the deletion of the URL:

```
    $query = "UPDATE $category_tablename
            SET num_item = num_item - 1
            WHERE category_id = '$category_id'";
    $result = mysql_query($query);
    if(!$result) error_message(sql_error());
```

Then next step is the actual URL deletion. We perform a DELETE query, which eliminates any URL in the directory whose ID matches the ID of the URL to delete:

```
$query = "DELETE FROM $directory_tablename WHERE url_id = '$url_id'";
$result = mysql_query($query);
if(!$result) error_message(sql_error());
```

Then we check that at least one (but only one) record has been modified:

```
$num_rows = mysql_affected_rows($link_id);
if($num_rows != 1) error_message(sql_error());
```

If this is true, we display a deletion confirmation message, and refresh the browser window:

```
else echo
    "<SCRIPT>alert(\"$title($url) has been successfully deleted!\");
self.location.href='$PHP_SELF?action=show_list
                             &category_id=$category_id';</SCRIPT>";
}
```

## top_menu()

Finally, the `top_menu()` function displays a set of administration links:

```
function top_menu() {
  global $PHP_SELF;
```

The body of the function basically displays a number of hyperlinks. Clicking on each link calls the script (`$PHP_SELF`) again, with the value of the `$action` variable or `$mode` variable passed through the URL. The values of these variables are used to decide which function the program should jump to next:

```
echo "<A HREF=\"$PHP_SELF\">Admin</A> ";
echo "| <A HREF=\"javascript:open_window('$PHP_SELF?action=update_db');\">
                         Update DB</A> ";
echo "| <A HREF=\"$PHP_SELF?mode=edit_category\">
                         Edit Category Mode</A> ";
echo "| <A HREF=\"$PHP_SELF?mode=add_category\">Add Category Mode</A>\n";
echo "| <A HREF=\"$PHP_SELF?action=view_new\">New Listings</A>\n";
echo "| <A HREF=\"$PHP_SELF?action=show_list\">View Listings in Admin
Mode</A>\n";
echo "<P>\n";
}
```

The "View Listings in Admin Mode" link uses the `show_list()` function, just like when users view listings. The `show_list()` function sets the `$admin` flag after comparing the name of the calling script with the filename provided in `$admin_script`.

We have now dealt with all of the functions in the administrator script. At the end of the script, we have a `switch` statement which causes the program to jump to the function implied by the `$action` state variable. We jump to the `list_categories()` function by default:

```
switch($action) {
  case "add_category_form":
     add_category_form();
  break;
  case "add_category":
     add_category();
  break;
  case "edit_category_form":
     edit_category_form();
  break;
  case "edit_category":
     edit_category();
  break;
  case "delete_category":
     delete_category();
  break;
  case "view_new":
     view_new();
  break;
  case "edit_new_form":
     edit_new_form();
  break;
  case "edit_new":
     edit_new();
  break;
  case "add_url_form":
     add_url_form();
  break;
  case "add_url":
     add_url();
  break;
  case "modify_url_form":
     modify_url_form();
  break;
  break;
  case "modify_url":
     modify_url();
  break;
  case "go_url":
     go_url();
  break;
  case "delete_url":
     delete_url();
  break;
  case "update_db":
     update_db();
  break;
  case "show_list":
     directory_header();
     top_menu();
     show_list();
     directory_footer();
  break;
  default:
     list_categories();
```

```
      break;

   }
   ?>
```

And that's the end of the script!

# User Feedback

Now we have a working application. After creating an application, you should release it as a beta test version and gather feedback from other developers, designers, and users. Later you may want to add additional features, or modify existing ones. User feedback is very important. An application can't be considered complete if its users are not satisfied with it.

If you want to add an additional feature, how about a [Report Bugs] link, for example, that opens up either a local e-mail client just like the [Report Broken Link] link does, or a new window with a bug report form. That way, you'll have solid debugging support from the actual users.

# Summary

In this case study chapter, we created a full-blown Yahoo-like directory indexing script. During the course of developing the application, we guided you through a usual process of creating an application: identifying the features we need, finding the best way to implement these features, then finally writing and testing the code to do the job.

We also learned how a modular approach helps make your source-code more readable and scalable (easy to build upon).

The directory management application we created lacked a few advanced features that could come in handy:

❏    Allow users to view the listings ordered by hits or registered dates.

❏    Allow administrators to move a URL from under the current category to another.

❏    Allow administrators to move a category from one branch of the category tree to another.

We'll leave these features for you to add. Have fun!

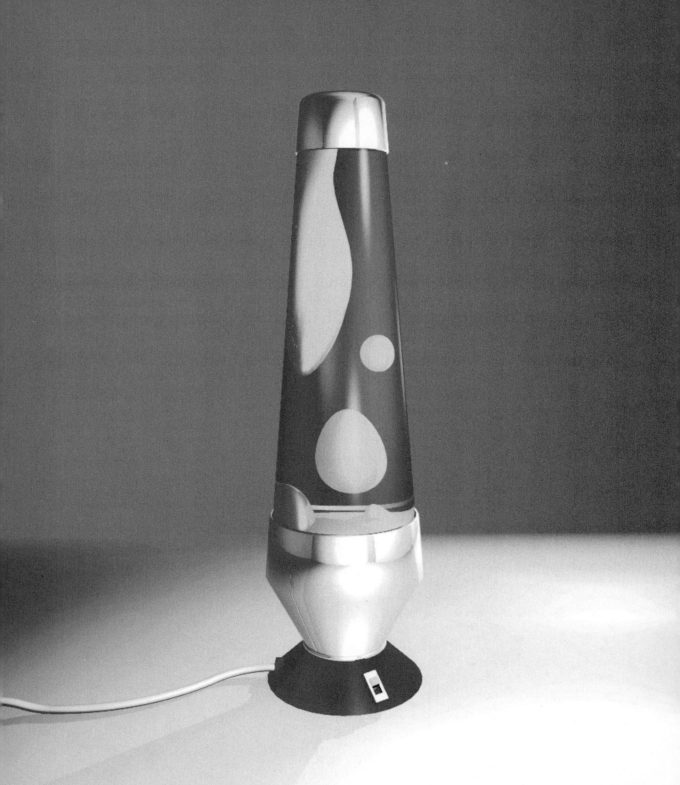

# ODBC

In the body of this book, we worked exclusively with MySQL as our database management system. That's fine if you're able to build the database for your web application, but what if you have some pre-existing data that you want to access from PHP? Alternatively, you may want to be able to manage the data in your database using a visual tool such as Microsoft Access, rather than using the command-line functionality of MySQL's basic database client. In this appendix, we're going to look at how we can use PHP to access data stored in many different database systems, particularly those running on Microsoft Windows servers, and including those created with Microsoft Access. To do it, we'll be using PHP's Unified ODBC functions.

## What is ODBC?

ODBC stands for Open Database Connectivity, and it's a standard developed by Microsoft which allows programmers to connect to databases running under different systems through a common set of functions. It does this by providing a connectivity layer, which manages different data sources, through which programs can talk to different database management systems.

A Windows machine can provide any number of **ODBC Data Sources**, which can be connected to by programs running on that machine. Data sources on a given machine are identified by their data source name, or **DSN**.

Each DSN has three things associated with it:

❑   An **ODBC Driver**, which is a program that knows how to establish a connection with a specific type of data source, for example a SQL Server database, or a Microsoft Access `.mdb` file. There are even ODBC drivers that allow you to open an ODBC connection to an Excel spreadsheet, or a plain text file, and use them as if they were a database.

❑   A set of connection settings, which tell the driver which data source to connect to, what password to use (if one is required), and so on.

❑   Some security settings, such as a username and password, which can be used to prevent unauthorized programs or users from opening connections to the data source.

So, for example, you could configure one DSN to identify a connection to a specific Access database on your hard drive, and another to represent a connection to a Microsoft SQL Server running on a workgroup server on the network. Those two data sources would then be available for any software running on your computer that knows how to open an ODBC connection (and knows the right passwords).

So from PHP, using the Unified ODBC commands, we can connect to any local ODBC data source to which we know the DSN, username and password (if required).

To use an ODBC data source, then, a program connects to the ODBC system, and requests a connection to a specific DSN. The ODBC system launches the appropriate driver, which might either open a file on the local machine to use as a data source, or open a connection to an already-running database server, such as SQL Server or Oracle (much as we did with MySQL). This server could be running on a different, locally networked machine, if necessary, so having a local ODBC data source provides a way for our PHP scripts to connect to remote SQL Server systems.

It's worth making a special point about how Microsoft Access databases are handled by ODBC. The Microsoft Access program itself, which is part of the Microsoft Office suite, isn't a database server (like MySQL's `mysqld`), nor is it a database client (like MySQL's `mysql`). In fact it's a sort of hybrid of the two. When you run Microsoft Access, the program starts up a database engine called Jet, which provides the core database functionality, much like `mysqld` does (although you can't connect directly to Jet across a network). The graphical user interface that Access provides is a sort of database client to the Jet engine.

Say you create an ODBC source that uses the Microsoft Access driver to make the contents of an Access `.mdb` database file available via ODBC. The driver will use exactly the same Jet database engine to provide the database functionality to ODBC clients like our PHP scripts. Consequently, we don't actually have to *run* Microsoft Access (or even leave it in the background) to make Access databases available through ODBC.

# What ODBC Isn't

ODBC is **not** a full database abstraction layer – that is to say, it manages the *mechanics* of connecting to databases, but doesn't provide a translation service. Think of the ODBC data source manager as a telephone switchboard: it can put you through to the DSN you request, but once you're connected, it doesn't get involved in helping you talk to the server. This means you'll still need to know the specifics of the SQL syntax used by the server you're connecting to, and that's going to be different from one server to the next.

### Try It Out – Creating an ODBC data source

Windows provides an ODBC data source manager, which you'll either find in Control Panel (Win9x) under the name **ODBC Data Sources (32bit)**, or in the Administrative Tools menu (Win2K) under the name **Data Sources (ODBC)**. When you start it, you'll see a window like the one shown at the top of the opposite page:

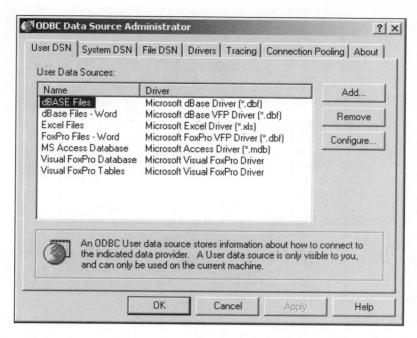

We need to create our data source under the **System DSN** tab. This will make it available to all programs running on the computer, including PHP. When you're on the **System DSN** page, click **Add...** and you'll see the following dialog box:

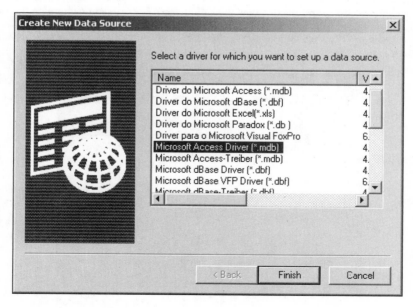

We'll use the Access driver for our example. Click **Finish**, and the next dialog box appears:

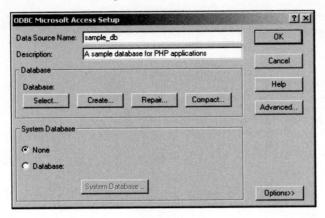

The precise form this dialog takes will depend on the driver you've selected. For Access, we'll need to choose a .mdb file that will hold the data. For SQL Server, we would have to specify connection parameters to use in connecting to a running SQL Server system. Regardless of what driver we're using, we must specify the DSN by which the data source will be known. We've given our data source the name **sample_db**, and add a suitable description.

Now, for most of the drivers that use a file as their data store, the next step would always be to click the **Select...** button and choose a file from the local file system. We could do that here, selecting an existing .mdb file which we've created using Microsoft Access. But note though that there's also a **Create...** button, which gives us the option of creating a new .mdb file without even having to start Access. Such a file is no different to a normal Access database file – indeed, you'd be able to open it using Access at a later date if you wanted to. We click **Create...**, and make a new file called sample.mdb somewhere on the local hard disk.

So, having created a new Access database, we click **OK** and return to the System DSN screen, where our new data source is now listed:

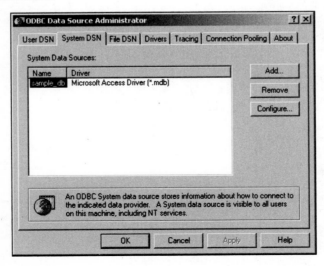

Any ODBC-aware application can now connect to this data source. The application will have access to all tables in the database: it will be able to see the data they contain, manipulate that data, add new records, and even create or delete tables from the database – just as we were able to using MySQL. If we created a new database to store the data for our ODBC data source, it would contain no tables to begin with, but we could in fact create tables to store data without ever having to run Access itself.

Remember that any connection to this database is being run by the ODBC driver under the Jet database engine; we'll therefore need to send commands to manipulate the database using Jet's SQL syntax. Most SQL commands are pretty similar to those we've used under MySQL, but when it comes to manipulating the structure of databases, there are some important differences to be aware of. Use Microsoft Access's help system and look up Microsoft Jet SQL Reference if you want to find out the detailed syntax of these commands. Note that we must also pay attention to the different data types used by Jet. Remember the following MySQL command we used to set up our user table?

```
CREATE TABLE user (
    usernumber MEDIUMINT(10) DEFAULT '0' NOT NULL AUTO_INCREMENT,
    userid VARCHAR(8) BINARY NOT NULL,
    userpassword VARCHAR(20) BINARY NOT NULL,
    username VARCHAR(30) NOT NULL,
    usercountry VARCHAR(50) NOT NULL,
    useremail VARCHAR(50) NOT NULL,
    userprofile TEXT NOT NULL,
    registerdate DATE DEFAULT '0000-00-00' NOT NULL,
    lastaccesstime TIMESTAMP(14),
    PRIMARY KEY (userid),
    UNIQUE usernumber (usernumber)
);
```

Jet wouldn't accept that statement. What we'd need to do instead is:

```
CREATE TABLE user (
    usernumber COUNTER NOT NULL UNIQUE,
    userid VARCHAR(8) NOT NULL PRIMARY KEY,
    userpassword VARCHAR(20) NOT NULL,
    username VARCHAR(30) NOT NULL,
    usercountry VARCHAR(50) NOT NULL,
    useremail VARCHAR(50) NOT NULL,
    userprofile TEXT NOT NULL,
    registerdate DATE NOT NULL,
    lastaccesstime DATETIME
);
```

There are a few key differences to note here:

❑ Keys are specified using a constraint clause in the field definition itself, rather than separately at the end.

❑ Rather than specifying a MEDIUMINT and telling it to AUTO_INCREMENT to create our usernumbers, we use the Jet data type COUNTER. MEDIUMINT is a MySQL specific data type that doesn't exist in most other databases. Conversely, COUNTER is a Jet data type that doesn't exist in most other databases.

❑ Jet doesn't understand TIMESTAMP – instead, it uses the keyword DATETIME.

# PHP and ODBC

PHP's ODBC connectivity functions are slightly different to those used with MySQL, but the principles are the same. We need to:

- ❑ Connect to a data source.
- ❑ Execute a query against the data source.
- ❑ Retrieve data from the result a row at a time.
- ❑ Repeat as required.
- ❑ If necessary, close the connection.

As you might have guessed, just as the names of the MySQL functions in PHP begin `mysql_`, PHP's ODBC functions all begin `odbc_`.

# Connecting to a Data Source

Connecting to an ODBC data source is achieved with a call to `odbc_connect()`. As you would probably expect, the connection requires three arguments, one to specify the DSN, one for the username, and one for the password. The default username and password for an ODBC data source are empty strings, but if you set up security when you created your DSN, you'll have to pass the correct values here.

Just like the MySQL equivalent, and the file commands we used earlier, `odbc_connect()` returns either a connection ID, or zero if the connection fails. As you'd expect, we test this returned value to see whether the connection succeeded:

```
if(!($db=odbc_connect("sample_db","","")))
        die("could not connect to database");
```

You should now have a connection handle stored in `$db` which can be used to perform queries on the server.

# Executing SQL commands

PHP has two main functions for performing SQL operations on an ODBC data source – `odbc_do()` and `odbc_exec()` – and they are completely interchangeable. There's no particular reason for PHP having two identical functions to do the same thing, except perhaps to confuse us. Both simply take a connection handle and SQL query as arguments. Note that the order of these arguments is different from that used in `mysql_query()`, and that both are required.

The following commands are therefore equivalent, and which you use is entirely up to you:

```
$result = odbc_do($db, "SELECT now()");
```

```
$result = odbc_exec($db, "SELECT now()");
```

Just as with MySQL, we're returned a pointer to the result set generated. The form of the result set is slightly different, though, so we'll need to take a look at handling ODBC query results before getting too involved. However, we can still use the familiar test to see if the query succeeded or not:

```
if(!($result = odbc_do($db, "SELECT now")))
        die("Query was invalid");
```

In this case, the query will fail, because we forgot to put brackets after the call to the database server's now() function, so the script will die with the specified error message.

As well as executing SQL queries, we can also call several other functions that return the same sort of ODBC result sets, with information about the database to which we are connected. odbc_tables() returns information about all of the tables in the specified database, while odbc_tableprivileges() returns a table of access control data, much the same as MySQL's privilege tables. All you need to provide these commands with is an ODBC connection identifier.

There are several other ODBC functions that return similar metadata – refer to the reference material at the back of this book (Appendix C), and the online PHP manual at http://www.php.net/manual for more information.

# Handling Query Results

ODBC result sets differ from MySQL result sets in several crucial ways. Principally, it's not always possible to move through the returned records in any order other than from start to finish, as we could with MySQL. This will depend on the ODBC driver.

Instead, we have two basic ways to handle the result data:

- ❏ Read the data one row at a time.
- ❏ Automatically display the data as an HTML table.

First of all, let's see how we can find out some facts about the returned result set.

We can get information about the result set by passing the result identifier to the following functions:

- ❏ odbc_num_fields() returns the number of columns in the result set.
- ❏ odbc_num_rows() returns the number of rows affected by an INSERT or UPDATE query – *not the number of rows in the result set*. More often than not, the result of a SELECT query will return -1 when passed to this function.

We can find out about the columns that the result set contains using these functions:

- ❏ odbc_field_name() takes a result ID and a column number, and returns the name of the field
- ❏ odbc_field_num() takes a result ID and a column name, and returns the numerical index of that column across the result set, counting from 1
- ❏ odbc_field_type() takes a result identifier and a column number, and returns a string containing the data type that fields in that column contain

❑ `odbc_field_len()` takes a result identifier and a column number, and returns an integer representing the maximum length of data permitted in that field

Armed with all this metadata, we've got everything we need to start iterating through the result set, and retrieving the actual data.

ODBC result sets have an internal record pointer called a **cursor**. When a result set is first retrieved, its cursor is not pointing to any of the records. You can think of it as pointing initially to row zero, with row one containing the first row of data (assuming the query returned any rows at all).

The `odbc_fetch_row()` function takes the result set ID as its argument, and looks to see if the next row on from the cursor exists; if it does, it moves the cursor on a line and returns `True`. If the row doesn't exist, it moves the cursor off the end of the result set (effectively pointing into empty space) and returns `False`.

This sounds rather like `mysql_fetch_row()`, except that `mysql_fetch_row()` returns an array containing actual data from the row, whereas `odbc_fetch_row()` requires us to work a little harder for our information.

To retrieve the contents of a specific cell, then, we must use `odbc_result()`, which takes a result ID and either a column name or number as arguments, and returns the data as a string.

So, without further ado, let's take a look at how we can display the data from an ODBC result set in an HTML table.

## Try It Out – Querying An ODBC Data Source

What we're going to do is simply run a query against an ODBC data source, and display the returned data (if any) in an HTML table. There are two parts to the process of creating the table: first, create a header row containing the names for all the columns; second, fill in the rows of data underneath. We'll use some of the metadata functions we saw above to do the first, and iterate through the result set with `odbc_fetch_row()` to achieve the second.

**1.** First of all, we need to start off the HTML page with a standard header.

```
<HTML>
<HEAD><TITLE>Try It Out - An ODBC Data Source</TITLE></HEAD>
<BODY>
```

**2.** Now we start off the PHP code by setting up some variables to identify the data source, user ID and password we need to access the database. We're using the database we set up under the DSN `sample_db` earlier, which doesn't need a User ID or password. We also create a variable, `$query`, to hold the SQL statement we're going to execute. In this case, we've used Microsoft Access to create and populate a table called `user` in our database, and we simply `SELECT` all the data from it.

```
<?php
//odbc_query.php
    $odbc_dsn = "sample_db";
    $odbc_userid = "";
    $odbc_password = "";

    $query = "SELECT * FROM user";
```

**3.** Now we connect to the ODBC data source, using the values we've stored, and die() if the operation fails. The connection handle is stored in $odbc_db.

```
if(!($odbc_db = odbc_connect($odbc_dsn, $odbc_userid, $odbc_password)))
        die("Could not connect to ODBC data source $odbc_dsn");
```

**4.** We can now use this handle to execute the query against the data source. We place the result set handle in $odbc_rs, or die() if the operation fails.

```
if(!($odbc_rs = odbc_do($odbc_db, $query)))
        die("Error executing query $query");
```

**5.** If we've got this far, we know that $odbc_rs contains a reference to our result set. We now use odbc_num_fields() to find out how many columns of data have been returned. If the query resulted in an empty set, there will be no columns and we die(). This would be the case if we'd run an INSERT or UPDATE query, or created a table, for example.

```
$num_cols = odbc_num_fields($odbc_rs);
if($num_cols < 1) die("Query returned an empty set");
?>
```

**6.** In order to display the results, we drop out of PHP mode and open up a <TABLE> tag in HTML. We also declare the start of our first row, which will contain the column headings. Then it's simply a case of using a for loop that counts from 1 up to the number of columns, and putting the value returned by odbc_field_name() for each column into a table header cell.

```
<TABLE>
  <TR> <?php

   for($a = 1; $a <= $num_cols; $a++) {

?>

   <TH><B> <?php
        echo odbc_field_name($odbc_rs, $a);
      ?> </B></TH>

<?php

   }

?> </TR>
```

At the end of the loop, we use the </TR> tag to complete the row.

**7.** Now we need to iterate through the rows of results. Each time we call odbc_fetch_row() it moves the cursor on a row and returns True if there is data there. We can therefore make use of this fact by making it the condition in a while loop. The code inside this loop will therefore execute repeatedly until odbc_fetch_row() returns False, which it will do once we've looked at the last row. If the query returned no rows of data, odbc_fetch_row() will return False the first time it's called, and the contents of the while loop will never be executed.

Each time we execute the `while` loop, we want to create a new table row, display all the values in that row, and then close it. We display the values by means of a `for` loop, identical to the one we used to display column headings, but calling `odbc_result()` for each cell rather than `odbc_field_name()`.

```php
<?php

    while(odbc_fetch_row($odbc_rs)) {

?> <TR> <?php

        for($a = 1; $a <= $num_cols; $a++) {

            $data = odbc_result($odbc_rs, $a);
            echo "<TD>$data</TD>";

        }

?> </TR> <?php

    }
```

**8.** Finally, we finish off the page by closing our table and HTML body tags.

```php
?>
</TABLE>
</BODY>
</HTML>
```

**9.** Save the file as `odbc_query.php`, and call it up in a browser:

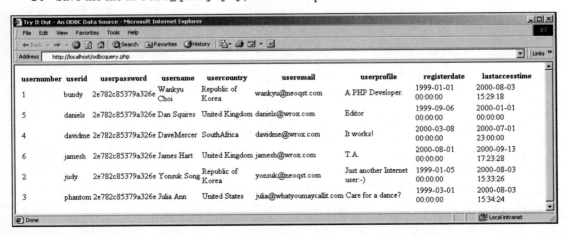

Now that we've done this the hard way, it's only fair to mention that the PHP ODBC API provides another useful function in the form of `odbc_result_all()`. Change the `odbcquery.php` script as follows:

```
<HTML>
<HEAD><TITLE>Try It Out - An ODBC Data Source</TITLE></HEAD>
<BODY>

<?php
//odbc_query.php
   $odbc_dsn = "sample_db";
   $odbc_userid = "";
   $odbc_password = "";

   $query = "SELECT * FROM user";

   if(!($odbc_db = odbc_connect($odbc_dsn, $odbc_userid, $odbc_password)))
            die("Could not connect to ODBC data source $odbc_dsn");


   if(!($odbc_rs = odbc_do($odbc_db, $query)))
            die("Error executing query $query");

   odbc_result_all($odbc_rs);

?>

</TABLE>
</BODY>
</HTML>
```

And execute the script, and you'll see the following result:

| usernumber | userid | userpassword | username | usercountry | useremail | userprofile | registerdate | lastaccesstime |
|---|---|---|---|---|---|---|---|---|
| 1 | bundy | 2e782c85379a326e | Wankyu Choi | Republic of Korea | wankyu@neoqst.com | A PHP Developer. | 1999-01-01 00:00:00 | 2000-08-03 15:29:18 |
| 5 | daniels | 2e782c85379a326e | Dan Squires | United Kingdom | daniels@wrox.com | Editor | 1999-09-06 00:00:00 | 2000-01-01 00:00:00 |
| 4 | davidme | 2e782c85379a326e | DaveMercer | SouthAfrica | davidme@wrox.com | It works! | 2000-03-08 00:00:00 | 2000-07-01 23:00:00 |
| 6 | jamesh | 2e782c85379a326e | James Hart | United Kingdom | jamesh@wrox.com | T.A. | 2000-08-01 00:00:00 | 2000-09-13 17:23:28 |
| 2 | judy | 2e782c85379a326e | Yonsuk Song | Republic of Korea | yonsuk@neoqst.com | Just another Internet user:-) | 1999-01-05 00:00:00 | 2000-08-03 15:33:26 |
| 3 | phantom | 2e782c85379a326e | Julia Ann | United States | julia@whatyoumaycallit.com | Care for a dance? | 1999-03-01 00:00:00 | 2000-08-03 15:34:24 |

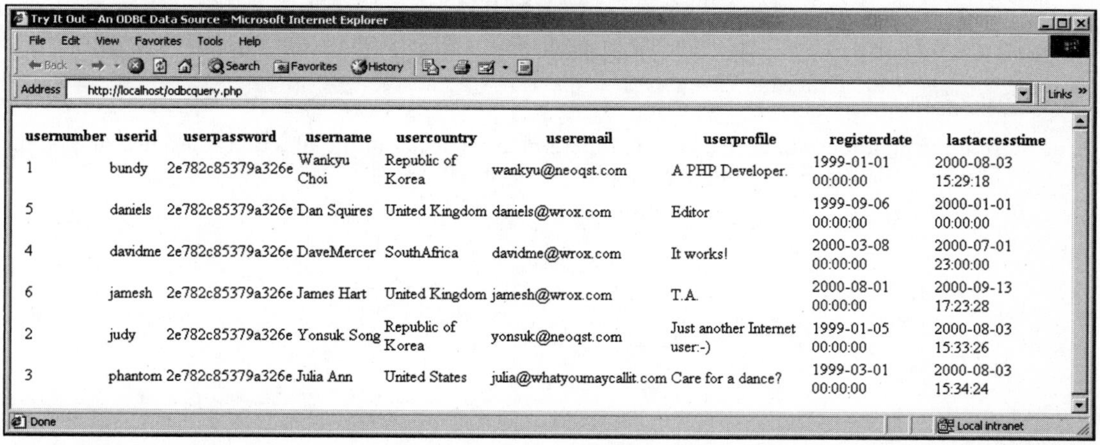

As you can see, `odbc_result_all()` performs exactly the same operation we just did the long way – formatting the whole of a returned result set as an HTML table. For quickly checking your SQL logic, it's an invaluable tool. Using CSS (Cascading Stylesheets – an HTML formatting technology supported by most modern browsers), it's even possible to pretty up the results somewhat, which might make it possible to use the function in an actual production web page. Add the following to the head part of the script:

```
<HTML>
<HEAD>
  <TITLE>Try It Out - An ODBC Data Source</TITLE>
  <STYLE TYPE="text/css">
    TH {color: white; background-color: gray}
    TD {background-color: silver}
  </STYLE>
</HEAD>
<BODY>

<?php

  ...
```

And the output will look like this:

For more information about PHP's ODBC functionality, check out the function reference in Appendix C, and also the PHP manual at http://www.php.net/manual.

# B

# PHP Functions

This appendix is intended as a quick reference to the syntax of the most useful PHP4 functions. The exhaustive reference material at http://www.php.net/manual should be your next port of call for information about the specific behavior of PHP's functions.

Note that not all of these are compiled into PHP4 by default, and you may need to add libraries or modules to your system to enable their functionality.

## Apache-Specific Functions

| Function | Returns | Description |
|---|---|---|
| apache_lookup_uri (*filename*) | Class | Returns a class of information about the URI specified in *filename* |
| apache_note(*note_name* [, *note_value*]) | String | Retrieves or (if the second parameter is included) sets values from the notes tables |
| getallheaders() | Array | Returns an array of the HTTP request headers |
| virtual(*filename*) | Integer | Performs an Apache sub-request such as including a CGI script |

## Array Functions

| Function | Returns | Description |
|---|---|---|
| array([...]) | Array | Creates and returns an array from the supplied parameters |
| array_count_values (*array*) | Array | Returns an array containing the values of the *array* as keys and their frequency as values |

*Table continued on following page*

| Function | Returns | Description |
| --- | --- | --- |
| `array_diff(arrays)` | Array | Returns an array containing the values from `array1` that do not occur in subsequent arrays |
| `array_flip(array)` | Array | Returns the elements of the `array` with their values and their keys switched |
| `array_intersect(arrays)` | Array | Returns an array containing all the values of `array1` that are present in all of the arrays supplied |
| `array_keys(array [, search_value])` | Array | Returns an array containing all the keys of the supplied `array`, or just those specified in `search_value` |
| `array_merge(arrays)` | Array | Merges and returns the supplied `arrays` and where the input arrays have the same string keys, then the later value for that key will overwrite the previous one; if, however, the arrays have the same numeric key, the later value will not overwrite the original value, but will be appended |
| `array_merge_recursive(arrays)` | Array | Merges and returns the elements of two or more arrays so that the values of one are appended to the end of the previous one; if the input arrays have the same string keys, then the values for these keys are merged together into an array, and this is done recursively, so that if one of the values is an array itself, the function will merge it with a corresponding entry in another array too |
| `array_multisort(array [, mixed])` | Boolean | Sorts several arrays at once or a multi-dimensional array |
| `array_pad(array, pad_size, pad_value)` | Array | Returns a copy of the `array` padded to the size specified by `pad_size` with value `pad_value` |
| `array_pop(array)` | Mixed | Removes and returns the last element from the end of the `array` |
| `array_push(array, variables)` | Integer | Pushes the supplied `variables` onto the end of the `array` and returns the number of elements in the array |
| `array_rand(array [, num_req])` | Mixed | Selects and returns one (or more if `num_req` is specified) random entries from the `array` |
| `array_reverse(array)` | Array | Returns the elements of the `array` in reverse order |

| Function | Returns | Description |
|---|---|---|
| array_shift(*array*) | Mixed | Removes and returns the first element from the beginning of the *array* |
| array_slice(*array*, *offset* [, *length*]) | Array | Returns a sub-array from the specified *array* starting at the *offset*, containing the number of elements specified in *length* |
| array_splice(*array*, *offset* [, *length*] [, *replacement*]) | Array | Removes a sub-array from the *array* and replaces it with the elements of the *replacement* array and returns an array containing the removed elements |
| array_unique(*array*) | Array | Removes duplicate values from the *array* |
| array_unshift (*array*, *variables*) | Integer | Adds the supplied *variables* to the beginning of the *array* and returns the new number of elements in the *array* |
| array_values(*array*) | Array | Returns an array containing all the values of the supplied *array* |
| array_walk (*array*, *function* [, *parameter*]) | Integer | Applies the named *function* to every element of the *array*, passing parameter as a third argument to funtion |
| arsort(*array*) | Nothing | Sorts the supplied *array* in descending order, retaining the correlation between keys and values |
| asort(*array*) | Nothing | Sorts the supplied *array* in ascending order, retaining the correlation between keys and values |
| compact(*varnames*) | Array | Merges the variables and/or arrays named in the *varnames* argument into a single array |
| count(*array*) | Integer | Returns the number of elements in the supplied *array* |
| current(*array*) | Mixed | Returns the current element in the supplied *array* |
| each(*array*) | Array | Returns a four-element sub-array containing the key and value of the current element from the specified *array* |
| end(*array*) | Nothing | Sets the last element of the supplied *array* as the current element |

*Table continued on following page*

| Function | Returns | Description |
|---|---|---|
| extract(*array* [, *extract_type*] [, *prefix*]) | Nothing | Import variables into the symbol table from the supplied *array*. The *extract_type* parameter specifies the action to take in case of a collision, and *prefix* specifies a string to be prefixed to the variable names |
| in_array(*value*, *array*) | Boolean | Indicates if the specified *value* exists in the supplied *array* |
| key(*array*) | Mixed | Returns the key for the current element in the *array* |
| krsort(*array*) | Integer | Sorts the *array* by key in reverse order, retaining the correlation between keys and values |
| ksort(*array*) | Integer | Sorts the *array* by key, retaining the correlation between keys and values |
| list(*variables*) | Nothing | Assigns the supplied *variables* as if they were an array |
| natsort(*array*) | Nothing | Implements a sort algorithm that orders alphanumeric strings as a human being would ("natural ordering") |
| natcasesort(*array*) | Nothing | A case-insensitive version of natsort() |
| next(*array*) | Mixed | Moves the *array* pointer one element forward and returns the next element, or false if the end of the array is reached |
| pos(*array*) | Mixed | Returns the current element from the supplied *array* |
| prev(*array*) | Mixed | Moves the internal array pointer backwards one element and returns the new current element, or false if there are no more elements |
| range(*low*, *high*) | Array | Creates and returns an array of integers between *low* and *high* inclusive |
| reset(*array*) | Mixed | Returns the first element of the supplied *array* and sets it as the current element |
| rsort(*array*) | Nothing | Sorts the supplied *array* in descending order |
| shuffle(*array*) | Nothing | Puts the supplied *array* into random order |
| sizeof(*array*) | Integer | Returns the number of elements in the *array* |

| Function | Returns | Description |
|---|---|---|
| sort(*array*) | Nothing | Sorts the supplied *array* in ascending order |
| uasort(*array*, *function*) | Nothing | Sorts the supplied *array* using the specified user-defined *function*, retaining the correlation between keys and values |
| uksort(*array*, *function*) | Nothing | Sorts the supplied *array* by key using the specified user-defined *function* |
| usort(*array*, *function*) | Nothing | Sorts the supplied *array* by value using the specified user-defined *function* |

# Aspell Functions

| Function | Returns | Description |
|---|---|---|
| aspell_check(*link*, *word*) | Boolean | Checks the spelling of the supplied *word* in the dictionary with the specified *link* |
| aspell_check-raw (*link*, *word*) | Boolean | Checks the spelling of the supplied *word* in the dictionary with the specified *link* without trimming or changing case |
| aspell_new (*master*, *personal*) | Integer | Loads the specified dictionary and returns a link identifier for the new dictionary |
| aspell_suggest (*link*, *word*) | Array | Returns an array of suggested spellings for the specified *word* from the dictionary with the specified *link* |

# Calendar Functions

| Function | Returns | Description |
|---|---|---|
| easter_date([*year*]) | Integer | Returns the UNIX timestamp for midnight on Easter Day of the specified *year*, or, if no year is specified, of the current year |
| easter_days([*year*]) | Integer | Returns the number of days after March 21 on which Easter Day falls in the specified *year*, or, if no year is specified, in the current year |
| frenchtojd(*french*) | Integer | Converts a French Republican Calendar date to a Julian Day Count |

*Table continued on following page*

| Function | Returns | Description |
|---|---|---|
| gregoriantojd(*gregorian*) | Integer | Converts a Gregorian Calendar date to a Julian Day Count |
| Jddayofweek (*julianday, mode*) | Mixed | Returns the day of the week for a Julian Day Count in the format supplied by *mode* |
| Jdmonthname (*julianday, mode*) | String | Returns the month name for a Julian Day Count in the format and calendar specified by *mode* |
| jdtofrench(*julianday*) | String | Converts a Julian Day Count to a French Republican Calendar date |
| jdtogregorian(*julianday*) | String | Converts a Julian Day Count to a Gregorian Calendar date |
| jdtojewish(*julianday*) | String | Converts a Julian Day Count to a Jewish Calendar date |
| jdtojulian(*julianday*) | String | Converts a Julian Day Count to a Julian Calendar date |
| jdtounix(*julianday*) | Integer | Converts a Julian Day Count to a UNIX timestamp |
| jewishtojd(*jewish*) | Integer | Converts a Jewish Calendar date to a Julian Day Count |
| juliantojd(*julian*) | Integer | Converts a Julian Calendar date to a Julian Day Count |
| unixtojd(*timestamp*) | Integer | Converts a UNIX timestamp to a Julian Day Count |

# Class/Object Functions

| Function | Returns | Description |
|---|---|---|
| call_user_method (*method_name, object [, parameters]*) | Mixed | Calls a user method from the *object* and passes the optional *parameters* |
| class_exists(*class_name*) | Boolean | Checks if *class_name* has been defined |
| get_class(*object*) | String | Returns the name of the class of *object* |
| get_class_methods (*class_name*) | Array | Returns an array of method names for *class_name* |

| Function | Returns | Description |
|---|---|---|
| get_class_vars (*class_name*) | Array | Returns an array of default properties of *class_name* |
| get_declared_classes() | Array | Returns an array of defined classes for the current script |
| get_object_vars(*object*) | Array | Returns an associative array of defined properties for *object* |
| get_parent_class(*object*) | String | Returns the name of the parent class for *object* |
| is_subclass_of (*object*, *superclass*) | Boolean | Checks if *object* belongs to a subclass of *superclass* |
| method_exists (*object*, *method_name*) | Boolean | Checks if *method_name* has been defined for *object* |

# CURL, Client URL Library Functions

| Function | Returns | Description |
|---|---|---|
| curl_close(*handle*) | Nothing | Closes the specified CURL session |
| curl_exec(*handle*) | Boolean | Executes the CURL session specified by *handle* |
| curl_init([*url*]) | Integer | Initializes a new CURL session and returns a handle for use with other CURL functions |
| curl_setopt (*handle*, *option*, *value*) | Boolean | Sets an *option* with given *value* for a CURL session identified by *handle* |
| curl_version() | String | Returns the current CURL version |

# Database Functions

## Database Abstraction Layer Functions

| Function | Returns | Description |
|---|---|---|
| dba_close(*handle*) | Nothing | Closes the database specified by *handle* |
| dba_delete(*key*, *handle*) | Boolean | Deletes the entry specified by *key* from the database specified by *handle* |

*Table continued on following page*

| Function | Returns | Description |
|---|---|---|
| dba_exists(*key*, *handle*) | Boolean | Checks if the specified *key* exists in the database specified by *handle* |
| dba_fetch(*key*, *handle*) | String | Returns the data specified by *key* from the database specified by *handle* |
| dba_firstkey(*handle*) | String | Returns the first key in the database specified by *handle* and resets the database pointer to the first entry |
| dba_insert(*key*, *value*, *handle*) | Boolean | Inserts an entry with the specified *key* and *value* into the database specified by *handle* |
| dba_nextkey(*handle*) | String | Returns the next key from the database specified by *handle* and increments the database pointer |
| dba_open (*path*, *mode*, *handler*) | Integer | Opens a database instance for *path* with *mode* using *handler* |
| dba_optimize(*handle*) | Boolean | Optimizes the database with the specified *handle* and returns *true* on success |
| dba_popen (*path*, *mode*, *handler*) | Integer | Establishes a persistent database instance for *path* with *mode* using *handler* and returns False if it fails |
| dba_replace (*key*, *value*, *handle*) | Boolean | Replaces or inserts the entry specified by *key* and *value* into the database specified by *handle* and returns *true* on success |
| dba_sync(*handle*) | Boolean | Synchronizes the database with the specified *handle* and returns *true* on success |

## dBase Functions

| Function | Returns | Description |
|---|---|---|
| dbase_add_record (*dbase_id*, *record*) | Boolean | Adds a *record* to the dBase database |
| dbase_close(*dbase_id*) | Boolean | Closes the dBase database specified by *dbase_id* |

| Function | Returns | Description |
|---|---|---|
| dbase_create (*filename*, *fields*) | Integer | Creates a dBase database specified by filename with the field formats specified by fields and returns an identifier (*dbase_id*) for the database on success |
| dbase_delete_record (*dbase_id*, *record*) | Boolean | Marks the specified *record* for deletion from the dBase database |
| dbase_get_record (*dbase_id*, *record*) | Array | Returns the specified *record* from the dBase database in an array |
| dbase_get_record_with_names (*dbase_id*, *record*) | Array | Returns the specified *record* from the dBase database in an associative array |
| dbase_numfields(*dbase_id*) | Integer | Returns the number of fields in the dBase database |
| dbase_numrecords(*dbase_id*) | Integer | Returns the number of records in the dBase database |
| dbase_open(*filename*, *flags*) | Integer | Opens the dBase database specified by filename in the mode specified by flags and returns an identifier (*dbase_id*) for the database on success |
| dbase_pack(*dbase_id*) | Boolean | Packs (deletes records marked for deletion) the dBase database specified by *dbase_id* |
| dbase_replace_record (*dbase_id*, *record*, *record_num*) | Boolean | Replaces the data specified by *record_num* in the dBase database with the data specified by *record* |

## DBM Functions

| Function | Returns | Description |
|---|---|---|
| dblist() | String | Describes the DBM-compatible library in use |
| dbmclose(*dbm_id*) | Boolean | Closes the dbm database specified by *dbm_id* |
| dbmdelete(*dbm_id*, *key*) | Boolean | Deletes the value specified by *key* from the dbm database |
| dbmexists(*dbm_id*, *key*) | Boolean | Indicates whether a value exists for the specified *key* in the dbm database specified by *dbm_id* |

*Table continued on following page*

| Function | Returns | Description |
|---|---|---|
| dbmfetch(*dbm_id*, *key*) | String | Returns the value for the specified *key* from the dbm database |
| dbmfirstkey(*dbm_id*) | String | Returns the first key in the dbm database |
| Dbminsert (*dbm_id*, *key*, *value*) | Integer | Inserts the specified *key*/*value* pair into the dbm database |
| dbmnextkey(*dbm_id*, *key*) | String | Returns the next key after the specified *key* in the dbm database |
| dbmopen(*filename*, *flags*) | Integer | Opens a dbm database with the specified *filename*. Returns an identifier for the database |
| Dbmreplace (*dbm_id*, *key*, *value*) | Boolean | Replaces with *value* the value associated with the specified *key* in the dbm database |

## Informix Functions

| Function | Returns | Description |
|---|---|---|
| ifx_affected_rows(*result_id*) | Integer | Returns the number of rows affected by the query |
| ifx_blobinfile_mode(*mode*) | Nothing | Sets the default BLOB mode for SELECT queries |
| ifx_byteasvarchar(*mode*) | Nothing | Sets the default byte mode for SELECT queries |
| ifx_close([*link_identifier*]) | Integer | Closes the connection |
| ifx_connect([*database*] [, *userid*] [, *password*]) | Integer | Opens a connection to an Informix database and returns a connection identifier |
| ifx_copy_blob(*bid*) | Integer | Copies the specified BLOB object |
| ifx_create_blob (*type*, *mode*, *param*) | Integer | Creates a BLOB object |
| ifx_create_char(*param*) | Integer | Creates a char object |
| ifx_do(*result_id*) | Integer | Executes a previously prepared SQL statement |
| ifx_error() | String | Returns the last occurring error |
| ifx_errormsg([*error_code*]) | String | Returns the error message for the last occurring error or for the specified *error_code* |

| Function | Returns | Description |
|---|---|---|
| ifx_fetch_row(*result_id* [, *position*]) | Array | Fetches a row as an enumerated array |
| ifx_fieldproperties (*result_id*) | Array | Returns an associative array of the field names and the SQL field properties |
| ifx_fieldtypes(*result_id*) | Array | Returns an associative array of the field names and the SQL field types |
| ifx_free_blob(*bid*) | Integer | Deletes the BLOB object specified by *bid* |
| ifx_free_char(*bid*) | Integer | Deletes the char object specified by *bid* |
| ifx_free_result(*result_id*) | Integer | Frees the resources used by the specified query |
| ifx_free_slob(*bid*) | Integer | Deletes the specified SLOB object |
| ifx_get_blob(*bid*) | Integer | Returns the content of the specified BLOB object |
| ifx_get_char(*bid*) | Integer | Returns the content of the specified char object |
| ifx_getsqlca(*result_id*) | Array | Returns the contents of sqlca.sqlerrd[0..5] after a query |
| ifx_htmltbl_result (*result_id* [, *html_table_options*]) | Integer | Formats the rows of a query specified by result_id as an HTML table |
| ifx_nullformat(*mode*) | Nothing | Sets the default return value for NULL values on a fetched row |
| ifx_num_fields(*result_id*) | Integer | Returns the number of fields in the query |
| ifx_num_rows(*result_id*) | Integer | Returns the number of rows already fetched for the query |
| ifx_pconnect([*database*] [, *userid*] [, *password*]) | Integer | Opens a persistent connection to an Informix database and returns a link identifier |
| ifx_prepare(*query* [, *link_identifier*] [, *cursor_type*] [, *blobidarray*]) | Integer | Prepares a SQL statement for execution, returns a result_id for use by ifx_do() |

*Table continued on following page*

| Function | Returns | Description |
|---|---|---|
| `ifx_query(query,`<br>`[, link_identifier]`<br>`[, cursor_type],`<br>`[, blobidarray])` | Integer | Executes the specified *query* against the Informix database |
| `ifx_textasvarchar(mode)` | Nothing | Sets the default text mode for `SELECT` queries |
| `ifx_update_blob(bid, content)` | Integer | Updates the content of the specified BLOB object |
| `ifx_update_char(bid, content)` | Integer | Updates the specified char object with *content* |
| `ifxus_close_slob(bid)` | Integer | Deletes the specified SLOB object |
| `ifxus_create_slob(mode)` | Integer | Creates and opens a SLOB object |
| `ifxus_open_slob(bid, mode)` | Integer | Opens the specified SLOB object |
| `ifxus_read_slob(bid, bytes)` | Integer | Reads the specified number of *bytes* of the specified SLOB object |
| `ifxus_seek_slob`<br>`(bid, mode, offset)` | Integer | Sets the current position of the specified SLOB object to *offset* |
| `ifxus_tell_slob(bid)` | Integer | Returns the current position of the SLOB object specified |
| `ifxus_write_slob`<br>`(bid, content)` | Integer | Writes the specified *content* into the specified SLOB object |

## InterBase Functions

| Function | Returns | Description |
|---|---|---|
| `ibase_close([connection_id])` | Integer | Closes a connection to the specified InterBase database, or the last opened link |
| `ibase_connect(database`<br>`[, username [, password`<br>`[, charset [, buffers`<br>`[, dialect [ ,role]]]]]])` | Integer | Opens a connection to an InterBase database |
| `ibase_execute`<br>`(query [,bind_args])` | Integer | Executes a query prepared by `ibase_prepare()` |
| `ibase_fetch_object(result_id)` | Object | Returns a row as an object from *result_id* |

| Function | Returns | Description |
| --- | --- | --- |
| ibase_fetch_row (result_identifier) | Array | Returns the next row specified by result_identifier (obtained from ibase_query) |
| ibase_free_query(query) | Integer | Frees a prepared query |
| ibase_free_result(result_id) | Integer | Frees the result set specified by result_id |
| ibase_num_fields(result_id) | Integer | Returns the number of fields in the specified result set |
| ibase_pconnect(database [, username [, password [, charset [, role]]]]) | Integer | Creates a persistent connection to an InterBase database |
| ibase_prepare([link_identifier, query]) | Integer | Prepares a query for later binding of parameter placeholders and execution |
| ibase_query ([link_identifier, query] [, bind_args]) | Integer | Executes a query on an InterBase database and returns a result_identifier |
| ibase_timefmt(format, [columntype]) | Integer | Sets the format of timestamp, date or time type columns returned from queries |

## Microsoft SQL Server Functions

| Function | Returns | Description |
| --- | --- | --- |
| mssql_close(link_id) | Boolean | Closes the specified SQL Server connection |
| mssql_connect ([server_name] [, username] [, password]) | Integer | Opens an SQL Server connection and returns a link_id |
| mssql_data_seek (result_id, row_number) | Boolean | Moves to the specified row_number in the resultset |
| mssql_fetch_array(result_id) | Array | Returns the next row in the resultset as an array |
| mssql_fetch_field(result_id [, field_offset]) | Object | Returns an object representing the specified field |
| mssql_fetch_object (result_id) | Object | Returns the next row in the resultset as an object |

*Table continued on following page*

| Function | Returns | Description |
| --- | --- | --- |
| mssql_fetch_row(*result_id*) | Array | Returns the next row in the resultset as an enumerated array |
| mssql_field_length (*result_id* [, *offset*]) | Integer | Returns the length of a field |
| mssql_field_name (*result* [, *offset*]) | Integer | Returns the name of a field |
| mssql_field_seek (*result_id*, *field_offset*) | Integer | Moves to the field specified in *field_offset* |
| mssql_field_type (*result_id* [, *offset*]) | String | Returns the field type |
| mssql_free_result(*result_id*) | Integer | Frees the memory used by the resultset |
| mssql_get_last_message() | String | Returns the last message from the server |
| mssql_min_error_severity (*severity*) | Nothing | Sets the lower error severity |
| mssql_min_message_severity (*severity*) | Severity | Sets the lower message severity |
| mssql_num_fields(*result_id*) | Integer | Returns the number of fields in the specified resultset |
| mssql_num_rows(*result_id*) | Integer | Returns the number of rows in the specified resultset |
| mssql_pconnect([*servername*] [, *username*][, *password*]) | Integer | Opens a persistent SQL connection and returns a *link_id* |
| mssql_query(*query*, [*link_id*]) | Integer | Executes the specified *query* and returns a *result_id* |
| mssql_result (*result_id*, *row*, *field*) | Integer | Fetches the contents of the cell specified by the *row* and *field* arguments |
| mssql_select_db (*database*, *link_id*) | Integer | Sets the specified SQL Server database as the current database |

## mSQL Functions

| Function | Returns | Description |
| --- | --- | --- |
| Msql (*database*, *query*, *link_id*) | Integer | Executes the specified mSQL query and returns a *query_id* |

| Function | Returns | Description |
|---|---|---|
| msql_affected_rows(*query_id*) | Integer | Returns the number of rows affected by the specified query |
| msql_close(*link_id*) | Boolean | Closes the mSQL connection |
| msql_connect([*hostname*]) | Integer | Opens a connection to the specified mSQL server and returns a *link_id* |
| msql_create_db (*name*, [*link_id*]) | Integer | Creates an mSQL database with the specified *name* |
| msql_createdb (*name*, [*link_id*]) | Integer | Creates an mSQL database with the specified *name* |
| msql_data_seek (*query_id*, *row_number*) | Boolean | Moves to the specified row of a resultset |
| msql_dbname(*query_id*, *index*) | String | Returns the name of the mSQL database with the specified index position |
| msql_drop_db(*name*, *link_id*) | Boolean | Deletes the named mSQL database |
| msql_dropdb(*name*, *link_id*) | Boolean | Deletes the named mSQL database |
| msql_error() | String | Returns any error message resulting from the last mSQL operation |
| msql_fetch_array (*query_id* [, *result_type*]) | Array | Fetches the next row in the resultset as an array |
| msql_fetch_field (*query_id*, *field_offset*) | Object | Returns an object representing the field with the specified position |
| msql_fetch_object (*query_id* [, *result_type*]) | Object | Fetches the next row in the resultset as an object |
| msql_fetch_row(*query_id*) | Array | Fetches the next row in the resultset as an enumerated array |
| msql_field_seek (*query_id*, *field_offset*) | Integer | Moves to the field specified by *field_offset* |
| msql_fieldflags (*query_id*, *field*) | String | Returns the flags for the specified *field* |
| msql_fieldlen (*query_id*, *field*) | Integer | Returns the length of the specified *field* |
| msql_fieldname (*query_id*, *field*) | String | Returns the name of the specified *field* |

*Table continued on following page*

| Function | Returns | Description |
|---|---|---|
| msql_fieldtable (*query_id*, *field*) | Integer | Returns the name of the table that *field* was fetched from |
| msql_fieldtype(*query_id*, *field*) | String | Returns the field type for the specified *field* |
| msql_free_result(*query_id*) | Integer | Frees the memory used by the resultset |
| msql_freeresult(*query_id*) | Integer | Frees the memory used by the resultset |
| msql_list_dbs() | Integer | Lists the database on the specified mSQL server; returns a result identifier |
| msql_list_fields (*database*, *table*) | Integer | Lists the fields in the specified table; returns a result identifier |
| msql_list_tables(*database*) | Integer | Lists tables in the specified mSQL database; returns a result identifier |
| msql_listdbs() | Integer | Lists the database on the specified mSQL server; returns a result identifier |
| msql_listfields (*database*, *table*) | Integer | Lists the fields in the specified table; returns a result identifier |
| msql_listtables(*database*) | Integer | Lists tables in the specified mSQL database; returns a result identifier |
| msql_num_fields(*query_id*) | Integer | Returns the number of fields in the resultset |
| msql_num_rows(*query_id*) | Integer | Returns the number of rows in the resultset |
| msql_numfields(*query_id*) | Integer | Returns the number of fields in the resultset |
| msql_numrows(*query_id*) | Integer | Returns the number of rows in the resultset |
| msql_pconnect([*hostname*]) | Integer | Opens a persistent connection to the specified mSQL server and returns a link_id |
| msql_query(*query*, *link_id*) | Integer | Executes the specified mSQL query and returns a query_id |
| msql_regcase(*string*) | String | Generates a regular expression for a case-insensitive match |

| Function | Returns | Description |
|---|---|---|
| msql_result (*query_id*, *row*, *field*) | Integer | Fetches the contents of the cell specified by the *row* and *field* arguments |
| msql_select_db (*database*, *link_id*) | Boolean | Sets the current database to the one specified |
| msql_selectdb (*database*, *link_id*) | Boolean | Sets the current database to the one specified |
| msql_tablename(*query_id*, *field*) | String | Returns the table name for the specified field |

## MySQL Functions

| Function | Returns | Description |
|---|---|---|
| mysql_affected_rows([*link_id*]) | Integer | Returns the number of rows affected by the query |
| mysql_change_user (*user*, *password* [, *database*] [, *link_id*]) | Integer | Changes the logged in user of the active connection |
| mysql_close([*link_id*]) | Boolean | Closes the MySQL connection |
| mysql_connect ([*hostname* [:*port*] [:/*path/to/socket*]] [, *username*] [, *password*]) | Integer | Opens a connection to the specified MySQL server |
| mysql_create_db (*database* [, *link_id*]) | Integer | Creates a MySQL database with the name *database* |
| mysql_data_seek (*result_id*, *row_number*) | Boolean | Moves to the specified row of a resultset |
| mysql_db_name (*result_id*, *row* [, *field*]) | Integer | Obtains result data |
| mysql_db_query (*database*, *query* [, *link_id*]) | Integer | Executes the specified *query* on the specified *database* and returns a result_id |
| mysql_drop_db (*database_name* [, *link_id*]) | Integer | Deletes the specified MySQL database |
| mysql_errno([*link_id*]) | Integer | Returns the error number for the previous MySQL operation |
| mysql_error([*link_id*]) | String | Returns the error message for the previous MySQL operation |

*Table continued on following page*

| Function | Returns | Description |
|---|---|---|
| mysql_fetch_array (*result_id*, [*result_type*]) | Array | Fetches the next row in the resultset as an array |
| mysql_fetch_field (*result_id* [, *field_offset*]) | Object | Returns an object representing the specified field |
| mysql_fetch_lengths(*result_id*) | Array | Returns an array consisting of the length of each field in the resultset |
| mysql_fetch_object (*result_id* [, *result_type*]) | Object | Fetches the next row in the resultset as an object |
| mysql_fetch_row(*result_id*) | Array | Fetches the next row in the resultset as an enumerated array |
| mysql_field_flags (*result_id*, *field*) | String | Returns the field flags of the specified field |
| mysql_field_len (*result_id*, *field*) | Integer | Returns the length of the specified field |
| mysql_field_name (*result_id*, *field*) | String | Returns the name of the specified field |
| mysql_field_seek (*result_id*, *field_offset*) | Integer | Moves to the specified *field_offset* |
| mysql_field_table (*result_id*, *field*) | String | Returns the name of the table that the specified *field* is in |
| mysql_field_type (*result_id*, *field*) | String | Returns the type of the specified *field* |
| mysql_free_result(*result_id*) | Integer | Frees the memory used by the resultset |
| mysql_insert_id([*link_id*]) | Integer | Returns the ID generated by an AUTO_INCREMENT field in a previous INSERT query |
| mysql_list_dbs([*link_id*]) | Integer | Lists the database on the specified MySQL server and returns a result_id |
| mysql_list_fields (*database*, *table*, [*link_id*]) | Integer | Lists the fields in the specified table and returns a result_id |
| mysql_list_tables(*database*) | Integer | Lists the database in the specified MySQL database; returns a result_id |
| mysql_num_fields(*result_id*) | Integer | Returns the number of fields in the resultset |

| Function | Returns | Description |
|---|---|---|
| mysql_num_rows(result_id) | Integer | Returns the number of rows in the resultset |
| mysql_pconnect ([hostname [:port] [:/path/to/socket]] [, username] [, password]) | Integer | Opens a persistent connection to the specified MySQL server |
| mysql_query(query, [link_id]) | Integer | Executes the specified MySQL query |
| mysql_result (result_id, row, [field]) | Mixed | Fetches the contents of the cell specified by the row and field arguments |
| mysql_select_db (database, [link_id]) | Boolean | Sets the current database to the one specified |
| mysql_tablename(result_id, index) | String | Returns the table name from which the specified field was taken |

## Unified ODBC Functions

| Function | Returns | Description |
|---|---|---|
| odbc_autocommit (connection_id, [OnOff]) | Boolean | Sets or returns the auto-commit behavior for the specified connection |
| odbc_binmode(result_id, mode) | Integer | Sets the mode for converting binary data |
| odbc_close(connection_id) | Nothing | Closes the specified ODBC connection |
| odbc_close_all() | Nothing | Closes all ODBC connections |
| Odbc_columnprivileges (connection_id [, qualifier [, owner [, table_name [, column_name]]]]) | Integer | Lists columns and associated privileges for the specified table and returns a result_id |
| odbc_columns(connection_id [, qualifier] [, owner] [, table_name] [, column_name]) | Integer | Lists all columns in the specified range and returns a result_id |
| odbc_commit(connection_id) | Integer | Commits all pending transactions on the specified connection |

*Table continued on following page*

| Function | Returns | Description |
|---|---|---|
| odbc_connect (*DSN*, *userID*, *password* [, *cursor_type*]) | Integer | Connects to the ODBC data source with the specified Data Source Name and returns a connection_id |
| Odbc_cursor(*result_id*) | String | Returns the cursorname for the specified resultset |
| odbc_do(*connection_id*, *query*) | Integer | Prepares and executes the specified SQL *query* |
| odbc_exec(*connection_id*, *query*) | Integer | Prepares and executes the specified SQL *query* and returns a result_id |
| odbc_execute (*result_id*, [*parameters*]) | Integer | Executes a prepared SQL statement |
| odbc_fetch_into (*result_id* [, *row_number*], *result*) | Integer | Fetches the specified row from the resultset into the *result* array |
| odbc_fetch_row (*result_id* [, *row_number*]) | Boolean | Fetches the specified row from the resultset |
| odbc_field_len (*result_id*, *field_number*) | Integer | Returns the length of the specified field |
| odbc_field_name (*result_id*, *field_number*) | String | Returns the name of the specified field |
| odbc_field_num (*result_id*, *field_name*) | Integer | Returns the column number for the specified *field_name* |
| odbc_field_precision (*result_id*, *field_number*) | Integer | Returns the length of the specified field |
| odbc_field_scale (*result_id*, *field_number*) | String | Returns the scale of the specified field |
| odbc_field_type (*result_id*, *field_number*) | String | Returns the data type of the specified field |
| odbc_foreignkeys(*connection_id*, *pk_qualifier*, *pk_owner*, *pk_table*, *fk_qualifier*, *fk_owner*, *fk_table*) | Integer | Retrieves information about foreign keys in the specified table and returns a result_id |
| odbc_free_result(*result_id*) | Boolean | Releases the resources used by the specified resultset |

| Function | Returns | Description |
|---|---|---|
| odbc_gettypeinfo (connection_id, [data_type]) | Integer | Retrieves information about data types supported by the data source and returns a result_id |
| odbc_longreadlen (result_id, length) | Integer | Determines the number of bytes returned to PHP from fields of type LONG |
| odbc_num_fields(result_id) | Integer | Returns the number of fields in the resultset |
| odbc_num_rows(result_id) | Integer | Returns the number of rows in the resultset |
| odbc_pconnect (DSN, userID, password, [cursor_type]) | Integer | Opens a persistent connection to the ODBC data source with the specified Data Source Name |
| odbc_prepare (connection_id, query) | Integer | Prepares the specified SQL statement for execution |
| odbc_primarykeys(connection_id, qualifier, owner, table) | Integer | Obtains the column names that comprise the primary key for a table and returns a result_id |
| odbc_procedurecolumns (connection_id [, qualifier [, owner [, proc [, column]]]]) | Integer | Retrieves information about parameters for procedures and returns a result_id |
| odbc_procedures (connection_id [, qualifier [, owner [, name]]]) | Integer | Obtains the list of procedures in the requested range and returns a result_id |
| odbc_result(result_id, field) | String | Returns the contents of the specified field |
| odbc_result_all (result_id [, format]) | Integer | Prints the entire resultset as an HTML table |
| odbc_rollback(connection_id) | Integer | Aborts all pending transactions on the specified connection |
| odbc_setoption (ID, function, option, parameter) | Integer | Sets the specified ODBC option |
| odbc_specialcolumns (connection_id, type, qualifier, owner, table, scope, nullable) | Integer | Returns either the optimal set of columns that uniquely identifies a table row, or columns that are automatically updated |

*Table continued on following page*

| Function | Returns | Description |
|---|---|---|
| odbc_statistics (*connection_id*, *qualifier*, *owner*, *table_name*, *unique*, *accuracy*) | Integer | Retrieves statistics about the specified table and it's indexes and returns a `result_id` |
| odbc_tableprivileges (*connection_id* [,*qualifier*] [,*owner*] [,*name*]) | Integer | Lists tables and privileges associated with each table and returns a `result_id` |
| odbc_tables (*connection_id* [,*qualifier*] [,*owner*] [,*name*][,*types*]) | Integer | Lists table names in the specified data source |

## Oracle 8 Functions

| Function | Returns | Description |
|---|---|---|
| OCIBindByName (*statement*, *ph_name*, &*variable*, *length* [, *type*]) | Integer | Binds the specified PHP variable to the Oracle Placeholder specified by *ph_name* |
| OCIColumnIsNULL (*statement*, *column*) | Boolean | Indicates whether the specified *column* contains a NULL value |
| OCIColumnName (*statement*, *column_number*) | String | Returns the name of the specified *column_number* |
| OCIColumnSize (*statement*, *column*) | Integer | Returns the size of the specified *column* |
| OCIColumnType (*statement*, *column_number*) | Mixed | Returns the data type of the specified *column* |
| OCICommit(*connection*) | Integer | Commits all pending transactions on the specified *connection* |
| OCIDefineByName (*statement*, *column_name*, &*variable* [, *type*]) | Integer | Fetches the specified SQL column into the supplied PHP variable |
| OCIError ([*statement*\|*connection*\|*global*]) | Integer | Returns the code for the last occurring error |
| OCIExecute(*statement*, [*mode*]) | Integer | Executes the specified SQL statement |
| OCIFetch(*statement*) | Integer | Fetches the next row from the resultset |
| OCIFetchInto (*statement*, *result*, [*mode*]) | Integer | Returns the next row from the resultset into the *result* array |

| Function | Returns | Description |
|---|---|---|
| OCIFetchStatement (*statement*, *result*) | Integer | Returns all rows from the resultset into the *result* array |
| OCIFreeCursor(*statement*) | Boolean | Frees all resources used by the cursor for the specified *statement* |
| OCIFreeStatement (*statement*) | Integer | Frees all resources used by the specified *statement* |
| OCIInternalDebug(*OnOff*) | Nothing | Turns internal debugging on or off |
| OCILogOff(*connection*) | Integer | Closes the specified Oracle connection |
| OCILogon (*username*, *password*, [*database*]) | Integer | Opens a connection to an Oracle database and returns a connection identifier |
| OCINewCursor(*connection*) | Integer | Returns a new cursor for the specified *connection* |
| OCINewDescriptor (*connection* [,*type*]) | String | Initializes a new empty LOB (the default) or FILE descriptor |
| OCINLogon (*username*, *password*, [*database*]) | Integer | Connects to an Oracle database using a new connection |
| OCINumCols(*statement*) | Integer | Return the number of columns in the resultset |
| OCIParse (*connection*, *query*) | Integer | Validates the specified *query* |
| OCIPLogon (*username*, *password*, [*database*]) | Integer | Opens a persistent connection to an Oracle database |
| OCIResult (*statement*, *column*) | Mixed | Returns the data for the specified *column* for a fetched row |
| OCIRollback(*connection*) | Integer | Aborts all pending transactions on the specified *connection* |
| OCIRowCount(*statement*) | Integer | Returns the number of affected rows in the resultset |
| OCIServerVersion (*connection*) | String | Returns information about the server version |
| OCIStatementType (*statement*) | String | Returns the type of the specified OCI *statement* |

## Oracle Functions

| Function | Returns | Description |
|---|---|---|
| ora_bind(*cursor*, *&variable*, *SQLparameter*, *length* [,*type*]) | Boolean | Binds the specified PHP *variable* to the specified Oracle *parameter* |
| ora_close(*cursor*) | Boolean | Closes the specified Oracle *cursor* |
| ora_columnname (*cursor*, *column*) | String | Returns the name of the specified *column* |
| ora_columnsize (*cursor*, *column*) | Integer | Returns the size of the specified *column* |
| ora_columntype (*cursor*, *column*) | String | Returns the data type of the specified *column* |
| ora_commit(*connection*) | Boolean | Commits a transaction |
| ora_commitoff(*connection*) | Boolean | Disables automatic committing of transactions |
| ora_commiton(*connection*) | Boolean | Enables automatic committing of transactions |
| ora_do(*connection*, *query*) | Integer | Parses and executes a statement, then fetches the first result row |
| ora_error(*cursor*\|*connection*) | String | Returns the message for the last occurring error |
| ora_errorcode (*cursor*\|*connection*) | Integer | Returns the code for the last occurring error |
| ora_exec(*cursor*) | Boolean | Executes a parsed statement on the specified *cursor* |
| ora_fetch(*cursor*) | Boolean | Fetches a row from the specified *cursor* |
| ora_fetch_into (*cursor*, *result* [,*flags*]) | Integer | Fetches a row into the specified *result* array |
| ora_getcolumn(*cursor*, *column*) | Mixed | Returns the contents from the specified *column* for the current row |
| ora_logoff(*connection*) | Boolean | Close the specified Oracle *connection* |
| ora_logon(*user*, *password*) | Integer | Opens a connection to Oracle and returns a connection index |
| ora_numcols(*cursor_ind*) | Integer | Returns the number of columns in a resultset |

| Function | Returns | Description |
|---|---|---|
| ora_numrows(*cursor_ind*) | Integer | Returns the number of rows in a resultset |
| ora_open(*connection*) | Integer | Opens a cursor on the specified *connection* and returns a cursor_index |
| ora_parse(*cursor*, *SQL_statement*, *defer*) | Boolean | Validates the specified SQL statement |
| ora_plogon(*user*, *password*) | Boolean | Opens a persistent connection to an Oracle database |
| ora_rollback(*connection*) | Boolean | Aborts a transaction |

## PostgreSQL Functions

| Function | Returns | Description |
|---|---|---|
| pg_client_encoding([*connection*]) | String | Returns the client encoding as a string |
| pg_close(*connection*) | Boolean | Closes a PostgreSQL connection |
| pg_cmdtuples(*result_id*) | Integer | Returns the number of affected tuples |
| pg_connect(*host*, *port*, *options*, *tty*, *dbname*) | Integer | Connects to a PostgreSQL database and returns a connection_index |
| pg_dbname(*connection*) | String | Returns the name of the database for the specified *connection* |
| pg_end_copy([connection]) | Boolean | Syncs PostgreSQL frontend with the backend after doing a copy operation |
| pg_errormessage(*connection*) | String | Returns the error message for the specified *connection* |
| pg_exec(*connection*, *query*) | Integer | Executes the specified *query* |
| pg_fetch_array(*result*, *row* [,*result_type*]) | Array | Fetches a row as an array |
| pg_fetch_object(*result*, *row* [,*result_type*]) | Object | Fetches a row as an object |
| pg_fetch_row(*result*, *row*) | Array | Fetches a row as an enumerated array |

*Table continued on following page*

| Function | Returns | Description |
|---|---|---|
| pg_fieldisnull<br>(*result_id*, *row*, *field*) | Integer | Indicates whether the specified *field* in the given *row* has a NULL value |
| pg_fieldname<br>(*result_id*, *field_number*) | String | Returns the name of the specified field |
| pg_fieldnum<br>(*result_id*, *field_name*) | Integer | Returns the number of the specified field |
| pg_fieldprtlen<br>(*result_id*, *row_number*,<br>*field_name*) | Integer | Returns the printed length of the specified field |
| pg_fieldsize<br>(*result_id*, *field_number*) | Integer | Returns the internal storage size of the specified field |
| pg_fieldtype<br>(*result_id*, *field_number*) | String | Returns the type of the specified field |
| pg_freeresult(*result_id*) | Integer | Frees the memory used by the resultset |
| pg_getlastoid(*result_id*) | Integer | Returns the last object identifier |
| pg_host(*connection*) | String | Returns the host name associated with the connection |
| pg_loclose(*file_descriptor*) | Nothing | Closes the large object specified by the *file_descriptor* |
| pg_locreate(*connection*) | Integer | Creates a large object and returns the object_id |
| pg_loexport<br>(*object_id*, *file*<br>[,*connection_id*]) | Boolean | Exports a large object to the specified *file* |
| pg_loimport<br>(*file*, [*connection_id*]) | Integer | Imports a large object from the specified *file* and returns an object_id |
| pg_loopen<br>(*connection*, *object_id*,<br>*mode*) | Integer | Opens a large object and returns a file descriptor for the object |
| pg_loread<br>(*file_descriptor*, *len*) | String | Reads up to *len* bytes from the specified large object |
| pg_loreadall<br>(*file_descriptor*) | Nothing | Reads an entire large object and passes it through to the browser |
| pg_lounlink<br>(*connection*, *object_id*) | Nothing | Deletes the large object with the specified identifier |

| Function | Returns | Description |
|---|---|---|
| pg_lowrite (*file_descriptor*, *buf*) | Integer | Writes to the specified large object from the variable *buf* |
| pg_numfields(*result_id*) | Integer | Returns the number of fields in the specified resultset |
| pg_numrows(*result_id*) | Integer | Returns the number of rows in the specified resultset |
| pg_options(*connection*) | String | Returns the options associated with the specified *connection* |
| pg_pconnect(*connection*) | Integer | Open a persistent connection to a PostgreSQL database using the quoted string *connection*, and returns a connection index |
| pg_port(*connection*) | Integer | Returns the port number for the specified *connection* |
| pg_put_line ([*connection*, *data*]) | Boolean | Sends a NULL-terminated string to the PostgreSQL backend server |
| pg_result (*result_id*, *row_number*, *field_name*) | Mixed | Returns values from a result identifier |
| pg_set_client_encoding ([*connection*, *encoding*]) | Boolean | Sets the client encoding |
| pg_trace (*filename* [,*mode* [,*connection*]]) | Boolean | Enables tracing of a PostgreSQL connection |
| pg_tty(*connection*) | String | Returns the tty name associated with the *connection* |
| pg_untrace([*connection*]) | Boolean | Disables tracing of a PostgreSQL connection |

## Sybase Functions

| Function | Returns | Description |
|---|---|---|
| sybase_affected_rows ([*link_id*]) | Integer | Returns the number of rows affected by the query |
| sybase_close(*link_id*) | Boolean | Closes the Sybase connection |
| sybase_connect (*server_name*, *username*, *password*) | Integer | Opens a connection to the specified Sybase server and returns a link_id |

*Table continued on following page*

| Function | Returns | Description |
|----------|---------|-------------|
| sybase_data_seek (*result_id*, *row_number*) | Boolean | Moves to the specified row of a resultset |
| sybase_fetch_array (*result_id*) | Integer | Fetches the next row in the resultset as an array |
| sybase_fetch_field (*result_id*, *field_offset*) | Object | Returns an object containing field information for the field with the specified position |
| sybase_fetch_object (*result_id*) | Object | Fetches the next row in the resultset as an object |
| sybase_fetch_row(*result_id*) | Array | Fetches the next row in the resultset as an enumerated array |
| sybase_field_seek (*result_id*, *field_offset*) | Integer | Moves to the specified *field_offset* |
| sybase_free_result (*result_id*) | Integer | Frees the memory used by the resultset |
| sybase_num_fields (*result_id*) | Integer | Returns the number of fields in the resultset |
| sybase_num_rows(*result_id*) | Integer | Returns the number of rows in the resultset |
| sybase_pconnect (*servername*, *username*, *password*) | Integer | Opens a persistent connection to the specified Sybase server and returns a link_id |
| sybase_query (*query*, [*link_id*]) | Integer | Executes the specified Sybase *query* |
| sybase_result (*result_id*, *row*, *field*) | Integer | Fetches the contents of the cell specified by the *row* and *field* arguments |
| sybase_select_db (*database* [,*link_id*]) | Boolean | Sets the current database to the one specified |

# Date and Time Functions

| Function | Returns | Description |
|----------|---------|-------------|
| Checkdate (*month*, *day*, year) | Boolean | Validates the specified date |
| date(*format* [,*timestamp*]) | String | Formats a local time/date |

| Function | Returns | Description |
|---|---|---|
| getdate(*timestamp*) | Array | Returns an associative array with date/time settings for the specified timestamp |
| gettimeofday() | Array | Returns an associative array containing settings for the current time |
| Gmdate (*format* [,*timestamp*]) | String | Formats a GMT date/time |
| Gmmktime ([*hour*] [,*minute*] [,*second*] [,*month*] [,*day*] [,*year*] [,*is_dst*]) | Integer | Returns the UNIX timestamp for the GMT time/date. using current values for missing parameters |
| Gmstrftime (format, timestamp) | String | Formats a GMT/CUT time/date according to the current locale |
| Localtime ([*timestamp* [,*is_associative*]) | Array | Returns the local time as an array |
| microtime() | String | Returns a string containing the microseconds and seconds since the epoch |
| Mktime ([*hour*] [,*minute*] [,*second*] [,*month*] [,*day*] [,*year*] [,*is_dst*]) | Integer | Returns the UNIX timestamp for the specified date, using current values for missing parameters |
| Strftime (*format* [,*timestamp*]) | String | Formats a local time/date according to the current locale |
| strtotime(*time* [,*now*]) | Integer | Parses an English datetime format into a UNIX timestamp |
| time() | Integer | Returns current UNIX timestamp |

# Directory Functions

| Function | Returns | Description |
|---|---|---|
| chdir(*directory*) | Boolean | Sets the specified *directory* as the current directory |
| closedir(*dir_handle*) | Nothing | Closes the directory stream specified by *dir_handle* |
| dir(*directory*) | Directory object | Returns an object representing the specified *directory* |

*Table continued on following page*

| Function | Returns | Description |
|---|---|---|
| getcwd() | String | Returns the current working directory |
| opendir(*path*) | Integer | Opens the specified directory stream and returns a directory_handle |
| readdir(*dir_handle*) | String | Returns the next entry from the directory with the specified handle |
| rewinddir(*dir_handle*) | Nothing | Resets the directory stream specified by *dir_handle* to the beginning of the directory |

# DOM XML Functions

| Function | Returns | Description |
|---|---|---|
| xmldoc(*str*) | Object | Creates a DOM object from an XML document |
| xmldocfile(*filename*) | Object | Creates a DOM object from an XML file |
| xmltree(*str*) | Object | Creates a tree of PHP objects from an XML document |

# Error Handling and Logging Functions

| Function | Returns | Description |
|---|---|---|
| error_log (*message*, *message_type* [,*destination* [,*extra_headers*]]) | Integer | Sends an error message |
| error_reporting([*level*]) | Integer | Sets which PHP errors are reported |
| restore_error_handler() | Nothing | Restores the previous error handler function |
| set_error_handler (*error_handler*) | String | Sets a user defined error handler function |
| trigger_error (*error_msg* [,*error_type*]) | Nothing | Generates a user level error message |
| user_error (*error_msg* [,*error_type*]) | Nothing | Generates a user level error message |

# Filesystem Functions

| Function | Returns | Description |
|---|---|---|
| basename(*path*) | String | Returns the filename component of *path* |
| chgrp(*filename*, *group*) | Integer | Assigns the file with the specified *filename* to the specified *group* |
| chmod(*filename*, *mode*) | Integer | Changes the *mode* of the specified file |
| chown(*filename*, *user*) | Boolean | Changes the *filename* owner to *user* |
| clearstatcache() | Nothing | Clears the file stat cache |
| copy(*source*, *destination*) | Boolean | Copies the file from *source* to *destination* |
| dirname(*path*) | String | Returns the directory name component from *path* |
| diskfreespace(*directory*) | Float | Returns the free space in the specified *directory* |
| fclose(*file_pointer*) | Boolean | Closes the file with the specified *file_pointer* |
| feof(*file_pointer*) | Boolean | Tests for end-of-file on the *file_pointer* |
| fgetc(*file_pointer*) | String | Reads the next character from the file specified by *file_pointer* |
| Fgetcsv (*file_pointer*, *length* [,*delimiter*]) | Array | Returns an array from the next line of the file specified by *file_pointer* |
| fgets(*file_pointer*, *length*) | String | Reads a line of up to *length* - 1 bytes from the file specified by *file_pointer* |
| Fgetss (*file_pointer*, *length* [,*allowable_tags*]) | String | Reads a line of up to *length* - 1 bytes from the file specified by *file_pointer*, stripping off any HTML and PHP tags other than *allowable_tags* |
| File (*filename* [,*use_include_path*]) | Array | Reads an entire file into an array, each line in the file corresponding to an element in the array |
| file_exists (*filename*) | Boolean | Checks whether the specified file exists |

*Table continued on following page*

| Function | Returns | Description |
|---|---|---|
| fileatime(*filename*) | Integer | Returns the time that the specified file was last accessed |
| filectime(*filename*) | Integer | Returns the time that the specified file was last changed |
| filegroup(*filename*) | Integer | Returns the ID for the file owner's group |
| fileinode(*filename*) | Integer | Returns the specified file's inode number |
| filemtime(*filename*) | Integer | Returns the time that the specified file was last modified |
| fileowner(*filename*) | Integer | Returns the user ID of the file owner |
| fileperms(*filename*) | Integer | Returns the file permissions |
| filesize(*filename*) | Integer | Returns the size of the file |
| filetype(*filename*) | String | Returns the file type |
| Flock (*file_pointer, operation* [,*wouldblock*]) | Boolean | Sets or releases a lock on the file specified by *file_pointer* |
| Fopen (*filename, mode* [,*use_include_path*]) | Integer | Opens the specified file |
| fpassthru(*file_pointer*) | Integer | Outputs all remaining data from the file specified by *file_pointer* |
| Fputs (*file_pointer, string* [,*length*]) | Integer | Writes the supplied *string* up to *length* characters to the file specified by *file_pointer* |
| Fread(*file_pointer, length*) | String | Reads up to *length* characters from the file specified by *file_pointer* |
| Fscanf(*handle, format* [,*var1...*]) | Mixed | Parses input from the file associated with *handle* according to the specified *format* |
| Fseek (*file_pointer, offset* [,*whence*]) | Integer | Moves the internal pointer in the file specified by *file_pointer* by *offset* places from *whence* |
| fstat(*file_pointer*) | Array | Returns information about a file as an array |

| Function | Returns | Description |
|---|---|---|
| ftell(*file_pointer*) | Integer | Returns the position of the internal pointer in the file specified by *file_pointer* |
| Ftruncate (*file_pointer*, *size*) | Integer | Truncates the file specified by *file_pointer* to the length specified by *size* |
| Fwrite (*file_pointer*, *string* [,*length*]) | Integer | Writes the supplied *string* up to *length* characters to the file specified by *file_pointer* |
| is_dir(*filename*) | Boolean | Indicates whether the specified file is a directory |
| is_executable (*filename*) | Boolean | Indicates whether the specified file is executable |
| is_file(*filename*) | Boolean | Indicates whether the specified file is a regular file |
| is_link(*filename*) | Boolean | Indicates whether the specified file is a symbolic link |
| is_readable(*filename*) | Boolean | Indicates whether the specified file is readable |
| is_writeable(*filename*) | Boolean | Indicates whether the specified file is writeable |
| is_uploaded_file(*filename*) | Boolean | Indicates whether the file was uploaded via HTTP POST |
| link(*target*, *link*) | Integer | Creates a hard link |
| linkinfo(*path*) | Integer | Returns information about the specified link |
| lstat(*filename*) | Array | Returns information about the specified file or symbolic link |
| mkdir(*pathname*, *mode*) | Integer | Creates the directory specified by *pathname* with the specified *mode* |
| move_uploaded_file (*filename*, *destination*) | Boolean | Moves an uploaded file to a new location |
| pclose(*file_pointer*) | Integer | Closes a *file_pointer* to a pipe opened by popen() |
| popen(*command*, *mode*) | Integer | Opens a pipe by forking the specified *command* |

*Table continued on following page*

| Function | Returns | Description |
| --- | --- | --- |
| Readfile (*filename* [,*use_include_path*]) | Integer | Reads and outputs a file |
| readlink(*path*) | String | Returns the target of a symbolic link |
| realpath(*path*) | String | Returns canonicalized absolute pathname |
| rename(*oldname*, *newname*) | Integer | Renames the specified file from *oldname* to *newname* |
| rewind(*file_pointer*) | Integer | Rewinds *file_pointer* to the beginning of the file stream |
| rmdir(*directory*) | Integer | Removes the specified *directory* |
| set_file_buffer (*file_pointer*, *buffer*) | Integer | Sets the size of the buffer for the file specified by *file_pointer* |
| stat(*filename*) | Array | Returns information about the specified file |
| symlink(*target*, *link*) | Integer | Creates a symbolic link |
| tempnam(*directory*, *prefix*) | String | Creates a unique temporary filename in the specified *directory* |
| tmpfile() | Nothing | Creates a temporary file |
| touch(*filename* [,*time*]) | Integer | Sets the modification time of the specified file |
| umask(*mask*) | Integer | Changes the current umask |
| unlink(*filename*) | Integer | Deletes the specified file |

## Forms Data Format Functions

| Function | Returns | Description |
| --- | --- | --- |
| fdf_close(*fdf_document*) | Nothing | Closes the specified FDF document |
| fdf_create() | Integer | Creates a new FDF document |
| fdf_get_file(*fdf_document*) | String | Returns the value of the /F key in the specified FDF document |
| fdf_get_status(*fdf_document*) | String | Returns the value of the /STATUS key in the specified FDF document |
| fdf_get_value (*fdf_document*, *fieldname*) | String | Returns the value of the named field in the specified FDF document |

| Function | Returns | Description |
| --- | --- | --- |
| fdf_next_field_name<br>(*fdf_document*, *fieldname*) | String | Returns the name of the field following the specified field |
| fdf_open(*filename*) | Integer | Opens the specified FDF document with form data |
| fdf_save(*filename*) | Integer | Saves the FDF document to the specified file |
| fdf_set_ap<br>(*fdf_document*, *field_name*,<br>*face*, *filename*, *page_number*); | Nothing | Sets the appearance of the named field in the specified FDF document |
| fdf_set_file<br>(*fdf_document*, *filename*) | Nothing | Sets the value of the /F key in the specified FDF document |
| fdf_set_flags<br>(*fdf_document*, *fieldname*,<br>*whichFlags*, *newFlags*) | Nothing | Sets flags of the specified field |
| fdf_set_javascript_action<br>(*fdf_document*, *fieldname*,<br>*trigger*, *script*) | Nothing | Sets a JavaScript action for the specified field |
| fdf_set_opt<br>(*fdf_document*, *fieldname*,<br>*element*, *string1*, *string2*) | Nothing | Sets options of the specified field |
| fdf_set_status<br>(*fdf_document*, *status*) | Nothing | Sets the value of the /STATUS key in the specified FDF document |
| fdf_set_submit_form_action<br>(*fdf_document*, *fieldname*,<br>*trigger*, *script*, *flags*) | Nothing | Sets a submit form action for the given field |
| fdf_set_value<br>(*fdf_document*, *fieldname*,<br>*value*, *is_name*) | Nothing | Sets the *value* of the named field in the specified FDF document |

# Function Handling Functions

| Function | Returns | Description |
| --- | --- | --- |
| call_user_func<br>(*function_name* [,*parameter*<br>[,…]]) | Mixed | Calls a user defined function specified by *function_name* |
| create_function(*args*, *code*) | String | Creates an anonymous function from the parameters passed and returns a unique name for it |

*Table continued on following page*

| Function | Returns | Description |
|---|---|---|
| func_get_arg(*arg_num*) | Mixed | Returns an item from the argument list |
| Func_get_args() | Array | Returns an array comprising a function's argument list |
| Func_num_args() | Integer | Returns the number of arguments passed into the function |
| function_exists (*function_name*) | Boolean | Checks if *function_name* has been defined |
| register_shutdown_function (*function*) | Integer | Registers *function* to be executed when script processing is complete |

# HTTP Functions

| Function | Returns | Description |
|---|---|---|
| header(*string*) | Integer | Sends the specified HTTP header |
| header_sent() | Boolean | Checks if headers have been sent |
| Setcookie (*name*, [*value* [,*expire* [,*path* [,*domain* [,*secure*]]]]]) | Integer | Sends a cookie with the specified *name* and *value* |

# Image Functions

| Function | Returns | Description |
|---|---|---|
| Getimagesize (*filename* [,*image_info*]) | Array | Returns the size of the image with the specified filename |
| Imagearc (*im*, *cx*, *cy*, *width*, *height*, *start*, *end*, *col*) | Integer | Draws a partial ellipse in image *im* centred at *cx*, *cy* with the specified *width* and *height*, from the *start* angle to the *end* angle, in the color *col* |
| Imagechar (*im*, *font*, *x*, *y*, *c*, *col*) | Integer | Draws a character *c* horizontally in image *im* |
| Imagecharup (*im*, *font*, *x*, *y*, *c*, *col*) | Integer | Draws a character vertically |
| Imagecolorallocate (*im*, *red*, *green*, *blue*) | Integer | Allocates a color for an image and returns a color identifier |

| Function | Returns | Description |
|---|---|---|
| imagecolorat(*im*, *x*, *y*) | Integer | Returns the index of the color of the pixel at the specified point in the image |
| Imagecolorclosest (*im*, *red*, *green*, *blue*) | Integer | Returns the index of the closest color to the specified color in the pallete of the specified image |
| Imagecolordeallocate (*im*, *index*) | Integer | De-allocates a color for an image |
| Imagecolorexact (*im*, *red*, *green*, *blue*) | Integer | Returns the index of the specified color in the palette of the specified image |
| Imagecolorresolve (*im*, *red*, *green*, *blue*) | Integer | Returns the index of the specified color or its closest possible alternative |
| Imagecolorset (*im*, *index*, *red*, *green*, *blue*) | Boolean | Sets the color for the specified palette *index* |
| Imagecolorsforindex (*im*, *index*) | Array | Returns an associative array containing the red, green and blue values for the specified color *index* |
| imagecolorstotal(*im*) | Integer | Returns the total number of colors in the specified image's palette |
| Imagecolortransparent (*im* [, *col*]) | Integer | Sets *col* as the transparent color |
| Imagecopy (*dst_im*, *src_im*, *dst_x*, *dst_y*, *src_x*, *src_y*, *src_w*, *src_h*) | Integer | Copies part of an image *src_im* to *dst_im*, from the *src_* coordinates to the *dst_* coordinates |
| Imagecopyresized (*dst_im*, *src_im*, *dstX*, *dstY*, *srcX*, *srcY*, *dstW*, *dstH*, *srcW*, *srcH*) | Integer | Copies and resizes part of an image, using *dstX* and *dstY* as top left coordinates |
| imagecreate(*width*, *height*) | Integer | Creates a new image with the specified *height* and *width* |
| imagecreatefromgif(*filename*) | Integer | Creates a new image from the specified GIF file |
| imagecreatefromjpeg(*filename*) | Integer | Creates a new image from the specified JPEG file |
| imagecreatefromPNG(*filename*) | Integer | Creates a new image from the specified PNG file |
| Imagedashedline (*im*, *x1*, *y1*, *x2*, *y2*, *col*) | Integer | Draws a dashed line in the specified image |

*Table continued on following page*

| Function | Returns | Description |
|---|---|---|
| imagedestroy(*im*) | Integer | Destroys the image specified by *im* |
| imagefill(*im*, *x*, *y*, *col*) | Integer | Flood fills the image specified by *im* with color *col* |
| Imagefilledpolygon (*im*, *points*, *num_points*, *col*) | Integer | Draws a filled polygon in the image specified by *im* between the points in the *points* array |
| Imagefilledrectangle (*im*, *x1*, *y1*, *x2*, *y2 col*) | Integer | Draws a filled rectangle in the image specified by *im* |
| Imagefilltoborder (*im*, *x*, *y*, *border*, *col*) | Integer | Performs a flood fill in the image specified by *im*, with a border color of *border* |
| imagefontheight(*font*) | Integer | Returns the height of the specified *font* in pixels |
| imagefontwidth(*font*) | Integer | Returns the width of the specified *font* in pixels |
| Imagegammacorrect (*im*, *inputgamma*, *outputgamma*) | Integer | Applies a gamma correction to a GD image *im* |
| imagegif(*im* [,*filename*]) | Integer | Sends the GIF image *filename* to a file or browser as image *im* |
| Imageinterlace (*im* [,*interlace*]) | Integer | Turns interlacing on or off for the specified image |
| Imagejpeg (*im* [,*filename* [,*quality*]]) | Integer | Sends the JPEG image to a file or browser; use an empty string (' ') to replace no filename when specifying *quality* |
| Imageline (*im*, *x1*, *y1*, *x2*, *y2*, *col*) | Integer | Draws a line in the image *im* |
| imageloadfont(*filename*) | Integer | Loads a bitmap font from the specified *filename* |
| imagepng(*im* [,*filename*]) | Integer | Sends the PNG image to a file or browser |
| Imagepolygon (*im*, *points*, *num_points*, *col*) | Integer | Draws a polygon in the image *im* between the points in the array *points* |
| Imagepsbbox (*text*, *font*, *size*, *space*, *width*, *angle*) | Array | Calculates the coordinates for the bounding box of a text rectangle using a PostScript font |
| Imagepsencodefont (*encodingfile*) | Integer | Loads the specified character encoding vector for a PostScript font |

| Function | Returns | Description |
|---|---|---|
| Imagepsextendfont (*font_index*, *extend*) | Boolean | Extends or condenses a font |
| imagepsfreefont (*fontindex*) | Nothing | Releases the PostScript font with the specified *fontindex* from memory |
| imagepsloadfont (*filename*) | Integer | Loads the PostScript from the specified font file |
| Imagepsslantfont (*font_index*, *slant*) | Boolean | Slants the specified font |
| Imagepstext (*im*, *text*, *font*, *size*, *foreground*, *background*, *x*, *y* [,*space*] [,*tightness*] [,*angle*] [,*antialias_steps*]) | Array | Draws a text string on the specified image using a PostScript font |
| Imagerectangle (*im*, *x1*, *y1*, *x2*, *y2 col*) | Integer | Draws a rectangle in the specified image |
| imagesetpixel(*im*, *x*, *y*, *col*) | Integer | Draws a pixel in the specified image |
| Imagestring (*im*, *font*, *x*, *y*, *s*, *col*) | Integer | Draws a string *s* horizontally in the specified image |
| Imagestringup (*im*, *font*, *x*, *y*, *s*, *col*) | Integer | Draws a string *s* vertically in the specified image |
| imagesx (*im*) | Integer | Returns the width of the specified image |
| imagesy (*im*) | Integer | Returns the height of the specified image |
| Imagettfbbox (*size*, *angle*, *fontfile*, *text*) | Array | Returns the bounding box for a TypeType font string |
| Imagettftext (*im*, *size*, *angle*, *x*, *y*, *col*, *fontfile*, *text*) | Array | Draws the specified *text* to the image using a TrueType font |
| imagetypes() | Integer | Returns the image types supported by this PHP build |
| read_exif_data (*filename*) | Array | Returns the EXIF headers from a JPEG image file |

# Mail Functions

| Function | Returns | Description |
|---|---|---|
| ezmlm_hash(*addr*) | Integer | Calculates the hash value needed by EZMLM mailing lists |
| mail(*to, subject, message* [*,additional_headers*]) | Boolean | Sends the specified email |

# Mathematical Functions

| Function | Returns | Description |
|---|---|---|
| abs(*number*) | Mixed | Returns the absolute value of *number* |
| acos(*arg*) | Float | Returns the arc cosine of *arg* in radians |
| asin(*arg*) | Float | Returns the arc sine of *arg* in radians |
| atan(*arg*) | Float | Returns the arc tangent of *arg* in radians |
| atan2(*y, x*) | Float | Returns the arc tangent of *y* and *x* |
| base_convert (*number, frombase, tobase*) | String | Converts a *number* between specified bases |
| bindec(*binary_string*) | String | Converts the specified *binary_string* to decimal |
| ceil(*number*) | Integer | Rounds fractions up to the next highest integer |
| cos(*arg*) | Float | Returns the cosine of *arg* in radians |
| decbin(*number*) | String | Converts the specified decimal *number* to binary |
| dechex(*number*) | String | Converts the specified decimal *number* to hexadecimal |
| decoct(*number*) | String | Converts the specified decimal *number* to octal |
| deg2rad(*number*) | Double | Converts the *number* in degrees to the radian equivalent |
| exp(*arg*) | Float | Returns e to the power of *arg* |
| floor(*number*) | Integer | Rounds fractions down to the next lowest integer |

| Function | Returns | Description |
|---|---|---|
| getrandmax() | Integer | Shows the greatest random value that can be returned from rand() |
| hexdec(*hex_string*) | Integer | Converts the specified *hex_string* to decimal |
| lcg_value() | Double | Returns a pseudo random number between 0 and 1 |
| log(*arg*) | Float | Returns the natural logarithm of *arg* |
| log10(*arg*) | Float | Returns the base 10 logarithm of *arg* |
| max(*arg1*, *arg2*, ...) | Mixed | Returns the greatest of the passed-in arguments |
| min(*arg1*, *arg2*, ...) | Mixed | Returns the lowest of the passed-in arguments |
| mt_getrandmax() | Integer | Returns the largest value than can be returned from a call to mt_rand() |
| mt_rand([*min*] [,*max*]) | Integer | Returns a Mersenne Twister random value |
| mt_srand(*seed*) | Nothing | Seeds the Mersenne Twister random number generator |
| number_format (*number* [,*dec_places*] [,*dec_point*] [,*thousands*]) | String | Formats the specified *number* to the given number of decimal places using the supplied decimal point and *thousands* separator |
| octdec(*octal_string*) | Integer | Converts the specified *octal_string* to decimal |
| pi() | Float | Returns the value of pi |
| pow(*base*, *exp*) | Float | Returns *base* to the power of *exp* |
| rad2deg(*number*) | Double | Converts the radian *number* to degrees |
| rand([*min*] [,*max*]) | Integer | Generates a random integer |
| round(*number* [,*precision*]) | Integer | Returns float *number* to the nearest integer |
| sin(*arg*) | Float | Returns the sine of *arg* in radians |
| sqrt(*arg*) | Float | Returns the square root of *arg* |
| srand(*seed*) | Nothing | Seeds the random number generator |
| tan(*arg*) | Float | Returns the tangent of *arg* in radians |

# Miscellaneous Functions

| Function | Returns | Description |
|---|---|---|
| connection_aborted() | Boolean | Indicates whether the client has aborted the connection |
| connection_status() | Integer | Returns the connection status |
| connection_timeout() | Boolean | Indicates whether the script has timed out |
| define(name, value [,case_insensitive]) | Integer | Defines a named constant |
| defined(name) | Boolean | Checks whether the named constant exists |
| die(message) | Nothing | Outputs the specified message and terminates the script |
| eval(string) | Mixed | Evaluate the specified string as PHP code |
| exit() | Nothing | Terminates the current script |
| get_browser([user_agent]) | Object | Indicates what the user's browser is capable of |
| highlight_file(filename) | Nothing | Prints out a syntax highlighted version of the specified file |
| highlight_string(str) | Nothing | Prints out a syntax highlighted version of the specified string |
| ignore_user_abort ([setting]) | Integer | Sets whether a client disconnecting will terminate the execution of the script |
| iptcparse(iptcblock) | Array | Parses the specified IPTC block into an array |
| leak(bytes) | Nothing | Leaks the specified amount of memory |
| pack(format [,args...]) | String | Packs the supplied arguments into a binary string using the specified format |
| show_source(filename) | Nothing | Prints out a syntax highlighted version of the code contained in filename |
| sleep(seconds) | Nothing | Pauses the script for the specified number of seconds |

| Function | Returns | Description |
|---|---|---|
| uniqid(*prefix* [,*lcg*]) | Integer | Generates a unique ID based on the current time in microseconds and the supplied *prefix* |
| unpack(*format*, *data*) | Array | Unpacks the specified *data* from a binary string into an array using the specified *format* |
| usleep(*microseconds*) | Nothing | Pauses the script for the specified number of *microseconds* |

# Network Functions

| Function | Returns | Description |
|---|---|---|
| Checkdnsrr (*host* [,*type*]) | Integer | Searches the DNS records of the specified *host* for records of the specified *type* |
| closelog() | Integer | Closes the connection to the system log |
| debugger_off() | Integer | Disables the internal PHP debugger |
| debugger_on(*server*) | Integer | Enable the internal PHP debugger and connects it to *server* |
| define_syslog_ variables() | Nothing | Initializes all syslog related constants |
| Fsockopen ([udp://]*hostname*, *port* [,*errno* [,*errstr* [,*timeout*]]]) | Integer | Opens a socket connection |
| Gethostbyaddr (*ip_address*) | String | Returns the hostname corresponding to the specified IP address |
| Gethostbyname (*hostname*) | String | Returns the IP address corresponding to the specified *hostname* |
| Gethostbyname1 (*hostname*) | Array | Returns an array of IP addresses corresponding to the specified *hostname* |
| getmxrr(*hostname*, *mxhosts* [,*weight*]) | Integer | Returns the MX records corresponding to the specified *hostname* |
| getprotobyname(*name*) | Integer | Returns the protocol number associated with the protocol *name* |
| Getprotobynumber (*number*) | String | Returns the protocol name associated with the protocol *number* |
| Getservbyname (*service*, *protocol*) | Integer | Returns the port number associated with the specified *service* and *protocol* |

*Table continued on following page*

| Function | Returns | Description |
|---|---|---|
| Getservbyport (*port, protocol*) | String | Returns the Internet service associated with the specified *port* and *protocol* |
| ip2long (*ip_address*) | Integer | Converts a string containing an Internet Protocol dotted address into a proper address |
| long2ip (*proper_address*) | String | Converts a proper address into a string in Internet standard dotted format |
| Openlog (*ident, option, facility*) | Integer | Opens a connection to the system logger |
| Pfsockopen (*hostname, port* [,*errno*] [,*errstr*] [,*timeout*]) | Integer | Opens a persistent socket connection |
| socket_set_blocking (*socket, mode*) | Integer | Sets the blocking mode for the specified *socket* |
| socket_set_timeout (*socket_descriptor, seconds, microseconds*) | Boolean | Sets the timeout period on a socket |
| Syslog (*priority, message*) | Integer | Writes the specified *message* to the system log |

# Output Control Functions

| Function | Returns | Description |
|---|---|---|
| flush() | Nothing | Flushes the output buffers |
| ob_start() | Nothing | Turns on output buffering |
| ob_get_contents() | String | Returns the contents of the output buffering |
| ob_get_length() | String | Returns the length of the output buffer |
| ob_end_flush() | Nothing | Sends the contents of the output buffer and turns off output buffering |
| ob_end_clean() | Nothing | Erases output buffer and turns off output buffering |
| ob_implicit_flush ([*flag*]) | Nothing | Turns implicit flushing on or off |

# PHP Options and Information

| Function | Returns | Description |
|---|---|---|
| assert(*assertion*) | Integer | Will check if an *assertion* is false |
| assert_options (*what* [,*value*]) | Mixed | Gets or sets the various assert flags |
| dl(*library*) | Integer | Loads the PHP extension *library* at runtime |
| extension_loaded(*name*) | Boolean | Indicates whether the specified extension is loaded |
| get_cfg_var(*var*) | String | Returns the value of the PHP configuration option *var* |
| get_current_user() | String | Returns the name of the owner of the current PHP script |
| get_extension_funcs (*module_name*) | Array | Returns the names of the functions of a module |
| get_included_files() | Array | Returns an associative array of the names of all the files that have been loaded into a script using include_once() |
| get_loaded_extensions() | Array | Returns the names of all modules compiled and loaded |
| get_magic_quotes_gpc() | Long | Returns the current setting for magic_quotes_gpc |
| get_magic_quotes_runtime () | Long | Returns the current setting for magic_quotes_runtime |
| get_required_files() | Array | Returns an associative array of the names of all the files that have been loaded into a script using require_once() |
| getenv(*var*) | String | Returns the value of the specified environment variable |
| getlastmod() | Integer | Returns the time when the page was last modified |
| getmyinode() | Integer | Returns the inode of the current script |
| getmypid() | Integer | Returns the current process ID for PHP |
| getmyuid() | Integer | Returns the user ID for the PHP script's owner |
| getrusage([*who*]) | Array | Returns the current resource usages |

*Table continued on following page*

| Function | Returns | Description |
|----------|---------|-------------|
| ini_alter (*varname*, *newvalue*) | String | Changes the value of a configuration option |
| ini_get (*varname*) | String | Returns the value of a configuration option |
| ini_restore (*varname*) | String | Restores the value of a configuration option |
| ini_set (*varname*, *newvalue*) | String | Sets the value of the specified configuration option |
| php_logo_guid() | String | Returns the logo GUID |
| php_sapi_name() | String | Returns the type of interface between web server and PHP |
| php_uname() | String | Returns information about the operating system that PHP is built on |
| phpcredits(*flag*) | Nothing | Prints out the credits for PHP |
| phpinfo() | Integer | Outputs information about the current state and configuration of PHP |
| phpversion() | String | Returns the current version of PHP |
| putenv(*setting*) | Nothing | Sets the value of an environment variable by adding *setting* to the server environment |
| set_magic_quotes_runtime (*new_setting*) | Long | Enables or disables magic_quotes_runtime |
| set_time_limit(*seconds*) | Nothing | Sets the limit for the maximum length of time that a PHP script can take to execute |
| zend_logo_guid() | String | Returns the Zend GUID |

# POSIX Functions

| Function | Returns | Description |
|----------|---------|-------------|
| posix_ctermid() | String | Returns the path name of the controlling terminal |
| posix_getcwd() | String | Returns the pathname of the current directory |
| posix_getegid() | Integer | Returns the effective group ID of the current process |
| posix_geteuid() | Integer | Returns the effective user ID of the current process |

| Function | Returns | Description |
|---|---|---|
| `posix_getgid()` | Integer | Returns the real group ID of the current process |
| `posix_getgrgid(gid)` | Array | Returns information about a group by group ID |
| `posix_getgrnam(name)` | Array | Returns information about a group by `name` |
| `posix_getgroups()` | Array | Returns the group set of the current process |
| `posix_getlogin()` | String | Returns the login name of the user owning the current process |
| `posix_getpgid(pid)` | Integer | Returns the process group identifier for the process `pid` |
| `posix_getpgrp()` | Integer | Returns the current process group identifier |
| `posix_getpid()` | Integer | Returns the process identifier of the current process |
| `posix_getppid()` | Integer | Returns the parent process identifier of the current process |
| `posix_getpwnam(username)` | Array | Returns information about the user `username` |
| `posix_getpwuid(uid)` | Array | Returns information about a user by user ID |
| `posix_getrlimit()` | Array | Returns information about system resource limits |
| `posix_getsid(pid)` | Integer | Returns the sid of the process `pid` |
| `posix_getuid()` | Integer | Returns the real user ID of the current process |
| `posix_isatty(fd)` | Boolean | Indicates whether the file descriptor `fd` is an interactive terminal |
| `posix_kill(pid, sig)` | Boolean | Sends the signal specified by `sig` to the process specified by `pid` |
| `posix_mkfifo (pathname, mode)` | Boolean | Creates a fifo special file |
| `posix_setgid(gid)` | Boolean | Sets the effective group ID of the current process |
| `posix_setpgid(pid, pgid)` | Integer | Lets the process `pid` join the process group `pgid` |
| `posix_setsid()` | Integer | Makes the current process a session leader |

*Table continued on following page*

| Function | Returns | Description |
|---|---|---|
| posix_setuid(uid) | Boolean | Sets the effective user ID of the current process |
| posix_times() | Array | Returns process times |
| posix_ttyname(fd) | String | Returns the terminal device name |
| posix_uname() | Array | Returns the system name |

# Program Execution Functions

| Function | Returns | Description |
|---|---|---|
| escapeshellarg(arg) | String | Escapes a string to be used as a shell argument |
| escapeshellcmd(command) | String | Escapes shell metacharacters in the specified command |
| Exec (command [,array [,return_var]]) | String | Executes the specified command and returns the last line from the result of that command |
| Passthru (command [,return_var]) | Nothing | Executes the specified command and displays the raw output |
| system(command [,return_var]) | String | Executes the specified command and displays any output |

# Pspell Functions

| Function | Returns | Description |
|---|---|---|
| pspell_add_to_personal (dictionary_link, word) | Integer | Adds the word to a personal wordlist |
| pspell_add_to_session (dictionary_link, word) | Integer | Adds the word to the wordlist in the current session |
| pspell_check (dictionary_link, word) | Boolean | Checks the spelling of a word |
| pspell_clear_session (dictionary_link) | Integer | Clears the current session and makes the current wordlist blank |
| pspell_config_create (language [,spelling [,jargon [,encoding]]]) | Integer | Creates a config used to open a dictionary |

| Function | Returns | Description |
|---|---|---|
| pspell_config_ignore (*dictionary_link*, *n*) | Integer | Ignores words less than *n* characters long |
| pspell_config_mode (*dictionary_link*, *mode*) | Integer | Changes the number of suggestions returned to *mode* |
| pspell_config_personal (*dictionary_link*, *file*) | Integer | Sets a file that contains a personal wordlist |
| pspell_config_repl (*dictionary_link*, *file*) | Integer | Sets a file that contains replacement pairs |
| pspell_config_runtogether (*dictionary_link*, *flag*) | Integer | Considers run-together words as valid compounds |
| pspell_config_save_repl (*dictionary_link*, *flag*) | Integer | Determines whether to save a replacement pairs list along with the wordlist |
| pspell_new (*language* [,*spelling* [,*jargon* [,*encoding* [,*mode*]]]]) | Integer | Loads a new dictionary |
| pspell_new_config(*config*) | Integer | Loads a new dictionary with settings based on a given config |
| pspell_new_personal (*personal*, *language* [,*spelling* [,*jargon* [,*encoding* [,*mode*]]]]) | Integer | Loads a new dictionary with a personal wordlist |
| pspell_save_wordlist (*dictionary_link*) | Integer | Saves the personal wordlist to a file |
| pspell_store_replacement (*dictionary_link*, *misspelled*, *correct*) | Integer | Stores a replacement pair for a word |
| pspell_suggest (*dictionary_link*, *word*) | Array | Suggests an array of spellings for the specified *word* |

# Perl-Compatible Regular Expression Functions

| Function | Returns | Description |
|---|---|---|
| preg_grep(*pattern*, *input*) | Array | Returns an array of the entries from the *input* array that match the *pattern* |
| preg_match(*pattern*, *subject* [,*matches*]) | Integer | Performs a regular expression match for *pattern* in *subject* and will fill *matches* with the result |

*Table continued on following page*

| Function | Returns | Description |
|---|---|---|
| preg_match_all(*pattern*, *subject*, *matches* [,*order*]) | Integer | Performs a global regular expression match, putting the results in *matches* in the order specified by *order* |
| preg_quote(*string* [,*delimiter*]) | String | Puts a backslash in front of every regular expression character in *string*, along with any *delimiter* specified |
| preg_replace(*pattern*, *replacement*, *subject* [,*limit*]) | Mixed | Performs a regular expression search for *pattern* in *subject* and replaces it with *replacement* |
| preg_split(pattern, subject [,*limit* [,*flags*]]) | Array | Splits the specified *string* using the regular expression *pattern* |

# Regular Expression Functions (POSIX Extended)

| Function | Returns | Description |
|---|---|---|
| Ereg (*pattern*, *string* [,*regs*]) | Integer | Searches the specified *string* for matches to the regular expression *pattern*. The matches can be stored in the *regs* array |
| ereg_replace (*pattern*, *replacement*, *string*) | String | Replaces matches to the specified *pattern* in *string* with the *replacement* string |
| Eregi (*pattern*, *string* [,*regs*]) | Integer | Performs a case-insensitive search against *string* for matches to the regular expression *pattern*. The matches can be stored in the *regs* array |
| eregi_replace (*pattern*, *replacement*, *string*) | String | Performs a case-insensitive search and replaces matches to the specified *pattern* in *string* with the *replacement* string |
| Split (*pattern*, *string* [,*limit*]) | Array | Splits the specified *string* into an array using the regular expression *pattern* |
| Spliti (*pattern*, *string*, [*limit*]) | Array | Splits the specified *string* into an array using the regular expression *pattern* and is case-insensitive |
| sql_regcase(*string*) | String | Returns a regular expression for a case-insensitive match of the specified *string* |

# Session Handling Functions

| Function | Returns | Description |
|---|---|---|
| session_cache_limiter ([*cache_limiter*]) | String | Sets or returns the current cache limiter |
| session_decode (*string*) | Boolean | Decodes the specified session data |
| session_destroy() | Boolean | Destroys all session data |
| session_encode() | String | Encodes the data for the current session as a string |
| session_get_cookie_ params() | Array | Returns an array with the current session cookie information |
| session_id([*id*]) | String | Sets or returns the current session ID |
| session_is_registered (*name*) | Boolean | Indicates whether the variable specified by *name* is registered with the current session |
| session_module_name ([*module*]) | String | Sets or returns the name of the current session module |
| session_name([*name*]) | String | Sets or returns the name of the current session |
| session_register (*name* [,...]) | Boolean | Registers one or more variables with the current session |
| session_save_path ([*path*]) | String | Sets or returns the path where data for the current session is saved |
| session_set_cookie_ params(*lifetime* [,*path*] [,*domain*]) | Nothing | Sets the session cookie parameters |
| session_set_save_ handler(*open*, *close*, *read*, *write*, *destroy*, *gc*) | Nothing | Sets user-level session storage function |
| session_start() | Boolean | Initializes a session |
| session_unregister (*name*) | Boolean | Unregisters a session variable |
| session_unset() | Nothing | Frees all session variables |

# String Functions

| Function | Returns | Description |
|---|---|---|
| Addcslashes (*string*, *charlist*) | String | Returns *string* with slashes before characters listed in *charlist* |
| addslashes(*string*) | String | Adds escape slashes to characters in the specified *string* that need to be quoted in database queries |
| bin2hex(*string*) | String | Converts the specified binary data into an ASCII hexadecimal representation |
| chop(*string*) | String | Removes trailing whitespace from the specified *string* |
| chr(*ascii*) | String | Returns the character represented by the specified ASCII code |
| chunk_split (*string* [,*chunklen*] [,*end*]) | String | Splits *string* into smaller chunks by inserting the string *end* every *chunklen* characters |
| convert_cyr_string (*string*, *from*, *to*) | String | Converts the specified *string* from one Cyrillic character set to another |
| count_chars (string, [mode]) | Mixed | Returns information about characters used in a string |
| crc32(*string*) | Integer | Calculates the cyclic redundancy checksum (crc32) polynomial of 32-bit lengths of *string* |
| crypt(*string* [,*salt*]) | String | DES-encrypts the specified *string* using the two-character *salt* |
| echo(*string*) | | Outputs one or more strings |
| Explode (*separator*, *string* [,*limit*]) | Array | Splits the specified *string* into an array containing *limit* entries, using the *separator* parameter as a delimiter |
| flush() | Nothing | Flushes the output buffer |
| get_html_translation_table (*table* [,*quote_styles*]) | String | Returns the translation table used by htmlspecialchars() and htmlentities() |
| get_meta_tags (*filename* [,*use_include_path*]) | Array | Returns an array of all the <META> tag content attributes from the specified file |
| Hebrev (*hebrew_text* [,*max_chars_per_line*]) | String | Converts logical Hebrew text to visual text |

| Function | Returns | Description |
|---|---|---|
| Hebrevc (*hebrew_text* [,*max_chars_per_line*]) | String | Converts logical Hebrew text to visual text with newline conversion |
| Htmlentities (*string* [,*quote_style*]) | String | Converts all applicable characters in *string* into HTML entities |
| Htmlspecialchars (*string* [,*quote_style*]) | String | Converts any special characters in the supplied *string* to HTML entities |
| Implode (*glue*, *pieces*) | String | Joins the *pieces* array into a single string using *glue* as a delimiter |
| Join(*glue*, *pieces*) | String | Joins the *pieces* array into a single string using *glue* as a delimiter |
| Levenshtein(*str1*, *str2*) | Integer | Calculates Levenshtein distance between two strings |
| Ltrim(*string*) | String | Strips whitespace from the beginning of the specified *string* |
| md5(*string*) | String | Calculates the MD5 hash of the specified *string* |
| Metaphone(*str*) | String | Calculates the metaphone key of a string, similar sounding words having the same metaphone key |
| nl2br(*string*) | String | Inserts "<BR>" before all line breaks in the specified *string* |
| ord(string) | Integer | Returns the ASCII value of the first character of the specified *string* |
| Parse_str(*string* [,*arr*]) | Nothing | Parses *string* into variables as if it were a query string, storing variables in the array *arr* if supplied |
| Print(*string*) | | Outputs the specified *string* |
| Printf(*format* [,*args...*]) | Integer | Outputs a formatted string |
| Quoted_printable_decode (*string*) | String | Converts a quoted-printable string to an 8-bit string |
| quotemeta(*string*) | String | Escapes meta characters in the specified *string* |
| rawurldecode(*string*) | String | Decodes URL-encoded strings |
| rawurlencode(*string*) | String | URL-encodes the specified *string* according to RFC1738 |

*Table continued on following page*

| Function | Returns | Description |
|---|---|---|
| rtrim(*string*) | String | Removes trailing whitespace |
| Setlocale (*category*, *locale*) | String | Sets the locale information for functions of the specified *category* |
| Similar_text (*string1*, *string2* [,*percent*]) | Integer | Calculates the similarity between *string1* and *string2* |
| soundex(*string*) | String | Calculates the soundex key of the specified *string*, where similar sounding words have the same soundex key |
| sprintf(*format* [,*args…*]) | String | Returns a formatted string |
| Sscanf (*string*, *format* [,*var1…*]) | Mixed | Parses input from *string* according to *format* |
| str_pad (*input*, *pad_length* [,*pad_string*] [,*pad_type*]) | String | Pads the *string* input to the length of *pad_length* with another string |
| str_repeat (*input*, *multiplier*) | String | Repeats a string *multiplier* times |
| str_replace (*needle*, *replacement*, *haystack*) | String | Replaces all occurrences of *needle* in *haystack* with *replacement* |
| Strcasecmp (*string1*, *string2*) | Integer | Binary safe case-insensitive string comparison |
| Strchr (*haystack*, *needle*) | String | Finds the first occurrence of *needle* in *haystack* |
| Strcmp (*string1*, *string2*) | Integer | Performs a binary safe string comparison |
| Strcspn (*string1*, *string2*) | Integer | Returns the number of characters at the beginning of *string1* which do not match *string2* |
| strip_tags(*string*) | String | Removes HTML and PHP tags from a string |
| Stripcslashes (*string*) | String | Returns a string with C style backslashes stripped off |
| Stripslashes(*string*) | String | Removes escape slashes in the specified *string* |
| stristr(*haystack*, *needle*) | String | Returns all occurrences of *needle* in *haystack* in a case-insensitive manner |

| Function | Returns | Description |
|---|---|---|
| strlen(*string*) | Integer | Returns the length of the specified *string* |
| Strnatcasecmp (*string1*, *string2*) | Integer | Performs a case-insensitive comparison using a "natural order" algorithm |
| Strnatcmp (*string1*, *string2*) | Integer | Compares strings using a "natural order" algorithm |
| Strncmp (*string1*, *string2*, *n*) | Integer | Performs a binary safe string comparison of the first *n* characters |
| strpos(*haystack*, *needle*) | Integer | Returns the numeric position of the first occurrence of *needle* in *haystack* |
| strrchr(*haystack*, *needle*) | String | Returns the end of *haystack* from the last occurrence of *needle* in *haystack* |
| strrev(*string*) | String | Returns the specified *string* in reverse order |
| strrpos(*haystack*, *needle*) | Integer | Finds the numeric position of the last occurrence of *needle* in *haystack* |
| strspn(*string1*, *string2*) | Integer | Returns the number of characters at the beginning of *string1* which match *string2* |
| strstr(*haystack*, *needle*) | String | Returns all of *haystack* from the first occurrence of *needle* to the end |
| strtok(*string1*, *string2*) | String | Tokenizes (breaks down) *string1* into segments separated by *string2* |
| strtolower(*string*) | String | Converts the specified *string* to lower case |
| strtoupper(*string*) | String | Converts the specified *string* to upper case |
| strtr(*string*, *from*, *to*) | String | Replaces all occurrences of each character in the string *from* in *string* with the corresponding character in the string *to* |
| Substr (*string*, *start* [,*length*]) | String | Returns *length* characters in *string* from the position specified by *start* |
| substr_count (*haystack*, *needle*) | Integer | Returns the number of times the substring *needle* occurs in the string *haystack* |

*Table continued on following page*

| Function | Returns | Description |
|---|---|---|
| substr_replace (*string*, *replacement*, *start* [,*length*]) | String | Replaces with *replacement* text within a portion of *string*, starting from *start* for *length* characters |
| trim(*string*) | String | Strips whitespace from the beginning and end of the specified *string* |
| ucfirst(*string*) | String | Converts the first character of the specified *string* to upper case |
| ucwords(*string*) | String | Converts the first character of each word in the specified *string* to upper case |
| wordwrap(*string* [,*width* [,*break* [,*cut*]]]) | String | Wraps a *string* to a given number of characters using a string break character |

# URL Functions

| Function | Returns | Description |
|---|---|---|
| base64_decode(*string*) | String | Decodes the specified base-64 encoded *string* |
| base64_encode(*string*) | String | Base-64 encodes the specified *string* |
| parse_url(*url*) | Array | Parses the specified URL into its separate components |
| rawurldecode(*string*) | String | Decodes the specified URL-encoded *string* |
| rawurlencode(*string*) | String | URL-encodes the specified *string*, replacing every alphanumeric character except -_ and . with a percentage sign and the hex code for the character |
| urldecode(*string*) | String | Decodes the specified URL-encoded *string* |
| urlencode(*string*) | String | URL-encodes the specified *string* |

# Variable Functions

| Function | Returns | Description |
| --- | --- | --- |
| doubleval(*variable*) | Double | Returns the double value of *variable* |
| empty(*variable*) | Integer | Indicates whether *variable* has been set and has a non-zero value |
| gettype(*variable*) | String | Returns the data type of the specified *variable* |
| intval(*variable* [,*base*]) | Integer | Returns the integer value of *variable* using the specified *base* |
| is_array(*variable*) | Boolean | Indicates whether *variable* is an array |
| is_bool(*variable*) | Boolean | Indicates whether *variable* is a boolean |
| is_double(*variable*) | Boolean | Indicates whether *variable* is a double |
| is_float(*variable*) | Boolean | Indicates whether *variable* is a floating point number |
| is_int(*variable*) | Boolean | Indicates whether *variable* is an integer |
| is_integer(*variable*) | Integer | Indicates whether *variable* is an integer |
| is_long(*variable*) | Boolean | Indicates whether *variable* is an integer |
| is_numeric(*variable*) | Boolean | Indicates whether *variable* is a number or a numeric string |
| is_object(*variable*) | Boolean | Indicates whether *variable* is an object |
| is_real(*variable*) | Boolean | Indicates whether *variable* is a real number (double) |
| is_resource(*variable*) | Boolean | Indicates whether *variable* is a resource |
| is_string(*variable*) | Boolean | Indicates whether *variable* is a string |
| isset(*variable*) | Boolean | Indicates whether a value has already been assigned to the specified *variable* |
| print_r(*expression*) | Nothing | Prints human-readable information about a variable |
| serialize(*value*) | String | Generates a storable representation of a *value* |
| settype(*variable*, *type*) | Integer | Converts a *variable* to the specified data *type* |
| strval(*variable*) | String | Returns the string value of the specified *variable* |

*Table continued on following page*

| Function | Returns | Description |
|---|---|---|
| unserialize(*string*) | Mixed | Creates a PHP value from a stored representation |
| unset(*variable*) | Boolean | Destroys the specified variable |
| var_dump(*expression*) | Nothing | Dumps information about an *expression* |

# WDDX Functions

| Function | Returns | Description |
|---|---|---|
| wddx_add_vars (*packet_id*, *variable* [,...]) | Nothing | Serializes the specified variables and adds this string to the packet specified by *packet_id* |
| wddx_deserialize (*packet*) | Mixed | Deserializes a WDDX *packet* |
| wddx_packet_end (*packet_id*) | Integer | Ends the WDDX packet specified by *packet_id* |
| wddx_packet_start ([*comment*]) | Integer | Starts a new WDDX packet |
| wddx_serialize_value (*var* [,*comment*]) | String | Serializes a single value into a WDDX packet |
| wddx_serialize_vars (*var_name* [,...]) | String | Serializes variables into a WDDX packet |

# XML Parser Functions

| Function | Returns | Description |
|---|---|---|
| utf8_decode(*string*) | String | Converts the supplied UTF-8 encoded *string* to ISO-8859-1 |
| utf8_encode(*string*) | String | Encodes the supplied ISO-8859-1 *string* to UTF-8 |
| xml_error_string (*code*) | String | Returns the error message associated with the supplied error *code* |
| xml_get_current_ byte_index(*parser*) | Integer | Returns the current byte index for an XML *parser* |
| xml_get_current_ column_number(*parser*) | Integer | Returns the current column number for the specified *parser* |

| Function | Returns | Description |
|----------|---------|-------------|
| xml_get_current_line _number(*parser*) | Integer | Returns the current line number for the specified *parser* |
| xml_get_error_code (*parser*) | Integer | Returns the error code for the last occurring XML parser error |
| xml_parse (*parser*, *data* [,*is_final*]) | Boolean | Parses the specified *data* |
| xml_parse_into_struct (*parser*, *data*, *values*, *index*) | Integer | Parses XML *data* into an array structure of two arrays, *values* and *index* |
| xml_parser_create ([*encoding*]) | Integer | Creates an XML parser |
| xml_parser_free (*parser*) | Boolean | Frees the specified XML *parser* |
| xml_parser_get_option (*parser*, *option*) | Mixed | Returns the value for the specified *option* for the specified *parser* |
| xml_parser_set_option (*parser*, *option*, *value*) | Boolean | Sets the *option* for an XML *parser* to the specified *value* |
| xml_set_character_ data_handler(*parser*, *handler*) | Integer | Registers the character data handler |
| xml_set_default_ handler(*parser*, *handler*) | Boolean | Registers the default handler |
| xml_set_element_ handler(*parser*, *start_element_handler*, *end_element_handler*) | Integer | Registers the start and end element handlers |
| xml_set_external_ entity_ref_handler (*parser*, *handler*) | Integer | Registers the external entity reference handler |
| xml_set_notation_ decl_handler(*parser*, *handler*) | Boolean | Registers the notation declaration handler |
| xml_set_object (*parser*, *object*) | Nothing | Allows the use of XML *parser* inside *object* |
| xml_set_processing_ instruction_handler (*parser*, *handler*) | Integer | Registers the processing instruction handler |
| xml_set_unparsed_entity_ decl_handler(*parser*, *handler*) | Boolean | Registers the unparsed entity declaration handler |

# Zlib Functions

| Function | Returns | Description |
|---|---|---|
| gzclose(*zp*) | Boolean | Closes an open gz-file pointer |
| Gzcompress (*data* [,*level*]) | String | Returns a gzip-compressed version of *data* |
| gzeof(*zp*) | Boolean | Test for end-of-file on a gz-file pointer |
| Gzfile (*filename* [,*use_include_path*]) | Array | Reads an entire gz-file into an array |
| gzgetc(*zp*) | String | Returns a character from gz-file pointer |
| gzgets(*zp*, *length*) | String | Returns a line from gz-file pointer up to *length*-1 bytes |
| Gzgetss (*zp*, *length* [,*allowable_tags*]) | String | Returns a line from gz-pointer and strips any HTML and PHP tags not in *allowable_tags* |
| Gzopen (*filename*, *mode* [,*use_include_path*]) | Integer | Opens a gz-file |
| gzpassthru(*zp*) | Integer | Outputs all remaining data on a gz-file pointer |
| Gzputs (*zp*, *string* [,*length*]) | Integer | Writes to a gz-file pointer |
| gzread(*zp*, *length*) | String | Binary-safe gz-file read; reads up to *length* bytes from *zp* |
| gzrewind(*zp*) | Integer | Rewinds the position of a gz-file pointer to the beginning of the file stream |
| gzseek(*zp*, *offset*) | Integer | Seeks on a gz-file pointer |
| gztell(*zp*) | Integer | Returns the position of the gz-file pointer *zp* |
| Gzuncompress (*data* [,*length*]) | String | Uncompresses a gz-compressed string |
| Gzwrite (*zp*, *string* [,*length*]) | Integer | Binary-safe gz-file write |
| Readgzfile (*filename* [,*use_include_path*]) | Integer | Outputs a gz-file |

# Index

## Functions Index

### A

abs() function, 722
acos() function, 722
addcslashes() function, 734
addslashes() function, 451, 641, 734
apache_lookup_uri() function, 683
apache_note() function, 683
array() function, 166, 683
array_count_values() function, 683
array_diff() function, 684
array_flip() function, 684
array_intersect() function, 684
array_keys() function, 684
array_merge() function, 684
array_merge_recursive() function, 684
array_multisort() function, 188, 684
array_pad() function, 684
array_pop() function, 180, 353, 684
array_push() function, 180, 467, 684
array_rand() function, 684
array_reverse() function, 684
array_shift() function, 685
array_slice() function, 685
array_unique() function, 685
array_unshift() function, 685
array_values() function, 685
array_walk() function, 685
arsort() function, 179, 685
asin() function, 722
aspell_check() function, 687
aspell_check-raw() function, 687
aspell_new() function, 687
aspell_suggest() function, 687
assert() function, 727
assert_options() function, 727
atan() function, 722
atan2() function, 722

### B

base_convert() function, 722
base64_decode() function, 738
base64_encode() function, 738
basename() function, 347, 365, 713
bin2hex() function, 734
bindec() function, 722

### C

call_user_func() function, 717
call_user_method() function, 688
ceil() function, 722
chdir() function, 359, 711
checkdate() function, 710
checkdnsrr() function, 725
chgrp() function, 713
chmod() function, 713
chop() function, 734
chown() function, 713
chr() function, 734
chunk_split() function, 530, 734
class_exists() function, 688
clearstatcache() function, 713
closedir() function, 358, 711
closelog() function, 725
compact() function, 685
connection_aborted() function, 724
connection_status() function, 724
connection_timeout() function, 724
convert_cyr_string() function, 734
copy() function, 347, 713
cos() function, 722
count() function, 433, 624, 656, 685
crc32() function, 734
create_function() function, 717
crypt() function, 635, 641, 734
curl_close() function, 689
curl_exec() function, 689
curl_init() function, 689
curl_setopt() function, 689
curl_version() function, 689
current() function, 173, 685

# D

date() function, 710
dba_close() function, 689
dba_delete() function, 689
dba_exists() function, 690
dba_fetch() function, 690
dba_firstkey() function, 690
dba_insert() function, 690
dba_nextkey() function, 690
dba_open() function, 690
dba_optimize() function, 690
dba_popen() function, 690
dba_replace() function, 690
dba_sync() function, 690
dbase_add_record() function, 690
dbase_close() function, 690
dbase_create() function, 691
dbase_delete_record() function, 691
dbase_get_record() function, 691
dbase_get_record_with_names() function, 691
dbase_numfields() function, 691
dbase_numrecords() function, 691
dbase_open() function, 691
dbase_pack() function, 691
dbase_replace_record() function, 691
dblist() function, 691
dbmclose() function, 691
dbmdelete() function, 691
dbmexists() function, 691
dbmfetch() function, 692
dbmfirstkey() function, 692
dbminsert() function, 692
dbmnextkey() function, 692
dbmopen() function, 692
dbmreplace() function, 692
debugger_off() function, 725
debugger_on() function, 725
decbin() function, 722
dechex() function, 722
decoct() function, 722
define() function, 724
define_syslog_variables() function, 725
defined() function, 724
deg2rad() function, 722
die() function, 404, 724
dir() function, 711
dirname() function, 360, 480, 713
diskfreespace() function, 713
dl() function, 727
doubleval() function, 739

# E

each() function, 175–76, 685
easter_date() function, 687
easter_days() function, 687
echo() command, 42, 734
empty() function, 68, 739
end() function, 685
ereg() function, 244, 366, 732
eregi() function, 466, 732
eregi_replace() function, 466, 732
error_log() function, 257, 712

error_reporting() function, 404, 406, 712
escapeshellarg() function, 730
escapeshellcmd() function, 730
eval() function, 724
exec() function, 730
exit() function, 724
exp() function, 722
explode() function, 180–81, 353, 467, 734
extension_loaded() function, 727
extract() function, 686
ezmlm_hash() function, 722

# F

fclose() function, 327, 334, 713
fdf_close() function, 716
fdf_create() function, 716
fdf_get_field_name() function, 717
fdf_get_file() function, 716
fdf_get_status() function, 716
fdf_get_value() function, 716
fdf_open() function, 717
fdf_save() function, 717
fdf_set_ap() function, 717
fdf_set_file() function, 717
fdf_set_flags() function, 717
fdf_set_javascript_action() function, 717
fdf_set_opt() function, 717
fdf_set_status() function, 717
fdf_set_submit_form_action() function, 717
fdf_set_value() function, 717
feof() function, 331, 713
fgetc() function, 331, 713
fgetcsv() function, 713
fgets() function, 332, 713
fgetss() function, 713
file() function, 333, 713
file_exists() function, 339, 713
fileatime() function, 340, 714
filectime() function, 340, 714
filegroup() function, 343, 714
fileinode() function, 714
filemtime() function, 340, 714
fileowner() function, 343, 714
fileperms() function, 714
filesize() function, 339, 714
filetype() function, 343, 714
flock() function, 714
floor() function, 722
flush() function, 726, 734
fopen() function, 325–27, 714
fpassthru() function, 334, 714
fputs() function, 333, 714
fread() function, 327, 714
frenchtojd() function, 687
fscanf() function, 714
fseek() function, 335, 714
fsockopen() function, 725
fstat() function, 714
ftell() function, 335, 715
ftruncate() function, 715
func_get_arg() function, 718
func_get_args() function, 718
func_num_args() function, 718
function_exists() function, 718
fwrite() function, 327, 715

# G

get_browser() function, 724
get_cfg_var() function, 727
get_class() function, 688
get_class_methods() function, 688
get_class_vars() function, 689
get_current_user() function, 727
get_declared_classes() function, 689
get_extension_funcs() function, 727
get_html_translation_table() function, 734
get_included_files() function, 727
get_loaded_extensions() function, 727
get_magic_quotes_gpc() function, 727
get_magic_quotes_runtime() function, 727
get_meta_tags() function, 734
get_object_vars() function, 689
get_parent_class() function, 689
get_required_files() function, 727
getallheaders() function, 683
getcwd() function, 712
getdate() function, 340, 711
getenv() function, 727
gethostbyaddr() function, 725
gethostbyname() function, 725
gethostbynamel() function, 725
getimagesize() function, 718
getlastmod() function, 727
getmxrr() function, 725
getmyinode() function, 727
getmypid() function, 727
getmyuid() function, 727
getprotobyname() function, 725
getprotobynumber() function, 725
getrandmax() function, 723
getrusage() function, 727
getservbyname() function, 725
getservbyport() function, 726
gettimeofday() function, 711
gettype() function, 67, 739
gmdate() function, 42, 711
gmmktime() function, 711
gmstrftime() function, 711
gregoriantojd() function, 688
gzclose() function, 742
gzcompress() function, 742
gzeof() function, 742
gzfile() function, 742
gzgetc() function, 742
gzgets() function, 742
gzgetss() function, 742
gzopen() function, 742
gzpassthru() function, 742
gzputs() function, 742
gzread() function, 742
gzrewind() function, 742
gzseek() function, 742
gztell() function, 742
gzuncompress() function, 742
gzwrite() function, 742

# H

Header() function, 718
header_sent() function, 364, 560, 718
hebrev() function, 734
hebrevc() function, 735
hexdec() function, 723
highlight_file() function, 724
highlight_string() function, 724
htmlentities() function, 735
htmlspecialchars() function, 143–44, 735

# I

ibase_close() function, 694
ibase_connect() function, 694
ibase_execute() function, 694
ibase_fetch_object() function, 694
ibase_fetch_row() function, 695
ibase_free_query() function, 695
ibase_free_result() function, 695
ibase_num_fields() function, 695
ibase_pconnect() function, 695
ibase_prepare() function, 695
ibase_query() function, 695
ibase_timefmt() function, 695
ifx_affected_rows() function, 692
ifx_blobinfile_mode() function, 692
ifx_byteasvarchar() function, 692
ifx_close() function, 692
ifx_close_slob() function, 694
ifx_connect() function, 692
ifx_copy_blob() function, 692
ifx_create_blob() function, 692
ifx_create_char() function, 692
ifx_create_slob() function, 694
ifx_do() function, 692
ifx_error() function, 692
ifx_errormsg() function, 692
ifx_fetch_row() function, 693
ifx_fieldproperties() function, 693
ifx_fieldtypes() function, 693
ifx_free_blob() function, 693
ifx_free_char() function, 693
ifx_free_result() function, 693
ifx_free_slob() function, 693
ifx_get_blob() function, 693
ifx_get_char() function, 693
ifx_getsqlca() function, 693
ifx_htmltbl_result() function, 693
ifx_nullformat() function, 693
ifx_num_fields() function, 693
ifx_num_rows() function, 693
ifx_open_slob() function, 694
ifx_pconnect() function, 693
ifx_prepare() function, 693
ifx_query() function, 694
ifx_read_slob() function, 694
ifx_seek_slob() function, 694
ifx_tell_slob() function, 694
ifx_textasvarchar() function, 694
ifx_update_blob() function, 694
ifx_update_char() function, 694

ifx_write_slob() function, 694
ignore_user_abort() function, 724
imagearc() function, 560, 718
imagechar() function, 718
imagecharup() function, 718
imagecolorallocate() function, 557, 587, 589, 718
ImageColorAt() function, 587, 719
ImageColorClosest() function, 589, 719
imagecolordeallocate() function, 719
ImageColorExact() function, 719
imagecolorresolve() function, 719
imagecolorset() function, 589, 719
ImageColorsForIndex() function, 588, 719
ImageColorsTotal() function, 590, 719
ImageColorTransparent() function, 587, 719
imagecopy() function, 719
ImageCopyResized() function, 581, 586, 719
ImageCreate() function, 556, 719
imagecreatefromgif() function, 719
imagecreatefromjpeg() function, 719
ImageCreateFromPNG() function, 577, 719
imagedashedline() function, 719
ImageDestroy() function, 560, 720
ImageFill() function, 578, 720
imagefilledpolygon() function, 720
imagefilledrectangle() function, 720
imagefilltoborder() function, 720
imagefontheight() function, 720
imagefontwidth() function, 720
imagegammacorrect() function, 720
imagegif() function, 720
imageinterlace() function, 720
ImageJPEG() function, 559, 720
ImageLine() function, 558, 720
imageloadfont() function, 720
imagepng() function, 720
imagepolygon() function, 720
imagepsbbox() function, 720
imagepsencodefont() function, 720
imagepsextendfont() function, 721
imagepsfreefont() function, 721
imagepsloadfont() function, 721
imagepsslantfont() function, 721
imagepstext() function, 721
ImageRectangle() function, 562–63, 721
imagesetpixel() function, 721
ImageString() function, 578, 721
imagestringup() function, 721
ImageSX() function, 586, 721
ImageSY() function, 586, 721
imagettfbbox() function, 721
imagettftext() function, 721
imagetypes() function, 721
implode() function, 180–81, 354, 517, 735
in_array() function, 686
ini_alter() function, 728
ini_get() function, 728
ini_restore() function, 728
ini_set() function, 728
intval() function, 739
ip2long() function, 726
iptcparse() function, 724
is_arrayl() function, 739
is_bool() function, 739
is_dir() function, 344, 715

is_double() function, 739
is_file() function, 344, 715
is_float() function, 739
is_int() function, 739
is_integer() function, 739
is_link() function, 715
is_long() function, 739
is_numeric() function, 739
is_object() function, 739
is_readable() function, 715
is_real() function, 739
is_resource() function, 739
is_string() function, 739
is_subclass_of() function, 689
is_uploaded_file() function, 715
is_writeable() function, 715
isset() function, 68, 739

## J

jddayofweek() function, 688
jdmonthname() function, 688
jdtofrench() function, 688
jdtogregorian() function, 688
jdtojewish() function, 688
jdtojulian() function, 688
jdtounix() function, 688
jewishtojd() function, 688
join() function, 735
juliantojd() function, 688

## K

key() function, 173, 686
krsort() function, 686
ksort() function, 179, 686

## L

lcg_value() function, 723
leak() function, 724
levenshtein() function, 735
link() function, 715
linkinfo() function, 715
list() function, 175–76, 686
localtime() function, 711
log() function, 723
log10() function, 723
long2ip() function, 726
lstat() function, 715
ltrim() function, 735

## M

mail() function, 515, 722
max() function, 432, 723
md5() function, 529, 735
metaphone() function, 735
method_exists() function, 689
microtime() function, 711
min() function, 433, 723
mkdir() function, 360, 715
mktime() function, 711
move_uploaded_file() function, 715

msql() function, 696
msql_affected_rows() function, 697
msql_close() function, 697
msql_connect() function, 697
msql_create_db() function, 697
msql_createdb() function, 697
msql_data_seek() function, 697
msql_dbname() function, 697
msql_drop_db() function, 697
msql_dropdb() function, 697
msql_error() function, 697
msql_fetch_array() function, 697
msql_fetch_field() function, 697
msql_fetch_object() function, 697
msql_fetch_row() function, 697
msql_fetch_seek() function, 697
msql_fieldflags() function, 697
msql_fieldlen() function, 697
msql_fieldname() function, 697
msql_fieldtable() function, 698
msql_fieldtype() function, 698
msql_free_result() function, 698
msql_freeresult() function, 698
msql_list_dbs() function, 698
msql_list_fields() function, 698
msql_list_tables() function, 698
msql_listdbs() function, 698
msql_listfields() function, 698
msql_listtables() function, 698
msql_num_fields() function, 698
msql_num_rows() function, 698
msql_numfields() function, 698
msql_numrows() function, 698
msql_pconnect() function, 698
msql_query() function, 698
msql_regcase() function, 698
msql_result() function, 699
msql_select_db() function, 699
msql_selectdb() function, 699
msql_tablename() function, 699
mssql_close() function, 695
mssql_connect() function, 695
mssql_data_seek() function, 695
mssql_fetch_array() function, 695
mssql_fetch_field() function, 695
mssql_fetch_length() function, 696
mssql_fetch_name() function, 696
mssql_fetch_object() function, 695
mssql_fetch_row() function, 696
mssql_fetch_seek() function, 696
mssql_fetch_type() function, 696
mssql_free_result() function, 696
mssql_get_last_message() function, 696
mssql_min_error_severity() function, 696
mssql_min_message_severity() function, 696
mssql_num_fields() function, 696
mssql_num_rows() function, 696
mssql_pconnect() function, 696
mssql_query() function, 696
mssql_result() function, 696
mssql_select_db() function, 696
mt_getrandmax() function, 723
mt_rand() function, 723
mt_srand() function, 723
mysql_affected_rows() function, 401, 454, 699
mysql_change_user() function, 699

mysql_close() function, 400, 699
mysql_connect() function, 400, 538, 699
mysql_create_db() function, 412, 699
mysql_data_seek() function, 426, 699
mysql_db_name() function, 699
mysql_db_query() function, 412, 699
mysql_drop_db() function, 412, 699
mysql_errno() function, 404, 699
mysql_error() function, 404, 699
mysql_fetch_array() function, 424, 612, 700
mysql_fetch_field() function, 461, 700
mysql_fetch_lengths() function, 700
mysql_fetch_object() function, 424, 700
mysql_fetch_row() function, 402, 700
mysql_field_flags() function, 459, 700
mysql_field_len() function, 459, 700
mysql_field_name() function, 459, 700
mysql_field_seek() function, 700
mysql_field_table() function, 700
mysql_field_type() function, 459, 700
mysql_free_result() function, 700
mysql_insert_id() function, 450, 700
mysql_list_dbs() function, 400, 700
mysql_list_fields() function, 458, 700
mysql_list_tables() function, 401, 700
mysql_num_fields() function, 458, 700
mysql_num_rows() function, 401, 444, 701
mysql_pconnect() function, 701
mysql_query() function, 411, 412, 701
mysql_result() function, 425, 701
mysql_select_db() function, 401, 414, 538, 701

# N

natcasesort() function, 686
natsort() function, 686
next() function, 173–75, 686
nl2br() function, 735
number_format() function, 627, 723

# O

ob_end_clean() function, 726
ob_end_flush() function, 726
ob_get_contents() function, 726
ob_get_length() function, 726
ob_implicit_flush() function, 726
ob_start() function, 726
OCIBindByName() function, 704
OCIColumnIsNULL() function, 704
OCIColumnName() function, 704
OCIColumnSize() function, 704
OCIColumnType() function, 704
OCICommit() function, 704
OCIDefineByName() function, 704
OCIError() function, 704
OCIExecute() function, 704
OCIFetch() function, 704
OCIFetchInto() function, 704
OCIFetchStatement() function, 705
OCIFreeCursor() function, 705
OCIFreeStatement() function, 705
OCIInternalDebug() function, 705
OCILogOff() function, 705
OCILogon() function, 705

OCINewCursor() function, 705
OCINewDescriptor() function, 705
OCINLogon() function, 705
OCINumCols() function, 705
OCIPLogon() function, 705
OCIResult() function, 705
OCIRollback() function, 705
OCIRowCount() function, 705
OCIServerVersion() function, 705
OCIStatementType() function, 705
odbc_autocommit() function, 701
odbc_binmode() function, 701
odbc_close() function, 701
odbc_close_all() function, 701
odbc_columnprivileges() function, 701
odbc_columns() function, 701
odbc_commit() function, 701
odbc_connect() function, 674, 702
odbc_cursor() function, 702
odbc_do() function, 674, 702
odbc_exec() function, 674, 702
odbc_execute() function, 702
odbc_fetch_into() function, 676, 702
odbc_fetch_row() function, 702
odbc_field_len() function, 676, 702
odbc_field_name() function, 675, 702
odbc_field_num() function, 675, 702
odbc_field_precision() function, 702
odbc_field_scale() function, 702
odbc_foreignkeys() function, 702
odbc_free_result() function, 702
odbc_gettypeinfo() function, 703
odbc_longreadlen() function, 703
odbc_num_fields() function, 675, 703
odbc_num_rows() function, 675, 703
odbc_pconnect() function, 703
odbc_prepare() function, 703
odbc_primarykeys() function, 703
odbc_procedurecolumns() function, 703
odbc_procedures() function, 703
odbc_result() function, 676, 703
odbc_result_all() function, 678, 703
odbc_rollback() function, 703
odbc_setoption() function, 703
odbc_specialcolumns() function, 703
odbc_statistics() function, 704
odbc_tableprivileges() function, 675, 704
odbc_tables() function, 675, 704
opendir() function, 358, 712
openlog() function, 726
ora_bind() function, 706
ora_close() function, 706
ora_columnname() function, 706
ora_columnsize() function, 706
ora_columntype() function, 706
ora_commit() function, 706
ora_commitoff() function, 706
ora_commiton() function, 706
ora_do() function, 706
ora_error() function, 706
ora_errorcode() function, 706
ora_exec() function, 706
ora_fetch() function, 706
ora_fetch_into() function, 706
ora_getcolumn() function, 706
ora_logoff() function, 706

ora_logon() function, 706
ora_numcols() function, 706
ora_numrows() function, 707
ora_open() function, 707
ora_parse() function, 707
ora_plogon() function, 707
ora_rollback() function, 707
ord() function, 735

## P

pack() function, 724
parse_str() function, 735
parse_url() function, 738
passthru() function, 730
pclose() function, 715
pfsockopen() function, 726
pg_client_encoding() function, 707
pg_close() function, 707
pg_cmdtuples() function, 707
pg_connect() function, 707
pg_dbname() function, 707
pg_end_copy() function, 707
pg_errormessage() function, 707
pg_exec() function, 707
pg_fetch_array() function, 707
pg_fetch_object() function, 707
pg_fetch_row() function, 707
pg_fieldisnull() function, 708
pg_fieldname() function, 708
pg_fieldnum() function, 708
pg_fieldprtlen() function, 708
pg_fieldsize() function, 708
pg_fieldtype() function, 708
pg_freeresult() function, 708
pg_getlastoid() function, 708
pg_host() function, 708
pg_loclose() function, 708
pg_locreate() function, 708
pg_loexport() function, 708
pg_loimport() function, 708
pg_loopen() function, 708
pg_loread() function, 708
pg_loreadall() function, 708
pg_lounlink() function, 708
pg_lowrite() function, 709
pg_numfields() function, 709
pg_numrows() function, 709
pg_options() function, 709
pg_pconnect() function, 709
pg_port() function, 709
pg_put_line() function, 709
pg_result() function, 709
pg_set_client_encoding() function, 709
pg_trace() function, 709
pg_tty() function, 709
pg_untrace() function, 709
php_logo_guid() function, 728
php_sapi_name() function, 728
php_uname() function, 728
phpcredits() function, 728
phpinfo() function, 68, 728
phpversion() function, 728
pi() function, 723
popen() function, 715

pos() function, 686
posix_ctermid() function, 728
posix_getcwd() function, 728
posix_getegid() function, 728
posix_geteuid() function, 728
posix_getgid() function, 729
posix_getgrgid() function, 343, 729
posix_getgrnam() function, 729
posix_getgroups() function, 729
posix_getlogin() function, 729
posix_getpgid() function, 729
posix_getpgrp() function, 729
posix_getpid() function, 729
posix_getppid() function, 729
posix_getpwnam() function, 729
posix_getpwuid() function, 342, 729
posix_getrlimit() function, 729
posix_getsid() function, 729
posix_getuid() function, 729
posix_isatty() function, 729
posix_kill() function, 729
posix_mkfifo() function, 729
posix_setgid() function, 729
posix_setpgid() function, 729
posix_setsid() function, 729
posix_setuid() function, 730
posix_times() function, 730
posix_ttyname() function, 730
posix_uname() function, 730
pow() function, 723
preg_grep() function, 731
preg_match() function, 731
preg_match_all() function, 732
preg_quote() function, 732
preg_replace() function, 732
preg_split() function, 732
prev() function, 686, 173–75
print() function, 735
print_r() function, 739
printf() function, 735
pspell_add_to_personal() function, 730
pspell_add_to_session() function, 730
pspell_check() function, 730
pspell_clear_session() function, 730
pspell_config_create() function, 730
pspell_config_ignore() function, 731
pspell_config_mode() function, 731
pspell_config_personal() function, 731
pspell_config_repl() function, 731
pspell_config_runtogether() function, 731
pspell_config_save_repl() function, 731
pspell_new() function, 731
pspell_new_config() function, 731
pspell_new_personal() function, 731
pspell_save_wordlist() function, 731
pspell_store_replacement() function, 731
pspell_suggest() function, 731
putenv() function, 728

## Q

quoted_printable_decode() function, 735
quotemeta() function, 735

## R

rad2deg() function, 723
rand() function, 113, 723
range() function, 686
rawurldecode() function, 735, 738
rawurlencode() function, 738
read_exif_data() function, 721
readdir() function, 358, 712
readfile() function, 334, 716
readgzfile() function, 742
readlink() function, 716
realpath() function, 716
register_shutdown_function() function, 718
rename() function, 347-49, 716
reset() function, 686
restore_error_handler() function, 712
rewind() function, 336, 716
rewinddir() function, 359, 712
rmdir() function, 360, 716
round() function, 723
rsort() function, 179, 686
rtrim() function, 736

## S

serialize() function, 739
session_cache_limiter() function, 733
session_decode() function, 733
session_destroy() function, 733
session_encode() function, 733
session_get_cookie_params() function, 733
session_id() function, 733
session_is_registered() function, 733
session_module_name() function, 733
session_name() function, 733
session_register() function, 288, 733
session_save_path() function, 733
session_set_cookie_params() function, 733
session_set_save_handler() function, 733
session_start() function, 733
session_unregister() function, 733
session_unset() function, 733
set_error_handler() function, 712
set_file_buffer() function, 716
set_magic_quotes_runtime() function, 728
set_time_limit() function, 728
setcookie() function, 281, 718
setlocale() function, 736
settype() function, 67, 739
show_source() function, 724
shuffle() function, 686
similar_text() function, 736
sin() function, 723
sleep() function, 724
socket_set_blocking() function, 726
socket_set_timeout() function, 726
sort() function, 177, 359, 687
soundex() function, 736
split() function, 732
spliti() function, 732
sprintf() function, 736
sql_regcase() function, 732
sqrt() function, 723
srand() function, 723

sscanf() function, 736
stat() function, 716
str_pad() function, 736
str_repeat() function, 736
str_replace() function, 524, 736
strcasecmp() function, 736
strchr() function, 736
strcmp() function, 736
strcspn() function, 736
strftime() function, 711
strip_tags() function, 524, 736
stripcslashes() function, 736
stripslashes() function, 451, 736
stristr() function, 736
strlen() function, 611, 737
strnatcasecmp() function, 737
strnatcmp() function, 737
strncmp() function, 737
strpos() function, 737
strrchr() function, 737
strrev() function, 737
strrpos() function, 737
strspn() function, 737
strstr() function, 737
strtok() function, 737
strtolower() function, 737
strtotime() function, 711
strtoupper() function, 737
strtr() function, 737
strval() function, 739
substr() function, 427, 613, 737
substr_count() function, 737
substr_replace() function, 738
sybase_affected_rows() function, 709
sybase_close() function, 709
sybase_connect() function, 709
sybase_data_seek() function, 710
sybase_fetch_array() function, 710
sybase_fetch_field() function, 710
sybase_fetch_object() function, 710
sybase_fetch_row() function, 710
sybase_field_seek() function, 710
sybase_free_result() function, 710
sybase_num_fields() function, 710
sybase_num_rows() function, 710
sybase_pconnect() function, 710
sybase_query() function, 710
sybase_result() function, 710
sybase_select_db() function, 710
symlink() function, 716
syslog() function, 726
system() function, 730

## T

tan() function, 723
tempnam() function, 716
time() function, 284, 529, 711
tmpfile() function, 716
touch() function, 716
trigger_error() function, 712
trim() function, 517, 738

## U

uasort() function, 687
ucfirst() function, 357, 738
ucwords() function, 738
uksort() function, 687
umask() function, 716
uniqid() function, 529, 725
unixtojd() function, 688
unlink() function, 348–49, 716
unpack() function, 725
unserialize() function, 740
unset() function, 68, 740
urldecode() function, 738
urlencode() function, 577, 738
user_error() function, 712
usleep() function, 725
usort() function, 687
utf8_decode() function, 740
utf8_encode() function, 740

## V

var_dump() function, 740
virtual() function, 683

## W

wddx_add_vars() function, 740
wddx_deserialize() function, 740
wddx_packet_end() function, 740
wddx_packet_start() function, 740
wddx_serialize_value() function, 740
wddx_serialize_vars() function, 740
wordwrap() function, 738

## X

xml_error_string() function, 740
xml_get_current_byte_index() function, 740
xml_get_current_column_number() function, 740
xml_get_current_line_number() function, 741
xml_get_error_code() function, 741
xml_parse() function, 502, 741
xml_parse_into_struct() function, 741
xml_parser_create() function, 502, 741
xml_parser_free() function, 502, 741
xml_parser_get_option() function, 741
xml_parser_set_option() function, 741
xml_set_character_data_handler() function, 502, 741
xml_set_default_handler() function, 741
xml_set_element_handler() function, 502, 741
xml_set_external_entity_ref_handler() function, 741
xml_set_notation_decl_handler() function, 741
xml_set_object() function, 741
xml_set_processing_instruction_handler() function, 741
xml_set_unparsed_entity_decl_handler() function, 741
xmldoc() function, 712
xmldocfile() function, 712
xmltree() function, 712

## Z

zend_logo_guid() function, 728

# Index

## A Guide to the Index

The index is arranged hierarchically, in alphabetical order, with symbols preceding the letter A. Most second-level entries and many third-level entries also occur as first-level entries. This is to ensure that users will find the information they require however they choose to search for it.

## Symbols

$ (dollar sign), 52
& (ampersand)
  passing variables by reference, 307
. (period), 56
.= operator, 614
@ notation for suppressing error messages, 257
[ ] (square brackets), arrays, 165–67
++ increment operator, 160
< (less than character), using within tags, 498
<= (less than equals operator), 105
7bit encoding, 527
8bit encoding, 527

## A

<A> tag
  TARGET attribute, 372
absolute paths, 326
Access databases
  ODBC handling of, 670
access_log table example, 410
  creating, 411
  populating, 420
accessor methods, 304
  passing variables by reference, 307–11
  passing variables by value, 307–11
  variables in multiple instances of a class, 306
  variables that belong to a class, referring to within
    functions, 313
ACTION attribute
  <FORM> tag, 72
actions
  reporting results of with alert() method, 520
add_category() function
  URL directory manager case study, 651
add_category_form() function
  URL directory manager case study, 649–51
add_url() function
  URL directory manager case study, 634–37
add_url_form() function
  URL directory manager case study, 630, 631–34

addition operator, 59
  replaces spaces in name/value pairs, 74
  URL encoding, 75
addslashes() function, 451, 641, 734
admin_mailer.php
  newsletter mailing list manager, 544–52
administration scripts, newsletters, 544–52
  where to place, 601
administrators
  authentication of, 602
  determining if current user is, 619
  of directory managers, 595
aggregate functions, MySQL, 432–33
  applying to specific groups of records, 434
alert() method
  reporting errors, 350, 520
  reporting results of actions, 520
aliases, 434, 486
  accessing virtual fields using, 489
ALT attribute
  <IMG> element, 579
ALTER statement, 392
ALTER TABLE command, 415–17
anchors, 246
AND logical operator, 119, 430
Apache, 28–36
  configuring, 32
  configuring and starting with PHP4, 31–34
  finding, 31
  htdocs directory, 32
  httpd.conf file, 32
  information gathering, 32
  running PHP scripts on, 33
  starting, 33
Apache web server, 44
  PHP functions, 683
<AREA> tag, 579
  shape attribute, 580
arguments, 194
  default parameter values
    pitfalls of, 206
    setting, 204
  errors, 236
  functions, 203–6
  parameter order, 204–5
  passing by reference, 203
  passing by value, 203

**arithmetic operators.** *See* **mathematical operators**
**array data type, 55**
**array() function, 166, 683**
  multi-dimensional arrays, 182–83
**array_multisort() function, 188**
**array_pop() function, 180, 353, 684**
**array_push() function, 180, 467, 684**
**arrays, 165–88.** *See also* **loops; code**
  array_pop() function, 180
  array_push() function, 180
  arsort() function, 179
  asort() function, 178
  associative arrays, 165
    iterating through, 176–77
    returning, 424
    sorting, 178
    sorting according to the index, 179
  check boxes, creating with, 88
  contents of, displaying, 175–76
  correspondence between two, 168–72
  current() function, 173
  data types, assigning to values in, 165
  each() function, 175–76
  elements
    adding, 180
    removing, 180
  explode() function, 180–81
  filling, 612
  functions, 180
  HTTP_GET_VARS, 182
  HTTP_POST_VARS, 182
    using for persistence, 269–72
  implode() function, 180–81
  indexes, 95, 165
    explicit values, 166
    linking several through, 168–72
    linking several after one has been sorted, 186
    passing information on between pages, 171
    setting first index value, 166
  initializing, 165–67
  iterating through, 167–77
  key() function, 173
  ksort() function, 179
  list() function, 175–76
  listboxes, creating with, 94
  listboxes, populating, 170
  loops, using with, 167–77
  multi-dimensional, 182–83
  multisorting, 188
  navigating through, 173–75
  next() function, 173–75
  non-sequential
    iterating through, 172
  persistence, 276
  PHP functions, 683
  placing strings into, 180–81
  pointers, 173
  prev() function, 173–75
  pushing items into, 180
  returned by queries, 391
  rsort() function, 179
  sort() function, 177
  sorting, 177–79
    in reverse alphabetical order, 179
  storing contents of as a string, 180–81
  string-indexed, iterating through, 176–77
  text boxes, retrieving contents of, 182
  using, 183–88
  variables, assigning to values in, 165

**arsort() function, 179, 685**
**AS keyword, 415**
**asort() function, 178, 685**
**assignment operator, 116**
**associative arrays, 165**
  indexing, 167
  iterating through, 176–77
  returning, 424
  sorting, 178
  sorting according to the index, 179
  using, 172
**attachments, e-mail, 525–36**
  attaching files, 529–32
  encoding file contents as long string, 530
**ATTLIST declaration, XML, 501**
**attributes, database fields, 408**
    returning, 459
**attributes, XML, 496**
  quotes, using consistently, 498
**authentication**
  administrators, 602
  function for, 477
  users, 474, 595
**AUTO_INCREMENT fields, 408**
**auto_prepend_file, 478**
**avg() function, 433**

# B

**backing up, 347**
**backslash as escape character, 418, 450**
  addslashes() function, 451
  stripslashes() function, 451
**bank example.** *See* **loan application form example**
**base64_encode() function, 530**
**basename() function, 347, 365, 713**
**Bcc: header field, 519**
**Berners-Lee, Tim, 262**
**BIGINT data type, 389**
**BINARY fields, 408**
**Blind Carbon Copies, e-mail, 519**
**BLOB data type, 389**
**<BLOCKQUOTE> tag, 627**
**BODMAS, 61**
**body parts, multipart media type messages, 528**
**body, HTTP**
  request, 48
  response, 49
**Boolean operators, 112–23**
  assignment, 116
  combining, 123–27
  equality, 116
  greater than, 112–16
  greater than or equal to, 122
  inequality, 116
  less than, 112–16
  less than or equal to, 122
**Boolean values, 112**
**boundary delimiter lines, 528**
  generating with md5() function, 529
**branching statements.** *See* **conditional statements**
**break command, 136**

**browsers**
caching, 51–52
as clients, 44
determining type of, 69
PHP not dependent upon, 51
printing files to, 334
refreshing, 52, 642
returning to previous page, 350, 608
sending image canvases to, 559
sending non-HTML data to, 560
**bugs.** *See* **errors; debugging**
**business logic, 295**
**buttons, 355**

# C

**caches, browsers, 51–52**
**Calculator object example, 298**
Calculator class, 311–13
how it works, 313
memory functions, 304–7
scientific calculator, 314–17
variables in multple instances of, 306
**calendar functions, 687**
**callback functions**
character data handler, 510
defining on page before parsing, 504
elements, 509
event driven parsing, 501
**canvases, images, 556**
creating, 577
sending to browsers, 559
**capitalizing first character of strings, 357**
**Carbon Copies, e-mail, 518**
**Cascading Stylesheets, 679**
**case folded names, 503**
**case keyword, 135**
**casting, 67**
settype() function, 67
**category hierarchies, 594**
adding categories, 649–51
associative array of metadata, returning, 609–15
category trees, 598
deleting categories, 649, 654–55
deriving depth of category, 613
editing categories, 652–54
expanded family names of categories, 613
metadata, retrieving, 655
searching, 616–17
**Cc: header field, 518**
**CHANGE keyword, 416**
**CHAR data type, 389**
**character classes, 246**
**character data handler callback, 510**
**character data type, 388**
**character sets**
specifying for e-mail messages, 526
**character strings, extracting from files, 327**
**chdir() function, 359, 711**
**check boxes, 82–88**
arrays, creating, 88
multiple, 85–88
**chunk_split() function, 530, 734**
**circles, drawing, 560–62**
**Clark, James, 493**
**class/object functions, 688**

**classes, 296**
accessor methods, 304
building, 302–4
Calculator object example, 298
constructors, 313
creating, 311–13
defining methods, 302
example class for inserting images and hyperlinks, 317–21
extending, 314–17
interfaces, 299
Reference class example, 318
using, 297
variables in multiple instances of, 306
**clauses, SQL queries, 393**
**client-server database model, 383–84**
benefits of, 383
**client-server relationship, 44**
**closedir() function, 358, 711**
**code**
arrays, 165–88
commenting, 237–38
conditional statements, 110–44
debugging, 255–58
detrimental effect of usury on, 154
functions, 238
good practice, 236–40
hackers, protecting from, 242
indenting, 129, 237
JavaScript, incorporating in, 601
loops, 148–64
modularization of, 194, 601
organizing, 193, 279–80
patterns, 243
quotation marks, 42
reuse, 194
include files, 219
scripts, 50
semicolons, terminating lines with, 42
testing, 240–41
types of, 41
variable names, 239–40
**colors, 556–57.** *See also* **images**
allocating, 557, 589
array of red, green and blue components, returning, 588
palette limitations, 589–90
of specific pixel, returning, 587
**comments, 237–38**
**common include files, 351**
**common_mail.inc**
newsletter mailing lists, 538–39
**comparison operators, 112–16**
**compression**
lossless, 556
lossy, 555
**concat() function, 454**
**concatenation, 56**
implicit type conversions, 611
with .= operator, 614
with echo() command, 56
with period (.), 56
**conditional includes, 219**
**conditional statements, 110–44.** *See also* **code**
assignment operator, 116
Boolean operators, 112–23
Boolean values, 112
combining operators, 123–27

**conditional statements (cont'd)**
comparison operators, 112–16
day to day example, 110
else statement, 127–29
elseif statement, 127–29
equality operator, 116
form validation, 140–44
greater than or equal to operator, 122
if statement, 111–35
nesting, 129–35
inequality operator, 116
less than or equal to operator, 122
logical operators, 119–22
multiple conditions, 127–35
switch statements, 135–39
**confirm() method, 350, 628**
**confirmation e-mails, newsletter mailing lists, 543**
**constants, 63–64**
define keyword, 64
displaying, 64
do not need to declare, 64–65
**constructors, 313**
**container tags, 508**
**Content-transfer-encoding header field, 527**
**Content-type header field, 526**
header() function, 364
multipart/mixed parameter, 530
**controls.** *See also* **forms**
arrays, creating with check boxes, 88
check boxes, 82–88
hidden, 95–99
HTML, 76–99
listboxes, 91–95
multiple check boxes, 85–88
passwords, 99
radio buttons, 88–91
retrieving contents of from HTTP_GET_VARS, 182
text areas, 80–82
text boxes, 76–79
**converting between data types, 65–68**
**cookies, 264, 280–87**
accessing, 282
deleting, 282
displaying contents of, 69
setcookie() function, 281
setting, 281
storing user preferences, 282–87
using, 281–87
**co-ordinate system, images, 557–58**
**copy() function, 347, 713**
**count() function, 433, 624, 656, 685**
**CREATE statement, 392**
**CREATE TABLE command, 411**
**crypt() function, 635, 641, 734**
**CSS, 679**
**curdate() function, 419, 427, 455**
**current() function, 173, 685**
**cursors, 676**
**curtime() function, 427, 455**

# D

**data.** *See also* **data types**
deleting, 392–93
manipulating, 396–97
replacing, 392–93
retrieving, 392–93 (*See also* **user record viewer**)
complex retrievals, 433–37
duplicate entries, eliminating, 433
fields, 427–32
from several tables, 435–37
indexes, 390
limiting number of results, 396, 428–30
ordering results, 430–31
PHP functions for, 423–26
specific row, 426
SQL statements for, 426–46
summaries, 432–33
tables, inserting into, 417–20
updating, 392
validation, 105, 140–44
**data members, objects, 296**
**data source names.** *See* **DSN**
**data sources.** *See* **ODBC Data Sources**
**data storage models, 379, 380**
**data types**
arrays, assigning to values in, 165
conversions, 65–68
forced by concatenation, 611
date and time, 454–58
gettype() function, 67
in PHP, 55–63
in SQL, 388
numeric, 58–63
settype() function, 67
specifying for body of e-mails, 526, 532
string, 55–58
**database management systems.** *See* **DBMS**
**databases, 379–84.** *See also* **relational databases;**
**MySQL; tables**
architecture, 382–84
client/server model, 383–84
closing connection to, 403
complex retrievals, 433–37
creating, 392, 412
with MySQL, 407–11
with PHP, 411–15
deleting data, 392–93
dropping, 392, 407, 412
entities, 381
fields, 380
information on, 461
retrieving, 427–32
returning number of, 458
functions, 689
imagemaps, generating from, 580
indexes, 390
inserting into, 392–93
joins, 382, 436
limiting number of results, 428–30
manipulating data in, 396–97
normalization, 380–82
ODBC, 669
ordering results, 430–31
pattern matching, 431–32
primary keys, 381

**databases (cont'd)**
privileges (See **privileges**)
records, 380
    inserting using PHP, 449–52
    retrieving rows, 402
redundancy in, 380–82
relational (See **relational databases**)
replacing, 392–93
retrieving data, 392–93, 423–26
retrieving specific rows, 426
schemas, 597
searches, increasing the speed of, 390
selecting, 394, 401, 414
server errors, 403–7
showing names of available, 400
SQL (See **SQL**)
standalone model, 383
summaries, 432–33
tables, 380
    altering structure of, 392, 415–17, 425
    creating, 407–11
    data, inserting into, 417–20
    information on, 458–68
    populating, 419–20
    viewing list of, 394–96, 401, 412
unique fields, 381, 598
updating data, 392
user record viewer example, 437–46
users, 396
**date and time functions, 710**
    formatted date and time, returning, 626
**DATE data type, 389, 455**
**date strings**
    format of, specifying, 42
    gmdate() function, 42
    retrieving date, 427
    returning, 352, 443
**date/time data type, 388, 454–58**
**date_format() function, 456, 626**
**DATETIME data type, 389, 455**
**dayname() function, 457**
**db_connect() function, 424, 538**
    connection failures, 406
    default database, selecting, 406
    URL directory manager case study, 607
**dBase, 383**
    functions, 690
**DBM, 383**
    functions, 691
**DBMS, 380**
**debugging, 255–58.** See also **errors; error messages**
    checking HTML source, 257
    echo() command, 256
    error log, 257–58
    supressing error messages, 257
**DECIMAL data type, 389**
**declaration**
    not needed in PHP, 64–65
**DEFAULT fields, 408, 464**
**default parameter values**
    pitfalls of, 206
    setting, 204
**define keyword, 64**
**DELETE statement, 392**
    deleting records, 452
    using with WHERE clause, 397, 452
**delete_category() function**
    URL directory manager case study, 654–55

**delete_url() function**
    URL directory manager case study, 628, 664–65
**deleting files, 348–49**
**DESC keyword, 395, 431**
**die() function, 724**
    exiting after connection failures, 404
**dir object, 360**
**directories, 323, 358–71.** See also **files.**
    absolute paths, 326
    changing, 359
    chdir() function, 359
    closing, 358
    creating, 360, 364
    dir() function, 360
    directory handles, 358
    dirname() function, 360
    entries
        arranging in order, 359
        moving back to first, 359
        returning, 358
    functions, 711
    mkdir() function, 360
    name, returning, 360
    navigator, 363–67
    next entry, returning, 358
    object-oriented methods, 360
    paths in UNIX and Windows, 323
    relative paths, 326
    removing, 360
    rewinddir() function, 359
    rmdir() function, 360
    sort() function, 359
    splitting filenames from directory paths, 347
    traversing, 361–63
**directory managers**
    administrators, 595
        authentication of, 602
        determining if current user is, 619
    category hierarchies, 594
    correcting inconsistencies between tables, 655–57
    data storage, 596–601
    deleting URLs, 664–65
    designing, 594
    errors, 605
    modifying URLs, 637–42
    most-visited sites, listing, 642–44
    new records, inserting, 635
    newly added URLs
        viewing, 657–60
    searching, 616–17
    state information, 645
    user authentication, 595
    user interfaces, 596
    user requirements, 594–96
**directory tree**
    stopping users going up, 253–55
**directory_footer() function**
    URL directory manager case study, 606
**directory_header() function**
    URL directory manager case study, 606
**dirname() function, 360, 713**
    returns nothing when used on root directories, 480
**DISTINCT keyword, 433**
**division operator, 59**
    whole numbers, returning from division
        operations, 104

**do while loops, 155–59**
  example, 156
  infinite loops, 234
  iterating through arrays, 168
**DOCTYPE declaration, XML, 500**
**Document Type Definition.** *See* **DTDs**
**dollar sign ($), 52**
**DOM XML functions, 712**
**double data type, 55, 58–63, 389**
**double quotes around strings, 418**
**DROP statement, 392**
  being cautious with, 407
**dropdown listboxes.** *See* **listboxes**
**DSN, 669**
**DTDs, 499–501**
  ATTLIST declaration, 501
  DOCTYPE declaration, 500
  ELEMENT declaration, 500
  external, 501
    linking to, 508
  format of, 500
**duplicate entries, eliminating, 433**
**duplicate entry error, 418**
**dynamic generation of web pages, 50**

# E

**each() function, 175–76, 685**
**echo() command, 42, 734**
  concatenation of variables, 56
  constants, displaying, 64
  displaying variables on web pages, 53
  forms, creating, 98
  hidden controls, 95–99
  use of in debugging, 256
  values returned by functions, displaying, 195
**edit command, 410**
**edit_category() function**
  URL directory manager case study, 653–54
**edit_category_form() function**
  URL directory manager case study, 652–53
**edit_new() function**
  URL directory manager case study, 662–64
**edit_new_form() function**
  URL directory manager case study, 660–62
**ELEMENT declaration, XML, 500**
**elements**
  arrays, 165
  callback functions, 509
  XML, 496
**elements, arrays, 165**
**ellipses, graphics, 561**
**else statement, 127–29.** *See also* **conditional statements**
**elseif statement, 127–29.** *See also* **conditional statements**
**e-mail, 515**
  address checking, 249–51
  advanced e-mailer program, 532
  anatomy of, 518–19, 525–29
  attachments, 525–36
    attaching files, 529–32
    encoding file contents as long string, 530
  boundary delimiter lines, 528
  character sets, specifying, 526
  custom e-mail function, 519–25

  empty mail, 524
  enabling file uploads to attach to e-mails, 532
  encoding transformation, specifying, 527
  ensuring only text is used in e-mail messages, 524
  functions, 722
  header fields, 518
    adding extra, 519
  mail() function
    arguments, 515
  MIME handling, 525
  multiple components, 528–29
  newsletter mailing list manager, 536–52
  non-textual data, 528–29
  sending to several addresses, 517
  Sendmail program, 516
  spam mailers, 517
  specifying remote SMTP server to relay, 516
  specifying type and subtype of data, 526, 532
**empty tags, 497**
**empty() function, 68, 739**
**encapsulation, 300**
**encoding transformation, e-mail, 527**
**encryption**
  passwords, 396, 635, 641
**ENCTYPE attribute**
  <FORM> tag, 367
**end of files, 331**
**entities, relational databases, 381**
**Entity category**
  HTTP request header, 47
  HTTP response header, 48
**ENUM data type, 390, 464–68**
**environment variables, 68–69**
**equality operator, 116**
  errors, 236
  MySQL, 429
**ereg() function, 244, 366, 732**
  e-mail address checking, 250
**ereg_replace() function, 365**
**eregi() function, 466, 732**
**eregi_replace() function, 466, 732**
  in URL directory manager case study, 634, 640
**error code values, 48**
**error handling, 227.** *See also* **errors; debugging; error messages**
  functions, 712
  messages sent to browser, 228
**error log, 257–58**
**error messages.** *See also* **errors; debugging**
  inconspicuous, 228
  level of error reporting, setting, 404
  sent to browser, 228
  supressing, 257, 348, 404
  user record viewer example, 439
**error_log() function, 257, 712**
**error_message() function**
  URL directory manager case study, 608
**error_reporting() function, 404, 406, 712**
**errors.** *See also* **error messages; debugging**
  arguments in wrong order, 236
  avoiding, 236–40
    by indenting code, 237
    by using comments, 237–38
    by using functions, 238
    by using include files, 239
    by using sensible variable names, 239–40
  division by zero, 232

**errors (cont'd)**
  equality operator, 236
  fatal, 232
  form validation, 241–43
  functions with no return value, 235
  infinite loops, 234
  logical, 232–36
  loops, 230
  MySQL, 403–7
  mysql_errno() function, 404
  mysql_error() function, 404
  opening files and directories, 325
  parse, 229
  program assumptions, 235
  reporting with alert() method, 350, 520
  returned by PHP engines, 50
  runtime, 232
  semicolons, 231
  suppressing MySQL error reporting, 538, 404
  syntax, 229–32
  types of, 229
  unexpected output, 232, 235
  URL directory manager case study, 607
**escape characters, 418, 450**
  addslashes() function, 451
  htmlspecialchars() function, 451
  not used  between double quotes, 57
  stripslashes() function, 451
**event driven parsing, 501**
**exam results example, 183–88**
**execution of PHP script, 50.** See also **code**
**exit statement, 140**
  infinite loops, escaping from, 154
**expat parser, 493**
**explode() function, 180–81, 353, 467, 734**
  lists, breaking up, 571
**extends keyword, 315**
**Extensible Markup Language.** See **XML**
**external DTDs, 501**

# F

**fatal errors, 232**
**fclose() function, 327, 713**
  not called after using fpassthru(), 334
**feof() function, 331, 713**
**fgetc() function, 331, 713**
**fgets() function, 332, 713**
**fields, databases, 380.** See also **tables**
  adding, 415
  attributes, 408
    returning, 459
  changing definition of, 415
  date/time data type, 454–58
  default values, 416, 464–68
    function for, 464
  definition of, changing, 416
  deleting, 415
  ENUM type, 464–68
    listing options available, 465
  granting privileges to, 398
  information on, 461
  inserting values into, 417
  listing, 458
  position of, altering, 416
  properties of, 459
  renaming, 415

  retrieving, 427–32
  specifying as holding indexes, primary keys and
    unique values, 409
**file position indicator, 326**
**file() function, 333, 713**
  holds file path, 324
  sending e-mail to several addresses, 517
**file_exists() function, 339, 713**
**fileatime() function, 340, 714**
**filectime() function, 340, 714**
**filegroup()  function, 343, 714**
**filemtime() function, 340, 714**
**fileowner() function, 343, 714**
**files, 323, 324–58.** See also **directories.**
  absolute paths, 326
  attaching to e-mail, 529–32
  backing up, 347
  basename() function, 347
  character strings, extracting from, 327
  closing, 325, 327
  copying, 347
  deleting, 348–49
  determining if file exists, 339
  encoding contents as long string, 530
  end of, 331
  file handles, 324
  file position indicator
    moving, 335
    resetting to beginning of file, 336
    returning offset of, 335
  fopen() function, 325–27
  functions, 713
  group ID, returning, 343
  hit counter example, 328–30
  include path, 326
  information on, 339–46, 353
  last access time, 340
  loading existing, 356
  mode, specifying, 326
  names
    breaking up with explode() function, 353
    splitting from directory path, 347
  navigating within, 336
  opening, 325
    detecting errors when, 325
    on remote hosts, 333, 508
  ownership, 342–44
  path names, 326
  permissions, 342–44
  printing, 334
    to a window, 364
  printing to web browsers, 334
  random access to data in, 335–38
  readfile() function, 334
  reading, 333–35
  reading one character at a time, 331
  reading sets of characters, 332
  relative path notation, 326
  renaming, 347-49
  rewind() function, 336
  saving, 355
  sensitive, stopping users accessing, 253–55
  time-related properties, 340–42
  type, returning, 343
  unlink() function, 348–49
  uploading, 367–71
  uploads, enabling, 532
  user ID, returning, 343
  writing data to, 327

filesize() function, 339, 714
filetype() function, 343, 714
FIRST keyword, 416
FLOAT data type, 389
floating point numbers, 58–63
flood-filling images, 578
flushing privileges, 397
footers
    handling with include files, 222
fopen() function, 325–27, 714
    how file is to be used, specifying, 326
    include paths, 326
    name of file, specifying, 325
    remote files, 325, 333, 508
for loops, 159–64
    increment operator ++, 160
    iterating through arrays, 167
    using, 160
for() statement, 571
foreach loops, 188–91
    using, 189
<FORM> tag, 72–76
    ACTION attribute, 72
    ENCTYPE attribute, 367
    METHOD attribute, 73–76
        which to use, 75
forms, 71–105
    check boxes, 82–88
    directing server to a page after submission of, 72
    echo() command, creating with, 98
    empty fields, 241
    exit statement, 140
    GET method, 73–75
        example, 76
    hidden controls, 95–99
    listboxes, 91–95
    loan application form example, 100–105
    multiple check boxes, 85–88
    passwords, 99
    persistence, 265–72
    POST method, 75
        example, 80
    radio buttons, 88–91
    reset buttons, 99
    script, preventing from being entered into, 143–44, 242
    sending information to server, 73–76
    submit buttons, 99
    text areas, 80–82
    text boxes, 76–79
    validation, 140–44, 241–43
        htmlspecialchars() function, 143–44
    values returned from, using in PHP scripts, 100–105
Forms Data Format functions, 716
fpassthru() function, 334, 714
fputs() function, 333, 714
fread() function, 327, 714
freshmeat
    parsing external XML files example, 508–12
FROM clause, 435
From: header field, 518
FrontPage, 13
fseek() function, 335, 714
ftell() function, 335, 715
full moon, 148
function keyword, 195

functions, 193. See also variables; code; specific functions and functions index
Apache, 683
arguments, 194, 203–6
    parameters with unset values, 204–5
    passing by reference, 203
    passing by value, 203
arrays, 683
Aspell, 687
calender, 687
callback functions, 501
calling, 195
class/object, 688
conditional includes, 219
constructors, 313
CURL, 689
database, 689
date and time, 710
dBase, 690
DBM, 691
defining, 195–201
directory, 711
DOM XML, 712
end of, denoting, 195
error handling, 712
errors, 235
filesystem functions, 713
forms data format, 716
function handling functions, 717
HTTP, 718
images, 718
include files, 218–23
    common uses of, 221
    using cautiously, 222
Informix, 692
InterBase, 694
mail, 722
mathematical, 722
mSQL, 696
MySQL, 699
nesting, 213–15
network, 725
objects, passing as parameters, 296
ODBC, 701
Oracle, 706
Oracle 8, 704
output control, 726
parameters, 194
    default values, setting, 204
    optional, 205
    order, 204–5
    with unset values, 204–5
passing values, 203–6
passing variables by reference, 307–11
passing variables by value, 307–11
Perl-compatible regular expression functions, 731
in PHP, 42
PHP options and information, 727
POSIX, 728
PostgreSQL, 707
program execution functions, 730
Pspell, 730
putting in common include files, 351
recursion, 215–18
regular expression functions, 243–55, 732
returning values from, 195
session handling, 733
SQL Server, 695
strings, 734

**functions (cont'd)**
switching, 201–2
Sybase, 709
URLs, 738
using is good coding practice, 238
values returned
assigning to variables, 202
displaying, 195
variables, 739
definitions of, 196
global, 207–9
global, using inside functions, 208
local, 207
making value persisting between function calls, 209–10
scope of, 206–13
that belong to a class, referring to, 313
WDDX functions, 740
XML parser functions, 740
Zlib, 742
**fwrite() function, 327, 715**
file handles, 324

# G

**gd graphics library, 17, 555**
**gdImageColorAllocate, 589**
**General category**
HTTP request header, 47
HTTP response header, 48
**GET method command, HTTP, 47**
example, 76
forms, 73–75
not used for passwords, 99
query strings
using for persistence, 272–80
retrieving contents of controls from HTTP_GET_VARS, 182
**get_category_info() function**
URL directory manager case study, 609–15
**get_url_info() function**
URL directory manager case study, 615–16, 641
**getdate() function, 340, 711**
**getters.** *See* **accessor methods**
**gettype() function, 67, 739**
**GIF file format, 556**
**global keyword, 208**
**global variables, 207–9, 301**
example, 210
MySQL database connections, 604
namespace conflicts, 302
putting in common include files, 351
using inside functions, 208
**$GLOBALS array, 208**
using, 209
**gmdate() function, 42, 711**
**Gnotepad+, 35**
**go_url() function, 627**
URL directory manager case study, 642
**GOTO statement, 194**
**GRANT command, 398–99**
**graphics, 555–91.** *See also* **images**
advanced manipulation of, 585–89
circles, 560–62
color of specific pixel, returning, 587
colors, 556–57
file formats, 555

image canvases, 556
images
co-ordinate system, 557–58
creating, 556
destroying, 560
drawing, 558–66
resizing, 582
specifying quality of, 559
text, writing onto, 578
interactive maps, 566–84
lines, 558–60
palette limitations, 589–90
rectangles, 562–63
with rounded corners, 563–66
shading polygons, 578
thumbnails, 581–84
tool tips, 579
transparent backgrounds, 587
use of loops, 571
**greater than operator, 112–16**
**greater than or equal to operator, 122**
**GROUP BY clause, 434**
**groups in UNIX, 342**
ID returning, 343

# H

**hackers, 242**
**handle property**
dir object, 360
**hangman, 273–78**
**hard links, 349**
**HEAD method command, HTTP, 47**
**header fields, e-mail, 518**
adding extra to e-mail messages, 519
Content-transfer-encoding, 527
Content-type, 526
MIME-Version, 527
parameters, 526
**Header() function, 364, 718**
sending non-HTML data to browsers, 560
**headers**
handling with include files, 222
HTTP, 46
request, 47
response, 48
**hidden controls, 95–99**
passing variables as, 98
URL directory manager case study, 638
using for persistence, 265–69
**history.go(-1) method, 350**
URL directory manager case study, 608
**hit counters, 328–30**
graphical, 330
last access time, 340
using fgetc() function, 331
using file() function, 333
using sessions, 289–91
**holiday example, functions, 198**
**htdocs directory, Apache, 32**
**HTML.** *See also* **forms**
controls, 76–99
echo() command, creating forms with, 98
example class for inserting images and hyperlinks, 317–21
forms, 71–105
imagemaps, 579–81

**HTML (cont'd)**
  interactivity, 262–64
  limitations of, 494
  markup, 41
  scripts, inserting into, 50
**HTML entities, 451**
**htmlspecialchars() function, 242, 451, 488**
  preventing malicious script from being entered into
    forms, 143–44
**HTTP, 45–49**
  body, 46
  environment variables, 68–69
  functions, 718
  header, 46
  interactivity, 262–64
  POST method, 75
  preventing pages from being cached, 52
  request body, 48
  request header, 47
  request/response line, 46, 48
  requests, 45, 46
  response body, 49
  response header, 48
  responses, 45, 48
  statelessness of, 261
  status codes, 48
**$HTTP_ACCEPT environment variable, 69**
**$HTTP_COOKIE_DATA environment variable, 68**
**HTTP_GET_VARS, 182**
**$HTTP_FROM environment variable, 69**
**HTTP_POST_VARS, 182**
  using for persistence, 269–72
**$HTTP_USER_AGENT  environment variable, 69**
**httpd.conf file, Apache, 32**
**hyperlinks**
  broken links, 618
  example class for inserting, 317–21
  TARGET attribute, 372
**Hypertext Transfer Protocol.** See **HTTP**

**I**

**ID numbers, users, 342**
  changing, 484
**if statement, 111–35.** See also **conditional**
  **statements; code**
  assignment operator, 116
  Boolean values, 112
  combining operators, 123–27
  equality operator, 116
  form validation, 140–44
  greater than operator, 112–16
  inequality operator, 116
  less than operator, 112–16
  logical operators, 119
  multiple conditions, 127–35
  nesting, 129–35
**IIS, 19**
  installing from NT4.0 option pack, 20–22
  installing IIS 5.0 on Windows 2000, 23–24
  installing PHP4 alongside, 24–28
**image canvases, 556**
  creating, 577
  sending to browsers, 559
**image functions, 718-21**
  gd graphics library, 555

**ImageArc() function, 560, 718**
**ImageColorAllocate() function, 557, 587, 589, 718**
**ImageColorAt() function, 587, 719**
**ImageColorClosest() function, 589, 719**
**ImageColorExact() function, 589, 719**
**ImageColorsForIndex() function, 588, 719**
**ImageColorsTotal() function, 590, 719**
**ImageColorTransparent() function, 587, 719**
**ImageCopyResized() function, 581, 586, 719**
**ImageCreate() function, 556, 719**
**ImageCreateFromPNG() function, 577, 719**
**ImageDestroy() function, 560, 720**
**ImageFill() function, 578, 720**
**ImageJPEG() function, 559, 720**
**ImageLine() function, 558, 720**
**imagemaps, 579–81**
  generating from databases, 580
**ImageRectangle() function, 562–63, 721**
**images**
  circles, 560–62
  color of specific pixel, returning, 587
  colors, 556–57
  co-ordinate system, 557–58
  creating, 556
  destroying, 560
  drawing, 558–66
  example class for inserting, 317–21
  functions, 718
  height of, returning, 586
  lines, 558–60
  palette limitations, 589–90
  rectangles, 562–63
    with rounded corners, 563–66
  resizing, 582
  shading, 578
  specifying quality of, 559
  text, writing onto, 578
  thumbnails, 581–84
  tool tips, 579
  transparent backgrounds, 587
  use of loops, 571
  width of, returning, 586
**ImageString() function, 578, 721**
**ImageSX() function, 586, 721**
**ImageSY() function, 586, 721**
**<IMG> element**
  ALT attribute, 579
  USEMAP attribute, 580
**implode() function, 180–81, 354, 517, 735**
  joining elements in array into a string, 577
**.inc files, 221**
**include files, 218–23**
  conditional includes, 219
  minimize errors, 239
  uses of, 219, 221
  using cautiously, 222
**include paths, files, 326**
**include statement, 218**
**increment operator (++), 160**
**incrementing variables, 60**
**indexed color images, 588**

indexes, 390
  adding, 415, 416
  arrays, 95, 165
    explicit index values, 166
    linking several through index, 168–72
    linking several after one has been sorted, 186
    multisorting, 188
    passing index information between pages, 171
    setting first index value, 166
  associative arrays, 165, 167
  deleting, 415, 416
  interactive maps, 566
  primary keys as, 391
  specifying fields to hold, 409
  usefulness of, 566
inequality operator, 116
infinite loops, 154, 234
informix functions, 692
inheritance, 314–17
initialization of variables not needed in PHP, 64–65
inodes, 349
<INPUT> form tag, 76–79
  check boxes, 82–88
  hidden controls, 95–99
  NAME attribute, 78
  passwords, 99
  radio buttons, 88–91
  text boxes, 76–79
  TYPE attribute, 76–79
  uploading files, 367
INSERT statement, 392, 396
  auto-incremented value generated by query,
    returning, 450
  difference from REPLACE, 419
  inserting values into fields, 417
  inserting values into tables, 417–20
installation of PHP, 11–36
INT data type, 389
integer data type, 55, 58–63
integers as unique identifiers, 598
interactive maps, 566–84
  adding data, 568
  database, 568
  drawing shopping mall map, 569–73
  framework, 573–79
  imagemaps, 579–81
  layout, 574–79
  shop detail, 581–84
  testing data, 569–73
interactivity, 262–64
InterBase functions, 694
interfaces, classes, 299
internet protocols, 44
Internet Explorer. See also browsers
  cache, 52
  refreshing, 52
Internet Information Server. See IIS
Internet Services Manager, 25
is_dir() function, 344, 715
is_file() function, 344, 715
ISPs, 182
isset() function, 68, 739
iterations of loops, 148
  specifying number of, 159

J

JavaScript. See also scripts; code
  confirm() method, 628
  history.go(-1) method, 608
  incorporating lines of into PHP code, 601
  open_window() function, 649
Jet database engine, 670
joins, 382, 436
  indexes, 391
JPEG file format, 555
  specifying quality of images, 559

K

KEdit, 35
key() function, 173, 686
keys, databases, 436
keyword searches, implementing, 623
  multiple keywords, 624
ksort() function, 179, 686

L

LAMP, 28
last access time, returning, 340
  with date_format() function, 457
Lerdorf, Rasmus, 295
less than equals operator (<=), 105
less than operator, 112–16
less than or equal to operator, 122
lifetime of variables, 206
LIKE operator, 431–32
  multiple keyword searches, 624
LIMIT clause, 428–30, 658
lines, drawing, 558–60
link identifiers, 400, 605
  in mysql_list_dbs() function call, 403
links, UNIX, 349
Linux
  case-sensitvity, 394
  installing MySQL, 386–88
    from source, 387
    using RPMs, 386
  installing PHP, 28–36
    choosing method, 29
list() function, 175–76, 686
list_categories() function
  URL directory manager case study, 646–49
list_sites() function
  URL directory manager case study, 642–44
listboxes, 91–95
  arrays, creating, 94
  populating using arrays and loops, 170
  variables, 104
lists
  ordering, 643
loan application form example, 100–105
  improvements, 105
  processing claim, 104
  with while loop, 149
local mail server
  needs to be specified for mail() function, 516

**local variables, 207**
  example, 210
  making value persisting between function
    calls, 209–10
**localhosts, 34**
**logging users, 478**
  do_authentication() function, 481
  functions, 712
**logical errors, 232–36**
**logical operators, 119–22**
  AND operator, 119
  combining, 123–27
  MySQL, 429
  NOT operator, 119
  OR operator, 119
  using, 120
**login script, 474–82**
  auth_user() function, 477
  do_authentication() function, 481
  logging users, 478
  login_form() function, 477
**LONGBLOB data type, 389**
**LONGTEXT data type, 390**
**loop index, 460**
**loops, 148–64.** *See also* **arrays; code**
  arrays, iterating through, 167–77
  do while, 155–59
  errors, 230
  for, 159–64
  foreach, 188–91
  increment operator ++, 160
  infinite, 154, 234
  iterations, 148
    specifying number of, 159
  listboxes, populating, 170
  use of in drawing images, 571
  while, 148–55
**Lord of the Rings, XML example, 498–99**
  DTD, 499–501
  parsing, 503–7
**lossless compression, 556**
**lossy compression, 555**

# M

**mail() function, 515, 722**
  custom e-mail function, 519–25
  empty mail, 524
  failures, 516
  header fields, adding extra, 519
  local mail server specification, 516
  sending mail to several addresses, 517
  URL directory manager case study, 636
  using, 516
**mail_charset input field, 532**
**mail_encoding input field, 532**
**mail_type input field, 532**
**Malaysia, 233**
**management systems, 593**
  category hierarchies, 594
  data storage, 596–601
  new records, inserting, 635
  user interfaces, 596
**<map> tag, 579–81**

**maps**
  interactive, 566–84
    adding data, 568
    database, 568
    drawing shopping mall map, 569–73
    framework, 573–79
    imagemaps, 579–81
    layout, 574–79
    shop detail, 581–84
    testing data, 569–73
  stylized, 585–89
**Mars probes, how to loose, 235**
**mathematical functions, 722**
  recursion, 215–18
**mathematical operators, 59**
  precedence, 61
  whole numbers, returning from division operations,
    104
**max() function, 432, 723**
**md5() function, 529, 735**
**MEDIUMBLOB data type, 389**
**MEDIUMINT data type, 389**
**MEDIUMTEXT data type, 390**
**messages, displaying to users, 608**
**metacharacters, 244–48**
  alternatives, 247
  anchors, 246
  character classes, 246
  qualifiers, 247
  quantifiers, 248
  word boundaries, 247
**METHOD attribute**
  <FORM> tag, 73–76
  GET value, 73–75
    example, 76
  POST value, 75
    example, 80
    passwords, 99
  which to use, 75
**method command, HTTP, 46**
**methods, objects, 297**
  calling, 299
  defining, 302
  passing variables by reference, 307–11
  passing variables by value, 307–11
**MIME handling, 525**
  headers, setting up, 535
**MIME-Version header field, 527, 530**
**min() function, 433, 723**
**mkdir() function, 360, 715**
**mode, files, 326**
**modifier variables, 133**
**MODIFY keyword, 416**
**modify_url() function**
  URL directory manager case study, 640–42
**modify_url_form() function**
  URL directory manager case study, 628, 637–40
**modularization of code, 194, 601**
**modulus operator, 59, 100, 156**
**mSQL functions, 696**
**multi-dimensional arrays, 182–83**
**multipart media type, 528–29**
**MULTIPLE attribute**
  <SELECT> tag, 92
**multiple check boxes, 85–88**
  variables, 87

multiple keyword searches, 624
multiple mail components, 528–29
multiplication operator, 59
Multipurpose Internet Mail Extensions. See MIME handling
MySQL, 384–88. See also databases
  aggregate functions, 432–33
  aliases, 434
  avg() function, 433
  case-sensitvity on UNIX, 394
  closing connection to, 400, 403
  connecting to MySQL Server, 400, 424, 538, 607
  count() function, 433
  curdate() function, 427
  curtime() function, 427
  databases, creating, 407–11
  DESC keyword, 395
  equality operators, 429
  features, 384
  functions, 699
  global variables associated with database connection, 604
  GRANT command, 398–99
  installing
    from source, 387
    on Linux, 386–88
    on Windows, 385–86
    using RPMs, 386
  joins, 436
  logical operators, 429
  max() function, 432
  min() function, 433
  NULL values, 392, 429
  ordering results, 430–31
  passwords, 396
  pattern matching, 431–32
  PHP connectivity, 400–403
    example, 402
  queries, 392–93
  records, inserting using PHP, 449–52
  resources, 421, 447, 491
  result identifiers, 423
  REVOKE command, 399
  root account, 387
  selecting database, 401
  server errors, 403–7
  server functions, 426
  sum() function, 432
  summaries, 432–33
  suppressing error reporting, 538
  supressing error reporting, 404
  tables
    creating, 407–11
    viewing list of, 394–96
  testing, 388
  USE command, 394
  user record viewer example, 437–46
  winmysqladmin.exe tool, 385
mysql client program, 393
  arguments, 393
  database, selecting, 394
  running, 393
mysql_affected_rows() function, 401, 454, 699
  URL directory manager case study, 636
mysql_close() function, 400, 699
mysql_connect() function, 400, 538, 699
mysql_create_db() function, 412, 699
mysql_data_seek() function, 426, 699
mysql_db_query() function, 412, 699

mysql_drop_db() function, 412, 699
mysql_errno() function, 404, 699
mysql_error() function, 404, 699
mysql_fetch_array() function, 424, 612, 700
mysql_fetch_field() function, 461, 700
  bug, 463
mysql_fetch_object() function, 424, 700
mysql_fetch_row() function, 402, 700
mysql_field_flags() function, 459, 700
mysql_field_len() function, 459, 700
mysql_field_name() function, 459, 700
mysql_field_type() function, 459, 700
mysql_insert_id() function, 450, 700
mysql_list_dbs() function, 400, 700
  link identifiers, 403
mysql_list_fields() function, 458, 700
mysql_list_tables() function, 401, 700
  link identifiers, 403
mysql_num_fields() function, 458, 700
mysql_num_rows() function, 401, 444, 701
mysql_query() function, 411, 412, 701
mysql_result() function, 425, 701
mysql_select_db() function, 401, 414, 538, 701
mysqld, 387

## N

NAME attribute
  <INPUT> tag, 78
name/value pairs, 73. See also URLs; query strings
  spaces, replacing with addition operator, 74
  URL encoding, 75
namespace conflicts, 302
NAMLLU. See loan application form example
navigating within files, 336
navigator, directories, 363–67
  creating a directory, 364
  display() function, 364
  main function, 364
  mkdir_form() function, 363
nesting functions, 213–15
nesting if statements, 129
nesting tags, 496
Netscape Navigator. See also browsers
  cache, 52
  refreshing, 52
network functions, 725
networking protocols, 44
newline character
  on Windows and UNIX platforms, 518
newsletter mailing list manager, 536–52
  admin_mailer.php, 544–52
  administration script, 544–52
  common_mail.inc, 538–39
  confirmation e-mails, 543
  creating new, 547
  displaying list of subscribers, 549
  listing currently available newsletters, 541
  newsletter.php, 539–44
  removing subscribers, 550
  sending newsletter, 551
  specific formats, querying number of subscribers that want, 545
  subscription scripts, 537, 542
  switching between different functions, 551
  unsubscribing from, 543, 550

next() function, 173–75, 686
non-sequential arrays
  iterating through, 172
normalization, 380–82
NOT LIKE operator, 431–32
NOT logical operator, 119
NOT NULL fields, 408
now() function, 427, 455, 675
NULL fields, 408
NULL values, 391, 429
  arithmetic operations involving, 392
number_format() function, 627, 723
numeric data type, 58–63, 388

## O

object data type, 55
object oriented programming
  advantages of, 300
  creating classes, 311–13
  encapsulation, 300
  inheritance, 314–17
  terminology, 296–97
object/class functions, 688
objects, 295–321
  accessor methods, 304
  advantages of using, 300
  Calculator object example, 298
  classes, 296
    building, 302–4
    using, 297
  creating classes, 311–13
  instances, 296
  methods, 297
    calling, 299
    defining, 302
  passing as parameters, 296
  passing variables by reference, 307–11
  properties, 296
  returning from result sets, 424
  variables, 302
    in multiple instances of object, 306
octet streams, 527
ODBC, 669
  Access databases, 670
  cursors, 676
  functions, 701
  PHP connectivity, 674
  PHP ODBC API, 678
  result sets, 675
ODBC Data Sources, 669
  connecting to, 674
  creating, 670
  executing SQL commands, 674
  querying, 676
ODBC Drivers, 669
odbc_connect() function, 674, 702
odbc_do() function, 674, 702
odbc_exec() function, 674, 702
odbc_fetch_row() function, 676, 702
odbc_field_len() function, 676, 702
odbc_field_name() function, 675, 702
odbc_field_num() function, 675, 702
odbc_field_type() function, 675
odbc_num_fields() function, 675, 703
odbc_num_rows() function, 675, 703
odbc_result() function, 676, 703

odbc_result_all() function, 678, 703
odbc_tableprivileges() function, 675, 704
odbc_tables() function, 675, 704
offset of file position indicator, returning, 335
Open Database Connectivity. See ODBC
open_window() function, 438, 649
opendir() function, 358, 712
<OPTION> tag, 91–95
OR logical operator, 119, 430
Oracle
  functions, 706
  Oracle 8 functions, 704
ORDER BY clause, 430–31, 643
output control functions, 726
ownership of files, 342–44

## P

palettes, 589–90
parameters
  default values
    pitfalls of, 206
    setting, 204
  functions, 194
  header fields, 526
  optional, 205
  order, 204–5
  with unset values, 204–5
parse errors, 229
parsing, 50
  external files, 508–12
  XML, 501–2
    begin and end elements, 502
    character data, handling, 502
    freeing memory, 502
    parser, creating, 502
    parsing, starting, 502
password() function, 396, 419
passwords, 99, 342
  authentication, 474
  changing, 453
  database users, 396
  encrypting, 635, 641
  two fields, 470
  URL directory manager case study, 633
path property
  dir object, 360
pattern matching, MySQL, 431–32
patterns in code, 243
PCDATA, 501
performance
  client/server database model, 383
period (.), 56
Perl
  not suitable for web sites with heavy traffic, 597
  Perl-compatible regular expression functions, 731
permissions
  files, 342–44
persistence, 261
  changing script functionality with query
    strings, 279–80
  cookies, 280–87
  forms, 265–72
  hidden fields, 265–69
  HTTP_POST_VARS, 269–72
  query strings, 272–80
  sessions, 287–91

Personal Web Server. *See* **PWS**
**personalization of web sites, 280**
**PHP**
    Apache, configuring and starting, 31–34
    arrays, 165–88
    commands, 42
    conditional statements, 110–44
    constants, 63–64
    databases, creating, 411–15
    directories (*See* **directories**)
    e-mail, 515
    errors, 50
        handling, 228
        reporting, 404
    execution of, 50
    files (*See* **files**)
    functions, 42, 683
    graphics, 555–91
    inserting records, 449–52
    installing, 11–36
        alongside IIS, 24–28
        alongside PWS, 17–19
        on Linux, 28–36
        on Windows 95 and 98, 13–19
        on Windows NT and 2000, 19–28
        RPM packages needed, 30–31
        RPMs, obtaining, 29–30
        testing installation, 34–36
    interactivity, 262–64
**JavaScript, incorporating in, 601**
    loops, 148–64
    MySQL connectivity, 400–403
        example, 402
    MySQL queries, issuing, 411–15
    objects, 295–321
    ODBC, 669
    parsing, 50
    programming with, 39
    sessions, 264, 288–91
    tables, creating, 411–15
    users, information from, 71–105
    variables, 52–63
    web page requests, 49–50
    XML, 493–512
**<?php ... ?> tags, 41, 51**
**PHP ODBC API, 678**
**PHP script, 41.** *See also* **scripts; code**
    changing functionality with query strings, 279–80
    debugging, 255–58
    identifying, 51
    running on Apache, 33
    using values returned from forms in, 100–105
**.php suffix, 40**
    include files, 221
**PHP variables. See environment variables**
**php.ini file**
    auto_prepend_file, 478
    local mail server specification, 516
    register_globals configuration setting, 182
**PHP4 ISAPI filter, 26**
**phpinfo() function, 68, 728**
**PNG file format, 555**
**pointers, arrays, 173**
**POSIX functions, 728**
**posix_getgrgid() function, 343, 729**
**posix_getpwuid() function, 342, 729**

**POST method command, HTTP, 47**
    example, 80
    forms, 73, 75
    passwords, 99
    retrieving contents of controls from HTTP_GET_VARS, 182
**PostgreSQL functions, 707**
**precedence in mathematical operations, 61**
**prepending files to web pages, 478**
**presentation logic, 295, 321**
**prev() function, 686, 173–75**
**primary keys, 381**
    adding, 416
    as indexes, 391
    deleting, 416
    specifying fields as holding, 409
**privilege tables, 395**
**privileges**
    changing, 396
    flushing, 397
    granting, 398–99
    granting to other users, 399
    revoking, 399
**program execution functions, 730**
**properties of objects, 296**
**protocols, 44**
    HTTP, 45
    TCP/IP, 44
**Pspell functions, 730**
**PWS, 13**
    installing from NT option pack onto Windows 95, 14–15
    installing from Windows 98 CD, 15
    installing PHP4 alongside, 17–19
    Personal Web Manager, 18
    setting up, 15–16

# Q

**qualifiers, regular expression functions, 247**
**quantifiers, regular expression functions, 248**
**queries.** *See also* **SQL statements**
    clauses, 393
    commands, 392–93
    granting privilege to issue, 398
    PHP, issuing from, 411–15
    result identifiers, 423
    specifying name of database, 412
    SQL, 391
    when not to use semicolons to terminate, 411
**query strings.** *See also* **URLs**
    changing script's functionality with, 279–80
    name/value pairs, 74
    using for persistence, 272–80
**quotes**
    displaying value of variable, 55
    escape characters not used between double quotes, 57
    escaping, 418–19, 450
    stripping single quotes, 466
    in tag attributes, 498
    when assigning values to variables, 53
    when to use in code, 42

# R

radio buttons, 88–91
  variables, 104
rand() function, 113, 723
  using, 115
random access to data in files, 335–38
random numbers, generating, 113
RDBMS, 382
RDF, 508
read only mode, files, 326
readdir() function, 358, 712
readfile() function, 334, 716
REAL data type, 389
records, databases, 380
  deleting, 452–54
  inserting using PHP, 449–52
  populating tables with, 419–20
  retrieving rows, 402
  updating, 452–54
rectangles, drawing, 562–63
  with rounded corners, 563–66
recursion, 215–18
  traversing directories, 361–63
redundancy in databases, 380–82
Reference class example, 318
refreshing browsers, 52, 642
regexp. See regular expression functions
register_globals configuration setting, 182
registration. See user registration script
regular expression functions, 243–55, 732
  alternatives, 247
  anchors, 246
  character classes, 246
  e-mail address checking, 249–51
  ereg() function, 244
  escaping special characters, 245
  qualifiers, 247
  quantifiers, 248
  security, 253–55
  special characters, 244–48
  URL checking, 251–53
  word boundaries, 247
Relational Database Management Systems. See
  RDBMS
relational databases, 436. See also Databases; MySQL
  client/server model, 383–84
  directory management systems, 596–601
  entities, 381
  indexes, 390
  joins, 382
  normalization, 380–82
  primary keys, 381
  SQL (See SQL)
  standalone model, 383
  tables, 600
  unique fields, 381, 598
relative path notation, 326
relays, when server needs to be configured to allow,
  516
reliability of client/server database model, 384
remote files
  opening with fopen() function, 325, 333, 508
rename() function, 347-49, 716

REPLACE statement, 392
  difference from INSERT, 419
  difference from UPDATE, 397
  using to overwrite records, 397
Reply-to: header field, 518
Request category
  HTTP request header, 47
request/response line, HTTP, 46
requests, 44. See also HTTP
  body, 48
  environment variables, 68–69
  HTTP, 45, 46
  POST method, 75
  request line, 46
reset buttons, 99
resizing images, 582
Resource Description Framework. See RDF
Response category
  HTTP response header, 48
responses, 44. See also HTTP
  body, 49
  environment variables, 68–69
  header, 48
  HTTP, 45, 48
  response line, 48
restaurant example. See also persistence; sessions
  persistence with $HTTP_POST_VARS, 269–72
  persistence with hidden fields, 265–69
result identifiers, 423
result sets, 391
  iterating through, 621
  multiple, 403
  number of rows in, determining, 401
  ODBC, 675
$result variable, 423
retrieving data, 392–93. See also user record viewer
  complex retrievals, 433–37
  duplicate entries, eliminating, 433
  from several tables, 435–37
  indexes, 390
  limiting number of results, 396, 428–30
  ordering results, 430–31
  PHP functions for, 423–26
  SQL statements, 426–46
  summaries, 432–33
  WHERE clause, 396
return keyword, 195
REVOKE command, 399
rewind() function, 336, 716
rewinddir() function, 359, 712
RGB mode color, 557
rmdir() function, 360, 716
root account, MySQL, 387
rows, retrieving, 402
RPMs
  finding out which packages are installed, 31
  packages needed, 30–31
  PHP installation, 29–30
rsort() function, 179, 686
runtime errors, 232
  division by zero, 232
  infinite loops, 234

## S

SAX, 501
schemas, databases, 597
scope of variables, 206–13
    example, 210
script engines, 50
scripting languages, 50
scripts, 50. *See also* **PHP script; code**
    debugging, 255–58
    PHP script, identifying, 51
    preventing from being entered into forms, 143–44,
        242
    server-side scripting, 50–51
search engines
    keyword searches, implementing, 623
    multiple keyword searches, implementing, 624
    URL directory manager case study, 616–17
search_form() function
    URL directory manager case study, 616–17
security
    authentication, 474–82
        function for, 477
    client/server database model, 383
    errors, 228
    privileges (*See* **privileges**)
    stopping users going up directory tree, 253–55
    URL directory manager case study, 601
SELECT statement, 392, 424
    aliases, 434
    complex retrievals, 433–37
    data retrieval, 426–46
    duplicate entries, eliminating, 433
    fields, retrieving, 427–32
    joins, 436
    limiting number of results, 428–30
    retrieving feilds from several tables, 435–37
<SELECT> tag, 91–95
    MULTIPLE attribute, 92
semicolons, 17. *See also* **code**
    errors, 231
    terminating lines with, 42
    when not used to terminate query strings, 411
Sendmail program, 516
server functions, MySQL, 426
servers, 11
    client/server database model, 383
    requests, 44
    responses, 44
    web, 44
server-side scripting, 50–51
session handling functions, 733
session identifier. *See* **SIDs**
session variables, 288–91
    registering, 288
session_register() function, 288, 733
sessions, 264, 287–91 *See also* **persistence**
    cookies, 280–87
    page access, counting, 289–91
    PHP4, 288–91
        registering, 288
    SIDs, 288
SET data type, 390
setcookie() function, 281, 718
setters. *See* **accessor methods**
settype() function, 67, 739

shape attribute
    <AREA> tag, 580
shopping example. *See also* **loops**
    do while loops, 155
    while loops, 148
SHOW DATABASES command, 394
SHOW TABLES command, 394–96
show_list() function
    URL directory manager case study, 617–31
SIDs, 288
signals, event driven parsing, 501
Simple API for XML. *See* **SAX**
simplicity in user interfaces, 596
SMALLINT data type, 389
SMTP, specifying remote SMTP server to relay e-mail,
    516
sort() function, 177, 359, 687
sorting order, 440
spam mailers, 517
special characters in regular expression functions,
    244–48
    alternatives, 247
    anchors, 246
    character classes, 246
    qualifiers, 247
    quantifiers, 248
    word boundaries, 247
SQL, 388–93. *See also* **SQL statements**
    clauses, 393
    data types, 388
    NULL values, 391
SQL Server functions, 695
SQL statements, 388
    ALTER, 392
    CREATE, 392
    data retrieval, 426–46
    DELETE, 392, 397
    DROP, 392
    from text files, 410
    GRANT, 398–99
    granting privilege to issue, 398
    INSERT, 392, 417–20
    ODBC data sources, executing on, 674
    PHP, issuing from, 411–15
    queries, 391
    REPLACE, 392, 397
    REVOKE, 399
    rows affected by, determining, 401, 454
    SELECT, 392
    UPDATE, 392
    WHERE clause, 396, 397
sql_error() function
    URL directory manager case study, 607
square brackets [], arrays, 165–67
stacks, 180
standalone database model, 383
state information, 645
States of USA example, 168–72. *See also* **arrays**
    improvements, 172
static keyword, 209
static variables, 209–10
status codes, HTTP, 48
str_replace() function, 736
    use of in preparing e-mail headers, 524
string data type, 55–58
string-indexed arrays
    iterating through, 176–77

**strings**
  concat() function, 454
  concatenation, 56
    with .= operator, 614
  functions, 734
  images, writing onto, 578
  placing into arrays, 180–81
  storing contents of arrays as strings, 180–81
  string variables, 57
  substrings, extracting, 613
  writing to files, 327
**strip_tags() function, 736**
  ensuring only text is used in e-mail messages, 524
**stripslashes() function, 451, 736**
**strlen() function, 611, 737**
**Structured Query Language.** *See* **SQL**
**stylized maps, 585–89**
**Subject: header field, 518**
**submit buttons, 99**
**subscription scripts, newsletters, 537, 542**
**substr() function, 427, 613, 737**
  formatted date string, retrieving, 443
**substring() function, 427**
**substrings, extracting from strings, 613**
**subtraction operator, 59**
**subtypes of data**
  specifying for body of e-mails, 526
**sum() function, 432**
**summaries, MySQL, 432–33**
**switch statements, 135–39.** *See also* **conditional**
  **statements; code**
  break command, 136
  changing script's functionality with, 279–80
  shorthand version, 136
  switching functions, 201–2
**syntax errors, 229–32**

# T

**tables, 380.** *See also* **databases; MySQL**
  altering structure of, 392, 415–17, 425
  correcting inconsistencies between, 655–57
  creating
    with MySQL, 407–11
    with PHP, 411–15
  data, inserting into, 417–20
    duplicate entry error, 418
    escaping quotes, 418–19
  fields
    adding, 415
    information on, 461
    specifying as holding indexes, primary keys and unique
      values, 409
  indexes, 390
    adding or dropping, 416
  information on, 458–68
  populating, 419–20
  primary keys (*See* **primary keys**)
  privileges
    granting, 398–99
  records
    deleting, 452–54
    inserting using PHP, 449–52
    updating, 452–54
  relational databases, 600
  renaming, 415
  retrieving fields from several, 435–37

  summaries of data, 432–33
  viewing list of, 394–96, 401, 412
  viewing structure of, 395
**tags, 41**
  < (less than character), using within, 498
  container tags, 508
  empty, 497
  nesting, 496
  setting state of, 509
**TARGET attribute, 372**
**TCP, 45**
**TCP/IP, 44**
**text**
  images, writing onto, 578
**text areas, 80–82**
  setting size of, 82
**text boxes, 76–79**
  retrieving contents of from HTTP_GET_VARS, 182
  testing user has entered something in, 576
**TEXT data type, 390**
**text editor, 350–58.** *See also* **web text editor**
  button, 355
  common include file, 351
  date string, 352
  error message, 352
  footer, 352
  form, 353
  header, 352
  information relating to files, 353
  main function, 356
  PHP script, 353
  saving files, 355
**<TEXTAREA> tag, 80–82, 350**
  setting size of text area, 82
**$this keyword, 313**
**thumbnails, 581–84**
**time.** *See also* **date strings**
  curtime() function, 427
  format of, specifying, 42
  gmdate() function, 42
  now() function, 427
**TIME data type, 389, 455**
**time() function, 284, 529, 711**
**time-related properties of files, 340–42**
**TIMESTAMP data type, 389, 455**
  working with, 455
**timestamps, 282**
**TINYBLOB data type, 389**
**TINYINT data type, 389**
**TINYTEXT data type, 390**
**TITLE attribute, 579**
**To: header field, 518**
**to_days() function, 457**
**tool tips, 579**
**top_menu() function**
  URL directory manager case study, 665–67
**touch command**
  hit counter example, 329
**track_vars setting, 182**
**transparent backgrounds, images, 587**
**traversing directories, 361–63**
**trim() function, 517, 738**
**TYPE attribute**
  <INPUT> element, 76–79
**type casting, 67**

## U

**U.S. nuclear defense system, 235.** *See also* **Mars probes, how to loose**
**ucfirst() function, 357, 738**
**uniqid() function, 529, 725**
**unique fields, relational databases, 381, 598**
   specifying, 409
**UNIX.** *See also* **Linux**
   case-sensitvity, 394
   directory paths, 323
   newline character, 518
   Sendmail program, 516
   unlinking files, 349
   user groups, 342
**UNIX timestamp format, 282, 340**
**unknown data type, 55**
**unlink() function, 348–49, 716**
**unset() function, 68, 740**
**unsubscribing from newsletters, 543, 550**
**UPDATE statement, 392**
   difference from REPLACE, 397
   incrementing visitcount field, 453
   updating records, 452–54
   using with WHERE clause, 397, 452
**update_db() function**
   URL directory manager case study, 655–57
**uploads, 367–71**
   directory paths, 324
   enabling to attach to e-mails, 532
   preventing user from uploading to a place above the
      default directory, 374
   size limit, 368
   web text editor example, 374
**URL directory manager case study, 593**
   add_category(), 651
   add_category_form(), 649–51
   add_url(), 634–37
   add_url_form(), 630, 631–34
   administration code, 646–67
   administrator, 595
      authentication of, 602
      determining if current user is, 619
   administrator script, 603
   associative array of category metadata, returning,
      609–15
   broken links, 618
   categories, adding, 649–51
   categories, editing, 652–54
   category hierarchies, 594
   category tree, 598
   code implementation, 604
   code layout, 601–4
   common script, 603, 604–44
   correcting inconsistencies between tables, 655–57
   data storage, 596–601
   database
      connecting to, 597
      schema, 597
      tables, 600
   db_connect(), 607
   delete_category(), 654–55
   delete_url(), 628, 664–65
   deleting categories, 649, 654–55
   deleting URLs, 664–65
   deriving depth of category, 613
   designing, 594

   dir_manager.php, 646–67
   directory functions, 602
   directory_footer(), 606
   directory_header(), 606
   edit_category(), 653–54
   edit_category_form(), 652–53
   edit_new(), 662–64
   edit_new_form(), 660–62
   error_message(), 608
   errors, 605, 607
   expanded family names of categories, 613
   feedback, 667
   functionality, 602
   get_category_info(), 609–15
   get_url_info(), 615–16, 641
   go_url(), 642
   hidden fields, 638
   history object, 608
   hypertext links, 614
   keyword searches, implementing, 623
   list_categories(), 646–49
   list_sites(), 642–44
   modify_url(), 640–42
   modify_url_form(), 628, 637–40
   modifying URLs, 637–42
   most-visited sites, listing, 642–44
   multiple keyword searches, implementing, 624
   navigation links, 629, 658
   new records, inserting, 635
   newly added URLs
      approving, deleting or editing, 660–62
   newly added URLs, viewing, 657–60
   passwords, 633
   php_directory.inc, 604–44
   php_directory.php, 644–45
   root, preventing users from submitting at, 619
   search engine, 616–17
   search_form(), 616–17
   security issues, 601
   show_list(), 617–31
   sql_error(), 607
   submitting URLs, 631–34
   substrings, extracting from category ID, 613
   top_menu(), 665–67
   update_db(), 655–57
   URLs, information on, 615–16
   user authentication, 595
   user code, 644–45
   user interface, 596
   user requirements, 594–96
   user script, 603
   user_message(), 608
   variables, 605
   view_new(), 657–60
**URL encoding, 75**
**urlencode() function, 577, 738**
**URLs.** *See also* **query strings**
   format of, checking with regular expression functions,
      251–53
   functions, 738
   name/value pairs, appending, 73
   query strings
      using for persistence, 272–80
**USE command, 394**
**USEMAP attribute**
   <IMG> tag, 580
**user groups**
   ID, returning, 343
   UNIX, 342

**user interfaces**
simplicity, 596
**user managers, 482–91**
deleting records, 483
editing records, 483, 486
listing records, 483
reporting results of operations, function for, 482
updating user access records, 485
**user record viewer example, 437–46.** *See also* **user managers**
choosing an action to take, 445
common_db.inc, 437
error message, 439
footer, 438
global variables, 437
header function, 438
navigation links, 442
registered users, displaying list of, 439
script, 439
user information, displaying, 443
using, 446
**user registration script, 468–73**
checking if user ID is in use, 469
choosing actions to take, 472
displaying form, 469
global variables, 468
new records, inserting, 471
register.php, 468
**user requirements, 594–96**
**user table example**
creating, 411
new records, inserting, 471
populating, 419
structure, 409
**user_message() function**
URL directory manager case study, 608
**userfile input field, 532**
**users**
authentication, 474, 595
database users, creating, 396
displaying messages to, 608
getting confirmation from, 350
getting information from, 71–105
granting privileges, 398–99
ID
changing, 484
returning, 343
input from, 243–55
interactivity, 262–64
logging, 478
preferences, storing, 282–87
privileges, 396
registering (See user registration script)
revoking privileges, 399
tracking, 474–82
validation of data from, 140–44
**usury, detrimental effect on code of, 154**

**V**

**valid XML documents, 499–501**
**validation of data, 105, 140–44, 241–43**
exit statement, 140
htmlspecialchars() function, 143–44
**VARCHAR data type, 389**

**variables, 52–63.** *See also* **functions**
accessor methods, 304
adding to itself, 60
arrays, creating with check boxes, 88
assigning to values in arrays, 165
case-sensitivity of names, 53, 79
check boxes, 85
concatenation, 56
converting between data types, 65–68
destroying, 68
determining if name is created or not, 68
displaying on web page, 53
do not need to declare, 64–65
from HTML forms, 76
functions, 739
definitions of variables in, 196
values returned by, assigning to variables, 202
global, 207–9, 301
using inside functions, 208
hidden controls, passing as, 98
incrementing, 60
lifetime, 206
limits on naming, 53
listboxes, 104
local, 207
making value persisting between function calls, 209–10
modifiers, 133
multiple check boxes, 87
in multiple instances of a class, 306
names, 239–40
namespace conflicts, 302
objects, 302
passing by reference, 307–11
passing by value, 307–11
radio buttons, 104
scope, 206–13
session variables, 288–91
static, 209–10
string, 57
submit buttons, 99
that belong to a class, referring to within functions, 313
type casting, 67
**view source**
use of in debugging, 257
**view_new() function**
URL directory manager case study, 657–60
**view_record() function, 456**
**virtual fields**
accessing with aliases, 489
**visitcount field**
incrementing, 453
**Visual InterDev, 13**

**W**

**WDDX functions, 740**
**web browsers.** *See* **browsers**
**web pages**
caching, 51–52
displaying variables on, 53
dynamically generating, 50
forms, 71–105
graphical hit counters, 330
hit counters, 289–91, 328–30
logging visits to, 478

**webpages (cont'd)**
navigation links, 629
passing information between, 95–99
prepending files to, 478
preventing from being cached, 52
requests, 49–50
viewing, 44
**web servers.** *See* **servers**
**web sites**
consistency through object oriented programming, 321
interactivity, 262–64
last access time, 471
login script, 474–82
number of days since last visit, calculating, 457
personalization, 280
search engines (*See* **search engines**)
simplicity, 596
stopping users accessing sensitive files, 253–55
user registration script, 468–73
**web text editor, 371–77**
editor.inc, 373
file upload form, 374
frame page, 373
navigator.inc, 372
script, 373
uploading files, 374
**weekday name , returning, 457**
**well-formed XML, 496–99**
empty tags, 497
nesting tags, 497
**WHERE clause, 396, 428–30**
using with SQL commands, 397
**while loops, 148–55.** *See also* **loops; code**
conditional statements, 152
infinite loops, 234
iterating through arrays, 168
using, 149
usurious transaction example, 149
**$WINDIR environment variable, 346**
**Windows.** *See also* **Linux**
browser caches, 52
directory paths, 323
installing IIS 5.0 on Windows 2000, 23–24
installing IIS from Windows NT 4.0 option pack, 20–22
installing MySQL, 385–86
installing PHP on Windows 95 and 98, 13–19
installing PHP on Windows NT and 2000, 19–28
newline character, 518
PWS, 13

**winmysqladmin.exe tool, 385**
**WITH GRANT OPTION clause, 399**
**word boundaries, 247**
**World Wide Web**
HTTP, 45–49

# X

**XHTML, 41**
**XML, 493–512**
< (less than character), using within tags, 498
ATTLIST declaration, 501
attributes, 496
DOCTYPE declaration, 500
document structure, 496
DTDs, 499–501
ELEMENT declaration, 500
elements, 496
empty tags, 497
external DTDs, 501
linking to, 508
nesting tags, 497
parsing, 501–2
begin and end elements, 502
character data, handling, 502
external files, 508–12
freeing memory, 502
parser, creating, 502
starting, 502
PCDATA, 501
SAX, 501
valid documents, 499–501
well-formed, 496–99
**XML parser functions, 502, 740**
**xml_parse() function, 502, 741**
**xml_parser_create() function, 502, 741**
**xml_parser_free() function, 502, 741**
**xml_set_character_data_handler() function, 502, 741**
**xml_set_element_handler() function, 502, 741**

# Y

**Yahoo, 593**
reason for its success, 596
**YEAR data type, 389, 455**

# Z

**zero, division by, 232**
**Zlib functions, 742**